THE COMING
OF
POST-INDUSTRIAL
SOCIETY

THE COMING OF

OF

POST–INDUSTRIAL

SOCIETY

A Venture in Social Forecasting

DANIEL BELL

Basic Books, Inc., Publishers

NEW YORK

FOR

Jordy Bell Jacoby

AND

Stephen Jacoby

CONTENTS

Contents

CHAPTER
4

CHAPTER
5

CHAPTER
6

CODA

FOREWORD: 1976

The phrase "post-industrial society" has passed quickly into the sociological literature—whether for better or worse remains to be seen. In one sense, the reception was logical and understandable. Once it was clear that countries with diverse social systems could be defined commonly as "industrial societies," it was inevitable that societies which were primarily extractive rather than fabricating would be classified as "pre-industrial," and, as significant changes in the character of technology took place, one could think about "post-industrial" societies as well. Given, too, the vogue of "future schlock," in which breathless prose is mistaken for the pace of change, a hypothesis about the lineaments of a new society is bound to provoke interest. If I have been a beneficiary of fashion, I regret it.

As I indicate in the book, the idea of a post-industrial society is not a point-in-time prediction of the future but a speculative construct, an *as if* based on emergent features, against which the sociological reality could be measured decades hence, so that, in comparing the two, one might seek to determine the operative factors in effecting societal change. Equally, I rejected the temptation to label these emergent features as the "service society" or the "information society" or the "knowledge society," even though all these elements are present, since such terms are only partial, or they seek to catch a fashionable wind and twist it for modish purposes.[1]

I employed the term "post-industrial" for two reasons. First, to emphasize the interstitial and transitory nature of these changes. And second, to underline a major axial principle, that of an intel-

---

[1] Perhaps the major misconception is to identify the idea of the post-industrial society with the expansion of the service (or tertiary) sector of the economy and dispute its importance. Some writers using the term (e.g., Herman Kahn) have emphasized this feature. To the extent that some critics identify me with the centrality of a service sector, it is either ignorance or a willful misreading of my book.

lectual technology. But such emphasis does not mean that technology is the primary determinant of all other societal changes. No conceptual scheme ever exhausts a social reality. Each conceptual scheme is a prism which selects *some* features, rather than others, in order to highlight historical change or, more specifically, to answer certain questions.

One can see this by relating the concept of post-industrial society to that of capitalism. Some critics have argued that post-industrial society will not "succeed" capitalism. But this sets up a false confrontation between two *different* conceptual schemata organized along two different axes. The post-industrial schema refers to the socio-technical dimension of a society, capitalism to the socio-economic dimension.

The confusion between the two arose in the first place because Marx thought that the mode of production (the sub-structure of a society) determines and encompasses *all* other dimensions of a society. Since capitalism is the prevailing mode of production in Western society, Marxists sought to use that concept to explain all realms of social conduct, from economics through politics to culture. And since Marx felt that industrialization as the advanced feature of capitalist production would spread throughout the world, there would be, ultimately, global uniformity in the mode of production, and a uniformity in the conditions of life. National differences would disappear, and in the end only the two classes, capitalists and proletariat, would be left in stark, final confrontation.

I think this is demonstrably not so. Societies are not unified entities. The nature of the polity—whether a nation is democratic or not—rests not on the economic "foundation" but on historic traditions, on value systems, and on the way in which power is concentrated or dispersed throughout the society. Democracy cannot be easily "discarded," even when it begins to hobble the economic power of capitalists.[2] Equally, contemporary Western culture is not the "bourgeois" culture of the eighteenth or nineteenth century, but a modernism, hostile to the economizing mode, that has been absorbed by a "cultural mass" and transformed into a materialistic hedonism which is promoted, paradoxically, by capitalism itself.

For Marx, the mode of production united *social relations* and *forces* of production under a single historical rubric. The social relations were primarily property relations; the forces of production, technological. Yet the same forces of production (i.e., technology)

---

[2] For Marxists, fascism was the "last" stage of monopoly capitalism. While many capitalists did support fascism, the character of the system derived from the déclassé who led the movement, and the lower middle class which formed its mass base. Fascism is a cultural-political phenomenon. Curiously, we still have no comprehensive Marxist anlaysis of fascism, nor even a "Marxist analysis" of the new class structure of the Soviet Union itself.

exist within a wide variety of different systems of social relations. One cannot say that the technology (or chemistry or physics) of the Soviet Union is different from the technology (or chemistry or physics) of the capitalist world.

Rather than assume a single linkage between the social relations and the forces of production, if we *uncouple* the two dimensions, we can get different "answers" to the question of the relation between different social systems. Thus, if one asks: Is there a "convergence" between the Soviet Union and the United States? the answer would depend on the axis specified. This can be indicated, graphically, by Figure 1.

FIGURE 1

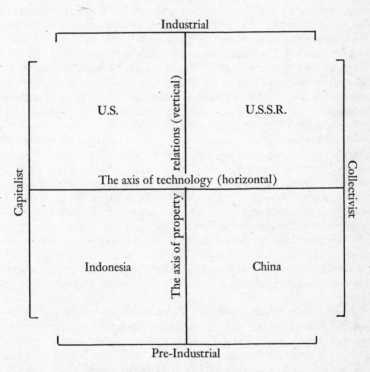

Thus, if one divides the countries by the horizontal axis of technology, both the United States and the U.S.S.R., are industrial societies, whereas Indonesia and China are not. Yet if one divides the countries along the vertical axis of property relations, there is a divergence, in that the United States and Indonesia are capitalist while the Soviet Union and China are both "socialist" or state collectivist.

(Yet *that* congruence does not explain why there is such fierce rivalry and tension between the two communist countries.)

And if we uncouple the concepts, we can also specify different schemata of social development: feudal, capitalist, and socialist; or pre-industrial, industrial, and post-industrial; or, within the Weberian framework of political authority, that of patriarchical, patrimonial, and legal-rational bureaucracy—so long as one does not claim that the particular conceptual scheme is exhaustive, and subsumes all others. Within a given historical period, it may well be that a specific axial principle is so important that it becomes determinative of most other social relations. I think it is quite evident that in the nineteenth century the capitalist mode of social relations (i.e., private property, commodity production, etc.) become the prevailing ethos and substantially shaped much of character and culture. But that is different from the claim that the mode of production always determines the "superstructure" of a society.

The mode of production does not unify a society. National differences have not disappeared. There are no unilineal sequences of societal change, no "laws of social development." The most grievous mistake in the social sciences is to read the character of a society through a single overriding concept, whether it be *capitalism* or *totalitarianism*, and to mislead one as to the complex (overlapping and even contradictory) features of any modern society, or to assume that there are "laws of social development" in which one social system succeeds another by some inexorable necessity. Any society, since it mingles different kinds of economic, technological, political, and cultural systems (some features of which are common to all, some of which are historical and idiosyncratic), has to be analyzed from different vantage points, depending on the question one has in mind. My focus has been on the influence of technology, not as an autonomous factor but as an analytical element, in order to see what social changes come in the wake of new technologies, and what problems the society, and its political system, must then attempt to solve.

The concept "post-industrial" is counterposed to that of "pre-industrial" and "industrial." A pre-industrial sector is primarily *extractive*, its economy based on agriculture, mining, fishing, timber, and other resources such as natural gas or oil. An industrial sector is primarily *fabricating*, using energy and machine technology, for the manufacture of goods. A post-industrial sector is one of *processing* in which telecommunications and computers are strategic for the exchange of information and knowledge.

In recent years, the world has become dramatically aware of the strategic role of energy and natural resources as limiting factors of industrial growth, and the question is raised whether these limitations do not modify the onset of a post-industrial sector.

To this, there is an empirical and a theoretical answer. As a practical fact, the introduction of post-industrial elements, which are capital intensive, does depend—in the timing, rate of diffusion, and extensivity of use—on the productivity of the other sectors. The development of an industrial sector depends in considerable measure on the economic surplus of an agrarian sector; yet once industrialization is under way, the productivity of the agrarian sector itself is increased through the use of fertilizer and other petro-chemical products. Similarly, the introduction of new information and processing devices may be delayed by rising costs in the industrial sector or lagging productivity, but once introduced they may be the very means of raising that productivity.

Theoretically, one can say that post-industrial society is, *in principle*, different from the other two. As a theoretical principle, the idea of industrialism did not derive from an agrarian mode. And similarly, the strategic role of theoretical knowledge as the new basis of technological innovation, or the role of information in re-creating social processes, does not derive from the role of energy in creating a manufacturing or fabricating society. In short, these are, *analytically*, independent principles.

Broadly speaking, if industrial society is based on machine technology, post-industrial society is shaped by an intellectual technology. And if capital and labor are the major structural features of industrial society, information and knowledge are those of the post-industrial society.[3] For this reason, the social organization of a post-industrial sector is vastly different from an industrial sector, and one can see this by contrasting the economic features of the two.

Industrial commodities are produced in discrete, identifiable units, exchanged and sold, consumed and used up, as are a loaf of bread or an automobile. One buys the products from a seller and takes physical possession of it. The exchange is governed by specific legal rules of contract. But information and knowledge are not consumed or "used

---

[3] By information I mean, broadly, the storing, retrieval, and processing of data, as the basis of all economic and social exchanges. This would include:

(a) Records: payrolls, government benefits (e.g., social security), bank clearances, credit clearances, and the like

(b) Scheduling: airline reservations, production scheduling, inventory analysis, product-mix information, and so forth.

(c) Demographic and library: census data, opinion surveys, market research, knowledge storage, election data, and so forth.

By knowledge, I mean an organized set of statements, of facts or ideas, presenting a reasoned judgment or an experimental result that is transmitted to others through communication media in some systematic form. (For an elaboration, see p. 174 et seq.)

up." Knowledge is a *social* product and the question of its costs, price, or value is vastly different from that of industrial items.

In the manufacture of industrial goods, one can set up a "production function," (i.e., the relative proportions of capital and labor to be employed) and determine the appropriate mix, at the relative costs, of each factor. If capital is embodied labor, one can talk of a labor theory of value.

But a post-industrial society is characterized not by a labor theory but by a knowledge theory of value.[4] It is the codification of knowledge that becomes directive of innovation. Yet knowledge, even when it is sold, remains also with the producer. It is a "collective good" in that, once it has been created, it is by its character available to all, and thus there is little incentive for any single person or enterprise to pay for the production of such knowledge unless they can obtain a proprietary advantage, such as a patent or a copyright. But, increasingly, patents no longer guarantee exclusiveness, and many firms lose out by spending money on research only to find that a competitor can quickly modify the product and circumvent the patent; similarly, the question of copyright becomes increasingly difficult to police when individuals or libraries can Xerox whatever pages they need from technical journals or books, or individuals and schools can tape music off the air or record a television performance on video disks.

If there is less and less incentive for individual persons or private enterprises to produce knowledge without particular gain, then the need and effort falls increasingly on some social unit, be it university or government, to underwrite the costs. And since there is no ready market test (how does one estimate the value of "basic research?") there is a challenge to economic theory to design a socially optimal policy of investment in knowledge (e.g., how much money should be spent for basic research; what allocations should be made for education, and for what fields; in what areas do we obtain the "better re-

---

[4] A parallel argument has been made by the German Marxist scholar Jurgen Habermas, who has written:

. . . technology and science [have] become a leading productive force, rendering inoperative the conditions for Marx's labor theory of value. It is no longer meaningful to calculate the amount of capital investment in research and development on the basis of the value of unskilled (simple) labor power, when scientific-technical progress has become an independent source of surplus value, in relation to which the only source of surplus value considered by Marx, namely the labor power of the immediate producers, plays an ever smaller role. Jurgen Habermas, *Toward a Rational Society* (Boston: Beacon Press, 1970) p. 104.

To that extent, too, one can say that *knowledge*, not labor, is a social product, and that Marx's analysis of the social character of production applies more fully to knowledge than to the production of goods.

turns" in health; and so on), and how to "price" information and knowledge to users.[5]

In a narrower, technical sense, the major problem for the post-industrial society will be the development of an appropriate "infra-structure" for the developing *compunications* networks (the phrase is Anthony Oettinger's) of digital information technologies that will tie the post-industrial society together. The first infra-structure in society is transportation—roads, canals, rail, air—for the movement of people and goods. The second infra-structure has been the energy utilities—oil pipeline, gas, electricity—for the transmission of power. The third infra-structure has been telecommunications, principally the voice telephone, radio, and television. But now with the explosive growth of computers and terminals for data (the number of data terminals in use in the United States went from 185,000 in 1970 to 800,000 in 1976) and the rapid decrease in the costs of computation and information storage, the question of hitching together the varied ways information is transmitted in the country becomes a major issue of economic and social policy.

The "economics of information" is not the same character as the "economics of goods," and the social relations created by the new net-works of information (from an interactive research group communicating through computer terminals to the large cultural homogenization created by national television) are not the older social patterns—or work relations—of industrial society.[6] We have here—if this kind of society develops—the foundations of a vastly different kind of social structure than we have previously known.

---

[5] The seminal work on this question of collective goods is Mancur Olson's *The Logic of Collective Action* (Cambridge: Harvard University Press, 1965). The question of the "economics of information" has come to absorb the attention of the Harvard economists Kenneth Arrow and Michael Spence. For some initial reflections, see, Kenneth Arrow, "Limited Knowledge and Economic Analysis," *American Economic Review*, March 1974, and Michael A. Spence, "An Economist's View of Information," in *Annual Review of Information Science and Technology*, Vol. 9, edited by Carlos A. Cuadra and Ann W. Luke (Washington, D.C. 1974). American Society for Information Science.

[6] One intriguing way in which cheap communications technology creates new social patterns is the use of citizens' band radio as a form of coordinated action. In 1974, independent truckers could create vast slowdowns on a thousand-mile chain of roads in the midwest by radio communication from selected blockade points. In one sense, this is little different from the pattern of riverboat pilots exchanging information which Mark Twain described so hilariously in *Life on the Mississippi*, but in this, as in so many instances, the characteristic of modernity is not the nature of the action but its scale, rapidity, and coordination.

For an authoritative elaboration of these technical questions, see the monograph *The Medium and the Telephone: The Politics of Information Resources*, by Paul J. Berman and Anthony Oettinger, Working Paper 75-8, Harvard Program on Information Technology and Public Policy. For this and other materials on information technology I am indebted to my colleague Professor Oettinger.

The post-industrial society, as I have implied, does not *displace* the industrial society, just as an industrial society has not done away with the agrarian sectors of the economy. Like palimpsests, the new developments overlie the previous layers, erasing some features and thickening the texture of society as a whole. In orienting a reader to the detailed arguments in this book, therefore, it might be useful to highlight some of the new dimensions of post-industrial society.

1. *The centrality of theoretical knowledge.* Every society has always existed on the basis of knowledge, but only now has there been a change whereby the codification of theoretical knowledge and materials science becomes the basis of innovations in technology. One sees this primarily in the new science-based industries—computers, electronics, optics, polymers—that mark the last third of the century.

2. *The creation of a new intellectual technology.* Through new mathematical and economic techniques—based on the computer linear programming, Markov chains, stochastic processes and the like—we can utilize modeling, simulation and other tools of system analysis and decision theory in order to chart more efficient, "rational" solutions to economic and engineering, if not social, problems.

3. *The spread of a knowledge class.* The fastest growing group in society is the technical and professional class. In the United States this group, together with managers, made up 25 percent of a labor force of eight million persons in 1975. By the year 2000, the technical and professional class will be the largest single group in the society.

4. *The change from goods to services.* In the United States today more than 65 out of every 100 persons are engaged in services. By 1980, the figure will be about 70 in every 100. A large service sector exists in every society. In a pre-industrial society this is mainly a household and domestic class. (In England, it was the single largest class in the society until about 1870.) In an industrial society, the services are transportation utilities, and finance, which are auxiliary to the production of goods, and personal service (beauticians, restaurant employees, and so forth). But in a post-industrial society, the new services are primarily human services (principally in health, education and social services) and professional and technical services (e.g., research, evaluation, computers, and systems analysis). The expansion of these services (as I indicated on pp. 154–164) becomes a constraint on economic growth and a source of persistent inflation.

5. *A change in the character of work.* In a pre-industrial world, life is a game against nature in which men wrest their living from the soil, the waters, or the forests, working usually in small groups, subject to the vicissitudes of nature. In an industrial society, work is a game against fabricated nature, in which men become dwarfed by machines as they turn out goods and things. But in a post-industrial

world, work is primarily a "game between persons" (between bureaucrat and client, doctor and patient, teacher and student, or within research groups, office groups, service groups). Thus in the experience of work and the daily routine, nature is excluded, artifacts are excluded, and persons have to learn how to live with one another. In the history of human society, this is a completely new and unparalleled state of affairs.

6. *The role of women.* Work in the industrial sector (e.g., the factory) has largely been men's work, from which women have been usually excluded. Work in the post-industrial sector (e.g., human services) provides expanded employment opportunities for women. For the first time, one can say that women have a secure base for economic independence. One sees this in the steadily rising curve of women's participation in the labor force, in the number of families (now 60 percent of the total) that have more than one regular wage earner, and in the rising incidence of divorce as women increasingly feel less dependent, economically, on men.

7. *Science as the imago.* The scientific community, going back to the seventeenth century, has been a unique institution in human society. It has been charismatic, in that it has been revolutionary in its quest for truth and open in its methods and procedures; it derives its legitimacy from the credo that knowledge itself, not any specific instrumental ends, is the goal of science. Unlike other charismatic communities (principally religious groups and messianic political movements), it has not "routinized" its creeds and enforced official dogmas. Yet until recently, science did not have to deal with the bureaucratization of research, the subordination of its inquiries to state-directed goals, and the "test" of its results on the basis of some instrumental payoff. Now science has become inextricably intertwined not only with technology but with the military and with social technologies and societal needs. In all this—a central feature of the post-industrial society—the character of the new scientific institutions—will be crucial for the future of free inquiry and knowledge.

8. *Situses as political units.* Most of sociological analysis has focused its attention on classes or strata, horizontal units of society that exist in superior-subordinate relation to each other. Yet for the post-industrial sectors, it may well be that *situses* (from the Latin *situ*, location), a set of vertical orders, will be the more important loci of political attachment. On pp. 374–375 I sketch the possible situses of the post-industrial order. There are four *functional* situses—scientific, technological (i.e., applied skills: engineering, economics, medicine), administrative and cultural—and five *institutional* situses—economic enterprises, government bureaus, universities and research complexes, social complexes (e.g., hospitals, social-service centers), and the mili-

tary. My argument is that the major interest conflicts will be between the situs groups, and that the attachments to these situses might be sufficiently strong to prevent the organization of the new professional groups into a coherent class in society.[7]

9. *Meritocracy.* A post-industrial society, being primarily a technical society, awards place less on the basis of inheritance or property (though these can command wealth or cultural advantage) than on education and skill. Inevitably the question of a meritocracy becomes a crucial normative question. In this book I attempt to define the character of meritocracy and defend the idea of a "just meritocracy," or of place based on achievement, through the respect of peers.

10. *The end of scarcity?* Most socialist and utopian theories of the nineteenth century ascribed almost all the ills of society to the scarcity of goods and the competition of men for these scarce goods. In fact, one of the most common definitions of economics characterized it as the art of efficient allocation of scarce goods among competing ends. Marx and other socialists argued that abundance was the precondition for socialism and claimed, in fact, that under socialism there would be no need to adopt normative rules of just distribution, since there would be enough for everyone's needs. In that sense, the definition of communism was the abolition of economics, or the "material embodiment" of philosophy. Yet it is quite clear that scarcity will always be with us. I mean not just the question of scarce resources (for this is still a moot point) but that a post-industrial society, by its nature, brings new scarcities which nineteenth- and early-twentieth-century writers had never thought of. The socialists and liberals had talked of the scarcities of goods; but in the post-industrial society, as I point out, there will be scarcities of information and of time. And the problems of allocation inevitably remain, in the crueler form, even, of man becoming *homo economicus* in the disposition of his leisure time.

11. *The economics of information.* As I pointed out earlier, information is by its nature a collective, not a private, good (i.e., a property). In the marketing of individual goods, it is clear that a "competitive" strategy between producers is to be preferred lest enterprise become slothful or monopolistic. Yet for the optimal social investment in knowledge, we have to follow a "cooperative" strategy in order to increase the spread and use of knowledge in society. This new problem regarding information poses the most fascinating chal-

---

[7] What is striking is that in the communist world, it is quite clear that *situses* play the major role in politics. One analyzes the play of power, not in class terms, but on the basis of the rivalries among the party, the military, the planning ministries, the industrial enterprises, the collective farms, the cultural institutions—all of which are *situses*.

lenges to economists and decision makers in respect to both theory and policy in the post-industrial society.

Most of the examples in this book are taken from the United States. The question that arises is whether other industrial nations in Western Europe, Japan, and the Soviet Union will become post-industrial as well. As I indicated (see p. 59), Marx took England as the chief illustration of his theoretical ideas and assumed, as against the German reader who might shrug off the transformation of England, that capitalism would spread everywhere, because of "natural laws" working themselves out "with iron necessity towards inevitable results." I do not believe that any social system is subject to such a causal trajectory. Yet the very features of post-industrial society indicate that, *as tendencies*, they are emergent in all industrial societies, and the extent to which they do appear depends upon a host of economic and political factors that have to do with the balance of world power, the ability of "third world" countries to organize effectively for a political and economic redistribution of wealth, the tensions between the major powers which might erupt into war or not. But it is clear that, as a theoretical construct, the continuing economic growth of all these societies necessarily involves the introduction of post-industrial elements.

The two large dimensions of a post-industrial society, as they are elaborated in this book, are the centrality of theoretical knowledge and the expansion of the service sector as against a manufacturing economy. The first means an increasing dependence on science as the means of innovating and organizing technological change. Most of the industrial societies are highly sensitive to the need for access to scientific knowledge, the organization of research, and the increasing importance of information as the strategic resource in the society. And to that extent a shift in the sociological weight of the sectors within the advanced societies, and the increasing role of science-based industries, are a crescive fact.[8]

The second change—the expansion of services in the economic sector—has been most striking in the United States, but has occurred in Western Europe as well. In 1960, a total of 39.5 percent of the workers in the enlarged Common Market area were in services (de-

---

[8] As I indicated in the text (p. 117), the national power of industrial societies was once rated on the basis of steel capacity. Two years ago, the Soviet Union passed the United States in the steel tonnage it produces, a fact that received only passing mention in the business pages of the *New York Times*. Yet in the development of computers, both in degree of sophistication and numbers, the Soviet Union is far, far behind the United States, a fact that was made vividly clear when the Soyuz and Apollo capsules were linked and the quality of their equipment could be compared.

fined broadly as transport, trade, insurance, banking, public administration, personal service). Thirteen years later, in 1973, the proportion had risen to 47.6 percent. A change of this kind usually goes in two phases. The first—the observation of Colin Clark who first decribed the phenomenon thirty years ago—was a shift to services at the expense of agriculture, but with industrial employment growing as well. But in Denmark, Sweden, Belgium and the United Kingdom, the service-oriented sectors have now grown at the relative expense of *industrial* employment (since agriculture has reached almost rock-bottom), and this is beginning to take place throughout Europe as well.[9]

The Soviet Union is an industrial society, and it is likely that post-industrial features will appear in that country as well. The striking fact, however, is that this book, *The Coming of Post-Industrial Society*, has been the object of an extraordinary range of attacks in the Soviet press, from serious discussions in academic journals, such as *Problems of Philosophy*, or intellectual weeklies such as the *Literary Gazette*, to ideological polemics in the official Party theoretical magazine *Kommunist* and vulgar and highly distorted accounts in *Pravda*. It would seem as if a decision had been made by the Party's ideological committee to attack this book as an ideological threat to Party doctrine. The reasons are quite clear. From the Soviet point of view there is a "historic" conflict between capitalism and communism in which the "objective laws of history" prove the ultimate victory of communism. And this is still a central tenet of the faith—at least for export purposes. On a theoretical level, my discussion denies the idea that one can use monolithic concepts such as capitalism or socialism to explain the complex structure of modern societies. More directly, since the Party doctrine bases its view of history on the inevitable victory of the proletariat (and justifies the repressive rule of the Party in the name of the "dictatorship of the proletariat"), how can one sustain that dogma when the proletariat is no longer the major occupational class of a post-industrial society?

---

[9] It is striking that Italy, Germany and France are the countries where industrial employment has increased; the largest increase was in Italy, which had lagged furthest in industrialization in Europe. But in the other countries, the proportion of those in industry has begun to shrink in relation to services. (For some detailed statistics on these occupational shifts, see *The Economist* [London], November 29, 1975, p. 17.)

Japan, too, has been following a similar trajectory in which the expansion in services has been at the expense of industry. For a detailed discussion, see Henry Rosovsky, "Japan's Economic Future," *Challenge*, July/August, 1973. In this essay Rosovsky develops a definition of "economic maturity" which is interesting in the light of sector changes that have taken place in the industrializing countries in the last fifty years. He writes: "Economic maturity is a difficult term to define but as used here it has a narrow meaning. Let us call it that state in which the incentives of sectoral labor force reallocation have become minimal—in the extreme case, impossible" (p. 16).

This was precisely the problem of a remarkable book by some members of the Czechoslovak Academy of Science, *Civilization at the Crossroads: Social and Human Implications of the Scientific and Technological Revolution*, which appeared during the "Prague Spring," in 1967, under the sponsorship of the social-science director Radovan Richta. In this book, the Czechoslovak sociologists explored the possibility of new "interest conflicts," if not "class conflicts," between the new scientific and professional strata and the working class in socialist society. Clearly, such a discussion was highly embarrassing to Marxist doctrine, and the theme a threat to the ideological justification of the Party. After 1968, Richta, who remained in Czechoslovakia after the Soviet occupation, abjectly and ignominiously repudiated the implications of his work.

The theme of post-industrialism applies primarily to changes in *the social structure* (the techno-economic order) and only indirectly to those in the polity and the culture, which comprise the other major realms of societal structure. One consequence of this is to widen the disjunction between the realms, since each now operates under axial principles that are contrary to the other.

When capitalism arose as a socio-economic system, it had a tenuous unity: an ethos (individualism), a political philosophy (liberalism), a culture (a bourgeois conception of utility and realism), and a character structure (respectability, delayed gratification, and the like). Many of these elements have withered or remain as pale ideologies. What is left is a technological engine, geared to the idea of functional rationality and efficiency, which promises a rising standard of living and promotes a hedonistic way of life. A post-industrial change begins to rework the stratification system of the society, to provide a more sophisticated technology, and to harness science more directly to instrumental purposes. Yet it is not at all clear that science, as a "republic of virtue," has the power to provide a new ethos for the society; more likely it is science itself that may become subverted. What this means is that the society is left with no transcendent ethos to provide some appropriate sense of purpose, no anchorages that can provide stable meanings for people.

In effect, what a post-industrial transformation means is the enhancement of *instrumental* powers, powers over nature and powers, even, over people. In the nineteenth century, utopian and socialist thinkers believed that any enhancement of man's power would necessarily be progressive, since it would mean the decline of religion and superstition and a proof of the greater powers and self-consciousness of Man. Yet this has proved to be a delusion. Instruments can be put to varied use. The kinds of use depend upon the values of a society, the entrenched nature of a privileged class, the openness of the society, its sense of decency or—as we have learned so viciously in the twentieth century—its bestiality.

A post-industrial transformation provides no "answers." It only establishes new promises and new powers, new constraints and new questions—with the difference that these are now on a *scale* that had never been previously imagined in world history.

DANIEL BELL

PREFACE

Since the rise of human settlements (or of our written records of these), there have been, according to Arnold Toynbee, twenty-one different civilizations, of which Western society, as a cultural unity, is one. But Western society alone is a huge historical canvas. Within Western society there has been a bewildering variety of interweaving elements, whether these be the differentiation of religions, the rise and fall of political empires, or the succession of socio-economic systems. The task for the sociologist or historian is to devise an intelligible unit of study.

One can, within a time-space frame, identify the structural features common to diverse societies and the more enduring and consistent patterns of change. Necessarily, these are on some level of abstraction.

Such an analytic approach, however, risks flattening out what may be distinctive and meaningful in the history of a particular society and generation. (Trotsky once remarked that fifty years is a short time in the life span of a social system; but it is almost the entire conscious lifetime of a particular person.) So, one can take the vicissitudes of a particular society (a territorial unit bound by a common past and ethos, and organized in a political sovereignty) and trace its rich yet idiosyncratic fate on the basis of its history, the character of its people, its "national will," and the like.

Yet it is also obvious that while its history may be individual, every society shares elements with other societies—religion, culture, economy, technology—that cut across the particular social organization of a people and influence them in specific ways. Spanish Catholicism is like, yet different from, Irish Catholicism. For some purposes we may focus on the common elements in Catholicism, for others on the national characteristics that create the differences. American capitalism is like, yet unlike, Japanese capitalism (in such crucial dimensions as managerial practices and responsibility for the worker); one's purpose dictates the focus of attention.

In this book, I have taken "industrial society" as my intelligible unit of study. Industrial society is a concept that embraces the experiences of a dozen different countries and cuts across the contrasting political systems of such antagonistic societies as the United States and the Soviet Union. Industrial society is organized around the axis of production and machinery, for the fabrication of goods; pre-industrial society is dependent on raw labor power and the extraction of primary resources from nature. In its rhythm of life and organization of work, industrial society is the defining feature of the social structure—i.e. the economy, the occupational system, and the stratification system —of modern Western society. The social structure, as I define it, is separate analytically from the two other dimensions of society, the polity and the culture.

But when used statically, the phrase "industrial society," like "capitalism," is deceiving, because these are not fixed social forms. Just as the corporate and managerial capitalism of the twentieth century is vastly different from the family capitalism of the eighteenth and nineteenth centuries, so the industrial society of the twentieth century, with its dependence on technology and science, is far different from the manufacturing society of the previous two centuries. No social system—or national society—has a patent on the future, and the sociological problem is to identify the character, and if possible the trajectory, of change: the initiating and resisting forces, the reinforcing and disintegrating elements.

The thesis advanced in this book is that in the next thirty to fifty years we will see the emergence of what I have called "the post-industrial society." As I emphasize, this is primarily a change in the social structure, and its consequences will vary in societies with different political and cultural configurations. Yet as a social form it will be a major feature of the twenty-first century, in the social structures of the United States, Japan, the Soviet Union, and Western Europe. The concept of post-industrial society is on the level of abstraction.

I take the United States as my singular unit of illustration, not only because it is the one I know best, but because the processes of change are more advanced and visible here. It also allows me to deal with the particular, and gain the advantages of immediacy and recognition while retaining the context of sociological generalization.

Unlike Marx, however, who believed that the fate of England (his example of capitalist industrial society) foreshadowed the fate of all such societies, I do not believe in a deterministic trajectory. A post-industrial society is not a "substructure" initiating changes in a "superstructure." It is one important dimension of a society whose changes pose management problems for the political system that arbitrates the society, just as changes in culture and life-style bring about confrontations with tradition, or the rise of new social groups, and the visibility of disadvantaged groups, raises issues of power and distribution of privilege in a society.

This, then, is a view from the twenty-first century. It is an attempt, methodologically, to use a new kind of conceptual analysis, that of axial principles and axial structures, as a way of "ordering" the bewildering number of possible perspectives about macro-historical change. It is an effort, empirically, to identify the substantive character of structural changes in the society as these derive from the changing nature of the economy, and the new and decisive role of theoretical knowledge in determining social innovation and the direction of change. It is a venture into the future.

"In any experiment of thinking," John Dewey wrote in *Art As Experience*, "premises emerge only as conclusions become manifest." This was the case with the concept of the post-industrial society. The chapters that make up this book were written in the last five years, and I had been struggling with the idea for some five years before that. Since the concept is a speculative one, and deals with possibilities in the alternative futures of society, there could be no linear development of the argument but only an exploration of diverse themes. Each essay was composed on a separate occasion, yet each was thought of as part of a mosaic. I have rewritten the essays in the last two years to emphasize these interrelationships and to identify the five dimensions of the concept post-industrial society. All of this is elucidated in detail in my Introduction. In addition, I have written a forty-thousand-word Coda to explore the major questions that a post-industrial society will have to confront in the decades ahead. The purpose of this preface is to express my gratitude to the persons and institutions that made this work possible.

The original formulation of the concept of the post-industrial society was presented at a forum on technology and social change in Boston in 1962 in a long, unpublished paper. Robert Heilbroner chaired that forum, and I want to thank him for his comments at the time and for intermittent discussions over the decade.

In 1965, a small grant from the Carnegie Corporation, to explore the idea, enabled me to acquire some research materials and the part-time help for a year of Dr. Virginia Held of the Philosophy Department of Hunter College. Dr. Held prepared a number of memoranda, some of which were incorporated into the working papers of the Commission on the Year 2000, and some of which I have used in Chapter 5. The discussions with Dr. Held were important to my early formulations.

The idea of the post-industrial society became one of the "baselines" of the Commission on the Year 2000, of the American Academy of Arts and Sciences, and is reflected in the five volumes of Working Papers circulated by the academy and in the book *Toward the Year 2000* (1967), a selection of materials from the commission. I am indebted to John Voss, the executive director of the American Academy of Arts and Sciences, for his generous help, and to Stephen Graubard, editor of *Daedalus* and a long-time intellectual companion, with whom I discussed many of these ideas and tested them against his broad historical knowledge.

My greatest debt, institutionally, is to the Russell Sage Foundation and its president, Orville Brim. A grant from the foundation in 1967 at first released me from one-third of my teaching schedule at Columbia and allowed me to organize an experimental graduate seminar at Columbia on modes of forecasting. The foundation also subsidized my research in the next few years. In 1969–1970 I spent a sabbatical year as a visiting fellow at the foundation, where this book began to take shape. Chapter 3, in somewhat different form and entitled "The Measurement of Knowledge and Technology," appeared in the volume *Indicators of Social Change*, edited by Eleanor Bernert Sheldon and Wilbert Moore, of the Russell Sage Foundation. I want to thank Dr. Sheldon, especially, for her editorial comments on that essay.

During the past decade I have pursued several overlapping and divergent intellectual interests: the work on the post-industrial society, the development of social indicators, the interest in long-range social forecasting and the year 2000, an assessment of theories of social change and the idea of axial structures as a way of organizing the field of macro-sociology, and a large concern with what I have called the disjunction of culture and social structure. The Russell Sage Foundation has been tolerant with me as I rattled about from one theme to another, occasionally publishing small chips from these rough-hewn blocks of manuscript. This book is the first of several, to be published in the next years, that will give these concerns coherence. I want to thank Orville Brim for his patience, and trust he will find some reward in this book.

In June 1970, Ralf Dahrendorf and I organized a small international seminar in Zurich, sponsored by the International Association for Cultural Freedom, for a discussion of the idea of the post-industrial society. Chapter 6 is the essay that formed the basis for the discussion. Subsequently, a number of critical and dissenting papers were written by Dr. Jean Floud of Nuffield College, Oxford, Professor Francois Bourricaud of the Sorbonne, Professor Giovanni Sartori, rector of the Faculty of Law at the University of Florence, Professor Peter Wiles of the London School of Economics, and Professor Ken'ichi Tominaga of the University of Tokyo. These papers were published in *Survey* (London), Winter 1971, and the interested reader may find them profitable.[1]

More personally, I have an enduring obligation to my friend Irving Kristol who, though suspicious of all social science and particularly of large-scale generalization, brought an astringent mind to every essay and insisted on an esthetic order in their presentation.

My secretary at the Russell Sage Foundation, Vivian Kaufman, and my secretary at Harvard, Mrs. Ann Merriman, have all the virtues that writers pray their secretaries may have. Miss Mari Tavitian did the typing of the Coda. Neal Rosenthal, of the Bureau of Labor Statistics, was unflaggingly helpful in providing some of the statistical data in Chapter 2. Mrs. Judith Burbank brought some of the statistics in Chapter 3 up to date. Mrs. Anne Freedgood, both friend and former editor, read the manuscript and made useful textual suggestions. Regina Schachter of Basic Books was most patient with me as she shepherded the manuscript through galleys and page proofs.

No writer is ever a proper judge of his own prose, and my most severe yet loving critic has been my wife, Pearl Kazin Bell, who edited the manuscript in its entirety.

March 1973
Cambridge, Mass.

---

[1] The other participants included S. N. Eisenstadt of Hebrew University, Reinhard Bendix of Berkeley, Zbigniew Brzezinski of Columbia, Michel Crozier of Paris, Zygmunt Bauman of Tel Aviv, Helio Jaguaribe of Brazil, Juan Linz of Yale, Ota Sik of Basle, Andrew Shonfield of Chatham House, David Lockwood of Essex, Stanley Hoffmann of Harvard, and Stephen Graubard of Cambridge, Mass.

INTRODUCTION

T HIS is an essay in social forecasting. But can one predict the future? The question is misleading. One cannot, if only for the logical reason that there is no such thing as "the future." To use a term in this way is to reify it, to assume that such an entity is a reality.[1] The word *future* is a relational term. One can only discuss the future of *something*.[2] This essay deals with the future of advanced industrial societies.

Forecasting differs from prediction. Though the distinction is arbitrary, it has to be established. Predictions usually deal with events —who will win an election, whether or not a country will go to war, who will win a war, the specification of a new invention; they center on decisions. Yet such predictions, while possible, cannot be formalized, i.e. made subject to *rules*. The prediction of events is inherently difficult. Events are the intersect of social vectors (interests, forces, pressures, and the like). While one can to some extent assess the strength of these vectors individually, one would need a "social physics" to predict the exact crosspoints where decisions and forces

---

[1] In his essay, "Has Futurology a Future?" Robert Nisbet writes: "The essence of futurology is that the future lies in the present just as our present once lay in the past. . . . Fundamental, it seems to me, to futurology is the attractive, but utterly fallacious, assumption *that the continuity of time is matched by the continuity of change or the continuity of events." Encounter* (November 1971. Emphasis in original). To use an old Russian proverb, Mr. Nisbet is knocking down an open door. He has set up a group of metaphors—the future, time, change—with no reference to content or relationships, so that incongruities between the words as words can easily be created. The methodological issue is the *kinds* of forecasting about different sorts of social phenomena. That is why I have never liked or used the term *futurology;* it is essentially meaningless.

[2] This is a common confusion. For example, one hears much talk of *consciousness,* or *consciousness-raising.* Yet as William James pointed out long ago, there is no such thing as consciousness, only consciousness *of* something. See "The Stream of Consciousness," chap. 2 of *Psychology: The Briefer Course* (New York, 1961; originally published in 1892).

combine not only to make up the event but, more importantly, its outcome. Prediction, therefore (and Kremlinology is a good example), is a function largely of the detailed inside knowledge and judgment that come from long involvement with the situation.

Forecasting is possible where there are regularities and recurrences of phenomena (these are rare), or where there are persisting trends whose direction, if not exact trajectory, can be plotted with statistical time-series or be formulated as historical tendencies. Necessarily, therefore, one deals with probabilities and an array of possible projections. But the limitations of forecasting are also evident. The further one reaches ahead in time with a set of forecasts, the greater the margin for error, since the fan of the projections widens. More important, at crucial points these trends become subject to choice (and increasingly in modern societies these are conscious interventions by men with power) and the decision (to accelerate, swerve or deflect the trends) is a policy intervention which may create a turning point in the history of a country or an institution.

To put it a different way: forecasting is possible only where one can assume a high degree of rationality on the part of men who influence events—the recognition of costs and constraints, the common acceptance or definition of the rules of the game, the agreement to follow the rules, the willingness to be consistent. Thus, even when there is conflict, the situation can be mediated through bargaining and trade-offs, if one knows each party's schedule of acceptable costs and order of priorities. But in many human situations—and particularly in politics—privileges and prejudices are at stake, and the degree of rationality or consistency is low.

What use, then, do forecasts have? Though they cannot predict results, they can specify the *constraints*, or limits, within which policy decisions can be effective. Given men's desire to control their history, this is a distinct gain in social self-consciousness.

Forecasting has many different modes. Social forecasting differs from other modes in its scope and techniques. The most important distinction is that the sociological variables are usually the independent, or exogenous, variables which affect the behavior of the other variables. And, while having the largest sweep—and potentially the greatest power, compared to the other modes of forecasting—they are the least precise.

A quick review of these various modes of forecasting will illustrate what is at stake.

Technological forecasting deals with rates of change or permutations and combinations of factors within *classes of events*. Just as one cannot predict events, one cannot predict specific inventions. One can, however, forecast the necessary next steps of a succession of changes within a closed system. Thus it is possible to project speed trend curves—an important factor in transportation—from jets to supersonic speeds; one can take computer memories, extrapolate the next level of capacities, and fit these within "envelope curves." [3] Such projections can be made because technology has finite parameters which are defined by physical constraints. Thus, the maximum speed on earth is 16,000 miles an hour; higher speeds take one into orbit. Or, in computer speeds, one is limited by the character of the transmitting units: originally vacuum tubes, then transistors, now integrated circuits. Theoretically, one can specify the kinds of materials (new tensile strengths or lightness) or the processes (e.g. miniaturization) necessary to achieve the next level of speed or capacity that is sought. Then one looks for these materials or processes. But this, however, is a matter of economics—the costs of the search, the assessment of possible gains, the amounts already invested in existing technologies, the scope of markets for new products, and the like. And this is outside the technological system.

Demographic forecasting—population statistics are the foundation of most economic and social analysis—is a curious mixture of indeterminacy and a modified closed system. The number of children born in any particular time period is subject to changes in values, the fluctuations of economic conditions, and the like. But once a given number are born we can predict from actuarial tables, with a high degree of probability, the numbers that will survive, and the rate of the cohort's diminution over time. From this one can estimate such social needs as education, health, and so on. But the original decisions are indeterminate and sociological.

There are three kinds of economic forecasting. The first is the simple market survey, based on income data, age distributions, household formations, and anticipated needs, which firms use for anticipating consumer demand, the amount of inventory to carry, and the acceptance of new products. The second, and most standardized, is the creation of time series of macrovariables—e.g. wholesale and consumer price indexes, industrial output, agricultural productivity, rate of unemployment, and a hundred other items—that serve as indicators of business activity and which are combined to make forecasts about the state of the economy. The third, and most sophisticated, is the econometric model which, by defining the actual interaction of the crucial variables in the system, seeks to simulate the reality of the economic system as a whole.

Again, there are limitations. Market surveys are subject to the

---

[3] The specific techniques are discussed in the section on technological forecasting in chap. 3.

usual hazards of discrepancy between individuals' attitudes and behavior, and this widens when there is a high level of discretionary income, since an individual can postpone purchases or be "indifferent" (in the technical economic sense of the word) to alternative items (a second car, a long vacation, a swimming pool) depending on price. Trend extrapolation is subject to a "system break" which comes exogenously. Thus, from 1910 to 1940, the index of agricultural productivity went from a base of 100 to about 125; if it had continued at the same rate for the next twenty years as it had for the previous thirty, it would have reached about 140 in 1960. Yet in 1960 the actual mark was about 400. During the 1940s a system break was created by huge wartime demand, loss of manpower, and a revolution in farm technology because of new fertilizers. The output per man-hour almost quadrupled in the forties and fifties, and at the same time there was a huge reduction in the number of farms and a large migration to the cities after the war.[4] The econometric model has the virtue of being a closed system, but its finite parameters are established by the analyst, rather than by physical laws. Its difficulties, of course, lie in the correct identification of the relevant variables and of the exact order in which they interact so that the actual economic flows can be simulated. The Brookings model which makes quarterly forecasts, completed in 1965, contains over 300 equations and endogenous variables and more than 100 exogenous variables—at which point the authors conclude that, "having examined the composite equation system, it should be clear to the reader that the task of building a large-scale quarterly econometric model of the U.S. economy has only begun." [5]

Political forecasting is the most indeterminate of all. In some societies, certain structural features have a high degree of stability. Thus I can *predict* (with a fair degree of certainty) that in 1976, 1980, and 1984 there will be presidential elections in the United States, or that within every five years there will be at least one parliamentary election in Great Britain—no mean feat, since one cannot make such predictions about many countries. (Can one equally assess the political

---

[4] The illustration is taken from Kenneth Boulding, "Expecting the Unexpected: The Uncertain Future of Knowledge and Technology," in *Prospective Changes in Society by 1980*, Designing Education for the Future, vol. 1 (Colorado Department of Education, 1966).

[5] *The Brookings Quarterly Econometric Model of the United States*, ed. James S. Duesenberry, Gary Fromm, Lawrence R. Klein, and Edwin Kuh (Chicago, 1965), p. 734.

The Brookings model breaks down the economy into 36 producing sectors and government plus 18 other major components (such as consumer demand, twenty variables; labor force and marriage, eighteen variables; residential construction, 23 variables; foreign trade, nine variables, etc.). See chap. 18, "The Complete Model: A First Approximation."

stability of Italy, let alone African or Latin-American countries?) Through public-opinion polling, I can make some fair forecasts about political events in the stable democracies. But the most important political issues involve conflict situations in which the chief players must make uncertain or risky calculations about each other.[6] A game theorist might order the array of choices, but only specific information about motives can permit one to say which choice will be made. And the degree to which crucial political decisions are carried out often depends on qualities of leadership and strength of will; such aspects of personality are not easy to calculate, especially in crisis situations.

There are also three kinds of social forecasting: the extrapolation of social trends, the identification of historical "keys" that turn new levers of social change, and projected changes in major social frameworks.

The most common, especially for short-run forecasting, is the projection of social indicators: crime rates, the number who will be educated, health and mortality data, migration, and the like. But such data have serious drawbacks. First, it is difficult to aggregate many of the indicators in a meaningful way. What does it mean, for example, to say that "crime" is increasing? The "crime rate" used by the FBI jumbles together the number of murders, rapes, assaults, burglaries, car thefts, etc., but these figures are not weighted and have no common metric. One can take a pound of potatoes and a pound of automobile and convert them into a common metric of dollar costs, and one can weight different kinds of purchases in a consumer price index. But how does one construct a common crime rate, or a general health index, or extent-of-education rate? The second difficulty is that even when there are fairly unambiguous rates, the time periods for the data are very short, and we do not know how meaningful some of the changes are. (For example, the decline in marriage age which began in the mid-fifties seemed to stop by 1970 and even to reverse itself. As for rates of divorce, are the numbers increasing, or have the rates simply levelled off?) Third, we do not know exactly what relates to what and how. In a general way, we know that residential segregation of races and classes widens the disparity of educational competences; that the amount and character of education affects occupational choices and social mobility in the society; that

---

[6] The paradigm for this is the "second-degree lie" exemplified in the Minsk-Pinsk joke. Two men are standing in a railroad station. The first asks: "Where are you going?" "To Minsk," the other replies, "to buy some cotton goods." "Huh," snorts the first, "you're telling me you are going to Minsk to buy some cotton goods to make me think you are going to Pinsk to buy some woolen goods, but I know you are going to Minsk to buy some cotton goods; so why do you tell me lies!"

7

there are correlations between heavy migration and the rates of crime. But we do not have a "model" of the society analogous to our model of the economy, and so we lack precision in relating rates of social change to each other.[7]

Changes in values and the rise of new social processes herald major societal changes whose drift can be charted roughly along historical time. Tocqueville's *Democracy in America*, published in 1835, is a powerful work that still seems fresh today because he identified one of the major "irresistible" forces transforming society: the drive for equality. In a different vein, Max Weber identified the process of bureaucratization as transforming the organization and administrative structures of society, but he also saw this change, which has revolutionized the work life and social relations of most persons in society, as part of a more pervasive process of the rationalization of all life in modern society.[8]

In the last hundred and fifty years, the social tensions of Western society have been framed by these contradictory impulses towards equality and bureaucracy, as these have worked themselves out in the politics and social structure of industrial society. Looking ahead to the next decades, one sees that the desire for greater participation in the decision-making of organizations that control individual lives (schools, hospitals, business firms) and the increasing technical requirements of knowledge (professionalization, meritocracy) form the axes of social conflict in the future.

But the identification of historical "keys" is quite tricky. It is the fashion these days to read into many social tendencies or new social movements portents that may not be there, or which are quickly erased (since the pace of change in intellectual fashion is often greater than in other fields). There are, therefore, few sure guides as to which new ideas, values or processes are genuine turning points in social history. Failing this—or at least guarding against such overestimation—we turn to changes in social frameworks.

Social frameworks are the structures of the major institutions that order the lives of individuals in a society: the distribution of persons

---

[7] For a general survey of social trend analysis, see Otis Dudley Duncan, "Social Forecasting: The State of the Art," *The Public Interest*, no. 17 (Fall 1969).

[8] For Tocqueville, see *Democracy in America*, translated by George Lawrence and edited by J.P. Mayer and Max Lerner (New York, 1966), Author's Introduction, pp. 5–6. For Weber, see chap. 11, "Bureaucracy," in *Economy and Society*, vol. 3 (New York, 1968). Written between 1914 and 1920, it was uncompleted on Weber's death in that year. (The first German edition appeared in 1922.) As Weber wrote, "The United States still bears the character of a polity which, at least in the technical sense, is not fully bureaucratized. But the greater the zones of friction with the outside and the more urgent the needs for administrative unity at home become, the more this character is inevitably and gradually giving way formally to the bureaucratic structure." Ibid., p. 971.

by occupation, the education of the young, the regulation of political conflict, and the like. The change from a rural to an urban society, from an agrarian to an industrial economy, from a federalized to a centralized political state, are major changes in social frameworks. Because such frameworks are structural, invariably they are crescive and difficult to reverse. For this reason they can be more readily identified. But such changes in frameworks are on a large scale, and they do not allow us to specify the exact details of a future set of social arrangements. When such changes are under way, they allow us not to predict the future but to identify an "agenda of questions" that will confront the society and have to be solved. It is this agenda that itself can be forecast.

The idea of the post-industrial society, which is the subject of this book, is a social forecast about a change in the social framework of Western society.

A Methodological Excursus

Social frameworks are not "reflections" of a social reality but conceptual schemata. History is a flux of events and society a web of many different kinds of relations which are known not simply by observation. If we accept the distinction between matters of fact and matters of relation, then knowledge, as a combination of the two, depends on the correct sequence between factual order and logical order. For experience, the factual order is primary; for meaning, the logical order. Mind knows nature by finding some language in which to express an underlying pattern. Knowledge, thus, is a function of the categories we use to establish relationships just as perception, as in art, is a function of the conventions we have accepted in order to see things "correctly." As Einstein once put it: "It is the theory which decides what we can observe." [9]

Nomen est numen, to name is to know, is an ancient maxim. In the contemporary philosophy of science, *nomen* are not merely names but concepts, or prisms. A conceptual schema selects particular attributes from a complex reality and groups these under a common rubric in order to discern similarities and differences. As a logical ordering device, a conceptual schema is not true or false but either useful or not.

A conceptual schema—in the way I use the device—rests on

---

[9] Quoted in Werner Heisenberg, *Physics and Beyond: Encounters and Conversations* (New York, 1971), p. 63.

an axial principle and has an axial structure. My purpose is to restore some of the informing power of older modes of social analysis.

To set a problem, as Dewey observed, is the most effective way of influencing subsequent thought. Marx set the problem of how to define society by positing the idea of a substructure based on economic relations, and a superstructure that was determined by it. Subsequent writers inverted the relationship by insisting on the primacy of ideological or cultural or political factors or, as the convention became accepted, emphasized the interaction of all factors and denied that any one of them was primary. Thus the attack on monocausal theory ended by denying a general theory of social causation or even the effort to search for primacies. As one sociologist puts it: "Contemporary systems theory sees society as a total unaggregated system whose dynamic nature stems from the interplay of its component subsystems with each other as well as with the external environment." [10] One posits a set of subsystems—the educational, the occupational, the political, the religious, the socialization—which influence each other, yet there are no clues as to which is the most important, or why. Everything is dissolved into interacting forces.

The idea of axial principles and structures is an effort to specify not causation (this can only be done in a theory of empirical relationships) but centrality. Looking for the answer to the question how a society hangs together, it seeks to specify, within a conceptual schema, the *organizing* frame around which the other institutions are draped, or the *energizing* principle that is a primary logic for all the others.

Many of the masters of social science used the idea of axial principles or axial structures implicitly in their formulations. Thus for Tocqueville, in his *Ancien Régime*, the entire interpretative structure of his work—the emphasis on the continuity of French society before and after the Revolution—rests on an axial structure, the centralization of administration in the hands of the state. In *Democracy in America*, equality is the axial principle that explains the spread of democratic feeling in American society. For Max Weber, the process of rationalization is an axial principle for understanding the transformation of the Western world from a traditional to a modern society: rational accounting, rational technology, the rationalistic economic ethic and the rationalization of the conduct of life.[11] For Marx, the production of commodities is the axial principle of capitalism, as the business firm is its axial structure; and for Raymond Aron machine

---

[10] Walter Buckley, *Sociology and Modern Systems Theory* (Englewood Cliffs, N.J., 1967), pp. 42–45, *passim*.
[11] For Weber's formulation, see the *General Economic History* (London, n.d.), chap. 30, esp. p. 354.

technology is the axial principle of industrial society and the factory its axial structure.

Conceptual prisms are logical orders imposed by the analyst on the factual order. But since the factual order is so multifarious and complex, many different logical orders—each with its own axial principle—can be imposed on the same time or social frame, depending on the questions one has in mind. A shortcoming of eighteenth- and nineteenth-century social thought (and of physics) was its naive scientism. Reality existed "out there," and the only problem was to get a true reflection of it, undistorted by bias, habit, received prejudices, and the like. (In Francis Bacon's classic formulation, distortions were caused by the idols of the tribe, the idols of the cave, the idols of the marketplace, and the idols of the theater.) Or the mapping of the social world was conceived as being like a Mercator projection in which the map is drawn as a "plan," no different than an architect's blueprint, in which the viewpoint is at *infinity*; i.e. one is not over a particular point on the map, but over all points simultaneously. But even the invariable placing of North at the top of the map is a geographical convention (of relatively modern date), and one can learn much more about economic (and strategic) geography by looking at *perspective* maps, which are drawn from the standpoint of an observer at a finite point. Seeing Europe "from the East," i.e. in a map drawn from the standpoint of an observer in the Pacific looking east, gives a more compelling view of the land mass of Russia than any conventional map.[12]

Conceptual prisms and axial structures are valuable because they allow one to adopt a multi-perspective standpoint in trying to understand social change, but they do not forgo the value of perceiving the "primary logic" of key institutions or axial principles within a particular scheme. Thus the terms feudalism, capitalism, and socialism are a sequence of conceptual schemes, in the Marxist framework, along the axis of property relations. The terms pre-industrial, industrial, and post-industrial societies are conceptual sequences along the axis of production and the kinds of knowledge that are used. Depending on the axis, we can highlight similarities or differences. Thus along the axis of property there is a contradictory relation between the United States and the Soviet Union, in that one is a capitalist and the other a (statist) socialist society. Along the axis of production and technology, both the Soviet Union and the United States are industrial societies and thus somewhat congruent. In this respect, when

---

[12] For a vivid illustration of these differences, see the beautiful maps of Richard Edes Harrison, *Look at the World* (New York, 1944).

one looks at the Soviet Union and the United States one need not depend exclusively on a principle of convergence or of inherent conflict, but one can specify the rotating axes along which the distinctions are made. In this fashion, one can avoid a single-minded determinism, such as an economic determinism or a technological determinism, in explaining social change, yet single out a primary logic within a given conceptual scheme. One forgoes causality but emphasizes significance (or in Dilthey's sense, meaning). One is able, also, to create a principle of "complementarity" in social explanation.[13]

The Dimensions of Post-Industrial Society

Analytically, society can be divided into three parts: the social structure, the polity, and the culture. The social structure comprises the economy, technology, and the occupational system. The polity regulates the distribution of power and adjudicates the conflicting claims and demands of individuals and groups. The culture is the realm of expressive symbolism and meanings. It is useful to divide society in this way because each aspect is ruled by a different axial principle. In modern Western society the axial principle of the social structure is *economizing*—a way of allocating resources according to principles of least cost, substitutability, optimization, maximization, and the like. The axial principle of the modern polity is *participation*, sometimes mobilized or controlled, sometimes demanded from below. The axial principle of the culture is the desire for the *fulfillment and enhancement of the self*. In the past, these three areas were linked by a common value system (and in bourgeois society through a common

---

[13] There is an inherent risk in taking a concept derived from one field bodily into another, and the social sciences particularly have been bedeviled by such borrowing. For example, the use of the terms force and power from physics, and structure and function from biology. Complementarity was used by Niels Bohr to explain the contradictory behavior of light as wave and particle, but Bohr did feel, according to my colleague, the physicist Gerald Holton, that the principle applied to many phenomena in nature and society. This may have been the *hubris* of a great man infatuated with the discovery of a compelling principle. Since the concept is suggestive, let me say only that I use it simply as a metaphor and not as an explanatory device.

This discussion of axial structures and conceptual schemata is elaborated in my essay "Macro-Sociology and Social Change," in *Theories of Social Change: A Stock-taking*, which I have edited for the Russell Sage Foundation, to be published in 1974. A different use of the idea of conceptual schemata appears in Georges Gurvitch's *The Social Frameworks of Knowledge* (Oxford, 1971; published originally in French in 1966). Gurvitch seeks to define a succession of historical social types and the kinds of cognitive systems associated with each. To that extent he is elaborating the kind of sociology of knowledge developed by Max Scheler in his *Die Wissenformen und die Gesellschaft* (1926).

character structure). But in our times there has been an increasing disjunction of the three and, for reasons I discuss in the Coda, this will widen.

The concept of the post-industrial society deals primarily with changes *in the social structure*, the way in which the economy is being transformed and the occupational system reworked, and with the new relations between theory and empiricism, particularly science and technology. These changes can be charted, as I seek to do in this book. But I do not claim that these changes in social structure *determine* corresponding changes in the polity or the culture. Rather, the changes in social structure pose *questions* for the rest of society in three ways. First, the social structure—especially the social structure—is a structure of roles, designed to coordinate the actions of individuals to achieve specific ends. Roles segment individuals by defining limited modes of behavior appropriate to a particular position, but individuals do not always willingly accept the requirements of a role. One aspect of the post-industrial society, for example, is the increasing bureaucratization of science and the increasing specialization of intellectual work into minute parts. Yet it is not clear that individuals entering science will accept this segmentation, as did the individuals who entered the factory system a hundred and fifty years ago.

Second, changes in social structure pose "management" problems for the political system. In a society which becomes increasingly conscious of its fate, and seeks to control its own fortunes, the political order necessarily becomes paramount. Since the post-industrial society increases the importance of the technical component of knowledge, it forces the hierophants of the new society—the scientists, engineers, and technocrats—either to compete with politicians or become their allies. The relationship between the social structure and the political order thus becomes one of the chief problems of power in a post-industrial society. And, third, the new modes of life, which depend strongly on the primacy of cognitive and theoretical knowledge, inevitably challenge the tendencies of the culture, which strives for the enhancement of the self and turns increasingly antinomian and anti-institutional.

In this book, I am concerned chiefly with the social structural and political consequences of the post-industrial society. In a later work I shall deal with its relation to culture. But the heart of the endeavor is to trace the societal changes primarily within the social structure.

"Too large a generalization," Alfred North Whitehead wrote, "leads to mere barrenness. It is the large generalization, limited by a happy particularity, which is the fruitful conception." [14] It is easy —and particularly so today—to set forth an extravagant theory which, in its historical sweep, makes a striking claim to originality. But when tested eventually by reality, it turns into a caricature— viz. James Burnham's theory of the managerial revolution thirty years ago, or C. Wright Mills's conception of the power elite, or W. W. Rostow's stages of economic growth. I have tried to resist that impulse. Instead, I am dealing here with *tendencies*, and have sought to explore the meaning and consequences of those tendencies if the changes in social structure that I describe were to work themselves to their logical limits. But there is no guarantee that they will. Social tensions and social conflicts may modify a society considerably; wars and recriminations can destroy it; the tendencies may provoke a set of reactions that inhibit change. Thus I am writing what Hans Vahinger called an "as if," a fiction, a logical construction of what *could* be, against which the future social reality can be compared in order to see what intervened to change society in the direction it did take.

The concept of the post-industrial society is a large generalization. Its meaning can be more easily understood if one specifies five dimensions, or components, of the term:

1. Economic sector: the change from a goods-producing to a service economy;
2. Occupational distribution: the pre-eminence of the professional and technical class;
3. Axial principle: the centrality of theoretical knowledge as the source of innovation and of policy formulation for the society;
4. Future orientation: the control of technology and technological assessment;
5. Decision-making: the creation of a new "intellectual technology."

Creation of a service economy. About thirty years ago, Colin Clark, in his *Conditions of Economic Progress,* analytically divided the economy into three sectors—primary, secondary, and tertiary —the primary being principally agriculture; the secondary, manufacturing or industrial; and the tertiary, services. Any economy is a mixture in different proportions of each. But Clark argued that, as nations became industrialized, there was an inevitable trajectory whereby, because of sectoral differences in productivity, a larger proportion of the labor force would pass into manufacturing, and as national incomes rose, there would be a greater demand for services and a corresponding shift in that slope.

---

[14] Alfred North Whitehead, *Science and the Modern World* (New York, 1960; original edition, 1925), p. 46.

By this criterion, the first and simplest characteristic of a post-industrial society is that the majority of the labor force is no longer engaged in agriculture or manufacturing but in services, which are defined, residually, as trade, finance, transport, health, recreation, research, education, and government.

Today, the overwhelming number of countries in the world (see Tables 1 and 2) are still dependent on the primary sector: agriculture, mining, fishing, forestry. These economies are based entirely on natural resources. Their productivity is low, and they are subject to wide swings of income because of the fluctuations of raw material and primary-product prices. In Africa and Asia, agrarian economies account for more than 70 percent of the labor force. In western and northern Europe, Japan, and the Soviet Union, the major portion of the labor force is engaged in industry or the manufacture of goods. The United States today is the only nation in the world in which the service sector accounts for more than half the total employment and more than half the Gross National Product. It is the first service economy, the first nation, in which the major portion of the population is engaged in neither agrarian nor industrial pursuits. Today about 60 percent of the United States labor force is engaged in services; by 1980, the figure will have risen to 70 percent.

The term "services," if used generically, risks being deceptive about the actual trends in the society. Many agrarian societies such as India have a high proportion of persons engaged in services, but of a personal sort (e.g. household servants) because labor is cheap and usually underemployed. In an industrial society different services tend to increase because of the need for auxiliary help for production, e.g. transportation and distribution. But in a post-industrial society the emphasis is on a different kind of service. If we group services as personal (retail stores, laundries, garages, beauty shops); business (banking and finance, real estate, insurance); transportation, communication and utilities; and health, education, research, and government; then it is the growth of the last category which is decisive for post-industrial society. And this is the category that represents the expansion of a new intelligentsia—in the universities, research organizations, professions, and government.

The pre-eminence of the professional and technical class. The second way of defining a post-industrial society is through the change in occupational distributions; i.e. not only *where* people work, but the *kind* of work they do. In large measure, occupation is the most important determinant of class and stratification in the society.

The onset of industrialization created a new phenomenon, the semi-skilled worker, who could be trained within a few weeks to do

15

TABLE 1

The World's Labor Force by Broad Economic Sector,
and by Continent and Region, 1960 *

REGION	TOTAL LABOR FORCE (MILLIONS)	PERCENTAGE DISTRIBUTION BY SECTOR		
		AGRICULTURE	INDUSTRY	SERVICES
World	1,296	58	19	23
Africa	112	77	9	14
Western Africa	40	80	8	13
Eastern Africa	30	83	7	10
Middle Africa	14	86	6	8
Northern Africa	22	71	10	19
Southern Africa [a]	6	37	29	34
Northern America [a]	77	8	39	53
Latin America	71	48	20	32
Middle America (mainland)	15	56	18	26
Caribbean	8	53	18	29
Tropical South America	37	52	17	31
Temperate South America [a]	12	25	33	42
Asia	728	71	12	17
East Asia (mainland)	319	75	10	15
Japan [a]	44	33	28	39
Other East Asia	15	62	12	26
Middle South Asia	239	71	14	15
South-East Asia	90	75	8	17
South-West Asia	20	69	14	17
Europe [a]	191	28	38	34
Western Europe [a]	60	14	45	41
Northern Europe [a]	34	10	45	45
Eastern Europe [a]	49	45	31	24
Southern Europe [a]	47	41	32	27
Oceania [b]	6	23	34	43
Australia and New Zealand	5	12	40	49
Melanesia	1	85	5	10
USSR [a]	111	45	28	27

SOURCE: *International Labour Review* (January–February, 1967); ILO estimates based on national censuses and sample surveys.

NOTE: Owing to independent rounding, the sum of the parts may not add up to group totals.

[a] More developed regions.

[b] Excluding Polynesia and Micronesia.

* An ILO survey for 1970 is due to be published later in the decade. In 1969, however, the OECD in Paris published a breakdown of the labor force in West Europe, by sectors, which provides for the comparisons in Table 2.

TABLE 2

Labor Force and GNP in Western Europe and United States by Sectors, 1969

COUNTRY	AGRICULTURE		INDUSTRY		SERVICES	
	PERCENT-AGE OF GNP	PERCENT-AGE OF LABOR	PERCENT-AGE OF GNP	PERCENT-AGE OF LABOR	PERCENT-AGE OF GNP	PERCENT-AGE OF LABOR
West Germany	4.1	10.6	49.7	48.0	46.2	41.4
France	7.4	16.6	47.3	40.6	45.3	42.8
Britain	3.3	3.1	45.7	47.2	51.0	49.7
Sweden	5.9	10.1	45.2	41.1	48.9	48.8
Netherlands	7.2	8.3	41.2	41.9	51.6	49.8
Italy	12.4	24.1	40.5	41.1	51.7	45.1
United States	3.0	5.2	36.6	33.7	60.4	61.1

SOURCE: Organisation for Economic Co-operation and Development (Paris, 1969).

the simple routine operations required in machine work. Within industrial societies, the semi-skilled worker has been the single largest category in the labor force. The expansion of the service economy, with its emphasis on office work, education, and government, has naturally brought about a shift to white-collar occupations. In the United States, by 1956, the number of white-collar workers, for the first time in the history of industrial civilization, outnumbered the blue-collar workers in the occupational structure. Since then the ratio has been widening steadily; by 1970 the white-collar workers outnumbered the blue-collar by more than five to four.

But the most startling change has been the growth of professional and technical employment—jobs that usually require some college education—at a rate twice that of the average. In 1940 there were 3.9 million such persons in the society; by 1964 the number had risen to 8.6 million; and it is estimated that by 1975 there will be 13.2 million professional and technical persons, making it the second-largest of the eight occupational divisions in the country, exceeded only by the semi-skilled workers (see Table 3). One further statistical breakdown will round out the picture—the role of the scientists and engineers, who form the key group in the post-industrial society. While the growth rate of the professional and technical class as a whole has been twice that of the average labor force, the growth rate of the scientists and engineers has been triple that of the working population. By 1975 the United States may have about 550,000 scientists (natural and social scientists), as against 275,000 in 1960, and almost a million and a half engineers, compared to 800,000 in 1960. Table 4 [15] gives

---

[15] In Table 3 the projected figure for the number of professional and technical persons in 1975 is given as 13.2 million and in Table 4 as 12.9 million. The discrep-

TABLE 3

*Employment by Major Occupation Group, 1964,
and Projected Requirements, 1975* [a]

MAJOR OCCUPATION GROUP	1964		1975		PERCENTAGE CHANGE, 1964–1975
	NUMBER (IN MILLIONS)	PERCENT	NUMBER (IN MILLIONS)	PERCENT	
Total employment	70.4	100.0	88.7	100.0	26
White-collar workers	31.1	44.2	42.8	48.3	38
Professional, technical, and kindred workers	8.6	12.2	13.2	14.9	54
Managers, officials, and proprietors, except farm	7.5	10.6	9.2	10.4	23
Clerical and kindred workers	10.7	15.2	14.6	16.5	37
Sales workers	4.5	6.3	5.8	6.5	30
Blue-collar workers	25.5	36.3	29.9	33.7	17
Craftsmen, foremen, and kindred workers	9.0	12.8	11.4	12.8	27
Operatives and kindred workers	12.9	18.4	14.8	16.7	15
Laborers, except farm and mine	3.6	5.2	3.7	4.2	b
Service workers	9.3	13.2	12.5	14.1	35
Farmers and farm managers, laborers, and foremen	4.4	6.3	3.5	3.9	−21

SOURCE: *Technology and the American Economy*, Report of the National Commission on Technology, Automation, and Economic Progress, vol. 1 (Washington, D.C., 1966), p. 30; derived from Bureau of Labor Statistics, *America's Industrial and Occupational Manpower Requirements, 1964–1975*.

NOTE: Because of rounding, sums of individual items may not equal totals.

a Projections assume a national unemployment rate of 3 percent in 1975. The choice of 3 percent unemployment as a basis for these projections does not indicate an endorsement or even a willingness to accept that level of unemployment.

b Less than 3 percent.

the breakdown of the professional and technical occupations—the heart of the post-industrial society.

The primacy of theoretical knowledge. In identifying a new and emerging social system, it is not only in the extrapolated social trends, such as the creation of a service economy or the expansion of the professional and technical class, that one seeks to understand fundamental social change. Rather, it is through some specifically defin-

ancies are due in part to the fact that the figure in Table 4 was calculated five years later, and also because different assumptions about the unemployment rate were made. I have let the figures stand to indicate the range.

TABLE 4

The Make-up of Professional and Technical Occupations,
1960 and 1975 (in thousands)

	1960	1975
Total labor force	66,680	88,660
Total professional and technical	7,475	12,925
Scientific and engineering	1,092	1,994
Engineers	810	1,450
Natural scientists	236	465
Chemists	91	175
Agricultural scientists	30	53
Geologists and geophysicists	18	29
Mathematicians	21	51
Physicists	24	58
Others	22	35
Social scientists	46	79
Economists	17	31
Statisticians and actuaries	23	36
Others	6	12
Technicians (Except medical and dental)	730	1,418
Medical and health	1,321	2,240
Physicians and surgeons	221	374
Nurses, professional	496	860
Dentists	87	125
Pharmacists	114	126
Psychologists	17	40
Technicians (Medical and dental)	141	393
Others	245	322
Teachers	1,945	3,063
Elementary	978	1,233
Secondary	603	1,160
College	206	465
Others	158	275
General	2,386	4,210
Accountants	429	660
Clergymen	200	240
Editors and reporters	100	128
Lawyers and judges	225	320
Arts and entertainment	470	774
Architects	30	45
Librarians	80	130
Social workers	105	218
Others (Airline pilots, photographers, personnel relations, etc.)	747	1,695

SOURCE: BLS Bulletin no. 1606, "Tomorrow's Manpower Needs," vol. IV (February 1969), Appendix E, pp. 28–29.

ing characteristic of a social system, which becomes the axial principle, that one establishes a conceptual schema. Industrial society is the coordination of machines and men for the production of goods. Post-industrial society is organized around knowledge, for the purpose of social control and the directing of innovation and change; and this in turn gives rise to new social relationships and new structures which have to be managed politically.

Now, knowledge has of course been necessary in the functioning of any society. What is distinctive about the post-industrial society is the change in the character of knowledge itself. What has become decisive for the organization of decisions and the direction of change is the centrality of *theoretical* knowledge—the primacy of theory over empiricism and the codification of knowledge into abstract systems of symbols that, as in any axiomatic system, can be used to illuminate many different and varied areas of experience.

Every modern society now lives by innovation and the social control of change, and tries to anticipate the future in order to plan ahead. This commitment to social control introduces the need for planning and forecasting into society. It is the altered awareness of the nature of innovation that makes theoretical knowledge so crucial.

One can see this, first, in the changed relationship between science and technology. Almost all the major industries we still have—steel, electric power, telegraph, telephone, automobiles, aviation—were nineteenth-century industries (although steel begins in the eighteenth century and aviation in the twentieth), in that they were mainly the creation of inventors, inspired and talented tinkerers who were indifferent to science and the fundamental laws underlying their investigations. Kelly and Bessemer, who (independently) created the oxidation process that makes possible the steel converter and the mass production of steel, were unaware of their contemporary, Henry Clifton Sorby, whose work in metallurgy disclosed the true microstructure of steel. Alexander Graham Bell, inventor of the telephone, was in Clerk Maxwell's opinion a mere elocutionist who "to gain his private ends [money] has become an electrician." Edison's work on "etheric sparks," which led to the development of the electric light and generated a vast new revolution in technology, was undertaken outside the theoretical research in electromagnetism and even in hostility to it. But the further development of electrodynamics, particularly in the replacement of steam engines, could only come from engineers with formal training in mathematical physics. Edison, as one biographer has written, lacked "the power of abstraction." [16]

---

[16] Matthew Josephson, *Edison* (New York, 1959), p. 361.

What might be called the first "modern" industry, because of its intricate linking of science and technology, is chemistry, since one must have a theoretical knowledge of the macromolecules one is manipulating in order to do chemical synthesis—the recombination and transformation of compounds.[17] In 1909 Walter Nerst and Fritz Haber converted nitrogen and hydrogen to produce synthetic ammonia. Working from theoretical principles first predicated by the Frenchman Henri Le Chatelier in 1888, the two German chemists provided a spectacular confirmation of Kant's dictum that there is nothing so practical as a good theory.[18] The irony, however, lies in the use of the result.

War is a technological forcing house, but modern war has yoked science to technology in a radically new way. Before World War I, every General Staff calculated that Germany would either win a quick, smashing victory or, if France could hold, the war would end quickly in a German defeat (either in the field or at the negotiating table). The reasoning was based on the simple fact that Chile was Germany's (and the world's) major source of the natural nitrates needed for fertilizer and for explosives and, in wartime, Germany's access to Chile would be cut off by the British Navy. In 1913 Germany used about 225,000 tons of nitrogen, half of which was imported. Stocks began to fall, but the Haber-Bosch process for the manufacture of synthetic ammonia developed so rapidly that by 1917 it accounted for 45 percent of Germany's production of nitrogen compounds. By the armistice Germany was almost self-sufficient in nitrogen,[19] and because she was able to hold out, the war became a protracted struggle of static trench warfare and slaughter.

In the latter sense, World War I was the very last of the "old" wars

---

[17] Aviation is an interesting transition. The first inventors were tinkerers, but the field could develop only through the use of scientific principles. Langley (1891) and Zahm (1902–1903) started the new science of aerodynamics by studying the behavior of air currents over different types of airfoils. At the same time, in 1900, the Wright brothers began tinkering with gliders, and in 1903 put a gasoline-powered engine into an airplane. But further work was possible only through the development, after 1908, of experiments (such as models in wind tunnels) and mathematical calculations (such as airflows over different angles of wings) based on physical laws.

[18] See Eduard Farber, "Man Makes His Materials," in Kransberg and Pursell, eds. *Technology and Western Civilization*, vol. 2 (New York, 1967).

[19] See L. F. Haber, *The Chemical Industry, 1900–1930* (Oxford, 1971), chap. 7, pp. 198–203. As Haber writes:

"The Haber process . . . was still largely an unknown factor when the Great War broke out. The synthesis of ammonia . . . represents one of the most important advances in industrial chemistry. . . . The process, discovered by Fritz Haber and developed industrially by Carl Bosch, was the first application of high-pressure synthesis; the technology of ammonia production, appropriately modified, was used later in the synthesis of methanol and the hydrogenation of coal to petroleum. Its influence extends to present-day techniques of oil refining and use of cracker gases from refining operations for further synthesis." Ibid., p. 90.

of human civilization. But with the new role of science it was also the first of the "new" wars. The eventual symbolic fusion of science and war was, of course, in World War II the atom bomb. It was a demonstration, as Gerald Holton has written, "that a chain of operations, starting in a scientific laboratory, can result in an event of the scale and suddenness of a mythological occurrence." Since the end of World War II the extraordinary development of scientific technology has led to hydrogen bombs, distant-early-warning networks coordinated in real time through computer systems, intercontinental ballistics missiles, and, in Vietnam, the beginning of an "automated" battlefield through the use of large-scale electronic sensing devices and computer-controlled retaliatory strikes. War, too, has now come under the "terrible" dominion of science, and the shape of war, like all other human activity, has been drastically changed.

In a less direct but equally important way, the changing relation between theory and empiricism is reflected in the formulation of government policy, particularly in the management of the economy. During the Great Depression of the 1930s, almost every government floundered about and had no notion of what to do with any confidence. In Germany in 1930, the socialist economists who determined government policy insisted that the depression would have to "run its course," meaning that the "overproduction" which caused it, by their Marxist reasoning, would be sopped up. In England, there was a similar sense of hopelessness. Tom Jones, a confidant of Stanley Baldwin and a member of the Unemployment Assistance Board, noted in a letter to Abraham Flexner on March 1, 1934: "On the home front we have favourable if slight evidence of improved trade, but nothing that will make any dent in the unemployment figures. It is slowly but surely being realized by more and more that the great majority of these will never work again, and people like Lindsay of Balliol, T.J., and that ilk, are facing up to big and permanent developments of these occupational and training centres." [20]

In the United States, Franklin D. Roosevelt tinkered with a wide variety of programs. Through the National Recovery Administration he set up an elaborate price-fixing and regulative set of codes which resembled a corporate state. On the advice of George Warren, he manipulated the gold content of the dollar in order to raise the price level. To do something for the idle, he began a large campaign of public works. Few of these policies derived from any comprehensive theory about economic recovery; there was none at hand. As Rexford Tugwell, one of Roosevelt's economic advisors, later observed,

---

[20] Thomas Jones, *A Diary with Letters* (New York, 1954), p. 125. Lindsay is A. D. Lindsay, Master of Balliol College for twenty-five years until 1949. T. J. is an ironic reference by Jones to himself.

Roosevelt simply was trying one "magical formula" after another in the hope of finding some combination that would get the economy moving.[21]

It was largely through the joining of theory and policy that a better understanding of economic management was achieved. Keynes provided the theoretical justification for the intervention of government into the economy as the means of bridging the gap between saving and investment.[22] The work of Kuznets, Hicks, and others in macro-economics gave government policy a firm framework through the creation of a system of national economic accounts—the aggregations of economic data and the fitting of such components as investment and consumption into product accounts and income accounts—so that one could measure the level of economic activity and decide which sectors needed government intervention.

The other major revolution in economics has been the attempted use of an increasingly rigorous, mathematically formalized body of economic theory, derived from the general equilibrium theory of Walras and developed in the last three decades by Leontief, Tinbergen, Frisch, and Samuelson [23] for policy purposes. In the past, these concepts and tools—production functions, consumption functions, time preferences, and discounting—though powerful as abstractions were remote from empirical content because there was no appropriate quantitative data for testing and applying this body of theory.[24]

---

[21] See Rexford G. Tugwell, *The Democratic Roosevelt* (New York, 1957), chap. 15, esp. pp. 312–313.

[22] The Keynesian revolution in economics actually occurred after most of the economies had recovered from the depression even though many policies, particularly so-called unbalanced budgets or deficit financing, were adopted by trial-and-error and had "Keynesian" effects. The most self-conscious effort to use the new economics was in Sweden, where the socialist finance minister, Ernest Wigforss, broke away from Marxist thinking and, on the advice of the economists Erik Lindahl and Gunnar Myrdal, pursued an active fiscal and public-works policy which was Keynesian before Keynes, i.e. before the publication of Keynes' *General Theory* in 1936.

[23] Thirty years ago few, if any, graduate schools taught mathematical economics. The turning point, probably, was the publication of Paul Samuelson's *Foundations of Economic Analysis* in 1947, which presented a mathematically formalized version of neoclassical economics. Today, no one can work in economic theory without a solid grounding in mathematics.

[24] It is striking that during the depression there was no real measure of the extent of unemployment because of the confusion over a conceptual definition and the lack of sample survey techniques to make quick counts; the government relied on the 1930 census and some estimates from manufacturing establishments. In 1921, when President Harding called a conference of experts to discuss the unemployment that accompanied the postwar depression, estimates ranged widely and the final figure published was decided, literally, by majority vote. The confusions about who should be counted, or what constituted the "labor force," continued through the 1930s and a settled set of definitions and figures emerged only in the 1940s. Nor were there, of course, the Gross National Product and national-income accounts to give a view of

The development of modern economics, in this respect, has been possible because of the computer. Computers have provided the bridge between the body of formal theory and the large data bases of recent years; out of this has come modern econometrics and the policy orientation of economics.[25] One major area has been the models of interdependencies among industries such as the input-output matrices developed by Wassily Leontieff, which simplify the general equilibrium system of Walras and show, empirically, the transactions between industries, or sectors, or regions. The input-output matrix of the American economy is a grid of 81 industries, from Footwear and other Leather Products (1) to Scrap, Used, and Secondhand Goods (81) grouped into the productive, distributive, and service sectors of the economy. A dollar-flow table shows the distribution of the output of any one industry to each (or any) of the other 80 sectors. The input-output matrix shows the mix and proportions of inputs (from each or several industries) which go into a specific unit of output (in dollar value or physical production terms). An inverse matrix shows the indirect demand generated by a product as well as the direct demand. Thus, one can trace the effect of the final consumer demand say for automobiles on the amount (or value) of iron ore, even though the automobile industry buys no iron ore directly. Or one can see what proportion of iron ore, as a raw material, goes into such final products as autos, ships, buildings, and the like. In this way, one can chart the changes in the nature of final demands in terms of the differential effects on each sector of the economy.[26] Input-output tables are now the basic tools for national economic planning and they have been applied in regional planning, through computerized models, to test the effect on trade of changes in population distributions.

The large econometric models of the economy, such as the Brookings model discussed earlier, allow one to do economic forecasting, while the existence of such computer models now enables economists to do policy "experiments," such as the work of Fromm and Taubman in simulating eight different combinations of fiscal and mone-

---

the economy as a whole. This came into public-policy use only in 1945. (I am indebted to an unpublished dissertation at MIT by Judith de Neufville, on social indicators, for the illustration on unemployment statistics.)

[25] Charles Wolf, Jr., and John H. Enns have provided a comprehensive review of these developments in their paper "Computers and Economics," Rand Paper P-4724. I am indebted to them for a number of illustrations.

[26] Mathematically speaking, an input-output matrix represents a set of simultaneous linear equations—in this case 81 equations with 81 variables which are solved by matrix algebra. See Wassily Leontieff, *The Structure of the American Economy: Theoretical and Empirical Explorations in Input-Output Analysis* (New York, 1953). Ironically, when the Bureau of Labor Statistics tried to set up an input-output grid for the American economy in 1949, it was opposed by business on the ground that it was a tool for socialism, and the money was initially denied.

tary policy for the period 1960–1962, in order to see which policy might have been the most effective.[27] With these tools one can test different theories to see whether it is now possible to do "fine tuning" of the economy.

It would be technocratic to assume that the managing of an economy is only a technical offshoot of a theoretical model. The overriding considerations are political, and set the frames of decision. Yet the economic models indicate the boundaries of constraint within which one can operate, and they can specify the consequences of alternative political choices.[28] The crucial point is that economic policy formulations, though not an exact art, now derive from theory, and often must find justification in theory. The fact that a Nixon administration in 1972 could casually accept the concept of a "full employment budget," which sets a level of government expenditures *as if* there were full utilization of resources (thus automatically accepting deficit financing) is itself a measure of the degree of economic sophistication that government has acquired in the past thirty years.

The joining of science, technology, and economics in recent years is symbolized by the phrase "research and development" (R & D). Out of this have come the science-based industries (computers, electronics, optics, polymers) which increasingly dominate the manufacturing sector of the society and which provide the lead, in product cycles, for the advanced industrial societies. But these science-based industries, unlike industries which arose in the nineteenth century, are primarily dependent on theoretical work prior to production.

---

[27] Their conclusions: that the largest impact on real GNP came from increases in government nondurable and construction expenditures. Income-tax cuts were less of a stimulant than increase in expenditures. Gary Fromm and Paul Taubman, *Policy Simulations with an Econometric Model* (Brookings Institution, Washington, D.C., 1968), cited in Wolf and Enns, op. cit.

[28] With modern economic tools, Robert M. Solow argues, an administration can, within limits, get the measure of economic activity it wants, for the level of government spending can redress the deficits of private spending and step up economic activity. But in so doing, an administration has to choose between inflation or full employment; this dilemma seems to be built into the market structure of capitalist economies. An administration has to make a trade-off—and this is a political choice. Democrats have preferred full employment and inflation, Republicans price stability and slow economic growth.

In the last few years, however, there has been the new phenomenon—simultaneous high unemployment and high inflation. For reasons that are not clear, unemployment no longer "disciplines" an economy into bringing prices down, either because of substantial welfare cushions (e.g. unemployment insurance), wage-push pressure in organized industries, or the persistent expectation of price rises that discounts inflation.

The two turning points in modern economic policy were President Kennedy's tax cut in 1964, which canonized Keynesian principles in economic policy, and President Nixon's imposition of wage and price controls in 1971. Though mandatory controls were relaxed in 1973, the option to use them now remains.

The computer would not exist without the work in solid-state physics initiated forty years ago by Felix Bloch. The laser came directly out of I.I. Rabi's research thirty years ago on molecular optical beams. (One can say, without being overly facile, that U.S. Steel is the paradigmatic corporation of the first third of the twentieth century, General Motors of the second third of the century, and IBM of the final third. The contrasting attitudes of the corporations toward research and development are a measure of these changes.)

What is true of technology and economics is true, albeit differentially, of all modes of knowledge: the advances in a field become increasingly dependent on the primacy of theoretical work, which codifies what is known and points the way to empirical confirmation. In effect, theoretical knowledge increasingly becomes the strategic resource, the axial principle, of a society. And the university, research organizations, and intellectual institutions, where theoretical knowledge is codified and enriched, become the axial structures of the emergent society.

The planning of technology. With the new modes of technological forecasting, my fourth criterion, the post-industrial societies may be able to reach a new dimension of societal change, the planning and control of technological growth.

Modern industrial economies became possible when societies were able to create new institutional mechanisms to build up savings (through banks, insurance companies, equity capital through the stock market, and government levies, i.e. loans or taxes) and to use this money for investment. The ability consistently to re-invest annually at least 10 percent of GNP became the basis of what W.W. Rostow has called the "take-off" point for economic growth. But a modern society, in order to avoid stagnation or "maturity" (however that vague word is defined), has had to open up new technological frontiers in order to maintain productivity and higher standards of living. If societies become more dependent on technology and new innovation, then a hazardous "indeterminacy" is introduced into the system. (Marx argued that a capitalist economy had to expand or die. Later Marxists, such as Lenin or Rosa Luxemburg, assumed that such expansion necessarily had to be geographical; hence the theory of imperialism. But the greater measure of expansion has been capital-intensive or technological.) Without new technology, how can growth be maintained? The development of new forecasting and "mapping techniques" makes possible a novel phase in economic history—the conscious, planned advance of technological change, and therefore the reduction of indeterminacy about the economic future. (Whether this can actually be done is a pregnant question, discussed in Chapter 3.)

But technological advance, as we have learned, has deleterious side effects, with second-order and third-order consequences that are often overlooked and certainly unintended. The increasing use of cheap fertilizers was one of the elements that created the revolution in agricultural productivity, but the run-off of nitrates into the rivers has been one of the worst sources of pollution. The introduction of DDT as a pesticide saved many crops, but also destroyed wildlife and birds. In automobiles, the gasoline engine was more effective than steam, but it has smogged the air. The point is that the introduction of technology was uncontrolled, and its initiators were interested only in single-order effects.

Yet none of this has to be. The mechanisms of control are available as well. As a number of studies by a panel of the National Academy of Science has shown, if these technologies had been "assessed" before they were introduced, alternative technologies or arrangements could have been considered. As the study group reported:

The panel believes that in some cases an injection of the broadened criteria urged here might have led, or might in the future lead, to the selection or encouragement of different technologies or at least modified ones —functional alternatives with lower "social costs" (though not necessarily lower total costs). For example, bioenvironmental rather than primarily chemical devices might have been used to control agricultural pests, or there might have been design alternatives to the purely chemical means of enhancing engine efficiency, or mass transit alternatives to further reliance upon the private automobile.[29]

Technology assessment is feasible. What it requires is a political mechanism that will allow such studies to be made and set up criteria for the regulation of new technologies.[30] (This question is elaborated in Chapter 4.)

The rise of a new intellectual technology. "The greatest invention

---

[29] *Technology: Processes of Assessment and Choice*, Report of the National Academy of Sciences, U.S. House of Representatives, Committee on Science and Astronautics, July 1969.

[30] To further the idea of technology assessment, the National Academy of Engineering undertook three studies in developing fields, that of computer-assisted instruction and instructional television; subsonic aircraft noise; and multiphasic screening in health diagnosis. The study concluded that technology assessment was feasible, and outlined the costs and scope of the necessary studies. In the case of technological teaching aids, the study considered eighteen different impacts they might have. In the case of noise, they examined the costs and consequences of five alternative strategies, from relocating airports or soundproofing nearby homes to modifying the airplanes or their flight patterns. See *A Study of Technology Assessment*, Report of the Committee on Public Engineering Policy, National Academy of Engineering, July 1969.

The idea of "technology assessment" grew largely out of studies made by the House Science and Astronautics Committee, and in 1967 a bill was introduced in the House by Congressman Daddario for a Technology Assessment Board. The bill was passed in 1972 and the Congress, not the Executive, is charged with setting up a Technology Assessment Office.

of the nineteenth century," Alfred North Whitehead wrote, "was the invention of the method of invention. A new method entered into life. In order to understand our epoch, we can neglect all the details of change, such as railways, telegraphs, radios, spinning machines, synthetic dyes. We must concentrate on the method itself; that is the real novelty, which has broken up the foundations of the old civilization." [31]

In the same spirit, one can say that the methodological promise of the second half of the twentieth century is the management of organized complexity (the complexity of large organizations and systems, the complexity of theory with a large number of variables), the identification and implementation of strategies for rational choice in games against nature and games between persons, and the development of a new intellectual technology which, by the end of the century, may be as salient in human affairs as machine technology has been for the past century and a half.

In the eighteenth and nineteenth centuries, scientists learned how to handle two-variable problems: the relationship of force to distance in objects, of pressure and volume in gases, of current versus voltage in electricity. With some minor extensions to three or four variables, these are the bedrock for most modern technology. Such *objects* as telephones, radio, automobile, airplane, and turbine are, as Warren Weaver puts it, problems of "complex simplicity." [32] Most of the models of nineteenth- and early-twentieth-century social science paralleled these simple interdependencies: capital and labor (as fixed and variable capital in the Marxist system; as production functions in neo-classical economics), supply and demand, balance of power, balance of trade. As closed, opposed systems, to use Albert Wohlstetter's formulation, they are analytically most attractive, and they simplify a complex world.

In the progression of science, the next problems dealt with were not those of a small number of interdependent variables, but the ordering of gross numbers: the motion of molecules in statistical mechanics, the rates of life expectancies in actuarial tables, the distribution of heredities in population genetics. In the social sciences, these became the problems of the "average man"—the distributions of intelligence, the rates of social mobility, and the like. These are, in Warren Weaver's term, problems of "disorganized complexity," but their solutions were made possible by notable advances in probability

---

[31] *Science and the Modern World*, p. 141.
[32] Warren Weaver, "Science and Complexity," in *The Scientists Speak*, ed. Warren Weaver (New York, 1947). I am indebted to a former special student at Columbia, Norman Lee, for this citation and for a number of other suggestions in this section.

theory and statistics which could specify the results in chance terms.

The major intellectual and sociological problems of the post-industrial society are, to continue Weaver's metaphor, those of "organized complexity"—the management of large-scale systems, with large numbers of interacting variables, which have to be coordinated to achieve specific goals. It is the *hubris* of the modern systems theorist that the techniques for managing these systems are now available.

Since 1940, there has been a remarkable efflorescence of new fields whose results apply to problems of organized complexity: information theory, cybernetics, decision theory, game theory, utility theory, stochastic processes. From these have come specific techniques, such as linear programming, statistical decision theory, Markov chain applications, Monte Carlo randomizing, and minimax solutions, which are used to predict alternative optimal outcomes of different choices in strategy situations. Behind all this is the development in mathematics of what Jagit Singh calls "comprehensive numeracy." [33] Average properties, linear relationships, and no feedback, are simplifications used earlier to make mathematics manually tractable. The calculus is superbly suited to problems of a few variables and rates of change. But the problems of organized complexity have to be described in probabilities—the calculable consequences of alternative choices, which introduce constraints either of conflict or cooperation—and to solve them one must go beyond classical mathematics. Since 1940, the advances in probability theory (once intuitive and now rigorous and axiomatic), sophisticated set theory, and game and decision theory have made further advances in application theoretically possible.

I have called the applications of these new developments "intellectual technology" for two reasons. Technology, as Harvey Brooks defines it, "is the use of scientific knowledge to specify ways of doing things in a *reproducible* manner." [34] In this sense, the organization of a hospital or an international trade system is a *social* technology, as the automobile or a numerically controlled tool is a *machine* technology. An *intellectual* technology is the substitution of algorithms (problem-solving rules) for intuitive judgments. These algorithms may be embodied in an automatic machine or a computer program or a set of instructions based on some statistical or mathematical for-

[33] Jagit Singh, *Great Ideas of Operations Research* (New York, 1968).
[34] Harvey Brooks, "Technology and the Ecological Crisis," lecture given at Amherst, May 9, 1971, p. 13 from unpublished text, emphasis added. For an application of these views, see the reports of two committees chaired by Professor Brooks, *Technology, Processes of Assessment and Choice*, Report of the National Academy of Science, published by the Committee on Science and Astronauticism, U.S. House of Representatives, July 1969; and, *Science Growth and Society*, OECD (Paris, 1971).

mula; the statistical and logical techniques that are used in dealing with "organized complexity" are efforts to formalize a set of decision rules. The second reason is that without the computer, the new mathematical tools would have been primarily of intellectual interest, or used, in Anatol Rappoport's phrase, with "very low resolving power." The chain of multiple calculations that can be readily made, the multivariate analyses that keep track of the detailed interactions of many variables, the simultaneous solution of several hundred equations—these feats which are the foundation of comprehensive numeracy—are possible only with a tool of intellectual *technology*, the computer.

What is distinctive about the new intellectual technology is its effort to define rational action and to identify the means of achieving it. All situations involve constraints (costs, for example) and contrasting alternatives. And all action takes place under conditions of certainty, risk, or uncertainty. Certainty exists when the constraints are fixed and known. Risk means that a set of possible outcomes is known and the probabilities for each outcome can be stated. Uncertainty is the case when the set of possible outcomes can be stipulated, but the probabilities are completely unknown. Further, situations can be defined as "games against nature," in which the constraints are environmental, or "games between persons," in which each person's course of action is necessarily shaped by the reciprocal judgments of the others' intentions.[35] In all these situations, the desirable action is a

---

[35] Most of the day-to-day problems in economics and management involve decision-making under conditions of certainty; i.e. the constraints are known. These are such problems as proportions of product mixes under known assumptions of cost and price, production scheduling by size, network paths, and the like. Since the objectives are clear (the most efficient routing, or the best profit yield from a product mix), the problems are largely mathematical and can be solved by such techniques as linear programming. The theory of linear programming derives from a 1937 paper by John von Neumann on the general equilibrium of a uniformly expanding closed economy. Many of the computational procedures were developed by the Soviet economist L.V. Kantorovich, whose work was ignored by the regime until Stalin's death. Similar techniques were devised in the late 1940s by the Rand mathematician G.B. Dantzig, in his simplex method. The practical application of linear programming had to await the development of the electronic computer and its ability (in some transportation problems, for example) to handle 3200 equations and 600,000 variables in sequence. Robert Dorfman has applied linear programming to the theory of the firm, and Dorfman, Samuelson and Solow used it in 1958 in an inter-industry model of the economy to allow for substitutability of supply and a criterion function that allows a choice of solutions for different objectives within a specified sector of final demand.

Criteria for decision-making under conditions of uncertainty were introduced by the Columbia mathematical statistician Abraham Wald in 1939. It specifies a "maximin" criterion in which one is guided by an expectation of the worst outcome. Leonid Hurwicz and L.J. Savage have developed other strategies, such as Savage's charmingly named "criteria of regret," whose subjective probabilities may cause one to increase or decrease a risk.

strategy that leads to the optimal or "best" solution; i.e. one which either maximizes the outcome or, depending upon the assessment of the risks and uncertainties, tries to minimize the losses. Rationality can be defined as judging, between two alternatives, which one is capable of yielding that preferred outcome.[36]

Intellectual technology makes its most ambitious claims in systems analysis. A system, in this sense, is any set of reciprocal relationships in which a variation in the character (or numerical value) of one of the elements will have determinate—and possibly measurable—consequences for all the others in the system. A human organism is a determinate system; a work-group whose members are engaged in specialized tasks for a common objective is a goal-setting system; a pattern of bombers and bases forms a variable system; the economy as a whole is a loose system.

The problem of the number of variables has been a crucial factor in the burgeoning fields of systems analysis for military or business decisions. In the design of an airplane, say, a single performance parameter (speed, or distance, or capacity) cannot be the measure of the intrinsic worth of a design, since these are all interrelated. Charles J. Hitch has used this to illustrate the problems of systems analysis for bombers. "Suppose we ruthlessly simplify aircraft characteristics to three—speed, range, altitude. What else do we have to consider in measuring the effectiveness of the bombers of 1965? At least the following: the formation they will use, their flight path to target, the base system, the target system, the bombs, and the enemy defenses. This may not sound like many parameters (in fact, it is far fewer than

---

Game theory has a long history but the decisive turn occurred in a 1928 paper of John von Neumann which provided a mathematical proof of a general minimax strategy for a two-person game. The 1944 book by von Neumann and Morgenstern, *Theory of Games and Economic Behavior* (Princeton), extended the theory of games with more than two persons and applied the theorem to economic behavior. The strategy proposed by von Neumann and Morgenstern—that of minimax, or the minimization of maximum loss—is defined as the rational course under conditions of uncertainty.

Games-and-decision theory was given an enormous boost during World War II, when its use was called "operations research." There was, for example, the "duel" between the airplane and the submarine. The former had to figure out the "best" search pattern for air patrol of a given area; the other had to find the best escape pattern when under surveillance. Mathematicians in the Anti-Submarine Warfare Operations Research Group, using a 1928 paper of von Neumann, figured out a tactical answer.

The game-theory idea has been widely applied—sometimes as metaphor, sometimes to specify numerical values for possible outcomes—in bargaining and conflict situations. See Thomas C. Schelling, *The Strategy of Conflict* (Cambridge, Mass., 1960).

[36] R. Duncan Luce and Howard Raiffa, *Games and Decisions* (New York, 1957). My discussion of rationality is adapted from the definition on p. 50; that of risk, certainty, and uncertainty from p. 13.

would be necessary) but if we go no higher than ten, and if we let each parameter take only two alternative values, we already have 2^{10} cases to calculate and compare (2^{10} 1000). If we let each parameter take four alternative values we have 4^{10} cases (4^{10} 1,000,000)." [37] The choice of a new kind of bomber system was thus not simply a question one could leave to the "old" air force generals. It had to be computed in terms of cost-effectiveness on the weighing of these many variables.

The crucial point is the argument of Jay Forrester and others, that the nature of complex systems is "counterintuitive." A complex system, they insist, involves the interaction of too many variables for the mind to hold in correct order simultaneously. Or, as Forrester also suggests, intuitive judgments respond to immediate cause-and-effect relations which are characteristic of simpler systems, whereas in complex systems the actual causes may be deeply hidden or remote in time or, more often, may lie in the very structure (i.e. pattern) of the system itself, which is not immediately recognizable. For this reason, one has to use algorithms, rather than intuitive judgments, in making decisions.[38]

The cause-and-effect deception is illustrated in Forrester's computer simulation model of how a central city first grows, then stagnates and decays. The model is composed of three major sectors, each containing three elements. The business sector has new, mature, and declining industries; the housing sector has premium, worker, and underemployed housing; and the population sector holds managerial-professionals, laborers, and underemployed. These nine elements are linked first with twenty-two modes of interaction (e.g. different kinds of migrations) and then with the outside world through multiplier functions. The whole, however, is a closed, dynamic system which models the life-history of the city. At first the vacant land fills up, different elements readjust, an equilibrium is attained, then stagnation develops as industries die and taxes increase. The sequence runs over a period of 250 years.

From this model, Forrester has drawn a number of policy conclusions. He argues that increased low-income housing in the central city has the negative effects of bringing in more low-income people, decreasing the tax base, and discouraging new industry. Job-training programs have the undesirable consequence of taking trained workers

[37] See Charles J. Hitch, "Analysis for Air Force Decisions," in *Analysis for Military Decisions: the Rand Lectures on Systems Analysis*, ed. E. S. Quade (Chicago, 1964). His illustration is conjectural. A more relevant but much more complicated illustration is Quade's case history, in the same volume, on the selection and use of strategic air bases.

[38] Jay W. Forrester, *Urban Dynamics* (Cambridge, Mass., 1969), pp. 10–11.

out of the city. None of this surprises Forrester because, as he points out, the direct approach is to say that if there is a need for more homes, build more housing, whereas the more difficult and complex approach would be to try to change the job patterns and population balances. In this sense, the policies which are wrong are the immediate cause-and-effect judgments, whereas the better policies would be the "counter-intuitive ones."

The decision-making logic which follows systems analysis is clear. In the case of Rand and the Air Force, it led to the installation of technocrats in the Defense Department, the creation of the Program Planning Budget Systems (PPBS), which was responsible in large measure for the realignment of strategic and tactical programs, and the imposition of cost-effectiveness criteria in the choice of weapons systems. In Forrester's illustration, it would lead to the substitution of economic rather than political judgments in the crucial policy decisions of city life.

The goal of the new intellectual technology is, neither more nor less, to realize a social alchemist's dream: the dream of "ordering" the mass society. In this society today, millions of persons daily make billions of decisions about what to buy, how many children to have, whom to vote for, what job to take, and the like. Any single choice may be as unpredictable as the quantum atom responding erratically to the measuring instrument, yet the aggregate patterns could be charted as neatly as the geometer triangulates the height and the horizon. If the computer is the tool, then decision theory is its master. Just as Pascal sought to play dice with God, and the physiocrats attempted to draw an economic grid that would array all exchanges among men, so the decision theorists seek their own *tableau entier* —the compass of rationality, the "best" solution to the choices perplexing men.

That this dream—as utopian, in its way, as the dreams of a perfect commonwealth—has faltered is laid, on the part of its believers, to the human resistance to rationality. But it may also be due to the very idea of rationality which guides the enterprise—the definition of function without a justification of reason. This, too, is a theme I explore in these essays.

The History of an Idea

No idea ever emerges full-blown from the head of Jove, or a secondary muse, and the five dimensions which coalesced in the concept of the post-industrial society (its intellectual antecedents are sketched in

Chapter 1) have had a long and complicated history. These may be of interest to the reader.

The starting point for me was a theme implicit in my book *The End of Ideology*—the role of technical decision-making in society. Technical decision-making, in fact, can be viewed as the diametric opposite of ideology: the one calculating and instrumental, the other emotional and expressive. The theme of *The End of Ideology* was the exhaustion of old political passions; the theories that developed into "The Post-Industrial Society" sought to explore technocratic thought in its relation to politics.[39]

The interest in the role of technical decision-making and the nature of the new technical elites was expressed in a section of a paper I wrote in the spring of 1955 for a conference of the Congress for Cultural Freedom, in Milan, "The Break-up of Family Capitalism." The argument was, briefly, that capitalism had to be understood not only as an economic system but also as a social system tied through the family enterprise, which provided the system's social cement by creating both a community of interest and a continuity of interest through the family dynasty. The rise of managerial capitalism, therefore, had to be seen not only as part of the professionalization of the corporation, but as a "crack" in that social cement. After describing the break-up of family capitalism in America (in part because of the intervention of investment banking), the essay argued that two "silent revolutions" in the relationship between power and social class were taking place: the decline of inherited power (but not necessarily of wealth) meant that the social upper class of wealthy businessmen and their descendants no longer constituted a ruling class; the rise of the managers meant that there was no continuity of power in the

---

[39] It may not be amiss at this point to clear up a misapprehension that derives, perhaps, from those who know a thesis only from the title of a book and never read its argument. In *The End of Ideology* I did not say that all ideological thinking was finished. In fact, I argued that the exhaustion of the old ideologies inevitably led to a hunger for new ones. So I wrote at the time:

Thus one finds, at the end of the fifties, a disconcerting caesura. In the West, among the intellectuals, the old passions are spent. The new generation, with no meaningful memory of these old debates, and no secure tradition to build upon, finds itself seeking new purposes within a framework of political society that has rejected, intellectually speaking, the old apocalyptic and chiliastic visions. In the search for a "cause," there is a deep, desperate, almost pathetic anger . . . a restless search for a new intellectual radicalism. . . . The irony . . . for those who seek "causes" is that the workers, whose grievances were once the driving energy for social change, are more satisfied with the society than the intellectuals. . . . The young intellectual is unhappy because the "middle way" is for the middle-aged, not for him; it is without passion and is deadening. . . . The emotional energies—and needs—exist, and the question of how one mobilizes these energies is a difficult one. *The End of Ideology* (Glencoe, Ill., 1960), pp. 374–375.

hands of a specific special group. The continuity of power was in the institutional position. Rule was largely in the hands of the technical-intellectual elite, including corporate managers, and the political directorate who occupied the institutional position at the time. Individuals and families pass; the institutional power remains.[40]

A second strand was a series of studies I did in *Fortune* magazine in the early 1950s on the changing composition of the labor force, with particular reference to the decline of the industrial worker relative to the non-production worker in the factory, and the technical and professional employee in the occupational system. Here the influence of Colin Clark's *Conditions of Economic Progress* was apparent. A more direct influence, however, was an article, unjustly neglected, by Paul Hatt and Nelson Foote, in the *American Economic Review* of May 1953, which not only refined Clark's "tertiary" category (setting forth quaternary and quinary sectors) but linked these sector changes to patterns of social mobility. In relating changes in sector distributions to occupational patterns, Hatt and Foote singled out as the most important development the trend toward professionalization of work and the crucial importance of the quinary or intellectual sector.

A third influence was Joseph Schumpeter's emphasis on technology as an open sea (ideas which were developed in the various studies by Arthur Cole, Fritz Redlich, and Hugh Aitken at the Harvard Center for Entrepreneurial Studies in the 1950s).[41] Schumpeter's argument, re-read in the early 1960s, turned my mind to the question of technological forecasting. Capitalist society had been able to regularize growth when it found the means to institutionalize the mechanisms of savings and credit which could then be transformed into investment. One of the problems of the post-industrial society would be the need to iron out the indeterminacy of the future by some means of "charting" the open sea. The various efforts at technological forecasting in the 1960s (summed up by Erich Jantsch in *Technological Forecasting in Perspective*, Paris, OECD, 1967) argued the feasibility of the proposition.

And finally, in this inventory of influences, I would single out an essay by the physicist and historian of science, Gerald Holton, in illuminating for me the significance of theoretical knowledge in its changing relation to technology, and the codification of theory as the basis for innovation not only in science, which Holton demonstrated, but in technology and economic policy as well. Holton's

---

[40] The essay appears as chap. 2 of *The End of Ideology*. The argument is expanded in the next chapter of that book "Is There a Ruling Class in America?"

[41] See Joseph Schumpeter, *Capitalism, Socialism and Democracy* (New York, 1942), p. 118.

paper is a masterly exposition of the development of science as a set of codifications and branchings of knowledge.[42]

I first presented many of these ideas, using the term "post-industrial society," in a series of lectures at the Salzburg Seminar in Austria in the summer of 1959. The emphasis then was largely on the shifts in sectors and the change from a goods-producing to a service society. In the spring of 1962, I wrote a long paper for a forum in Boston entitled, "The Post-Industrial Society: A Speculative View of the United States in 1985 and Beyond." Here the theme had shifted to the decisive role of "intellectual technology" and science in social change and as constituting the significant features of the post-industrial society. Though the paper was not published, it was widely circulated in academic and government circles.[43] A variant of this paper was presented in the winter of 1962–63 before the Seminar on Technology and Social Change at Columbia University, and printed in truncated form a year later in the papers of that seminar edited by Eli Ginzberg. The centrality of the university and of intellectual organizations as institutions of the post-industrial society was a theme I developed in my book, *The Reforming of General Education*, 1966 (and for that reason I have omitted a discussion of the university in this book). The emphasis on conceptual schemes arose in connection with my work as chairman of the Commission on the Year 2000, in developing frameworks for the analysis of the future of American society. A number of memoranda I wrote at that time dealt with the concepts of a national society, a communal society, and a post-industrial society as a means of understanding the changes in American society created by the revolutions in transportation and communication, the demand for group rights and the rise of non-market public decision-making, and the centrality of theoretical knowledge and research institutions. The idea of axial structures emerged from my efforts to deal more theoretically with problems of social change, and is the basis for a stock-taking of theories of social change that is underway for the Russell Sage Foundation.[44]

[42] See Gerald Holton, "Scientific Research and Scholarship: Notes Toward the Design of Proper Scales," *Daedalus* (Spring 1962).

[43] I did not want to publish the paper at that time because I felt that the idea was unfinished. Sections of the paper, which had been circulated at the forum in Boston, were printed without permission by the public-affairs magazine *Current* and by business publication *Dun's Review*, from which, inexplicably, it turned up as a citation in the volume published by the Czechoslovak Academy of Science on the scientific and technological revolutions which were creating a post-industrial society. The degree of circulation of the paper in government circles, particularly by the Office of Science and Technology, was noted in an article in *Science* (June 12, 1964), p. 1321.

[44] On these earlier versions, see *Technology and Social Change*, ed. Eli Ginzberg (New York, 1964), chap. 3; *The Reforming of General Education* (New York, 1966); *Toward the Year 2000*, ed. Daniel Bell, (Boston, 1968). Different aspects

The question has been asked why I have called this speculative concept the "post-industrial" society, rather than the knowledge society, or the information society, or the professional society, all of which are somewhat apt in describing salient aspects of what is emerging. At the time, I was undoubtedly influenced by Ralf Dahrendorf, who in his *Class and Class Conflict in an Industrial Society* (1959) had written of a "post-capitalist" society, and by W.W. Rostow, who in his *Stages of Economic Growth* had suggested a "post-maturity" economy.[45] The sense was present—and still is—that in Western society we are in the midst of a vast historical change in which old social relations (which were property-bound), existing power structures (centered on narrow elites), and bourgeois culture (based on notions of restraint and delayed gratification) are being rapidly eroded. The sources of the upheaval are scientific and technological. But they are also cultural, since culture, I believe, has achieved autonomy in Western society. What these new social forms will be like is not completely clear. Nor is it likely that they will achieve the unity of the economic system and character structure which was characteristic of capitalist civilization from the mid-eighteenth to the mid-twentieth century. The use of the hyphenated prefix *post-* indicates, thus, that sense of living in interstitial time.

---

of the nature of post-industrial society (incorporated in chaps. 5 and 6 of this volume) were presented at Syracuse in 1966, and at the seventy-fifth anniversary celebration of the California Institute of Technology. Those papers were included in the volumes *Scientific Progress and Human Values*, ed. Edward and Elizabeth Hutchings, Proceedings of the 75th Anniversary of the California Institute of Technology (New York, 1967); and *A Great Society*, ed. Bertram M. Gross, the Bentley Lectures at Syracuse University (New York, 1968). The "Notes on Post-Industrial Society" that appeared in *The Public Interest*, nos. 6 and 7 (Winter and Spring 1967) are abridgments of the Cal Tech and Syracuse papers.

[45] The question of intellectual priority always takes intriguing turns. In the notes and tables distributed to the Salzburg Seminar participants in 1959, I wrote: "The term post-industrial society—a term I have coined—denotes a society which has passed from a goods-producing stage to a service society." I was using "post-industrial" in contrast to Dahrendorf's "post-capitalist," since I was dealing with sector changes in the economy, while he was discussing authority relations in the factory. Subsequently, I discovered that David Riesman had used the phrase "post-industrial society" in an essay entitle "Leisure and Work in Post-Industrial Society," printed in the compendium *Mass Leisure* (Glencoe, Illinois, 1958). Riesman had used "post-industrial" to connote leisure, as opposed to work, but did not in any subsequent essay develop the theme or the phrase. I had quite likely read Riesman's essay at the time and the phrase undoubtedly came from him, though I have used it in a very different way. Ironically, I have recently discovered that the phrase occurs in the title of a book by Arthur J. Penty, *Old Worlds for New: A Study of the Post-Industrial State* (London, 1917). Penty, a well-known Guild Socialist of the time and a follower of William Morris and John Ruskin, denounced the "Leisure State" as collectivist and associated with the Servile State, and called for a return to the decentralized, small workshop artisan society, ennobling work, which he called the "post-industrial state"!

I have been using the idea of the post-industrial society for nearly a decade, and in recent years it has come into more common usage, though with shades of meaning that differ from mine. It may be useful to make note of some of these differences.

Herman Kahn and Anthony J. Wiener make the post-industrial society the pivot of their book *The Year 2000*,[46] but they give the term an almost entirely economic meaning (and in their descriptive table it is equated with a post-mass-consumption society). They depict a society so affluent (in which per-capita income is doubled every eighteen years) that work and efficiency have lost their meaning; and increase in the pace of change would produce an "acculturation" trauma or future shock. Kahn and Wiener almost assume a "post-economic" society in which there is no scarcity and the only problems are how to use abundance. Yet the concept "post-economic" has no logical meaning since it implies a social situation in which there are no costs for anything (for economics is the management of costs) or the resources are endless. Some five years ago there was euphoric talk of a triple revolution whereby "cybernation" would bring about a full cornucopia of goods. Now we hear of a devastated planet and the need for zero economic growth lest we completely pollute or hopelessly deplete all the resources of the world. Both of these apocalyptic visions, I think, are wrong.

Zbigniew Brzezinski thinks he has made an accurate "fix" on the future through his neologism the "technetronic" society: "a society that is shaped culturally, psychologically, socially, and economically by the impact of technology and electronics—particularly in the area of computers and communications." [47] But the formulation has two drawbacks. First, Brzezinski's neologism shifts the focus of change from theoretical knowledge to the practical applications of technology, yet in his exposition he refers to many kinds of knowledge, pure and applied, from molecular biology to economics, which are of critical importance in the new society. Second, the idea of the "shaping" nature or primacy of the "technetronic" factors implies a technological determinism which is belied by the subordination of economics to the political system. I do not believe that the social structure "determines" other aspects of the society but rather that changes in social structure (which are predictable) pose management problems or policy issues for the political system (whose responses

---

[46] The major discussion is in chap. IV, "Post-Industrial Society in the Standard World," esp. pp. 186–189. See Herman Kahn and Anthony J. Wiener, *The Year 2000* (New York, 1967). The work appeared originally as vols. II and IIa of the Working Papers of the Commission on the Year 2000 (privately printed, 1966).

[47] Zbigniew Brzezinski, *Between Two Ages: America's Role in the Technetronic Era* (New York, 1970), p. 9.

are much less predictable). And as I have indicated, I believe that the present-day autonomy of culture brings about changes in life styles and values which do not derive from changes in the social structure itself.

Another group of writers, such as Kenneth Keniston and Paul Goodman, have used the term post-industrial society to denote a major shift in values for a significant section of youth, among whom, as Keniston writes, there is "the quest for a world beyond materialism, the rejection of careerism and vocationalism." Goodman believes there is a turn toward "a personal subsistence economy," independent of the excesses of a machine civilization.[48] Whether there is any staying power to these impulses remains to be seen.[49] I think there is a radical disjunction between the social structure and the culture, but its sources lie deep in the anti-bourgeois character of a modernist movement and work themselves out in a much more differentiated way than simply the impulsiveness of a youth movement.[50]

Finally, the theme of the post-industrial society has appeared in the writings of a number of European neo-Marxist theoreticians such as Radovan Richta, Serge Mallet, Andre Gorz, Alain Touraine, and Roger Garaudy, who have emphasized the decisive role of science and technology in transforming the industrial structure and thus calling into question the "ordained" role of the working class as the historic agent of change in society. Their work has spawned a variety of theories that, in one way or another, emphasize the fusion of science and technical personnel with the "advanced" working class, or propose the theory of a "new working class" made up principally of technically skilled personnel.[51] While all these writers have sensed the urgency of the structural changes in the society, they become tediously theological in their debates about the "old" and "new" work-

---

[48] See Keniston's *Youth and Dissent* (New York, 1971), especially the chapter "You Have to Grow up in Scarsdale." For Goodman, see the introduction to Helen and Scott Nearing, *Living the Good Life* (New York, Shocken paper edition, 1971). Goodman is close to Penty's view of the artisan guild society. Recently a group of young political scientists have argued that "important groups among the populations of Western societies have passed beyond [subsistence] stages," and they use the concept of post-industrial society to denote a situation in which groups of persons "no longer have a direct relationship to the imperatives of economic security." See, for example, Ronald Inglehart, "The Silent Revolution in Europe: Intergenerational Change in Post-Industrial Societies," *American Political Science Review* (December 1971), pp. 991–1017.

[49] For evidence of the growing conservatism of each radical generation as the cohort gets older, see S.M. Lipset and E.C. Ladd, Jr., "College Generations—from the 1930s to the 1960s," *The Public Interest*, no. 25 (Fall 1971).

[50] This is a theme implicit in Lionel Trilling's conception of the "adversary culture." See Trilling, *Beyond Culture* (New York, 1965).

[51] The theory of Radovan Richta and his group in the Czechoslovak Academy of Science is discussed in chap. 1; that of Gorz and Mallet in chap. 2.

ing class, for their aim is not to illuminate actual social changes in the society but to "save" the Marxist concept of social change and the Leninist idea of the agency of change. For a real ideological crisis does exist. If there is an erosion of the working class in post-industrial society, how can Marx's vision of social change be maintained? And if the working class will not inherit the world (and is in fact shrinking), how does one justify the "dictatorship of the proletariat" and the role of the Communist Party as the "vanguard" of the working class? One cannot save the theory by insisting that almost everybody is a member of the "new working class." [52]

The Plan of the Book

The six chapters of this book are interrelated, as I have indicated, by an exploration of diverse themes that rotate, so to speak, like a pinwheel, rather than give a linear exposition of an argument.

Chapter 1 is a discussion of theories of social development in advanced industrial society. The starting point, necessarily, is Marx, but in two rather unfamiliar ways. The conventional view of the future of capitalism is derived from Volume I of *Capital*, in which Marx predicted the centralization of enterprise, the polarization of society into two classes, and the inevitable economic crisis of the capitalist system. But much less well known is a highly different and fascinating scheme of social development that Marx laid out piecemeal in Volume III; there he predicted the separation of ownership from control in the management of enterprises; the rise of a white-collar administrative class which would become disproportionate to the industrial working class; and new modes of the availability of capital through the centralization of the banking system. The development of capitalism has in fact followed Marx's second schema, not his first. The difference between the two is that in Volume I Marx was positing a "pure" theory of capitalism, as a simplified model, divorced from the complications of an existing reality; in Volume III he was dealing with actual empirical tendencies.

The second way in which Marx becomes relevant is that in his view of the economic substructure of society, the mode of production was divided into two parts—the social relations of production

---

[52] It is surely too simple-minded to insist that since there are fewer and fewer independent entrepreneurs or self-employed professionals, *all* wage and salaried workers are members of the working class. And since the majority of workers are now on salary, rather than piece- or time-work, how can one call for a "dictatorship of the salariat?" And over whom?

(property) and the forces or techniques of production (machinery). In the development of capitalism, he thought, the social relations would become most central, leading to a highly polarized class struggle. But that polarization has not taken place, and what has become most important is the emphasis on technique and industrialization. The theory of industrial society, which has been advanced most notably by Raymond Aron, takes off from the second of these two aspects of Marx's theory of the mode of production.

The theories of social development in the West—those of Werner Sombart, Max Weber, Emil Lederer, Joseph Schumpeter, Raymond Aron—are, as I try to show, "dialogues" with these different schemata of Marx. The essential point of difference comes in the theory of bureaucracy, of which Max Weber has been the master. For Weber, socialism and capitalism were not contradictory systems but, from the imperatives of functional rationality, two variants of the same social type, bureaucracy. Industrial development in the Soviet Union has followed Marx's dimension of "technique," but along the lines of bureaucratic development predicted by Weber. The confrontation with Bureaucracy, and the new class it spawns, was the problem for Trotsky in confronting the fruits of the Russian Revolution.

Today both systems, Western capitalist and Soviet socialist, face the consequences of the scientific and technological changes which are revolutionizing social structure. Communist theorists have shied away from the implications of these changes, except for the remarkable study of the Czechoslovak Academy of Science, under Radovan Richta, which emerged during the Prague "thaw." Contrary to most Communist theorists, Richta acknowledges the possibility of "interest" if not "class" conflicts between the new scientific-professional stratum and the working class in socialist society.

In accepting the model of industrial society as the common framework of Western social development, the first chapter sketches the major differences between pre-industrial, industrial, and post-industrial society as a basis for comparative analysis of social structures. The concluding section provides an overall view of the concept of post-industrial society which is developed in the subsequent chapters.

Chapter 2 explores, within the framework of the United States, two of the five major dimensions of the post-industrial society: the change from a goods-producing to a service economy, and the changes in the occupational slopes, wherein the professional and technical class emerges as the predominant occupational group in the post-industrial society. Within that context, a number of themes are explored, dealing largely with the future of the working class: the theories of the "new working class"; the historical strength of trade unionism as a blue-collar force and its increasing difficulties in achieving future goals, such as control of work, within the straits of a service economy and foreign competition.

The dimensions of knowledge and technology are the themes of Chapter 3. The initial problem, which arises from the changing nature of the two, has to do with the pace of change. There are multiple confusions about this idea because few people have ever been able to define exactly *what* is changing. In terms of technology, probably more substantial change was introduced in the lives of individuals in the nineteenth century by the railroad, steamship, electricity, and telephone, and in the early twentieth century by radio, automobiles, motion pictures, aviation, and high-speed vertical elevators, than by television and computers, the main technological items introduced in the last twenty-five years. The real effect of the "pace of change" has come not from the various technological items, but from a tightened social framework, which has brought isolated regions and classes of a nation into society, and has multiplied the degree of contact and interaction between persons through the revolutions in communication and transportation. But along with a greater degree of interdependence has come a change of scale—the spread of cities, the growth of organizational size, the widening of the political arena—which has made individuals feel more helpless within larger entities, and which has broadened the span of control over the activities of any organization from a center. The major social revolution of the latter half of the twentieth century is the attempt to master "scale" by new technological devices, whether it be "real-time" computer information or new kinds of quantitative programming.

Within this context, Chapter 3 seeks to define "knowledge": to analyze the nature of its exponential growth; to specify the actual ways in which knowledge develops through branching; and to define technology, measure its growth, and specify the modes of technological forecasting. The second half of the chapter is a detailed statistical effort to sketch the structure of the knowledge class—the distributions of professional occupations and the major trends among them —and the allocation of resources for a technical society, which is the distribution of money for research and development.

The private corporation in capitalist society (or the enterprise in socialist economies) is bound to remain the major organizational mode of society to the end of the century. Given the logic of the firm in both cases—the logic of functional rationality—it becomes less meaningful to talk about capitalism or socialism than about the "economizing" and "sociologizing" modes which are present in both systems. Each of these is a "logic" responsive to a different end. The "economizing" mode is oriented to functional efficiency and the management of things (and men treated as things). The sociologizing mode establishes broader social criteria, but it necessarily involves the loss of efficiency, the reduction of production, and other costs that follow the introduction of non-economic values. Within the context of the United States, Chapter 4 scrutinizes the logic of these two modes and argues that the balance between the two is a primary question for post-industrial society.

A post-industrial society is one in which there will necessarily be more conscious decision-making. The chief problem is the stipulation of social choices that accurately reflect the "ordering" of preferences by individuals. The Condorect paradox, as developed by Kenneth J. Arrow, argues that theoretically no such social-welfare choice can be created. What remains therefore is bargaining between groups. But in order to bargain, one has to know social benefits and social costs. At present the society has no such mechanisms to do social accounting and to verify social goals. Chapter 5 deals with the adequacy of our concepts and tools for social planning.

Finally, the significance of the post-industrial society is that:

1. It strengthens the role of science and cognitive values as a basic institutional necessity of the society;
2. By making decisions more technical, it brings the scientist or economist more directly into the political process;
3. By deepening existing tendencies toward the bureaucratization of intellectual work, it creates a set of strains for the traditional definitions of intellectual pursuits and values;
4. By creating and extending a technical intelligentsia, it raises crucial questions about the relation of the technical to the literary intellectual.

In sum, the emergence of a new kind of society brings into question the distributions of wealth, power, and status that are central to any society. Now wealth, power, and status are *not* dimensions *of* class, but values sought or gained *by* classes. Classes are created in a society by the fundamental axes of stratification. The two major axes of stratification in Western society are property and knowledge. Alongside them is a political system that increasingly manages the two and gives rise to temporary elites (temporary in that there is no necessary continuity of power of a specific social group through office, as there is continuity of a family or class through property and the differential advantage of belonging to a meritocracy).

Chapter 6 thus deals primarily with the relationship between technocratic and political decision-making. Against the dreams of the early technocrats such as Saint-Simon, who hoped that the savants would rule, it becomes clear that political decisions are the central ones in the society and that the relationship of knowledge to power is essentially a subservient one.

Any new emerging system creates hostility among those who feel threatened by it. The chief problem of the emerging post-industrial society is the conflict generated by a meritocracy principle which is central to the allocation of position in the knowledge society. Thus the tension between populism and elitism, which is already apparent, becomes a political issue in communities. A second set of problems arises from the historic independence of the scientific community and the contradictory problems generated by its tradition of autonomy, its increasing dependence on government for research funds, and the service it is called upon to perform. These questions come to a head in the university, which is the primary institution of the post-industrial society. And finally, the deepest tensions are those between the culture, whose axial direction is anti-institutional and antinomian, and the social structure which is ruled by an economizing and technocratic mode. It is this tension which is ultimately the most fundamental probem of the post-industrial society. These questions are sketched in the Coda.

What I am arguing in this book is that the major source of structural change in society—the change in the modes of innovation in the relation of science to technology and in public policy—is the change in the character of knowledge: the exponential growth and branching of science, the rise of a new intellectual technology, the creation of systematic research through R & D budgets, and, as the calyx of all this, the codification of theoretical knowledge.

The attitude to scientific knowledge defines the value system of a society. The medieval conception of natural science was that of "forbidden knowledge." The divines feared that "knowledge puffeth up" and that it "hath somewhat of the serpent." During the Christian centuries, "nature," in quite a special sense, had been consigned to the Satanic order. The Faustus legend used by Marlowe testified to the fascinated dread of natural science for the Middle Ages.[53] By the turn of the seventeenth century, the belief in man's expansive power had begun to replace the earlier vision of fear. In Francis Bacon's *New Atlantis*, which he intended to replace the mythical Atlantis of Plato's *Timaeus*, the King is no longer the philosopher but the research scientist. And on the frangible island of Bensalem, the most important building, Salomon's House, is not a church but a research institute, "the noblest foundation . . . that ever was upon the earth and the

---

[53] See Basil Willey, *The Seventeenth Century Background* (London, 1949), chap. II, "Bacon and the Rehabilitation of Nature," esp. p. 31.

lantern of this kingdom." Salomon's House, or the College of the Six Days Works, is a state institution created "for the production of great and marvelous works for the benefit of man." As one of the "Fathers" of Salomon's House describes its purpose: "The end of our foundation is the knowledge of causes, and secret motion of things; and the enlarging of the bounds of human empire, to the effecting of all things possible." [54]

Until now, this boundless ambition has ruled the quest for knowledge. At first man sought to conquer the natural order; and in this he has almost succeeded. In the last hundred years he has sought to substitute a technical order for the natural order; and in this he is well on his way.[55] The post-industrial society, at root, is a recasting of this technical quest in even more powerful form. But now there is a question whether man will or will not want to proceed. This is the openness of history.

---

[54] Francis Bacon, *New Atlantis*, in *Famous Utopias*, ed. Charles M. Andrews (New York, n.d.), p. 263.

[55] These are themes that I explore on the historical and philosophical levels in my essay, "Technology, Nature and Society: The Vicissitudes of Three World-Views and the Confusion of Realms," given as the Frank Nelson Doubleday Lecture at the Smithsonian National Museum of History and Technology in December 1972, and to be published by Doubleday & Co. in a collected volume of those lectures.

CHAPTER
I

---

*From Industrial to
Post-Industrial Society:
Theories of Social
Development*

THE sociologist is always tempted to play the prophet—and if not the prophet, the seer. From 1850 to 1860, as he sat each morning in the reading room of the British Museum, Marx thought he heard in every faint sound of riot or each creaking downturn of the business cycle the rumblings of revolution and the abrupt transformation of society. In this respect, Marx's anxious awaiting was squarely in the center of the preoccupation that attended the rise of sociology since its beginnings in the nineteenth century: namely, the scanning of the historical skies for the portents of "the new class" which would overturn the existing social order. Henri de Saint-Simon, the master of August Comte and one of the fathers of modern sociology, initiated this quest in 1816 when he began publishing, irregularly, the periodical *L'Industrie* (popularizing there the word *industrialism*) and describing in it the society of the future. Past society, said Saint-Simon, had been military society in which the chief figures were priests, warriors, and feudal lords—the "parasites" and consumers of wealth. The new industrial society, he said, would be ruled by the producers—the engineers and the entrepreneurs, the "coming men" of the times.

Different times, different men, different images. Writing in 1840, Tocqueville predicted the possible outcome of the new mass democracy he saw emerging in modern society:

A multitude of similar and equal individuals are working to procure themselves petty and vulgar satisfactions. . . . Above these men there rears a monstrous tutelary power [the state] which provides for their security, foresees and supplies their necessities, directs their industry, regulates the descent of property and subdivides their inheritances: what remains, but to spare them all the care of thinking and the trouble of living.[1]

---

[1] Alexis de Tocqueville, *Democracy in America* (New York, 1966), part IV, chap. 6, "The Sort of Despotisms that Democratic Nations Have to Fear," pp. 666–667. I am indebted to J. P. Mayer's *Alexis de Tocqueville: A Biographical Study in Political Science* (New York, 1960), pp. 121–122, for this and the following citation, but in both instances, in checking the original sources, I have extended his quotations.

Thirty years later, the historian Jacob Burckhardt, observing the transformation of German society, wrote in a letter to a friend:

the military machine . . . is bound to become the model of existence . . . the military state will have to turn "industrialist." These agglomerations of men in the great factories [will live under] a degree of definite and superintended poverty where everyone would wear the uniform and where the day would begin and end with the drum-roll; logically this is what should come.[2]

Fifty years after Burckhardt, Thorstein Veblen returned to the Saint-Simonian theme. Revolution in the twentieth century, he said, could only be an "industrial overturn," and *if* a revolution came in the United States—the *if* is italicized for as a practiced skeptic he was highly dubious of that prospect—it would not be led by a minority political party, as in Soviet Russia, which was a loose-knit and backward industrial region, nor by the trade unions, who were only "votaries of the dinner pail," but by the production engineers who were the indispensable "General Staff" of the industrial system. "These main lines of revolutionary strategy," he wrote in *The Engineers and the Price System*, "are lines of technical organization and industrial management; essential lines of industrial engineering; such as will fit the organization to take care of the highly technical industrial system that constitutes the indispensable material foundations of any modern civilized community." [3]

What is extraordinary about these efforts to sketch the contours of the new age is the glimpse of truth each contains but also the shadow of complexity which falsifies the prediction. As Burckhardt added wryly, immediately after his own prediction of what "logically" should come: "I know enough history to know that things do not always work out logically." [4]

Our time, too, has not lacked for sociological seers. The habits of the past have been compelling, and even though previous experience warns of caution, the sense of social change is so vivid and the changes in social structure so dramatic that each sociological theorist of any pretension carries a distinctive conceptual map of the social terrain and a set of signposts to the society ahead.

For the new states or underdeveloped countries the prognosis has been standard: they will become industrialized, modernized, and westernized, even though it is less clear that they will be communist or

---

[2] *The Letters of Jacob Burckhardt*, ed. Alexander Dru (London, 1955). Letter to Von Preen, April 26, 1872, pp. 151–152.

[3] Thorstein Veblen, *The Engineers and the Price System*, Harbinger edition with an introduction by Daniel Bell (New York, 1963), p. 4.

[4] Op. cit., p. 152.

socialist, socially transformed by elites (military or political) or revitalized by masses. One skeptic, Clifford Geertz, has remarked that the category "transitional society" may become a permanent category in the social sciences. Yet for the *tiers monde*, though development may be long and arduous, there is a sense of a turning point in history and the beginning of a new age.

For the advanced industrial societies however the picture is more clouded. Every seer has a sense that an age is ending (how many "crises," oh Lord, have we experienced), but there is little agreement as to what may be ahead. This common apocalyptic note of a "sense of an ending" is, as Frank Kermode has noted, the distinctive literary image of the time.

In sociology this sense of marking time, of living in an interregnum, is nowhere symbolized so sharply as in the widespread use of the word *post*—a paradox since it is a prefix denoting posteriority —to define, as a combined form, the age in which we are moving. —For Ralf Dahrendorf, we are living in a *post-capitalist society*. What counts in industrial society, he says, is not ownership but authority, and with the diminution in the legal ownership of the means of production, there is, in consequence, a break between the economic and the political orders. The old industrial conflicts of bourgeoisie and proletariat, he says, are "institutionally isolated" and there is little carry-over from the job to other areas of life. ("If it is correct that with industry itself industrial conflict has been institutionally isolated in post-capitalist societies, it follows that his occupational role has lost its comprehensive moulding force for the social personality of the industrial worker, and that it determines only a limited sector of his social behavior.") Authority is autonomous in each realm:

. . . in post-capitalist society the ruling and the subjected classes of industry and of the political society are no longer identical; that there are, in other words, in principle two independent conflict fronts. Outside the enterprise, the manager may be a mere citizen, the worker a member of parliament; their industrial class position no longer determines their authority position in the political society.

It is post-capitalist society, in short, because relation to the instruments of production no longer decides dominance or power or privilege in society. Economic or property relations, while still generating their own conflicts, no longer carry over or become generalized as the major center of conflict in society. Who, then, constitutes the ruling class of post-capitalist society? "We have to look for the ruling class," writes Dahrendorf, "in those positions that constitute the head of bureaucratic hierarchies, among those persons who are authorized to give directives to the administrative staff." But while there may be managerial or capitalist elites, real power is in the hands of the governmental elites. ("It is necessary to think of this elite in the first place, and never to lose sight of its paramount position in the authority structure of the state.") Conflicts occur primarily in the political arena; changes are introduced or prevented by the government elites; and when managerial or capitalist elites seek to exercise power outside their domains, they do so by seeking to influence governmental elites.

Who are the governmental elites? The administrative staff of the state, the government ministers in the cabinet, the judges. But since governments represent interests, there are "groups behind" the elites.

In abstract, therefore, the ruling political class of post-capitalist society consists of the administrative staff of the state, the governmental elites at its head and those interested parties which are represented by the governmental elite. This insistence on governmental elites as the core of the ruling class must be truly shocking to anybody thinking in Marxian terms, or, more generally, in terms of the traditional concept of class . . .

As Dahrendorf writes, "if it sounds strange . . . this strangeness is due to the strangeness of reality." [5]

"The reality is," according to George Lichtheim, that "the contemporary industrial society is increasingly 'postbourgeois', the nineteenth-century class structure tending to dissolve along with the institution of private entrepreneurship on which it is pivoted. Hence the uncertainty that afflicts so much of current political thinking." The reason is, says Lichtheim, that social welfare legislation and income redistribution "are aspects of a socialization process" that circumscribe the operation of a market economy, while at the same time the spread of public ownership creates a new balance between the public and private sectors. "Least of all does it follow that industrial society retains a 'bourgeois' complexion. There cannot be a bourgeoisie without a proletariat, and if the one is fading out, so is the other, and for the same reason: Modern industrial society does not require either for its operation." [6]

For Amitai Etzioni, we are in a "post-modern" era. He opens his book, *The Active Society*, with the portentous pronouncement, "The modern period ended with the radical transformation of the technologies of communication, knowledge and energy that followed the Second World War." But unhappily nowhere else, literally, in the 670 pages of text, notes, and glossary that follow, is there a dis-

---

[5] Ralf Dahrendorf, *Class and Class Conflict in an Industrial Society* (Stanford, 1959). See chaps. VII and VIII, "Classes in Post-Capitalist Society (I) Industrial Conflict, (II) Political Conflict." Quotations above are from pp. 272, 275–276, 301–303.

[6] George Lichtheim, *The New Europe: Today and Tomorrow* (New York, 1963), p. 194.

cussion of the technologies of communication, knowledge, and energy, or a specification of what, exactly, "post-modern societies" are like. In the end we have to return to the intention, at the opening lines of the preface:

A central characteristic of the modern period has been continued increase in the efficacy of the technology of production which poses a growing challenge to the primacy of the values they are supposed to serve. The post-modern period, the onset of which may be set at 1945, will witness either a greater threat to the status of these values by the surging technologies or a reassertion of their normative priorty. Which alternative prevails will determine whether society is to be the servant or the master of the instrument it creates.

So, the post-modern, period or society, is not a definition, but only a question.[7]

For Kenneth Boulding, we are at the start of the *post-civilized* era. Since civilization, as Mr. Boulding points out, has had a favorable connotation and post-civilization may strike one as unfavorable, one might use the word "technological or the term developed society." But the distinctive characteristic of this new period for Mr. Boulding is the consciousness of, using Teilhard's phrase, the *noösphere*, the sphere of knowledge, as the premise for the social direction of society and the achievement of social, as against individual, self-consciousness. Thus, the thrust of Boulding's term is to emphasize the possibility of the guidance of society in the new, emerging period of social or mental evolution rather than the adaptive biological or social evolution of the past.[8]

In the epilogue to the 1969 (Vintage) edition of his *British Politics in the Collectivist Age*, Sam Beer talks of a "post-collectivist" politics. He feels that the collectivist model of British politics which was party-divided, functionalist, and oriented to the welfare state may be coming to a close. The post-collectivist tendency is a "reaction to the increasing scale and intensity of rationalization in both government and society." And even though it would not create a basic rupture in the political mode, it could form a readjustment of the polity in England (p. 426).

And so it goes. It used to be that the great literary modifier was the word *beyond:* beyond tragedy, beyond culture, beyond society. But we seem to have exhausted the beyond, and today the sociological modifier is *post:* a theologian, Sydney E. Ahlstrom, has described the religious scene in the United States in the 1960s as "post-Puritan,

---

[7] Amitai Etzioni, *The Active Society* (New York, 1968), p. vii.

[8] Kenneth Boulding, *The Meaning of the Twentieth Century: The Great Transition* (New York, 1964).

post-Protestant, and post-Christian." [9] Lewis Feuer has subtitled his book on *Marx and the Intellectuals* as a "set of post-ideological essays." John Leonard in *The New York Times* has talked of the "post-Literature Culture" as being heralded by the McLuhanite age.[10] For S. N. Eisenstadt, the sociologist, the new states have become "post-traditional" societies for though they are no longer bound by the norms of the past and they seek consciously to change, they live in a suspended world with little approximation to the modern societies of the West.[11] Earlier, Roderick Seidenberg, foretelling the victory of rationalism, had described a *post-historic man* in which we move from prehistory, in which instinct dominated intelligence, through the transitional period of history into post-history, in which intelligence dominates instinct,[12] just as in *Zarathustra*, man— suspended on the rope above the abyss—is the transition between the animal of the past and the superman to come. And finally in this inventory (only by virtue of humility) we have the theme of the *post-industrial society*.[13]

The Two Schemata of Marx

We are all *epigones* of the great masters.[14] Edward Shils was quite right when he commented recently:

[9] Sydney Ahlstrom, "The Radical Turn in Theology and Ethics," *The Annals* (January 1970).

[10] *The New York Times*, November 26, 1970.

[11] This was the theme of a *Daedalus*-sponsored seminar in Paris, June 9–10, 1970. Eric Hobsbawm has written of "post-tribal societies," arguing that social classes only begin at such stages of social development. See his essay, "Social History and the History of Society," in *Daedalus* issue entitled *Historical Studies Today* (Winter 1971), p. 36.

[12] Roderick Seidenberg, *Post-Historic Man* (Chapel Hill, N.C., 1950).

[13] Tom Burns, of Edinburgh, though scoffing at the phrase "post-industrial" society, talks of the "post-market society and post-organization society phase of industrialism" in "The Rationale of the Corporate System" (p. 50), unpublished ms. for the Harvard Program on Technology and Society, 1970. To this litany we should add "post-economic," a possibility envisaged by Herman Kahn of a time when incomes will be so high that cost would be of little practical matter in any decision. (See his briefing paper, "Forces for Change in the Final Third of the Twentieth Century," Hudson Institute, 1970.) In the logic of the situation, some radicals (vide the discussions in *Social Policy*, vol. I, nos. 1, 4) have talked of a "post-scarcity" society, while Gideon Sjoberg and his collaborators have written of a "post-welfare" society. And in his new book *Freedom in a Rocking Boat*, Sir Geoffrey Vickers talks of a "post-liberal era." In all, this is a catalogue of twenty different uses of the word *post* to denote some new phase in our society.

[14] It would be unfair and presumptuous to assume that all the *epigones* of Saint-Simon or Marx have gathered under the banner of the word *post*. There have been more daring adventurers who have tried to define in more forthright fashion the character of the new age.

One of the great difficulties is that we cannot imagine anything beyond variations on the theme set by the great figures of nineteenth and twentieth century sociology. The fact that the conception of "post-industrial society" is an amalgam of what St. Simon, Comte, de Tocqueville and Weber furnished to our imagination is evidence that we are confined to an ambiguously defined circle which is more impermeable than it ought to be.[15]

The one figure Professor Shils left out, strangely, is Marx, perhaps because we have all become post-Marxists. St. Simon described stages of history in alternating spirals of organic and critical societies (which foreshadowed Sorokin's ideational and sensate mentalities), and Comte saw a rationalist progression of society from theological to metaphysical to a scientific stage. Both are insightful, if neglected theories, yet the source of our interest in social change is necessarily Marx. Marx rooted social change in social structure or institutions (rather than mentalities, even though he treated ideas too cavalierly or as epiphenomena), and he charted social change in determinate fashion seeking to lay bare the sources of that determinism in the social relations between men. Few of us would claim that the social changes we forecast arise out of the blue, or come solely from men's imaginative design. Even when they emerge first as ideas they have to be embodied in institutions; and to chart social change is to chart the changes in the character of axial institutions. If, then, there is some

---

Thus Ralf Dahrendorf, in a later foray, describes a "service class society." "Sociologists have given many names to this new society: post-capitalist and managerial, leisure-time and consumer's, advanced industrial and mass society are but a small selection. It cannot do much harm therefore to add one further name and claim that Europe is well under way toward a service class society." The service class, for Dahrendorf, is essentially the white-collar and particularly the professional and technical stratum in the society. (See "Recent Changes in Class Structure," *A New Europe?* ed. Stephen R. Graubard [Boston, 1964], esp. p. 328.)

Zbigniew Brzezinski writes of a "technetronic" age in which "technology and especially electronics—hence my neologism "technetronic"—are increasingly becoming the determinants of social change, altering the mores, the social structure, the values, and the global outlook of society." Brzezinski writes that he prefers the neologism "technetronic" to "post-industrial" because "it conveys more directly the character of the principal impulses for change in our time." (See *Between Two Ages: America's Role in the Technetronic Era* [New York, 1970], esp. p. 9.)

Jacques Ellul has called his vision the Technological Society, Marshall McLuhan the Global Village, and on a more trivial level Bertram Gross talks of the "mobiletic revolution," while popularizer Alvin Toffler, after hovering over "transindustrial" and "post-economic," settles on the term "super-industrial society." It is intended to mean, he writes, "a complex, fast-paced society dependent upon extremely advanced technology and a post-materialist value system." (*Future Shock* [New York, 1970], p. 434.) With Toffler it would seem that all the permutations and combinations of the "post" idea have been exhausted.

[15] Edward Shils, "Tradition, Ecology and Institutions in the History of Sociology," in *Daedalus* (Fall 1970), issue on *The Making of Modern Science: Biographical Studies*, p. 825.

pattern of determinism that one has to identify, one has to come to terms, again, with the ghost of Marx. If we seek to chart the stages of development of capitalist industrial society, we have to begin with the predictions of Marx. But in so doing we are confronted with a conundrum, for in this view of the future, there is not, as I shall try to show, one but two schemata, and it is to these two divergent schemata that most of the theories of social development are responsive.

In *Capital* (especially vol. I, chap. XXXIII, on the "Historical Tendency of Capitalistic Accumulation") Marx sketched his basic scheme of social development: the structure of the new society, he said, namely, the socialized organization of production, lay fully developed within the womb of the old; this new structure reflected the increasing contradiction between the socialized character of production and the "fetter upon the mode of production" created by the "monopoly of capital"; society was becoming polarized in two classes, a diminishing number of magnates of capital and a steadily growing working class; the character of the new society becomes incompatible with the capitalist form of the old, and finally, the "integument is burst asunder," and a socialist world has arrived. The metaphor is biological, the process is immanent, the trajectory of development unilateral.

And yet, of course, it did not turn out that way. Whatever the extraordinary power of Marxism as a social appeal, it was in backward countries, not advanced capitalist countries, that Marxist movements have been most successful. More importantly, the social structures of advanced capitalist societies have evolved in a fashion far different from that envisaged in the sketch in volume I. And yet Marx, in the later years, particularly in sections expressed in volume III of *Capital* did glimpse accurately the shape of things that did come. It is this set of differences between *two different schemes* of Marx which is the true, starting point for the analysis of social developments in capitalist and advanced industrial societies of the West.

Let us begin with *schema one*. Marx's analysis of the capitalist process rests, initially, on two spheres of production: large-scale manufacture and agriculture.[16] With the expansion of the capitalist system, however, the distinction between land and capital, and between the landowning and capitalist classes, disappears. The fusion of these two classes leaves in society two main classes: the capitalists, owners of the means of production, and the proletariat. Our assumption, says

---

[16] I follow here the argument laid out by Abram L. Harris in "Pure Capitalism and the Disappearance of the Middle Class," *Journal of Political Economy* (June 1939), with further elaboration from the passages in Marx he has identified. All page references to *Capital* indicated in the text are from the Kerr Edition, Chicago, 1906.

Marx, is the continuing spread of capitalist production to absorb the entire society; accordingly there are only these two classes (vol. II, p. 401). All *dritte personen* are excluded. As Abram Harris writes:

Dritte personen is a term which Marx used to designate two different but more or less related categories of people. The first category includes such independent producers as small farmers, independent handicraftsmen and all other hangovers of an earlier mode of production who function outside the capitalist process proper. The second category includes two groups (1) priests, shopkeepers, lawyers, state officials, professors, artists, teachers, physicians and soldiers who exist on the basis of the capitalist process but who do not participate in it; and (2) merchants, middle-men, speculators, commercial laborers (white-collar employees), managers, foremen, and all other officials who "command in the name of capital." [17]

Why should these *dritte personen* be excluded? For Marx, the independent farmers and artisans are outside the capitalist process, though they assume the character of the process. (As owners of their means of production they are capitalists; as owners of their labor power they are wage earners.) In any event, with the development of capitalism, as a class they will tend to disappear. The artists, physicians, professors, et al., are "unproductive workers." To be productive labor must replace the old value advanced by the capitalist by new value in the form of surplus product and new capital. A cook or a waiter working in a hotel is "productive" because he has created profit for the hotel owner; as house servants they are unproductive even when paid a wage. Unproductive labor receives its income from the expenditures of the two dominant classes involved in production. If the worker-capitalist relation were to spread to medical service, amusement and education, the physician, artist and professor would then be wage earners and "productive."

In all this, Marx assumed a model of "pure capitalism." [18] As Marx wrote:

---

[17] Ibid., pp. 339–340.

[18] The first writer to explicate this model of "pure capitalism," was Henryk Grossmann in his *Das Akkumulations und Zusammensbruchsgesetz des kapitalistichen Systems* (*The Law of Accumulation and Collapse of the Capitalist System*) (Leipzig, 1929). Paul Sweezey makes the same assumption about the use of abstraction in his *The Theory of Capitalist Development* (Oxford, 1946).

As Marx wrote in the author's preface to volume I of *Capital*:

. . . The value-form whose fully developed shape is the money-form, is very elementary and simple. Nevertheless, the human mind has for more than 2000 years sought in vain to get to the bottom of it, whilst on the other hand, to the successful analysis of much more composite and complex forms, there has been at least an approximation. Why? Because the body, as an organic whole, is more easy of study than are the cells of that body. In the analysis of economic forms, moreover, neither microscopes nor chemical reagents are of use. *The force of abstraction must replace both.* But in bourgeois society the commodity-form of the product of labor—or the value-form of the commodity—is the economic cell-form. To

Such a general rate of surplus-value—as a tendency, like all other economic laws—has been assumed by us for the sake of theoretical simplification. But in reality it is an actual premise of the capitalist mode of production, although it is more or less obstructed by practical fictions . . . in theory it is the custom to assume that the laws of capitalist production evolve in their pure form. In reality, however, there is always but an approximation (vol. III, p. 206).

This assumption of a "pure form" is fundamental, then, to Marx's analysis. It assumes that all non-capitalist spheres of production either would be eliminated by the expansion of the system or become subordinate to it. Whether the capitalist process is considered from the standpoint of commodities or from that of the distribution of income, "there are only two points of departure: the capitalist and the laborer. All third classes of persons must either receive money for their services from these two classes . . . or in the form of rent, interest, etc." (vol. II, p. 384).

Within the relation of capitalist and labor, a double process ensues, which is the "absolute, general law of capitalist accumulation." The progressive accumulation of capital leads to a concentration of capital and its centralization in the hands of the "gigantic industrial enterprises" at the expense, principally, of the "many small capitalists whose capital partly passes into the hands of their conquerors, partly vanishes" (vol. I, p. 687). On the other hand, there is a disproportionate employment of constant capital as compared with variable capital, or labor. This produces a relative "surplus population" through the displacement of labor and causes the rate of profit to sink. ("The rate of profit sinks, not because the laborer is less exploited, but because less labor is employed in proportion to employed capital in general," vol. III, p. 288.) Out of this comes the grand passion play of the economic apocalypse:

Hand in hand with this centralization, or this expropriation of many capitalists by few, develop, on an ever extending scale, the co-operative form of the labor process, the conscious technical application of science . . . the entanglement of all peoples in the net of the world-market. . . . Along with the constantly diminishing number of the magnates of capital . . . grows the revolt of the working-class, a class always increasing in numbers. . . . Centralization of the means of production and socialization of labor at last reach a point where they become incompatible with their

the superficial observer, the analysis of these forms seems to turn upon minutiae. It does in fact deal with minutiae, but they are of the same order as those dealt with in microscopic anatomy (p. 12, emphasis added).
Marx elaborated this idea in an unfinished essay, "The Method of Political Economy," which was published as an appendix to the *Contribution to the Critique of Political Economy* (Chicago, 1906).

capitalist integument. This integument is burst asunder (vol. I, pp. 836–837).[19]

In a famous passage in the author's preface to *Capital*, Marx argues that these results will work themselves out inevitably with iron necessity, and that the fate of England, the first country where this will happen, foreshadows the fate of all others. As Marx wrote:

The physicist either observes physical phenomena where they occur in their most typical form and most free from disturbing influence or, wherever possible, he makes experiments under conditions that assure the occurrence of the phenomenon in its normality. In this work I have to examine the capitalist mode of production, and the conditions of production and exchange corresponding to that mode. Up to the present time, their classic ground is England. That is the reason why England is used as the chief illustration in the development of my theoretical ideas. If, however, the German reader shrugs his shoulders at the condition of the English industrial and agricultural laborers, or in optimist fashion comforts himself with the thought that in Germany things are not nearly so bad, I must plainly tell him, "*De te fabula narratur!*"

Intrinsically, it is not a question of the higher or lower degree of development of the social antagonisms that result from the *natural laws of capitalist production*. It is a question of these laws themselves, of these tendencies *working with iron necessity towards inevitable results*. The country that is more developed industrially only shows, to the less developed, the image of its own future (pp. 12–13, emphasis added).

Marx's *first* schema of social development, it should be emphasized, is not an empirical description but is derived from his model of "pure capitalism." Yet "pure capitalism" itself was a theoretical simplification, and by the time Marx had begun to write the third volume of *Capital*, the growth of a large-scale investment banking system and the emergence of the corporation had begun to transform the social structure of capitalist society. If in the first stages of capitalist society there had been an "old" middle class of farmers, artisans, and independent professionals, what was one to say of the emerging "new" middle class of managers, technical employees, white-collar workers, and the like. This is the basis of *schema two*. Marx observed this phenomenon with extraordinary acuity.

Three crucial structural changes were taking place in the society. First, with the rise of a new banking system, the accumulation of

---

[19] Like all laws, Marx wrote, this "is modified in its working by many circumstances." There were, Marx wrote, various "counteracting tendencies" principally the rise of new industries created by the growth of luxuries, the refinement of wants, the creation of new ones, etc., and these new industries absorb displaced labor and expand "unproductive" employment. Modifying as these are, they do not alter the basic features and nature of the capitalist economy.

capital no longer rested on the thrift and savings of the individual entrepreneur engaging in self-financing, but on the savings of the society as a whole. Marx comments: "This social character of capital is promoted and fully realized by the complete development of the credit and banking system. It places at the disposal of the industrial and commercial capitalists all the available, or even potential capital of society" (vol. III, p. 712).

The second change was the revolution wrought by the corporation, the effect of which was to separate ownership from management and bring a new category of occupation—if not a new class —which Marx calls "the labor of superintendence" into society.

That not the industrial capitalists, but the industrial managers are "the soul of our industrial system," has already been remarked by Mr. Ure. . . . The capitalist mode of production itself has brought matters to such a point, that the labor of superintendence, entirely separated from the ownership of capital, walks the streets (vol. III, pp. 454–455).

And finally, the expansion of the banking and credit system and the growth of the corporation would necessarily mean the expansion of office personnel and white-collar work.

. . . it is clear that commercial operations increase to the extent that the scale of production is enlarged. . . . The more developed the scale of production is, the greater, if not in proportion, will be the commercial operations of industrial capital. . . . The calculation of prices, bookkeeping, managing funds (accounting), all these belong under this head. . . . This necessitates the employment of commercial wage workers who form the office staff (vol. III, p. 352).[20]

And yet, while these three structural changes would seem to modify considerably or challenge drastically the theory of polarization of classes which is so strong in the *Manifesto* and at the end of volume I of *Capital*—and which was the dominant idea of classical Marxism —Marx felt that the basic sociological tendency, the deepening of

---

[20] In the *Theorien über den Mehrwert*, the uncollected materials which Engels had not included in *Capital* but which was edited, after Engels's death, by Kautsky (and which is sometimes called vol. IV of *Capital*), Marx says explicitly, in fact, that the middle class, standing between labor on the one side and the capitalists on the other, constantly grow "[weighing] heavily on the labor sub-stratum and [increasing] the social security of the upper ten thousand." More specifically, he writes: "The size of the middle class increases and the proletariat will always form a comparatively small part of the populace (although it is still growing). This is indeed the true course of bourgeois society." Cited by Hans Speier, *The Salaried Employee in German Society*, mimeographed translation, W.P.A. Project No. 465-97-3-81 (New York, 1939), pp. 9–10.

A. L. Harris's essay (op. cit.) contains detailed references to these sections in the *Theorien* which contain Marx's discussion of the role of the middle class both outside and within the capitalist productive process.

economic crises and the spread of a socialized character to property, would force acute conflict in society.

Of the banking system, rather than seeing the institutionalization of credit as a source of stability in the system, he thought it would hasten crises.

By means of the banking system the distribution of capital as a special business, as a social function, is taken out of the hands of the private capitalists and usurers. But at the same time banking and credit thus become the most effective means of driving capitalist production beyond its own boundaries, and one of the most potent instruments of crises and swindle (vol. III, p. 713).

As for the managerial function, he saw this as much, if not more, an aspect of socialism as it is of capitalism. The managerial function, said Marx, "arises from the social form of the labor process" and "to say that this labor is a capitalistic one . . . amounts merely to saying that the vulgar economists cannot conceive of the forms developed in the womb of capitalist production separated and freed from their antagonistic capitalist character" (vol. III, p. 455). "A director of an orchestra need not be the owner of the instruments." "The cooperative factories furnish the proof that the capitalist has become just as superfluous as a functionary."

In fact, writes Marx shortly afterwards, in a startling analysis, the rise of the manager is one of the key elements in transforming profits into "social property," for with the introduction of the manager ("skilled labor the price of which is regulated in the labor market, like that of any other labor"), the capitalist becomes removed from the process of production, the manager is alienated from his own labor, and profits assume a social character. Marx writes:

. . . this total profit is henceforth received only in the form of interest, that is, in the form of mere compensation of the ownership of capital, which is now separated from its function in the actual process of reproduction in the same way in which this function, in the person of the manager, is separated from the ownership of capital. The profit now presents itself . . . as a mere appropriation of the surplus labor of others, arising from the transformation of means of production into capital, that is, from its alienation from its actual producer, from its antagonism as another's property opposed to the individuals actually at work in production, from the manager down to the last day laborer.

In the stock companies the function (of production) is separated from the ownership of capital, and labor, of course, is entirely separated from the ownership of the means of production and of surplus labor. This result of the highest development of capitalist production is a necessary transition to the reconversion of capital into the property of the producers, no longer as the private property of individual producers, but as the common property of associates, as social property outright (vol. III, p. 517).

As for the white-collar worker, Marx foresaw that the number of such employees would spread, but he felt that the extension of capitalism would lead to the proletarianization of the white-collar worker because the division of labor in the office and the growth of public education would depreciate their value. As he put it:

The commercial laborer, in the strict meaning of the term, belongs to the better paid class of wage workers: he belongs to the class of skilled laborers, which is above the average. However, wages have a tendency to fall, even in proportion to the average labor, with the advance of the capitalist mode of production. This is due to the fact that in the first place, division of labor in the office is introduced; this means that only a one-sided development of the laboring capacity is required. . . . In the second place, the necessary preparation, such as the learning of commercial details, languages, etc., is more and more rapidly, easily, generally, cheaply reproduced with the progress of science and popular education, to the extent that the capitalist mode of production organizes the methods of teaching, etc. in a practical manner. The generalization of public education makes it possible to recruit this line of laborers from classes that had formerly no access to such an education and that were accustomed to a lower standard of living. At the same time this generalization of education increases the supply and thus competition. With few exceptions, the labor-power of this line of laborers is therefore depreciated with the progress of capitalist development. Their wages fall, while their ability increases (vol. III, p. 354).

These new structural tendencies, therefore, were discounted because Marx believed, implicitly, that *schema one* would be decisive. Yet why the "integument" would have to burst is not clear. As Paul Sweezey writes: "In a real sense it can be said that Marx's entire theoretical system constitutes a denial of the possibility of indefinite capitalist expansion and an affirmation of the inevitability of the socialist revolution. But nowhere in his work is there to be found a doctrine of the specifically economic breakdown of capitalist production." [21] And as Sweezey comments further, efforts by later Marxist writers, including Rosa Luxemburg and Henryk Grossmann, to posit such a *necessary* breakdown are unconvincing.

On the historical evidence, the *tendency* Marx laid out in *schema one* has been modified, if not falsified, by the showing that there is no intrinsic tendency of the rate of profit to fall; that the state has been able to intervene and soften, if not prevent, economic crises; and that technology has been an open frontier for the reinvestment of capital.

---

[21] Paul Sweezey, op. cit., pp. 191–192. See chap. XI for "The Breakdown Controversy."

There is no evidence—in theory or empirical reality—that capitalism must collapse from *economic* contradictions within the system.

What, then, of the structure of the "new society" within the "womb" of the old—the changing character of the labor force, the role of the manager? What of the social developments which I have called *schema two?* What role have these elements played in social theory and the conceptions of social evolution since Marx? If one reads the sociological theories on the future of capitalism which were enunciated in the first half of the twentieth century, one sees that almost all were, in effect, a dialogue with *schema two* of Marx.

Post-Marxism: The Dialogue in the West

Few writers on capitalism have seen it as a "permanent" system of society. The very self-consciousness that attended the coinage of the term in the nineteenth century—the fact that it was associated principally with socialist theoreticians [22]—from the start led to the belief that capitalism was only a "stage" in the evolution of economic society and to the expectation that it would be replaced—shortly—by some successor economic system of some collectivist kind. (In fact, given all the predictions of an early demise, what is to be explained, if anything, is the relative longevity of the system.)

The writer who first sought to chart the transformation of capitalism in some set of qualitatively different sociological periods—the

---

[22] What is startling to realize is that, because of the origin of the word, the concept of capitalism was accepted so belatedly in economic literature and, in the article on "Capitalism" in the *Encyclopedia of the Social Sciences* printed in 1930, Werner Sombart could point out that major economic texts of the late nineteenth and early twentieth century ignored the term. He writes:

The concept of capitalism and even more clearly the term itself may be traced primarily to the writings of socialist theoreticians. It has in fact remained one of the key concepts of socialism down to the present time. . . . Despite the fact that capitalism tends to become the sole subject-matter of economics, neither the term nor the concept has as yet been universally recognized by representatives of academic economics. The older German economists and to a much greater extent the economists of other countries rejected entirely the concept of capitalism. In many cases the rejection was merely implicit; capitalism was not discussed at all except perhaps in connection with the history of economic doctrines, and when it was mentioned there was no indication that it was of particular importance. The term is not found in Gide, Cauwes, Marshall, Seligman, or Cassel, to mention only the best-known texts. In other treatises, such as those of Schmoller, Adolf Wagner, Richard Ehrenberg, and Philippovich, there is some discussion of capitalism but the concept is subsequently rejected. In the newer economics it is recognized as indispensable or at least useful, but the uncertainty as to its exact meaning is generally expressed by quotation marks about the word. "Capitalism," *Encyclopedia of the Social Sciences* (New York, 1930), vol. III, p. 195.

first, actually, to make capitalism the centerpiece of economic history and analysis—was the German economic historian Werner Sombart. In *Der Moderne Kapitalismus* (the final revisions of which were published from 1921 to 1927 in three volumes) Sombart sought to write a full-scale history of the transition of economic society from a pre-capitalist phase of a sustenance economy to the rise of modern capitalism and its deliquescence. While he dealt fully with the influence of technology and the creation of the capitalist enterprise as a distinctive social form, his emphasis was principally on the capitalist spirit (or mentality) as its most unique characteristic, and on the entrepreneur as the key figure in capitalist development.[23]

For Sombart, economic epochs could be understood only within the framework of other historical systems. Thus the early period of any system overlaps with the late period of a retreating or previous economic system; the period of full development reveals a system in its singular purity; and the last period is identified when one can show the onset of a new, oncoming system. Applying this division of epochs to capitalism Sombart distinguished between early capitalism, the period from the middle of the thirteenth century to the middle of the eighteenth; full capitalism (*Hochkapitalismus*) from about 1750 to 1914; and "late capitalism," the period after the First World War.

Early capitalism still bore the marks of the handicraft period. Traditionalism was still strong, economic life had a personal cast, buyer and seller allowed personal likes and dislikes to affect their relationships, and employers and workers were held together by patriarchal bonds.

In the period of full capitalism the principles of profit and eco-

---

[23] Sombart is an unjustly neglected figure today in sociological history in part because, in his last years, he expressed some sympathy with the Nazis, and in greater measure, perhaps, because his writings, though extraordinarily suggestive were quite careless. This is probably best exemplified in his "debate" with Max Weber on the spirit of capitalism. Where Weber emphasized the role of the "Protestant ethic," Sombart singled out the Jews as the major element basing himself on both the religious rules of Judaism and the migration patterns of Jews in the fifteenth century, arguing that the shift in the commercial center of the Western world from the Mediterranean basin to Antwerp and Holland followed the expulsion of the Jews from Spain. Yet his evidence about the Jews was sloppy.

Sombart's writings cover the rise of socialism, beginning with *Socialism and the Social Movement* (1896) and the development of capitalism from the first edition of *Der Moderne Kapitalismus* in 1902. There is no English translation of *Der Moderne Kapitalismus*, though a "free hand" adaptation was published by F. L. Nussbaum in 1933 as *A History of the Economic Institutions of Modern Europe: An Introduction to Der Moderne Kapitalismus of Werner Sombart* (New York, 1933). Sombart's fascinating history and psychology of the businessman, *Der Bourgeois*, was translated and edited by M. Epstein and published as *The Quintessence of Capitalism* (New York, 1915), and *Die Juden und das Wirtschaftsleben*, translated by M. Epstein as *The Jews and Modern Capitalism* (London, 1913) and reissued with a new introduction by Bert F. Hoselitz by the Free Press (Glencoe, Ill., 1951).

nomic rationalism permeated all economic relationships. Markets expanded, the size of business increased, scientific mechanistic technology was utilized, relationships became impersonal and institutionalized. "The capitalistic spirit at its prime," writes Sombart, "was characterized by psychological strains of peculiar intensity born of the contradictions between irrationality and rationality, between the spirit of speculation and that of calculation, between the mentality of the daring entrepreneur and the hard-working, sedate bourgeois." [24]

In the period of late capitalism two major changes are central. Within the society, "the strength of specifically capitalistic elements of economic life" declines, while "mixed" public-private undertakings, state and communal public works and non-capitalistic economic endeavors "increase in number, size and importance." Within the firm, "there is a gradual decay of the entrepreneurial mentality." In place of the entrepreneur comes the bureaucratic mentality, and the firm itself becomes bureaucratized.

In late capitalism, says Sombart—his model was the cartelization of German industry in the 1920s—the major desire is for stabilization. The striving for profit grows less intense ("witness such symptoms as the fixed dividend rate, the reinvestment of surplus—in the United States, for example, some concerns provide 30 to 35 percent of their new capital in this way"), the market mechanism is superseded by the price regulation by combinations or even by the government, the cyclical oscillations of the economic system become attenuated, and the interventions of government become more and more decisive. The features that had given capitalism its distinctiveness have begun to atrophy. If capitalism, as Sombart put it, could be characterized by three constituent elements, spirit, form, and technology, the spirit was now gone and only form and technology remain.

All these themes of Sombart, with subtle shifts of emphasis, are present in Schumpeter who, in his *Capitalism, Socialism and Democracy* (1942), predicted the end of capitalist civilization. The transformation is both on the level of mentality and social structure. For Schumpeter, three elements are at work to change the capitalist mentality. One is the fact that capitalism is too rationalistic. "I have no hesitation in saying," writes Schumpeter, "that all logic is derived from the pattern of economic decision or, to use a pet phrase of mine, that the economic pattern is the matrix of logic." The capitalist process, he continues, "rationalizes behavior and ideas and by so doing

---

[24] "Capitalism," *Encyclopedia of the Social Sciences* (New York, 1930), vol. III, p. 207.

chases from our minds, along with metaphysical beliefs, mystic and romantic ideas of all sorts." But such rationality, says Schumpeter, is too stringent for society. "The stock exchange is a poor substitute for the Holy Grail." Second is the "obsolescence of the entrepreneurial function." The entrepreneur was the man who unsettled things, who innovated and got things done. But today, "personality and will power" count for less in economic environments that have become routinized, where "bureau and committee work tends to replace individual action" and economic progress becomes "depersonalized and automatized." Third is the corrosion of all established beliefs. Rationalism and empiricism foster a critical attitude which begins to question everything. Traditions begin to crumble. The desire for change and novelty become built into the system. The intellectual—the man "who wields the power of the spoken and the written word" —becomes increasingly hostile to capitalism. ("Only a socialist or a fascist government is strong enough to discipline them.") Inevitably, thus, the social antagonism to capitalism grows.

On the level of social structure, what sustained capitalism, said Schumpeter, was an institutional framework built on twin pillars, the institution of property and the freedom of contract. The political support for this framework is maintained by a "host of small and medium-sized firms of owner-managers" who, "together with their dependants, henchmen and connections, count quantitatively at the polls." Yet for Schumpeter, this institutional framework has become brittle. Freedom of contract is hemmed in by various forms of regulation, from the powers of trade unions to that of government. The institution of property is undermined in two ways. One, the process of monopolization and the growth of the large corporation tend to eliminate the intermediate-sized firms. ("Economically . . . the case against concentration of economic control . . . misses the salient point [i.e.] the political consequences of concentration.") Second, the transformation of the owner-proprietor into the salaried executive diminishes the strength of property and the managerial group begins to adopt a set of social attitudes which are at variance with the stockholders' interests in the firm. Thus, for reasons parallel to Marx, Schumpeter, too, sees the walls of capitalism as crumbling and—in a century!—the "civilization that slowly works deep down below" may then emerge.[25]

---

[25] Joseph Schumpeter, *Capitalism, Socialism and Democracy* (New York, 1942). The quotations are taken from chaps. XI–XIV, in sequence, pp. 122–123, 127, 137, 132–133, 140, 150, 162.

Schumpeter, at the end, is careful to say that what he is describing is an historical tendency. As he says in the last paragraph of his section, "Can Capitalism Survive":

But what is the "civilization that slowly works deep down below"? Marx had thought it was socialism. But Marx's great antagonist, Max Weber, had a far different vision. For Weber, the master key of Western society was rationalization, the spread through law, economy, accounting, technology, and the entire conduct of life of a spirit of functional efficiency and measurement, of an "economizing" attitude (maximization, optimization, least cost) towards not only material resources but all life.[26] With the inevitability of rationalization, administration takes over, and the complete bureaucratization of all social institutions is inescapable: "The future belongs to bureaucratization. . . . Where once the modern trained official rules, his power is virtually indestructible, because the whole organization of the most basic provisions of life is fashioned to suit his performance." [27]

But while bureaucratization was a feature of capitalism, it would be, necessarily, a feature of socialism as well. In *Wirtschaft und Gesellschaft* Weber writes:

The primary source of bureaucratic administration lies in the role of technical knowledge which, through the development of modern technology and business methods in the production of goods, has become completely indispensable. In this respect, it makes no difference whether the economic system is organized on a capitalistic or a socialistic basis. Indeed, if in the latter case a comparable level of technical efficiency were to be achieved, it would mean a tremendous increase in the importance of professional bureaucrats. . . . capitalism in its modern stages of development requires the bureaucracy, though both have arisen from different historical sources . . . a socialistic form of organization would not alter this fact. It would be a question [Weber refers here to the rational calculation of the use of capital] whether in a socialistic system it would be possible to provide conditions for carrying out as stringent a bureaucratic organization as has been possible in a capitalistic order. For socialism would, in

Things have gone to different lengths in different countries but in no country far enough to allow us to say with any confidence precisely how far they will go, or to assert that their "underlying trend" has grown too strong to be subject to anything more serious than temporary reverses. . . . The middle class is still a political power. Bourgeois standards and bourgeois motivations though being increasingly impaired are still alive. Survivals of traditions—and family ownership of controlling parcels of stock—still make many an executive behave as the owner-manager did of old. The bourgeois family has not yet died; in fact, it clings to life so tenaciously that no responsible politician has as yet dared touch it by any method other than taxation. From the standpoint of immediate practice as well as for the purposes of short run forecasting—and in these things, a century is a "short run"—all this surface may be more important than the tendency toward another civilization that slowly works deep down below. Ibid., p. 163.

[26] See Max Weber, *General Economic History* (London, n.d.), chap. 30, esp. p. 354.
[27] Max Weber, *Gesammelte Politische Schriften* (Munich, 1921), pp. 149–150, cited by Richard Pipes, "Max Weber and Russia," *World Politics* (April 1955), p. 377.

fact, require a still higher degree of formal bureaucratization than capitalism. If this should prove not to be possible, it would demonstrate the existence of another of those fundamental elements of irrationality—a conflict between formal and substantive rationality of the sort which sociology so often encounters.[28]

As Richard Pipes points out:

Weber repeatedly criticized the Marxists for ignoring what to him seemed the central problem facing socialism: *who* will operate the nationalized enterprises? As for himself he felt certain that this function would be assumed by the groups technically best prepared for the task, that is, the bureaucracy "from which nothing is further removed than [a sense of] solidarity with the proletariat." [29]

The spread of technical knowledge, the rise of the manager in industry and the bureaucrat in government, rather than exemplifying for the new directors (in the St. Simonian image which Marx had taken over) a role analogous to the "director of the orchestra," meant for Weber a new form of domination:

. . . the edifice for the new bondage stands everywhere in readiness. . . . All the *economic* weather signs point in the direction of diminishing freedom. . . . He who desires to be a weather vane of a tendency of development had better abandon these old-fashioned ideals as quickly as possible.[30]

Thus, for Weber, capitalism and socialism were not two contradictory systems (which they might be conceived of if one used property as the axis of difference) but two faces of a common type—bureaucracy. And for Weber, bureaucracy was identical with rationalized administration and the class on which it was built, the clerical and managerial stratum in politics as well as in the economy. The future, then, belonged not to the working class but to the bureaucracy.

---

[28] Max Weber, *Economy and Society* (New York, 1968), vol. 1, pp. 223–225. This was composed in 1913–1914; Weber died in 1920.

[29] Pipes, op. cit., p. 378. The inner quote is from Weber's essay, *Der Sozialismus* (Vienna, 1918).

[30] Weber, *Zur Lage der burgerlichen Democratie in Russland*, cited by Richard Pipes, "Max Weber and Russia," *World Politics* (April 1955), p. 378. Ironically, Weber felt that there was only one rival to the bureaucrat, and that is the individual capitalist entrepreneur: "Superior to bureaucracy in the knowledge of techniques and facts is only the capitalist entrepreneur, within his own sphere of interest. He is the only type who has been able to maintain at least relative immunity from subjection to the control of rational bureaucratic knowledge. In large scale organizations, all others are inevitably subject to bureaucratic control, just as they have fallen under the dominance of precision machinery in the mass production of goods" (*Economy and Society*, op. cit., p. 225). Thus a socialist economy, by eliminating the capitalist entrepreneur, has no counterfoil to the bureaucrat.

Before the First World War orthodox socialist theory believed that the proletariat would expand and that the middle class was destined to perish. In Germany, the "old" middle class of independent entrepreneurs, small farmers, and self-employed professionals did begin to decline, but so, too, did the industrial working class: from 1895 to 1925, the proportion of wage laborers in industry as compared to the labor force as a whole dropped from 56.8 percent to 45.1 percent.[31] Between the two a new stratum was emerging—the white-collar salaried employee, clerical and professional; and their number was growing steadily. How was this to be explained?

The first person to call attention to this new sociological phenomenon and to study it consistently was Emil Lederer, the social analyst and editor of the influential *Archiv für Sozialwissenschaft und Sozialpolitik*. In an essay in 1912 Lederer called this group "the new middle class." Historically the bourgeoisie had been called the middle class because it stood between the land-owning class and the working class. With the decline of the gentry the grand bourgeoisie became the ruling class of great financiers and the industrialists; but between them and the working class—and now taking over the term middle class—was what Marx called the petty bourgeoisie: the small trader and independent small businessman, the self-employed professional and independent artisan. Now, within the enterprise, in the position between employers and workers was a new stratum. Lederer called it a "new middle class," less for its function than from its social evaluation which was based upon their own self-esteem and the esteem of others. "This middle position between the two classes," Lederer wrote, "a negative characteristic rather than definite technical function, is the social mark of the salaried employees and establishes their social character in their own consciousness and in the estimation of the community." [32]

---

[31] Hans Speier, *The Salaried Employee in German Society*, vol. I (New York, 1939), p. 9. In 1937 the New York State Department of Social Welfare, together with the Department of Sociology at Columbia, jointly sponsored a WPA project of translations of Foreign Social Science Monographs. In all, about 25 were translated, mimeographed, and deposited in the Columbia University Library as well as disseminated in limited distribution. One major topic was that of the "white collar worker" in Germany, and in all about ten such studies were translated including the major essays of Émil Lederer, Lederer and Marschak, Fritz Croner, Hans Speier, Carl Dreyfuss, Erich Engelhard, and Hans Tobias.

[32] Emil Lederer, *Die Privatangestellten in der modern Wirtschaftsentwicklung* (1912), translated as *The Problem of the Modern Salaried Employee: Its Theoretical and Statistical Basis*, WPA Project No. 465-97-3-81, Department of Social Science, Columbia University.

Lederer, who came to the United States after the rise of Hitler, became one of the founding members of the Graduate Faculty of the New School for Social Research in New York; he died in 1939. He is best known, in English, for his theory of

A year later, in an essay on "Zum sozialpsychischen Habitus der Gegenwert," Lederer spelled out the psychological differences between the classes, in the context of the changeover of society from a traditional to a rational mode of economic conduct. What was distinctive, he said, was the varied life "rhythms" of the different social strata in modern economic organization. For the manual worker life is irregular, his existence atomized by external forces such as business conditions; the week, at best, is the unit of his economic life. For the salaried worker there is a steadiness of life which is shaped by the expectation of a yearly salary; his "economic unit" is the month. The civil servant regards the year as the axis of his life, but in addition he looks forward to regular promotions as his horizon for the future. It is in these different "rhythms" that Lederer found the sociological distinctiveness of the different strata.[33]

The major theoretical analysis of this new phenomenon was made by Lederer and Jacob Marschak in a famous essay, "Der Neue Mittelstand," which appeared in 1926 in the *Grundriss der Sozialökonomik*.[34] Here the analysis was put in the framework of a "theory of historical development," and on the basis of revising existing theory of "historical classes." "The war and the revolution," the authors point out,

gave a tremendous impetus to the growth of the salaried employees' class . . . for war economy means the expansion of big business, as well as ex-

"mass society," which is discussed in his last book, *The State of the Masses* (New York, 1940).

[33] Emil Lederer, "Zum sozialpsychischen Habitus der Gegenwert," in the *Archiv für Sozialwissenschaft und Sozialpolitik*, vol. 46 (1918–19). (The essay, though written in 1913, was not published until five years later.) Translated as *On the Socio-Psychic Constitution of the Present Time*, WPA Project 465-97-3-81 (New York, 1937), pp. 8–9.

[34] Emil Lederer and Jacob Marschak, "Der Neue Mittelstand," in *Grundriss der Sozialökonomik*, IX Abteilung, I Teil (Tübingen, 1926), translated as "The New Middle Class," ibid., (New York, 1937).

Technically, it should be pointed out, the *neue Mittelstand* should not be translated as class, but estate. Marx himself, in generalizing the word class to cover all human history, has contributed a confusion about the meaning of the term. In precapitalist and pre-industrial society, social distinctions were ones of rank and position, reinforced by legal distinction and legitimized by tradition. Modern capitalist or industrial society swept away these distinctions, and created the bare, abstract materiality of "class" based on market position. This is the basis of the historic distinction of estate society and capitalist society. As Ralf Dahrendorf writes: "It is significant that in conversational German the word 'class' is even today restricted to the two strata of entrepreneurs and workers. Neither the nobility nor the professions nor the older groups of craftsmen and peasants are called classes. They are 'estates'—a concept which in the case of the 'middle estate' (*Mittelstand*) has been retained even for the newer groups of white-collar workers and civil servants. An estate, however, is something else than a stratum or class, not only in everyday language but for the sociologist as well." *Class and Class Conflict in an Industrial Society*, op. cit., pp. 6–7.

tensive "organization," or bureaucratization which multiplies the functions of the salaried employee. But neither the termination of the war . . . nor the abandonment of the war economy re-established the social stratification of the pre-war period.

In addition,

both state and municipalities have extended their activities by operating industrial enterprises under direct management. These tendencies towards municipalization and nationalization have brought into being legions of public servants which, properly speaking, are neither the consequence of the capitalistic system nor of the industrialization of the national economy.

These tendencies, the authors pointed out, derive from the "large expansion of the manifold functions which the modern 'service state' performs." [35]

After a detailed statistical analysis of the growth of the salaried employee—as a technical worker, clerical employee, salesperson, and public employee—the authors concluded:

It follows from the statistical data . . . that the rapid growth of the employees' class must be regarded as a consequence of a continuous economic development, particularly of big business, and of the new methods of business organization. . . . The rapid increase of the employees enhances their effective power and activity as a group, particularly in the large cities where we find them concentrated in large numbers. . . . All these facts have as a further consequence that the employees, by their sheer numbers, offer a counterweight to the increasing numerical strength of the laboring class.[36]

For more than a decade, a fierce debate raged in German sociology about the characterization of this "new middle class." Left-wing writers regarded the salaried employee as simply a "white-collar proletariat" whose "mass character" would lead to the adoption of working-class attitudes. Some optimistic sociologists saw in the "new middle class" a factor for social solidarity which would act as a balancing group between the employers and industrial workers and provide cohesion for the enterprise, if not the society. Theodor Geiger predicted that the new middle class would be "crushed" between the capitalist class and the industrial proletariat, while Schumpeter argued that because of the increase in the number of salaried employees, the world of the future would be a world of bureaucracy.[37]

[35] ibid., pp. 8–11.   [36] Ibid., p. 16.

[37] The article by Theodor Geiger, "Zur Theorie des Klassenbegriffs . . ." appeared in *Schmoller's Jahrbuch*, 54th Year, vol. I (1930); that of Schumpeter in *Bonner Mitteilungen*, no. 1, 1929. An influential book on the white-collar worker was Siegfried Kracauer's *Die Angestellten* (Frankfurt-am-Main, 1930), which portrayed the world of the white-collar worker in what we would call today Kafkaesque terms.

Those who saw the "new middle class" only in economic terms, as did Lederer and Marschak, predicted that a position "between the classes" was no longer possible and that in a society increasingly self-conscious of group interests so that employment relations were arbitrated by law, the new middle class would organize itself collectively and probably ally itself with the trade union movement.

But the growing number of empirical studies made one thing clear: that the new middle class, in part because of its social origins (most of the white-collar workers were recruited from the declining older middle class), in part because of the ethos of "clean cuff occupations" was stubbornly determined to maintain a self-image and a self-esteem which was "middle class." [38] And when the depression hit, and Hans Fallada asked the question in the title of his novel, *Little Man, What Now?*, the answer given by the new middle class, like the old middle class, when the center and liberal parties collapsed, was by and large to shift their support to the Nazis rather than to the working-class parties.[39] Thus, the "new middle class," an expected product of economic and social development, had an unexpected but distinctive political consequence which had not been anticipated either by the Marxists or by the sociologists in Germany.

Marx had defined the mode of production at any given historical stage as a correspondence between the forces of production (technical equipment and organization of labor) and the social relations derived from the character of the ownership of the means of production. The post-Marxist separation of manager from owner, the

---

fried Kracauer's *Die Angestellten* (Frankfurt-am-Main, 1930), which portrayed the world of the white-collar worker in what we would call today Kafkaesque terms. The debate in German sociology is summarized in Hans Speier's book *The Salaried Employee in German Society*, op. cit., especially chap. 1, and Erich Engelhard, "The Salaried Employee," loc. cit., chap. 2.

[38] Summarizing a number of different studies by Otto Suhr, Erich Engelhard comments:

. . . his white collar is and remains the direct expression of his particular mode of life. This life is esteemed by him and others. Employees do their utmost to preserve the accepted standard of living. Beginning from a certain income figure the poorer they are, the more money they spend for rent in proportion to their income. Basically, pro-capita family expenses increase with income, but expenses for existential needs—food, housing, clothing—increase at a slower rate than those for life's other needs. The commercial employee spends most for clothing and haberdashery; he economizes on food, probably [because he] wants to make a clean-cut impression. It is just this outward style of life, too well-known for further comment, which leads to positively-oriented esteem. The mode of living is a more deciding factor for the development of the group towards an estate than "occupation" as such. Erich Engelhard, "Die Angestellten," in *Kölner Vierteljahrsehefte für Soziologie*, translated as *The Salaried Employee*, WPA Project (1939), op. cit., pp. 57–59.

[39] The voting evidence is summarized by S. M. Lipset, *Political Man* (New York, 1960), chap. V, "Fascism—Left, Right and Center," esp. pp. 134–152.

bureaucratization of enterprise, the complication of occupational structure, all made the once clear-cut picture of property domination and social relations ambiguous. Marx had asserted, further, that the centralization of production and its concentration would act as a "fetter" upon the production of goods, but in the hundred years since *Capital* the Western world had seen a burst of productivity and technological growth undreamed of by any of the utopians of the time.

It was this very ambiguity of the character of the social relations, and the success of technology, which brought into focus the "forces" of production and revived the concept of industrial society as an alternative to the distinction between capitalism and socialism. Just as, in relation to the problem of authority, the concept of bureaucratization saw capitalism and socialism not as different but as variants of a common type, so too, on the issue of social development, the concept of industrial society subsumed the two social systems under a common rubric. As Raymond Aron, who, more than any other modern writer, is identified with the concept of industrial society, points out in his lectures:

The sociological problem which has provided the main theme of this book [*18 Lectures on Industrial Society*] is that posed by Marx and Marxism—especially as the latter is expounded in *Capital*. . . . [Marx] tried to understand the laws of its development . . . the central phenomenon in Marx's view was that of *accumulation*. He believed that the essence of capitalism was to be found in the accumulation of capital. By choosing economic growth as the central subject of this investigation I have taken up the Marxist theme of accumulation in the terminology and using the concepts of modern economics. . . .

Instead of capitalism I have chosen industrial society (or technical, scientific or rationalized society) as the principal historical concept. . . . Beginning with this concept of industrial society I have then distinguished several different types of industrial society and have introduced the ideas of models of growth and phases of growth. These four concepts, industrial society, types of industrial society, models of growth and phases of growth represent the successive stages of the theory.[40]

---

[40] Raymond Aron, *18 Lectures on Industrial Society* (London, 1967), p. 235. The book was published in France in 1962, but as Aron notes in his foreword to the French edition, the lectures were given as a course in the Sorbonne in 1955–1956 and, as is common with professorial courses at the Sorbonne, distributed in roneoed form by the Centre de Documentation Universitaire. The interest in the topic led to their book publication though as Aron points out the original form, as lectures, was maintained.

In effect, as Aron points out, those choosing to emphasize the idea of industrial society pay homage to Marx by emphasizing the forces of production as the central idea; those who wish to emphasize the distinction of capitalism and socialism focus on social relations. For Aron's discussion of the alternating emphases in social

If one focuses the problem on stages of development and economic growth, the paradox is compounded, for while there are communist states in the world today, none of them have replaced or succeeded any capitalist society (and none are socialist in the egalitarian sense envisaged by the founding fathers). And, having taken over power in economically backward countries, these communist regimes concentrate primarily on the function which Marx historically attributed to capitalism, namely, the development of the productive forces—the technological equipment—of the society, and usually by forced modes of capital accumulation. (In any precise sense, because these are hierarchically stratified and politically coordinated societies organized around profit, even though for the State rather than for private purposes, they come closest to Marx's glimpse of "state capitalism" as a possible social form, which he hinted at in volume III of *Capital*, than any other appropriate sociological designation.)

In that historical sense "communism," then, is not a "next" stage in history but simply one of a number of alternative modes of industrialization. What these regimes create are "industrial" societies, but through specifically political, rather than market, mechanisms.

The emergence since the end of the Second World War of more than fifty new states, most of them economically "underdeveloped," committed to the goal of economic growth, has tended to reinforce a distinction between pre-industrial and industrial societies. As Aron points out:

My visit to Asia helped to convince me that the major concept of our time is that of industrial society. Europe, as seen from Asia, does not consist of two fundamentally different worlds, the Soviet World and the Western World. It is one single reality: industrial civilization. Soviet and capitalist societies are only two species of the same genus, or two versions of the same social type, progressive industrial society.[41]

Aron organized the concept of industrial society around the axis of economic growth. If one takes a broader, societal view, the sociological concept of industrial society may be seen as a compound of four themes which are associated, principally, with four thinkers: St. Simon, Durkheim, Weber, and Colin Clark.

For St. Simon (and Comte who followed him) industrial society was to be contrasted to military society. The latter was organized around plunder, waste, display; the former around the orderly output of goods. For St. Simon, there were four dimensions to an industrial society: it was concerned with production; its methods were those of

thought on the "forces of production" and the "social relations of production," see ibid., pp. 2–3.

[41] Ibid., p. 42.

order, certainty and precision; it would be organized by "new men," engineers, industrialists, planners; and it would be based on knowledge. What one had here, in short, was the prescription of the "New Atlantis" that Francis Bacon had once prophesied.

For Durkheim, the world of "organic solidarity" was a world of specialization, complementarity, and interdependence. The ruling principle—in Talcott Parsons's emendation of Durkheim—is "structural differentiation." In industrial society, there is a separation of the economic system from the family system, the work place from the home. With the breakup of the traditional "collective conscience," core beliefs are to be organized around occupational codes and mediated through professional ethics.

For Weber, the theme is rationalization and universalism. A single ethic and style begins to pervade all society: these are the norms of impersonality, the emphasis on performance and achievement, the criteria of efficiency based on least cost, and the introduction of a rational calculus (a *Zweckrationalität*) in all areas of administration.

For Colin Clark (as first expressed in his *Conditions of Economic Progress*, 1940) economic sectors, as defined by the distribution of labor, could be classified as primary (extractive), secondary (manufacturing), and tertiary (services), and the weights of each sector in a society would be a function of the degree of productivity (output per capita) in each sector. Economic progress, thus, was defined as the rate of transfer of labor from one sector to the other, and this rate was a function of the differential productivity between the sectors. In this fashion Clark could account easily for the changeover to industrial society.

While the phrase "technological imperatives" is too rigid and deterministic, in all industrial societies there are certain common constraints which tend to shape similar actions and force the use of common techniques. For all theorists of industrial society (and to this extent Marx as well) the locus (or primary institution) of the society is the industrial enterprise and the axis of the society is the social hierarchy which derives from the organization of labor around machine production. From this point of view there are some common characteristics for all industrial societies: the technology is everywhere the same; the kind of technical and engineering knowledge (and the schooling to provide these) is the same; classification of jobs and skills is roughly the same. More broadly, one finds that the proportion of technical occupations increases in each society relative to other categories; that the spread of wages is roughly the same (so are the prestige hierarchies); and that management is primarily a technical skill.

Industrial societies are *economizing* societies, that is, they are organized around a principle of functional efficiency whose desideratum is to get "more for less" and to choose the more "rational" course of action. Thus a decision to use natural gas rather than coal as an energy fuel will be dictated by comparative costs, and the decision of how to schedule work will depend upon an appropriate combination of materials and skills available. Ideology, to this extent, becomes irrelevant and is replaced by "economics" in the guise of production functions, capital output ratios, marginal efficiency of capital, linear programming and the like. To that extent, too, the distinction between "bourgeois economics" and "socialist economics" fades; and if one is concerned with optimization and maximization, there is no distinction at all.[42]

Industrial society, as St. Simon insisted, was the application of technical knowledge to social affairs in a methodical, systematic way. With industrial society, thus, has come the *technicien*—the French usage is more apt than the English "technician," for its sense in French is much wider—the trained expert in the applied sciences. It has implied, too, that those who possessed such knowledge would exercise authority —if not power—in the society.

St. Simon's vision of industrial society, a vision of pure technocracy, was a system of planning and rational order in which society would specify its needs and organize the factors of production to achieve them. Industrial society was characterized by two elements,

[42] This does not mean that socialist and bourgeois economics *have* been the same. For political or ideological reasons, the Soviet economy has often denied economic rationality. The most famous example is that during Stalin's lifetime, the Soviet economy used no capital pricing because of the ideological dogma that only labor, not capital, created value and that the interest rate was exploitative. The idea that the interest rate could be used to measure the marginal efficiency of capital and was essential for any accounting only gradually came into Soviet planning. Similarly, though the technique of linear programming was invented first by a Russian economist Kantorovich in the late 1920s, the idea was denounced as "bourgeois economics" and not used until almost forty years later after the technique had been "reinvented" independently during the war by a Rand economist George Dantzig.

Some of this ideological dogmatism is present in the refusal of Russian planners to accept the market as a mechanism of economic allocation (though the major reasons today are primarily political). For many communists the market is associated with capitalism though actually it is only a technique whereby the user (consumer or intermediate producer) decides upon the basis of demand what is to be produced rather than the central planner. Paradoxically, in the 1930s discussion on the possibility of rational pricing under socialism, it was Marxist economists like Oskar Lange who insisted that only under socialism could the market freely operate to guide production whereas under capitalism the market was distorted by monopoly and unequal income distribution. (See Lange *et al., On the Economic Theory of Socialism* (Minneapolis, Minn., 1938.)

Perhaps the most startling remnant of ideological infantilism in this regard is Fidel Castro's announcement that he hopes—soon—to bring socialism into Cuba by abolishing money, and that everything would then be "free"—as if in so doing one does away with the problem of comparative costs of items, and the reasons for the differential prices—and exchange—of products.

knowledge and organization. Knowledge, he said, was objective. No one had "opinions" on chemistry or mathematics; one either had knowledge or not. The metaphors St. Simon used for organization were an orchestra, a ship and an army, in which each person fulfils a function in accordance with his competence. Although St. Simon clearly outlined the process whereby a nascent bourgeoisie had superseded the feudal nobility, and though he predicted the rise of a large working class, he did not believe that the working class would succeed the bourgeoisie in power. As he tried to show in his sketch of historical development, classes do not rule, for society is always governed by an educated elite. The natural leaders of the working class would therefore be the industrialists and the scientists. He foresaw the dangers of conflict, but did not regard it as inevitable. If an organic society were created, men would accept their place as a principle of justice. The division of labor meant that some men would guide and others would be guided. In a society organized by function and capacity, doctors and engineers and chemists would employ their skills according to objective needs, not in order to gain personal power. These men would be obeyed not because they are masters but because they have technical competence; to be obedient to one's doctor, after all, is a spontaneous but rational act. For this reason the St. Simonians, in a set of phrases that later were used by Engels, gave their new social hierarchy the slogan, "From each according to his capacity, to each according to his performance," and the industrial society, as they describe it, was no longer the "rule over men, but the administration of things."

The administration of things—the substitution of rational judgment for politics—is the hallmark of technocracy. The evolution of industrial society has emphasized a double aspect of this role, of function, and of method. "The technical employee," as Lederer and Marschak point out,

was known neither to the handicrafts nor to industry in its infancy. For the master craftsman of old, as the independent proprietor of a manufactory, was totally different from the technical official of today's mammoth concern. These modern industrial concerns have devised a whole superstructure or mechanism, of which the technical employee must form an integral part. This mechanism removes and draws in all possible brain and routine work from the shops; everything is centered on the planning and laying-out department.[43]

And in the society, the issues become technical. As Zbigniew Brzezinski states the case: ". . . social problems are seen less as the consequence of deliberate evil and more as the unintended by-products of

---

[43] Lederer and Marschak, op. cit., p. 7.

both complexity and ignorance; solutions are not sought in emotional simplifications but in the use of man's accumulated social and scientific knowledge." [44]

With the rise of the *technicien* has come the belief that advanced industrial society would be ruled by the technocrat. This is a belief held particularly in France where there has been a long tradition of administration from the Center (reinforced, as Tocqueville pointed out, by the French Revolution) and where the elite Corps de l'Etat is drawn from the Grandes Ecoles which were created for that purpose: the *Ecole Polytechnique*, founded in 1793 by the revolutionary government as a center of higher technical education, and, after the Second World War, the *Ecole Nationale d'Administration*. (August Comte, as Raymond Aron points out, is the "symbolic patron" of the polytechnician manager.) A number of writers, principally Jean Meynaud, have argued that "real power" has shifted out of the hands of the elected representatives to the technical experts and that there now "begins a new type of government, neither democracy nor bureaucracy but a technocracy."

The rise of technocracy, Meynaud argues, goes hand in hand with the expansion of the powers of the Executive, and already in France, "three important sectors have been taken over by the technocrats today: economic planning, national defense and the organization of scientific research." We can "safely postulate," he writes, "that technocratic power tended to increase under the Third and Fourth Republics, if only because of the extension and systematization of state intervention in social and economic fields." These powers were enlarged in the creation of the specialized bodies of the European Economic Community, such as the European Coal and Steel Community. The decline of parliamentary influence in the Gaullist Fifth Republic, and the expansion of ministerial power—with many of the ministers drawn from the civil service—spread the role of technocratic influence in the 1960s. "The technocrat's predominance in the Fifth Republic," writes Meynaud, "may be partly attributed to some of the ways in which the regime functions, notably its power to prepare certain decisions or interventions in secret." [45]

Much of the writing on the subject portrays technocracy as in contrast to, or undermining, the normal political framework of democracy; some of it borders on hysteria, vide the late Georges Gurvitch, who defined technocracy as

a formidable social power, absolutist and secretive in character, which threatens to devour the state. Organized, planned capitalism pushes this

---

[44] Brzezinski, op. cit. See part II, sec. IV, "Ideas and Ideals Beyond Ideology."
[45] Jean Meynaud, *Technocracy* (London, 1968), pp. 95, 140–141.

power in the direction of fascist structures, camouflaged or otherwise, which unite the system of trusts, cartels, the banks, employers, higher administrative personnel and the most senior career soldiers with a totalitarian state at their service.[46]

Much of the confusion on the problem arises from the failure to distinguish two functions and two kinds of technical intellectuals: the *technicien*, who corresponds to the application of knowledge; and the technocrat, who is engaged in the exercise of power.[47] Technical knowledge—the administration of things—is a necessary and growing component of many kinds of decisions, including political and strategic ones. But power—the relations between men—involves political choices that are a compound of values and interests and cannot always be "ordered" in a technical way. The technocrat in power is simply one kind of politician, not a *technicien*, no matter how much he employs his technical knowledge.[48]

It is clear that in the society of the future, however one defines it, the scientist, the professional, the *technicien*, and the technocrat will play a predominant role in the political life of the society. But if any meaningful generalizations are to emerge about these different roles, a discussion of the power of this stratum or a section of it will have to clarify four questions:

1. The scope and limits of technical expertise in solving problems in society;
2. An assessment of the new kinds of industries which sell "knowledge," not goods, and the weight of these industries (profit and nonprofit) in the economy of the country;
3. The basis of cohesiveness of any new social class based on skill, not property; and
4. The likelihood of the *techniciens* and technocrats becoming a new, dominant class[49] (like the bourgeoisie, who preceded the development of large-scale industry), replacing the older capitalist class.

These, then, are the strands of social development as they have arisen in the sociological writings in the West since Marx. As I pointed

---

[46] From *Quel Avenir attend l'homme?* (Paris, 1961), quoted in Meynaud, ibid., p. 146.

[47] This distinction is also made in an interesting book by two Marxist writers, Frederic Bon and Michel-Antonie Burnier, *Les Nouveaux Intellectuels* (Paris, 1966). See chaps. IV and V, "Les Intellectuels Technocrates," and "Les Intellectuels Techniciens."

[48] This argument is developed in chap. 6, "Technocracy and Politics."

[49] One is not restricted to the specific focus of *techniciens;* if I read Dahrendorf's term "service class" rightly (see footnote 14), he would include this group, and little more, as the core of what he sees as the ascending new class in society.

out, they are, implicitly, an unravelling of Marx's schema two, but in a direction he did not think it would go. In these conceptions, the forces of production (technology) replace social relations (property) as the major axis of society, and from this arises the concept of industrial society in the work of Raymond Aron and others. Capitalist society is seen as undergoing change, but in the visions of Weber and Schumpeter, not towards socialism but towards some form of statism and bureaucratic society. For the classical Marxian views, and for the societies and social movements which claim to be Marxist, these theories of social development pose a crucial intellectual challenge.

Marxism: The Problem of Bureaucracy

In the post-Marxist sociological writing in the West, then, two themes have emerged as central for the transformation of capitalist or industrial society, one the bureaucratization of the enterprise, if not of the society as a whole, the other the rise of new classes, particularly the technical and white-collar occupations, to predominance in the society, altering thus the sociological character of the stratification system. To put the issues in the Marxian framework, the social *forces* of production have become industrial, but are common to a wide variety of political systems; the social *relations* of production have become bureaucratic, in which ownership assumes a diminishing role.

Marx had foreseen many of these changes. The joint-stock company, he wrote, "is the abolition of capital as private property within the boundaries of capitalist production itself" (*Capital*, vol. III, p. 516). He thought, as I indicated earlier, that the separation of ownership and control, and the transformation of the capitalist into a manager of "other people's capital," were a step in the socialization of the enterprise. (For Marx's discussion, see *Capital*, vol. III, pp. 454–459, 515–521.) But he did not foresee the issue of the managers (of both capitalist and socialist enterprises) becoming a new class. Nor did he take up much the question of bureaucracy. In the mid-twentieth century, bureaucracy has become the central problem for all societies, socialist as well as capitalist.

Strange to say, in only one essay, in the *Critique of Hegel's Philosophy of Right*, written in 1843, did Marx squarely confront the subject. Afterwards, other than marginal references, the topic seems to vanish from the center of Marx's concerns.[50] The reason lies, per-

---

[50] Inevitably, Marxologues disagree on this, as on so many other interpretations of Marx's thought. Thus Martin Albrow, in his excellent little book, *Bureaucracy* (London, 1970), writes: "The section devoted to bureaucracy constituted an important part of the *Kritik des Hegelschen Staatsrechts*. It was a topic on which Marx had

haps, in Marx's fundamental vision of the relation of society to politics in modern times.

In the classical world, as Hegel had pointed out, there is no distinction between the social and the political, between society and the state. As Avineri writes: "When the political state is just a form of socio-economic life, of the material state, *res publica* means that public life is the real content of individual life. Therefore anyone whose private life lacks political status is a slave: political unfreedom means social servitude."

The Middle Ages reverses this relationship. Each person is defined by his sociological standing and is a member of a specific estate or *Stände* which defines his rights and obligations. It is a society which is the foundation of social as well as political status; the term *Stände* refers both to social stratification and to political organization.

In modern society, there is a fundamental distinction between state and civil society. As Marx writes, in his essays on *The Jewish Question:* "The political revolution [i.e. the shattering of Estates and guild privileges] abolished the political character of the civic society. . . . The political emancipation was at the same time the emancipation of civil society from politics, from even the semblance of a general content." [51]

---

clearly thought deeply. But thereafter he scarcely gave it any attention. He made occasional mention of the bureaucrats, but the *Kritik* was neither cited nor published and the Marxist theory of the state developed in independence of it" (p. 69).

Shlomo Avineri, however, in his *The Social and Political Thought of Karl Marx* (Cambridge, England, 1968) argues: ". . . an insistence on the importance of understanding bureaucracy both historically and functionally runs through all of Marx's writings after 1843. For Marx, bureaucracy is central to the understanding of the modern state" (p. 49).

How to mediate this stark difference? By making a distinction. In the *Critique* of Hegel, Marx discusses the role of bureaucracy as a quasi-independent force, standing between the State and Civil Society. In his later political writings, particularly in *The Eighteenth Brumaire* and *The Civil War in France*, bureaucracy is seen as identical with the state apparatus, and it is the state, even though "the instrument of the ruling class," which, at times, "strove for power on its own," under the guise of representing the *general* interest. The idea, however, that the bureaucracy could be an *independent* force in modern society disappears from Marx's writing. This discussion, it should be emphasized, is in the framework of western social development. Bureaucracy was for Marx a central feature of the "Asiatic mode of production," a theme that is developed in Karl Wittfogel's *Oriental Despotism* (Yale University Press, 1957).

Marx's Critique of Hegel's Philosophy of Right was published first only in 1927, by D. Riazanov, as part of his collection of Marx's early writings. A full English translation appeared only in 1971, edited by Joseph O'Malley (Cambridge, England). Excerpts appeared in the U.S. in the edition, *Writings of the Young Marx on Philosophy and Society*, ed. Lloyd Easton and Kurt H. Guddat (New York, 1967), pp. 152–202. The translations used below are from Easton and Guddat, modified in one instance by the use of a section from Avineri where it made more colloquial sense.

[51] Reprinted in *Selected Essays of Karl Marx*, ed. H. J. Stenning (London, n.d.), p. 82.

For Hegel, from whom this basic distinction derived, the civil society was an assemblage of special interests, each pursuing its own individual aims while the state represented the "general interest" ruling for "all." The responsibility for carrying out the monarch's decision—the monarch embodying the state—is the civil servant's; Hegel does not use the word bureaucracy. "The nature of the executive functions," he writes in *The Philosophy of Right*, "is that they are objective and that in their substance they have been explicitly fixed by previous decision." For that purpose a special kind of person is required.

Individuals are not appointed to office on account of their birth or native personal gifts. The *objective* factor in their appointment is knowledge and proof of ability. Such proof guarantees that the state will get what it requires; and since it is the sole condition of appointment, it also guarantees to every citizen the chance of joining the class of civil servants.

The misuse of power—the guarantee that officials will not overstep the bounds of the general interest—is guarded against by the "hierarchical organizations and answerability of the officials," and the independence given to corporate bodies, e.g. universities and local communities with their own powers.[52]

For Marx this is sheer mystification. As he says in the *Critique:* "What Hegel says . . . does not deserve the name of philosophical exposition. Most of the paragraphs could be taken verbatim from the Prussian Civil Code." The opposition between general interests and special interests is illusory for the state is itself a private purpose simply confronting other private purposes, and the impartiality of the bureaucracy—a word Marx does use, in a pejorative sense—is a mask for its own special interests. It is in this context that Marx develops his views about the nature of bureaucracy:

Hegel proceeds from the *separation* of the "state" and "civil" society, from "particular interests" and the "completely existent universal." And bureaucracy is indeed based on *this separation.* . . . Hegel develops no *content* for bureaucracy, only some general definitions of its "*formal*" organization. And indeed bureaucracy is only the "formalism" of a content lying outside. . . .

"Bureaucracy" is the "state formalism" of civil society. It is the "state's consciousness," the "state's will," the "state's power," as a *corporation*, hence a *particular*, closed society in the state. . . .

Bureaucracy is a circle no one can leave. Its hierarchy is a *hierarchy of information.* The top entrusts the lower circles with an insight into details, while the lower circles entrust the top with an insight into what is universal, and thus they mutually deceive each other. . . .

[52] *Hegel's Philosophy of Right*, trans. T. M. Knox (Oxford, 1949), pp. 190, 192. The discussions of "the executive" are in paragraphs 287–297, pp. 186–193.

Bureaucracy possesses the state's essence, the spiritual essence of society, as its *private property*. The general spirit of bureaucracy is the official *secret*, the mystery sustained within bureaucracy itself by hierarchy and maintained on the outside as a closed corporation. Conducting the affairs of the state in public, even political consciousness, thus appears to the bureaucracy as high treason against its mystery. Authority is thus the principle of its knowledge, and the deification of authoritarianism is its credo.

. . . within bureaucracy spiritualism becomes a crass materialism, the materialism of passive obedience, of faith in authority, of the mechanism of fixedly formal activities, fixed principles, views and traditions. For the individual bureaucrat the state's purpose becomes his private purpose of hunting for higher positions and making a career for himself. In one respect he views actual life as something material, *for the spirit of this life has its separate existence* in bureaucracy. . . . Bureaucracy has therefore to make life as materialistic as possible. . . . Hence the bureaucrat must always behave toward the real state in a Jesuitical fashion, be it consciously or unconsciously. . . . The bureaucrat sees the world as a mere object to be managed by him.[53]

Acute as this is, one has to attribute the subsequent lack of attention to bureaucracy—and the lack of a systematic discussion of the political order—to the evolution of Marx's thought, from politics to sociology so to speak, an evolution reflected in the subsequent writings in the *Economic Manuscripts* and *The German Ideology*. Out of this came Marx's distinctive conception of sociology: the focus on society, not the state; on the economy, not the polity.

For Marx all basic social relations derive not from politics, but from the mode of production. Class relations are economic relations: there could not be autonomous political classes, or orders, such as bureaucracy and the military. For him, what was distinctive about modern society was not the creation of a national state, or a bureaucracy, but the *capitalist* mode of production. The crises which would shake modern society were primarily economic, deriving from the "laws of motion" of the capitalist mode of production: the chronic underconsumption, the disproportion between the producers' goods and consumers' goods sectors with consequent overproduction, and the falling rate of profit—all derived from the murderous competition between capitalists, and the consequent changing ratios of the organic composition of capital in the society as a whole. What was unique about capitalism was the existence of an autonomous market society which was not dependent on the state.[54]

[53] See Easton and Guddat, op. cit., pp. 184, 185, 186; Avineri, op. cit., pp. 23–24.
[54] As Avineri well puts it:
Civil society is totally emancipated from political limitations; private life, including economic activity, becomes completely independent of any considerations relevant to the commonwealth; and all political restrictions on property and eco-

For Marx, then, it was not politics but social structure which was decisive. Politics is an arena where the social divisions of a society are fought out. Politics has no autonomy; it is a reflection of societal forces. What is the state? An instrument of force—the army, police, bureaucracy—used by the dominant classes. For Marx, there was no capitalist *state*, but a state used by capitalists. In fact, there is no theory or history of types of *political order* in Marx, as in Weber, with his distinctions of patriarchal, patrimonial and legal bureaucratic political orders, or types of political legitimacy. For Marx, the focus is on the *underlying* social structure whose actual relations are obscured by formal relations (so, in his discussion of the fetishism of commodities in *Capital*, vol. I, Marx points out that abstract exchange relations between commodities mask concrete social relations between men).

For Marx, the *capitalist* mode of production was possible in a wide variety of *political* states, democratic or authoritarian (vide England and Imperial Germany), but, inevitably, since the capitalist was the dominant class in the society, the state would reflect and support capitalist interests.

But not always. The most vivid and striking of all of Marx's analyses of the ebb and flow of political power is *The Eighteenth Brumaire of Louis Bonaparte*. Yet *The Eighteenth Brumaire* is a study of an adventurer who was "above" the classes, and used the state to manipulate one class against another. As Marx writes:

This contradictory task of the man explains the contradictions of his government, the confused groping hither and thither which seeks now to win, now to humiliate first one class and then another and arrays all of them uniformly against him. . . .
As the executive authority which has made itself an independent power, Bonaparte feels it to be his mission to safeguard "civil order." But the strength of this civil order lies in the middle class. He looks on himself, therefore, as the representative of the middle class and issues decrees in this sense. Nevertheless he is somebody solely due to the fact that he has broken the political power of this middle class and daily breaks it anew. Consequently, he looks on himself as the adversary of the political and literary power of the middle class. *But by protecting its material power, he generates its political power anew.*[55]

"But above all," as Marx writes, Bonaparte, in fact, as the chief of the Society of 10 December, is the "representative of the *lumpenproletariat* to which he himself, his entourage, his government and his

---

nomic activity are abolished. Economic individualism and *laissez faire* express this dichotomy between civil society and state, with human society now fully conscious of its alienation and of the division of human life into a private and public sphere. Ibid., pp. 20–21.
[55] Reprinted in Karl Marx, *Selected Works*, vol. II (Moscow, 1936), pp. 423, 424.

army belong," and their prime purpose is to enrich themselves. And so, the political character of a regime is transitory. And yet, for a short space in history the state *can be* politically against the "dominant" class and be run by men or groups, demagogues or the military, who stand against the bourgeoisie or the major economic classes; but for Marx, what counts in the end is the underlying economic system on which "material power" rests.

It is this theme, the underlying mode of production and the character of property relations, which is central and decisive for Marx; all the rest is secondary. Marx's early writings were the criticism of religion and politics. The writing on bureaucracy, written before he turned to economics, came when Marx was still a democrat and not yet a communist.[56] In those writings, bureaucracy appears as a quasi-independent force, developing its own mode of existence, ruling the rest of society in its own interests. Yet two years after his essay on bureaucracy, when Marx had completed his *Economic Manuscripts*, he turned scathingly on a former friend, Karl Heinzen, and comments: "The fatuous Heinzen connects the existence of classes with the existence of *political* privileges and *monopolies*." [57] Marx had become a believer in the primacy of economic power.

The idea that the bureaucracy could become an independent force above a society was a theme that was central to all the skeptics of nineteenth-century progress, from anarchists like Bakunin to conservatives like Burckhardt.[58] Yet for Marxists, this would only contradict the proposition that class relations were economic relations and economic relations were *au fond* property relations. It was an insight into history that became an ideological dogma; and like all ideology it served, in turn, to obscure reality. The irony of it was that the place where this paradox worked itself out—where politics replaced economics—was in the first socialist society where power was taken in the name of Marx, in the Soviet Union.

---

[56] For an authoritative discussion of this point, see Leonard Krieger, "The Uses of Marx for History," in the *Political Science Quarterly*, vol. LXXV, no. 3.

[57] The reference is in Albrow, op. cit., p. 70.

[58] As Bakunin observed in a famous passage:

. . . a strong State can have only one foundation; military and bureaucratic centralization. In this respect the essential difference between a monarchy and a democratic republic is reduced to the following: in a monarchy the bureaucratic world oppresses and plunders the people for the greater benefiit of the privileged propertied classes as well as for its own benefit, and all that is done in the name of the monarch; in a republic the same bureaucracy will do exactly the same, but —in the name of the will of the people. . . . every State, even the most Republican and the most democratic State—even the would-be popular State conceived by M. Marx—are in their essence only machines governing the masses from above, through an intelligent and therefore a privileged minority, allegedly knowing the general interests of the people better than the people themselves. *The Political Philosophy of Bakunin*, ed. G. P. Maximoff (Glencoe, Ill., 1953), p. 211.

The Soviet Union: Bureaucracy and the New Class

In Czarist Russia a socialist revolution had taken place: private ownership of the means of production had been abolished and property relations, and consequently class relations had been transformed. Thus, in the most unlikely of circumstances, a Marxian theory of society and social development was to be tested.

Before the First World War, all Marxian theorists had predicted a revolution in Russia. This was based on Marx's notion, derived from the revolutions of 1848, that the *political* course of capitalist development would fall into two stages: the democratic revolution and the social revolution. The democratic revolution was essentially bourgeois; it was the achievement of political rights, such as the right of assembly, of franchise, etc. which the bourgeoisie itself needed to establish power, but which, in struggle, could be grasped by the working class as well. The social revolution was the action by the working class, using its political rights, to transform the economic relations of society.

From this point of view, Marxists drew a continuum: England and France had gone farthest in the democratic revolution; Germany's revolution was incomplete; Russia had lagged most behind. The agenda of history, therefore, remained to be completed; Russia still had to go through its "1848." Thus all socialists expected a revolution in Russia as an historical inevitability—but a "bourgeois" revolution, February, not October.

Some Marxists, particulary Trotsky, thought it possible to make a socialist revolution in Russia on the basis of what Trotsky called "the law of combined development" for backward countries. "In the conditions of capitalist decline," wrote Trotsky, "backward countries are unable to attain that level which the old centers of capitalism have obtained," and since such countries could not develop on a capitalist basis, only socialization could "solve those problems of technique and productivity which were long ago solved by capitalism in the advanced industrial countries." [59]

But in the Soviet Union, after the October Revolution, a new social force had arisen which had increasingly assumed autonomy and independent power—the bureaucracy. In *State and Revolution* Lenin had argued that the old state machinery had to be smashed,

---

[59] Leon Trotsky, *The Revolution Betrayed* (New York, 1937), pp. 5–6. To save elaborate footnoting, further citations of pages are given in brackets after quotation; all references are to this edition. Except where otherwise indicated, emphases are added.

and the new administrative apparatus would be, as in the Paris Commune of 1871, directly in the hands of the people: there would be officials, but they would not become bureaucrats, "i.e. privileged persons divorced from the people and standing *above* the people. That is the *essence* of bureaucracy." Workers' deputies were to supervise the management of the apparatus. They were to be elected and subject to recall. Their pay was not to exceed a worker's. There was to be "immediate introduction of control and supervision by *all*, so that *all* may become 'bureaucrats' for a time and that therefore, *nobody* may be able to become a 'bureaucrat'." [60]

But Trotsky, even from the start, had a more realistic view. Bureaucracy, he argued, is inescapable ("the tendencies of bureaucratism . . . would everywhere show themselves even after a proletarian revolution") for the obvious reason that no transition to socialism is ever immediate ("A socialist state even in America on the basis of the most advanced capitalism could not immediately provide everyone with as much as he needs, and would therefore be compelled to spur everyone to produce as much as possible"), so that both a state and some "directing apparatus" in the society would still be necessary (pp. 53, 55).

A bureaucracy, he said, inevitably tends to develop its own vested interests. But the counterweight to the bureaucracy is the Party ("the Party was always in a state of open or disguised struggle with the bureaucracy"). It was Stalin, in seeking his own power, who brought the two together. What Stalin did was to "subject the Party to its own officialdom and merge the latter in the officialdom of the state. Thus was created the present totalitarian regime" (p. 279).

But bureaucracy has its own trajectory. "The unlimited power of the bureaucracy is a no less forceful instrument of social differentiation," Trotsky wrote (p. 133). It uses its power to guarantee its own well-being; it divides sectors of the population from each other, creating privileged strata in the working class and collective farms; it strangles criticism in order to reinforce its own power. In all respects it has "the specific consciousness of a ruling 'class', which, however, is still far from confident of its right to rule" (p. 135).

If a new ruling "class" has emerged, what then is the character of Soviet society? Is it still socialist; and if so, in what way? If not what

---

[60] See V. I. Lenin, *The State and the Revolution*, in *Selected Works* (Moscow, 1951, published in England 1953), vol. II, part I, pp. 249–250, 280. "Such a beginning," Lenin added, "on the basis of a large-scale production, will of itself lead to the gradual 'withering away' of all bureaucracy . . . to an order in which the functions of control and accounting—becoming more and more simple—will be performed by each in turn, will then become a habit and will finally die out as the special functions of a special section of the population" (ibid., p. 250).

is it? These were the questions with which Trotsky wrestled in the book, questions crucial to one's assessment of the revolution.

Trotsky sought to give two answers, one political, the other sociological. The Stalin regime itself Trotsky called a form of Bonapartism, though "of a new type not before seen in history." Bonapartism arises when "in moments of history" a sharp struggle between two camps allows state power to rise, momentarily, above the contending classes. But as a Marxist, Trotsky could not accept Bonapartism as more than a passing political phase of a deeper struggle, that of contending classes. What, then, was the sociological character, i.e. the *class character*, of Soviet society?

Was it "state capitalism"? Trotsky considered the question in detail, but rejected the formulation on two curious grounds: one that property had been "socialized" in the Soviet Union and two, that state capitalism was a device in declining capitalist states, such as Germany or Italy, to restrict the "productive forces" of the society in order to serve reactionary purposes. Since, in the Soviet Union, the regime's intention was to "develop the productive forces" of society, the society was historically progressive. How, then, could one group both fascist and communist under a common rubric of state capitalism?

Is the bureaucracy a new class? Trotsky had more difficulty with this question. In bourgeois society the bureaucracy "represents the interests of a possessing and educated class." The fascists, "when they find themselves in power, are united with the big bourgeoisie by bonds of common interest." In the Soviet Union "the means of production belong to the state. But the state, so to speak, 'belongs' to the bureaucracy. . . . It is in the full sense of the word the sole privileged and commanding *stratum* in the Soviet society" (pp. 248–249).

But Trotsky shies away from calling the bureaucracy a *class* and accepting the fact that a new and different kind of social system had been created in the Soviet Union. When he uses the phrase "ruling 'class'," the word *class* is in quotation marks, to indicate its ambiguity; so, too, is the word *belong* when he writes that the state "belongs" to the bureaucracy. His chief argument is that the bureaucracy lacks the essential and distinctive feature of a class, i.e. property rights, and so it cannot "transmit to [its] heirs its rights in the exploitation of the state apparatus."

The issue, says Trotsky, is still open. The question of the character of the Soviet Union, he declares, is not yet decided by history. It is a "workers state, torn by the antagonism between an organized and armed Soviet aristocracy and the unarmed toiling masses," a *"contradictory society halfway between capitalism and socialism"* (pp. 278, 255). The alternatives are either a new upsurge by the proletariat to eliminate the privileges of the bureaucracy, or a "bourgeois restoration." Trotsky also considers a third variant, that "the bureaucracy continues at the head of the state." But his orthodox Marxism leads him to reject this as a likely permanent form since he cannot envisage a class becoming a ruling class without becoming a "possessing class," and passing on its privileges "by right of testament."

And yet, in wrestling with these questions, Trotsky is led to a startling conclusion: "To define the Soviet regime as transitional, or intermediate, means to abandon such finished social categories as *capitalism* (and therewith 'state capitalism') and also *socialism*" (p. 254, emphasis in the original). Doctrinaires would not be satisfied, he notes, "sociological problems would certainly be simpler if sociological phenomena had always a finished character." But "there is nothing more dangerous, however, than to throw out of reality, for the sake of logical completeness, elements which today violate your scheme and tomorrow may wholly overturn it" (p. 255).

As an orthodox Marxist, Trotsky could only envisage the Soviet Union, in his time, as tending either to capitalism or socialism. And yet, Trotsky did not throw out of his scheme the possibility that the bureaucracy could become a new class, even though it violated the "logical completeness" of the dichotomy of capitalism and socialism. In *The Revolution Betrayed* he wrote:

If these as yet wholly new relations [i.e. bureaucratic privilege] should solidify, become the norm and be legalized, whether with or without resistance from the workers, they would, in the long run, lead to a complete liquidation of the social conquests of the proletarian revolution. But to speak of that now is at least premature (p. 249).

Three years later, in what was to be his last theoretical pronouncement, Trotsky acknowledged the distinct possibility of another *either/or*. Writing shortly after the Nazi-Soviet pact, Trotsky told his followers that a new historic caesura had been reached: since the "further persistence of the disintegrating capitalist world is impossible," either the proletariat would organize the world for socialism or a new social form, bureaucratic collectivism, would establish itself on the stage of history.

Trotsky took the phrase and the idea of bureaucratic collectivism from a book published in Paris in 1939 entitled *Le Bureaucratisation du Monde* by a man who signed it only Bruno R. No one knew Bruno R., although Trotsky called him "an Italian 'left-Communist' who formerly adhered to the Fourth International." Even more curious, no one seemed to be able to find the book which, for Trotsky, represented the only real challenge to his ideas; and the argument about "bureaucratic collectivism" became known only second-hand, through Trotsky's account.

The thesis of the book, as reported by Trotsky, was sweeping in its stark and powerful simplicity. Not only did the bureaucracy in Russia constitute a new class but the men of this class— bureaucrats, managers, technicians—were the forerunners of a social revolution which was creating a new type of ruling class throughout the entire Western world: Stalin's Russia, Hitler's Germany, Mussolini's Italy, even Franklin D. Roosevelt's New Deal were all part of a common historical phenomenon.

For Trotsky there was a direct political corollary to this new *either/or*. "However onerous the . . . perspective may be," he wrote, if the Stalin regime was not merely an "abhorrent relapse" on the road to socialism but a distinct new social form, with permanent exploitative features of its own, then the proletariat everywhere would have to repudiate the Soviet Union and refuse to defend it against its enemies as progressive. In the longer perspective, if the larger thesis were true, that socialism was not the necessary stage after capitalism, then the idea itself would have to be considered as a "utopia." [61]

Trotsky, at his death, was still not prepared to accept the second perspective, and for him and his followers Russia was still a "degenerated workers' state" which could yet be redeemed by a proletarian revolution. For left-wing schismatics, however, for whom the orthodox Marxist categories had become too constricting, the phrase "bureaucratic collectivism" was a felicitous one. It congealed the gropings of independent radicals who sought a sociological category that was realistic about the Soviet regime. The dissident Trotskyite faction, led by Max Shachtman, adopted the concept and in a series of articles from 1940 on Shachtman sought to develop the idea that the Soviet Union was neither socialist nor capitalist but a new kind of society. [62] Shachtman's co-leader in the Trotskyite split, James Burnham,

---

[61] The article by Trotsky, entitled "The USSR in War," appeared in *The New International* (November 1939). As he formulated the question:

However onerous the second perspective may be, if the world proletariat should actually prove incapable of fulfilling the mission placed upon it by the course of development, nothing else would remain except openly to recognize that the socialist program, based on the internal contradictions of capitalist society, ended as a utopia. It is self-evident that a new "minimum" program would be required— for the defense of the interests of the slaves of the totalitarian bureaucratic society.

[62] The major argument was first summarized by Shachtman in 1943 in his long introduction to the publication, then, of Trotsky's *The New Course*, Trotsky's initial statement on the develpment of bureaucracy in Russia which he wrote as an internal document for the Party in 1923, and which Shachtman translated to establish the beginnings of the revisionist doctrine. Shachtman published a collection of

generalized the idea as Bruno R. had, and proposed the theory of *The Managerial Revolution* as the necessary outcome of Western social development.

Burnham's *The Managerial Revolution*, which as an idea and a phrase, rather than as a specific set of definitions and categories, has had a continuing influence since its publication thirty years ago, has an artful simplicity. It was based on the assumption that *function* rather than *ownership* was the crucial category of power in a technical society, and it presented a seductive theory of historical class succession so that just as the oppressed peasantry did not succeed the oppressive feudal lords but both were displaced by an entirely different class, the bourgeoisie, who remade society to their own image, so the proletariat would not succeed the capitalist, but both would be replaced by "the managers," who would become a new ruling class, wielding power on the basis of their technical superiority.

Though the idea of *The Managerial Revolution* may have been suggested by Bruno R. (however there are no references to him in Burnham's book), the historical lineaments of the conception were clear, and Burnham moved quickly to establish a patrimony in his next book, two years later, *The Machiavellians*, which he subtitled defensively "Defenders of Freedom." These fathers were Gaetano Mosca, who proclaimed that all societies are divided into elites and masses and that the political process is always a "struggle for pre-eminence" on the part of determined minorities; Vilfredo Pareto, who saw political history as a "circulation of elites" wherein new vigorous forces in society manipulate the sentiments of the masses in order to gain power [63]; and Robert Michels, who argued that complex organi-

---

his own writings on the subject as *The Bureaucratic Revolution: The Rise of the Stalinist State* (New York, 1962).

Inasmuch as when radical sects split each circle becomes squared, in the ideological break-up of the American Trotskyite movement in the early 1940s, Shachtman declared that a new social form, bureaucratic collectivism, had emerged in the Soviet Union, but at the other end of the quadrille the Johnson-Forest "tendency" argued that the Soviet Union could only be a "state capitalist" society. Johnson was the black writer C. L. R. James, who later went back to his first love, writing about cricket, on which he was an acknowledged authority. Forest was the pseudonym of the theoretician Raya Dunayevskaya, who had once been Trotsky's secretary. Miss Dunayevskaya retreated to Detroit, where she founded a matriarchal sect whose major theoretical effort was to convince workers that a knowledge of Hegel's *Science of Logic* was necessary to understand Lenin. Her book arguing this thesis in part, *Marxism and Freedom* (New York, 1958), carries an appreciative introduction by Herbert Marcuse. The two other corners were occupied by James P. Cannon, who defended the "orthodox" Trotsky view of Russia as a "degenerated workers' state," and James Burnham, who generalized the idea of bureaucratic collectivism into the sweeping idea of the managerial revolution.

[63] As Pareto describes the mechanism of this process:

Revolutions come about through accumulations in the higher strata of society—

zation creates a need for technical specialization, that "organization implies a tendency to oligarchy," that the leadership places the defense of its interests ahead of its constituency, and that the extension of state bureaucracy "alone can [satisfy] the claim of the educated members of the population . . . the discontented members of the educated classes . . . for secure positions" in the society.[64]

While the *phrase* "the managerial revolution" had a large resonance, the analysis and categories proved feeble indeed. The central terms shifted constantly. By "managers" Burnham said he meant the "production managers," "administrative engineers," "supervisory technicians," but not the finance executives, this differentiation a bastard version of Veblen's distinction between industry and business. But the managers were also in government, where they were the administrators, commissioners, bureau heads, and so on. Presumably there was a community of interest between those in industry and those in government.

The managers "will exercise their control over the instruments of production . . . through their control of the state which in turn will own and control the instruments of production." In Germany and Italy there is a shift from capitalism to managerial society. In Russia, "the nation most advanced toward managerial structure," the managers, who are the managers of factories and state trusts and big collective farms, are already getting the largest proportion of the national income.

In the West the managerial revolution had to come because capitalism itself will break down.

Experience has already shown that there is not the slightest prospect of ridding capitalism of mass unemployment. . . . The volume of public and private debt has reached a point where it cannot be managed much longer . . . there has been in all major capitalist nations a permanent agricultural depression. . . . [And finally] Capitalism is no longer able to find uses for the available investment funds, which waste in idleness in the account books of the banks. This mass unemployment of private money is scarcely less indicative of the death of capitalism than the mass unemployment of human beings.

---

either because of a slowing-down in class-circulation, or from other causes—of decadent elements no longer possessing the residues suitable for keeping them in power, and shrinking from the use of force; while meantime in the lower strata of society elements of superior quality are coming to the fore, possessing residues suitable for exercising the functions of government and willing to use force.
Paragraph 2057, *The Mind and Society* (New York, 1935), vol. III, p. 1431, "Class-Circulation."

[64] Robert Michels, *Political Parties* (Glencoe, Illinois, reprint edition, 1949), pp. 31–37, 185–189.

In the same apocalyptic vein Burnham writes: "We are now in a position to understand the central historical meaning of the first two world wars of the twentieth century. . . . The war of 1914 was the last great war of capitalist society; the war of 1939 is the first great war of managerial society." And, he continues: "The general outcome of the second war is also assured. It is assured because it does not depend upon a military victory by Germany, which is in any case likely." The general outcome is the collapse of capitalism, the consolidation of Europe ("The day of a Europe carved into a score of sovereign states is over") and the victory of managerial society.[65]

Apart from the political predictions, which were quickly falsified, how viable is the theory of the managerial revolution? Although Burnham is quite fuzzy as to who are the managers, it is clear from the context out of which his theory developed that it is the economic administrators, not the political bureaucrats, who will dominate the society, though at one point he states that there is no sharp distinction between the economic managers and the political bureaucrats when he writes: "To say that the ruling class is the managers is almost the same thing as to say that it is the state bureaucracy." [66]

But in fact the economic managers and the state bureaucracy—if one thinks of managers as the men who run the economic *enterprises*—are often quite distinct and even often at odds with each other. As Kerr, Harbison, Dunlop, and Myers argue in their comparative study of management:

. . . in all industrializing societies, the managerial class has neither the capacity nor the will to become the dominant ruling group. The managers are characteristically the agents of stockholders, of state bureaucracies, or

---

[65] James Burnham, *The Managerial Revolution* (New York, 1941). Citations, successively, to pp. 80, 72, 236, 159, 221, 32–33, 176, 247.

[66] A striking juxtaposition with Burnham is provided by Max Weber in an essay written in 1917 which contains a section called "Bureaucratization and the Naïveté of the Literati." Said Weber:

A progressive elimination of private capitalism is theoretically conceivable, although it is surely not so easy as imagined in the dreams of some literati who do not know what it is all about; its elimination will certainly not be a consequence of this war. But let us assume that sometime in the future it will be done away with. What would be the practical result? The destruction of the steel frame of modern industrial work? No! The abolition of private capitalism would simply mean that also the *top management* of the nationalized or socialized enterprises would become bureaucratic. . . . State bureaucracy would rule *alone* if private capitalism were eliminated. The private and public bureaucracies, which now work next to, and potentially against, each other and hence check one another to a degree, would be merged into a single hierarchy.

From the essay "Parliament and Government in a Reconstructed Germany," reprinted as Appendix II, in *Max Weber: Economy and Society*, ed. Roth and Wittich, vol. 3, pp. 1401–1402.

in some cases of workers' councils. Since they are preoccupied with internal affairs of enterprise, which become ever more complex, the members of the managerial class are prone to become conformists rather than leaders in the larger affairs of society.[67]

To say all this is not to minimize the real changes which have taken place in the social structure of Western society—if one looks at the enterprise in functional rather than formal terms. The power of technical management has forced a decisive change in many of the basic goals of capitalist corporations. And there is a high degree of managerial autonomy.[68] The tasks of running a single enterprise in the "socialist" economies often bring such managers into direct conflict either with the economic planners at the center or the political controllers who make the key decisions about targets of planned growth, allocation between sectors, and the like. But this is to delimit the scope of a theory of managerial revolution rather than accept it as the *leitmotif* of all structural changes in Western society.

Although Burnham's schematic and sweeping theory of the managerial revolution (a "Marx for the Managers" was the biting appraisal by Gerth and Mills of Burnham's intentions) never took sociological root, the idea that the Soviet Union had become a new social form, neither capitalist nor socialist, was widely accepted by socialist and

[67] Clark Kerr, Frederick Harbison, John Dunlop, and Charles A. Myers, "Industrialism and Industrial Man," *International Labour Review* (September 1960), p. 10. As the writers say further, in their book on this theme: "Although professional management is destined to sweep aside its political or patrimonial predecessors, it seldom becomes a ruling elite in any society. In other words, the state does not become the property of the professional managers, as James Burnham envisioned in his "managerial revolution." Rather the managers may be as much servants as masters of the state, as much subordinate as controllers of the market. The managers are a part of the ruling elite but they are not *the elite*. In the Soviet Union, for example, the industrial managers are clearly subservient to the political and government elite. In Japan the heads of the great *zaibatsu* were always conscious of their prior obligation to serve nationalist objectives and the interests of the state. . . . In the modern industrializing society, it appears, management can be supreme only within the orbit of the enterprise, and even here it must share its authority with others who demand and obtain a share in the making of the web of rules which governs industrializing man." *Industrialism and Industrial Man* (Cambridge, Mass., 1960), pp. 145–146.

[68] The most important study of the changed practices of the private corporation is that of Robin Marris, *The Economic Theory of "Managerial Capitalism"* (New York, 1964), who argues that the major objective of managers is not profit maximization but a "sustainable growth rate" whose chief purpose is the maximization of assets. In effect the motivations of the managers, rather than the nature of the market, shape primary corporate objectives. Marris's work is the technical basis for the more popular argument, along the same line, by J. K. Galbraith in *The New Industrial State*. The Marris hypothesis is tested and elaborated by a number of prominent economists in the book *The Corporate Economy*, edited by Robin Marris and Adrian Wood (Cambridge, Mass., 1971). For the Soviet Union, the best study of the role of the managers vis-à-vis the political controllers is by Jeremy Azrael, *Managerial Power and Soviet Politics* (Cambridge, Mass., 1966).

non-Stalinist Marxists in the forties and fifties and was one of the elements that contributed to the disillusionment with the old ideologies that was characteristic of that period.

The theme of the transformation of Soviet society into a new social form was given popular expression in 1957 by the publication of Milovan Djilas's *The New Class*. The book lacked the theoretical sophistication of Trotsky and evaded the complexities of the analytical issues that had been posed by earlier Marxist writers (Hilferding, Solomon Schwarz, Yugow, Ciliga, Peter Meyer, Yvon), who had made the first statistical analyses of the class and occupational trends of Soviet society. Yet the book was a success for three reasons: it had been written in jail, and smuggled out, by one of the highest ranking former communists of the post-Second World War world, the vice-president of Yugoslavia, who had been expelled from the Party in 1954 for having called for its "democratization"; it was published shortly after the Hungarian Revolution which had given many socialists hope that the Soviet system might, surprisingly, begin to crack; and its simplified exposition was infused with a moral earnestness that was highly appealing.

Djilas was quick to say that his analysis was principally of the communist world, the only one he knew. ("I do not pretend to know any world outside the communist world, in which I had either the fortune or misfortune to live.") "It is very difficult, perhaps impossible, to define the limits of the new class and to identify its members," he writes. But "the new class may be said to be made up of those who have special privileges and economic preference because of the administrative monopoly they hold." However, since the source of the privilege is the power of the Party, the heart of the new class is not the economic managers but the political bureaucracy. The very pattern of the Party, as a cadre of professional revolutionaries, itself foreshadowed the new class. Whereas in previous societies new classes attained power *after* new economic patterns had taken shape, in the communist world the reverse had happened. The new class "did not come to power to *complete* a new economic order, but to *establish* its own and, in so doing, to establish its power over society."

With an eye to the question of the managerial revolution thesis, Djilas writes: "It is important to note the fundamental differences between the political bureaucracies mentioned here and those which arise with every centralization in modern economy." In every advanced society there arises a new white-collar class and "functionaries" who may be becoming a special stratum of society. Though "such functionaries have much in common with communist bureaucrats . . . they are not identical." Bureaucrats in non-communist countries "have political masters, usually elected, or owners over them, while communists have neither masters nor owners over them." In the communist world, "The government both administers and distributes national property. The new class, or its executive organ—the Party oligarchy—both acts as the owner and is the owner. The most reactionary and bourgeois government can hardly dream of such a monopoly in the economy." [69]

[69] Milovan Djilas, *The New Class* (New York, 1957). Citations, successively, to pp. v, 38–39, 43–44, 207.

In the long wash of the discussion of Djilas's theoretical analysis there came a strange denouement. In the November 1958 issue of *Le Contrat Social*, a political bi-monthly edited by Boris Souvarine in Paris, there appeared an article by Georges Henein entitled "Bruno R. and the 'New Class'," which traced back Djilas's idea to *Le Bureaucratisation du Monde*. Unfortunately, said Henein, Bruno R. was dead.

In the March 1959 issue of *Le Contrat Social*, two pertinent letters appeared on the subject—one from Bruno R. himself, very much alive, the other from Hal Draper, the former editor of *Labor Action*, the Shachtmanite paper. Bruno R., identifying himself as a man named Bruno Rizzi, tells only sketchily about the writing of the book, and nothing about himself. He remarks that he first told Trotsky, "who I loved and regarded even as my teacher," of his ideas in 1938. He also denounced Burnham for plagiarizing his book and in doing so taking only the "negative side."

But it is Draper's letter which, for the first time, provided some biographical detail about his elusive character. A member of the Shachtmanite faction, Draper had long sought and finally in 1948 had located a copy of Bruno R.'s book. That year, in *The New International*, he printed the only complete review of Bruno R.'s work. In 1956, out of the blue, Draper received a letter from Bruno Rizzi, identifying himself as the author. Eight years after the *The New International* article he had first read it and was astonished to find that a group of socialists were espousing his theory. In April 1958 Draper and his wife, then in Europe, paid a call on Rizzi. A strange picture emerged. Bruno R., according to Draper, was not an anti-fascist Italian refugee but a commercial traveller who before the war journeyed freely between France and Italy. Rizzi was never a Trotskyite. In Paris, before 1938, Rizzi had sought membership in the Party, but the refugee Italian Trotskyites feared that he might be a fascist spy or, at best, a political eccentric.

These fears were understandable. In 1937, in Milan, he had published under his own name a book entitled *Dove va URSS* which contained the seeds of his theory but which was allowed to circulate, said Draper, "because according to the theories of Rizzi, Fascism was in the line of social progress." Such a view was not completely aberrant among some Marxists. The former French communist Jacques Doriot, the leader of the left wing of the Belgian Socialists, Henri de Man, and a wing of the French Socialist party, led by Spinasse and Rives, had supported Hitler at the outbreak of the war on the grounds that his victory would destroy capitalism and unify Europe. This historical amoralism permeated Burnham's book, when he wrote that, "The general outcome of the second war is also assured. . . . There is no possible solution on a capitalist basis." How often people confuse history—and progress—with necessity!

About the charge of plagiarism there was no proof, as Souvarine noted in an editorial coda, that Burnham actually "plagiarized" Bruno R. Since no copy of the book was available, there could be no literal borrowing of text. The idea itself was "in the air." In fact, as Max Nomad often claimed, the source of many of these conceptions go back to the theories of the Polish anarcho-syndicalist Waclaw Machajski, who, in 1899, in his book *The Evolution of Social Democracy*, asserted that the messianism of socialism was a masked ideology of discontented intellectuals who were using the proletariat as a vehicle to gain power themselves. And even before this one can go back to the origins of Russian socialism in the 1870s and 1880s in the

For Djilas, the death of Stalin meant that an epoch had passed and that some "normalization" of life would now be possible. The new class, he said, would not give up its power, but it "is tired of dogmatic purges and training sessions. It would like to live quietly. It must protect itself even from its own authorized leader now that it has been adequately strengthened" (p. 52).

A decade later, the question was raised whether or not the new class was "divided" and whether the growth of a new scientific and technical intelligentsia, a group whose creative elite had a stake in the freedom of inquiry, might not undermine the power of the Party over the society. The theme of an inherent conflict between the scientific intelligentsia and the Party bureaucracy was stated most sharply by Albert Parry in the book *The New Class Divided* (New York, 1966). Parry used the phrase "the new class" to capitalize on Djilas, but where Djilas, with some ambiguity, thought of the "new class" as the ruling Party bureaucracy, with an admixture of other elites, Parry was simply equating "the new class" with the "intelligentsia," which, he stated, "constitute nearly one-fifth of all Soviet toilers." Within this stratum which, as a whole, is more privileged than the working class and peasantry, there are about 600,000 "scientific workers," and it is the demands of this group, symbolized for Parry by the career and the writings of the physicist Peter Kapitza, that would constitute the challenges to the Party's monolithic control.

How extensive or effective such an opposition can be is problematic. That such a mood of challenge exists is evident most clearly from the text circulated by Andrei Sakharov, one of the designers of the Soviet H-bomb, who has become the conscience of the intellectuals. In a section of his manifesto entitled "Intellectual Freedom is Essential," Sakharov states:

This position of the intelligentsia in society renders senseless any loud demands that the intelligentsia subordinate its strivings to the will and inter-

---

disputes between Paul Axelrod and Peter Tkachev on the dangers voiced by Axelrod of depending only on a militant minority" as the leader of the masses in the forging of a revolution. And earlier one can cite Michael Bakunin as predicting for the future "the reign of scientific intelligence . . . a new class, a new hierarchy of real and pretended scientists and scholars . . . of the State engineers who will constitute the new privileged scientific-political class."

For an earlier and more elaborate account of Bruno R. see my essay in *The New Leader*, "The Strange Tale of Bruno R." (September 28, 1959), and the correspondence in the issue of November 16, 1959. The statements from Bakunin can be found in his "Critique of Marxism," part 3, chap. 4, pp. 283–289 in *The Political Philosophy of Bakunin*, ed. G. P. Maximoff (Glencoe, Ill., 1953). Bakunin's predictions regarding the new forms of domination that would come in the wake of a victory of Marxian ideas are quite striking and worth reading for the whole.

ests of the working class (in the Soviet Union, Poland and other socialist countries). What these demands really mean is subordination to the will of the Party or, even more specifically, to the Party's central apparatus and its officials. Who will guarantee that these officials always express the genuine interests of the working class as a whole and the genuine interests of progress rather than their own caste interests? [70]

And yet it is unlikely that the demands of a small elite, even though a strategic one, can be decisive in forcing the reorganization of power that would be necessary to assure the independence of the scientific community in the Soviet Union. Yet the necessity for some major structural changes does confront the Party leadership, for these needs derive, as any Marxist would know, from the changed socio-economic nature of the society. Zbigniew Brzezinski, for example, has argued that the monolithic Party control on politics, and of the command system on the economy, while once, perhaps, necessary for the industrialization of the country, is now increasingly "disfunctional" because the heavily centralized structure is increasingly incapable of managing a complex "technetronic society" which requires plural initiatives in order to keep on growing.

Brzezinski identifies five alternative paths of Soviet political development which he sees as logically possible.

Oligarchic petrifaction: the Party maintains its dominant role; ideology remains dogmatic; political leadership remains collective since the absence of deliberately imposed change does not require major choices. In effect, this would be a continuation of the present tendency.

Pluralist evolution: the transformation of the Party into a less monolithic body, somewhat as in Yugoslavia, and the ideological erosion of the dogmatic Leninist-Stalinist tradition. In that situation the Party's "role would be more that of a moral-ideological stimulant than that of a ruler; the state as well as the society itself would become the more important source of innovation and change."

Technological adaptation: the transformation of the bureaucratic Party into a Party of technocrats. The state would be led by scientific experts, trained in the newer techniques, and look to scientific innovation for the preservation of Soviet security and industrial growth.

Militant fundamentalism: the rekindling of ideological fervor, a shake-up in the rigid bureaucratic structure, a smaller, more centralized leadership and a greater posture of hostility to the outside world "along the lines of Mao Tse-tung's 'Cultural Revolution'."

Political disintegration: an internal paralysis in the ruling elite occasioned by the rising self-assertiveness of key groups and splits in the armed forces and other major support sectors of the system.

---

[70] Andrei D. Sakharov, *Progress, Coexistence and Intellectual Freedom* (New York, 1968), p. 30.

"Looking approximately a decade ahead and using as a guide the present distribution of power in Soviet society," Brzezinski says the Soviet leadership will seek to strike a balance between the first and third variants. It would seek to maintain oligarchic control yet, as in East Germany, to bring more technocrats into the decision-making process. However, says Brzezinski, because of the Party "style," the hugeness of the country which makes integration difficult, and because of military demands, this course is likely to be impeded. Yet if it were followed, "the fusion of the first and third variants (striving to combine ideological rigidity with technological expertise) would . . . involve the transformation during the 1970s of the present communist Party dictatorship into a communist praetorian oligarchy." [71]

Social Development: The View from Moscow

If we review where we stand, three major changes have emerged in the last forty years in the development of Western industrial societies: the transformation of the industrial enterprise by the emergence of managers as controllers of the organization; the changing composition of the occupational structure by the relative shrinkage of the industrial proletariat and the expansion of a new technical and professional stratum; and the transformation of the political system through the extension of the state bureaucracy and the rise of political technocrats.

These processes are at work in both Western capitalist and Russian communist society. In the West, the extension of a state bureaucracy and the increasingly technical nature of political decisions create a problem of balance between those who manage the political system by responding to the major interests (the politicians representing business, labor and other constituencies) and the bureaucracies and technocrats. In the Soviet Union, the existence of a large bureaucracy which has transformed itself into a new class threatens the validity of communist ideology and the promise of a future classless society. For both systems, the common transformation of the occupational and class structures calls into question the "historic images" of the future of industrial society (if neither capitalists nor working class will "inherit the earth"), and raises the fundamental issue of the relation between the political systems of the societies—managerial, statist, bureaucratic, democratic—and the new-type social structure, be it

---

[71] Zbigniew Brzezinski, *Between Two Ages: America's Role in the Technetronic Era* (New York, 1970), part III, especially pp. 164–172.

"post-industrial," "post-capitalist" or whatever other label one uses to designate an emerging society which is dominated by an educated professional-technical science class.

In Western sociology there has been a sustained inquiry into these trends and a vigorous discussion of the social categories and social theories that might best serve to explain these changes. In the Soviet Union, until recently, there has been virtual silence. There have been few, if any, serious discussions of the structural changes in Western society. (The continuing designation of these societies as "capitalist" implies presumably that communist writers regard the characteristics of the system as defined by Marx and Lenin as still relevant.[72]) Discussion of the political nature of Soviet bureaucracy, and the theme of a "new class," is, of course, tabooed. Only the changing composition of the Soviet occupational structure is a subject Soviet sociologists have recently begun to investigate, and here there is a full realization of the delicate nature of the subject and the ideological hornet's nest it contains.

If one turns to Soviet sociology, there are three levels of discourse that one can discern.

There is, first, the tattered realm of official ideology. On that level, theoretical sociology is equated with historical materialism, "theory" consists of quotations from Marx and Lenin, and the standard textbooks repeat a simplified scheme of social development, vulgarizing Marx, as if nothing had changed in Western society in the last hundred years, or Soviet society in the last forty years, to modify the proclaimed schemes.

Thus, Grigori Glezerman, in a book entitled *The Laws of Social Development*, writes:

. . . modern bourgeois sociology denies the possibility of cognition and the very existence of the laws of social development and thereby denies in

---

[72] It is noteworthy however that the talk of the inevitable *economic* crisis and the *economic* breakdown of capitalism has largely disappeared from Soviet scholarly writings. This has been replaced by discussions of the social instability of Western society.

In 1969 the USSR Academy of Sciences created an Institute on the United States of America which, in January 1970, began the publication of its own journal, *USA: Economics, Politics and Ideology*. As Merle Fainsod notes in a review of the first six issues of the journal: "The articles on contemporary American foreign policy, as might be expected, faithfully mirror the current Party line. But, within these limits, one cannot fail to note that primitive sloganeering has given way to better-informed and more sophisticated analysis of the forces and factors that shape American foreign policy." On other matters, particularly technical subjects, including economics, the articles tend to be largely factual, while American management literature and management practices are now thoroughly scoured for materials which may be utilized in the training of Soviet managers. See Merle Fainsod, "Through Soviet Eyes," *Problems of Communism* (November–December 1970).

most cases the possibility of prevision in social life. . . . . Their arguments about the impossibility of penetrating the veil of the future are primarily levelled against Marxism which has proved that communism will triumph. Marx proclaimed his thesis on the unavoidable downfall of capitalist society and its replacement by a socialist society over a hundred years ago.[73]

For theoretician Glezerman, there are "general" laws and "specific" laws. The "general" law of social development is that socialism as a new socio-economic formation is inevitable. But since each country in passing through or bypassing capitalism is not predestined to follow the same path, there are also "specific" laws. Since in the course of history there are so many variants, in the logic of the argument we soon find that there is a specific "law" for each case! Such is the quality of theory.[74]

A second level is scholarly, but still identified with the Party. It is centered in the Academy of Sciences, rather than in the official Party bodies, and is more interested in balancing the defense of traditional dogma and the upsetting results of "concrete" social research. Much of this work has been under the direction of Aleksei Rumiantsev, vice-president of the USSR Academy of Sciences until 1971. Rumi-

---

[73] G. Glezerman, *The Laws of Social Development* (Moscow, n.d.), p. 79. This book is a set of lectures for postgraduate students in philosophy at Moscow University and of the Philosophy Department of the Academy of Social Sciences of the Central Committee of the Communist Party.

[74] With theoretician Glezerman, confusion abounds. On one page, with abundant quotations from Engels and Lenin, we are told laws "reflect an *essential* connection," "a *universal* connection," and "a *necessary* connection between phenomena" (p. 46, emphasis in the original). Yet some pages later we are told that "Every law is incomplete, is limited. . . . In order to foresee any concrete process it is not enough to know one law, for it does not take into account all conditions, of which there are an *infinite* number. In this connection Lenin wrote in his *Philosophical Notebooks* that only the *infinite* sum of general conceptions, laws, gives the concrete in its completeness" (p. 82, emphasis added). One is told that "Marxists are able to *foresee* the course of social development thanks to their skilful application of theory when analyzing specific historical conditions" (p. 86), for the general trend of scientific development "is in *the last analysis* determined by the requirements of production. . . ." (p. 80, emphasis added). Yet it is not clear whether the "last analysis" is by the analyst (which might mean the latest surviving analyst) or at the end of the historical epoch; but if the latter, how then could one know beforehand which of the many "infinite" elements determining social development is the true one?

And finally, in our effort to find out what is a "law," we are told that "lastly, the . . . peculiarity of a law is that it expresses the *stable, constant* connection between phenomena. The objective world, nature and society that surround man, are constantly changing. But for all that, definite, relatively stable, constant connections are preserved. As Lenin noted in his *Philosophical Notebooks*, a law is the enduring, persisting in phenomena" (p. 47, emphasis in the original). Mr. Glezerman's effort to define change and constancy is better answered by the remark of Professor Sidney Morgenbesser of Columbia who, when asked by a young radical in his philosophy class whether he believed in Mao's "law of contradiction," answered: "I do and I do not."

antsev has attacked "creeping empiricism," yet at the same time he supported work in social forecasting as a means of supplying more sophisticated information about the changing character of Soviet society. In a paper delivered at the 1970 Varna meetings of the Sixth World Congress of Sociology, a paper remarkable for its freedom from cant, Rumiantsev set forth the basis for the social forecasting movement which has become a prominent part of Soviet sociology. "The lack of adequate knowledge and comprehension of the present social situation destines the prevision of the coming changes to failure," he wrote.

The difficulty with prognostication . . . derives from the very nature of social processes that are multifactor, complex and probabilistic . . . we confront the necessity to study not only the objective economic factors, but a number of subjective factors as well: those of tastes, fashion, preferences, etc. . . . The effectiveness of social planning depends to a great extent on the adequate consideration of both economic and noneconomic factors, as well as upon the knowledge of interests, motives, needs and inclinations. All that vast information can be effectively utilized only if statistical and mathematical methods, simulation and computer machinery are extensively resorted to in the process of cognition, planning and management.[75]

Rumiantsev reflects the thinking of the "managerial communists" for whom the important change is the "scientific technological revolution" which they see as transforming Soviet society. For Igor Bestuzhev-Lada, a working futurologist, the "scientific-technological revolution" has "extraordinarily complicated the management of social processes." In his book, *A Window to the Future: The Present Day Problems of Social Forecasting*, Bestuzhev-Lada reviews the different approaches to social forecasting and concludes that the "stochastic approach . . . is the most effective, if not the only possible way of their truly scientific study." He makes the further point that in futurology there has been a lack of research on the developments of moral-ethical norms and the way these developments will shape the scientific-technological revolution.[76]

---

[75] A. M. Rumiantsev, "Social Prognostication and Planning in the Soviet Union," English language version, Moscow, 1970, presented by the Soviet Sociological Association at Varna, Bulgaria, pp. 9, 6, 12. While all of this is unexceptionable, it is clear that Rumiantsev's strictures are directed against the dogmatists in Soviet planning when he writes, after citing the need to study tastes, fashions and preferences: "A long-term plan based on scientific forecasting of population needs is much more adequate than plans neglecting the factors mentioned" (p. 6). Yet, as a party ideologist, Rumiantsev also argues that the basic texts of Marxism-Leninism are still correct. See *Categories and Laws of the Political Economy of Communism* (Moscow, 1969).

[76] I. B. Bestuzhev-Lada, *Okno v budushchee: sovremennye problemy sotsialnogo prognozirovaniya* (Moscow: "Mysl," 1970). In his comment on the need to take a probabilistic, rather than a deterministic, approach, Bestuzhev-Lada writes:

The third level of Soviet discourse is the large array of empirical social researches which take as their starting point the occupational divisions within the Soviet Union, and cautiously explore their meanings. As Leo Labedz points out, "Ever since Stalin said in 1931 that 'no ruling class has managed without its own intelligentsia,' there has been the awkward problem of how to define this group and relate it to the general social structure." [77]

The fact is, as Rumiantsev indicated in 1965, that the "intelligentsia," defined roughly as "mental labor," comprise 25 million persons, or about one-fifth of the Soviet labor force. More importantly, as a host of studies document, the inheritance of such a position (and of wealth) is becoming an important fact in the creation of the new class structure in the Soviet Union. [78]

A number of studies by Soviet sociologists indicate that in the land of "workers and peasants" few of the children of the proletariat want to be workers, much less peasants and that the great majority want to go to college and to be members of the "intelligentsia." As Zev Katz comments, "Though conducted independently in various parts of the Soviet Union, these studies show a remarkable uniformity in their major findings." In the rankings on prestige, scientists, airplane pilots, and ships' captains are at the top, jobs in agriculture and services are at the bottom. Moreover, the children of the intelligentsia are disproportionately represented in the universities, and the children of the peasantry find it exceedingly difficult to enter the universities at all. As N. M. Blinov of the sociological laboratory at Moscow University reported in 1966:

. . . . class differences still have a strong influence upon social advancement of the individual and, therefore, the class structure as a social element plays a leading part in the formation of individual personality. For example, the relatively small number of people in the village with higher

---

The stochastic principles of the method of approach to the problems of the future, although, apparently, theoretically indisputable, require extremely complex scientific researches in order to be accurately utilized. For this reason, often the temptation to take the path of the least resistance takes the upper hand. This is facilitated by the inertia of thinking and by firmly established traditions (and even biases) connected with equating forecasting with divination.

The citations here are from a précis of Mr. Bestuzhev-Lada's book made available to me by Fred Ikle. See, also, Mr. Ikle's "Social Forecasting and the Problem of Changing Values, with Special Reference to Soviet and East European Writings," *Rand Paper*, P-4450 (January 1971).

[77] Leo Labedz, "Sociology and Social Change," *Survey* (July 1966), p. 21.

[78] For a comprehensive review of these studies, see Zev Katz, "Hereditary Elements in Education and Social Structure in the USSR," University of Glasgow, Institute of Soviet and East European Studies (1969) and "Soviet Sociology: A Half-way House," (Russian Research Center, Harvard University, 1971). I am obliged to Dr. Katz for making these materials available to me and for several discussions which guided me to other relevant data.

education is explained, among other things, by the fact that the percentage of students from the country is ten times lower than students from the town.[79]

Under Khrushchev an effort was made to reverse this tendency by giving special preference for university places to children of workers and peasants and requiring those who sought to go on to the university to engage in a year of manual labor. By 1964 the "reforms" had been dropped and ideas of egalitarian education have been scrapped in favor of a new "meritocracy." In Novosibirsk, for example, where a new "scientific city" has been created, the Novosibirsk Physics and Mathematics School, an exclusive prep school, selects 200 students annually from 100,000 likely candidates. In 1968 more than 500 such special elite preparatory schools had been opened throughout the Soviet Union. Previously, students in academic high schools spent up to 13 hours a week in manual labor; by 1968 the program was halted. Previously, young people who held jobs or served in the army had been allotted 80 percent of the places in universities; now the figure is down to 30 percent.[80]

Communist theoreticians had held that a socially homogeneous society would emerge in the Soviet Union. But this idea—at least for the present—has been abandoned by almost all serious Soviet sociologists, and various Western ideas of stratification, based on occupational divisions, are now being admitted. At Minsk, in 1966, some Soviet sociologists declared that Lenin's definition of class does not apply to present-day Soviet society and participants at the conference presented various criteria for reshaping the official views. Some even argued that those who are professionally engaged in administrative functions constitute a separate social group. And some have even viewed the Party, not in the original Leninist terms, as the vanguard of the working class, but as an instrument for resolving conflicts of interest among different social groups.[81]

[79] Cited by Katz, Glasgow, p. 4.

[80] See the report from Novosibirsk on "Russia's New Elite," *Wall Street Journal* (October 15, 1968).

[81] About the Minsk conference, see *Voprosy Filosofii*, no. 5 (1966), *Filosofiya nauki*, no. 3 (1966), pp. 133–138, also (a) *Klassy, sotsial nye sloi i gruppy v SSSR*, (b) *Problemy izmeneniia sotsialnoi struktury sotsialisticheskogo obshchestva*, ed. Ts. A. Stepanyan, V. S. Semenov (Moscow, Nauka, 1968). For material on new occupational and class classifications, see M. N. Rutkevich (1) "The Social Sources of the Replenishment of the Soviet Intelligentsia," CDSP, no. 9 (1967); (2) "O poniatii intelligentsii kak sotsialnogo sloya sotsialisticheskogo obshchevtva," *Filosofiya nauki*, no. 4 (1966); (3) "Kolichestvennye izmeneniya v sotsialnoi strukture sovetskogo obshchestva v. 60-e gody," *Sotsialnye razlichya* Sverdlovsk, v. 3, pp. 5–19; Stepanyan and Semenov: (a) *Klassy*, (b) *Problemy*, op. cit.; O. I. Shkaratan, "The Social Structure of the Soviet Working Class," CDSP, vol. XIX, no. 12; *Sotsiologiya i ideologiya*, ed. E. A. Arab-Ogly et al. (Moscow, Nauka, 1969). These are cited from Zev Katz (Harvard paper, 1971).

Although Soviet sociologists have documented the expansion of a new stratum, most have shied away from exploring the consequences of this change for Party doctrine and ideological dogma. If there is a growth of a distinct intelligentsia and a relative shrinkage of the working class, what, then, is the role of the Communist Party as the vanguard of the "dictatorship of the proletariat." On the official level, no contradictions are admitted. V. Afanasyev writes fatuously: "The Soviet intelligentsia . . . is a genuine people's intelligentsia with its roots in the working class and the peasantry. Having come from the people it serves them with devotion and dedication." [82] Bestuzhev-Lada, in a popular article on "Utopias of Bourgeois Futurology" in *New Times*, a popular weekly for foreign consumption, discusses the post-industrial society and admits that the number of persons employed in agriculture and "some industries" is falling, while the proportion of persons "employed in the service of industries and research and development is rising." But this does not mean, he claims, the disappearance of the working class. "The working class has been and remains the principal, decisive social force of modern times, the mainstay of modern production. . . ." [83]

On a more serious level, sophisticated young ideologists such as Eduard Arab-Ogly argue that the nature of the scientific and technical revolution is creating a "new" working class of highly skilled or technical workers, especially in such industries as chemical, atomic energy, and machine tools, and that a new category of "worker-intelligentsia" is coming to the fore to replace the old manual worker. [84] But the larger sociological questions posed by Trotsky and popularized by Djilas are, themselves, never confronted.

The Czech View of the Future

In the East European communist world outside the Soviet Union, the period after the death of Stalin in 1953, the Khrushchev disclosures in 1956, and the Polish Thaw and the Hungarian Revolution in 1956–1957, were times of extraordinary intellectual as well as political ferment. Old practices were sharply debated: the adequacy of the Leninist model of the Party, the merits of collectivization, the drawbacks of centralized planning. Traditional doctrine was challenged: historical materialism, the theory of class, the nature of alien-

---

[82] V. Afanasyev, *Scientific Communism* (Moscow, 1967), p. 179.

[83] Reprinted in *The Futurist* (Washington, D.C., December 1970), pp. 216–217.

[84] Eduard Arab-Ogly, *Nauchno-tekhnicheskaya revolutsiya i obschestvennyi* [The Scientific and Technical Revolution and Social Progress] (Moscow, 1969).

ation. Meaningless ideological dogmas were quietly discarded: the rigid conceptions of dialectical materialism, the theory of the interest rate as exploitative, the view of science as part of the "superstructure" of society.[85]

In all this ferment, there was, curiously, little extended discussion of the vision of the "future society" and what the changing nature of industrial social structure portended for the traditional communist view. Only in the early 1960s did some discussion of these problems begin and then, because of the reintroduction of ideological discipline, much of this discussion was aborted.[86]

The most important document to come out of these latter inquiries was the remarkable study by Radovan Richta and a research team of the Czechoslovak Academy of Science, entitled *Civilization at the Crossroads: Social and Human Implications of the Scientific and Technological Revolution,* which appeared in 1967. The Czech and Slovak editions of 50,000 copies were quickly sold out. An English translation was printed in Czechoslovakia in October 1968, and is available through an American distributor, but curiously it has received little notice in the West. Yet the document, "conceived in an atmosphere of critical, radical searching and intensive discussion on the way forward for a society that has reached industrial maturity while passing through a phase of far-reaching socialist transformation" (p. 21) is of major importance for the discussion of the changing social structures of communists and Western society.[87]

The starting point of the discussion is the "scientific technological revolution" which has become the new hope of communist ideologists. But unlike the Russians, the Richta group see this as a process that includes Western society as well (most of the Russians shy away from discussing this question since it would challenge some of the assumptions about capitalism, and open the door to the concepts of industrial and post-industrial society), and more important, they do not burke the issue of the new class structure, and the rise of a new dominating class, which such a development portends.

---

[85] For a review of some of these currents, see *Revisionism,* ed. Leo Labedz (London, 1962), and Z. A. Jordan, *Philosophy and Ideology, A Review of Philosophy and Marxism in Poland* (Dordrecht, Holland, 1963).

[86] For example, the leading Polish communist Wladyslaw Bienkowski, the Minister of Culture briefly in 1956, wrote a book *Motory Socjalizmu* (The Motors of Socialism), dealing with the changes required in socialist ideology because of the new role of science. The book was offered to several publishing houses in Poland but was refused; it was published without the author's permission by the emigré publishing house, Kultura, in Paris, in 1969.

[87] Radovan Richta, *Civilization at the Crossroads,* English language edition, October 1968; printed in Czechoslovakia, distributed in the U.S. by International Arts and Sciences Press, White Plains, N.Y., 1969. Because the study is virtually unknown, yet of interest for theories of social development, I quote it at length here.

From Industrial to Post-Industrial Society

The inquiry begins by posing "an analytical contrast between the industrial revolution and the scientific and technological revolution," and asserts that the consequence of this change is the transformation not just of labor but of all productive forces into a continuous, mechanized production process in which man now stands "alongside" the production process where formerly "he was its chief agent." In effect, not labor power (and the working class) but science (and knowledge classes) is the "decisive factor" in the growth of the productive forces of society (pp. 27–28):

In place of simple, fragmented work, which has so far been the basis of production, we now have the entry of *science* and its application in the guise of technology, organization, skills, etc. The sphere that used to be separated from industry and was merely brought in now and then from without in small doses is now penetrating the heart of production and the entire life of the community. This sphere, which not so long ago engaged a few hundreds of thousands of people, is growing into a vast *material force* comprising, alongside its wide technical basis, an army of over three-and-a-half million specialists and 11 million associated workers throughout the world. Some experts estimate that in an historically short span of time (by the next century) 20 percent of the total labor force will be employed in science and research (p. 36).

In other words, science is emerging as the leading variable in the national economy and the *vital dimension* in the growth of civilization. There are signs of a *new* ("post-industrial") *type of growth* with a new dynamic stemming from continuing structural changes in the productive forces, with the amount of means of production and manpower becoming less important than their changing quality and degree of utilization. Herein lie the *intensive* elements of growth, the acceleration intimately linked with the onset of scientific and technological revolution (p. 39).

At a certain stage in the course of the technological revolution and of the changes in growth models evoked by it, all the laws and proportions of society's development appear in a new light. This is primarily true of the relationship between *science, technology and production proper;* one may say that a divide is reached beyond which these relationships assume a role as vital as that occupied between Departments I and II of the production proper in the age of industrialization [i.e. the schemes outlined by Marx in *Capital*]. In the circumstances of the scientific and technological revolution, growth of the productive forces follows a law of higher priority, that is, the *precedence of science over technology and of technology over industry* (p. 41).

The distinction the authors accept between the industrial society and the post-industrial, or scientific-technological society, means, in effect, that some simplified Marxian categories no longer hold. The most important, clearly, is that of the leading role of the working class:

An entirely new phenomenon, demonstrating the disparity between the scientific and technological revolution and industrialization, is the turn to

a *relative* decline in the amount of labor absorbed by industry and associated activities—accompanied by a strong shift from the traditional
branches to the progressive within industry. This tendency clearly refutes
the standpoint giving absolute validity to the industrialization process and
the structure of "the industrial society" . . . (p. 120).

In general, we can assume that in the course of the scientific and technological revolution the volume of "services" will grow to the point of oc-
cupying 40–60 percent of national labor in coming decades, with a still
bigger share in the long term. The civilization to which we are advancing
might accordingly quite well be called "post-industrial civilization," "tertiary civilization," "services civilization," etc. (pp. 121–122).[88]

The most striking effect is, however, induced by the growing numbers
of *technical and professional* personnel in all sectors of the economy outside immediate production. In the fifties and sixties this group outpaced
all others in the United States in its rate of growth, which was twice that
for clerical workers (the category that held the lead in the forties) and
seven times more than the overall rate for workers (p. 131).

But, perhaps, most important of all, the older Marxist conception
of "laws of social development" is no longer valid:

The laws by which society develops are not predestined, they follow no
set scheme. Flowing always from the matter of history, from the motion
of society itself, they change with every turn in this essential substratum.
The profound intervention in the civilization base of human life signified
by the scientific and technological revolution in its entirety—viewing it
in its intrinsic correlation with the whole complex of social revolution of
our day—cannot fail to impinge on the *elementary laws of history*. In
many respects the course of civilization acquires a new logic and time
scale (p. 210).

At least in the long view, we would then be led to expect history to
lose the aspect of a natural process which in the traditional industrial civilization has obscured the unchallenged course of events, interrupted only
from time to time by a convergence of change in civilization (p. 277).[89]

Even the ideas of planning, and the time cycle of planning, based
as these were on the rhythms of capital formation and the turnover
of capital, now comes into question.

The rhythm of civilization is always determined by the decisive subjects
of its development. Time was when the natural reproduction of the prim-

---

[88] The references given at this point are to J. Fourastié, *Le Grand Espoir du XXe
Siècle* (Paris, 1958); and D. Bell, "The Post-Industrial Society," in *Technology and
Social Change* (New York-London, 1964).

[89] A footnote to the text at this point makes reference to the idea of history as a
natural process as follows: "Thus past history proceeds in the manner of a natural
process and is also essentially subject to the same laws of movement" (Letter from
Engels to J. Bloch, September 21, 1890, in Marx, *Selected Works*, vol. 1 [Moscow,
1933], p. 382.)

itive community set the tone and to this day the natural yearly cycle of subsistence in these enclosed units provides the dominant time scale over a great part of the world. In the classical industrial civilization, the period of *capital turnover* in the process of expanded reproduction is known to have been the starting point for all surmises about the future and for speculations usually calculated some years ahead. Similarly the five- or seven-year planning terms of socialism—although not often based on an awareness of the connection—correspond to the overall turnover period of *social labor*, of the assets concerned. Once *science* and its application start to determine growth, these outlooks based on the determinate subjectivity of stable economic relations are inevitably found wanting, although almost all practical perspectives continue to be drawn from them (p. 269).

Science itself has a distinct character which is different from other modes of activity, including labor; it is this character that sets apart a society based on science from industry:

Science owes its new status primarily to its exceptional power of *generalization*. In contrast to other products, a scientific finding is not consumed by use, on the contrary it is improved on—and then "it costs nothing." Moreover, science possesses a peculiar *growth* potential. Every finding is both a result and then a starting point for further research; the more we know, the more we can find out. This intrinsically exponential quality distinguishes science sharply from all traditional activities of the industrial type (p. 217).

From all this, three crucial sociological problems emerge; first, since the scientific and technological revolution cannot be led by the working class, what, then, is the role of the working class in the future society; second, the stratification system of the new society inevitably will emphasize the dominance of the professional and technical classes; and third, if the production and maintenance of the scientific mastery of the future society requires the presence of a highly trained research elite, supported by a large technical staff, does not all this define the attributes of a new potential ruling class?

Richta and his associates write:

Every revolution in production—including the industrial revolution —has hitherto been the work of the class that was instrumental in promoting it and which replaced another class in this role, carrying out the whole process at the expense of the class that represented the majority. If the model we have constructed of the scientific and technological revolution corresponds to reality, we should assume that, as a specific universal revolution in the productive forces, its progress will be impracticable— at least on the whole front—without the *positive*, independent participation of the *majority*, and ultimately of *all* members of the society (p. 245).

As the class structure under socialism changes . . . the dominant feature in the social stratification starts to be differentiation primarily according to the content of work. The long-term existence of two distinct strata working side by side—people performing exacting creative work and others occupied in simple operative jobs—will then have to be foreseen as a serious problem. . . .

So long as advances in science and technology are not rationally controlled in all their social and human implications, we shall be faced with a cleavage between the *professional* and *democratic* aspects. It may find expression in technocratic tendencies, which do not, however, stem from science and technology as such, but rather from conditions that heighten certain group and class interests to which science and technology are subordinated. The fact is that at the start of the scientific and technological revolution, the actual practice of management passes in many capitalist countries to a trained managerial elite, which under state monopoly acquires some degree of independence at least in relation to traditional capitalist groupings—although its status is still essentially one of servitude to capital (pp. 249–250).[90]

Under socialism this cleavage between professional elite and the mass will arise because the working class is not the leader of the new society:

Faced by the cleavage that industrial civilization has bestowed on us, one is led to the conclusion that even under socialism the working people will not be brought overnight into active participation in the scientific and technological revolution. The appropriate forms were lacking in previous social systems, and we cannot expect that the process will now be automatic and without problems, as indeed no stage of revolution has ever been (p. 252).

The problem of social differentiation will arise anew because of the new scientific and technical elites that might be created, and the efforts of these elites to consolidate their positions of privilege:

---

[90] This problem of characterizing the new managerial class, the scientific elite, and the new middle class clearly bedevils the Czech group even though they have moved away from dogmatic Marxist categories. Earlier, in describing the changing social stratification of capitalism, the writers remark of the tendency, described by a number of sociologists, of the rise of a "new middle class," the "levelling of the middle estate," the changing transformation of professional and technical personnel, and the like. This, however, they claim, is not a real change. Apart from a "small section comprising executives living mainly from profit—that is a product of class differentiation within the intelligentsia" [*sic*], the rise of a new specialist class is largely the expansion of a new working class. Yet clearly, when the writers turn to the discussion of socialism, as above, the problem of the distinction comes through quite sharply (see p. 247). The writers cited in relation to social stratification changes under capitalism are Michael Young, in *The Rise of the Meritocracy* (London, 1958), D. Bell in *Dun's Review and Modern Industry*, 1/1962, and Helmut Schelsky, *Die Sozial Folgen der Automatieirung* (Düsseldorf-Köln, 1957), and *Auf der Suche nach Wirklichkeit* (Köln-Düsseldorf, 1965).

There is nothing to be gained by shutting our eyes to the fact that an acute problem of our age will be to close the profound cleavage in industrial civilization which, as Einstein realized with such alarm, places the fate of the defenseless mass in the hands of an educated elite, who wield the power of science and technology. Possibly this will be among the most complex undertakings facing socialism. With science and technology essential to the common good, circumstances place their advance primarily in the hands of the conscious, progressive agents of this movement—the professionals, scientists, technicians and organizers and skilled workers. And even under socialism we may find tendencies to elitism, a monopoly of educational opportunities, exaggerated claims on higher living standards and the like; these groups may forget that the emancipation of the part is always bound up with the emancipation of the whole (p. 250).

The age-old socialist dream of a harmonious new society, thus, is doomed to frustration. Instead, the new society itself will generate new conflicts and new struggles not necessarily along the old lines of class and power, but of attitudes to change and to science itself:

In confrontation with the scientific and technological revolution all visions of a future free of conflict and struggle are doomed to disappointment. The idea that with socialism humanity will enter an epoch in which personal strain and individual effort will no longer be required, where society will care for all wants, is one of those illusions of industrial life that simply abstract from the two-edged manipulatory power of the industrial mechanism. . . . Frictions may emerge among the most varied groups of people, primarily—probably in their most persistent form—engendered by differences in work content and the resultant disagreement in ideas on life apart from work. . . . There may equally be a sharpening of misunderstandings among the generations, evoked by the widening gap between modes of life in the course of two to three decades.

The signs are that society will undergo a repeated and ever stronger polarization between *progressive* and *conservative* attitudes. This throws into relief the role of social conditions under which this divergence of forces and opening up of paths for progressive trends are linked with an inexorable lifelong division of people by attributes of class, property and power, where, moreover, irreconcilable antagonisms no longer breed ruthless struggles. This calls for conditions allowing this divergence to assume mobile, functional forms adequate to the actual dialectic of conflict. The drama of pioneering efforts by individuals and groups will, of course, involve risk, genuine collisions, with real victors and losers—although arbitrary power for the victors and humiliation for the defeated can and must disappear from the scene. And, indeed, the historic mission of socialism lies just there—in meeting such opening and closing of social splits that are not founded in conflicts among classes with a system of new, appropriate forms of motion, while employing for this purpose all suitable instruments of former social forms—economic instruments, democratic, social and political institutions, etc. (pp. 257–258).

With the Richta study, we come full circle. The vision here, out of Marxist theory, is what might be called a post-socialist society. That society is one which is also post-industrial. But such a society merges—*in its problems, not necessarily in its outcomes*—with the post-capitalist societies in that the new determining feature of social structure (but not necessarily of politics and culture) is the scientific and technological revolution, or what I have called in my writings the centrality of theoretical knowledge as the axial principle of social organization, while the character of the new stratification system will be the division between the scientific and technical classes and those who will stand outside.

The term *post* is relevant in all this, not because it is a definition of the new social form, but because it signifies a transition. What the new society will be remains to be seen, for the controlling agency is *not* the technology but the character of the political managers who will have to organize this new strategic resource and use it to buttress their political system.

In all this—if we face a new and puzzling kind of social change—we have to retreat from *theory*—if by theory one means a model of social structure that specifies the determinate interaction of the crucial variables of a system, establishes empirical regularities that predict future states of relation, and provides an explanatory principle of its history and operation. What we are forced back to is the creation of new paradigms in the sense that Thomas Kuhn has used the term, i.e. conceptual schemes which themselves are neither models nor theories but *standpoints* from which models can be generated and theories developed.

The Post-Industrial Society: A Conceptual Schema

The concept "post-industrial society" emphasizes the centrality of theoretical knowledge as the axis around which new technology, economic growth and the stratification of society will be organized. Empirically one can try to show that this axial principle is becoming more and more predominant in advanced industrial societies.

This is not to suggest a principle of convergence. The idea of convergence is based on the premise that there is *one* overriding institution that can define a society. Thus, years ago, Pitirim Sorokin and C. Wright Mills thought that the Soviet Union and the United States were coming to be "alike" because both were becoming centralized, bureaucratic societies mobilized around the single purpose of war. In a different way, Jan Tinbergen and his associates have argued that, because of the nature of economic rationality, both communist and capitalist countries are veering toward a common model of modified planning (direct or indirect) tied to the use of markets. And Marion Levy and, to some extent, Wilbert Moore, have argued that in their central features all industrial societies were becoming "alike" because of the common requirements of factory production, the relation of education to occupation, and the character of technical knowledge.[91] But few societies, as distinct historic and political entities, can be defined completely around a single institution as Marx believed, i.e. that one could define a system as capitalist and that *all other relations*, cultural, religious, political, derived from that foundational base. Societies differ in the way they relate their political systems to social structure and culture. And within the social structure (as in the political order and culture) there are different axes around which institutions are built. And even when different societies may be compared in their economy or social structure along one axis, they may differ markedly along another. Thus, along the axis of property, different societies could be defined as capitalist, but along the axis of, say, po-

---

[91] On the thesis of a convergence of the Soviet Union and the United States as centralized, bureaucratized societies, see C. Wright Mills, *The Causes of World War Three* (New York, 1958), part I, section 3; Pitirim Sorokin, *The Basic Trends of Our Times* (New Haven, 1964). For a contrary view, see Bertram D. Wolfe, "Russia and the U.S.A.: A Challenge to the Convergence Theory," *The Humanist* (September–October 1968). On the question of economic convergence, see Jan Tinbergen, "Do Communist and Free Economies Show a Converging Pattern?" *Soviet Studies* (April 1961); and H. Linnemann, J. P. Pronk and J. Tinbergen, "Convergence of Economic Systems in East and West" (Rotterdam, Netherlands Economic Institute, 1965). For a contrary view, see "Will Market Economies and Planned Economies Converge?," by George N. Halm in *Essays in Honor of Friedrich A. von Hayek*, ed. Streissler, Haberler et al. (London, 1969).

On the question of industrial societies, the literature is vast. A major statement on convergence is that of Marion Levy, Jr., *Modernization and the Structure of Societies* (Princeton, N.J., 1966). A more cautious statement is by Arnold Feldman and Wilbert Moore, "Industrialization and Industrialism: Convergence and Differentiation" in *Transactions* of the Fifth World Congress of Sociology (Washington, D.C., September 1962).

Though the concept of "industrial society" is interpreted by Soviet writers as a prime example of convergence theory (for a short review of this issue, see Cyril Black, "Marx and Modernization," *Slavic Review*, June 1970), and Raymond Aron is identified as the father of the theory of industrial society, Aron has voiced considerable doubts about the convergence thesis: see, *The Industrial Society* (New York, 1967), pp. 105–130.

For two major reviews of the literature and controversy on convergence, see Ian Weinberg, "The Problem of Convergence of Industrial Societies: A Critical Look at the State of a Theory," in *Comparative Studies in Society and History* (January 1969); and Alfred G. Meyer, "Theories of Convergence," in *Change in Communist Systems*, ed. Chalmers Johnson (Stanford, 1970).

litical consensus, these societies would differ as democratic and authoritarian.

In a different sense, one can say that the sequences of feudalism, capitalism and socialism, and pre-industrial and post-industrial society both proceed from Marx. Marx defined a mode of production as including both the social relations and the "forces" (i.e., techniques). He called the present mode of production capitalist, but if we restrict the term capitalist to social relations and industrial to techniques, then we can see, analytically, how the different sequences unfold. In this sense there can be socialist post-industrial societies as there could be capitalist, just as both the Soviet Union and the United States, though separated along the axis of property, are both industrial societies.

Further, one has to make a distinction between convergence and internationalization. One may have an internationalization of style, in painting or music or architecture, so that a "modern" artist may paint the same way in France, England, Japan, and Mexico. And there may be an internationalization of scientific knowledge and technological processes, but *societies*, as specific historical entities, represent distinct *institutionalized* combinations which are difficult to match directly to each other. On different dimensions (technology, architecture) they may resemble each other, or draw from a common fund of knowledge or style, yet on other dimensions (values, political systems, traditions)—and the ways these become formulated, say, in educational systems—they may differ. If there is a meaning to the idea of convergence it is that societies resemble each other somewhat along the same dimensions, or they may confront a *similar core of problems*. But this in no way guarantees *a common or like response*. The response will be relative to the different political and cultural organization of the specific society.

The idea of a post-industrial society, like that of industrial society, or capitalism, has meaning only as a conceptual scheme. It identifies a new axial principle of social organization and defines a common core of problems which societies that become more and more post-industrial have to confront. The idea of a post-industrial society does not rest, as Jean Floud seems to think, on the concept of a social system. I do not believe that societies are organic or so integrated as to be analyzable as a single system. In fact, my major theoretical preoccupation today is the disjunction, in Western society, between the culture and the social structure, the one becoming increasingly anti-institutional and antinomian, the other oriented to functional rationality and meritocracy. The concept of post-industrialism is an effort to identify a change in the *social structure*. But there is no necessary correlate, as I have argued repeatedly, between the changes in that realm as against changes in the other two analytical dimensions of a society, that of politics and culture.

I do believe that the major orders, or realms, of societies can best be studied by trying to identify *axial* institutions or principles, which are the major lines around which other institutions are draped, and which pose the major problems of solution for the society. In capitalist society the axial institution has been private property and in the post-industrial society it is the centrality of theoretical knowledge. In Western culture in the last one hundred years the axial thread has been "modernism" with its onslaught on tradition and established institutions. In the Western political systems the axial problem is the relation between the desire for popular participation and bureaucracy.

One of the difficulties for social analysis is the overlapping and conflicting nature of these principles vis-à-vis one another, and within a single system itself. Thus, in the stratification system, which sociologists take as basic for any society, the historic base of power has been property, and the means of access through inheritance. Yet while property remains as an important base, technical skill becomes another, sometimes rival, base with education the means of access to the attainment of technical skill. But equally, a political office becomes a base for power and privilege (particularly for groups such as ethnic groups that find barriers in the other two modes), and political mobilization or cooptation becomes the means of access to political office. It is the contradictory nature of the three modes that makes identification of consistent social groups and political interests so difficult.[92] Culture has replaced technology as a source of change in the society, and the tensions between the adversary culture and the eroded Protestant ethic have created a remarkable contradiction in the value system of American society.[93]

In what way does a post-industrial society differ from previous society? In an historical sense, Professor Tominaga is right: the post-industrial society is a continuation of trends unfolding out of industrial society, and many of the developments were foreseen long ago. Both St. Simon and Marx, for example, were obsessed with the crucial role of engineers (in the one case) and science (in the other) in transforming society, though neither of them had, or could have, any sense of the change in the fundamental relation of science to economic and technological development, the fact, for instance, that most of the

---

[92] See *Survey* (London), Winter 1971, vol. 16, no. 1, for the comments of Dr. Floud, and those referred to subsequently of Professors Bourricaud and Tominaga.

[93] These themes are elaborated in the Coda, in the section on culture and consciousness.

major industries of the nineteenth and early twentieth centuries—
steel, telegraph, telephone, electricity, auto, aviation—were developed largely by talented tinkerers who worked independently of the
fundamental work in science; while the first modern industry is
chemistry, since one has to have a theoretical *a priori* knowledge of
the properties of the macromolecules one is manipulating in order to
create new products.

Yet for *analytical* purposes, one *can* divide societies into pre-industrial, industrial, and post-industrial and see them in contrast along
many different dimensions. Thus, I have tried to show in the accom-
panying schematic table how, along different dimensions, the three
kinds of societies differ radically. (See Table 1–1, General Schema
of Social Change.) These are, of course, ideal-type constructions, yet
the purpose of such constructs is to illuminate essential differences.
Thus, the "design" of pre-industrial society is a "game against nature": its resources are drawn from extractive industries and it is subject to the laws of diminishing returns and low productivity; the "design" of industrial society is a "game against fabricated nature" which
is centered on man-machine relationships and uses energy to
transform the natural environment into a technical environment; the
"design" of a post-industrial society is a "game between persons" in
which an "intellectual technology," based on information, rises
alongside of machine technology. Because of these different designs,
there are vast differences in the character of economic sector distribution and the slopes of occupations. The methodology of each society differs and, most important, there are distinctly different axial
principles around which the institutional and organizational features
of the society are draped.

Because of all this, there are crucial differences in the kinds of
structural problems that engage each kind of society. In industrial society the chief economic problem has been the problem of capital:
how to institutionalize a process of creating sufficient savings and the
conversion of these moneys into investment areas; and this has been
done through the equity market, investment banks, self-financing,
and state taxation. The locus of social relations has been the enterprise or firm and the major social problem that of industrial conflict
between employer and worker. To the extent that the investment
process has been routinized and the "class conflicts" encapsulated so
that the issue of class strife no longer acts to polarize a country
around a single issue, those older problems of an industrial society
have been muted if not "solved."

In the post-industrial society, the chief problem is the organization
of science, and the primary institution the university or the research
institute where such work is carried out. In the nineteenth and early

From Industrial to Post-Industrial Society

TABLE 1-1

General Schema of Social Change

	PRE-INDUSTRIAL	INDUSTRIAL	POST-INDUSTRIAL	
Regions:	Asia Africa Latin America	Western Europe Soviet Union Japan	United States	
Economic sector:	Primary Extractive: Agriculture Mining Fishing Timber	Secondary Goods producing: Manufacturing Processing	Tertiary Transportation Utilities Quinary Health Education Research Government Recreation	Quaternary Trade Finance Insurance Real estate
Occupational slope:	Farmer Miner Fisherman Unskilled worker	Semi-skilled worker Engineer	Professional and technical Scientists	
Technology:	Raw materials	Energy	Information	
Design:	Game against nature	Game against fabricated nature	Game between persons	
Methodology:	Common sense experience	Empiricism Experimentation	Abstract theory: models, simulation, decision theory, systems analysis	
Time perspective:	Orientation to the past Ad hoc responses	Ad hoc adaptiveness Projections	Future orientation Forecasting	
Axial principle:	Traditionalism: Land/resource limitation	Economic growth: State or private control of investment decisions	Centrality of and codification of theoretical knowledge	

twentieth centuries the strength of nations was their *industrial* capacity, the chief index of which was steel production. The strength of Germany before the First World War was measured by the fact that she had overtaken Great Britain in steel production. After the Second World War, the *scientific* capacity of a country has become a determinant of its potential and power, and research and development (R & D) has replaced steel as a comparative measure of the strength of the powers. For this reason the nature and kinds of state support for science, the politicization of science, the sociological problems of the organization of work by science teams all become central policy issues in a post-industrial society. (See Table 1–2, Structure and Problems of the Post-Industrial Society.)

A major social change brings a major reaction. The student revolts of the late 1960s were, in part, a reflection of the new power of an adversary culture reacting against the growth of a science-based society. But in greater measure the student revolt was a reaction to the "organizational harnesses" a post-industrial society inevitably drops on intellectual work, and this was signified by the increasing pressures on young people, at an earlier and earlier age, to choose a good college, the pressure to choose a main subject, and the anxiety about graduate school and a career.

Politically, the problem of a post-industrial society, as François Bourricaud rightly points out, is the growth of a non-market welfare economics and the lack of adequate mechanisms to decide the allocation of public goods. For technical and conceptual reasons one cannot measure the value of such goods in market terms; because such goods are distributed to all, there is a disincentive on the part of a citizenry to support such expenditures. Most important, the nature of non-market political decisions invites direct conflict: as against the market which disperses responsibility, in politics the decision points are open and visible, and the consequences of political decisions, as to who would lose and who would gain, are clear. Because there is such a focal point, conflict flares more readily when such decisions are to be reached.

TABLE 1–2

Structure and Problems of the Post-Industrial Society

AXIAL PRINCIPLE:	THE CENTRALITY OF AND CODIFICATION OF THEORETICAL KNOWLEDGE
Primary institutions:	University Academy institutes Research corporations
Economic ground:	Science-based industries
Primary resource:	Human capital
Political problem:	Science policy Education policy
Structural problem:	Balance of private and public sectors
Stratification: Base— Access—	Skill Education
Theoretical issue:	Cohesiveness of "new class"
Sociological reactions:	The resistance to bureaucratization The adversary culture

In the broadest sense, the most besetting dilemma confronting all modern society is bureaucratization, or the "rule of rules." Historically, bureaucratization was in part an advance of freedom. Against the arbitrary and capricious power, say, of a foreman, the adoption of impersonal rules was a guarantee of rights. But when an entire world becomes impersonal, and bureaucratic organizations are run by mechanical rules (and often for the benefit and convenience of the bureaucratic staff), then inevitably the principle has swung too far.

All of these changes take place in the context of a society that is multiplying its constituencies (especially the scientific and technical claimants), that mixes technocratic and political decisions, and that sees the rise of a new class which may or may not be struggling to establish a corporate cohesiveness as a new ruling class in society. It is all these issues that frame the problems of a post-industrial society.

The concept of a post-industrial society is not a picture of a complete social order; it is an attempt to describe and explain an axial change in the social structure (defined as the economy, the technology and the stratification system) of the society. But such a change implies no specific determinism between a "base" and a "superstructure"; on the contrary, the initiative in organizing a society these days comes largely from the political system. Just as various industrial societies—the United States, Great Britain, Nazi Germany, the Soviet Union, post-World War II Japan—have distinctively different political and cultural features, so it is likely that the various societies that are entering a post-industrial phase will have different political and cultural configurations. The essential division in modern society today is not between those who own the means of production and an undifferentiated "proletariat" but the bureaucratic and authority relations between those who have powers of decision and those who have not, in all kinds of organizations, political, economic, and social. It becomes the task of the political system to manage these relations in response to the various pressures for distributive shares and social justice.

What the concept of a post-industrial society suggests is that there is a common core of problems, hinging largely on the relation of science to public policy, which will have to be solved by these societies; but these can be solved in different ways and for different purposes. The sociologist seeks those "ordering devices" that allow one to see the way social change takes place in a society. The concept of the post-industrial society is one such "ordering device" to make more intelligible the complex changes in Western social structure.

CHAPTER
2

From Goods to Services:
The Changing Shape
of the Economy

IN *The Communist Manifesto*, which was completed in February 1848, Marx and Engels envisaged a society in which there would
be only two classes, captialist and worker—the few who owned
the means of production and the many who lived by selling their
labor power—as the last two great antagonistic classes of social history, locked in final conflict. In many ways this was a remarkable
prediction, if only because at that time the vast majority of persons in
Europe and the United States were neither capitalist nor worker but
farmer and peasant, and the tenor of life in these countries was overwhelmingly agrarian and artisan.

England was the evident model for industrialization, but despite
Manchester, Leeds, Birmingham, and Sheffield, Great Britain at the
mid-century mark was not at all industrial, a fact which is clearly
demonstrated in the occupational statistics. As David Landes writes:

The British census of 1851—for all its inaccuracies—shows a country
in which agriculture and domestic service were far and away the most
important occupations; in which most of the labour force was engaged in
industries of the old type: building trades, tailoring, shoemaking, unskilled
work of all sorts. Even in the cotton manufacture, with over three-fifths
of its working force of over half a million (of a total of almost sixteen millions) in mills, almost two-thirds of the units making returns employed
less than fifty men; the average mill in England employed less than 200;
and tens of thousands of hand looms were still at work in rural cottages.[1]

If Britain was barely advanced, at mid-century, continental Europe
was about a generation behind her in industrial development. In Belgium, the most industrialized nation on the continent, about half the
labor force was engaged in agriculture (in Britain it was only one-

---

[1] David Landes, *The Unbounded Prometheus: Technological Change and Industrial Development in Western Europe from 1750 to the Present* (Cambridge, England, 1969), pp. 119–120.

fourth). Germany took another twenty-five years just to reach that 50 percent industrial mark; indeed, as late as 1895 there were more people engaged in agriculture than in industry. And in France the number of persons in industry was outnumbered by those in agriculture until the Second World War! To return to Marx's day, in the Prussia of 1852, which in this respect was representative of all of Germany, 72 percent of the population was classified as rural. As Sir John Clapham comments: "German industry in general could in no sense be called capitalistic; and before 1840 large enterprises of the factory type were extraordinarily rare." In France in 1851, only 10½ percent of the population lived in towns and, writes Clapham, "the number of concerns employing more than a hundred people in 1848 was so small that they could not much affect the average for the whole country; outside mining and metallurgy they hardly existed [and] true factory conditions were exceptional in the France of 1848." In the United States in 1850, of a population of 23 million persons, 19.6 million lived in rural territory (defined as places with under 2,500 persons), and of a labor force of 7.7 million, 4.9 were engaged in agriculture, 1.2 in manufacturing and construction combined (it was only in 1870 that the two figures were separated), and almost one million in domestic service.[2]

Marx's vision of the inexorable rise of industrial society was thus a bold one. But the most important social change in Western society of the last hundred years has been not simply the diffusion of industrial work but the concomitant disappearance of the farmer—and in a Ricardian world of diminishing returns in land, the idea that agricultural productivity would be two or three times that of industry (which it has been in the United States for the last thirty years) was completely undreamed of.

The transformation of agrarian life (whose habits had marked civilization for four thousand years) has been the signal fact of the time. In beholding the application of steam power to a textile mill, one could venture predictions about the spread of mechanization and the extension of factory work. But who would, with equal confidence, have made similar predictions following the invention by Cyrus McCormick of the reaper in 1832 and its exhibition at the Crystal Palace in London in 1851? Yet in the United States today, only 4 percent of the labor force is engaged in agriculture; the work of little more than three million persons (as against more than twice that number two decades ago) feeds 207 million persons, and if all crop

---

[2] Sources for the above are Landes, op. cit., p. 187; J. H. Clapham, *The Economic Development of France and Germany, 1815–1914* (Cambridge, England, 1945; original edition, 1921), pp. 82, 84, 54, 70–71; *Historical Statistics of the United States* (Washington, D.C., 1960), pp. 14, 74.

restraints were released, they could probably feed fifty million more.

In place of the farmer came the industrial worker, and for the last hundred years or so the vicissitudes of the industrial worker—his claims to dignity and status, his demand for a rising share of industrial returns, his desire for a voice in the conditions which affected his work and conditions of employment—have marked the social struggles of the century. But beyond that, in the utopian visions of Marx and the socialist movement, the working class, made conscious of its fate by the conditions of struggle, was seen as the agency not only of industrial but of human emancipation; the last great brakes on production and abundance would be removed when the working class took over control of the means of production and ushered in the socialist millennium.

Yet if one takes the industrial worker as the instrument of the future, or, more specifically, the factory worker as the symbol of the proletariat, then this vision is warped. For the paradoxical fact is that as one goes along the trajectory of industrialization—the increasing replacement of men by machines—one comes logically to the erosion of the industrial worker himself.[3] In fact, by the end of the century the proportion of factory workers in the labor force may be as small as the proportion of farmers today; indeed, the entire area of blue-collar work may have diminished so greatly that the term will lose its sociological meaning as new categories, more appropriate to the divisions of the new labor force, are established. Instead of the industrial worker, we see the dominance of the professional and technical class in the labor force—so much so that by 1980 it will be the second largest occupational group in the society, and by the end of the century the largest. This is the new dual revolution taking place in the structure of occupations and, to the extent that occupation determines other modes of behavior (but this, too, is diminishing), it is a revolution in the class structure of society as well. This

---

[3] In Marx's writings, there are many contradictory views of this situation. In the *Grundrisse*, the outline sketch for the master work which preceded *Capital*, and which was never published by Marx, he envisaged a time when almost all work would be replaced by the machine, and science, not labor power, would be considered the main productive force. In *Capital*, when he is working out the logic of the changing organic composition of capital, Marx describes a dual process resulting, on the one hand, in an increasing concentration of firms, and, on the other, an increase in the "industrial reserve army," i.e. the unemployed. Yet Marx could never escape the power of his own rhetoric, and in the penultimate chapter of *Capital*, when he is describing, nay sounding, the death-knell of capitalism, he writes: "Along with the constantly diminishing number of the magnates of capital . . . grows the revolt of the working-class, a class always increasing in numbers. . . . Centralization of the means of production and socialization of labor at last reach a point where they become incompatible with their capitalist integument. This integument is burst asunder." (*Capital*, vol. 1, p. 837.)

change in the character of production and of occupations is one aspect of the emergence of the "post-industrial" society.

The concept of a post-industrial society gains meaning by comparing its attributes with those of an industrial society and pre-industrial society.

In pre-industrial societies—still the condition of most of the world today—the labor force is engaged overwhelmingly in the extractive industries: mining, fishing, forestry, agriculture. Life is primarily a game against nature. One works with raw muscle power, in inherited ways, and one's sense of the world is conditioned by dependence on the elements—the seasons, the nature of the soil, the amount of water. The rhythm of life is shaped by these contingencies. The sense of time is one of *durée*, of long and short moments, and the pace of work varies with the seasons and the storms. Because it is a game against nature, productivity is low, and the economy is subject to the vicissitudes of tangible nature and to capricious fluctuations of raw-material prices in the world economy. The unit of social life is the extended household. Welfare consists of taking in the extra mouths when necessary—which is almost always. Because of low productivity and large population, there is a high percentage of underemployment, which is usually distributed throughout the agricultural and domestic-service sectors. Thus there is a high service component, but of the personal or household sort. Since individuals often seek only enough to feed themselves, domestic service is cheap and plentiful. (In England, up to the mid-Victorian period, the single largest occupational class in the society was the domestic servant. In *Vanity Fair*, Becky Sharp and Captain Rawdon Crawley are penniless, but they have a servant; Karl Marx and his large family lived in two rooms in Soho in the 1850s and were sometimes evicted for failing to pay rent, but they had a faithful servant, Lenchen, sometimes two.) Pre-industrial societies are agrarian societies structured in traditional ways of routine and authority.

Industrial societies—principally those around the North Atlantic littoral plus the Soviet Union and Japan—are goods-producing societies. Life is a game against fabricated nature. The world has become technical and rationalized. The machine predominates, and the rhythms of life are mechanically paced: time is chronological, methodical, evenly spaced. Energy has replaced raw muscle and provides the power that is the basis of productivity—the art of making more with less—and is responsible for the mass output of goods which characterizes industrial society. Energy and machines transform the nature of work. Skills are broken down into simpler components, and the artisan of the past is replaced by two new figures

—the engineer, who is responsible for the layout and flow of work, and the semi-skilled worker, the human cog between machines—until the technical ingenuity of the engineer creates a new machine which replaces him as well. It is a world of coordination in which men, materials, and markets are dovetailed for the production and distribution of goods. It is a world of scheduling and programming in which the components of goods are brought together at the right time and in the right proportions so as to speed the flow of goods. It is a world of organization—of hierarchy and bureaucracy—in which men are treated as "things" because one can more easily coordinate things than men. Thus a necessary distinction is introduced between the role and the person, and this is formalized on the organization chart of the enterprise. Organizations deal with the requirements of roles, not persons. The criterion of *techne* is efficiency, and the mode of life is modeled on economics: how does one extract the greatest amount of energy from a given unit of embedded nature (coal, oil, gas, water power) with the best machine at what comparative price? The watchwords are maximization and optimization, in a cosmology derived from utility and the felicific calculus of Jeremy Bentham. The unit is the individual, and the free society is the sum total of individual decisions as aggregated by the demands registered, eventually, in a market. In actual fact, life is never as "one-dimensional" as those who convert every tendency into an ontological absolute make it out to be. Traditional elements remain. Work groups intervene to impose their own rhythms and "bogeys" (or output restrictions) when they can. Waste runs high. Particularism and politics abound. These soften the unrelenting quality of industrial life. Yet the essential, technical features remain.

A post-industrial society is based on services. Hence, it is a game between persons. What counts is not raw muscle power, or energy, but information. The central person is the professional, for he is equipped, by his education and training, to provide the kinds of skill which are increasingly demanded in the post-industrial society. If an industrial society is defined by the quantity of goods as marking a standard of living, the post-industrial society is defined by the quality of life as measured by the services and amenities—health, education, recreation, and the arts—which are now deemed desirable and possible for everyone.

The word "services" disguises different things, and in the transformation of industrial to post-industrial society there are several different stages. First, in the very development of industry there is a necessary expansion of transportation and of public utilities as auxiliary services in the movement of goods and the increasing use of energy, and an increase in the non-manufacturing but still blue-collar force.

Second, in the mass consumption of goods and the growth of populations there is an increase in distribution (wholesale and retail), and finance, real estate, and insurance, the traditional centers of white-collar employment. Third, as national incomes rise, one finds, as in the theorem of Christian Engel, a German statistician of the latter half of the nineteenth century, that the proportion of money devoted to food at home begins to drop, and the marginal increments are used first for durables (clothing, housing, automobiles) and then for luxury items, recreation, and the like. Thus, a third sector, that of personal services, begins to grow: restaurants, hotels, auto services, travel, entertainment, sports, as people's horizons expand and new wants and tastes develop. But here a new consciousness begins to intervene. The claims to the good life which the society has promised become centered on the two areas that are fundamental to that life—health and education. The elimination of disease and the increasing numbers of people who can live out a full life, plus the efforts to expand the span of life, make health services a crucial feature of modern society; and the growth of technical requirements and professional skills makes education, and access to higher education, the condition of entry into the post-industrial society itself. So we have here the growth of a new intelligentsia, particularly of teachers. Finally, the claims for more services and the inadequacy of the market in meeting people's needs for a decent environment as well as better health and education lead to the growth of government, particularly at the state and local level, where such needs have to be met.

The post-industrial society, thus, is also a "communal" society in which the social unit is the community rather than the individual, and one has to achieve a "social decision" as against, simply, the sum total of individual decisions which, when aggregated, end up as nightmares, on the model of the individual automobile and collective traffic congestion. But cooperation between men is more difficult than the management of things. Participation becomes a condition of community, but when many different groups want too many different things and are not prepared for bargaining or trade-off, then increased conflict or deadlocks result. Either there is a politics of consensus or a politics of stymie.

As a game between persons, social life becomes more difficult because political claims and social rights multiply, the rapidity of social change and shifting cultural fashion bewilders the old, and the orientation to the future erodes the traditional guides and moralities of the past. Information becomes a central resource, and within organizations a source of power. Professionalism thus becomes a criterion of position, but it clashes, too, with the populism which is generated by the claims for more rights and greater participation in the society.

If the struggle between capitalist and worker, in the locus of the factory, was the hallmark of industrial society, the clash between the professional and the populace, in the organization and in the community, is the hallmark of conflict in the post-industrial society.

This, then, is the sociological canvas of the scheme of social development leading to the post-industrial society.[4] To identify its structural lineaments and trend lines more directly, let me turn now to the distribution of jobs by economic sector and the changing profile of occupations in the American economy.

The Sectors of Work and Occupations

Shortly after the turn of the century, only three in every ten workers in the country were employed in service industries and seven out of ten were engaged in the production of goods. By 1940, these proportions were more evenly balanced. By 1960, the proportions had shifted so that six out of every ten were in services. By 1980, with the rising predominance of services, close to seven in every ten workers will be in the service industries. (See Tables 2–1, 2–2, and 2–3.) Between 1900 and 1980, in exact reversal of the proportions between the sectors, there occurred two structural changes in the American economy, one, the shift to services, and two, the rise of the public sector as a major area of employment.

In historic fact, the shift of employment to services does not represent any sudden departure from previous long-run trends. As Victor Fuchs points out, "For as long as we have records on the industrial distribution of the labor force, we find a secular tendency for the percentage accounted for by the Service sector to rise." [5] From 1870 to 1920, the shift to services could be explained almost entirely by the movement from agricultural to industrial pursuits; employment in services rose as rapidly as industry and the major increases in services were in the *auxiliary* areas of transportation, utilities, and distribution. This was the historic period of industrialization in American life. After 1920, however, the rates of growth in the non-agricultural sector began to diverge. Industrial employment still increased numerically, but already its *share* of total employment tended to decline, as employment in services began to grow at a faster rate, and from 1968 to 1980, if we take manufacturing as the key to the industrial sector, the growth rate will be less than half of the labor force as a whole.

---

[4] The larger theoretical questions of the nature of class position and power, and the changes in the stratification system, are discussed in chap. 6.

[5] Victor Fuchs, *The Service Economy* (New York, 1968), p. 22.

TABLE 2–1

Sector Distribution of Employment by Goods and Services, 1870–1940
(in thousands)

	1870	1900	1920	1940
Total	12,900	29,000	41,600	49,860
Goods-producing total	10,630	19,620	23,600	25,610
Agriculture, forestry, and fishing	7,450	10,900	11,400	9,100
Manufacturing	2,250	6,300	10,800	11,900
Mining	180	760	1,230	1,100
Construction	750	1,660	2,170	3,510
Service-producing total	2,990	9,020	15,490	24,250
Trade, finance, and real estate	830	2,760	4,800	8,700
Transportation and utilities	640	2,100	4,190	4,150
Professional service	230	1,150	2,250	4,000
Domestic and personal service	1,190	2,710	3,330	5,710
Government (Not elsewhere classified)	100	300	920	1,690

SOURCE: Adapted from *Historical Statistics of the United States: 1820–1940*, series D57–71, p. 74.

NOTE: The totals do not always add up because of small numbers not allocated, and rounding of figures.

The great divide began in 1947, after World War II. At that time, overall civilian employment (inclusive of agriculture, self-employed and household domestics) was still close to the pre-war balance. But from then on, the growth rates began to diverge in new, accelerated fashion: only ten years later, the goods-producing industries provided less than 42 percent of all jobs and, by 1968, the proportion was down to 35.9 percent (Table 2–3). Despite the rising output of goods, this fall in *proportion* will persist. Altogether the goods producing industries accounted for about 29 million jobs in 1968 and this number is expected to increase to 31.6 million by 1980. However, those jobs will then represent less than 32 percent of total employment.

Within the goods-producing sector, employment in agriculture and mining will continue to decline in absolute terms. The major change—and the impetus to new jobs in that sector—will come in construction. The national housing goals for the 1968–1978 decade call for the building of 20 million new housing units in the private market and 6 million new and rehabilitated units through public subsidy. If these goals were to be met, employment in construction would rise by 35 percent in this decade.

---

[6] All statistical data in this section are from *The U.S. Economy in 1980*, U.S. Department of Labor Bulletin 1673 (1970).

Manufacturing is still the single largest source of jobs in the economy. It grew at 0.9 percent a year during the 1960s largely because of increased employment in defense industries—aircraft, missiles, ordnance, communications equipment and the like—which have higher labor components because the work is more "custom-crafted" than in mass production industries. But the shift away from defense spending—with its consequent unemployment in aircraft, missiles, and communications—means a slower rate of growth for manufacturing in the future. Any increase will appear largely in the manufacture of building materials for housing construction.

To return to the larger picture, the most important growth area in employment since 1947 has been government. One out of every six American workers today is employed by one of the 80,000 or so en-

TABLE 2–2

Sector Distribution of Employment by Goods and Services, 1968
Projected to 1980 (in thousands)

	1968	1980	PERCENTAGE CHANGE 1968–1980
Total	80,780	99,600	23
Goods-producing total	28,975	31,600	9
Agriculture, forestry, and fisheries	4,150	3,180	(−23)
Mining	640	590	(−9)
Construction	4,050	5,480	35
Manufacturing	20,125	22,358	11
Durable	11,850	13,275	12
Non-durable	8,270	9,100	10
Service-producing total	51,800	67,980	31
Transportation and utilities	4,500	5,000	10
Trade (Wholesale and retail)	16,600	20,500	23
Finance, insurance, and real estate	3,725	4,640	24
Services (Personal, professional, business)	15,000	21,000	40
Government	11,850	16,800	42
Federal	2,735	3,000	10
State and local	9,110	13,800	52

SOURCE: *The U. S. Economy in 1980*, Bureau of Labor Statistics Bulletin 1673 (1970). The data for 1968 and 1980 are from Table A–16, p. 49.

NOTE: The figures for 1980 assume a 3 percent unemployment. At a 4 percent unemployment, there would be a drop in the labor force of one million (i.e. from 99,600 to 98,600), and this loss is distributed between goods-producing (31,600 to 31,000) and service-producing (67,980 to 67,300) employment.

Figures are not always exact because of rounding.

TABLE 2-3

Sector Distribution of Employment by Goods
and Services Projected to 1980,
Distribution by Percentages

	1968	1980
Total	100	100
Goods-producing total	35.9	31.7
Agriculture, forestry, and fisheries	5.1	3.2
Mining	0.8	0.6
Construction	5.0	5.5
Manufacturing	24.9	22.4
Durable	14.7	13.3
Non-durable	10.2	9.1
Service-producing total	64.1	68.4
Transportation and utilities	5.5	5.0
Trade (Wholesale and retail)	20.5	20.6
Finance, insurance, real estate	4.6	4.7
Services (Personal, professional, business)	18.6	21.2
Government	14.6	16.9
Federal	3.3	3.0
State and local	11.2	13.9

SOURCE: *The U. S. Economy in 1980*, Bureau of Labor Statistics Bulletin 1673 (1970); conversion of figures into percentages.

tities which make up the government of the United States today. In 1929, three million persons worked for the government, or about 6.4 percent of the labor force. Today, twelve million persons work for the government—about 16 percent of the labor force. By 1980 that figure will rise to seventeen million, or 17 percent of the labor force.

Government to most people signifies the federal government. But state and local agencies actually account for eight out of every ten workers employed by the government. The major reason has been the expansion of schooling both in numbers of children and in the amount of schooling and thus of the number of teachers employed. Today about 85 percent of all pupils complete high school as against 33 percent in 1947. Educational services have been the area of fastest growth in the country and comprised 50 percent of state and local governmental activities in 1968 (as measured by employment).

General services were the second fastest growth area for employment between 1947 and 1968, and about 10 percent of employment in general services is in private educational institutions. Thus education as a whole, both public and private, represented 8 percent of total employment in the United States. Within general services, the largest category is medical services, where employment rose from 1.4 million in 1958 to 2.6 million a decade later.

The spread of services, particularly in trade, finance, education, health, and government, conjures up the picture of a white-collar society. But all services are not white collar, since they include transportation workers and auto repairmen. But then, not all manufacturing is blue-collar work. In 1970 the white-collar component *within* manufacturing—professional, managerial, clerical, and sales—came to almost 31 percent of that work force, while 69 percent were blue-collar workers (6,055,000 white-collar and 13,400,000 blue-collar). By 1975 the white-collar component will reach 34.5 percent. Within the blue-collar force itself there has been a steady and distinct shift from direct production to non-production jobs as more and more work becomes automated and in the factory, workers increasingly are employed in machine-tending, repair, and maintenance, rather than on the assembly line.[7]

In 1980 the total manufacturing labor force will number about 22 million, or 22 percent of the labor force at that time. But with the continuing spread of major technological developments such as numerical-control machine tools, electronic computers, instrumentation and automatic controls, the proportion of direct production workers is expected to go down steadily. Richard Bellmann, the Rand mathematician, has often been quoted as predicting that by the year 2000 only 2 percent of the labor force will be required to turn out all necessary manufactured goods, but the figure is fanciful and inherently unprovable. Automation is a real fact, but the bogey of an accelerated pace has not materialized.[8] But even a steady advance of 2 to 3 percent in productivity a year, manageable though it may be economically and socially (people are usually not fired, but jobs are eliminated through attrition), inevitably takes its toll. What is clear is that if an industrial society is defined as a goods-producing society— if manufacture is central in shaping the character of its labor force— then the United States is no longer an industrial society.

---

[7] There are no figures available for industry as a whole on the proportion of direct production to non-production workers. On the proportion of white-collar to blue-collar workers in manufacturing for 1960 and projections to 1975, see *Tomorrow's Manpower Needs* (Bureau of Labor Statistics Bulletin 1606), vol. IV.

[8] See *Technology and the American Economy*, Report of the President's Committee on Technology, Automation and Economic Progress, (Washington, D.C.: U.S. Government Printing Office, 1966); also my discussion "The Bogey of Automation," *New York Review of Books* (April 26, 1965).

The changeover to a post-industrial society is signified not only by the change in sector distribution—the places *where* people work —but in the pattern of occupations, the *kind* of work they do. And here the story is a familiar one. The United States has become a white-collar society. From a total of about 5.5 million persons in 1900 (making up about 17.6 percent of the labor force), the white-collar group by 1974 came to 41.7 million (148.6 percent) and will rise to 48.3 million in 1980, when it will account for *half* (50.8 percent) of all employed workers. (See Tables 2–4 and 2–5.)

TABLE 2–4

Percentage Distribution by Major Occupation Group, 1900–1960

MAJOR OCCUPATION GROUP	1900	1910	1920	1930	1940	1950	1960
Total	100.0	100.0	100.0	100.0	100.0	100.0	100.0
White-collar workers	17.6	21.3	24.9	29.4	31.1	36.6	42.0
Professional and technical	4.3	4.7	5.4	6.8	7.5	8.6	10.8
Managers, officials, and proprietors	5.8	6.6	6.6	7.4	7.3	8.7	10.2
Clerical and kindred	3.0	5.3	8.0	8.9	9.6	12.3	14.5
Sales workers	4.5	4.7	4.9	6.3	6.7	7.0	6.5
Manual workers	35.8	38.2	40.2	39.6	39.8	41.1	37.5
Craftsmen and foremen	10.5	11.6	13.0	12.8	12.0	14.1	12.9
Operatives	12.8	14.6	15.6	15.8	18.4	20.4	18.6
Laborers, except farm and mine	12.5	12.0	11.6	11.0	9.4	6.6	6.0
Service workers	9.0	9.6	7.8	9.8	11.7	10.5	12.6
Private household workers	5.4	5.0	3.3	4.1	4.7	2.6	3.3
Service, except private household	3.6	4.6	4.5	5.7	7.1	7.9	9.3
Farm workers	37.5	30.9	27.0	21.2	17.4	11.8	7.9
Farmers and farm managers	19.9	16.5	15.3	12.4	10.4	7.4	4.0
Farm laborers and foremen	17.7	14.4	11.7	8.8	7.0	4.4	3.9

SOURCE: Computed from Historical Statistics of the United States.
NOTE: Percentages may not add to 100 because of rounding.

Since 1920, the white-collar group has been the fastest-growing occupational group in the society, and this will continue. In 1956, for the first time, this group surpassed the employment of blue-collar workers. By 1980 the ratio will be about 5:3 in favor of the white-collar workers.

Stated in these terms, the change is dramatic, yet somewhat deceptive, for until recently the overwhelming number of white-collar workers have been women, in minor clerical or sales jobs; and in American society, as in most others, family status is still evaluated on the basis of the man's job. But it is at this point—in the changing nature of the male labor force—that a status upheaval has been tak-

TABLE 2-5

Occupational Distribution of Employed Persons: 1958–1974 (Actual); 1980 (Projected)

OCCUPATIONAL GROUP	1958 NUMBERS (THOUSANDS)	1958 PERCENTAGE	1974 NUMBERS (THOUSANDS)	1974 PERCENTAGE	1974 OVER 1958 PERCENTAGE INCREASE	1980 NUMBERS (THOUSANDS)	1980 PERCENTAGE
Total	63,000	100	85,935	100	36.4	95,000	100
White-collar workers	26,835	42.6	41,740	48.6	55.5	48,300	50.8
Professional and Technical	6,950	11	12,340	14.4	77.5	15,500	16.3
Managers and Officials	6,785	10.7	8,940	10.4	31.8	9,500	10
Clerical	9,115	14.5	15,000	17.5	64.6	17,300	18.2
Sales	3,985	6.3	5,400	6.3	35.5	6,000	6
Blue-collar workers	23,350	37.1	29,775	34.9	27.5	31,100	32.7
Craftsmen and foremen	8,460	13.4	11,470	13.4	35.5	12,200	12.8
Operatives (semi-skilled)	11,400	18.1	13,920	16.2	22.1	15,400	16.2
Laborers (unskilled)	3,485	5.5	4,380	5.1	25.6	3,500	3.7
Service Workers	7,490	11.9	11,370	13.2	51.8	13,100	13.8
Private Household	1,975	3.1	1,230	1.4	(37.7)		
Others	5,500	8.7	10,140	11.8	84.3		
Farm Workers	5,360	8.5	3,050	3.5	(43.1)	2,600	2.7
Farmers and Farm Managers	3,070	4.8	1,640	1.9	(46.6)		
Farm Laborers	2,280	3.6	1,400	1.6	(38.6)		

SOURCES: The figures for 1958 and 1974 are from *The Manpower Report of the President, 1975* Table A-15, p. 225. The projections for 1980 are from the U.S. Department of Labor, Bulletin 1673 (1970). Numbers and Percentages have been rounded.

ing place. In 1900 only 15 percent of American men wore white collars (and most of these were independent small businessmen). By 1940 the figure had gone up to 25 percent (and these were largely in administrative jobs). In 1970 almost 42 percent of the male labor force —some twenty million men—held white-collar jobs (as against twenty-three million who wore blue collars), and of these, almost fourteen million were managerial, professional, or technical—the heart of the upper middle class in the United States.[9]

The total blue-collar occupations, which numbered about 12 million in 1900, rose to 29.7 million in 1974 and will rise at a slower rate to 31.1 million in 1980. In 1900, the blue-collar workers formed about 35 percent of the total labor force, a figure which reached 40 percent in 1920 and again, after World War II, in 1950, but by 1974 it was down to about 34.9 percent of the total labor force and by 1980 will reach an historic low of 32.7 percent.

The most striking change, of course, has been in the farm population. In 1900 farming was still the single largest occupation in the United States, comprising 12.5 million workers and about 37.5 percent of the labor force. Until about 1930, the absolute number of farmers and farm workers continued to rise though their share of employment began to decline. In 1940, because of the extraordinary agricultural revolution, which shot productivity to spectacular heights, the number of farm laborers began its rapid decline. In 1974, employment on the farms numbered 3.0 million, and this will decline to 2.6 million in 1980; from 3.5 percent of the work force in 1974 it will fall to 2.7 percent in 1980.

The service occupations continue to expand steadily. In 1900 there were about three million persons in services, more than half of whom were domestics. In 1974, there were almost 11.4 million persons in services, only 10 percent of whom were domestics. The major rises were in such occupations as garage workers, hotel and restaurant workers, and the like. Through the 1970s, service occupations will increase by two-fifths or a rate one and one-half times the expansion for all occupations combined.

The category of semi-skilled worker (called operatives in the census classification) from 1920 on was the single largest occupational category in the economy, comprising more workers than any other group. Semi-skilled work is the occupational counterpart of mass production, and it rose with the increased output of goods. But the introduction of sophisticated new technologies has slowed the growth of this group drastically. Total employment will rise from 14

---

[9] For the current figures, see Statistical Abstract of the United States, 1971, table no. 347, "Employed Persons by Major Occupation Group and Sex," p. 222.

million in 1974 to 15.4 million in 1980, but the rate of increase is half the increase projected for all employment.

As a share of total employment, the percentage of semi-skilled will slide downward from 18.4 percent in 1968 to 16.2 percent in 1980 and will at that time be *third* in size ranking, outpaced by clerical, which will be the largest, and by professional and technical workers. Equally, the proportion of factory workers among the semi-skilled will probably drop. In 1968, six out of every ten semi-skilled workers were employed as factory operatives. Large numbers of them now work as inspectors, maintenance men, operators of material-moving equipment such as powered forklift trucks, and the like. Among the non-factory operatives, drivers of trucks, buses, and taxi-cabs make up the largest group.

The central occupational category in the society today is the professional and technical. Growth in this category has outdistanced all other major occupational groups in recent decades. From less than a million in 1890, the number of these workers has grown to 12.3 million in 1974. Within this category, the largest group was teachers (more than 2 million), the second largest professional health workers (about 2 million), scientists and engineers (about 1.4 million), and engineering and science technicians (about 900,000). Despite the momentary slowdown in the demand for education, and the immediate unemployment in engineering because of the shift away from defense work in 1970–1971, requirements in this category continue to lead all others, increasing half again in size (about twice the employment increase among all occupations combined) between 1968 and 1980. With 15.5 million workers in 1980, this will comprise 16.3 percent of total employment as against 11 percent in 1958. (For a graphic representation of the changes in the occupational categories, see Figures 2–1 and 2–2.)

These historic shifts pose a serious problem for the trade-union movement, which in the United States has historically been a blue-collar phenomenon. On the record, the trade-union movement (AFL–CIO plus the major independents) is stronger than it has ever been since the beginning of mass organizing in 1935. In 1970, the total American membership rose to 19,381,000, its all-time high. In the 1960s it gained 2,300,000 members, though the major increase came in the mid-years and the gains of the last two years were only half those of the major period of increase from 1964–1966.[10]

Yet this is a superficial way of looking at the problem, for the extraordinary fact is that, as a percentage of the total labor force, the

[10] All statistical data in this section, except as otherwise noted, are from *Labor Unions in the United States, 1969,* Bureau of Labor Statistics Bulletin 1665 (1970) and preliminary estimates for 1968–1970 in the BLS release, "Labor Union and Employee Association Membership, 1970" (September 13, 1971).

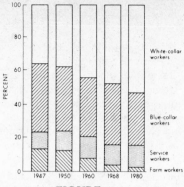

FIGURE 2–1

Employment Trends among Major Occupational Categories, 1947–1968 *(Actual)*
and 1980 *(Projected for a Services Economy with 3 Percent Unemployment)*
* Farm workers include farm managers.

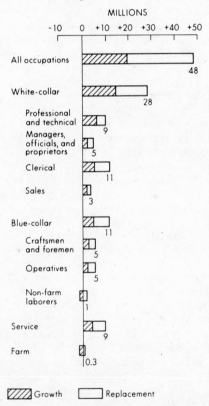

FIGURE 2–2

Net Job Openings in Major Occupational Categories and Groups, 1968–1980
(Projected for a Services Economy with 3 Percent Unemployment)
SOURCE: *The U. S. Economy in 1980,* Bureau of Labor Statistics Bulletin 1673
(1970).

number of members today is *exactly the same* as in 1947; and as a percentage of workers in non-agricultural establishments, the sector where most members are found and most organizing efforts are made, the percentage of union members is *less today* than in 1947. In effect, trade unionism in the United States has made no real advance in nearly a quarter of a century. (See Table 2–6.)

TABLE 2–6
Union Membership As a Proportion of the Labor Force, 1947–1970

		TOTAL LABOR FORCE		EMPLOYEES IN NON-AGRICULTURAL ESTABLISHMENTS	
YEAR	TOTAL UNION MEMBERSHIP (THOUSANDS)	NUMBER (THOU-SANDS)	PERCENTAGE UNION MEMBERS	NUMBER (THOU-SANDS)	PERCENTAGE UNION MEMBERS
1947	13,782	60,168	22.9	43,438	31.7
1952	15,805	62,966	23.7	48,306	30.9
1956	17,490	69,409	25.2	52,408	33.4
1960	17,049	72,142	23.6	54,234	31.4
1964	16,841	75,830	22.2	58,332	28.9
1968	18,916	82,272	23.0	67,860	27.9
1970	19,381	85,903	22.6	70,644	27.4

SOURCES: 1947 and 1952 figures by Leo Troy, Bureau of National Research; 1956–1968 data in Bureau of Labor Statistics, Bulletin 1665; 1970 data in release, BLS (September 13, 1971).

NOTE: In percentage of employees organized, the United States ranks among the lowest of Western industrial nations. In Belgium/Luxembourg, more than 65 percent of employees are organized, in Italy more than 55 percent, in Great Britain more than 45 percent, in Holland more than 40 percent, in Germany almost 40 percent, and France about 20 percent. (Data from European Economic Community, reported in *The Economist* [June 19, 1971], p. 46.)

After the Wagner Act was passed in 1935 and until the end of World War II, union membership made a four-fold gain. In subsequent years, the membership became stabilized. In 1953–1954, I wrote a series of studies for *Fortune* and elsewhere predicting that the labor movement would stop growing, and describing the kind of plateau it would reach.[11] My reasoning was based on the argument that unionism had come to the saturation point in manufacturing and construction simply because it had organized almost all the major employers, and it was too costly to tackle the small units of under a hundred that remained unorganized. There would be an expansion in the distributive trades (teamsters, retail clerks) since these were ex-

[11] See "The Next American Labor Movement," *Fortune* (April 1953), and my discussion, "Union Growth," in the Proceedings of the Seventh Annual Meeting of the Industrial Relations Research Association (December 1954).

panding areas of the labor force, but such gains would be offset by declines in railroad and mining. The unions had shown themselves incapable of organizing the white-collar and technical workers; the only major area for union growth was government employment and this depended on favorable government support.

Union growth in the United States has always been dependent on favorable government support. While it is clear that the upsurge of unionism in the 1930s was indigenous, its *institutionalization* was possible only under the umbrella of the National Labor Relations Board. The union gains could later be consolidated only when the War Labor Board virtually enacted union-shop clauses in collective-bargaining contracts during World War II.

The only real growth in American trade unionism in the last decade has been among government workers, and here the same forces have been at work. In January 1962, President Kennedy issued Executive Order 10988, which encouraged unionism in the federal service. This order gave clear and unequivocal support to public unionism, just as the Wagner Act of 1935 had supported unions and collective bargaining in private business. It declared that "the efficient administration of the government and the well-being of employees require that orderly and constructive relationships be maintained between employee organizations and management." In New York City, earlier executive orders by Mayor Robert F. Wagner resulted in the "breakthrough" of unionism, in 1961, among 44,000 teachers. Similar orders were issued in Philadelphia and other cities with evident results.[12]

In 1970, in some measure because of the economic downturn, in other measure because of the facilitating role of government, there began a movement for the unionization of college teachers. The growth of bargaining in the public sector was facilitated by the passage of public employee relations laws or similar measures in 19 states. The prospects for unionization at private institutions were enhanced when the National Labor Relations Board in 1970 assumed jurisdiction at private colleges and universities with gross incomes of more than $1 million a year.

By the end of 1971, collective bargaining agents for professors had been recognized at 133 of the country's 2,500 colleges and universities. These were principally in six states, New York, Michigan, New Jersey, Wisconsin, Illinois, and Massachusetts. But half the total number of the faculty covered were employees of two New York systems, those of the State University and the City University.

---

[12] See Everett M. Kassalow, "Trade Unionism Goes Public," in *The Public Interest*, no. 14 (Winter 1969).

In most areas of the country, teachers are organized, but usually in such professional associations as the National Education Association for elementary and secondary school teachers, or the American Association of University Professors. In the past, both have eschewed direct bargaining roles and contented themselves, particularly the NEA, with lobbying activities. In the 1970s, given the competition of teachers' unions, it is likely that both organizations will turn more aggressively to the economic defense of teachers' interests.

In 1956, when the Bureau of Labor Statistics first started collecting data on union membership by industry, 915,000 persons, or 5.1 percent of a total union membership of 18.1 million, were in government. By the end of 1962, the number had grown to 1.2 million, or 7 percent of the total membership, and by 1968 union membership had climbed to 2.2 million, or 10.7 percent of the total membership.[13]

The main push had been in the federal government, where about *half* the employees have been organized. But in the larger area of state and local government, less than 10 percent of their employees are unionized. The proportion of government employees organized at different levels is shown in Table 2–7.

TABLE 2–7

Proportion of Government Employees Organized

YEAR	GOVERNMENT		FEDERAL GOVERNMENT		STATE AND LOCAL	
	TOTAL EMPLOYMENT (THOUSANDS)	PERCENTAGE ORGANIZED	TOTAL EMPLOYMENT (THOUSANDS)	PERCENTAGE ORGANIZED	TOTAL EMPLOYMENT (THOUSANDS)	PERCENTAGE ORGANIZED
1956	7,277	12.6	2,209	—	5,069	—
1960	8,353	12.8	2,270	—	6,083	—
1964	9,596	15.1	2,348	38.2	7,248	7.7
1966	10,792	15.9	2,564	41.8	8,227	7.8
1968	11,846	18.2	2,737	49.4	9,109	8.8

SOURCE: *Monthly Labor Review* (July 1970).
NOTE: Dashes indicate data not available.

The relatively large advance in government unionism has changed the sector distribution of unionism in the United States. Following the big drive of the CIO, more than half of American unionism by 1949 was in manufacturing, but as shown in Table 2–8, that proportion has slowly begun to change in recent years and we can look for greater shifts in the years ahead.

---

[13] Harry P. Cohany and Lucretia M. Dewey, "Union Membership among Government Employees," *Monthly Labor Review* (July 1970).

TABLE 2–8

Union Membership by Sector, 1956 and 1968
(In Thousands)

YEAR	TOTAL	MANUFACTURING		NON-MANUFACTURING		GOVERNMENT	
		NUMBER	PERCENTAGE	NUMBER	PERCENTAGE	NUMBER	PERCENTAGE
1956	18,104	8,839	48.8	8,350	46.1	915	5.1
1968	20,210	9,218	45.6	8,837	43.7	2,155	10.7

Since 1956, union membership in manufacturing and non-manufacturing has continued to shrink as a proportion of total membership (union membership in manufacturing declined 44,000 between 1968 and 1970), and only membership in the public sector has moved upward. It is estimated that about 60 percent of manufacturing employment is organized, compared to one-quarter in non-manufacturing and a little less than 20 percent in government employment.

It is the white-collar field, of course, that is crucial for the future of organized labor, and here trade unionism has done poorly (see Table 2–9). According to reports from 167 unions and estimates

TABLE 2–9

White-Collar Unionism
(In Thousands)

YEAR	NUMBER OF WHITE-COLLAR MEMBERS	PERCENTAGE OF ALL UNION MEMBERS
1956	2,463	13.6
1968	3,176	15.7

for 22, total white-collar membership in 1968 stood at 3.2 million. This is about 15 percent of all union members. The highest ratio of white-collar union workers, more than 40 percent, was in government service, followed by 22 percent in non-manufacturing and 4 percent in manufacturing. Sixty-two unions reported a total of 982,-000 professional and technical members, but a large proportion of this group consisted of unions exclusively representing professional employees such as actors and artists, musicians, airline pilots, and, of those in government, mainly teachers. The major white-collar areas —in trade, finance, and insurance—remain largely unorganized, as does the entire area of science and engineering technicians and engineers.

Some Labor Problems of the Post-Industrial Society

The structural changes I have been delineating pose some crucial, long-run problems for the organized trade-union movement in the United States. But long-run, in this context, means thirty years or so before these tendencies work themselves out in detail, and numbers or proportions are not always a reliable index of influence. The number of farmers has been dwindling steadily, but the politics of agriculture still plays a major role in the calculations of the political parties, and the influence of the agricultural bloc casts a far longer shadow than its size. In that same respect, a movement with about 20 million members, even in a labor force of 100 million persons, is one that will exercise considerable influence for a long time.

A full-scale analysis of the problems of labor in a post-industrial society would have to include the structure of trade unionism, the problem of bureaucracy and democracy in unions, and the like; but these are outside the scope of this essay. The issues I shall deal with, some of them theoretical in nature, derive largely from the analysis of the changes in the composition of the work force, and the nature of the post-industrial society that I have sketched earlier.

EDUCATION AND STATUS

The most striking aspect of the new labor force is the level of formal educational attainment. By 1980, only 1 in 16 adult workers (25 years and over)—about 5 million—will have had less than 8 years of schooling, while 7 in every 10 adult workers, about 52 million, will at least have completed 4 years of high school. In 1968, by contrast, 1 in 10 (about 7 million) had completed less than 8 years of schooling and 6 in 10 (about 37 million) had completed 4 years of high school.

Many will have gone further. Nearly 1 in 6 persons, 25 years and over (about 13 million) will have completed at least four years of college, as against 1 in 7, or about 8.5 million, in 1968. Moreover, in 1980 about 9.2 million adults, 1 in 8, will have some college training, though less than four years.

Not only is there a much greater degree of educational attainment, but there is also a greater degree of cultural homogeneity. The American labor movement, particularly the blue-collar class, has always had a large component of foreign-born or first-generation workers, many of whom accepted a lower status as a matter of course. In 1950, about 34 percent of the blue-collar labor force (skilled, semi-skilled and unskilled) were either foreign-born or of foreign or mixed parentage. By 1960, this figure had fallen to 26 percent.[14] It is likely to fall further.

For the first time, therefore, historically speaking, the American blue-collar labor force is approaching the "classical" Marxist image of a relatively well-educated, culturally homogeneous force. To what extent does this change create the basis for a new consciousness or a new militancy? Those entering into plant and factory work today step into conditions far better than those their parents experienced. But, as we all know from generational experiences the gains of the past count little in the present. The crucial point is that however much an improvement there may have been in wage rates, pension conditions, supervision, and the like, the conditions of work themselves—the control of pacing, the assignments, the design and layout of work—are still outside the control of the worker himself. The trade-union movement, including the UAW, has never really challenged the organization of work itself, though it has modified the arbitrary authority over the workers. To what extent, then, the entry of a new, young, educated work force creates a very different psychology and new kinds of demands about the character of work, remains to be seen.

In a modern society, few groups remain unorganized for long. The professionals in the United States—engineers, doctors, teachers—are organized. These are primarily professional organizations, though in the case of teachers in the large urban centers, a number of these unions are affiliated with the AFL–CIO. The major question in the next two decades will be the character of these organizations: will they retain their traditional guild form, or become more militant and aggressive labor unions? One force that will seek to turn these organizations or newly formed professional groups in a more militant direction is the younger professionals, particularly in medicine and community-affairs activities, many of whom learned their organizational skills in the student protest movements of the 1960s. In addition, these professionals are increasingly subject to budgetary constraints, and while the income of professionals rose steadily in the 1960s, in the next decade that rise will be levelling off. Much depends, in this instance, on government policy, particularly its willingness or unwillingness to

---

[14] These figures are computed from the 1950 Census, Subject Report 3A, *Characteristics of the White Population 14 years old and over*, and 1960 Census, Subject Report 1 A, *Social and Economic Characteristics of the Population 14 years and over*. I am indebted to Mrs. Jordy Bell Jacoby for the breakdowns and computations. The figures of 34 and 26 percent are not an averaging; as it turns out, the distribution of native and foreign-born is equal across the skilled, semi-skilled, and unskilled classifications.

fund social programs, and on the extent of unemployment among intellectuals. The organization of professionals will be a major feature of post-industrial society, as the organization of skilled and semi-skilled workers was characteristic of industrial society. What form these organizations will take remains to be seen.

THE BLACKS

In an essay of almost a decade ago, in which I formulated the theme of the post-industrial society, I wrote: "Insofar as education is today —and tomorrow—the chief means of social mobility, by charting the school dropout rates and matching them against future skill requirements by education one can sketch a rough picture of class society in the United States thirty years from now. . . . By that criterion, thirty years hence, class society in the United States will be predominantly color society." [15]

The situation today is not as bleak as it was a dozen years ago. Blacks were 4 percent of the professional and technical group in 1960, but the proportion had almost doubled to 7 percent in 1970. They were 5 percent of the clerical group in 1960, and 8 percent in 1970. Thus, in these key sectors, the pace of gain has been striking. But the total numbers are still small. Only 22 percent of black males are professional, technical, and clerical, as against 43 percent of white males. (Thirty-six percent of black females are professional, technical, and clerical, as against 64 percent of white females.) Eighteen percent of black males are unskilled laborers as against 6 percent of whites, and 18 percent of black females are domestics as against 3 percent white. [16]

The single largest group of black workers are semi-skilled (28 percent of the males, as against 19 percent of white males). For this group, the problem of better jobs lies with the trade union movement which, while formally accepting the principle of help, has been quite slow, particularly in the construction and skilled trades (14 percent of blacks are skilled as against 21 percent of whites) in upgrading black workers. Whether the blacks maintain an alliance with the labor movement, particularly in the political field, depends more on the behavior and response of labor than on that of the blacks. The political independence of the blacks—at least of the top leadership —is one of the realities of the politics of the seventies.

[15] "The Post-Industrial Society" (June 14, 1962).

[16] All data are from *The Social and Economic Status of Negroes in the United States*, 1970, Current Population Reports, Series P-23, no. 38.

WOMEN

The fact is that a service economy is very largely a female-centered economy—if one considers clerical, sales, teaching, health technicians, and similar occupations. In 1960, 80 percent of all workers in the goods-producing area were men, and 20 percent women; conversely, in the services sectors only 54 percent of all workers were men and 46 percent women. Looked at along a different axis, 27 percent of all employed females worked in the goods-producing sector, while 73 percent of all women worked in the services sector.[17]

The fact that the service industries are so largely unorganized creates a special problem for the labor movement in its relation to women. In 1958, women unionists totaled 3.1 million, or 18.2 percent of total union membership; by 1968, their number had risen to 3.7 million, or 19.5 percent of all members. During these 10 years, unions added over 2 million new members to their ranks, and women made up 30 percent of that increase; since 1958, 600,000 more women in the United States have joined unions.

During those same ten years, however, the number of women in the labor force grew from 32.7 percent to 37.1 percent. Thus the ratio of women union members to employed women has declined over the decade from 13.8 to 12.5 percent. Moreover, most women are grouped into a few unions. A considerable number are blue collar and belong to such unions as the International Ladies Garment Workers, the Amalgamated Clothing, Service Employees (formerly Building Service), the Teamsters and the Auto Workers. The bulk of the others are in communication-workers, teachers, and government-workers unions.

For a variety of sociological reasons, women have been more difficult to organize than men. Fewer women have thought of their jobs as "permanent," and have been less interested in unions; many female jobs are part-time or "second jobs" for the family, and the turnover of the number of women at work has been much higher than that of men. Since the proportion of women in the labor force is bound to rise—the efforts of women's lib apart—simply because of the expansion of the service industries, the problem for the organized trade-union movement in recruiting more union members will be an increasingly difficult one.

THE NON-PROFIT SECTOR

The services industries, as I indicated earlier, can be divided into many different kinds: those which are directly auxiliary to industry,

---

[17] Victor R. Fuchs, *op. cit.*, table 66, p. 185.

such as transportation and utilities; those which handle distribution
and trade, as well as finance and insurance; those which provide professional and business services, such as data-processing; those which
derive from leisure demands, such as travel, entertainment, sports,
recreation, including the media; and those which deal with communal services, particularly health, education, and government. The
latter has been the largest-growing area since the end of World War
II.

The growth, in effect, has been taking place in the *non-profit* sector of society. In 1929, according to estimates of Eli Ginzberg and
his associates, the non-profit sector accounted for 12.5 percent of all
goods and services purchased. By 1963 it stood above 27 percent, and
it is still rising.[18] In 1929, 4,465,000 persons were employed by government and non-profit institutions, or about 9.7 percent of the labor
force. By 1960, 13,583,000, or 20 percent of everyone employed,
were in the non-profit sector; at that time, the number employed by
government was 8,300,000. Government employment has risen
rapidly (a rate of 4.5 percent a year), reaching 11.8 million in 1968,
and an estimated 16.8 million in 1980. (While there are no immediate
figures for the rise of the remaining non-profit sector, principally
health, one can assume a substantial rise there, too.)

More important, the non-profit sector is the major area of net *new*
jobs, i.e. actual expansion as against replacement. From 1950 to 1960,
the non-profit sector accounted for more than 50 percent of new
jobs, and in the period from 1960 to 1970, government alone contributed one-third of the *new* jobs in the service areas.

Are there significant differences in the ethos of those engaged in
the profit and non-profit sectors? There have been almost no studies
in this field. Yet, since the heart of the non-profit sector is health, education, and research, which by 1975 will comprise about 6,000,000
persons,[19] one can assume there is a core of middle-class and upper-
middle-class persons who not only form a large market for culture,
but whose political and social attitudes, in the main, will be more liberal than that of the society as a whole. It is in this area that the
greatest pressure for social change will come.

[18] Ginzberg, Hiestand and Reubens, *The Pluralistic Economy* (New York, 1965),
p. 86.
[19] Detailed projections by occupations are available only to 1975. *Tomorrow's
Manpower Needs,* Bureau of Labor Statistics Bulletin 1606, vol. IV, The National
Industry-Occupational Matrix, makes the following estimates (p. 28):

Medical and Health	2,240
Teachers	3,063
Natural Scientists	465
Social Scientists	79
Clergymen	240
Editors and Reporters	128

THE "NEW" WORKING CLASS

In a recent dialogue, the romantic French Marxist, Regis Debray, tested Chile's President Salvador Allende on his revolutionary purity:

> DEBRAY: . . . the main question is which sector of society is the motive force behind the process [of revolution], which class is in charge of the administration of the process.
> ALLENDE: The proletariat; that is, the working class.

But the problem for an advanced industrial society is: What is the working class? Is it the "factory worker," the "industrial worker," or, even more widely, the "blue-collar worker?" (For Marx, the proletariat was not identical with the masses of poor working people, and certainly not the *lumpenproletariat*, who he thought had lost the ability to function in human terms in society. The classical proletariat consisted of factory workers whose class-consciousness was created by the conditions of their work.) But even at its most comprehensive definition, the blue-collar group is in an increasing minority in advanced or post-industrial society. Is the proletariat, or the working class, *all* those who work for wages and salaries? But that so expands the concept as to distort it beyond recognition. (Are all managers workers? Are supervisors and administrators workers? Are highly paid professors and engineers workers?)

For a long time, Marxist sociologists simply ignored the issue, and argued that the "inevitable" economic crises of capitalism would force a revolutionary conflict in which "the working class" would win. In Germany in the 1920s, where the phenomenon of the new technical and administrative class was first noticed, it was categorized as "the new middle class," and it was in this sense that C. Wright Mills also used the idea in his 1951 book, *White Collar*. For the German sociologists, particularly Emil Lederer and Jacob Marschak, who first analyzed the phenomenon in detail, the "new middle class" could not be an autonomous independent class, but would eventually have to support either the working class or the business community. This was also Mills's argument: "Insofar as political strength rests upon organized economic power, the white-collar workers can only derive their strength from 'business' or from 'labor.' Within the whole structure of power, they are dependent variables. Estimates of their political tendencies, therefore, must rest upon larger predictions of the manner and outcomes of the struggles of business and labor." [20]

The German sociologists, and Mills, had been writing principally

---

[20] C. Wright Mills, *White Collar* (New York, 1951), p. 352.

about managerial, administrative, and clerical personnel. But when it became evident, particularly in the 1950s, that there was a large-scale transformation in the character of skilled work itself, with the expansion of engineering and technicians in the advanced technological fields—aerospace, computers, oil refining, electronics, optics, polymers—and that this new stratum was becoming occupationally more important as well as replacing the skilled workers as the crucial group in the industrial process, the problem of sociological definition became crucial.

The first Marxist to seek a theoretical formulation was the independent French radical Serge Mallet, who, in a series of articles in *Les Temps Modernes* and the magazine *La Nef* in 1959, wrote an analysis of the new industrial processes in France's petit counterpart to IBM, La Compagnie des machines Bull, and in the heavily automated oil refinery, Caltex. These studies, plus a long essay, "Trade Unionism and Industrial Society," were published in France in 1963 under the title *La Nouvelle Classe Ouvrière* (*The New Working Class*). Though untranslated, the book had a definite influence on some young American radicals, particularly in SDS (after all, they could eat their working-class cake and have it, too). For a while "the new working-class tendency," as it was called, seemed to be making its way among independent Marxists until it was swamped, on the one hand, by the revolutionary adventurism of the Weathermen, and, on the other, by the heavy-handed dogmatism of the young Progressive Labor Party groups. The breakup of the SDS left the tendency without a home.

The Mallet thesis is quite simple. The engineers and technicians are a "new" working class, in part replacing the old, with a potential for revolutionary leadership and the ability to play a role far beyond their numbers. They are a "new" working class, even though well paid, because their skills are inevitably broken down, compartmentalized, and routinized, and they are unable to realize the professional skills for which they were educated. Thus they are "reduced" to the role of a highly trained working class. The fact that they are better paid does not make them a new "aristocracy of labor," but in fact provides a model for the other workers. As Mallet writes:

The "new working class" is, in effect, tied to the most highly developed industrial capitalists, and the standard of living which they have is due entirely to the high degree of productivity of these enterprises. It is, however, a situation which could change according to the economic situation and it is a superficial analysis which permits one to assimilate these modern industrial technicians to a "working class aristocracy." It is true that there exists between them and the masses of workers an appreciable difference in the level of living. But, as we shall see, far from having negative consequences on the behavior of the rest of the working class, the existence of this "avant garde" has, on the contrary, positive effects.[21]

In principle, the idea is not new. It is central, of course, to the writing of Thorstein Veblen (little known to the French), who, in *The Theory of Business Enterprises* (1903), made a fundamental distinction between industry and business—between the engineer, devoted largely to improving the practices of production, and the finance capitalist or manager, who restricts production in order to maintain process and profit. In *The Engineers and the Price System* (1920), Veblen wrote "A Memorandum on a Practicable Soviet of Technicians" which laid out the argument of the revolutionary potential of the production engineer as the indispensable "General Staff of the industrial system."

Without their immediate and unremitting guidance and correction the industrial system will not work. It is a mechanically organized structure of the technical processes designed, installed and conducted by the production engineers. Without them and their constant attention, the industrial equipment, the mechanical appliances of industry, will foot up to just so much junk.[22]

Veblen wrote in the first flush of excitement after the Russian Revolution, and he felt that a syndicalist overturn of society was possible—in fact, he thought it could be the only one, since political revolutions in advanced industrial society were passé. For half a century that idea has seemed strange indeed, but its revival by the French writers has been possible because the idea of a professional new class has meshed with the idea of alienation.

Where Mallet, like Veblen, restricted his analysis largely to the technicians, the French social critic André Gorz, an editor of *Les Temps Modernes*, has extended his thesis to the "alienated situation" of the entire professional class. Until now, he argues, the trade union movement has taken the necessary stand of fighting for "quantitative gains," but this continuing strategy has become increasingly dysfunctional because it has tied the workers into the productivity of the economic system and the consumption society. The new strategy for labor, as well as for all professionals, should be to fight for "qualitative" changes, and in particular for control of production. In Gorz's words:

. . . technicians, engineers, students, researchers discover that they are wage earners like the others, paid for a piece of work which is "good"

---

[21] Serge Mallet, *La Nouvelle Classe Ouvrière* (Paris, 1963), p. 69 (my translation).
[22] See Thorstein Veblen, *The Engineers and the Price System* (Harbinger edition, 1963), pp. 4–5.

only to the degree that it is profitable in the short run. They discover that long-range research, creative work on original problems, and the love of workmanship are incompatible with the criteria of capitalist profitability. . . . They discover that they are ruled by the law of capital not only in their work but in all spheres of their life, because those who hold power over big industry also hold power over the State, the society, the region, the city, the university—over each individual's future . . .

It then becomes immediately evident that the struggle for a meaningful life is the struggle against the power of capital, and that this struggle must proceed without a break in continuity from the company level to the whole social sphere, from the union level to the political realm, from technology to culture. . . . From then on everything is involved: jobs, wages, careers, the city, the regions, science, culture, and the possibility of developing individual creative abilities in the service of humanity. . . . This goal will not be reached merely through nationalization (which risks turning into no more than bureaucratic governmentalization) of the centers of accumulation of capital and credit: it also requires the multiplication of centers of democratic decision making and their autonomy; that is to say, a complex and coordinated network of regional and local autonomous bodies. This demand, far from being abstract, has or can have all the urgency of imperious necessity. . . . because once a certain level of culture has been reached, the need for autonomy, the need to develop one's abilities freely and to give a purpose to one's life is experienced with the same intensity as an unsatisfied physiological necessity.

The impossibility of living which appeared to the proletarians of the last century as the impossibility of reproducing their labor power becomes for the workers of scientific or cultural industries the impossibility of putting their creative abilities to work. Industry in the last century took from the countryside men who were muscles, lungs, stomach: their muscles missed the open spaces, their lungs the fresh air, their stomachs fresh food; their health declined, and the acuteness of their need was but the empty functioning of their organs in a hostile surrounding world. The industry of the second half of the twentieth century increasingly tends to take men from the universities and colleges, men who have been able to acquire the ability to do creative or independent work; who have curiosity, the ability to synthesize, to analyze, to invent, and to assimilate, an ability which spins in a vacuum and runs the risk of perishing for lack of an opportunity to be usefully put to work.[23]

The most serious efforts to apply Gorz's ideas to the American scene have been made by some radical young economists at Harvard, notably Herbert Gintis. Gintis sees a "new emergent social class in modern capitalism," a new working class which he broadly labels "educated labor." Drawing upon the standard work of Edward

[23] André Gorz, *Strategy for Labor* (Boston, 1968), pp. 104–106. The book was first published in France in 1964, under the title of *Stratégie Ouvrière et Néocapitalisme*.

Denison, and of his Harvard colleague Samuel Bowles, Gintis emphasizes the importance of "educated labor," because if one compares the
relative contribution of physical capital (machines and technology)
with "human capital" in the economic growth of the United States
between 1929 and 1957, labor is between five and eight times more
important than physical capital. But Gintis sees educated labor as
pressed into a mold by the requirements of the capitalist system. A
revolutionary outlook emerges because of the alienated desire of educated persons for a full life as producers, as against the fragmentation
and specialization which is their lot in the workaday world. For Gintis, the student rebellion against the university foreshadows the possible revolt of all "educated labor" against capitalism.

The weakness of this abstract analysis lies, first, in seeing the students as the model for the revolution of the future. The university,
even with required courses, is not the prototype of the corporate
world, and it is highly unlikely that even "raised student consciousness" was a consciousness of "oppression." Universities are a "hot
house" in which a student lives in a world apart, free largely, especially today, from the sanctions and reprisals of adult authority for
almost any escapades. After graduation students enter a different,
highly differentiated society and begin to take on responsibilities for
themselves and their new families. It is not so surprising, therefore,
that whatever the initial benchmark of radicalism, the college generation, as it grows older, becomes more conservative.[24]

A second weakness is the monolithic rhetoric about the requirements of "the system." Paradoxically (and perhaps tongue-in-cheek)
Gintis drew his analysis not from Marcuse but from the functionalist
school of sociology, particularly Talcott Parsons, which Marxists have
attacked as too simple a view of the "integration" of society. In any
event, both the functionalist and the Marcusian views are too con-
stricted in their understanding of the diversity and multiplicity of the
society and the culture. There is no "system" which "reproduces" the
existing division of labor in the next generation, but many different
trends deriving from the diverse sources of occupational trends in the
United States.

And third, Gintis sees bureaucratization as identical with capitalism
("The bureaucratization of work is a result of the capitalist control of

---

[24] For a comprehensive review of the evidence for this argument, see S. M. Lipset
and E. C. Ladd, Jr., "College Generations—From the 1930s to the 1960s," *The
Public Interest*, no. 25 (Fall 1971). What is also true, as Professors Lipset and Ladd
point out, is that each succeeding college generation starts out from a point further
left than the preceding one; while they end up more conservative than when they
began, the final resting point may be more liberal or left than even the starting point
of generations a long time ago. To that extent, there is a basic liberal or left drift
among the successive college-educated generations in the society.

the work process, as bureaucracy seems to be the sole organizational form compatible with capitalist hegemony"), rather than as a pervasive feature of the historic development of all technological and hierarchical societies, capitalist and communist.[25] And what he misses, in his abstract conception of bureaucracy, are the large number of changes taking place in organizations which are modifying the classic hierarchical structures of bureaucracy by encouraging committees and participation. While such changes, it is true, do not alter the fundamental character of authority, the modifications often serve to provide the individual with a greater degree of participation than before.

The sources of these critiques are the moral impulses of socialist humanism, but though one can sympathize with their values, it is folly to confuse normative with analytical categories and convert social tendencies into rhetorical wish fulfillment, as Gorz and Gintis do. The engineers, for example, fit many of the attributes of the alienated "educated worker." Few of them are allowed to decide how their skills and knowledge will be used; the transition from a defense economy, combined with the drastic slash in research-and-development spending, has made many of them aware, for the first time, of the precariousness of a "career." Yet they do not in the least identify themselves with the "working class." (As *Fortune* found in a recent study of engineers, in June 1971, "Many have moved up into engineering from blue-collar union families and don't want to slip back.") What counts for the engineer is the maintenance of a "professional status." They complain that the word engineer is now used to describe everyone from a salesman (a systems engineer at IBM) to a garbage collector (a sanitary engineer, in the Chicago euphemism). The effort to reassert their professional status—through membership in high-prestige associations, through stiffer requirements for professional certification, through changes in school curricula—is an effort at differentiation, not identification.[26]

This effort to maintain professional status—one aspect of a society in which individual social mobility is still a positive value—

[25] Gintis's major statement is to be found in the essay "The New Working Class and Revolutionary Youth," a supplement to *Continuum* (Spring–Summer 1970), vol. 8, nos. 1 and 2. The quotation in the text is from p. 167.

[26] One sees here, in particular, the sociological differences between English and American life. In England, where engineering has never been considered a true profession, and technical schools until recently never had the status of universities, the Association of Scientific, Technical and Managerial Staffs has grown from 9,000 members in 1947 to 220,000 members today. There are a dozen or so engineering unions in the U.S. today, and the independent federation, the Council of Engineers and Scientists Organizations, claims to represent 100,000 members in the U.S. and Canada, but there are few collective bargaining contracts in the U.S. that cover engineers.

comes into conflict, however, with the New Left populism, which derogates professionalism as "elitism." In the schools, in the hospitals, in the community, the New Left political impulse is to deplore professionalism and hieratic standing as means of excluding the people from decisions. Thus one finds today the paradox that "educated labor" is caught between the extremes of bureaucratization and populism. If it is to resist the "alienation" which threatens its achievement, it is more likely to assert the traditional professionalism (certainly on the ideological level) than go in either direction. To this extent, the phrase "new working class" is simply a radical conceit, and little more.

The Constraints on Change

There is little question, I believe, that in the next few decades we shall see some striking changes in the structure of occupations and professional work. Within the factories there will be new demands for control over the decisions of work as the new, younger and more educated labor force faces the prospect of long years in a mechanical harness and finds the monetary rewards (which their forebears struggled to achieve) less important. Within the professions there will be more social-mindedness as a newer generation comes to the fore and the structure of professional relationships changes. Within medicine, for example, one of the central occupations of a post-industrial society, the inevitable end of the "fee-for-service" relationship, replaced by some kind of insurance-cum-government payment scheme, means the end of the doctor as an individual entrepreneur and the increasing centrality of the hospital and group practice. A whole new range of issues opens up: who is to run the hospitals—the old philanthropic trustees, the municipal political nominees, the doctors, the "constituencies," or the "community"? How does one balance research and patient care in the distribution of resources? Should there be more big teaching hospitals with greater sophisticated facilities or more simple community medical services? Similarly, within the law, the greater role of government in welfare, services for the poor, education, consumer standards, and health provides a whole new area of public-interest law for the lawyer alongside the older areas of business, real estate, labor law, wills and trusts. The multiplication of junior and community colleges and the break-up of the standard curricula in most universities provide an arena for experiment and change.

And yet, ironically, at a time when many needed reforms seem about to be made in the area of work and in the professions—in part out of the upheavals of the 1960s, in greater part because of the deeper forces of structural changes of a post-industrial society—there will be stronger objective constraints on such changes (apart from the vested and established interests which are always present) than in the previous several decades of American economic and social development.

There is, first, the constraint of productivity. The simple and obvious fact is that productivity and output grow much faster in goods than in services. (This is crucial in the shift in the relative shares of employment: men can be displaced by machines more readily in goods-production than in services.) Productivity in services, because it is a relation between persons, rather than between man and machine, will inevitably be lower than it is in industry. This is true in almost all services. In retailing, despite self-service, supermarkets, and pre-packaging, the rising proportion of the labor force engaged in marketing reaches a ceiling of productivity. In personal services, from barbering to travel arrangements, the nature of the personal relations is fixed by time components. In education, despite programmed learning and television instruction and large lecture classes (which students resent), the costs of education have been increasing at five to seven percent a year, while productivity for all services (including education) has shuffled upward at 1.9 percent a year. In health, despite multiphasic screens and similar mechanized diagnostic devices—a gain in numbers examined, but a loss in personal care—there is only so much of a physician's time to be distributed among patients. And, at the extreme, the example of live musical performances, where, as William J. Baumol is fond of pointing out, a half-hour quintet calls for the expenditure of 2½ man hours in its performance, and there can be no increase in productivity when the musician's wage goes up.[27]

This problem comes to a head in the cities whose budgets have doubled and tripled in the last decades (apart from welfare) because the bulk of municipal expenditures—education, hospitals, police, social services—falls into the non-progressive sector of the economy, and there are few real economies or gains that can halt these rises. Yet it is productivity which allows the social pie to expand.

The second constraint is an inflation which has been built into the structure of the economy itself by the *secondary* effects of bilateral actions of strong unions and oligopolistic industries. The inflation which has wracked the American economy since 1968 has been due,

---

[27] For a comprehensive scrutiny of the technical problems of measurement, see *Production and Productivity in the Service Industries*, ed. Victor R. Fuchs (New York, 1969).

in great measure, to the deceptions of President Johnson, who masked the costs of the Vietnam War from the country and who was afraid to raise the necessary taxes to finance the war. The bill, inevitably, will be paid for in the later years. But the Vietnam War apart, inflation has become a structural problem for the economy. The major alarums and noise of collective bargaining in such major industries as steel and auto, electric products and rubber, have been, in reality, mimetic combats in that an unstated but nonetheless real accommodation has been worked out between the contending parties. The unions receive substantial wage increases, and these increases become the occasion for even more substantial price increases which the industries, with their ability to "administer" prices, are able (until recently) to pass on to the public without protest either from the unions or from government.[28]

As a result of this system, the unions have been able to force wages up at an average rate of 7 percent annually for the past four years (while in some industries, such as printing and the construction trades, the rate has been 12 percent a year). Meanwhile productivity has been growing at only 3 percent a year. If the economy were only a manufacturing economy, this would be manageable. The labor costs in goods manufacturing are about 30 percent of the total costs. A 10 percent wage increase means, then, only a 3 percent increase in the cost of production, which can be offset by productivity. But in the services sectors, the wage proportion may run 70 percent or more of the total costs of the services, so a parallel 10 percent increase in wages adds 7 percent to the cost of services; productivity in the services sector, however, averages between 1.2 and 1.9 percent. The gap between these rates is a rough measure of the secondary effects of the cost-push factor of inflation that is being built into the system.

It is the changed nature of the service economy which is responsible for the structural elements of inflation that have become built into the economy. According to John Kenneth Galbraith's view of the "new industrial state," inflation is maintained by negotiated wages and ever rising administered prices in the corporate sectors of the economy. But the experience of 1965 to 1970 showed a different pattern. In those years, the price index rose 30 percent. The price of automobiles, one of the most highly-concentrated industries, rose 15 percent. Durable goods—television, appliances, furniture—rose

---

[28] For a detailed discussion of the origin of this system, and how the play was worked out, see my essay "The Subversion of Collective Bargaining," *Commentary* (March 1960).

18 percent. But the price of services—medical care, schooling, recreation, insurance—had gone up 42.5 percent. Some of that price rise was due to strong demand; yet in greater measure it was due to the increases in wages and prices in those areas with little corresponding gains in productivity.

When the pattern of steadily rising wages becomes so fixed, one finds an exacerbation in the governmental or communal services sector, for the higher "prices" become, necessarily, higher "taxes"— and more political grumbling. One can extend the urban problem to the society as a whole. As a larger portion of the labor force shifts into services, there is inevitably a greater drag on productivity and growth, and the costs of services, private and governmental, increase sharply. And yet there is, also inevitably, a greater demand for government activities and government goods to meet the social needs of the populace. But one then faces a painful contradiction, for if the wages in the service sectors, especially government, rise without compensating gains in productivity, they become additional claimants on social resources, competing for money needed for hospitals, schools, libraries, houses, clean water, clean air, etc.

In the nature of post-industrial society, the government has become the single largest employer in the society. But winning wage increases from the government is a far different problem from winning increases from private industry. Increasingly there looms what James O'Connor has called "the fiscal crisis of the state." The multiplication of government functions creates a need for new revenues. The concomitant expansion of the government bureaucracy increases costs. But government budgets are subject to constraints far different from those of private corporations, which can try to pass on their costs through price increases. Government revenues can increase in three ways. One is to step up the rate of economic growth and use the resulting gains in GNP for government purposes rather than private consumption. (This was how the government social programs were financed in the early 1960s.) But such acceleration risks inflation, and at the moment no Western society seems to know how to bring inflation under control. The second is to increase productivity in the government and service sectors, but while some gains are possible, intrinsically these will always lag behind the "progressive" industrial sectors. A third way is to raise taxes. But there is an increasing public outcry against rising taxes. The alternative is to cut government programs and hold down spending, but given the multiple pressures from different groups—business wants to cut social programs but maintain subsidies; labor wants higher budgets in all areas; reform groups want to cut the defense budget but expand social programs—this is not easy. And in all likelihood the fiscal problems will increase. This may well be an intractable problem of post-industrial society.[29]

A third constraint, more peculiar to the United States, is the evident fact that (from a businessman's point of view) American manufactured goods are pricing themselves out of the world market. From the view of theoretical economics, in the inevitable "product cycle" of goods production a more advanced industrial society finds itself at a price disadvantage when a product becomes standardized, inputs are predictable, price elasticity of demand is higher, and labor costs make a difference, so that less advanced but competing nations can now make the product more cheaply. And this is now happening in American manufacture. In the world economy the United States is now a "mature" nation and in a position to be pushed off the top of the hill by more aggressive countries, as happened to England at the end of the first quarter of this century.

If one looks at the position of the United States today in the world economy, three facts are evident:

1. Only in technology-intensive products does the United States have a favorable commercial balance in its trade with the rest of the world. In agricultural products, in minerals, fuels, and other non-manufactured and non-agricultural products, and in non-technology-intensive manufactured products, the balance is heavily the other way. In textiles, in such technological products as transistor radios, typewriters, and expensive cameras, which have now become standardized, the United States market has been swept by foreign goods. Even in technology-intensive products (computers, lasers, instruments) there has been a decline: in 1962 the favorable balance was 4:1 (exports of 10.2 billion and imports of 2.5 billion dollars); in 1968 it was 2:1 (exports of 18.4 billion against imports of 9.4 billion). In 1971 the unfavorable balance of trade as a whole was running at a deficit rate of $12 billion when President Nixon moved to force the revaluation of competing currencies and tighten the quotas of foreign goods to be sold in the United States.

2. The reduction in costs of transport, and the differential in

[29] For a theoretical model of this problem see William J. Baumol, "Macroeconomics of Unbalanced Growth: The Anatomy of Urban Crisis," *American Economic Review* (June 1967). As Professor Baumol writes:

Since there is no reason to anticipate a cessation of capital accumulation or innovation in the progressive sectors of the economy, the upward trend in real costs of municipal services cannot be expected to halt; inexorably and cumulatively, whether or not there is inflation, budgets will almost certainly continue to mount in the future. . . . This is a trend for which no man and no group should be blamed, for there is nothing that can be done to stop it (ibid., p. 423).

For a neo-Marxist view of this problem, see James O'Connor, "The Fiscal Crisis of the State," in *Socialist Revolution*, vol. 1, no. 1 (January–February 1970), and vol. 1, no. 2 (March–April 1970).

wages, has made it increasingly possible for American multi-national corporations to manufacture significant proportions of components abroad and bring them back here for assembly. The Ford Motor Company could only bring out its low-priced Pinto by having most of the components manufactured abroad, and Chrysler has announced that an increasing proportion of the parts for all its cars will be manufactured abroad rather than in Detroit.

3. Increasingly the United States is becoming a *rentier* society, in which a substantial and increasing proportion of the balance of trade consists of the return on investments abroad by American corporations, rather than exports.

All of this poses a very serious problem for American labor. The area where it is best organized, manufacture, faces a serious erosion of jobs. In response, American labor, which has traditionally been committed to free trade, is now heavily protectionist. This may save jobs in some sectors (textiles, electronics, steel, automobiles), but at a higher price to the consumer.

In effect, because of the constraints in two major areas—in the changing ratios between goods- and service-producing industries, and in the newly threatened position of American manufactures in the world economy—there may be less margin for social experiment. Thus, at a time when workers may be asking for more control over the conditions of work—which will inevitably increase costs— the squeeze may be greatest because of the changed condition of the economy.

The largest constraint is the very multiplicity of competing demands in the polity itself. A post-industrial society, as I pointed out earlier, is increasingly a communal society wherein public mechanisms rather than the market become the allocators of goods, and public choice, rather than individual demand, becomes the arbiter of services. A communal society by its very nature multiplies the definition of rights—the rights of children, of students, of the poor, of minorities—and translates them into claims of the community. The rise of externalities—the effects of private actions on the commonweal—turns clean air, clean water, and mass transit into public issues and increases the need for social regulations and controls. The demand for higher education and better health necessarily expands greatly the role of government as funder and setter of standards. The need for amenities, the cry for a better quality of life, brings government into the arena of environment, recreation, and culture.

But all this involves two problems: we don't really know, given our lack of social-science knowledge, how to do many of these things effectively; equally important, since there may not be enough money to satisfy all or even most of the claims, how do we decide what to do first? In 1960 the Eisenhower Commission on National Goals formulated a set of minimum standards for the quality of life—standards which already seem primitive a decade later—and when the National Planning Association projected these goals to 1975 and sought to cost them out (assuming a 4 percent growth rate, which we have not maintained), it found that we would be $150 billion dollars short in trying to achieve all those goals. So the problem is one of priorities and choice.

But how to achieve this? One of the facts of a communal society is the increased participation of individuals and groups in communal life. In fact, there is probably more participation today, at the city level, than at any other time in American history.[30] But the very increase in participation leads to a paradox: the greater the number of groups, each seeking diverse or competing ends, the more likelihood that these groups will veto one another's interests, with the consequent sense of frustration and powerlessness as such stalemates incur. This is true not only locally but nationally, where, in the last twenty years, new constituencies have multiplied. The standard entities of interest-group politics used to be corporate, labor, and farm, with the ethnic groups playing a role largely in state and city politics. But in the last two decades we have seen the rise of scientists, educators, the intelligentsia, blacks, youth, and poor, all playing a role in the game of influence and resource allocation.[31] And the old coalitions are no longer decisive. What we have been witnessing in the last decade, in fact, is the rise of an independent component, committed to neither of the two parties, whose swing vote becomes increasingly important. Thus the problem of how to achieve consensus on political questions will become more difficult. Without consensus there is only conflict, and persistent conflict simply tears a society apart, leaving the way open to repression by one sizeable force or another.

Industrial society in the West was marked by three distinctive features: the growth of the large corporation as the prototype of all business enterprise; the imprint of the machine and its rhythms on the character of work; and labor conflict, as the form of polarized class

---

[30] For an elaboration of this argument, and a documentation of these assertions, see Daniel Bell and Viginia Held, "The Community Revolution," *The Public Interest*, no. 16 (Summer 1969).

[31] Does business always have the disproportionate influence? It depends on the issue. One has to distinguish between the underlying *system* of the society, which is still capitalist, and the actual "ecology of games" wherein, on different issues, there are different coalitions, and even sizeable disagreements within the business community on specific political issues.

conflict, which threatened to tear society apart. All three of these elements are markedly changed in the post-industrial society.

The modern business corporation was a social invention, fashioned at the turn of the century, to implement the "economizing mode" which had become the engine of social change in the society.[32] It was a device which differed markedly from the army and the church (the two historic forms of large-scale organization) in its ability to coordinate men, materials and markets for the mass production of goods. In the first half of this century, beginning symbolically with the formation of the first billion-dollar corporation, United States Steel Company in 1901 by J. P. Morgan, the role of the corporation grew steadily and the economy came to be dominated by such familiar giants as General Motors, General Electric, Standard Oil, and the other monoliths that make up the banner listing of *Fortune*'s 500 industrials. Yet by 1956 the corporation seemed to reach a plateau in the economy, when incorporated businesses accounted for over 57 percent of the total national income, and since then the proportion has remained stable.

The modern business corporation is marked by large size: of assets, sales, and the number of employees. (General Motors, the largest corporation in the United States, in 1970 had 695,790 employees; Arvin Industries, the five-hundreth-largest, had 7,850.) But the distinctive character of the services sector is the small size of unit enterprise. Though one finds giant corporations in the services fields as large as any industrial corporation—in utilities (American Telephone and Telegraph), banking (Chase Manhattan), insurance (Metropolitan Life), retail trade (Sears Roebuck)—most of the firms in retail trade, personal and professional services, finance and real estate, and hospitals employ less than a thousand persons. The word government conjures up a picture of huge bureaucracy, but employment at the local level of government exceeds that of state and federal, and half of this local employment is in governmental units with fewer than 500 employees.[33]

Even where unit size is larger, in hospitals and in schools, what is different about these enterprises is the larger degree of autonomy of smaller units (the departments in the hospitals and colleges) and the

---

[32] For an elaboration of the "economizing mode," see chap. 4, "The Subordination of the Corporation."

[33] The data on unit size of enterprise are woefully inadequate, and even such recent accounts as Victor Fuchs's *The Service Economy* (1968) are forced to use data a decade old. Fuchs has used a unit size of 500 employees as the cut-off point in his own calculations. Assuming an increase in unit sizes in the decade, I have arbitrarily used a thousand employees as a cut-off point to emphasize the difference in the distribution of employment between the goods-producing and the services sectors. For Fuchs's data see chap. 8, particularly pp. 190–192.

greater degree of professional control. Surely this is an "organizational society" in that the organization rather than the small town is the locus of one's life, but to make this observation, as many sociologists do, is to miss the fact that what has been appearing is a multiplicity of diverse types of organization and that the received model we have, that of the large business corporation, while still pre-eminent, is not pervasive. New forms of small professional firms, research institutes, diverse kinds of government agencies, plus schools and hospitals, which are subject to professional and community control, become the locus of life for more and more persons in the society.

The change has come not only in place, but also in character of work. In an essay I published in 1956 *Work and Its Discontents*, I wrote: "The image of tens of thousands of workers streaming from the sprawling factories marks indelibly the picture of industrial America, as much as the fringed buckskin and rifle marked the nineteenth-century frontier, or the peruke and lace that of Colonial Virginia. The majority of Americans may not work in factories, as the majority of Americans never were on the frontier, or never lived in Georgian houses; yet the distinctive ethos of each time lies in these archetypes." I argued, further, that while a large variety of occupations and jobs were far removed from the factory, "the factory is archetypal because its rhythms, in subtle fashion, affect the general character of work the way a dye suffuses a cloth." [34]

The rhythms of mechanization are still pervasive in the United States. The nature of materials handling has been revolutionized by the introduction of mechanized devices. Office work, particularly in large insurance companies, banks, utilities, and industrial corporations has the same mechanical and dronelike quality, for routing procedures serve the same pacing functions as assembly lines. And yet, the distinctive archetype has gone. Charlie Chaplin's *Modern Times* at one time symbolized industrial civilization, but today it is a period piece. The rhythms are no longer that pervasive. The beat has been broken.

Does a new archetype exist today? The fact that in services relations are between persons led C. Wright Mills twenty years ago to declare that the white-collar world had become a "personality market," in which each person "sold himself" in order to impress another and get ahead. Mills's prototype was the salesman and the setting was "the big store." [35] But even at that time his argument was not entirely convincing (especially to those who tried to get service in some of these stores), and it is even less so today. New stereotypes abound.

---

[34] *Work and Its Discontents* (Boston, 1956), pp. 3, 36. The essay was reprinted in 1971 by the League for Industrial Democracy, with an introduction by Lewis Coser.

[35] C. Wright Mills, *White Collar*, op. cit., chap. 8.

An important one—to judge from some of the television commercials—is the researcher or the laboratory technician in a white coat, carrying out an experiment (usually to prove that the sponsor's product is better than the rival's). But this is more an effort to catch the reflected authority of science than the mimesis of a new civilization.

If there are no primary images of work, what is central to the new relationship is encounter or communication, and the response of ego to alter, and back—from the irritation of a customer at an airline-ticket office to the sympathetic or harassed response of teacher to student. But the fact that individuals now talk to other individuals, rather than interact with a machine, is the fundamental fact about work in the post-industrial society.

Finally, for more than a hundred years, the "labor issue" dominated Western society. The conflict between worker and boss (whether capitalist or corporate manager) overshadowed all other conflicts and was the axis around which the major social divisions of the society rotated. Marx had assumed, in the logic of commodity production, that in the end both bourgeoisie and worker would be reduced to the abstract economic relation in which all other social attributes would be eliminated so that the two would face each other nakedly—as would all society—in their class roles.[36] Two things, however, have gone awry with this prediction. The first has been the persistent strength of what Max Weber called "segregated status groups"—race, ethnic, linguistic, religious—whose loyalties, ties, and emotional identifications have been more powerful and compelling than class at most times, and whose own divisions have overridden class lines. In advanced industrial countries such as Belgium or Canada, no less than in tribal societies such as Africa or com-

---

[36] Marx's view is laid out most starkly in *The Communist Manifesto*. At various points he writes:

> The bourgeoisie cannot exist without incessantly revolutionising the instruments of production; and, consequently, the relations of production; and, therefore, the totality of social relations. . . . All stable and stereotyped relations, with their attendant train of ancient and venerable prejudices and opinions, are swept away, and the newly formed becomes obsolete before it can petrify. All that has been regarded as solid, crumbles into fragments; all that was looked upon as holy is profaned; at long last, people are compelled to gaze open-eyed at their position in life and their social relations (p. 29).

> Those who have hitherto belonged to the lower middle-class—small manufacturers, small traders, minor recipients of unearned income, handicraftsmen, and peasants—slip down, one and all, into the proletariat (p. 35).

> . . . the development of large-scale industry severs all family ties of proletarians, and . . . proletarian children are transformed into mere articles of commerce and instruments of labor. . . . National distinctions and contrasts are already tending to disappear more and more as the bourgeoisie develops . . . (pp. 48, 50).

The Communist Manifesto, ed. D. Ryazanoff (reprinted edition, New York, 1963).

munal societies such as India, the "status groups" have generated conflicts that have torn the society apart more sharply, often, than class issues. Second, the labor problem has become "encapsulated." An interest conflict and a labor issue—in the sense of disproportionate power between manager and worker over the conditions of work—remain, but the disproportions have shifted and the methods of negotiation have become institutionalized. Not only has the political tension become encapsulated, there is even the question whether the occupational psychology which Veblen and Dewey made so central to their sociology carries over into other aspects of a man's behavior as well. (A bourgeois was a bourgeois by day and a bourgeois by night; it would be hard to say this about some of the managers who are executives by day and swingers at night.) The crucial fact is that the "labor issue" *qua* labor is no longer central, nor does it have the sociological and cultural weight to polarize all other issues along that axis.

In the next decade, the possible demands for the reorganization of work, the decline in productivity, and the persistent threat of inflation because of the disproportionate productivity in the goods and services sectors, the threats of foreign competition, and other issues such as the recalcitrance of some unions on race, or the bilateral monopolies of unions and builders in the construction trades, all may make labor issues increasingly salient and even rancorous. The fact that some unions may even turn from concern with income and consumption to problems of production and the character of work is all to the good. But it is highly unlikely that these will become ideological or "class" issues, although they may become politicized.

The politics of the next decade is more likely to concern itself, on the national level, with such public-interest issues as health, education, and the environment, and, on the local level, crime, municipal services, and costs. These are all communal issues, and on these matters labor may find itself, on the national level, largely liberal, yet, on the local level, divided by the factious issues that split community life.

But all this is a far cry from the vision of *The Communist Manifesto* of 1848 and the student revolutionaries of 1968. In the economy, a labor issue remains. But not in the sociology and culture. To that extent, the changes which are summed up in the post-industrial society may represent a historic metamorphosis in Western society.[37]

---

[37] The owl of Minerva, as Hegel observed, flies at dusk, and the irony may be that labor, particularly in Europe, may become more aggressively class minded at a time of structural decline and when the economic constraints on achieving gains are greatest.

CHAPTER

3

*The Dimensions of
Knowledge and Technology:
The New Class Structure
of Post-Industrial Society*

L ET us begin with a parable: all the rest is exegesis.

. . . the Library is composed of an indefinite, perhaps an infinite number of hexagonal galleries, with enormous ventilation shafts in the middle, excluded by very low railings. . . .

Everything is there: the minute history of the future, the autobiographies of the archangels, the faithful catalogue of the Library, thousands and thousands of false catalogues, a demonstration of the fallacy of these catalogues, a demonstration of the fallacy of the true catalogue, the Gnostic gospel of Basilides, the commentary on this gospel, the veridical account of your death, a version of each book in all languages, the interpolations of every book in all books.

When it was proclaimed that the Library comprised all books, the first impression was one of extravagant joy. All men felt themselves lords of a secret, intact treasure. There was no personal or universal problem whose eloquent solution did not exist—in some hexagon. The universe was justified, the universe suddenly expanded to the limitless dimension of hope. . . .

The uncommon hope was followed, naturally enough, by a deep depression. The certainty that some shelf in some hexagon contained precious books and that these books were inaccessible seemed almost intolerable. A blasphemous sect suggested that all searches be given up and that men everywhere shuffle letters and symbols until they succeeded in composing, by means of an improbable stroke of luck, the canonical books. . . .

Other men, inversely, thought that the primary task was to eliminate useless works. They would invade the hexagons, exhibiting credentials which were not always false, skim through a volume with annoyance, and then condemn entire bookshelves to destruction: their ascetic, hygienic fury is responsible for the senseless loss of millions of books. Their name is execrated; but those who mourn the "treasures" destroyed by this frenzy overlook two notorious facts. One: the Library is so enormous that any reduction undertaken by humans is infinitesimal. Two: each book is unique, irreplaceable, but (inasmuch as the Library is total) there are always several hundreds of thousands of imperfect facsimiles—of works which differ only by one letter or one comma. . . .

The Library is limitless and periodic. If an eternal voyager were to traverse it in any direction, he would find, after many centuries, that the same volumes are repeated in the same disorder (which, repeated, would constitute an order: Order itself). My solitude rejoices in this elegant hope.[1]

Jorge Luis Borges
"The Library of Babel"

THE PACE OF CHANGE

Few men have sought to understand contemporary society so desperately as Henry Adams, a scion of one of the most distinguished families in American life. His grandfather, John Quincy Adams, had been the last representative of the patriciate in politics, and had fallen, finally, before the onslaught of Jacksonian populism. In a mass democracy there was little room, Henry Adams felt, for the natural aristocracy to which he belonged. In order to understand himself and his times, he turned to history.

For forty-five years Henry Adams pondered the past. He wrote a massive *History of the United States,* which is today unread; he traveled widely, retracing the steps of Gibbon through Rome. In the end, in that remarkable autobiography written in the third person, *The Education of Henry Adams,* he admitted his failure. "The human mind," he wrote, "has always struggled like a frightened bird to escape the chaos which caged it. . . ." He found himself in the same cage. "Never before had Adams been able to discern the working of law in history, which was the reason of his failure in teaching it; for chaos cannot be taught. . . ."

Yet he would not give up his search for the hidden order of history; and thus it happened, as he wrote, that "after ten years of pursuit, he found himself lying in the Gallery of Machines at the Great Exposition of 1900, his historical neck broken by sudden eruption of forces totally new." It was in the great hall of dynamos that this revelation took place.

In the energy churning from the dynamo, Henry Adams felt he had caught a glimpse of the secret that could unravel the complexities men had begun to note about their time. In the nineteenth century, he wrote, society by common accord measured its progress by the output of coal. The ratio of increase in the volume of coal power, he

---

[1] Jorge Luis Borges, "The Library of Babel," in *Labyrinths,* trans. James E. Irby (New York, 1962) © 1962 by New Directions Publishing Corporation. Reprinted by permission of New Directions Publishing Corporation and Laurence Pollinger Limited.

now said exultantly, might serve as a "dynamometer." Between 1840 and 1900, he pointed out, coal output had doubled every ten years; in the form of utilized power, each ton of coal yielded three or four times as much power in 1900 as it had in 1840. The gauge on the dynamometer of history had started out with arithmetical ratios; but new forces emerging around 1900—Adams had in mind the cracking of the world of appearances by the discovery of x-rays and radium—were creating new "supersensual" forces. What all this revealed, he said, was the foundation for a new, social physics, for a dynamic law of history, the fundamental secret of social change—the law of acceleration.

Impossibilities no longer stood in the way, he wrote in the *Education*, with a strange mingling of exultation and dismay.

One's life had fattened on impossibilities. Before the boy was six years old, he had seen four impossibilities made actual—the ocean steamer, the railway, the electric telegraph and the Daguerrotype. . . . He had seen the coal output of the United States grow from nothing to three hundred million tons or more. What was far more serious, he had seen the number of minds engaged in pursuing force—the true measure of its attraction—increase from a few score or hundreds in 1838, to many thousands in 1905, trained to a sharpness never before reached, and armed with instruments amounting to a new sense of indefinite power and accuracy while they chase force into hiding places where nature herself had never known it to be. . . . If science were to go on doubling or quadrupling its complexities every ten years, even mathematics would soon succumb to unintelligibility. An average mind [i.e. Adams] had succumbed already . . . it could no longer understand [science] in 1900.[2]

Henry Adams had sought to write a "social physics," a computation of the rates of change that would be as exact as the laws of velocity. That he could not—and that no one may ever be able to do so—may be a tribute to the cantankerousness of the human being who resists being reduced to a plotted line on a paper. Yet what Henry Adams had caught—and he was, perhaps, the first man of his time to do so—was a sense of the quickening change of pace that drives all our lives. When one turns the page of his essay on "The Rule of Phase Applied to History" and confronts, for the first time in a book of history, a soaring J-curve to illustrate the exponential growth of knowledge, one feels a little as Balboa did when he climbed a peak and saw for the first time the endless expanse of the Pacific before him.

The idea of exponential curves—the acceleration of doubling rates of all kinds—has now become commonplace. We know that

[2] Henry Adams, *The Education of Henry Adams: An Autobiography* (Boston and New York, 1918), pp. 494–495.

the time for circumnavigating the globe decreased exponentially every quarter of a century by a factor of two between Nelly Bly's voyage around the world in 1889 and the first transworld airplane flight in 1928, and by a factor of 10 since then. Derek Price claims (in a problem we will examine later) that the amount of scientific work since Newton has doubled every fifteen years, or presumably about three times in the course of the working life of a scientist.

It is crucial to grasp that such exponential curves not only signify a rapid change in time scales, but more and more quickly transform the character of our knowledge and our lives. Caryl Haskins, the President of the Carnegie Institution of Washington, wrote (in his presidential report of 1965–1966) that as late as 1920, "it was still widely believed that the Milky Way really comprehended our entire universe. Only within the last 10 years have we become fully aware that this galaxy of ours is in fact but one among millions or perhaps billions of such galaxies, lacing the heavens, stretching to distances of which the world of 1920 or even 1950 could have had little conception. . . ."

Only in the past decade have we become aware of quasars (quasi-stellar radio sources), one of which, identified little more than two years ago, was reckoned to be about two and a half trillion times as luminous as our sun. Such findings have radically altered our ideas about the nature and extent of the universe. In fact, the rate of discovery itself in the three hundred years since Galileo has accelerated so greatly that insights attained only within the past few years have combined and welded together partial visions that required many earlier decades to achieve.

From the outer reaches of astronomy to the biological world within, the same story is repeated. A hundred years ago, the monk Gregor Mendel laid the foundation for the science of genetics. A few years later, a young biochemist named Friedrich Miescher broke down the cytoplasm of living cells with enzymes to discover the basic bonds of the nucleus. It took seventy-five years from Miescher's work to the theoretical proposals of Linus Pauling and Robert Corey in the 1950s about the molecular structure of genes, and from there it was less than a decade before Crick and Watson deciphered the basic genetic code of life itself.

Important as any of these examples may be, the simple and crucial fact Henry Adams had so poignantly grasped in 1900 was that no longer would any child be able to live in the same kind of world— sociologically and intellectually—as his parents and grandparents had inhabited. For millennia—and this is still true in some sections of the globe, but they are shrinking—children retraced the steps of their parents, were initiated into stable ways and ritualized routines, had a common book of knowledge and morality, and maintained a basic familiarity with place and family. Today, not only does a child face a radical rupture with the past, but he must also be trained for an unknown future. And this task confronts the entire society as well.

THE CHANGE OF SCALE

The second salient fact that distinguishes our time from the past is the "change of scale" in our lives. Consider, first, the matter of numbers. It is startling to recall that when the Constitution which still guides American society was ratified, there were less than four million persons in the thirteen states of the Union. Of these, 750,000 were Negro slaves, outside society. It was a young population— the median age was only sixteen—and at that time fewer than 800,000 males had reached voting age. When George Washington was inaugurated as the first President of the United States, New York City, then the capital of the country, had a population of only 33,000.

Few people lived in cities. About 200,000 persons were settled in what were then called "urban areas"—that is, places with more than 2,500 inhabitants. Living in isolated clumps of small communities, or in sparsely inhabited areas, people rarely traveled great distances, and a visitor from afar was a rarity. Because it was an agricultural world, and artificial illumination came mainly from candles and kerosene lamps, daily life followed the orbit of the sun ("Good day" is, after all, a greeting from agricultural times), and there was little night life in the land. News meant local gossip, and the few news sheets that existed concentrated on parochial events. The ordinary citizen's image of the world and its politics was exceedingly circumscribed.

Consider the present. Today the population of the United States is over 200 million, and more than 110 million persons live in metropolitan areas (that is, within a county containing a city of at least 50,000 residents). Few persons live or work in social isolation. (Sixty percent of the manufacturing force works in enterprises that employ more than 500 workers each.) Even those who work on farms are tied to the national society by the mass media and the popular culture.

But the most striking difference—and this is the real change of scale between 1798 and today—has to do with the number of persons each one of us *knows* and the number each of us *knows of*— in short, the way in which we *experience* the world. An individual today, on the job, in school, in the neighborhood, in a professional or social milieu, knows immediately hundreds of persons and, if one considers the extraordinary mobility of our lives—geographical, occupational, and social—during a lifetime one comes to know, as acquaintances or friends, several thousand. And through the windows of the mass media, and because of the enlargement of the political world and the multiplication of the dimensions of culture—the number of persons (and places) that one *knows of* accelerates at a steeply exponential rate.

What happens when the world's population begins to experience this leap—in social awareness, contact, and interaction? Consider the quantum jumps in population simply in the past century. It was only in 1859, after thousands of years of social life, that the world achieved a population of one billion persons. The second billion took seventy-five years more (from 1850 to 1925), and the third billion was added only thirty-five years later, in 1960. In all likelihood, a world population of four billion will have been reached by 1980; and, if the present rates continue unchecked, a fifth billion will be added only ten years later, by 1990. As Roger Revelle points out, given present birthrates and deathrates, the population increase between 1965 and 2000 will be larger than the entire existing population. Or, to look at the doubling rates in a different light, it is estimated that, of all the people who have ever lived, one-fifth are alive today.

But a change of scale is not simply the original institution writ large. No biological organism or human institution which undergoes a change in size and a consequent change of scale does so without changing its form or shape. It was Galileo, more than three hundred and fifty years ago, who laid down this "general principal of similitude." The great biologist D'Arcy Wentworth Thompson, who described this problem in his classic *On Growth and Form*, put it thus:

[Galileo] said that if we tried building ships, palaces or temples of enormous size, yards, beams and belts would cease to hold together; nor can Nature grow a tree nor construct an animal beyond a certain size while retaining the proportions and employing the materials which suffice in the case of smaller structure. The thing will fall to pieces of its own weight unless we . . . change the relative proportions. . . .[3]

For Galileo, changes in proportion followed a mathematical principle, defined in normal spatial geometry as the square-cube law: as volume increases by cubic function, the surface enclosing it increases only by a square. Social institutions do not follow a fixed spatial law but, although the metaphor is biological, there is a process of *structural differentiation* "whereby *one* unit or organization differentiates into *two* which differ from each other in structure and in function

[3] D'Arcy Thompson, *On Growth and Form* (Cambridge, Eng., 1963), vol. I, p. 27.

for the system but which together are in certain respects 'functionally equivalent' to the earlier less differentiated unit." [4]

The concept of structural differentiation, as derived from Durkheim and Max Weber, and elaborated by Talcott Parsons and his students, is probably the key sociological concept today in the analysis of crescive social change. It points to the phenomenon that as institutions grow in size and in the functions they have to perform, specialized and distinct subsystems are created to deal with these functions. With the growth of specialized subsystems one finds as well new, distinct problems of coordination, hierarchy, and social control.

Within the context of social change, the processes of differentiation can be traced far back to early human societies in which, for example, sacerdotal and political functions that were conjoined (the Pharaonic powers of the old Egyptian kingdom) became differentiated into separate religious and political institutions (though symbolically the two were conjoined in post-Meiji Japan or even England today). Or the family, which was once the primary social institution, combining economic, welfare, recreational, and other functions, was sundered, resulting in a separation between the family and the occupational system, so that the family farm, the family business, or the family trade began to erode.

In contemporary industrial society, it has been the economic institutions that have shown the most marked form of internal differentiation. When firms and communities that were essentially alike began to meet, competition and a "heightened struggle for existence" took place. In the past, such competition often led to—in fact, was the prime cause of—war between communities. In contemporary society, because of the possibilities of economic growth through productivity, rather than through exploitation or plunder, such competition has led to a division of labor and to interdependent relationships. In order to meet competition, or to avoid going under, social units (regions, cities, firms) began to specialize, to narrow their activities, and to become complementary to one another. Just as, say, the complex process of supplying goods to larger and larger markets forced the division of trade into wholesale and retail components, so similar processes of differentiation were at work in the specialization of jobs that accompanied the growth of the economy, and of firms, as a whole. Just as one found a differentiation between ownership and management, so one found a differentiation in the tasks of management, so

---

[4] Talcott Parsons and Neil J. Smelser, *Economy and Society* (London, 1956), pp. 255–256.

that production, finance, marketing, research, personnel, and the like, each became the subject of new and professionalized vocations.[5]

But what has been so marked and pervasive a feature of economic life now begins to appear in the once simple structures of educational and intellectual life. The growth of a university from 5,000 to 50,000 students is clearly not just a linear increase in size but a massive upheaval in structure as well. Where in the past (and this is still somewhat true of colleges in Oxford and Cambridge) one could find economic investment, administration, admissions, and teaching in the hands of one academic body, now one finds the complex hierarchy of business officials, administrators, deans, institute heads, admissions officers, and teachers existing in new and difficult bureaucratic relationships to one another. Within scientific institutions and academies of research one finds the same processes of differentiation—and strain —at work. If there is anything which, in this sense, marks off the second half of the twentieth century from the first half, it is the extension of the specialization of function from the economic to the intellectual realm.

These two concepts—the pace of change and the change of scale —are the organizing ideas for the discussion of the central structural components of the post-industrial society, the dimensions of knowledge and technology.

The Dimensions of Knowledge

THE DEFINITION OF KNOWLEDGE

When does one date a social change; when does one identify the onset of a trauma? In the case of the character of knowledge, I would place it arbitrarily in the year 1788. The trauma: being unable to master all the relevant knowledge one needs. As the Prefatory Note to the 11th edition of the *Encyclopaedia Britannica* reveals: "These earliest editions of the *Encyclopaedia Britannica* [1745–1785] . . . like all their predecessors . . . had been put together by one or two men who were still able to take the whole of human knowledge for their province. It was with the Third Edition [1788] that the plan of drawing on specialist learning was first adopted." Thus we know when the unity of knowledge was fragmented. The 1967 edition, it may be noted, had 10,000 "recognized experts" involved in its preparation.

---

[5] For a discussion of the concept of "structural differentiation," see Talcott Parsons, "Some reflections on the Institutional Framework of Economic Development," in *Structure and Process in Modern Societies* (Glencoe, Ill., 1960), pp. 98–132.

What does one mean by knowledge? An *encyclo-paedia* means the whole circle, and one could take everything known (recorded or stated) as the province of this definition. For the purposes of this chapter, I shall define knowledge as *a set of organized statements of facts or ideas, presenting a reasoned judgment or an experimental result, which is transmitted to others through some communication medium in some systematic form.* Thus, I distinguish knowledge from news and from entertainment. Knowledge consists of new judgments (research and scholarship) or new presentations of older judgments (textbook and teaching).

This definition is broader than some established philosophical efforts. Thus Max Scheler distinguished three classes of knowledge: *Herrschaftswissen, Bildungswissen,* and *Erlösungswissen,* or, knowledge for the sake of action or control, knowledge for the sake of non-material culture, and knowledge for the sake of salvation (in Fritz Machlup's translation: instrumental knowledge, intellectual knowledge, and spiritual knowledge).

My definition is narrower, however, than Machlup's own comprehensive classification, which argues in *The Production and Distribution of Knowledge in the United States* that "an objective interpretation according to *what* is known will be less satisfactory than a subjective interpretation according to the meaning which the knower attaches to the known, that is *who* knows and *why* and *what for.*" [6] Using then "the subjective meaning of the known to the *knower* as the criterion," Machlup distinguishes five types of knowledge:

1. Practical knowledge: useful in a man's work, his decisions, and actions; can be subdivided, according to his activities into: (a) Professional knowledge; (b) Business knowledge; (c) Workman's knowledge; (d) Political knowledge; (e) Household knowledge; (f) Other practical knowledge.
2. Intellectual knowledge: Satisfying a man's intellectual curiosity, regarded as part of liberal education, humanistic and scientific learning, general culture; acquired as a rule in active concentration with an appreciation of the existence of open problems and cultural values.
3. Small-talk and pastime knowledge: Satisfying the non-intellectual curiosity or his desire for light entertainment and emotional stimulation, including local gossip, news of crimes and accidents, light novels, stories, jokes, games, etc.; acquired as a rule in passive relaxation from "serious" pursuits; apt to dull his sensitiveness.
4. Spiritual knowledge: related to his religious knowledge of God and of the ways to the salvation of the soul.

---

[6] Fritz Machlup, *The Production and Distribution of Knowledge in the United States* (Princeton, N.J., 1962), p. 21.

5. Unwanted knowledge: outside his interests, usually accidentally acquired, aimlessly retained.[7]

Robert Lane, who has put forth the idea of "a knowledge society," seeks to establish an epistemological foundation for his conception. Like Machlup, Lane includes both the "known" and the "state of knowing," but he also seeks to emphasize the increased self-consciousness about society which such knowledge provides. Lane writes:

As a first approximation to a definition, the knowledgeable society is one in which, more than in other societies, its members: (a) inquire into the basis of their beliefs about man, nature and society; (b) are guided (perhaps unconsciously) by objective standards of veridical truth, and, at upper levels of education, follow scientific rules of evidence and inference in inquiry; (c) devote considerable resources to this inquiry and thus have a large store of knowledge; (d) collect, organize and interpret their knowledge in a constant effort to extract meaning from it for the purposes at hand; (e) employ this knowledge to illuminate (and perhaps modify) their values and goals as well as to advance them. Just as the "democratic" society has a foundation in governmental and interpersonal relations, and the "affluent society" a foundation in economics, so the knowledgeable society has its roots in epistemology and the logic of inquiry.[8]

Definitions of this kind are neither right nor wrong; they are, rather, boundaries of usage. An effort to deal with comprehensive societal change would need to take these definitions into account. For the purposes of social policy, however—the need to determine the allocation of societal resources for some specified purpose of social utility—I would propose a restricted definition: Knowledge is that which is objectively known, an *intellectual property*, attached to a name or a group of names and certified by copyright or some other form of social recognition (e.g. publication). This knowledge is paid for—in the time spent in writing and research; in the monetary compensation by the communication and educational media. It is subject to a judgment by the market, by administrative or political decisions of superiors, or by peers as to the worth of the result, and as to its claim on social resources, where such claims are made. In this sense, knowledge is part of the social overhead investment of society; it is a coherent statement, presented in a book, article, or even a computer program, written down or recorded at some point for transmission, and subject to some rough count. Such a utilitarian definition, needless to say, shuns the relevant questions of a "sociology of

[7] Ibid., pp. 21–22.
[8] Robert E. Lane, "The Decline of Politics and Ideology in a Knowledgeable Society," *American Sociological Review*, vol. 21, no. 5 (October 1966), p. 650.

knowledge": the social setting of ideas, their interconnections, their relation to some structural foundation, and the like. Any evaluation of the specific character of particular sets of knowledge would, of course, have to take up such questions; these, however, are outside my purview here.[9]

THE MEASUREMENT OF KNOWLEDGE

Patterns of growth. In recent years we have become accustomed to the statement that the "amount" of knowledge is increasing at an exponential rate. The first rough count—the first flag of warning on the growth of knowledge as a coming storage and retrieval problem—came in 1944, when Fremont Rider, the Wesleyan University librarian, calculated that American research libraries were, on the average, doubling in size every sixteen years. Taking ten representative colleges, Rider showed that between 1831 (when each college had on the average about 7,000 books in its library) and 1938, their holdings had doubled every twenty-two years; taking comparable growth figures of larger American universities from 1831, the doubling rate was about sixteen years.[10] Rider chose Yale as an example of what the problem would be like in the future:

It appears that, along in the early part of the eighteenth century, the Yale library possessed somewhere around 1,000 volumes. If it had continued from this start to double every sixteen years it should, in 1938, have grown to about 2,600,000 volumes. In 1938, it actually did have 2,748,000 volumes, i.e. an amazingly close correspondence with the "standard" rate of growth. . . . It takes but a few moments' computation to work out that the Yale University library in 1849 occupied approximately 1¼ miles of shelving, and that its card catalog—if it then had a card catalog— would have occupied approximately 160 card drawers. In 1938 its 2,-748,000 volumes occupied perhaps eighty miles of shelving, and its card catalog of all sorts in all locations must have occupied a total of somewhere around ten thousand drawers. To service this library required in 1938 a staff of over two hundred persons, of whom probably half were catalogers.[11]

Rider speculated—whimsically, it seemed at the time—what would happen if the Yale Library continued to grow "at a rate no greater than the most conservative rate" at which library holdings

---

[9] For a comprehensive paradigm which sets forth the kinds of questions a sociology of knowledge would have to answer, see Robert K. Merton, "The Sociology of Knowledge," in *Social Theory and Social Structure*, rev. ed. (Glencoe, Ill., 1957), esp. pp. 460–461.
[10] Fremont Rider, *The Scholar and the Future of the Research Library* (New York, 1944).
[11] Ibid., pp. 11–12.

have been growing. In the year 2040, he estimated the Yale Library would have

approximately 200,000,000 volumes, which will occupy over 6,000 miles of shelves. Its card catalog file—if it then has a card catalog—will consist of nearly three-quarters of a million catalog drawers, which will of themselves occupy not less than eight acres of floor space. New material will be coming in at the rate of 12,000,000 volumes a year; and the cataloging of this new material will require a cataloging staff of over six thousand persons.[12]

Rider's findings on the growth of American research libraries were generalized by Derek Price to include almost the entire range of scientific knowledge. In *Science Since Babylon*, the first of his book publications to deal with this problem,[13] Price sought to chart the growth of the scientific journal and the learned paper as the two major indicators of knowledge. The scientific journal and the learned paper were innovations of the scientific revolution of the late seventeenth century. They allowed for the relatively rapid communication of new ideas to the growing circle of persons interested in science. The earliest surviving journal was the *Philosophical Transactions of the Royal Society of London*, first published in 1665, followed by some three or four similar journals published by other national academies in Europe. Thereafter, the number of journals increased, reaching a total of about one hundred by the beginning of the nineteenth century, one thousand by mid-century, and some ten thousand by 1900. Price concluded:

If we make . . . a count extending in time range from 1665 to the present day, it is immediately obvious that the enormous increase in the population of scientific periodicals has proceeded from unity to the order of a hundred thousand with an extraordinary regularity seldom seen in any man-made or natural statistic. It is apparent to a high order of accuracy, that the number has increased by a factor of ten during every half-century starting from a state in 1750 when there were about ten scientific journals in the world.[14]

In subsequent publications, Price has defended the counting of papers as a relevant indicator of scientific knowledge. In an essay published in 1965, he wrote:

---

[12] Ibid. None of this takes into account, of course, the technological substitution of micro-fiche cards for books. But that is a problem of storage, not of the growth of knowledge.

[13] Derek Price, *Science Since Babylon* (New Haven, 1961). His first publication on the subject was in the *Archives Internationales d'Histoire des Sciences*, no. 14 (1951). This was extended and republished in more popular form in *Discovery* (London, June 1956).

[14] Derek Price, *Science Since Babylon*, op. cit., p. 96.

To the scientist himself, the publication represents some mysteriously powerful, eternal, and open archive of the Literature into which he is reading his findings. Only in very rare and special instances does one have to consider pure scientific work in which there is no end product of literature. These would include pathological cases such as that of Henry Cavendish, who researched diligently but did not publish the bulk of his findings, which were therefore lost for a century until they were disinterred by Clerk Maxwell only a few years after the valuable results had been discovered independently by others. Is unpublished work like this, or work that is suppressed and unpublished because it is a national secret, a contribution to science? I find, in general, that it is fair enough to say it is not. Science is not science that communication lacks! . . .

Our definition holds, then, that science is that which is published in scientific journals, papers, reports and books. In short it is that which is embodied in the Literature. Conveniently enough, this Literature is far easier to define, delimit and count than anything else one might deal with. Because of its central function for scientists, it has been subjected to centuries of systematization by indexes, classifications, journals of abstracts and retrieval systems. . . . All such literature can be, and in very many cases has actually been counted, classified, and followed through the years as a time series. The chief component of the Research Literature, for example, can be defined as the papers published in the scientific serials included in the *World List of Scientific Periodicals*—a familiar tool of all reference librarians.[15]

By 1830, when it became obvious, with about three hundred journals being published in the world, that the cultivated man of science could no longer keep abreast of new knowledge, a new device appeared, the abstract journal, which summarized each article so that the interested individual could then decide which article to consult in full. But, as Price points out, the number of abstract journals has also increased, following the same trajectory, multiplying by a factor of ten every half-century. Thus, by 1950 the number of abstract journals had attained a "critical magnitude" of about three hundred.

Out of these figures, Price has sought to draw a "law of exponential increase." He considers that the most remarkable conclusion is that the number of new journals has grown exponentially rather than linearly. "The constant involved is actually about fifteen years for a doubling, corresponding to a power of ten in fifty years and a factor of a thousand in a century and a half. . . ."

If this is true, it is remarkable that not only do we find such a rapid growth but that the particular curve should be exponential, the mathematical consequence of having a quantity that increases in such a way that the bigger it is the faster it grows. "Why should it be," asks

---

[15] Derek Price, "The Science of Science," in *New Views of the Nature of Man*, ed. John R. Platt (Chicago, 1965), pp. 47–70, esp. pp. 58–59.

Price, "that journals appear to breed more journals at a rate proportional to their population at any one time instead of at any particular constant rate?" It must follow, he says, "that there is something about scientific discoveries or the papers by which they are published that makes them act in this way. It seems as if each advance generates a new series of advances at a reasonably constant birth rate, so that the number of births is strictly proportional to the size of the population of discoveries at any given time." [16]

This "law of exponential increase," which applies to the number of scientific journals, is also "obeyed," Price argues, by the actual number of scientific papers in those journals. Taking the papers recorded in the *Physics Abstracts* from 1918 to the present day, the total number, he claims, has followed an exponential growth curve, the accuracy of which does not vary by more than 1 percent of the total. At the beginning of the 1960s, there were about 180,000 physics papers recorded in those volumes, and the number has steadily doubled at a rate even faster than once every fifteen years. On the basis of about thirty such analyses since 1951, Price concludes that "it seems beyond reasonable doubt that the literature in any normal, growing field of science increases exponentially, with a doubling in an interval ranging from about ten to about fifteen years." [17]

A later study of mathematical publications by Kenneth O. May [18] confirms the general pattern sketched by Price for physics, but finds that "the rate of growth for mathematics is only *half* that found by Price." The doubling intervals cited by Price "correspond to an annual increase of from about 7 to 5 percent, whereas we have found for mathematics, an annual increase of about 2.5 percent and doubling about every 28 years."

The difference arises from the choice of a starting point. As May points out: "Before jumping to the conclusion that mathematics has a different growth rate than other sciences, note that although Price speaks of 'the literature' as though he were referring to the total literature his data are actually for the literature in each field after a certain time, in each case the beginning of an abstracting service: 1900 for physics, 1908 for chemistry, 1927 for biology, and 1940 for mathematics."

Professor May, in his inquiry, went back to 1868, to the *Jahrbuch über die Fortschritte der Mathematik*, tracing the growth through 1940 and from 1941 to 1965 in the *Mathematical Reviews*. He also points out that in mathematics, by successively ignoring the literature

---

[16] Derek Price, *Science Since Babylon*, op. cit., pp. 100–101.

[17] Ibid., p. 102n.

[18] Kenneth O. May, "Quantitative Growth of the Mathematical Literature," *Science*, vol. 154 (December 30, 1966), pp. 1672–1673.

prior to 1900, 1920, and 1940, one could achieve a series of growth curves similar to Price's higher findings. "It appears likely," May concludes, "that if Price and others took into account the literature prior to their statistical series, they would obtain substantially lower growth rates. This analysis supports the conjecture that the over-all total scientific literature has been accumulating at a rate of about 2.5 percent per year, doubling about four times a century."

Limits of growth. Any growth which is exponential must at some point level off, or we would reach a point of absurdity. Published figures on the electrical industry, for example, show that if we start with a single man, circa 1750—the time of Franklin's experiments with lightning—the exponential increase would bring us to two hundred thousand persons employed in 1925, an even million by 1955 and at that rate, the entire working population would be employed in this one field by 1990.[19] At some point, necessarily, there is a saturation and levelling-off. In the measurement of the growth of knowledge, as in other fields which have shown similar patterns, the questions revolve around the definition of that saturated state and the estimation of its arrival date.

The exponential pattern which has been described, the approach to some ceiling, is a sigmoid or $\int$-shaped curve in which the rate below and above its middle is often quite symmetrical. Because this is so, it lends itself easily to prediction, since one assumes that the rate above the mid-point will match that below and then level off. It is, in fact, the beauty of this curve that has seduced many statisticians into believing almost that it is the "philosopher's stone" for the charting of human behavior.

The phenomenon of saturation, as applied to a general law of human population, was first proposed in the 1830s by the statistician Adolphe Quetelet, the formulator of social physics, in his reflections on Malthus. A typical population grows slowly from an asymptotic minimum, multiplies quickly, and draws slowly to an ill-defined asymptotic maximum, the curve passing through a point of inflection to become $\int$-shaped. In 1838, a mathematical colleague of Quetelet's, P. F. Verhulst, sought to give a mathematical shape to the same general conclusions, to find a *"fonction retardatrice"* which would turn the Malthusian curve of geometrical progression into the $\int$-shaped or, as he called it, the logistic curve, which would constitute the true "law of population," and indicate the limit above which the population was not likely to grow.[20]

---

[19] The example is taken from Derek Price, *Science Since Babylon*, op. cit., p. 108.

[20] The account here is drawn from D'Arcy Thompson, *On Growth and Form*, op. cit., pp. 142–150.

Verhulst was making a number of assumptions: that the rate of increase could not be constant; that the rate must be some function, a linear one, of the population for the time being; and that once the rate begins to fall, or saturation sets in, it will fall more as the population begins to grow. Thus the growth factor and the retardation factor are proportional to one another so that, because of the "symmetry" of the curve, one can project or forecast the future.[21]

In 1924, the mathematical biologist Raymond Pearl came across Verhulst's papers and formulated the Verhulst-Pearl law. In seeking to draw an f-shaped population growth curve, Pearl stated that the rate of growth will depend upon the population at the time, and on "the still unutilized reserves of population-support" existing in the available land. Pearl had earlier formulated equations to describe the population growth of fruit flies in a closed environment, and in 1925 on the basis of similar equations, he predicted an American population in 1950 of 148.7 million and in 1960 of 159.2 million. The 1950 prediction came within 3 million persons of the actual count, but the 1960 prediction was already off by more than 25 million. Pearl's estimate of an upper limit of 197 million in the population of the United States has already been surpassed within this decade, and the population seems to be heading toward the 275 million mark by the year 2000.

The key problem in the use of f-curve analysis is that it works only within some "closed system," based either on fixed resources or physical laws or some concept of an absolute. In other words, the "ceiling conditions" force the levelling off of the curve. We do not have a "closed system" in human populations, or society, thus there is always a risk in using such curves for purposes of prediction. Yet there is some value in considering such a model as a "baseline" or fiction against which to test a social reality. The late Louis Ridenour, the former chief scientist of the air force, who was the first person to comment on the Fremont Rider data (in a 1951 paper printed in *Bibliography in an Age of Science*), pointed out that the phenomenon of the doubling rates of university libraries could be found as well in the assets of life insurance companies, the number of long-distance telephone messages and radio-telephone conversations, the time for circumnavigating the globe, the gross weight of aircraft in common use, airline-passenger miles flown, passenger-car registrations, and so forth. Ridenour, assuming the exponential law to be empirically es-

[21] "The point where a struggle for existence first sets in, and where *ipso facto* the rate of increase begins to diminish, is called by Verhulst the *normal level* of the population; he chooses it for the origin of his curve, which is so defined as to be symmetrical on either side of this origin. Thus Verhulst's law, and his logistic curve, owe their form and their precision and all their power to forecast the future to certain hypothetical assumptions." Ibid., p. 146.

tablished, argued, in fact, that there was a "law of social change" paralleling the "autocatalytic processes," such as chemical reaction or cell growth, which are found in chemistry and biology. In seeking to establish an explanation, Ridenour argued that the rate of public acceptance of a new product or service (such as long-distance telephoning or airline travel) will be proportional to the number of people who are familiar with it through exposure. Since at some point there has to be a saturation, Ridenour, like Verhulst, proposed a differential equation to indicate the rate of slowdown when the curve would begin to reach an absolute upper limit.[22]

The difficulty with Ridenour's proposed "law of social change" is that such curves are plotted only for single variables and presume a saturation. But what may be true of beanstalks, or yeast, or fruit flies, or similar organisms whose logistic growths have been neatly plotted in *fixed* ecological environments may not hold for social situations where decisions may be postponed (as in the case of births) or where substitutions are possible (as in the case of bus or subway transit for passenger cars), so that the growths do not develop in some fixed, "immanent" way. It is for this reason that the use of logistic curves may be deceptive.

Yet one advantage of this technique remains: by the use of mathematical language, one can often discern identical underlying structures in highly diverse phenomena. One may not think of people marrying and having children as the same kind of phenomenon as replacing capital equipment in a plant, but Richard Stone, the Cambridge, England economist, finds an exact mathematical analogy between the two. Stone discerns an equally striking analogy between epidemics in a population and the demand for education.[23] In charting the demand for education, the simple extrapolation of past trends is clearly unacceptable, for as we have seen, at some point there is a "system break," and a jump in the trend. (If one had projected the

---

[22] See Louis Ridenour, R. R. Shaw, and A. G. Hill, *Bibliography in an Age of Science* (Urbana, Ill., 1952). Ridenour introduces the mathematical equations on the "law of social change" by saying (p. 34):

Since so many aspects of human activity seem to be governed by the same general type of growth curve, it is of interest to inquire whether we can find a rationalization for the empirical law of social change.

One is, in fact, immediately accessible. It depends on the seemingly reasonable assumption that the rate of further public acceptance of a new device or service will, at any time, be proportional to the extent to which the device or service is already used. To take a specific example, this assumption claims that the number of people who will buy and register automobiles, per unit time, will depend upon the extent of the opportunity for those who do not own cars to ride in a car that is owned by someone else. The extent of this opportunity will be proportional to the number of automobiles that are already registered.

[23] Richard Stone, "A Model of the Educational System," in *Mathematics in the Social Sciences and Other Essays* (Cambridge, 1966), esp. p. 105.

demand for American universities on the basis of the trends in the 1950 decade, one would have assumed that only by 1975 would 40 percent of the age eighteen to twenty-two cohort be in college; actually that figure was reached in 1965.) Stone suggests that higher education can be regarded as an "epidemic process." "At each stage, the number who catch the infection and decide to go to a university depends partly on the numbers who have gone and so are available to be infected." In time, the "contagion" spreads until everyone susceptible to it is infected. The pattern is definable by a differential equation whose product, again, is the *f*-shaped or logistic curve.

To the extent that one can use logistic-curve analysis, even as baselines rather than for actual forecasts, a number of difficult problems present themselves, for at crucial points in the trajectory of the *f*-curve, "critical magnitudes" are reached and the logistic curve "reacts" to the approaching ceiling conditions in different ways. Pearl and Ridenour posited a simple saturation and a levelling off. In *Science Since Babylon*, Derek Price seemed to accept the same simplistic view:

It is a property of the symmetrical sigmoid curve that its transition from small values to saturated ones is accomplished during the central portion in a period of time corresponding to only the middle five or six doubling periods (more exactly 5.8), independent of the exact size of the ceiling involved. . . . For science in the United States, the accurate growth figures show that only about thirty years must elapse between the period when some few percent of difficulty is felt and the time when that trouble has become so acute that it cannot possibly be satisfied. . . . We are already, roughly speaking, about halfway up the manpower ceiling.[24]

Two years later, however, Price had begun to change his mind. It seems that the knowledge curves were not simple *f*-shaped or logistic curves. Under the influence of the writings of Gerald Holton, the Harvard physicist, Price sought to identify more differentiated modes of change. In rather exuberantly hypostasized language, Price now wrote:

. . . growths that have long been exponential seem not to relish the idea of being flattened. Before they reach a mid-point they begin to twist and turn, and, like impish spirits, change their shapes and definitions so as not to be exterminated against that terrible ceiling. Or, in less anthropomorphic terms, the cybernetic phenomenon of hunting sets in and the curve begins to oscillate wildly. The newly felt constriction produces restorative reaction, but the restored growth first wildly overshoots the mark and then plunges to greater depths than before. If the reaction is successful, its value usually seems to lie in so transforming what is being mea-

---

[24] Derek Price, *Science Since Babylon*, pp. 115–116.

sured that it takes a new lease on life and rises with a new vigor until, at last, it must meet its doom.

One therefore finds two variants of the traditional logistic curve that are more frequent than the plain ∫-shaped curve. In both cases the variant sets in some time during the inflection, presumably at a time when the privations of the loss of exponential growth become unbearable. If a slight change of definition of the thing that is being measured can be so allowed as to count a new phenomenon on equal terms with the old, the new logistic curve rises phoenixlike on the ashes of the old, a phenomenon first adequately recognized by Holton and felicitously called by him "escalation." Alternatively, if the changed conditions do not admit a new exponential growth, there will be violent fluctuations persisting until the statistic becomes so ill-defined as to be uncountable, or in some cases the fluctuations decline logarithmically to a stable maximum. At times death may even follow this attainment of maturity, so that instead of a stable maximum there is a slow decline back to zero, or a sudden change of definition making it impossible to measure the index and terminating the curve abruptly in midair.[25]

So much, then, for the symmetry of the sigmoid curve! Price proposes: "Now that we know something about the pathological afterlife of a logistic curve, and that such things occur in practice in several branches of science and technology, let us reopen the question of the growth curve of science as a whole."[26] What Price finally discovers is that after the "breakdown" of the exponential growth of knowledge, the curve (after tightening its sinews for a jump!) may move "either toward escalation or toward violent fluctuation." But in which direction we do not know. So where are we then? The idea of "escalation," or the renewal of an upward curve, may have some meaning where there is a deterministic path, following some physical laws, and in this sense it has found a place in technological forecasting, where it appears under the rubric of "envelope curve" forecasting. But to talk of "violent fluctuations" provides little help in charting measurable changes, for such fluctuations have no determinate pattern.

We find, in sum, that the "gross" measures of scientific knowledge, plotted as growth curves, are, so far at least, of little help, other than as metaphors, or as a means of alerting us generally to the problems we may have to face in the future because of such growths. To plan for social policy on the basis of such plotted curves would be highly misleading. To deal with such questions, we have to turn to less "exact" but sociologically more meaningful observations on the patterns of the development of knowledge.

---

25 Derek Price, *Big Science, Little Science* (New York, 1963), pp. 23–25.
26 Ibid., p. 30.

THE DIFFERENTIATION OF KNOWLEDGE

The idea of exponentiality, the idea that scientific knowledge accumulates "linearly" in some compound fashion, has obscured the fact that the more typical, and important, pattern is the development of "branching," or the creation of new and numerous subdivisions or specialties within fields, rather than just growth.

Contrary to the nineteenth-century image of science as a bounded or exhaustible field of knowledge whose dimensions would eventually be fully explored, we now assume an openness to knowledge which is marked by variegated forms of differentiation. Each advance opens up, sometimes rapidly, sometimes slowly, new fields which, in turn, sprout their own branches. Thus, to take the illustration cited by Gerald Holton, the field of "shock waves" initiated in 1848 by the British mathematician and physicist G. C. Stokes and the astronomer J. Challis, with their theoretical equations of motion in gases, led not only to significant contributions in mathematics and physics along this general line (by Mach, and later by von Neumann and Bethe, among others), but to the branching off of shock tube, aerodynamics, detonations, and magnetohydrodynamics, as four distinct fields. The last field, developed in 1942 by Alfven, plays a fundamental part in both basic and applied fusion research.[27]

Sometimes a stasis is reached and it seems that a field has been explored as far as possible, then some new discoveries suddenly create a series of new "spurts." In 1895, Röntgen seemed to have exhausted all the major aspects of x-rays, but in 1912 the discovery of x-ray diffraction in crystals by von Laue, Friedrich, and Knipping transformed two separate fields, that of x-rays and crystallography. Similarly the discovery in 1934 of artificial radioactivity by the Joliot-Curies created a qualitative change which gave rise, in one branching point to the work of Hahn and Strassman, which Lise Meitner successfully interpreted as the splitting of the uranium atom, and in another branch to Enrico Fermi's work on the increased radioactivity of metals bombarded with slow neutrons, work which led directly to controlled atomic fission and the bomb.

Much of the phenomenon of branching derives not simply from the "immanent" logic of intellectual development, but from the social organization of science itself. In the nineteenth century, science was a small but worthy profession for individuals in its own right. But in the twentieth century, the way in which scientists have come to organize and coordinate their individual research "into a fast-growing

---

[27] Gerald Holton, "Scientific Research and Scholarship: Notes Toward the Design of Proper Scales," *Daedalus* (Spring 1962), pp. 362–399. In this discussion of branching, I have largely followed Holton's account.

commonwealth of learning," as Holton puts it, has spurred individuals to develop their own work, subsequently, with their own teams. Holton illustrates this phenomenon with a drawing of a "tree" and its "branches," which traces, among other things, the work of Nobel laureate I. I. Rabi. In 1929, at Columbia, Rabi made a "breakthrough" in pure physics—sending molecular beams through a magnetic field—which gave rise to branching in several different directions, in optics, solid state masers, atomic structures, and a half-dozen other fields. Rabi not only developed the original molecular beam techniques—the trunk of the tree—but he also stimulated a group of productive associates and students to originate new questions, to move into neighboring parts of the same field, and to provoke a rapid branching into several new areas, some of which then developed branches of their own.[28]

One can find some indicators of the extraordinary proliferation of fields in the breakdown of specializations listed in the National Register of Scientific and Technical Personnel, a government-sponsored inventory of all persons with competence in scientific work. (The National Register is a cooperative undertaking of the National Science Foundation with the major professional scientific societies in the country.) The Register began shortly after World War II, with about 54 specializations in the sciences; 20 years later there were over 900 distinct scientific and technical specializations listed. To a considerable extent, the proliferation of fields arises out of a system of reclassifications, as more and more fine distinctions are made; but in many instances, the increase is due to the creation of new specializations and branchings. In physics, for example, the 1954 roster listed 10 distinct subfields with 74 specializations; in 1968, there were 12 fields with 154 specializations. In 1954, for example, Theoretical Physics (Quantum) was listed as a distinct field, with subspecializations headed as nuclear, atomic, solids, field; in 1968 the field was no longer listed as such and a more differentiated classification had appeared. In 1954, however, solid-state physics was broken down into 8 subspecializations; in 1968 there were 27 subspecializations under the solid-state classification, a proliferation which was the consequence of the additional "branching" of the field.

None of the scientific societies which are responsible for the maintenance of the rosters have made any studies seeking to chart the growth of their subjects either on the basis of the reclassification or addition of fields. A consistent monitoring of each field might reveal some useful and significant indicators of the rates of change in the development of fields of knowledge.

---

[28] Ibid., pp. 386–387.

The Measurement of Technological Change

MODERNITY AND TECHNOLOGICAL CHANGE

The claim of being "new" is the distinctive hallmark of modernity, yet many of these claims represent not so much a specifically new aspect of human experience as a change in scale of the phenomenon. The syncretism of culture was already a distinctive feature of the age of Constantine, with its mingling of the Greek and Asiatic mystery religions. The bifurcation of sensibility is as old, if not older, than Plato's separation of the rational from the spirited. But the revolutions in transportation and communication which have banded together the world society into one great *Oikoumenē* (ecumene) have meant the breakdown of older, parochial cultures and the overflowing of all the world's traditions of art, music, and literature into a new, universal container, accessible to all and obligatory upon all. This very enlargement of horizon, this mingling of the arts, this search for the "new," whether as a voyage of discovery or as a snobbish effort to differentiate oneself from others, is itself the creation of a new kind of modernity.

At the heart of the issue is the meaning of the idea of culture. When one speaks of a "classical culture" or a "Catholic culture" (almost in the sense of a "bacterial culture"—a breeding of distinctly identifiable strains), one thinks of a long-linked set of beliefs, traditions, rituals, and injunctions which in the course of its history has achieved something of a homogeneous style. But modernity is, distinctively, a break with the past *as* past, catapulting it into the present. The old concept of culture is based on continuity, the modern on variety; the old value was tradition, the contemporary ideal is syncretism.

In the radical gap between the present and the past, technology has been one of the chief forces in the diremption of social time, for by introducing a new metric and by enlarging our control over nature, technology has transformed social relationships and our ways of looking at the world. To be arbitrary, we can list five ways by which technology wrought these transformations:

1. By producing more goods at less cost, technology has been the chief engine of raising the living standards of the world. The achievement of technology, the late Joseph Schumpeter was fond of saying, was that it brought the price of silk stockings within the reach of every shopgirl, as well as of a queen. But technology has not only been the means of raising levels of living, it has been the chief mecha-

nism of reducing inequality within Western society. In France, writes Jean Fourastié, "the Chief Justice of the Court of Accounts . . . earned in 1948 not more than four and a half times as much as his office boy *by hour of work*, although the difference between these two positions was of the order of 50 to 1 in 1800." The simple reason for this, as Fourastié points out, is the cheapening of goods and the rise of real wages of the working class in Western life.[29]

2. Technology has created a new class, hitherto unknown in society, of the engineer and the technician, men who are divorced from the site of work but who constitute a "planning staff" for the operations of the work process.

3. Technology has created a new definition of rationality, a new mode of thought, which emphasizes functional relations and the quantitative. Its criteria of performance are those of efficiency and optimization, that is, a utilization of resources with the least cost and least effort. This new definition of functional rationality has its carryover in new modes of education, in which the quantitative techniques of engineering and economics now jostle the older modes of speculation, tradition, and reason.

4. The revolutions in transportation and communication, as a consequence of technology, have created new economic interdependencies and new social interactions. New networks of social relationships have been formed (pre-eminently the shift from kinship to occupational and professional ties); new densities, physical and social, become the matrix of human action.

5. Esthetic perceptions, particularly of space and time, have been radically altered. The ancients had no concept of "speed" and motion in the way these are perceived today: nor was there a synoptic conception of height—the view from the air—which provides a different standard of assessing a landscape or a cityscape. It is in art, especially in painting, that such a radical change of sensibility has taken place.[30]

MEASURES OF ECONOMIC CHANGE

It is with the economy that we are first concerned because technology is the foundation of industrial society. Economic innovation and change are directly dependent upon new technology. Yet the awareness of this fact is relatively recent. The founding fathers of contemporary economics were preoccupied with a "dismal science"

---

[29] Jean Fourastié, *The Causes of Wealth* (Glencoe, Ill., 1960), chap. I, esp. pp. 30–31.
[30] For an elaboration of this point, see Daniel Bell, "The Disjunction of Culture and Social Structure," in Gerald Holton, ed., *Science and Culture* (Boston, 1965), pp. 236–251.

because of their belief that capital accumulation could not continue indefinitely. These conclusions were based on three assumptions: the law of diminishing returns; the Malthusian principle, in which an increase in real wages would simply lead to faster population growth and the "dilution" of that increase; and, implicitly, an invariant state of technology. This was the basis of Ricardian economics.[31] It was elaborated by John Stuart Mill in the conception of "The Stationary State."

Even Marx, in this sense a post-Ricardian economist, came to a pessimistic conclusion. Though he was far more sensitive to the revolutionary role of machinery than his contemporaries, Marx felt that the chief consequence of the substitution of machinery for labor would be the centralization of capital, at the expense of other capitalists, the increased exploitation of labor (through longer working days) as more backward capitalists sought to meet competition, and, finally, a set of crises when the system reached a ceiling limit. Arguing from a labor theory of value, Marx felt that the expansion of the "organic composition of capital" could lead only to a decline in the average rate of profit and the continuing impoverishment of labor.

Yet this earlier pessimism has been belied. Real wages have risen consistently in the past hundred years; the increase in the per capita income in the United States has averaged more than 2 percent a year since 1870. How did the classical economists err so badly? As Professor Lester Lave writes: "Had Ricardo been asked whether increased productivity were possible, he would probably have answered that productivity would increase if capital per worker, including land per worker, were increased." [32] But he could not give a quantitative formulation of this effect. The standard capital-output ratios (known as the Cobb-Douglas function) which have been typically used assume that output will rise 1 percent for every 3 percent of capital increase, holding labor constant. Between 1909 and 1949, the capital per man-hour employed in the private nonfarm sector of the U.S. economy rose by 31.5 percent. On this basis, the increase in goods (per capita output) should have been about 10 percent. But the startling fact is that during this period, with a capital input of 31.5 percent, output

---

[31] As Ricardo wrote in his *Principles of Political Economy and Taxation*: "With a population pressing against the means of subsistence, the only remedies are either a reduction of people or a more rapid accumulation of capital. In rich countries, where all the fertile land is already cultivated, the latter remedy is neither very practicable nor very desirable, because its effect would be, if pushed very far, to render all classes equally poor." Cited in Lester B. Lave, *Technological Change: Its Conception and Measurement* (Englewood Cliffs, N.J., 1966), p. 3. In the paragraph above, I have followed Lave's formulations.

For Mill's discussion of the stationary state, see *Principles of Political Economy* (Toronto, 1965), book IV, chap. 6, pp. 752–758.

[32] Lave, op. cit.

per man-hour rose not 10 percent but 104.6 percent. In short, there was an increase in productivity of 90 percent that is unexplained by the increase in capital per worker. The explanation, simple in conception but complex in detail and proof, was supplied by Robert M. Solow in a now classical (or should one say neo-classical?) article, namely, *technological change*.[33] Technology, as we now know, is the basis of increased productivity, and productivity has been the transforming fact of economic life in a way no classical economist could imagine.

The simple answer, however, begs a complex question. What is technological change? One can say that technological progress consists of all the better methods and organization that improve the efficiency (i.e. the utilization) of both old capital and new. But this can be many things. It can be a machine to forge car engines replacing old hand-casting methods. It can be a physical technique, such as building a ramp to move stones up a pyramid. It can be a simple sociological technique such as a rough division of labor in the construction of a shoe or a sophisticated technique of industrial engineering such as time-and-motion studies. It can be a logical analysis embodied in operations research or a mathematical formula such as linear programming which specifies new queuing tables or the production schedules in which orders are to be filled. Clearly, all of these are incommensurate. How do we combine all these different things under one rubric and seek a measurement?

What makes the problem all the more vexing is that we are repeatedly told that we are living in a time of "constantly accelerating rate of technological change," which is creating new and "explosive" social problems. Now, no one can deny that a good deal of technologi-

---

[33] Robert M. Solow, "Technical Change and the Aggregate Production Function," *Review of Economics and Statistics*, vol. 39 (August 1957).

In his analysis, Solow postulated technology as a *residual* factor, after the computation of capital and labor inputs. But economists like to account for everything in terms of costs, and often do not like residual factors as explanations. Jorgenson and Griliches, accordingly, sought to recompute the data to show that changes in labor and capital inputs could account for the entire productivity increase. They write: "In explaining economic growth, we suggest greater reliance than heretofore on the twin pillars of human and nonhuman capital, each supporting an important part of the capital structure. Perhaps the day is not far off when economists can remove the intellectual scaffolding of technical change altogether." See Zvi Griliches and D. W. Jorgenson, "Sources of Measured Productivity Changes: Capital Input," *American Economic Review* (May 1966).

If the "right wing" questions the meaning of technology, the "left wing" argues that Solow's framework is too neo-classical and pays insufficient attention to structural factors. In her analysis of production functions, Joan Robinson has been more interested in the capitalist framework as the setting which dictates the choice of techniques in production, rather than the general conditions of equilibrium. For a review of those issues, see G. C. Harcourt, "Some Cambridge Controversies in the Theory of Capital," *The Journal of Economic Literature*, vol. VII, no. 2 (June 1969).

cal change has taken place since World War II: atomic energy, electronic computers, jet engines are three of the more spectacular introductions of new products and processes. But the difficulty with the publicistic (and political) argument is that the word "rate" implies a measurement, that somehow the changes that are being introduced now can be measured, say, against the introduction of the steam engine, the railroad, the telephone, the dynamo, and similar technological devices of the nineteenth century. How does one distinguish the change wrought by electricity from that created by atomic energy? We cannot. Both are "revolutionary" innovations. But there is no way of matching their effects in a comparable way. More than that, many social changes are occurring simultaneously, and writers often lump these together as part of the idea of rapid technological change.

The question of what constitutes *the* accelerating revolution of our time is too broad and vague. Clearly, it is in part technological. But it is also political in that, for the first time, broadly speaking, we are seeing the inclusion of the vast masses of people into society, a process that involves the redefinition of social, civil, and political rights. It is sociological in that it portends a vast shift in sensibility and in mores: in sexual attitudes, definitions of achievement, social ties and responsibilities, and the like. It is cultural, as we have already noted. Clearly there is no simple conceptual way to group all these together and find a common mensuration. It is simply impossible—if we restrict ourselves to the idea of "change"—to measure "the pace of change." There is no composite index; we have to be more delimited.

If we are to restrict ourselves to measuring the technological dimension, and ask about the rate of change, we have, first, to return to the realm where its values (beginning first in the monetary sense) are expressed—to economics.

For the economist, a technological change is a change in the "production function." [34] Simply stated, the production function is a relationship between inputs and outputs which shows, at any point in time, the *maximum* output rate which can be obtained from the given amounts of the factors of production. In the simplest cases, the factors of production are assumed to be capital and labor, and the production function would show the most effective combination (the optimal proportions) of factors at given costs. [35] Increases in real in-

---

[34] The definition here is based on the paper "Technological Change: Measurement Determinants and Diffusion," by Edwin Mansfield, prepared for the National Commission on Technology, Automation and Economic Progress, and published in Appendix 1 to the report of the Commission, *Technology and the American Economy* (Washington, D.C., 1966).

[35] Richard R. Nelson, Merton J. Peck, and Edward D. Kalachek, in their interesting book *Technology, Economic Growth and Public Policy*, The Brookings Institu-

come per man-hour are a function of both relative increases in capital and the more efficient utilization of resources. Classical economic theory emphasized that the higher levels of real income are generated by increasing the capital stock. But real wages might also be increased by an upward shift in the production function as a result of research that leads to better combinations of resources, new techniques, and so on. In fact, we assume today that technological change, rather than capital stock, is the more effective determinant of higher real wages. Robert Solow, for example, in his aforementioned 1957 paper created an "aggregate production function" (which has been criticized for its assumptions of homogeneity and high elasticity of substitution of capital for labor and capital for capital), which sought to separate the increase in productivity caused by growth in capital from that due to technological change. He found that in the period from 1909 to 1949 the capital increase accounted for approximately 12.5 percent of increased productivity, while technological change accounted for 88 percent.[36]

In the broader context, we have to move from production functions to the measures of productivity computed in regular time-series. Conventionally, the gross measurement of technological change is the year-by-year change in the output per man-hour of labor, or what economists call a partial productivity index. It is arrived at by dividing the market value of goods and services produced during a given year (in the economy as a whole, or in a particular industry) by the number of man-hours it has taken to produce them. Productivity so defined in no way identifies whether the increased efficiency has been brought about by new machinery or by a more skilled labor force, or even by a speed-up of work done on the job. Still, if we are to consider the question whether technological change has been vastly accelerating in recent years and at what rate, this is the only consistent measure we have.

The most comprehensive study of labor productivity in recent years, by John W. Kendrick,[37] draws the following conclusions:

tion (Washington, D.C., 1967), present a more disaggregated theory of a production function for technological progress. Seeking to designate the kinds and quantities of research-and-development inputs needed to make a design idea operational, they argue that the quantity of resources required depends on three key variables: (1) the magnitude of the advance sought over existing comparable products; (2) the nature of the product field, in particular the size and complexity of the system; and (3) the stock of relevant knowledge that permits new techniques to be derived or deduced, as well as the stock of available materials and components with which designers can work (p. 23).

[36] Recalculations of Solow's model disclosed some errors, and the share of capital in increasing productivity should have been 19 percent, not 12½ percent. See Lave, op. cit., p. 34.

[37] John Kendrick, *Productivity Trends in the United States*, National Bureau of Economic Research and Princeton University Press (Princeton, N.J., 1961).

First, during 1889–1957, the nation's real output per man-hour of work rose at an average rate of between 2 and 2.5 percent. These gains have been widely diffused, resulting in a rapid increase in real hourly earnings and a decline in working hours of between 20 and 30 percent since the turn of the century. According to Kendrick, there was a break after World War I. During 1889–1919, output per man-hour rose at an average rate of 1.6 percent; during 1920–1957, it grew at an average rate of 2.3 percent per year. The reasons for this increase are by no means clear. Kendrick suggests that it may have been due to the spread of scientific management, the expansion of college and graduate work in business administration, the spread of organized research and development, and the change in immigration policy. A similar picture is obtained if one uses the "total" productivity index for computations. The total productivity index, developed by Evsey Domar, relates changes in both labor and capital inputs rather than in labor inputs alone. Kendrick, using this index, estimated that during 1889–1957, total productivity for the entire domestic economy increased by 1.7 percent and that in the period following World War I, this rose to 2.1 percent.

In these measures, the usual assumption is that technological change is essentially "organizational," i.e. that technological progress consists of better methods and organization that improve the efficiency of both old capital and new. If one tries to measure that aspect of change that is due directly to machinery, rather than just to methods (i.e. time-and-motion studies, linear programming, etc.), these changes must be capital-embodied if they are to be utilized. For example, the introductions of the continuous wide strip mill in the steel industry and the diesel locomotive in railroads necessitated large capital investments, and we can thus "factor out" those proportions of productivity due to machinery. In a study based on capital-embodied change, published in 1959, Solow estimated that the rate of technological change in the private economy during 1919–1953 was 2.5 percent per year.[38]

Most of the analytical and specialized estimates stop at a period of ten years ago. Has there been a recent increase? In the early 1960s, the seemingly persistent high unemployment rates (averaging about 6 percent) gave rise to fears that a rapid increase in automation (which necessarily would be reflected in an accelerating rate of productivity) was responsible for the unemployment. A number of economic writers prophesied so dazzling a rate of productivity increase that the economy would be unable to absorb the new production without making

---

[38] Robert M. Solow, "Investment and Technical Change," in *Mathematical Models in the Social Sciences*, ed. Kenneth J. Arrow, Samuel Karlin, and Patrick Suppes (Stanford, 1959).

a sharp separation between income and work. In 1965, President Johnson appointed a National Commission on Technology, Automation, and Economic Progress to report on the question, and after a year of study, the Commission concluded that the arguments had been greatly exaggerated. The report stated: "In the 35 years before the end of the Second World War, output per man-hour in the private economy rose at a trend rate of 2 percent a year. But this period includes the depression decade of the 1930s. Between 1947 and 1965 productivity in the private economy rose at a trend rate of about 3.2 percent a year, or an increase of more than 50 percent. If agriculture is excluded, the contrast is less sharp, with the rate of increase 2 percent a year before the war and 2.5 percent after." [39]

If one moves to the more refined indexes, Kendrick and Sato found that the average annual rate of increase of *total* productivity in the private domestic economy during the 1948–1960 period was 2.14 percent as compared with a rate of 2.08 percent for the larger 1919–1960 period. Richard Nelson, assuming that technological change was organizational, estimated the average rate of technological change as 1.9 percent in 1929–1947; as 2.9 percent in 1947–1954 and 2.1 percent in 1954–1960. Thus, while there is some evidence that the rate of technological change has been higher since World War II, the difference is much smaller than that indicated by the behavior of output per man-hour. [40]

As the President's Automation Commission concluded:

Our study of the evidence has impressed us with the inadequacy of the basis for any sweeping pronouncements about the speed of scientific and technological progress. . . . Our broad conclusion is that the pace of technological change has increased in recent decades and may increase in the future, but a sharp break in the continuity of technical progress has not occurred, nor [since most major technological discoveries which will have a significant economic impact within the next decade are already in a readily identifiable stage of commercial development] is it likely to occur in the next decade. [41]

---

[39] *Technology and the American Economy*, p. 2.

[40] The data are cited in Mansfield, "Technological Change," op. cit., p. 105.

[41] *Technology and the American Economy*, p. 1. The words in brackets are from page 4 of the report. The Commission attributed the high unemployment rate of the period 1958–1966 to a low growth rate in the economy, as a result of a lagging aggregate demand, and the doubling of the entry rates of youths into the labor force, as the "baby boom" of the post-World War II period began to reach a crest.

Since some of the conclusions of the Commission's report may be subject to challenge, it is prudent to "declare one's interest." I was a member of the Commission, participated in the studies, and signed the conclusions. The principal drafter of the sections on the pace of technological change was Professor Robert M. Solow of Massachusetts Institute of Technology.

THE FORECASTING OF TECHNOLOGY

Even though it is difficult to demonstrate that the "rate" of technological change has leaped ahead substantially in the past decades, it is undeniable that something substantially *new* about technology has been introduced into economic and social history. It is the changed relationship between science and technology, and the incorporation of science through the institutionalization of research into the ongoing structure of the economy, and, in the United States, as a normal part of business organization. Two things, therefore, are new: the systematic development of research and the creation of new science-based industries.

Classical economists, even as late as John Stuart Mill, held that population and land were the limiting variables on economic growth and that eventually a prudent economy would end in a "stationary state." [42] Marx, to the contrary, saw that the dynamic of capitalist society was, necessarily, accumulation but that monopoly would inevitably slow down the rate of growth and that the system itself might even break down because of its "contradictions." Several generations of post-Marxian economists have, in turn, expected a new state of "economic maturity" based either on the exhaustion of markets and investment opportunities in new lands (the theme of imperialism), the slowdown of population growth (a favorite theme of economic pessimists of the 1930s, vide Alvin Hansen [43]), or the ending of new technological advances as the "long waves" of business activity because of the waning impetus of the railroad, electricity, and the automobile.

The bogey of "economic maturity" has by now been largely dispelled. And the principal reason is the openness of technology. In his *Capitalism, Socialism and Democracy*, published in 1942, Joseph Schumpeter wrote: "We are now in the downgrade of a wave of enterprise that created the electrical power plant, the electrical industry, the electrified farm and home and the motorcar. We find all that

---

[42] See John Stuart Mill, *Principles of Political Economy* (New York, 1886), vol. II, book IV, chap. 6. As Mill says, so appealingly:

I cannot . . . regard the stationary state of capital and wealth with the unaffected aversion so generally manifested towards it by political economists of the old school. I am inclined to believe that it would be, on the whole, a very considerable improvement on our present condition. I confess I am not charmed with the ideal of life held out by those who think that the normal state of human beings is that of struggling to get on; that the trampling, crushing, elbowing and treading on each other's heels, which form the existing type of social life, are the most desirable lot of human kind, or anything but the disagreeable symptoms of one of the phases of industrial progress. It may be a necessary stage in the progress of civilization, and those European nations which have hitherto been so fortunate as to be preserved from it, may have it yet to undergo (p. 328).

[43] Alvin Hansen, *Fiscal Policy and Business Cycles* (New York, 1941).

very marvelous, and we cannot for our lives see where opportunities of comparable importance are to come from."

Though Schumpeter was pessimistic about the future of capitalism (because of the bureaucratization of enterprise and the hostility of the intellectual), he did have a clear view of the promise of technology. Thus he added: "As a matter of fact, however, the promise held out by the chemical industry alone is much greater than what was possible to anticipate in, say, 1880. . . . Technological possibilities are an uncharted sea . . . there is no reason to expect slackening of the rate of output through exhaustion of technological possibilities." [44]

In the quarter of a century since Schumpeter made those prophetic remarks, two changes have occurred. One has been the systematic joining of science to invention, principally through the organization of research and development efforts. The second, more recent change has been the effort to "chart the sea" of technology by creating new techniques of technological forecasting which will lay out the future areas of development and which will allow industry, or society, to plan ahead systematically in terms of capital possibilities, needs, and products. This new fusion of science with innovation, and the possibility of systematic and organized technological growth, is one of the underpinnings of the post-industrial society.

Earlier inventions and innovations were not tied to scientific research. As Nelson, Peck, and Kalachek have observed:

Compare Watt's utilization of the theory of latent heat in his invention of the separate condensing chamber for steam engines, or Marconi's exploitation of developments in electromagnetism with Carothers' work which led to nylon, Shockley's work which led to the transistor, or recent technological advances in drugs and military aircraft. In the earlier cases the scientific research that created the breakthrough was completely autonomous to the inventive effort. In the later cases, much of the underlying scientific knowledge was won in the course of efforts specifically aimed at providing the basic understanding and data needed to achieve further technological advances. Carothers' basic research at Du Pont which led to nylon was financed by management in the hope that improvements in the understanding of long polymers would lead to important or new improved chemical products. Shockley's Bell Telephone Laboratories project was undertaken in the belief that improved knowledge of semiconductors would lead to better electrical devices. [45]

But, they continue, the new industries of the 1970s—the polymers and plastics, electronics and optics, chemicals and synthet-

---

[44] Joseph Schumpeter, *Capitalism, Socialism and Democracy* (New York, 1942), pp. 117–118.

[45] Nelson, Peck, and Kalachek, *Technology, Economic Growth and Public Policy*, op. cit., p. 41.

ics, aerospace and communications—are all integrally science-based.

The science-based technologies and industries have a great advantage in achieving major advances in products and processes. Research aimed at opening up new possibilities *has substituted both for chance development* in the relevant sciences, *and* for the classical major inventive effort aimed at *cracking open a problem through direct attack*. The post World War II explosion of major advances in electronics, aircraft, missiles, chemicals, and medicines, reflects the maturing of the science base in these industries, as well as the large volume of resources they employ to advance technology. Many of the products of the science-based industries are the materials used by other industries, and their improvement has led to rapid productivity growth in many sectors of the economy. The more important new consumer goods have come either directly from these industries or through incorporation into new products by other industries of the materials and components created by the science-based sector.[46]

The role of "research and development" as a component of scientific and economic activity will be discussed in a later section. In this discussion on the measurement of technology, we can turn to the new kinds of knowledge represented by technological forecasting.

Can we predict today better than before—at least in relatively chartable fields such as technology? Three factors distinguish the prediction of today from that of the past: (1) the awareness of the complex differentiation of society and the need, therefore, to define the different kinds of systems and their interrelations; (2) the development of new techniques, primarily statistical and often mathematical, which facilitate the ordering and analysis of data so as to uncover the different rates of change that obtain in different sectors of society; and (3) the sheer quantity of empirical data which allow one to see the detailed components of sectors and to plot their trends in consistent time-series.

The simplest and perhaps most important advantage is the sheer amount of statistical data. In 1790, it was debated in the English Parliament whether the population of England was increasing or decreasing. Different people, speaking from limited experiential evidence, presented completely contradictory arguments. The issue was resolved only by the first modern census. An important corollary is the number of competent persons who can work with the data. As J. J. Spengler said, tongue not altogether in cheek, "Not only can economists devote to the population question more attention than they gave it in the past eighty years when they devoted only about 1 to 1½ percent of their articles to population, but there are many more

---

[46] Ibid., p. 43 italics added.

economists to do the job. Today more economists are practicing than lived and died in the past four thousand years, and their number is growing even faster than the world's population." [47]

In simple terms, the more data you have (look at the total number of entries needed to build up a picture of the national product accounts), the easier it is to chart the behavior of variables and to make forecasts. Most, if not all, of our basic economic and social projections today are built around the concept of Gross National Product. Yet it is startling to realize how recent are the government gathering and publication of such macroeconomic data, going back only to Franklin D. Roosevelt's budget message in 1944. And systematic technological forecasting is still in its infancy. As Erich Jantsch writes, in a comprehensive survey of technological forecasting for the Organization for Economic Cooperation and Development (OECD),

The bulk of technological forecasting today is done without the explicit use of special techniques. . . . The need for formal techniques was not felt until a few years ago. While the beginning of systematic technological forecasting can be situated at around 1950, with forerunners since 1945, the existence of a more widespread interest in special techniques first made itself felt about a decade later, in 1960, with forerunners already experimenting in the late 1950s. Now, in the mid-1960s, a noticeable interest is developing in more elaborate multi-level techniques and integrated models that are amenable to computer programing.[48]

Most technological forecasting is still based on what an imaginative engineer or writer can dream up as possible. In 1892, a German engineer, Plessner, forecast technological developments (supercritical steam and metal vapor turbines) and functional capabilities (television and voice-operated typewriters) which were—and to some extent still are—far in the future. Arthur C. Clarke, who has made some of the more speculative forecasts in his serious science fiction, has argued that anything that is theoretically possible will be achieved, despite the technical difficulties, if it is desired greatly enough. "Fantastic" ideas, he says, have been achieved in the past and only by assuming that they will continue to be achieved do we have any hope of anticipating the future.[49] Much of this kind of expectation is "poetry," because little attention is paid to constraints, especially economic ones. Fantasy may be indispensable, but only if it is disciplined by technique. With his pixyish gift for paradox, Marshall McLuhan has said that the improvement of intuition is a highly technical matter.

Much of the early impetus to disciplined technological forecasting

[47] J. J. Spengler, Presidential Address, *American Economic Review* (May 1966).

[48] Erich Jantsch, *Technological Forecasting in Perspective*, Organization for Economic Cooperation and Development (Paris, 1967), p. 109.

[49] Arthur C. Clarke, *The Promise of Space* (New York, 1968).

came in the recognition of its necessity by the military and was pioneered by Theodor von Karman, the eminent Cal Tech scientist in the field of aerodynamics. His report in 1944 on the future of aircraft propulsion is often referred to as the first modern technological forecast.[50] Von Karman later initiated the concentrated technological forecasting, at five-year intervals, of the U.S. Air Force and the technological forecasting in NATO. His innovations were fairly simple. As described by Jantsch: von Karman looked at basic potentialities and limitations, at functional capabilities and key parameters, rather than trying to describe in precise terms the functional technological systems of the future; he emphasized the evaluation of alternative combinations of future basic technologies—i.e. the assessment of alternative technological options; and he sought to place his forecasts in a well-defined time-frame of fifteen to twenty years.

In this respect, as James Brian Quinn has pointed out, technological forecasts are quite similar to market or economic forecasts. No sophisticated manager would expect a market forecast to predict the precise size or characteristics of individual markets with decimal accuracy. One could reasonably expect the market analyst to estimate the most likely or "expected" size of a market and to evaluate the probabilities and implications of other sizes. In the same sense, as Mr. Quinn has put it,

Except in immediate direct extrapolations of present techniques, it is futile for the forecaster to predict the precise nature and form of the technology which will dominate a future application. But he can make "range forecasts" of the performance characteristics a given use is likely to demand in the future. He can make probability statements about what performance characteristics a particular class of technology will be able to provide by certain future dates. And he can analyze the potential implications of having these technical-economic capacities available by projected dates.[51]

The "leap forward" in the 1960s was due, in great measure, to the work of Ralph C. Lenz, Jr., who is in the Aeronautical Systems Division of the Air Force Systems Command at the Wright-Patterson Air Force Base in Ohio. Lenz's small monograph, *Technological Forecasting*, based on a Master's thesis done ten years before at MIT, is the work most frequently cited for its classification and ordering of technological forecasting techniques.[52] Lenz divided the types of

[50] Theodor von Karman, *Towards New Horizons*, report submitted on behalf of the U.S. Air Force Scientific Advisory Group (November 7, 1944).

[51] James Brian Quinn, "Technological Forecasting," *Harvard Business Review* (April 1967).

[52] R. C. Lenz, Jr., *Technological Forecasting*, Air Force Systems Command (June 1962).

forecasting into *extrapolation, growth analogies, trend correlation,* and *dynamic forecasting* (i.e. modeling), and sought to indicate the applications of each type either singly or in combination. Erich Jantsch, in his OECD survey, listed 100 distinguishable techniques (though many of these are only variations in the choice of certain statistical or mathematical methods), which he has grouped into *intuitive, explorative, normative,* and *feedback* techniques.

Of those broad approaches that have demonstrated the most promise, and on which the greatest amount of relevant work seems to have been done, four will be illustrated here: ʃ-curves and envelope curves (*extrapolation*); the Delphi technique (*intuitive*); morphological designs and relevance tree methods (*matrices and contexts*); and the study of *diffusion times,* or the predictions of the rates of change in the introduction of new technologies that have already been developed.

Extrapolation. The foundation of all forecasting is some form of extrapolation—the effort to read some continuing tendency from the past into a determinate future. The most common, and deceptive, technique is the straight projection of a past trend plotted on a line or curve. Linear projections represent the extension of a regular time series—population, or productivity, or expenditures—at a constant rate. The technique has its obvious difficulties. Sometimes there are "system breaks." As I pointed out earlier, if one had computed agricultural productivity from the mid-1930s for the next twenty-five years at the rate it had followed for the previous twenty-five, the index (using 1910 as a base) would in 1960 have been about 135 or 140, instead of its actual figure of 400. In a different sense, if the rate of expenditures on research and development for the past twenty years were extrapolated in linear fashion for the next twenty, this would mean that by then, most of the Gross National Product would be devoted to that enterprise.

Most economic forecasting is still based on linear projections because the rates of change in the economy seem to be of that order. In other areas, such as population or knowledge or sudden demand, where the growth seems to be exponential, various writers, from Verhulst to Price, have sought to apply ʃ-shaped or logistic curves. The difficulty with these curves, as we have seen, is either that they presume a fixed environment, or that in an open environment they become erratic. Recently, however, particularly in the field of technological forecasting, writers have been attracted to the idea of "escalation"; that is, as each curve in a single trajectory levels off, a new curve "takes off" following a similar upward pattern.

The notion of "escalation" has been taken up in recent years by Buckminster Fuller, Ralph Lenz, and Robert U. Ayres to become the most striking, if not the most fashionable, mode of technological forecasting, under the name of "envelope-curve" extrapolation.[53] In this technique, the best performance of the parameters of any *particular* invention (say, the speed of aircraft), or a *class* of technology, is plotted over a long period of time until one reaches the maximum limit of performance—which is called the *envelope*. There is an assumption here of a final fixed limit, either because it is an *intrinsic* theoretical limit (e.g. of terrestrial flight 16,000 miles an hour, the point at which the increase of speed in flight sends a vehicle into atmospheric orbit), or because it is an *extrinsic* stipulation (e.g. because of rate of resource use, a trillion and a half GNP figure for the economy as a ceiling by 1985). Having stipulated a final saturation, then one plots previous escalations and presumed *new* intermediate escalations by the *tangents* along the "backs" of the individual curves. In effect, envelope curves are huge $\int$-curves, made up of many smaller ones, whose successive decreases in the rate of growth occur as the curve approaches upper limits of intrinsic or extrinsic possibilities.

In other words, for any class of technology, one has to know, or assume, the absolute finite limits, and then estimate some regular rate of growth toward that limit. The fact that, *at the existing moment*, the engineering possibilities of moving beyond the present do not exist is, in and of itself, no barrier; it is assumed that the engineering breakthrough will occur.

Envelope-curve analysis, as Donald Schon points out, is not, strictly speaking, a forecast of invention, but rather the presumed effects of *sequential* inventions on some technological parameters.[54] It assumes that since there is some intrinsic logic in the parameter— e.g. the increasing efficiency of external combustion energy conversion systems, the accelerating rate of increase of operating energy in high-energy physics particle accelerators, in aircraft power trend or speed trend curves (see Figure 3–1)—there will necessarily be an immanent development of the parameter. It also assumes that some invention inevitably will come along which will send the curve shooting up along the big $\int$.

Robert U. Ayres of the Hudson Institute, the most enthusiastic proponent of envelope-curve extrapolation, has argued that the technique works, even when one extrapolates beyond the current "state of the art" in any particular field, because the rate of invention which has characterized the system in the past may be expected to continue until the "absolute" theoretical limits (e.g. velocity of light, absolute

---

[53] I follow here largely the work of Robert Ayres and have drawn upon a number of memoranda he has prepared for the Hudson Institute.

[54] Donald Schon, "Forecasting and Technological Forecasting," in *Toward the Year 2000: Work in Progress*, ed. Daniel Bell (Boston, 1968).

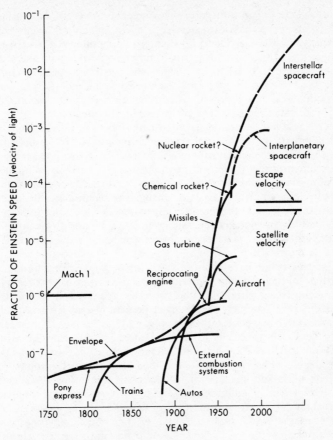

FIGURE 3–1

Speed Trend Curve

SOURCE: Courtesy Robert U. Ayres, Hudson Institute.

zero temperature) are reached for any particular parameter. One therefore should not judge the existing performance capacity of a parameter (e.g. operating energy in a particle accelerator) by the limits of a *particular* kind of component, but should look at the broad "macrovariable" in a historical context. By aggregating the particular types one can see its possible growth in a "piggy-back" jump which takes off from the previous envelope point.

Technological forecasters have claimed that in most instances it is useful to extrapolate from such envelope curves in terms of continued logarithmic growth, and to deviate from this assumption only when persuasive reasons are found for doing so. For example, forecasts projecting the existing trend at any time after 1930 would have produced a more accurate forecast about the maximum speed of aircraft than those based on the existing technological limitations. The singular point about envelope-curve extrapolation is that it cannot deal with individual technologies but with performance characteristics of "macrovariables." Ayres remarks that the more disaggregative (component-oriented) the analysis, the more it is likely to be biased intrinsically on the conservative side. In fact, it is almost normal for the maximum progress projected on the basis of analysis of components to be, in effect, the lower limit on actual progress, because it assumes no new innovations will come to change the technology. By dealing with a single *class* of technology, upper limits of growth can be readily stated for envelope curves, although these cannot be given for *individual* techniques, since these are subject to innovation, substitutability, and escalation.

Macrovariables have their obvious limits as well.[55] Thus in the plotting of the maximum energy curve in a thermal power plant since 1700 (see Figure 3–2), the curve has escalated in typical fashion from 1 or 2 percent to about 44 percent where it stands today. Increases have occurred rather sharply, and have been of the order of 50 percent each time, but at steadily decreasing intervals. Ayres predicts, on this basis, a maximum operating efficiency of 55–60 percent around 1980. In view of the long lead time of a commercial power plant, many persons might doubt this prediction. But since efficiencies of this magnitude are feasible by several means (fuel cells, gas turbines, magnetohydrodynamics) which are being explored, such a forecast may be realizable. However, increases after 1980 would pose a question for the curve since only one improvement factor of 1.5 would bring efficiencies up to 90 percent and improvement beyond that at the same rate is clearly impossible.

It is important to understand the central logic of envelope-curve projections. What the method assumes is that, for any class of technology, there is somewhere a set of fixed limits (such as the absolute velocity of light). Then, having stipulated that outer point, they seek

---

[55] If in forecasting parameters, one seeks to reduce the margin of error for particular techniques by grouping the "microvariables" into larger classes of relationships, there is the logical problem of classification: one may be arbitrarily selecting items to put together because they form a neat curve. The effort here to simplify may only distort. Most models, to be useful—and one sees this in economics —are highly cumbersome, involving hundreds of variables and equations. And yet this complexity is necessary if the predictions are to have a meaningful purchase on reality.

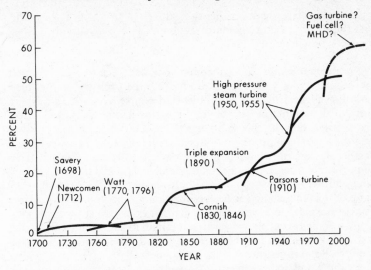

FIGURE 3–2

Efficiency of External Combustion Energy Conversion Systems

SOURCE: From *Energy for Man* by Hans Thirring, copyright 1958 by Indiana University Press, published by Harper & Row Torchbooks. Reproduced by permission of Indiana University Press and George C. Harrap and Company.

to estimate the intermediate trajectory of the technological development as a series of escalated ∫-curves moving toward that upper limit.

The weakness in the theory is, in part, the problem of any forecasting; namely, the choice of parameters and the estimation of their place in the curve, relative to the present, at which successive leveling-offs will occur, and relative to the presumed final limit, whether intrinsic or extrinsic. More generally, when one takes performance characteristics of variables (such as aircraft speed) there is no developed theory why progress *should* occur in this fashion, other than the argument that certain engineering parameters tend to grow logarithmically, or the crucial assumption that *some* invention will be forthcoming to produce the next escalation. As to the latter point, forecasters come more and more to rely on the observation, first made by William F. Ogburn and refined considerably by Robert K. Merton, that invention is a "multiple" or simultaneous affair. Because invention is, increasingly, an impersonal social process and not dependent on the genius of individual inventors, such inventions are responses to social need and economic demand. The assumption is made that where there is a demand, the new process will be found. But there may be little reason to assume that such inventions will appear "on schedule."

Intuitive technique. In most common-sense forecasting, the simplest procedure is to ask the expert, presumably the man who knows most and best about a field. The problem, of course, is who is an expert, how to determine the test of reliability for his forecasts, and, if experts differ, how to choose among them. To deal with this problem of "the epistemology of the inexact sciences," Olaf Helmer, then a mathematician at the Rand Corporation, devised the "Delphi technique" as an orderly, planned, methodological procedure in the elicitation and use of expert opinion. The rudiments of the procedure are simple: it involves the successive questioning individually of a large panel of experts in any particular field and the arrival by confrontations at some range, or consensus, of opinion in later rounds. Together with Theodore Gordon, Helmer conducted a long-range forecasting study at Rand to test the efficacy of the method.[56]

In the Rand forecasting study, six broad areas were selected for investigations—scientific breakthroughs, population growth, automation, space progress, probability and prevention of war, and future weapons systems—and a panel of experts was formed for each of the six areas.

In the panel on inventions and scientific breakthroughs, individuals were asked by letter to list those innovations which appeared urgently needed and realizable in the next fifty years. A total of forty-nine possibilities were named. In the second round, again by letter, the panel was asked to estimate the fifty-fifty probability of the realization of each of the items within a specified time period. From the results, the median year and quartile range for each item were established. (Thus it was predicted that economically useful desalination of sea water would come between 1965 and 1980, with 1970 as the median year, that controlled thermonuclear power would be available between 1978 to 2000, with 1985 as the median year.) In this second round the investigators found a considerable consensus for ten breakthroughs. They selected seventeen of the remaining thirty-nine for further probing. In a third round, the experts were asked to consider the probable time of these seventeen breakthroughs; if the individual opinion fell outside the range established by the middle 50 percent of the previous responses, the expert was asked to justify his answer. In the fourth round, the range of times was narrowed even

---

[56] The exposition of the Delphi technique, as well as the results of the Rand study, are contained in Olaf Helmer, *Social Technology* (New York, 1966).

further, thirty-one items were included in the final list on which reasonable consensus had been obtained, and majority and minority opinions were stated.

Laborious as all this may be, the panel technique was adopted for a double reason: it eliminates or lessens undue influence that would result from face-to-face discussion (e.g. the bandwagon effects of majority opinion, embarrassment in abandoning a publicly expressed opinion, etc.) and it allows a feedback, through successive rounds, which gives the respondents time to reconsider an opinion and to reassert or establish new probabilities for their choices.

With what "state of confidence" can we accept the method and these predictions? The major difficulty lies not in any single prediction but in the lack of defined contexts. Each prediction is made as a single instance, isolated from the others, though all participants easily recognize that the realization of any one prediction is not only dependent on many others but, even more, is dependent on the state of the nation itself. The implicit premise underlying all these predictions is that the context of the United States and the world will not change. But the social systems and the relationships between them are bound to change, and these changes, more than the technical feasibility of any of the individual breakthroughs, will determine the possibility of these breakthroughs being realized. In short, if forecasting is to advance, it has to be within a system context that specifies the major social, political, and economic relationships that will obtain at any given time. In the Rand use of the Delphi technique, what we are given is a set of possibilities, but the way in which these possibilities are combined depends upon the system in which they are embedded. And the art—or science—of forecasting can be extended only when we are able to advance in the creation of models of the social system itself.

Matrices and contexts. The effort to provide an orderly way of looking at possibilities underlies most of the work now going on under the headings of "morphological research" and "relevance trees." In principle these amount to a systematic effort to explore all possible solutions of a large-scale problem. What is novel is the means of ordering and the use of mathematical techniques to assign values to the different parameters of the problem.[57]

The morphological method was developed by Fritz Zwicky, a Swiss astronomer working at the Mount Wilson and Mount Palomar observatories while he was engaged in rocket research at the Aerojet Engineering Corporation in California.[58]

---

[57] Erich Jantsch, *Technological Forecasting*, op. cit., p. 175.
[58] Ibid., p. 176.

In his early work on rocket research and jet engines, a morphological box setting forth the different combinations of eleven classes of variables, each class with its own range of possibilities (e.g. propellants would be a class and gaseous, liquid, and solid state, would be the three possibilities; motion the class and translatory, rotatory, and oscillatory as the possibilities) produced a total of 25,344 possible kinds of engines. A previous evaluation, in 1943, on the basis of fewer parameters, derived 576 possibilities which included, however, the then-secret German pulse-jet powered aerial V-1 bomb and V-2 rocket, at a time when Professor Lindemann, Churchill's scientific advisor, failed to recognize the potential of the V-2, even when he was shown photographs, because he rejected the idea of liquid propellants.

As Jantsch has observed, "the full-scale application of [the morphological scheme] as it has been practiced by Zwicky in rocket and jet fuel development, apparently has had considerable success and was decisive in producing an unbiased approach in the early stages." The idea of morphological charts, as Jantsch points out, is used by a number of companies to map out, or even to block, possible future inventions by trying to patent, in a rather abstract way, combinations of basic parameters. ("For example, one could observe a 'rush' for patents which would fit into hitherto unpatented fields of a coolant/moderator chart of nuclear reactors.") [59]

The need to relate forecasting to specific objectives at different levels has given rise to the idea of "relevance trees," sometimes called reliance trees or simply decision trees. The concept of a relevance tree was first proposed by Churchman and Ackoff in 1957 [60] and is also an ordering device, like a company organization chart, for the mapping out of the program elements of a task and relating them to specific objectives. What is novel again is the effort to provide weights and scores for the different functional subsystems to see which patterned combinations provide the best payoffs.

While the "relevance tree" itself is simply a mapping device, the forecasting arises in the effort to deal with the unfolding of problems and new technologies over a five-, ten-, or fifteen-year sequence. North American Aviation's Autonetics division in Anaheim, California, has a "tree" called SCORE (Select Concrete Objectives for Research Emphasis) to relate objectives five to fifteen years ahead to specific strategies. The most prominent example of a decision tree is that of the Program Planning Budget System (PPBS) used by the Defense Department.

[59] Ibid., pp. 178–180.
[60] C. W. Churchman, R. L. Ackoff, and E. L. Arnoff, *Introduction to Operations Research* (New York, 1957).

Norbert Wiener once defined a system as "organized complexity." But when one has, as in the NASA Tree, 301 tasks, 195 systems, 786 sub-systems, and 687 functional elements, the job of keeping track of these, of evaluating performance, of calculating the effect of new technologies in one system on all the others, is quite obviously an awesome one. What these matrices and morphology schemes attempt to do, then, is to provide some charts for these relationships.

Diffusion times. Paul Samuelson has made the fundamental observation that the output that can be obtained from a given stock of factors "depends on the state of technology" existing at the time.[61] Some knowledge of the direction and spread of technologies therefore is crucial for the survival of any enterprise. But the important point is that technological forecasting rarely predicts, nor can it predict, specific inventions. Inventions, like political events, are subject to surprise, and often represent an imaginative breakthrough by the investigator. No one predicted the transistor of Shockley or the laser of Townes. Most technological forecasts *assume* invention—this is the crucial point—and then go on to predict the rate of extension through new escalations as in the case of the envelope curves, or the rate of diffusion as the new invention spreads throughout an industry. Our chief *economic* method of technological forecasting is the rate of diffusion.

What is true is that the rate at which technology is diffused through our economy has accelerated somewhat in the past seventy-five years, and this is one measure of the popular conception of the increase in the rate of change. A study by Frank Lynn for the President's Commission on Automation reported:

• The average lapsed time between the initial discovery of a new technological innovation and the recognition of its commercial potential decreased from thirty years, for technological innovations introduced during the early part of this century (1880–1919), to sixteen years, for innovations introduced during the post-World War I period, and to nine years for the post-World War II period.

• The time required to translate a basic technical discovery into a commercial product or process decreased from seven to five years during the sixty-to-seventy year time period investigated.[62]

In effect, the incubation time for new products has decreased drastically, principally because of the growth of research and development; but the marketing time, while shorter, has not decreased so substantially. What does stand out is Lynn's conclusion, stated "with reasonable confidence," that "those technological innovations which

---

[61] Paul Samuelson, *Problems of the American Economy* (New York, 1962).
[62] See, *Technology and the American Economy*, op. cit., Appendix 1.

will have a significant impact on our economy and society during the next five years have already been introduced as commercial products, and those technological innovations that will have a significant social and economic impact during the 1970–1975 period are now in a readily identifiable state of commercial development." It is on this basis that social and technological planning is possible.

Although that is a general conclusion, innovation and diffusion do vary considerably by sector and industry. In 1961, Edwin Mansfield studied how rapidly the use of twelve innovations spread from enterprise to enterprise in four industries—bituminous coal, iron and steel, brewing, and railroads. From the date of the first successful commercial application, it took twenty years or more for all major firms to install centralized traffic control, car retarders, by-product coke ovens and continuous annealing. Only in the case of the pallet-loading machine, the tin container, and continuous mining did it take ten years or less for their installation by all the major firms. In his study, Lynn concluded that the rate of diffusion for technological innovations with consumer applications is nearly twice that of innovations with industrial applications.

These studies have been ex post facto. Some efforts have been made to forecast the rate and direction of the diffusion of technology. Everett M. Rogers, in his *Diffusion of Innovations*,[63] uses historical diffusion curves (dollar volume and number of units in use are the measure) plotted against time in order to identify characteristic curve shapes. Mansfield has constructed a simple model [64] built largely around one central idea—the probability that a firm will introduce a new technique increases with the proportion of firms already using it and the profitability of doing so, but decreases with the size of the investment required. So far, these are all experimental.

With the question of diffusion one passes over from technology to economic and social forecasting, for the spread of a new invention or product clearly depends not only on its technical efficiency, but on its cost, its appeals to consumers, its social costs, by-products, and the like; the introduction of any new invention thus depends upon the constraints of the economy, the policies of government, and the values and social attitudes of the customers.

Technology, in a sense, is a game against nature, in which man's effort to wrest the secrets from nature comes up largely against the character of physical laws and man's ingenuity in mapping those hidden paths. But economic and social life is a game between persons in which forecasting has to deal with variable strategies, dispositions,

[63] Everett M. Rogers, *Diffusion of Innovations* (Glencoe, Ill., 1962).
[64] Edwin Mansfield, *Econometrica* (October 1961).

and expectations, as individuals seek, either cooperatively or antagonistically, to increase their individual advantage.

All of this takes place within social limits which it is the forecaster's task to define. No large-scale society changes with the flick of a wrist or the twist of a rhetorical phrase. There are the constraints of nature (weather and resources), established customs, habits and institutions, and simply the recalcitrance of large numbers. Those, for example, who made sweeping predictions about the radical impact of automation, based on a few spectacular examples, forgot the simple fact that even when a new industry, such as data processing or numerical control, is introduced, the impact of industries with sales mounting quickly even to several billion dollars is small compared to an economy which annually generates a trillion in goods.

The outer limit of a society is its economic growth rate, and theorists such as Robert M. Solow of MIT (whose development of an economic growth model, now called, with heavy responsibility, the Ricardo-Marx-Solow model, is one of the accomplishments of contemporary economics) have argued that each economy has its "natural" growth which is compounded of the rate of population increase and the rate of technological progress (the latter being defined as the rate of productivity, the rate of new inventions, the improvement in quality of organization, education, etc.).[65] Because of existing institutional arrangements (patterns of capital mobilization and spending, proportions of income used by consumers, etc.) and the large magnitudes of manpower, resources, and GNP in a society, even the revolutionary introduction of new technologies (such as in agriculture) will not increase the total productivity rate markedly. Some societies have a higher growth rate than others because of a later start and the effort to catch up. For short periods, advanced economies can speed up their growth rate within limits, but a shift in the "production function" to a greater utilization of capital leads later to replacement costs, lower marginal efficiency, and a flattening out of the rise until the "natural" rate again is resumed. According to studies of Edward Denison, for example, the "natural" rate of growth of the U.S. economy, because of institutional arrangements and technology, is about 3 percent a year.[66] Eventually—at least logically, though perhaps not sociologically—to the extent that technology, as a part of the common fund of knowledge, is available to all societies, the rate of increase of all economies may eventually tend to even out. But within any appreciable frame of time, the limit that frames the forecasts of

[65] Robert M. Solow, "Investment and Technical Change," op. cit.

[66] Edward Denison, *Sources of Economic Growth*, Committee on Economic Development (New York, 1962).

any economist or sociologist is the growth rate of an economy—which determines what is available for social use—and this is the baseline for any social forecasting.

We have said that technology is one axis of the post-industrial society; the other axis is knowledge as a fundamental resource. Knowledge and technology are embodied in social institutions and represented by persons. In short, we can talk of a knowledge society. What are its dimensions?

The Structure of the Knowledge Society

The post-industrial society, it is clear, is a knowledge society in a double sense: first, the sources of innovation are increasingly derivative from research and development (and more directly, there is a new relation between science and technology because of the centrality of *theoretical* knowledge); second, the weight of the society—measured by a larger proportion of Gross National Product and a larger share of employment—is increasingly in the knowledge field.

Fritz Machlup, in his heroic effort to compute the proportion of GNP devoted to the production and distribution of knowledge, estimated that in 1958 about 29 percent of the existing GNP, or $136,-436 million, was spent for knowledge.[67] (This total as distributed is shown in Table 3-1.) The definitions Machlup employs, however, are broad indeed. Education, for example, includes education in the home, on the job, and in the church. Communication media include all commercial printing, stationery, and office supplies. Information machines include musical instruments, signalling devices, and typewriters. Information services include moneys spent for securities brokers, real-estate agents, and the like. To that extent, the figure of 29 percent of GNP, which has been widely quoted, is quite misleading. Especially because of student attacks on Clark Kerr, who used this figure in *The Uses of the University*,[68] the phrases "knowledge industry" and "knowledge factory" have acquired a derogatory connotation.

Any meaningful figure about the "knowledge society" would be much smaller. The calculation would have to be restricted largely to research (the development side of R & D has been devoted largely to

---

[67] Fritz Machlup, op. cit., pp. 360–361. The figures on the proportion of educational expenditures to GNP are from the U.S. Government, *Digest of Educational Statistics* (U.S. Government Printing Office, 1970), p. 21.

[68] Clark Kerr, *The Uses of the University* (New York, 1966).

TABLE 3–1

Distribution of Proportion of Gross National Product
Spent on Knowledge, 1958

TYPE OF KNOWLEDGE AND SOURCE OF EXPENDITURES	AMOUNT IN MILLIONS OF DOLLARS	PERCENTAGE
Education	60,194	44.1
Research and development	10,990	8.1
Communication media	38,369	28.1
Information machines	8,922	6.5
Information services (Incomplete)	17,961	13.2
Total	136,436	100.0
Expenditures made by:		
Government	37,968	27.8
Business	42,198	30.9
Consumers	56,270	41.3
Total	136,436	100.0

SOURCE: Data from Fritz Machlup, *The Production and Distribution of Knowledge in the United States,* © 1962 by Princeton University Press, pp. 360–361, arranged in tabular form, by permission.

missiles and space, and is disproportionate to the total), higher education, and the production of knowledge, as I have defined it, as an intellectual property, which involves valid new knowledge and its dissemination. If one takes education alone, defining it more narrowly than Machlup as direct expenditures for public and private schools, the singular fact is that the proportion of GNP spent on education in 1969 was more than double that of 1949. In 1949, the expenditure on education was 3.4 percent of GNP (in 1939, it was 3.5 percent, and in 1929, it was 3.1 percent). In 1969, the figure had risen to .7.5 percent. This doubling can be taken as one indicator of the importance of education. (Other, limited indicators can be seen in the tables in the following sub-sections.)

DIMENSIONS OF THE KNOWLEDGE CLASS[69]

In the Republic of Plato, knowledge was vouchsafed only to one class, the philosophers, while the rest of the city was divided between warriors (guardians) and artisans. In the Scientific City of the future there are already foreshadowed three classes: the creative elite of scientists and the top professional administrator (can one call them the "new clerisy," in Coleridge's term?); the middle class of engineers

---

[69] In the sections that follow, all statistical data have been checked against available sources, and the latest year given is the one available as of mid-1972.

and the professorate; and the proletariat of technicians, junior faculty, and teaching assistants.

The metaphor can be carried too far, yet there is already an extraordinary differentiation within the knowledge society, and the divisions are not always most fruitfully explored along traditional class lines of hierarchy and dominance, important as these may be. There are other sociological differences as well. In the social structure of the knowledge society, there is, for example, the deep and growing split between the technical intelligentsia who are committed to functional rationality and technocratic modes of operation, and the literary intellectuals, who have become increasingly apocalyptic, hedonistic, and nihilistic. There are divisions between professional administrators and technical specialists, which sometimes result in dual structures of authority—for example, in hospitals and research laboratories. In the universities there are divisions between deans and faculty, and in the faculty between research and teaching. In the world of art there are complex relations between museum directors, curators, magazines, critics, dealers, patrons, and artists. The performing arts have different striations. Any further exploration of the knowledge class would have to explore in detail these varying patterns of vertical stratification and differentiation.

Conventionally, in social structure analysis, we begin with population. The gross figures are startling indeed. If one assumes, as does Abraham Moles, that by 1972, 5 percent of the population of the "advanced" countries and 3 percent of the total world population would be involved in intellectual work, then the global population of the Scientific City of tomorrow would number a hundred million persons! [70]

World comparisons are difficult, and the figure just cited was intended to indicate the change in scale that the growth of an intellectual class has produced. Because we have no figures for the past, such comparisons are difficult. One of our tasks, however, is to provide baselines for the future; and here we shall restrict ourselves to American data, and to the census categories that allow us to make some comparisons over time and some projections for the future.

The chief census category we are concerned with is that of "professional and technical persons." Between 1947 (the baseline after World War II) and 1964, the employment of professional and technical workers in the United States more than doubled, rising from about 3.8 million to over 8.5 million workers. By 1975, manpower requirements for this occupational group are expected to rise by more than half, to 13.2 million persons. If one assumes a total labor

---

[70] Abraham Moles, "La Cité Scientific dans 1972," *Futuribles* (Paris, 1964).

force at that time of 88.7 million, then the professional and technical group would make up 14.9 percent of the working population. If one adds, as well, an estimated 9.2 million managers, officials, and proprietors, then the total group would make up 25.3 percent of the working population. In effect, one out of every four persons would have had two to four years of college—the educational average for the group—and this 25.3 percent would comprise the educated class of the country.[71]

In the professional class, teachers make up the single largest group. The combined employment of public and private school teachers increased from about 1.3 million in the 1954–1955 school year to about 2.1 million in 1964–1965 and 2.8 million in 1970. Teachers comprised about 25 percent of all persons classified as professional and technical by the census. In the 1960 decade, half of all teachers were employed in elementary schools, more than a third in secondary schools, and about 20 percent in colleges and universities. The number of teachers is expected to rise by almost a third during the 1965–1975 decade, reaching almost 3 million in the 1974–1975 school year, but given the more rapid rise of other professional and technical groups, the proportion of teachers in this class will fall to about 20 percent.

Engineering is the second largest professional occupation, exceeded in size only by teaching, though for men it is the largest profession. Employment of engineers increased by more than 80 percent between 1950 and 1966, rising from an estimated 535,000 to about 1,000,000, the chief reason being the expansion in this period of the science-based industries such as electronics, space, missiles, scientific instruments, nuclear energy, and computer technology, and the longer time required to develop and produce products because of the increasing complexity of the production processes. About half of all engineers work in manufacturing, another quarter in construction, public utilities, and engineering services. A high number of engineers, about 150,000, are employed by the government, half of these by the federal government. Educational institutions employ about 35,000 engineers in research and teaching. The number of engineers is expected to rise by more than 50 percent between 1964 and 1975, to about 1.5 million; this group would then comprise more than 11 percent of the total professional and technical class.

---

[71] These figures and projections, and those that follow for the subclassifications, are taken from "America's Industrial and Occupational Manpower Requirements, 1964–1975," prepared by the Bureau of Labor Statistics for the National Commission on Technology, Automation and Economic Progress, and printed in the appendix to *Technology and the American Economy*. Later projections issued in *Tomorrow's Manpower Needs*, Bulletin 1606 (February 1969), modify these projections only fractionally.

Allied to the engineer is the engineering and science technician (excluding draftsmen and surveyors), whose numbers grew from 450,000 in 1960 to 650,000 in mid-1966, making up about 7 percent of all professional and technical workers. The number of engineering and science technicians is expected to rise by about two-thirds by 1975, bringing the total to more than a million.

The most crucial group in the knowledge society, of course, is scientists, and here the growth rate has been the most marked of all the professional groups. The number of engineers, for example, rose from 217,000 in 1930 to almost a million in 1964; in the same period, the number of scientists increased from 46,000 to 475,000. To put this growth in another context, whereas between 1930 and 1965 the work force increased by about 50 percent, the number of engineers increased by 370 percent, and that of scientists by 930 percent. By 1975, according to the Bureau of Labor Statistics, the number of natural scientists will rise to 465,000 and the number of social scientists to 80,000.[72] (See Table 3–2 and Figure 3–3.)

All this growth goes hand in hand with a democratization of higher education on a scale that the world has never seen before. No society has ever attempted to provide formal education for the bulk of its youth through age nineteen or twenty (the junior college level) or through age twenty-two, yet this has now become the explicit policy of the United States. Just as in the 1920s a decision was made to provide a secondary school education for every child in the country so, too, in the past two decades, the decision was made to provide a college education, or at least some years in college, for all capable youths in the country. At first this decision was made spontaneously through education for veterans, and then it spread through the various state systems as it became apparent that the new science-based industries would require more technically trained personnel. The change can be seen most graphically in Table 3–3, which shows the consistent rise in the proportion of the population aged eighteen to twenty-one attending college.

The table also shows a more rapid growth rate in the second decade than in the first. Total enrollments increased by 145 percent in the eighteen-year period 1946–1964 and by 104 percent during the last ten years of the period. Since 1964, the trend has continued upward. If one takes the data from the *Digest of Education Statistics*, then of the 18-19-year-old age group (the freshman age group), 46.3 percent of the group was in school in 1965, 47.6 percent in

---

[72] *Review of National Science Policy: United States*, Organisation for Economic Co-operation and Development (Paris, 1968), pp. 44–45, and U.S. Bureau of Labor Statistics, Bulletin 1606, ibid.

TABLE 3–2

Forecasts of Skilled Population and Scientific Personnel

	1963	1970	1975
Population of the United States (in millions)	190	209	227
Work force (millions)	76	86	
Civil employment (millions)	70.3 [a]		88.7
White-collar workers	31.12 [a]		42.8
(as percentage of civil employment)	(44.2%)		(48%)
Professional and technical	8.5 [a]		13.2
(as percentage of civil employment)	(12.2%)		(14.9%)
Scientific population (millions)	2.7	4	
(as percentage of active population)	(3.6%)	(4.7%)	
Scientists in the strict sense	0.5 ⎫ 1.43	0.74 ⎫ 2.14	
Engineers	0.93 ⎭	1.4 ⎭	
Technicians	1	1.6	
Science teachers in secondary schools	0.25	0.3	
Doctorate degrees (in thousands)	106	170	
In science	96	153	
In engineering	10	17	

SOURCE: Organisation for Economic Co-operation and Development, *Reviews of National Science Policy: United States* (Paris, 1968), p. 45.
[a] Based on 1964 data.

1967, 50.4 percent in 1968, and 50.2 percent in 1969. It is expected that the 50-percent mark will be the norm for some time.

Another statistical series used by the OECD reporting team provides a more useful definition than simple enrollment. A series measuring the growth of resident students in degree courses allows the growth in the number of students to be measured over a longer period, from 1869 to the present. Table 3–4 illustrates the different stages in university expansion.

Since 1879, American university population has doubled every twenty years. But compared with the corresponding age group, a very fast growth became apparent after World War II and was even more accentuated during the 1950s. This evolution reflects not only the growth in college enrollments but also the growth of graduates as well, their number doubling since 1950, whereas the number of undergraduates increased by 50 percent over the same period. Thus, not only is the total number of enrollments growing, but the number of more advanced students is increasing more than proportionately.

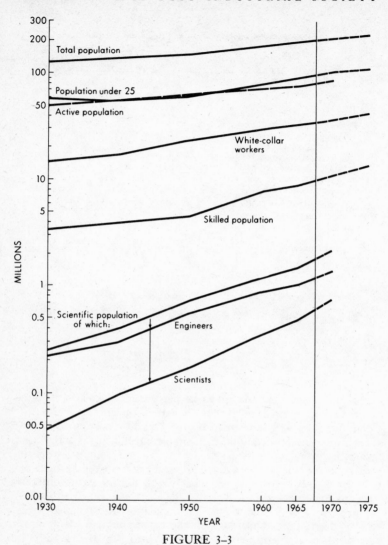

FIGURE 3–3

Trend of the Population Structure, 1930–1975
SOURCE: Organisation for Economic Co-operation and Development, *Reviews of National Science Policy: United States* (Paris, 1968), p. 43.

TABLE 3-3

Total Student Body and Corresponding Age Groups, 1946–1964

YEAR	POPULATION 18 TO 21	ENROLLMENTS	PERCENTAGE OF ENROLLMENTS TO POPULATION
1946	9,403,000	2,078,095	22.1
1947	9,276,000	2,388,226	25.2
1948	9,144,000	2,403,396	26.3
1949	8,990,000	2,444,900	27.2
1950	8,945,000	2,281,298	25.5
1951	8,742,000	2,101,962	24.0
1952	8,542,000	2,134,242	25.0
1953	8,441,000	2,231,054	26.4
1954	8,437,000	2,446,693	29.0
1955	8,508,000	2,653,034	31.2
1956	8,701,000	2,918,212	33.5
1957	8,844,000	3,036,938	34.3
1958	8,959,000	3,226,038	36.0
1959	9,182,000	3,364,861	36.6
1960	9,546,000	3,582,726	37.5
1961	10,246,000	3,860,643	37.7
1962	10,745,000	4,174,936	38.9
1963	11,129,000	4,494,626	40.4
1964	11,286,000	4,950,173	43.9

SOURCE: OECD, *Reviews of National Science Policy: United States*, p. 494.

TABLE 3-4

Student Population Studying for Degrees and Corresponding Age Groups, 1869–1963

ACADEMIC YEAR	STUDENT POPULATION TOTAL	UNDER-GRADUATE	GRADUATE	IN PERCENTAGE OF THE POPULATION 18–21 YEARS	18–24 YEARS
1869–70	52,286	—	—	1.68	1.14
1879–80	115,817	—	—	2.72	1.63
1889–90	156,756	154,374	2,382	3.04	1.78
1899–1900	237,592	231,761	5,831	4.01	2.29
1909–10	355,213	346,060	9,153	5.12	2.89
1919–20	597,880	582,268	15,612	8.09	4.66
1929–30	1,100,737	1,053,482	47,255	12.42	7.20
1939–40	1,494,203	1,388,455	105,748	15.59	9.08
1949–50	2,659,021	2,421,813	237,208	29.58	16.50
1959–60	3,215,544	2,873,724	341,820	34.86	20.49
Intake 1963	4,234,092	3,755,515	478,577	38.05	23.33

SOURCE: OECD, *Reviews of National Science Policy: United States*, p. 52.

By the end of the decade, the number of college students had advanced extraordinarily, literally doubling from 1960 to 1970. The major increase came, because of the population bulge, by the end of the decade, in the undergraduate sector. If one looks at the gross picture, one sees this striking increase. (See Table 3–5.)

TABLE 3–5

Enrollment in Institutions of Higher Learning,
Aged 18–24, 1964–1970

YEAR	POPULATION 18–24	ENROLLMENT	PERCENTAGE OF AGE GROUP
1964	18,722,000	4,950,000	26.4
1965	20,202,000	5,526,000	27.4
1966	21,346,000	5,928,000	27.8
1967	22,244,000	6,392,000	28.7
1968	22,787,000	6,928,000	30.4
1969	23,600,000	7,299,000	30.9
1970	24,500,000	7,612,000	31.1

SOURCE: *Digest of Educational Statistics*, Table 86, U.S. Office of Education, 1970.

The number of degrees has increased in proportion to the number of students, as shown in Table 3–6. Since 1947, the number of doctorates has tripled, the number of master's degrees or the equivalent has been multiplied by 2.4, and the number of bachelor's degrees or the equivalent by 1.8. By 1968, about 20 percent of the 22-year-old age group had completed a bachelor's degree (as against 14 percent in 1956). The percentage of those receiving master's degrees (at age 24) doubled from 3 to 6 percent of the age group, from 1956 to 1968, but the number of research doctorates, even though three times as great in 1970 as in 1960, still was about 1 percent of the 30-year-old age group in the United States.

If one breaks down the degrees by level and discipline, a startling fact is disclosed (Table 3–7). Both in 1954 and 1964 about 72 to 73 percent of the bachelors' degrees were taken in the social sciences and the humanities, and only 26 to 28 percent in the natural sciences and mathematics. Yet the figures for doctorates are reversed sharply. In both periods, almost 50 percent of the doctorates were in the natural sciences and mathematics. This figure itself reflects two main factors: first, the average time in achieving a doctorate in the sciences is considerably shorter than in the social sciences and humanities; and second, the employment opportunities in the sciences are more sharply defined by the possession of a doctorate than in the other fields. To take some specific figures on earned degrees conferred in

TABLE 3–6

Earned Degrees Conferred by Institutions of Higher Education,
1869–1870 to 1963–1964

YEAR	ALL DEGREES	BACCALAUREATES AND FIRST PROFESSIONAL	MASTERS EXCEPT FIRST PROFESSIONAL	DOCTORATES
		EARNED DEGREES CONFERRED		
1869–70	9,372	9,371	0	1
1879–80	13,829	12,896	879	54
1889–90	16,703	15,539	1,015	149
1899–1900	29,375	27,410	1,583	382
1909–10	39,755	37,199	2,113	443
1919–20	53,516	48,622	4,279	615
1929–30	139,752	122,484	14,969	2,299
1939–40	216,521	186,500	26,731	3,290
1941–42	213,491	185,346	24,648	3,497
1943–44	141,582	125,863	13,414	2,305
1945–46	157,349	136,174	19,209	1,966
1947–48	317,607	271,019	42,400	4,188
1949–50	496,661	432,058	58,183	6,420
1951–52	401,203	329,986	63,534	7,683
1953–54	356,608	290,825	56,788	8,995
1955–56	376,973	308,812	59,258	8,903
1957–58	436,979	362,554	65,487	8,938
1959–60	476,704	392,440	74,435	9,829
1961–62	514,323	417,846	84,855	11,622
1963–64	614,194	498,654	101,050	14,490
1965–66	709,832	551,040	140,555	18,237
1967–68	866,548	666,710	176,749	23,089
1968–69	984,129	764,185	193,756	26,188
1969–70	1,025,400	785,000	211,400	29,000

SOURCE: OECD, *Reviews of National Science Policy: United States,* p. 54. *Digest of Educational Statistics,* U.S. Office of Education, 1970. NOTE: Beginning in 1959–60, includes Alaska and Hawaii.

1968 (the latest available), 120,668 bachelor's degrees were taken in social science, but only 2,821 doctoral degrees; in the biological sciences, 31,826 students took bachelor's degrees and 2,784 received doctoral degrees; while in the physical sciences, 19,380 students took bachelor's degrees and 3,593 received doctorates! (U.S. Office of Education, "Earned Degrees Conferred, 1967–1968.")

SCIENTIFIC ELITE AND MASS

The chief resource of the post-industrial society is its scientific personnel. Their distribution, by sector (industry, government, university) and by function (production, research, teaching), forms the start

TABLE 3-7

Distribution of Degrees by Discipline, 1954-1964 (Percentages)

DISCIPLINES	1954			1964		
	BACHELOR AND EQUIVA-LENT	MASTER AND EQUIVA-LENT	DOCTOR AND EQUIVA-LENT	BACHELOR AND EQUIVA-LENT	MASTER AND EQUIVA-LENT	DOCTOR AND EQUIVA-LENT
Natural and mathematical sciences as percentage of whole	28.0	21.7	48.1	26.1	27.3	49.7
Mathematics	1.4	1.3	2.8	4.0	3.9	4.2
Engineering	7.9	7.7	6.8	6.9	11.0	12.3
Physics	3.7	4.4	19.4	3.5	4.5	16.9
Biology	3.2	2.8	11.2	4.6	3.3	11.1
Health	8.2	3.0	2.1	5.2	2.3	1.3
Social sciences and humanities	72.0	78.3	51.9	73.9	72.7	50.3
Social sciences	12.1	7.1	12.1	15.7	9.5	12.3
Education	18.6	47.5	16.6	18.0	37.6	14.8
Total number	287,401	58,204	8,840	529,000	111,000	15,300

SOURCE: OECD, *Reviews of National Science Policy: United States*, p. 56.

of any coherent science policy on the use of scarce resources in the society.[73] The definitions of such personnel are complicated, particularly in the case of engineers. Many persons are classified as engineers, especially in industry, who have not received formal training or do not possess a degree from a college; on the other hand, because of their training, many engineers are engaged in managerial activities outside their original specialization. The restrictions are less true of scientists, though some number in recent years have turned to administration and educational innovation. In general, scientific personnel is defined as persons engaging in any scientific work requiring knowledge or training equivalent to at least four years of college and specializing in one of the scientific disciplines. A similar definition applies to engineers.

We draw our first classification from the census. For 1960, the census of skilled personnel showed that there were 335,000 scientists and 822,000 engineers.[74]

We can show three basic classifications: by discipline, by sector,

---

[73] The statistical material in this section is drawn principally from two reports: the OECD *Review of Science Policies;* and *American Science Manpower 1966*, A Report of the National Register of Scientific and Technical Personnel, National Science Foundation NSF 68-7 (Washington, D.C., 1968) supplemented by updated statistics from the U.S. Office of Education.

[74] The 1970 census data will not be available until after 1972. Where updating has been possible for partial series, the text and tables reflect this.

and by function, and, following this, by specialty and function in industry, in universities, and in government.

Figure 3–4 shows the distribution of engineers and scientists by discipline. It is striking that while the distribution of engineers is fairly even throughout the four major components of engineering (industrial, civil, electrical, and mechanical), the greater proportion of scientists is concentrated in two fields—the biological sciences and chemistry.

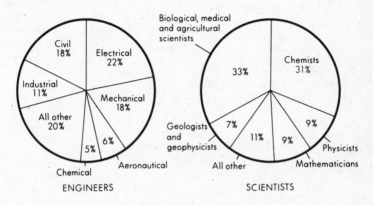

FIGURE 3–4

Distribution of Scientists and Engineers in 1960

SOURCE: OECD, *Reviews of National Science Policy: United States*, p. 207.

NOTE: Later figures show some slight change in proportions.

For engineers, figures cited for 1966 by the U.S. Department of Labor Bulletin 1606 (February 1969) show the following distribution: electrical, 20 percent; mechanical, 20 percent; civil, 20 percent; industrial, 11 percent; aeronautical, 6 percent; chemical, 5 percent.

As for scientists, a sampling by the National Science Foundation for 1970 (NSF 70-50) shows: chemists, 28 percent; physicists, 12 percent; mathematicians, 8 percent (plus 4 percent in computer sciences); biological and agricultural, 20 percent (excluding medical); earth and marine, 8 percent; atmosphere and space, 2 percent; other, 22 percent.

Table 3–8 shows the distribution of engineers and scientists by sector. Most engineers are still located primarily in manufacturing and secondarily in government; and while the single largest group of scientists is located in manufacturing, the universities and government combined employ the greater number.

If one takes the elite group and looks at the distribution of science and engineering doctorates by sector and area, one sees a heavy emphasis on the academic and research side and a concentration in the sciences. (See Tables 3–9, 3–10, and 3–11.)

TABLE 3–8

Distribution of Scientists and Engineers by Sector, 1960

SECTOR	SCIENTISTS AND ENGINEERS	ENGINEERS	SCIENTISTS
Total	1,157,300	822,000	335,300
Mining	31,600	19,100	12,400
Building and public works	55,100	52,700	2,400
Manufacturing industries	613,500	472,800	140,700
Transport, communications, and other services	61,500	58,800	2,800
Other industries	100,400	82,100	18,200
Government (Federal, state, and local)	170,100	109,400	60,700
Colleges and universities	125,100	27,000	98,100

SOURCE: OECD, *Reviews of National Science Policy: United States*, p. 208.

TABLE 3–9

Utilization of Science and Engineering Doctorates by Sector, 1969

SECTOR	PERCENTAGE
Academic	60
Private industry	26
Government	9
Other	5

SOURCE: National Science Foundation, *Science and Engineering Doctorates, Supply and Utilization* (NSF 71-20), May, 1971.

TABLE 3–10

Utilization of Science and Engineering Doctorates in Non-Academic Sector, 1969

SECTOR	PERCENTAGE
Research and Development	76
Other activities	24

SOURCE: National Science Foundation, *Science and Engineering Doctorates, Supply and Utilization*.

TABLE 3–11

*Distribution of Science
and Engineering Doctorates
by Field of Science, 1969*

FIELD	PERCENTAGE
Physical science	32
Life sciences	25
Mathematics	6
Engineering	15
Social sciences	22

SOURCE: National Science Foundation, *Science and Engineering Doctorates, Supply and Utilization.*

To illustrate the importance of the science-based industries, note the proportion of scientists and engineers to the total employment in each field. For 1962, the percentages were as follows: [75]

Manufacturing	3.0%
All chemicals	10.2%
Pharmaceuticals	16.9%
Electrical engineering	7.8%
Communications	12.3%
Aviation	12.4%
Scientific instruments	17.7%

The crucial question, of course, is what use is made of scientific personnel in each sector. The question, for example, of how many scientists are engaged in basic research compared to applied research (assuming one can draw these lines) can only be answered for smaller, more detailed samples. On the gross census level, we can deal with three main functions: production, research and development, and management and administration. All other functions, including teaching, are grouped as miscellaneous (Table 3–12).

A further classification of function by industry, university, and government is necessary to see the existing use of scientists and engineers.

Table 3–13 shows the distribution specialty and function of scientists and engineers employed in industry. Thirty percent of the total in industry are engaged in research and development. But 72.1 percent of the physicists and almost half of the mathematicians and

---

[75] By 1970, the figures had not changed significantly other than a shift to greater magnitudes in the proportion engaged in pharmaceuticals and instruments. NSF projections to 1975 indicate that 18.5 percent would be in pharmaceuticals and almost 26 percent in instruments.

TABLE 3-12

Distribution of Scientists and Engineers by Function, 1960 (Percentages)

PERSONNEL	PRODUCTION	RESEARCH AND DEVELOPMENT	MANAGEMENT AND ADMINISTRATION	MISCELLANEOUS
All scientists and engineers	35	34	7	24
Scientists	24	42	4	30
Engineers	41	30	8	21

SOURCE: OECD, *Reviews of National Policy: United States*, p. 210.

biologists are engaged in research. Yet the number of scientists doing work other than research is far from negligible. By the same token, half the mathematicians and half the chemists in industry are doing something far different from research.

Table 3-14 on universities uses a different set of figures. The data here are for 1965 and show that in that year higher education as a whole employed 261,000 scientists and engineers or more than twice the number employed in 1960 (see Table 3-8). The figures differ in part because of different counting techniques; that is, the 1960 figure was staff, while the 1965 figure included all persons employed at research centers in universities. Despite these differences, the figures reflect the sharp increase in half a decade in the number of scientists and engineers at universities. In 1965, in full-time equivalent, 61 percent of the personnel were engaged in teaching, 29 percent in research and development, and 10 percent in other activities (administration, etc.) Nearly all the personnel in the federal contract research centers attached to universities were doing research work, while only 29 percent of the 192,600 scientists and engineers who make up the university full-time personnel performed research as their major activity.

Finally we turn to the distribution of scientists and engineers employed in government. In 1962, approximately 144,000 scientists and engineers were employed by the government in federal laboratories or in administrative functions, representing 8 percent of federal employees. The Department of Defense employed the largest proportion of qualified persons, followed, surprisingly, by the Department of Agriculture. It is highly likely that later figures would show a considerable increase in the Department of Health, Education, and Welfare, reflecting the expansion of research in medicine and the life sciences in the past decade. In addition to direct government employment, one must count as well a total of 17,884 scientists and engineers employed (in 1965) in nonprofit organizations.

TABLE 3-13

Proportions of Scientists and Engineers Employed in Industry by Specialty and Principal Function, 1962

EMPLOYMENT	SCIENTISTS AND ENGINEERS	RESEARCH AND DEVELOPMENT	MANAGEMENT AND ADMINISTRATION		TECHNICAL COMMERCE, SALES AND MAINTENANCE SERVICES	PRODUCTION AND OPERATION	OTHER FUNCTIONS
			R & D	OTHER			
Total	100	30.1	5.5	12.6	10.9	34.3	6.5
Engineers	100	27.2	5.1	13.6	10.9	36.9	6.3
Physical sciences	100	44.9	7.6	8.4	8.0	24.6	6.5
Chemists	100	47.4	8.3	7.1	9.5	24.6	3.0
Physicists	100	72.1	12.6	2.8	3.0	7.0	2.4
Metallurgists	100	33.7	6.8	13.7	6.3	37.3	2.3
Geologists and geophysicists	100	6.8	2.3	16.3	2.8	38.1	33.6
Mathematicians	100	48.4	4.6	8.8	10.3	19.0	9.0
Life sciences	100	29.7	5.4	10.9	24.3	19.1	10.5
Medicine	100	17.8	5.0	9.0	44.2	7.8	16.1
Agriculture	100	18.7	5.3	20.0	13.3	27.3	15.4
Biology	100	48.0	5.9	4.7	18.5	20.7	2.2
Other scientists	100	33.4	13.6	10.6	9.3	12.1	21.0

SOURCE: OECD, *Reviews of National Science Policy: United States*, p. 211.

TABLE 3–14

Number of Scientists and Engineers, by Employment Status and by Field and Full-time Equivalent Number of Scientists and Engineers, by Function, in Universities and Colleges, 1965 (Thousands)

| ITEM | TOTAL | UNIVERSITIES AND COLLEGES PROPER | | OTHER INSTITUTIONS | FEDERAL CONTRACT RESEARCH CENTERS ATTACHED TO UNIVERSITIES |
		NUMBER	GRADUATE-DEGREE GRANTING INSTITUTIONS IN THE SCIENCES AND ENGINEERING		
Scientists and engineers, total	261.0	250.0	210.3	39.8	11.0
Employment status					
Full-time	158.9	148.8	118.1	30.6	10.1
Part-time	41.0	40.8	31.9	8.9	.2
Graduate students	61.1	60.4	60.2	.2	.7
Field					
Engineers	37.4	32.4	28.2	4.1	5.1
Physical scientists	67.6	62.4	49.6	12.7	5.2
Life scientists	101.2	100.7	93.6	7.1	.5
Psychologists	12.8	12.7	9.3	3.4	.1
Social scientists	40.8	40.7	29.0	11.7	.1
Other scientists	1.1	1.1	.5	.6	a
Full-time equivalent number of scientists and engineers, total	203.2	192.6	158.5	34.1	10.6
Function					
Teaching	117.7	117.7	85.1	32.6	a
Research and development	65.4	54.9	54.3	.6	10.5
Other activities	20.0	19.9	19.1	.9	.1

SOURCE: OECD, *Reviews of National Science Policy: United States*, p. 510.
a Less than 50.

The central group of the knowledge class are the individuals listed in the National Register of Scientific and Technical Personnel maintained by the National Science Foundation. These are the individuals who have the specialized talents that the government deems important to keep track of. They are, as the title of a NSF study indicates, America's Science Manpower. They are the upper class in the "Scientific City" of the day. As of 1968, they totalled 297,942 persons. In terms of disciplines, this is the breakdown:

Physical sciences	53 percent
Chemistry	32
Physics	11
Earth and marine	8
Atmosphere and space	2
Life sciences	20 percent
Biological	16
Agricultural	4
Mathematics and computer	11 percent
Mathematics	8
Computer	2
Statistics	1
Social sciences	17 percent
Psychology	8
Economics	4
Political science	2
Sociology	2
Linguistics	1
Anthropology	

The key figures are tabulated in Table 3–15. This provides a comprehensive overview of the scientific elite by numbers in each field, and the proportion of Ph.D. degree holders to all persons listed in the National Register.

This central group numbers 300,000 persons. One can say they have the crucial competences and the major talents of science. What is striking is that more than half of them are in the physical sciences, while only 17 percent are in the social sciences (half of these being psychologists). Since the end of World War II, the government has tended to concentrate its rewards in the physical sciences and the major graduate student aid has gone to those fields. Yet a change is now evident. In the recent years the major shift has been to the biological sciences and in the most recent period there has been an increase in the proportion of Ph.D. degrees in the life science field. Yet, inevitably, the necessary concerns with social policy will foster an increase in the number of economists and sociologists in the country.

If one looks at this central group, only 37 percent, as of 1968, possessed a Ph.D. An additional 29 percent had reached the master's level, and 30 percent held a bachelor's degree. These proportions can be expected to change over time, with a higher number, after the 1970s, holding higher degrees.

In the area of primary work activity, 32 percent are engaged in research and development, 21 percent in management and administration and 21 percent in teaching. Within the smaller group of Ph.D.

TABLE 3–15
Percentage of Ph.D. Degree Holders to Total NSF Registrants by Field, 1968

FIELD	TOTAL REGISTRANTS	PH.D. DEGREE HOLDERS		
		NUMBER	PERCENTAGE OF TOTAL	PERCENTAGE
All fields	297,942	111,206	37	100
Chemistry	93,788	28,973	31	26
Earth and marine	23,746	4,956	21	4
Atmosphere and space	5,745	514	9	—
Physics	32,491	14,311	44	13
Mathematics	24,477	6,929	28	6
Computer science	6,972	469	7	—
Agricultural science	12,740	2,332	18	2
Biological science	46,183	22,344	48	20
Psychology	23,077	14,794	64	13
Statistics	2,639	929	35	1
Economics	11,510	6,112	53	5
Sociology	6,638	3,396	51	3
Political science	5,176	3,034	59	3
Anthropology	1,219	1,158	95	1
Linguistics	1,541	955	62	1

SOURCE: *American Science Manpower, 1968.* A Report of the National Register of Scientific and Technical Personnel, National Science Foundation (Washington, D.C., 1970), NSF 70-50, p. 23.

holders some further refinements can be observed. Thus, the social sciences have a higher proportion of Ph.D. holders to total registrants than do the physical and natural sciences. For example, 95 percent of the anthropologists in the register have Ph.D.s, compared to 28 percent of the mathematicians or 53 percent of the economists. This difference reflects the fact that where employment opportunities are primarily in universities, as in the social sciences, the greater is the percentage of persons in those fields who hold a Ph.D. One-half (52 percent) of the doctorate scientists were in the physical and mathematical sciences, one-third were in the life sciences, and 11 percent were in the social sciences.

In terms of the type of employer (Table 3–16), more than half (58 percent) of the "upper class," the doctorate holders, were employed by educational institutions, and only 22 percent were employed by industry and business, a sharp contrast to the general occupational pattern of the "Scientific City" as a whole.

In terms of primary work activity of the "upper class" (Table 3–17), one-half (57 percent) of the doctorate holders were engaged primarily in some phase of research and development (compared to one-third of the "Scientific City"); and 30 percent of the doctorate holders reported teaching as their primary work activity.

TABLE 3-16

Percentage of Ph.D. Degree Holders to Total NSF Register by Type of Employer, 1968

| TYPE OF EMPLOYER | TOTAL REGISTRANTS | PH.D. DEGREE HOLDER | | TOTAL |
		NUMBER	PERCENTAGE OF REGISTRANTS	
All registrants	297,942	111,206	37	100
Educational institutions	117,746	64,624	55	58
Federal government	29,666	8,461	28	8
Other government	10,031	2,300	23	2
Non-profit organizations	11,204	4,937	44	4
Industry and business	95,776	24,099	25	22
Self-employed	6,462	1,945	30	2
Military	7,155	949	13	1
Other	1,729	549	32	—
No report	5,466	839	15	1

SOURCE: *American Science Manpower*, 1970, p. 23.

TABLE 3-17

Percentage of Ph.D. Degree Holders to Total NSF Register [a] by Primary Work Activity, 1968

| PRIMARY WORK ACTIVITY | PH.D. DEGREE HOLDER | |
	NUMBER	PERCENTAGE
All activities	111,206	100
Research and development	42,390	38
Basic Research	(26,727)	(24)
Applied research	(14,147)	(13)
Management or administration	21,069	19
Of research and development	(12,967)	(12)
Teaching	33,902	30
Production and inspection	782	1
Consulting	4,655	4
Exploration, forecasting, and reporting	1,099	1
Other	1,265	1
No report	3,541	3

SOURCE: *American Science Manpower*, 1970, p. 24.
NOTE: Subfigures are in parentheses. The totals of the subfigures do not always add up to the inclusive totals because of rounding.

[a] Total NSF Register is given in Tables 3-15 and 3-16.

In sum, we find that the place of the educated elite is at sharp variance with the population as a whole. Less than one-fourth are employed in business and more than half are in the universities; 24 percent are in basic research and half of them are involved in some form of research and development. While it would be too crude to say that business and the universities form completely different or even contrasting mentalities, it is clear that the *norms* of the two are different, and more importantly the social pressures (or to put the issue more technically, the "reference group") of the two differ. The ethos of the university is primarily liberal and while under that umbrella there is a wide spectrum of political differences, in most respects the elite is responsive largely to the ethos of its milieu. If one believes, as does Robert Heilbroner, that the expansion of science and scientifically based technology is creating the framework for a new social order that will erode capitalism, as the activities of the merchants and the bourgeois outside the landed economy undermined feudalism, then the significant fact is that most of the activities of science are outside the business system and the organization of science policy is not, in the first instance, responsive to business demand.[76] The necessary foundation for any new class is to have an independent institutional base outside the old dominant order. For the scientist this base has been the university. Whether the scientific community will be strong enough to maintain that independence remains to be seen. It is a question I return to in the Coda to this book.

THE FUTURE PROFILE OF THE HIGHER EDUCATED

The major problem for the post-industrial society will be adequate numbers of trained persons of professional and technical caliber. We assume, despite momentary dips, a continuing demand into the foreseeable future—and this is unique in human history. The expansion of the science-based industries will require more engineers, chemists, and mathematicians. The needs for social planning—in education, medicine, and urban affairs—will require large numbers of persons trained in the social and biological sciences. As the 1966 *Manpower Report* said:

Growth in research and development . . . can be expected to demand ever-rising number of experts in many professional and technical disciplines. In addition, greater number of city planners, engineers, and architects will be needed to rebuild and redesign blighted areas of many of our major metropolitan centers. Talents of a wide range of social scientists will be used to redeem human resources in these cities. Many more teachers will be needed. Among other occupations due for major increases are those involving personnel necessary to implement the new medicare pro-

[76] Robert Heilbroner, *The Limits of American Capitalism* (New York, 1966), pp. 114–120, 130–132.

gram and other programs developed by Federal, State and local government agencies to improve the health of the Nation's citizens.[77]

Short-range forecasts are fairly common. The college graduates of 1980 are already in high schools and one makes rough estimates of the proportion of college-age population who will go on to higher education—though the projections in the past have been notoriously faulty. On the basis of estimates by the U.S. Office of Education, the picture for 1977–1978 is shown in Table 3–18.

TABLE 3–18

Education in 1964 and 1967 Projected to 1977, Growth Rate, 1964–1977

	1964	1967	1977	GROWTH RATE 1964–1977 (percentage)
School population (in millions)	48.1	56.7	62.6	30
Enrollment in higher education (in millions)	5.0	6.9	10.6	112
Higher education degrees	635,300	856,000	1,297,600	104
Baccalaureates	529,000	685,000	980,000	85
Masters	111,000	148,800	273,700	147
Doctorates	15,300	22,000	43,900	187
Science	49.7%	51%	55.2%	—
Social science/humanities	50.3%	49%	44.8%	—
University staff (instructional)	420,000	478,000	665,000	58
Total educational expenditure (in billions)	38	54.3	76.3	101
Total expenditure on higher education (in billions)	11.9	18.8	30.3	155

SOURCE: *Projections of Educational Statistics to 1977*, HEW, 1969.
NOTES: The years given are academic years, thus, 1964 is 1964–1965, etc.
Degrees given include equivalents, thus are formally listed as Baccalaureates and the like, etc.
The dollar figures for 1964 are in 1963–1964 dollars, those for 1967 in 1967–1968 dollars, the projections in 1967–1968 dollars.

But how reliable are such projections? Our experience in the early 1970s, when the educational and research picture turned dim quite abruptly, provides some lessons in the hazards of forecasting. Most forecasters had simply projected the upward trends; yet they failed to take into account not only a set of political and sociological factors, but they had ignored crucial demographic indices as well. What was clear was that the period from 1955 to 1970 had been one of a

---

[77] U.S. Department of Labor, *Manpower Report of the President* (Washington, D.C., 1967), p. 44.

rapid and forced expansion of scientists and engineers, of research Ph.D.s and of college teachers as the universities struggled to keep up with the demand. What is equally clear is that the decade of 1970–1980 will be one of retrenchment. What had happened?

In the period from 1955 to 1970, three elements had conjoined. One was the extraordinary expansion of U.S. support for science following the launching by the Russians of their Sputnik spacecraft, and the consequent fear that U.S. scientific efforts were lagging. In 1955, slightly over $7 billion was spent for research and development, or about 1.65 percent of GNP. By 1960, the figure had risen to $13 billion, or 2.7 percent of GNP and by 1965 to $17.7 billion or 2.87 percent of GNP. Outlays for space research and technology went from $400 million in fiscal 1961 to $6 billion in 1966. By the mid-1960s, nearly 400,000 scientists and engineers, or about 30 percent the national total, were supported by federal funds, and more than half (55 percent) of all research and development scientists and engineers were dependent on federal monies for their work.

The second element was the sudden demographic upsurge in the college-age generation. From 1950 to 1960, the number of young persons aged 14 to 24 was almost constant, rising only slightly from 26.6 to 27.1 million. But in the 1960 decade, reflecting the postwar baby boom, the cohort jumped 44 percent, going from 27.1 million in 1960 to 39 million in 1969.

Added to this—the third element—was not only an increase in the total population who might seek to go to college, but a simultaneous rise in the *proportion* itself of the age cohort who would seek to enter college, a proportion rising from 27 percent in 1955 to 40 percent in 1965. For these two reasons, the colleges and the universities in the 1960s were swamped with new students, and they acted to expand accordingly.

To help meet the growing demand for college teachers and for scientists and engineers, the federal government, for the first time, heavily underwrote the support of graduate education. By the mid-1960s, of approximately 250,000 full-time graduate students, three out of five were receiving support in the form of a fellowship or scholarship. In the natural sciences, four out of every five graduate students received some such support; in the non-scientific fields the ratio was approximately one in two. As a result of this heavy demand and support—and also because the selective service gave students postponement from the draft—the proportion of college graduates who entered graduate or professional schools jumped enormously. In the fifteen years from 1950 to 1965, the proportion went from one in six to one in two. In most of the Ivy League schools, about 80 percent of the graduating classes went on to some form of post-graduate work.

The result of all this was an extraordinary upsurge in the number of persons with a doctorate degree in the society. As Dael Wolfle and Charles V. Kidd have pointed out, from 1861, when Yale became the first American university to grant the Ph.D. degree, through 1970, American universities awarded 340,000 doctorates; half of those degrees were earned in the last nine years of the period.[78]

By 1970, however, the market picture had changed. Many of the elements which conjoined to create the boom explain the decline. One was the demographic levelling-off of the rate of expansion of the college-age population. Though the absolute number continued to increase, *the bulge effect* had worn off. Second was the sharp cuts in federal spending in the three sectors which directly affected the universities: cuts in graduate support programs, cuts in research monies, and cuts in the space and defense-related industries which, for the first time, created heavy unemployment (running from 5 to 10 percent in different science and engineering disciplines) in educated manpower and reducing sharply the demand for scientists and engineers. And third was the combined effects of the recession and inflation which, together with the cuts in federal spending, created large deficits in almost all university budgets.

One result of all this is a set of very different employment prospects for the American educated elite and, for the first time, a real threat of "overproduction." More prolific than anyone had anticipated, graduate schools had been expanding degree output by nearly 14 percent a year rather than an anticipated 9 percent a year. As Allan M. Cartter has commented: "We have created a graduate education and research establishment in American universities that is about 30 to 50 percent larger than we shall effectively use in the 1970s and early 1980s." In the science area alone, according to Cartter, academic, research, and industry needs (based on replacement and 5 percent growth) would require between 210,000 and 255,000 new doctorates to 1985; at present levels we would be producing between 325,000 and 375,000 Ph.D.s in the next fifteen years.[79]

But what of beyond the 1980s? The future needs for educated manpower depend largely on three elements: the demographic balances; the demands of new technology; and the proportion of the age cohort that will go to college.

If one follows the reasoning of Wallace R. Brode, a former President of the American Association for the Advancement of Science, the surplus conditions of the 1970s and early 1980s will vanish by the

---

[78] Dael Wolfle and Charles V. Kidd, "The Future Market for Ph.D.'s," *Science*, vol. 173 (August 27, 1971), pp. 784–793.

[79] Allan M. Cartter, "Scientific Manpower for 1970–1985," *Science*, vol. 172 (April 9, 1971), pp. 132–140.

mid-1980s, and thereafter the country will face a real shortage of scientific and engineering manpower. Brode's reasoning is based on three factors: the continuation of the present technological growth rate, the peaking of the college-age population and then a down-turn in 1985, and a ceiling level in the proportion of scientists and engineers. Brode points out that since 1960, the annual number of college graduates in the natural sciences and engineering has been about 3.8 percent of the 22-year-olds. He considers this to be a natural ceiling set by the intellectual requirements of effective work in these fields. By computing the 3.8 percent against a projected trend of the number of students, he shows a surplus of bachelor's level scientists and engineers from 1968 to 1986 followed by a shortage lasting from 1987 to 2005. "After 1983," Brode writes, "the excess of scientists and engineers will taper off and by 1987 to the end of the century we are going to have a real shortage of scientists and engineers. If, by 1990, the scientist has maintained and improved his technical abilities, he can just about write his own ticket."

Since the surplus of scientists and engineers in the next decade will probably be not more than 10 percent of the supply by 1983, Brode advocates a "holding pattern" to preserve the temporary excess of technologists. "We should establish," he writes "through private, federal and state funding, technical programs in such areas as health, environmental improvement, pollution eradication, education, post-doctoral studies, updating courses, and basic research, in order to retain trained scientists and engineers and to expand their capability. In the period from 1970 to 1980, these workers will produce much of value and importance to the nation. In the decades after 1980, these scientists in the holding pattern would be prepared to fill important and much needed demands in industry, government and education." [80]

The overall picture, however, of the knowledge society depends on how far we go in completing the revolution in higher education which began after World War II. In the 1920s, the United States took the first major step in the expansion of education by making secondary education compulsory for almost all by abolishing child labor, raising the school-age-leaving level, and increasing vastly the monies available for education. Today 93 percent of all youths in their age cohort enter high school, and 80 percent of that total complete their high school education.

As regards higher education, until 1945, college was largely for a small elite. From 1945 to 1970 we moved to mass higher education. (Today about 50 percent of the high school graduates enter college

[80] Wallace R. Brode, "Manpower in Science and Engineering, Based on a Saturation Model," *Science*, vol. 173 (July 16, 1971), pp. 206–213; citation from pp. 208–209.

and 21 percent of all youths complete college.) The question is whether from 1970 to the year 2000 we will move to universal-*access* higher education.

We can turn to one set of detailed projections.

Between 1960 and 1980, the college-age population (18 to 21) will have increased by about 7 million; by the turn of the century it is likely to climb by another 7 million.[81] The crucial question is what proportion of this group will go on to college. Allan M. Cartter and Robert Farrell have made some estimates on higher education to the last third of the century.[82] Table 3–19 summarizes the historical relationship between the 18 to 21 age group and undergraduate enrollment. The pattern of college attendance has changed markedly in the first two-thirds of the century, for the attendance ratio has risen steadily from about .04 to .40, with only a minor break during war years. (In view of the age dispersion of college students noted in Note 81, these figures are expressed as attendance *ratios* rather than as percentages of the age group.) The lower half of the table projects five attendance ratios to the year 2000.

Applying various attendance rates to the population projections, Cartter and Farrell give a variety of estimates for future undergraduate enrollments (Table 3–20). These are baselines and can be employed as rough indicators, but as Alice Rivlin has remarked: "It does not seem likely that anything useful can be accomplished by fitting more trend curves to the same basic data on enrollment ratios. . . . It is time to begin looking at college enrollment as a dependent variable." [83]

The chief problem, in the past, has been that all projections vastly underestimated the proportion of high school youths who would go on to college, and planning was woefully inadequate. There was no "theory" about who would go to college; there was little expectation that the various states would respond so quickly to the postwar situation and expand the educational plant so rapidly.

If one is to look ahead to the year 2000 and consider the question of whether the number of educated persons will continue to match

[81] The 18–21 age group is not a completely reliable guide for purposes of projection, since about 33 percent of the present college and university students fall outside this range. According to the 1960 census, the age distribution of undergraduates was as follows:

Under 18	18–21	22–24	25–29	30 and over
2.2%	67.7%	13.9%	11.2%	5.0%

Yet for comparative purposes, over time, we use the 18–21 age group as a "convention."

[82] Allan M. Cartter and Robert Farrell, "Higher Education in the Last Third of the Century," *The Educational Record* (Spring, 1965), p. 121.

[83] Alice Rivlin, "The Demand for Higher Education," in *Microanalysis of Socio-Economic Systems* (New York, 1961), p. 216; cited by Folger, op. cit., p. 144.

TABLE 3-19
Historical and Projected Relationships of Undergraduates to the 18–21 Age Group

YEAR	18–21 AGE GROUP (MILLIONS)	RATIO OF UNDERGRADUATES TO 18–21 AGE GROUP
1889	5,160	.030
1899	5,931	.039
1909	7,202	.048
1919	7,312	.080
1929	8,901	.118
1935	9,236	.122
1945	9,558	.163
1955	8,508	.276
1960	9,546	.345
1964	11,282	.400

		PROJECTIONS				
		S_1	S_2	S_3	S_4	S_5
1965	12,282	.400	.416	.387	.412	.416
1970	14,278	.400	.459	.433	.468	.459
1975	16,107	.400	.483	.475	.519	.507
1980	16,790	.400	.483	.527	.566	.560
1985	16,957	.400	.483	.552	.607	.618
1990	18,880	.400	.483	.552	.645	.682
1995	21,570	.400	.483	.552	.679	.753
2000	23,730	.400	.483	.552	.710	.832

SOURCE: Allan M. Cartter and Robert Farrell, "Higher Education in the Last Third of the Century," *The Educational Record* (Spring, 1965), p. 121.

Derived from: Column 1: Historical data from the Bureau of the Census. Projections through 1980 appear in the Bureau of the Census, *Current Population Reports*, Series P-25, No. 286 (July 1964, Series B data). After 1980, data were supplied to the American Council on Education by the Bureau of the Census. Data are as of July of the year indicated.

Column 2: Ratios for 1889–1955 are based on resident degree-credit series presented in U.S. Office of Education, *Biennial Survey of Education, 1957–58*, chap. 4, sec. 1, p. 7. Ratios for 1960 and 1964 are derived from U.S.O.E. *Opening Fall Enrollment* series and *Enrollment for Advanced Degrees*.

NOTE: S_1 assumes a constant ratio at the 1964 level—an unlikely state of affairs, and one already disproved by the early reports of 1965 enrollments. S_2 assumes that the ratio will increase at a constant rate of 2 percent per year through 1970, then increase at a rate of 1 percent through 1975, and finally level off at its 1975 level. S_3 is based on Office of Education projections through 1975, then assumes a decline in the rate of increase until a constant ratio is achieved in 1985. S_4 is hyperbolic in form, rising at a constantly declining rate. S_5 assumes a constant 2 percent per year increase in the attendance ratio after 1965 (which would provide a statistically possible, but improbable, ratio of more than 1.0 by the year 2010).

TABLE 3-20

*Undergraduate Degree-Credit Enrollment, Fall 1960 and
Projected Through Fall 2000 (Thousands)*

YEAR	SERIES 1	SERIES 2	SERIES 3	SERIES 4	SERIES 5
1960	3,296	3,296	3,296	3,296	3,296
1965	4,829	5,021	4,675	4,973	5,021
1970	5,711	6,556	6,182	6,688	6,556
1975	6,443	7,773	7,655	8,366	8,166
1980	6,716	8,103	8,843	9,495	9,397
1985	6,783	8,183	9,367	10,296	10,478
1990	7,552	9,111	10,429	12,176	12,881
1995	8,628	10,410	11,915	14,648	16,249
2000	9,492	11,452	13,108	16,648	19,739

SOURCE: See Cartter and Farrell, "Higher Education in the Last Third of the Century," p. 122.

NOTE: Series 1 merely illustrates the effect of the growth in the size of the college-age population, indicating that undergraduate enrollments would grow from 3.3 million in 1960 to approximately 9.5 million by the end of the century even if there were no further change in attendance rates. Series 2 is a conservative estimate, rising to 11.4 millions. The authors hazard the guess that Series 3 and 4 are the more likely indicators of the magnitude of the impending expansion, with undergraduate enrollments rising to 10 million by the late 1980s, and to between 13 and 16 million by the year 2000. Series 5 is probably the outside limit for periods ten or more years ahead.

the demand, the central fact is that the college population, by and large, is still drawn principally from the middle class. As Martin Trow has remarked: "With all of the expansion of educational opportunities in the United States, there is still a very sizeable body of students who have the ability for college work but never get there. In [a study of the California state system, it was found] that nearly half (47 percent) of the high school graduates in the top 20 percent of academic ability whose fathers were manual workers did not go on to college (though some of them may after a period of working or in military service). This compares with 25 percent of the students in the same ability brackets from middle-class homes who did not go on to college."

A study by John K. Folger and his associates for the Russell Sage Foundation summarized the effects of socio-economic status on educational progress by comparing two *high school* groups who came equally from the top fifth of their age group in academic aptitude and differed only on socio-economic status, one in the top quintile of socio-economic status, the second in the bottom quintile. The groups graduated in 1960.

Of the high socio-economic status, high-ability group of 100 male, high school graduates: 9 did not go to college; 9 went to a junior college (3 of these also finished senior college); and 82 went to a senior college (63 of these graduated from senior college). Of the 66 who received a bachelor's degree, 36 continued immediately in graduate or professional school.

Of the low socio-economic status, high-ability group of 100 male high school graduates: 31 did not go to college; 17 went to a junior college (5 of these also finished senior college); and 52 went to a senior college (32 of these graduated from senior college). Of the 37 who received a bachelor's degree, 15 went on immediately to graduate or professional school.

Thus, in the early 1960s, a bright but poor boy had only about 55 percent as much chance of completing college within five years as his well-to-do counterpart, and only about 40 percent as much chance of doing post-graduate work.[84]

If there is going to be a continuing expansion of the proportion of high school graduates going on to college, it is clear that in the succeeding decades a larger number will have to be drawn from working class families. But why don't the children of working-class homes go on to college? The usual assumption has been that the failure is due largely to discriminatory barriers—that working-class children could not afford to go to college, were needed as early wage earners to contribute to the family, and so on. More recently, however, some sociologists have raised the question whether working-class children really want to go on to higher education. As John Porter has posed the issue:

One of the recurring questions is whether or not mobility values are part of a common values system for the whole society, or whether they are middle-class subcultural values. . . . In the light of the evidence that levels of aspiration and attitudes to education vary so much by class, one wonders how it could ever be claimed that, as part of the common value system, all Americans are achievement-oriented or share in a great quest for opportunity. . . . The notion of common values about mobility has serious implications when social policies assume—something like the old instinct theory—that by providing certain opportunities where they did not previously exist, latent mobility aspirations and achievement motives will be triggered and the previously deprived will be brought into

---

[84] Martin Trow, "The Democratization of Higher Education in America," *European Journal of Sociology*, vol. III, no. 2 (1962), p. 255. John K. Folger, Helen S. Austin, and Alan E. Bayer, *Human Resources and Advanced Education*, Russell Sage Foundation (1970), pp. 321–322.

the mainstream of an upwardly mobile and achievement-oriented society.[85]

Porter is dubious about this proposition, and argues that the new stage of major industrial societies (which he calls "postmodern") may face a shortage of highly trained manpower in consequence of these differences in values. The question is a relevant one and is not resolvable by opinion. If some of the data cited by Trow, however, are relevant, then it seems likely that going to college or not going to college is not the issue for working-class children, but *what kind of college* to go to. A study carried out both in the Midwest and in California on the effect of the availability of public institutions on the proportions of students from working-class families, compared to other class groups who attended college, showed that while students from professional and other white-collar backgrounds are much more likely to go to college out of town than working-class students, the students from working- and lower middle-class homes are about as likely to go to a local public junior college as are boys and girls from wealthier homes.

As Trow reports: "Where there is a local public junior college in the community, half of the boys from lower-class backgrounds went on to college, as compared with only 15% of boys from similar backgrounds living in communities with no local college. The presence of a four year state college (usually somewhat more selective, somewhat less vocational than the junior college) in the community raised college going rates among these lower-class boys to nearly a third." [86]

Predicting the future college enrollments has become increasingly hazardous. For one, now that births can be better controlled, the birth rate, paradoxically, is less predictable since couples can decide more easily if and at what time in their marriage they want children. The birth *rate* has been slowing down, but because of the broader base of the child-bearing group, the absolute number of the population may increase by about sixty to seventy million by the year 2000. The loosening of educational structures allows more persons to drop out for a while and then come back in. The shape of the labor market for college graduates itself is subject to uncertain change. Yet if a social policy decision is made to facilitate a minimum of 50 percent of all persons of college age to have access to higher education (it was about 2 percent in 1870), then certain rough predictions can be made. According to a 1971 report of the Carnegie Commission on Higher

---

[85] John Porter, "The Future of Upward Mobility," *American Sociological Review*, vol. 33, no. 1 (February 1968), pp. 12–13.
[86] Martin Trow, op. cit., pp. 255–256.

Education, the pattern from 1960 to the year 2000 will be one of Go-Stop-Go. In the decade from 1960 to 1970, enrollments doubled. From 1970 to 1980 it will have increased by one-half. From 1980 to 1990 there will be no change in enrollments, and from 1990 to 2000 the increase will be by one-third. By 1980, there would be 12,500,000 enrollments, by 1990, 12,300,000, and by 2000, about 16,000,000. The Carnegie Commission expects that the additional new students could be mostly absorbed by 1980 (and 1990) within the existing 2800 campuses. Nor is there any further need for more research-type universities granting the Ph.D. The major growth need for the year 2000 would be in community colleges and comprehensive colleges primarily in metropolitan areas.

What can we conclude from all this? By the year 2000, the United States will have become, in gross terms, a mass knowledge society. Thirty years hence, the enrollment in higher education will be roughly ten times greater than what it was thirty years before in 1940. And where in 1940, there were roughly 150,000 in the college faculty, thirty years from now the figure will probably be ten times as large as well. By the end of this decade, the number of Ph.Ds. granted will probably level off to about 40,000 to 45,000 annually so that by the end of the century there will be about a million persons in the society holding a Ph.D. degree.

And yet such a mass itself loses its distinction and the idea of higher education in and of itself loses its elite quality. What becomes most relevant are the distinctions within the knowledge society itself. And the fact that the educational system of the society is divided, as it is, among a community college, public university and small private college system, in effect tends to repeat and perpetuate the trifurcation of an elite, privileged, and educated mass and reinforce the class divisions within the structure of the "Scientific City" itself.

INSTITUTIONAL STRUCTURE

If one thinks of the major institutional sectors of the society as the polity, the economy, the intellectual system, the cultural and entertainment structures, the religious system, and the kinship system, then what is noteworthy is the high degree of dependence of the intellectual system—largely the educational system and the organization of basic research and scholarship—on government. In the economy, there is an indirect political management by government through the control of the levels of money and the rate of growth through fiscal policies, and there is, increasingly, a direct share of purchases of goods by government; yet in the economy there is also a high degree of independence of the operating units (corporations and firms), despite many government regulatory agencies. Similarly, the cultural and entertainment structures, despite the regulation of television and radio by government, are largely dependent on the market; and, in the case of serious works, to a small extent on foundations and patronage for support. The religious institutions are almost entirely dependent on private support and the family, except for welfare recipients, exists as an autonomous institution.

Educational institutions depend on the polity because of three factors: first, education has been traditionally a public function, in which the states have had primary responsibility for elementary and secondary education; second, the balance between private and public higher education in which, historically, the greater number of advanced students were educated in private schools (though a large number of the colleges were church-supported) has shifted so that today the larger number of students are in publicly supported institutions of higher learning; and third, the increasing dependence of the entire educational system on federal financing, particularly in higher education. This takes various forms—the dependence of private colleges on the government for student stipends, particularly in graduate work; the increasing use of loans from government for construction of college facilities; and the dependence of research on the federal government for its money—to the extent that about three-fourths of all research funds today are supplied by the federal government.

And yet, despite this extraordinary dependency on government, which, of course, is not unique to the United States, there is little or no centralized control of the education system. In France, for example, a centralized ministry is responsible for uniform curricula, examinations, and all (except denominational) universities. There is also in the United States little organized direction of research and planned allocations, such as, for example, the academy system provides in the Soviet Union. Instead, we have what is called "administrative pluralism," which is sometimes a euphemism for disorganization and disarray. There is no centralized research budget, or any set of coordinated policies. Responsibilities are distributed throughout the federal departments, in addition to a host of independent agencies such as the Atomic Energy Commission, the National Science Foundation, the Office of Science and Technology, and the like. In 1968, Alan Pifer summed up this high degree of decentralization in the organization of education:

Looking at the "structure" of higher education, [an outside] observer would discover some 2,200 institutions of widely varying types and wildly varying standards. He would find that some of these institutions are publicly controlled, some privately, with some of the latter church-related and some not. He would also find 50 separate state systems of higher education, all different, and with the exception of some regional coordination, not related to each other in such a way as to add up collectively to anything like a national system of education. . . . Our observer would be even more surprised when he looked at the role of the national government in regard to higher education. Here he would discover: that there is no clearly expressed and clearly understood federal role . . . that the federal role in higher education (with the exception of that mandated in the Land-Grant Acts) has over the years been only a by-product of other federal purposes, such as the support of research or discharge of responsibilities to war veterans or to the disadvantaged. . . . Only recently has the federal government begun to support higher education for its own sake and in so doing only on a hesitant, fragmented basis that could best be described as backing into a federal policy. . . . At the present time every federal department except the Post Office and Treasury and at least 16 independent agencies have direct relationships with institutions of higher education and that the Office of Education alone is responsible for administering over 60 separate programs in this area under the authorization of 15 different legislative enactments. Finally, he would find out that there is no single place in the federal government where all this activity is directed or coordinated, or its collective impact on the colleges and universities even assessed—no locus of concern about the health and welfare of higher education per se.[87]

This picture, which has become the conventional view of American higher education, fails, however, to indicate the degree of *concentration* of resources—that is, students and research money—in a comparatively *small* number of universities. If we trace the degree of concentration from the abundance of statistics, we find that of the 2,500 institutions of higher education in the United States, there are only 159 universities. Attending these 159 universities, however, were nearly one-third of all students in the United States and nearly one-half of all students in four-year degree institutions.[88]

The concentration can be traced by another measure. Between 1940 and 1960 college enrollment increased from 1.4 million to 3.6 million, but institutions which were founded after 1940 accounted for only about 10 percent of the increase. Thus existing institutions approximately doubled in size. But the large universities accounted for the greatest concentrations of all. In 1964, thirty-five universities, or only 1.6 percent of the number of all institutions, accounted for more than 20 percent of student enrollments. A hundred and four schools, or less than 5 percent of the total, accounted for 40 percent of the enrollments (Table 3–21).

[87] Alan Pifer, "Toward a Coherent Set of National Policies for Higher Education," address to the Association of American Colleges (January 16, 1968).

[88] *Digest of Educational Statistics, 1966*, U.S. Office of Education (Washington, D.C., 1966), table 99, p. 78.

TABLE 3–21

Number of Institutions of Higher Education, by Size of Degree-Credit Enrollment, United States and Outlying Areas, Fall 1969

NUMBER OF STUDENTS ENROLLED	INSTITUTIONS		ENROLLMENT	
	NUMBER	PERCENTAGE	NUMBER	PERCENTAGE
Total	2,525	100.0	7,917,000	100.0
Under 200	273	10.8	29,690	—
200–499	369	14.6	128,340	1.6
500–999	570	22.5	421,130	5.3
1,000–2,499	618	24.4	966,420	12.2
2,500–4,999	287	11.4	1,019,490	12.8
5,000–9,999	229	9.0	1,656,750	20.0
10,000–19,999	114	4.5	1,589,320	20.0
20,000–29,999	39	1.5	924,830	11.6
30,000 or more	26	1.0	1,180,980	14.9

SOURCE: *Digest of Educational Statistics, 1970*, U.S. Office of Education, 1970, p. 85.

Within the university world itself, there is a high degree of concentration. Of the 2,500 colleges and universities in the country, one hundred carry out more than 93 percent of the research. And, within this circle, twenty-one universities carried out 54 percent of all university research, and ten universities carried out 38 percent of university research.[89]

Given this degree of concentration, one can say that on the elite level, there is a national system of education and university research, characterized by a number of indicators. These are the universities which are most responsive to "national needs," in that they undertake such diverse work as the expansion of foreign-area training (Russian, Chinese, Latin American studies), oceanography, space, health, urban affairs; these are also the universities which have direct ties with government, often by the loan of personnel not only for high-level administrative jobs but also for such diverse tasks as foreign aid, economic development, technical assistance, and the like; within this university system there is a high degree of mobility and a strengthening of professional ties between key persons.

I have argued that the university increasingly becomes the primary

---

[89] The first ten, in order, are: University of California (combined), Massachusetts Institute of Technology, Columbia, University of Michigan, Harvard, University of Illinois, Stanford, University of Chicago, Minnesota, and Cornell.

The others, not in order are Yale, Princeton, Pennsylvania, North Carolina, Wisconsin, Michigan State, Ohio State, New York University, California Institute of Technology, Rochester, and Washington.

institution of the post-industrial society.[90] In the past twenty years, the university—and by "the university" I have in mind the elite group—has taken on a vast number of enlarged functions: in basic research, as a service institution, and in the expansion of general education. In one sense, none of the specific functions is new, since the university, when it first undertook the organization of graduate schools, going back to Johns Hopkins and Chicago, had these functions in mind. What is new is the vast change of scale. The majority of research scientists in basic research today are in the universities; the university serves as the source for the specialized intellectual personnel needed in government and public organizations; even the majority of critics and writers today are employed in the university. The university has become the center of establishment culture. The unrest of the students in the mid-1960s was itself a significant sign of protest against the neglect of traditional teaching functions and the inattention to the student. But the singular fact is that, lacking any organized academy system, the government has forced on the university, willy nilly, a huge array of tasks that in other countries are performed outside the university system. It is not the traditional dependence of the educational system on the polity which is the important dimension of the postwar society but the "scientific-administrative complex" which represents an intermingling of government, science and the university unprecedented in American history. While it is often mentioned that in his "farewell speech" President Eisenhower warned against the military-industrial complex, it is seldom recalled that in the same speech President Eisenhower balanced his sentence with an equal warning against the scientific-administrative complex which he felt also represented an undue concentration of influence.

If, as is projected to the end of the century, we may see a doubling of student enrollments in higher education, there is a very significant question whether the existing concentration of elite universities will continue. Much depends upon the source of the student body. If a significant proportion is recruited from the children of working-class parents, it is likely that the greater number will go on to junior colleges. The junior colleges have been the fastest-growing segment of the American education scene. In 1930, there were 217 junior colleges; by 1950 the number had jumped to 528; by 1968 there were 802 junior colleges in the country. The elite private schools, universities, and colleges have begun to limit enrollment, in contrast to the major state universities, such as Wisconsin, Ohio, Minnesota, Michigan, and the California schools, which have expanded enormously. As

---

[90] See Daniel Bell, *The Reforming of the General Education* (New York, 1966), chap. 3.

Jencks and Riesman have noted: "The private sector's share of the market, which had hovered around 50 percent from 1910 to 1950 started falling about 1 percent annually. It was 36 percent in 1964 and is expected to be about 20 percent in 1980. Limiting enrollment had two consequences. One, it raised the ability of the average student, making private colleges relatively more attractive to both students and faculty, and probably indirectly raising the cash value of their degrees. Two, it meant that the philanthropic income did not have to be spread so thin." [91]

Over the years, the number of elite schools has remained comparatively stable (though there have been changes of standing within the group). Whether this will continue is an open question.

Despite the enormous sums spent by the United States government on research (for details, see the next section), there is no central science or research budget in the government, no set of priorities or objectives, no evaluation, no long-range planning as to fields of necessary interest or kinds of manpower to be encouraged. Beginning with the Manhattan District, which produced the atomic bomb, American research policy has been overwhelmingly "mission-oriented," and each sector of the government—defense, health, atomic energy, space—determines its own missions, the monies being subject to some review by the Budget Bureau and the allocation by Congress. Because of this mission-orientation, there is no system in which existing laboratories or resources belonging to one agency or department are able to put their resources, manpower, and facilities at the service of another. As fresh needs, urgencies, and priorities develop, new research facilities, organizations, and laboratories, and new arrangements with universities are created to meet these fresh tasks. Because needs were often urgently defined, and capacities were unavailable within government, a whole host of "federal contract" devices, with newly established non-profit corporations and universities, was designed in which these tasks were performed outside of government. So scattered and dispersed are the institutional structures of science and research activities of the government that there is no single description extant of its range and structure!

Within the Executive Office of the President, there was the President's Special Assistant for Science and Technology, created in 1957. He served as chairman of the Office of Science and Technology (OST, created in 1962), the President's Science Advisory Committee (PSAC, 1957), the Federal Council for Science and Technology

[91] Christopher Jencks and David Reisman, *The Academic Revolution* (New York, 1968), p. 272. In 1970, the private colleges and universities enrolled less than 30 percent of all students.

(FCST, 1959) and as a member of the Defense Science Board of the Department of Defense.

The President's science advisor is supposed to have an overall view of federal science policy, but his position is weakened by the fact that almost 90 percent of the expenditures for research and development are expended by four agencies—defense, atomic energy, space, and health—and the science advisor has little say in their activities. The President's Science Advisory Committee is a government agency whose membership is drawn from outside the government. It is a policy advisory body charged with defining necessary new areas of science expenditures, and assessing the balance of science resources between science and technology and military and non-military uses. But on actual political issues, it has had little influence.

In the Nixon administration, the role of the science advisor was reduced considerably and in January 1973, the Office of Science and Technology was abolished; some of its functions were distributed among other agencies, principally the National Science Foundation. What it meant concretely was that the scientific community no longer had direct access to the President as it had from 1945 to 1968.

Because research budgets are primarily in the hands of the different federal agencies, a multifarious system has developed which varies from agency to agency. The National Aeronautics and Space Agency (NASA) built a large in-house technical capacity, but much of its development work was contracted with private industry. The Atomic Energy Commission (AEC) has created a large number of national laboratories, but in almost all instances these are managed, under contract, by universities (e.g. the Argonne laboratory at Chicago by the University of Chicago), a consortium of universities (e.g. the Brookhaven laboratory on Long Island) or a private corporation (Oak Ridge, managed by Union Carbide, or Sandia by Western Electric). The Defense Department has a wide variety of devices. Applied research and development may be evaluated by nonprofit corporations, such as Rand, or the Institute of Defense Analysis; exploratory research may be handled on contract with universities, such as the Lincoln Lab at MIT; design work may be handled by nonprofit corporations which had been created by universities, such as MITRE from MIT or the Riverside Institute from Columbia; development work would be handled by nonprofit corporations such as the Aerospace Corporation, and production by major corporations such as Lockheed, Boeing, etc. In the health field, there has been a move toward the setting up of government institutes, and the National Institutes of Health, created in 1948, today comprise nine institutes. The National Institutes of Health are responsible for nearly 40 percent of the total American expenditure on medical research. From the start, NIH was empowered to make research grants as well as to operate its own research facilities. At the start, these activities were in equal balance. Since then, the weight of activities has swung largely to research grants; and in 1966, about $912 million was disbursed in contracts and $218 million for in-house operations. (As a measure of the expansion of these activities, in 1950 some $30 million was spent in research and $15 million in direct operations.)

In general, the institutional structure of U.S. science policy until now has been marked by two features: where special tasks are defined, particularly in new fields, applied research and development, new institutional groupings and forms have been created ad hoc to meet these missions; in pure and basic research, money has been given, on a project basis, to individuals who have been able to convince juries or research panels of the worthiness of the project or their competence as researchers.

This double feature of *mission-orientation* and *project grants* has had the unique quality of encouraging a high degree of success, by concentrating on the specific mission and mobilizing large resources for the tasks, and by stimulating a high research productivity by individuals who can prove themselves very quickly (compared to the European pattern, where a research man may be "indentured" for a long time to a specific professor). The drawbacks are equally obvious: there is a loss of sustained institution-building, either as an in-house capacity of government, or even in a university, since in most cases research facilities are provided largely for individuals or small teams, not for the institution. (The university, Clark Kerr has remarked wryly, has as often as not simply been a hotel.) Nor is there the possibility for sustained, long-run research since the project system tends to emphasize specific and identifiable bits of research that can be completed in two or three years.

In the larger, political context, the lack of a unified science policy, or a major academy or ministerial system, has meant that the "technocratic potential" inherent in the growing influence of science and the nature of technical decision-making is minimized in the American system. Science itself has simply become a constituency, but with no inherent unity other than some major professional associations and the political role of older clique groups who had played influential roles during World War II and shortly after. As a constituency, it is one more claimant on the national resources, like industry, labor, farmers, or the poor, although much of its "business" is done with the executive agencies, rather than with Congress. But power, in science policy, has rested with the political and bureaucratic interests of the major agencies—Defense, Atomic Energy, and Space—rather than with the scientific community, or even an overall political policy body for science.

THE ALLOCATION OF RESOURCES

By common agreement, the "financial" measure of the growth of science and technology has become the expenditures on research and development (R & D). Efforts have been made to relate the expenditures of R & D to economic growth, to scientific productivity, to the acceleration of the pace of invention, to the shortening of time between invention and production, and the like. There are analytical problems in each of these alleged relationships. What we can take as the simple indicator, however, is the commitment of a country to its scientific and technological potential by the expenditures on R & D, and, to a secondary extent, on education.

The United States, by devoting 3 percent of the GNP to research and development, in the words of the OECD report on science in the United States, became "a symbol for other countries which now regard this as a target to be reached." [92] From the end of the war and for the next two decades R & D expenditures in America multiplied by 15 times, and the total expenditure on education by six, whereas GNP itself has only tripled. In 1965, the United States was spending more than 9 percent of the total GNP on R & D and education.[93]

While international comparisons in this area are quite risky, a comparison between the American effort and those of Western Europe, Canada, and Japan reveals a very large gap, indeed. As a percentage of national product, R & D expenditure amounted to 2.3 percent in the United Kingdom, which is the country nearest to the magic 3 percent mark, and about 1.5 percent for the other large industrialized nations. In comparing the number of researchers with population, the United States had about four times as many as Germany, France, Belgium, or Canada, and more than twice as many as the United Kingdom or Japan (Table 3–22).

What is striking about the pattern of R & D expenditures is that the federal government supplied most of the funds while the work · was performed principally by industry, universities, and the nonprofit organizations. Without the lead of the federal government, there probably would have been little expansion in R & D in the

---

[92] OECD, *Reviews of National Science Policy: United States*, p. 29.

[93] The statistical data in this section, unless otherwise noted, have been taken from reports of the National Science Foundation, *National Patterns of R & D Resources*, Funds & Manpower in the United States (NSF 67-7); and *Federal Funds for Research, Development and Other Scientific Activities*, fiscal years 1966, 1967, and 1968, vol. XVI (NSF 67-19). Statistics dealing with the 1967–1970 period are from further NSF reports in the series and are cited in text.

TABLE 3–22

Comparison of the R & D Effort of the United States with That of Other Western States and Japan

STATE	GNP IN BILLIONS OF DOLLARS 1964	GNP PER CAPITA IN DOLLARS	POPULATION (IN MILLIONS) 1964	R & D EXPENDITURE			QUALIFIED R & D PERSONNEL [a]		
				(IN MILLIONS OF DOLLARS)	AS PERCENTAGE OF GNP	YEAR	TOTAL	NUMBER PER 10,000 POPULATION	YEAR
Germany	103.98	1,774	58.2	1,436	1.4	1964	33,382	6	1964
France	88.12	1,674	48.4	1,299	1.6	1963	32,382	7	1963
Italy	49.58	897	51.1	290	0.6	1963	19,415	4	1963
Belgium	15.44	1,502	9.3	123	0.9	1963	5,536	6	1963
Netherlands	16.86	1,385	12.1	314	1.9	1964	9,227	8	1964
EEC, excluding Luxembourg	273.98	—	179.6	3,462	1.4	1963–64	99,942	—	1963–64
United Kingdom	91.90	1,700	54.2	2,159	2.3	1964–65	59,415	11	1965
Sweden	17.47	2,281	7.6	253	1.5	1964	16,425	22	1964
Japan	69.08	622	96.9	892	1.5	1963	114,839	12	1964
Canada	43.54	2,109	19.2	425	1.0	1963	13,525	7	1963
United States	638.82	3,243	192.1	21,323 [b]	3.4	1963–64	474,900	25	1965

Source: OECD, *Reviews of National Science Policy: United States*, p. 32.

[a] Full-time equivalent.

[b] Estimated according to OECD standards and not according to those of the NSF.

United States. Federal expenditures on R & D between 1940 and 1964 grew at the average annual rate of 24.9 percent. In 1965, a total of $20.5 billion was spent on R & D, of which the federal government financed 64 percent of the total; industry contributed 32 percent, universities spent 3.1 percent, and nonprofit institutions 1 percent.[94] Yet only 15 percent of the work was done by the federal government; 70 percent was performed by industry, 12 percent by universities (including 3 percent at federal contract research centers) and 3 percent by nonprofit institutions. For fundamental research, the federal government provided about 64 percent of the funds, but the universities were the principal performers. Of almost $3 billion spent for fundamental research in 1965, 58 percent was used by universities, 21 percent by industry, and 7 percent by non-profit institutions (Table 3–23).

TABLE 3–23
Expenditures of Fundamental Research, 1965

ORIGIN OF FUNDS (MILLIONS OF DOLLARS)	FEDERAL GOVERN- MENT	INDUSTRY	UNIVERSITIES PROPER	UNIVERSITIES FCRC [a]	NON- PROFIT ORGANI- ZATIONS	TOTAL	PERCENT- AGE ORIGIN OF FUNDS
Federal government	424	191	920	198	118	1,851	63.0
			1,118				
Industry		416	25		16	457	16.0
Universities			473			473	16.0
Nonprofit organizations			74		71	145	5.0
Total	424	607	1,492	198	205	2,926	100.0
			1,690				
Percentage of performers	14.0	21.0	51	7	7.0	100	
			58.0				

SOURCE: OECD, Reviews of National Science Policy: United States, p. 34.
[a] Federal contract research centers.

[94] The proportion of public funds in other countries is considerably lower. In 1964, according to the OECD, it was:

Country	Percentage
France	63.3
United Kingdom	56.6
Sweden	47.7
Germany	40.4
Netherlands	40.0
Japan	27.8
Italy	33.1

If we think of R & D not just as contributing to economic growth, or being the engine of science and technology, but in *political* terms, then a very different picture of the American effort in that period emerges. The largest proportion of total R & D expenditures was spent for defense purposes. These direct expenditures (Department of Defense and certain Atomic Energy Commission programs) have fluctuated around 50 percent from 1953 to 1961 but, according to the NSF, decreased to 32 percent in 1965. But much of this offset in proportions was due to relatively increased spending for space, rather than domestic needs, and if, with the OECD report on science policy in the United States, we consider "as a single category" all *expenditures connected with external challenge*, it appears, from Table 3–24, that this political reason dictated more than 80 percent of all federal expenditures and more than 60 percent of the total R & D expenditure. (Since a large proportion of the privately financed industrial R & D was also connected with defense, the proportion of the total R & D related to the political response to external challenge is undoubtedly higher than 60 percent.)

Given this pattern, the considerable lead of the United States over other countries in R & D assumes a different proportion. For the

TABLE 3–24
Research and Development Linked with External Challenge, 1954–1967

FISCAL YEAR	FEDERAL R & D EXPENDITURE IN MILLIONS OF DOLLARS	R & D EXPENDITURE LINKED WITH EXTERNAL CHALLENGE (MILLIONS OF DOLLARS)	COLUMN 2 AS PERCENTAGE OF COLUMN 1	COLUMN 2 AS PERCENTAGE OF TOTAL R & D EXPENDITURE
1954	3,147	2,768	87.9	49.4
1955	3,308	2,896	87.5	46.7
1956	3,446	2,947	85.5	35.4
1957	4,462	3,775	84.6	39.5
1958	4,990	4,155	83.2	38.4
1959	5,803	4,766	82.1	38.5
1960	7,738	6,548	84.6	48.1
1961	9,278	7,917	85.3	55.3
1962	10,373	8,711	83.9	55.8
1963	11,988	10,068	83.9	58.1
1964	14,694	12,440	84.7	66.5
1965	14,875	12,580	84.6	62.2
1966	15,963	13,208	82.7	—
1967	16,152	12,941	80.1	—

SOURCE: OECD, *Reviews of National Science Policy: United States*, p. 38.
NOTE: The figures in column 2 are obtained by adding the expenditure of the Departments of Defense, NASA and about 50 percent of the expenditure of the Atomic Energy Commission which can, in the view of most experts, be regarded as "defense-oriented."

United Kingdom devoted about 33 percent of its R & D expenditure to military research and defense (including military atomic research); Germany, 17 percent to atomic, space, and military research; Italy, 21 percent; Canada, 23 percent; Japan, 3 percent; and France, 45 percent (of which 22 percent is devoted to atomic research). To this extent it is clear that the driving force of the American government in financing R & D is primarily related to political objectives, as is, in fact, the proportions spent by the state in any country.

What of the future? Research and development expenditures rose at a compound annual rate of 12.1 percent, from $5.2 billion in 1953 to about $20.5 billion in 1965. Over the same period, GNP rose by a compounded rate of 5.3 percent. But the average growth rate in R & D, measured from the survey base year of 1953, has been falling since it peaked at 17.6 percent in 1953–1956. In the 1964–1965 period, while GNP moved upward to 7.8 percent, R & D slowed down to a 6.7 percent increase, the first period in which the percentage increase in research and development was less than that for the economy as a whole.

Research and development manpower, the most critical component of research, grew faster than the country's civilian labor force during the decade of 1954–1965, advancing from 237,000 to 504,000 persons, an annual rate of 7.1 percent compared with the 1.5 percent for the labor force as a whole. As a percentage of the labor force, the number of R & D scientists moved from 0.37 to 0.68 percent in that same period. Industry, in 1965, as in the past, was the largest employer of R & D scientists and engineers, reporting 351,200 in full-time equivalent numbers or around 70 percent of the 503,600 total. The federal government employed 69,000 professional scientific and engineering personnel or about 14 percent of the total. The universities and colleges employed 66,000 R & D scientists and engineers for 13 percent of the total, 54,900 of them in universities and colleges proper. Three percent of the R & D scientists worked in the other non-profit sector. This percentage distribution was close to the pattern of 1958 (Table 3–25).

Research and development data are classified by the National Science Foundation into funds allocated for *development, applied research,* and *basic research.* (Federal obligations for total research are shown in Table 3–26.) Development is defined as the design and testing of specific prototypes and processes to meet a specific functional (e.g. defense) or economic requirement. Applied research is defined as the first pilot steps in translating existing knowledge into applications. And basic research is defined "as primarily motivated by the desire to pursue knowledge for its own sake . . . free from the

TABLE 3–25

Scientists and Engineers Employed in Research and Development, By Sector, 1954, 1958, 1961, and 1965

SECTOR	1954	1958	1961	1965
Total	237,000	356,000	429,600	503,600
Federal government [a]	37,600	50,200	55,100	69,000 [b]
Industry [c]	164,100	256,100	312,000	351,200
Universities and colleges [c]	30,000	42,500	51,700	66,000
(Universities and colleges proper)	(25,000)	(33,900)	(42,700)	(54,900)
Other nonprofit institutions [c]	5,300	7,200	10,800	17,400

SOURCE: National Science Foundation.

[a] Numbers of civilian and uniformed military personnel; uniformed scientists and engineers (Department of Defense) were estimated at 7,000 in 1954, 8,400 in 1958, 9,200 in 1961, and 12,000 in 1965.

[b] Estimate.

[c] Numbers of full-time employees plus the full-time equivalent of part-time employees. Includes professional R & D personnel employed at federal contract research centers administered by organizations in the sector.

TABLE 3–26

Federal Obligations for Total Research by Field of Science (Millions of dollars)

FIELD OF SCIENCE	ACTUAL, 1966	ESTIMATES 1967	ESTIMATES 1968
Total	$5,271	$5,623	$6,390
Life sciences	1,290	1,431	1,584
Medical sciences	811	909	1,020
Biological sciences	370	406	441
Agricultural sciences	109	116	124
Psychological sciences	100	107	124
Physical sciences	3,641	3,817	4,382
Physical sciences proper	1,842	1,852	2,040
Engineering sciences	1,677	1,840	2,205
Mathematical sciences	123	124	137
Social sciences	166	178	209
Other sciences	74	90	91

SOURCE: National Science Foundation.

NOTE: Detail may not add to totals because of rounding.

need to meet immediate objectives and . . . undertake to increase the understanding of natural laws." Whether these distinctions, particularly between basic and applied research, are meaningful is an important theoretical question that needs to be pursued.[95] Inasmuch as these distinctions, however, are used by the National Science Foundation, one can follow certain trend lines and establish future baselines from their data. While the proportion of money spent for development and applied and basic research has remained relatively constant—about two-thirds of the money has gone for development and one-third for research—the balance between money spent for applied and basic research has changed somewhat. In 1965, basic research outlays amounted to 14 percent of total R & D and applied research about 22 percent; in the period between 1953 and 1958, the money spent for basic research was about 9 percent of the total.

If one examines the distribution between fields, it is seen that of the federal research total of $5.6 billion in 1967, approximately 68 percent, or $3.8 billion, went to the support of the physical sciences; 25 percent, or $1.4 billion, to the support of the life sciences; and 7 percent, or $0.4 billion, to support of the psychological, social, and other sciences (Table 3–26).

In the 1955–1965 decade, there were large increases in money outlays for research. The greatest absolute growth was in the physical sciences, followed by that of the life sciences. However, the social and psychological sciences, starting from smaller bases, showed faster relative gains. From 1956 to 1967 their combined average annual growth rate was 26 percent. These figures contrast with the other sciences whose average annual growth rates have been 20 percent in the decade. In the next decade it is expected that the major research emphases will be in the atmospheric sciences, marine science and technology, space, biomedical research, and, in the social sciences, in education and urban affairs.

The distribution of applied research funds among the major science fields is not very different from that for basic research. Funds for applied research were largely concentrated in the physical sciences because this was the area of prime interest to the Department of Defense and NASA. Physical sciences accounted for 69 percent of total obligations in 1967, life sciences 23 percent, and the behavioral sciences 8 percent. In basic research, the physical sciences received 65 percent of funds, the life sciences 29 percent and the behavioral sciences 6 percent.

It is in subdisciplines that important differences exist. Within phys-

---

[95] A useful set of questions along this line is posed by Michel D. Reagan, "Basic and Applied Research: A Meaningful Distinction," *Science* (March 17, 1967).

ical sciences, 46 percent of the applied research funds were channeled to the engineering sciences in 1967, as compared to only 10 percent of basic research funds. Within the life sciences, biology accounted for only 2 percent of the applied research effort; in basic research it represents 16 percent. The relative distribution of applied research funds by fields of science and discipline remained stable since 1956: more than 45 percent of the funding has been for engineering disciplines and approximately 20 percent for medicine. In the basic research area, significantly higher growth rates are expected for the behavioral and the life sciences (Table 3–27).

TABLE 3–27

Federal Obligations for Basic Research
by Field of Science, 1969

FIELD	OBLIGATIONS (IN MILLIONS)	PERCENTAGE
Total	$2,094	100
Life sciences	569	27
Psychology	55	3
Physical sciences	819	39
Astronomy	282	13
Chemistry	132	6
Physics	398	18
Other	7	b
Environmental sciences	319	15
Atmospheric sciences	171	8
Geological sciences	95	5
Oceanography	52	2
Other	a	b
Mathematics	57	3
Engineering	191	9
Social sciences	72	3
Other sciences	11	1

SOURCE: *Federal Funds for R & D and Other Scientific Activities*, NSF 70–30, Vol. XIX.
a Less than $500,000.
b Less than 0.5 percent.

Much of the basic research, of course, is done in universities. In 1966, universities and federal contract centers attached to them spent almost $2 billion dollars for research and development. (The universities spent $1.3 billion; the federal contract centers $640 million.) More than half (55 percent) went for basic research, two-fifths (39 percent) for applied research, and only 6 percent for development.

Five agencies—Health, Education, and Welfare, Defense, the National Science Foundation, NASA, and the Atomic Energy Commission—provide almost all the funds to universities and colleges. The single largest sum comes from HEW—more than 40 percent, primarily from the National Institutes of Health—and accounts for most of the medical, life sciences, and behavioral sciences programs.

This, then, is the picture of R & D in its golden years. During the Eisenhower and Kennedy administrations, R & D increased by an average of 15 to 16 percent a year. Under President Johnson the increases began at a 3 to 4 percent annual increase but during the tenure of President Nixon an actual decline set in. From 1960 to 1967, federal R & D obligations grew steadily, the expansion of the space program being the single largest element in the expansion. The 1967 high point of $16.5 billion marked the end of the long-term growth cycle.

Between 1967 and 1970, the R & D total fell steadily, declining in obligated dollars by 2 percent. When constant dollars are used, to account for the inflation, the average annual decline is actually 7 percent, and research shows a decline instead of an increase. (See Figure 3–5 and Table 3–28.)

TABLE 3–28

Average Annual Growth Rate of R & D
in Percentages, 1960–1972

CHARACTER OF WORK	60–67	67–70	70–71	71–72
Current dollars				
R & D total	12	—2	a	8
Research	15	2	7	11
Basic research	19	1	5	11
Applied research	14	3	8	11
Development	10	—5	—3	7
Constant dollars *				
R & D total	10	—7	—5	b
Research	13	—2	2	b
Basic research	17	—3	b	b
Applied research	12	—2	3	b
Development	9	—9	—8	b

SOURCE: National Science Foundation, *Federal Funds for R & D and Other Scientific Activities*, Vol. XX.
a Less than 0.5 percent.
b Not available.
* Based on the GNP implicit price deflator.

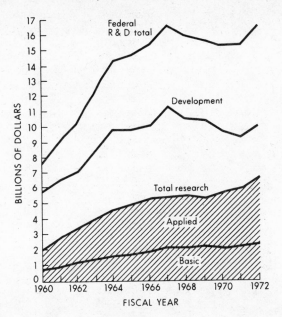

FIGURE 3–5
Trends in Federal R & D Obligations

If looked at as a proportion of the federal budget, in 1940 R & D expenditures were less than one percent of total U.S. budget outlays. By 1956 it had risen to almost 5 percent, by 1963 to more than 10 percent, and a peak was reached in 1965 when R & D accounted for 12.6 percent of total budget outlays. Since then, while the dollars figures have been relatively constant, the proportion by 1971 had fallen to an estimated 8 percent. (See Table 3–29.)

But the major point remains. During the large-scale expansion of R & D in the United States, the chief areas of federal funding have been defense, space, and atomic energy. In 1960, these three agencies spent 91 percent of all federal R & D money. By 1970, however, even though the monies for these three agencies had increased, the proportions as a whole had shifted; yet in 1970, the three agencies still accounted for 82 percent of federal R & D monies. Health, which in 1960 spent 4 percent of the total, by 1970 had doubled in percentage terms and accounted for 8 percent of the monies. (See Table 3–30.)

If one looks at product field, in 1969 over 70 percent of industrial R & D spending went into five fields: guided missiles and spacecraft, electrical equipment, aircraft, machinery, and chemicals. In effect,

TABLE 3–29
Three Decades of the U.S. Science and Technology Budget
(Millions of dollars)

FISCAL YEARS	TOTAL U.S. BUDGET OUTLAYS	RESEARCH, DEVELOPMENT, AND R & D PLANT	
		EXPENDITURES	EXPENDITURES AS PERCENT OF TOTAL BUDGET OUTLAYS
1940	9,589	74	0.8
1941	13,980	198	1.4
1942	34,500	280	0.8
1943	78,909	602	0.8
1944	93,956	1,377	1.5
1945	95,184	1,591	1.7
1946	61,738	918	1.5
1947	36,931	900	2.4
1948	36,493	855	2.3
1949	40,570	1,082	2.7
1950	43,147	1,083	2.5
1951	45,797	1,301	2.8
1952	67,962	1,816	2.7
1953	76,769	3,101	4.0
1954	71,138	3,148	4.4
1955	68,503	3,308	4.8
1956	70,461	3,446	4.9
1957	76,748	4,462	5.8
1958	82,575	4,991	6.0
1959	92,111	5,806	6.3
1960	92,230	7,744	8.4
1961	97,802	9,284	9.5
1962	106,830	10,381	9.7
1963	111,314	11,999	10.8
1964	118,585	14,707	12.4
1965	118,431	14,889	12.6
1966	134,654	16,018	11.9
1967	158,352	16,842	10.6
1968	178,862	17,030	9.5
1969	184,556	16,348	8.9
1970 Estimate	197,885	16,154	8.2
1971 Estimate	200,771	16,161	8.0

SOURCE: National Science Foundation.

the research and development pattern in the United States was badly skewed. The effects showed up in two ways: from an economic growth and productivity point of view—as a series of NSF studies in February 1971 showed—the United States was under-investing in the civilian sector; in terms of the evident social needs and social concerns, such as housing, pollution, environmental deterioration, and the like, there was almost no R & D effort to deal with these

TABLE 3–30

Federal Obligations for Research and Development by Federal Agency
(Dollars in Millions)

AGENCY	ACTUAL		ESTIMATES	
	1960	1970	1971	1972
Total	$7,552	$15,330	$15,387	$16,662
Department of Defense	5,712	7,360	7,420	8,332
National Aeronautics and Space Administration	369	3,800	3,248	3,189
Education, and Welfare	320	1,221	1,480	1,635
Department of Health, Atomic Energy Commission	762	1,346	1,307	1,251
Department of Transportation	—	317	437	483
National Science Foundation	75	289	345	494
Department of Agriculture	126	281	303	314
Department of the Interior	64	158	185	204
Department of Commerce	31	122	158	182
Environmental Protection Agency	—	89	116	144
Office of Economic Opportunity	—	123	116	100
All other	94	224	272	335

SOURCE: National Science Foundation: *An Analysis of Federal R & D Funding by Budget Function*, NSF 71-25.
NOTE: Detail may not add to total because of rounding.

questions. By 1966, Europeans already had 30 percent more scientists and engineers engaged in civilian oriented R & D or industrial and environmental fields than did the United States.

One can make a telling comparison by contrasting housing with defense. In 1968, for example, according to estimates of the National Planning Association, the total private and public outlays for urban facilities, including housing, were greater than the expenditures for national defense, $92 billion as compared with $81 billion. Yet while the Defense Department will have spent between $7 and $8 billion for research and development in 1970 and 1971, the Department of Housing and Urban Development will have spent a total of $22 *million* for R & D in 1970, increasing to $35 *million* in 1971. The projected 1971 spending, as Leonard Lecht of the National Planning Association points out, would amount to one-fourth of one percent of the overall federal expenditures for development.

These two basic changes—the leveling off and even decline of federal R & D, and the small and even hesitant changeovers to areas of health, housing, transportation—pose the clearest challenges. Will the allocative process simply be one of immediate responses to urgent definitions, either of defense or even of social needs, because of the "discovery" of pollution, poverty, urban chaos, and other social ills, or will there be an effort to spell out a coordinated set of policies based on some considerations of national goals defined in long-range terms? Is the present system of "administrative pluralism," in which the individual agencies hold power, to be maintained or will there be some unified science and educational agencies? Can science and research be funded largely on a project basis, or will there be a consideration of long-run institution building, either as a federal in-house capacity, or in independent institutes and agencies, or in conjunction with the universities themselves? If the research and development effort, in short, has been motivated largely by "external challenge" and the need to expand quickly the science complex of the country to help the defense posture, will there be a similar effort for sustained support of domestic social needs and the long-range interests of science and universities in a post-industrial society?

Conclusion

This chapter has undertaken three tasks: to delineate the fundamental structural trends in the society as they affect knowledge and technology; to analyze some problems in the measurement of knowledge and technology; and to put forth the present and future dimensions of the educated and technical class of the country. These tasks have been large ones, and necessarily many questions have been slighted. Moreover, a number of major questions have been ignored for reasons of space. Yet, in any full discussion of knowledge and technology they would have to be included: the changing organizational contexts of knowledge (e.g. the compatibility of hierarchical and bureaucratic work organization with collegial and associational modes of status); the norms of science (e.g. the compatibility of the idea of the autonomy of science with the call for service to national goals); communication patterns within knowledge structures (e.g. the problems of information retrieval, formal and informal networks of communication, etc.); the revolutionary nature of the new "intellectual technology" (e.g. the role of simulation, systems engineering, and the like linked to the computer).

Much of this chapter has been concerned with facts, data, measurement. David Hume, that skeptical Scotsman, once asked of knowledge: "If we take in our hand any volume of divinity or school metaphysics let us ask: Does it contain any abstract reasoning concerning quantity and number? No. Does it contain any experimental reasoning concerning matter of fact and existence? No. Commit it then to the flames: for it contains nothing but sophistry and illusion."

We can observe the skeptic's caution, yet reserve a realm of knowledge for that which cannot be weighed and measured, the realm of values and choice. The central point about the last third of the twentieth century, call it the post-industrial society, the knowledgeable society, the technetronic age, or the active society, is that it will require more societal guidance, more expertise.[96] To some extent, this is an old technocratic dream. But an earlier technocratic visionary like Saint-Simon felt that in such a technocratic society politics would disappear since all problems would be decided by the expert. One would obey the competence of a superior just as one obeys the instructions of a doctor or an orchestra conductor or a ship's captain.[97] It is more likely, however, that the post-industrial society will involve *more* politics than ever before, for the very reason that choice becomes conscious and the decision-centers more visible.[98] The nature of a market society is to disperse responsibility and to have "production" decisions guided by the multiple demands of the scattered consumer. But a decision to allocate money to one scientific project rather than another is made by a political center as against a market decision. Since politics is a compound of interests and values, and these are often diverse, an increased degree of conflict and tension is probably unavoidable in the post-industrial society.

Inasmuch as knowledge and technology have become the central resource of the society, certain political decisions are inescapable. Insofar as the institutions of knowledge lay claim to public resources, some public claim on these institutions is unavoidable.

We are, then, at a number of turning points, and both society and the knowledge community will have to confront a number of crucial decisions about its intertwined future.

The financing of higher education. It is clear that the balance in higher education is shifting from the private school to the public college, but even the private school can no longer continue without sub-

---

[96] A comprehensive effort to provide a conceptual framework in sociological terms for this new, different kind of society has been made by Amitai Etzioni in *The Active Society* (New York, 1968). Pointing out, quite accurately, that the historic language and received models of sociology, even when emphasizing process, lack a vocabulary to deal with direction and choice, he has attempted the task of providing a scaffolding for new sociological structures. What I find contradictory about Etzioni's effort is his employment of *consciousness* and *cybernetics* as his key terms. A cybernetic model, even though involving feedback and self-adjustment, is essentially mechanical and closed. Consciousness, and the implication of the enlargement of human vision and control over nature and society, can only operate in an open system.

[97] A more sophisticated version of this argument is made by Robert Lane in his essay, "The Decline of Politics and Ideology in a Knowledgeable Society," *American Sociological Review* (October 1966).

[98] This technocratic dream in such writers as Saint-Simon, Cournot, F. W. Taylor, and Veblen, and its limitations in a politicalized world are discussed in chap. 6.

stantial public aid; and in both cases the degree of aid requires a centralized federal effort.[99] The obvious question, then, is: for whom and how? Is every type of institution, large and small, public and private, religious and secular, undergraduate, graduate, and professional, to be helped regardless of quality? If not, who is to make the decision? And if new schools are to be created, are the decisions to be left largely to the states, with no consideration of regional or national needs? If there is to be public funding, what is to be the public voice?

The evaluation of knowledge. If public resources are employed, in what ways are the results of research to be evaluated as the basis for future expenditures, and by whom? If there is a choice, because of the limitation of resources, between expenditures of manpower and money on space and, say, on particle accelerators (whose total costs may run to more than a billion dollars), how are these decisions to be made?

The conditions of creativity. Is knowledge more and more a product of "social cooperation," a collaborative effort whose setting is the laboratory and the team, or is it the fruit of the individual cogitator working from his own genius? And if this is too rigid or even false an antinomy, what are the conditions and settings for creativity and productivity?

The transfer of technology. What are the processes whereby discoveries in the laboratory may be transferred more readily into prototypes and production? In part this is an information problem, and it raises the question, for example, of the responsibility of the federal government in establishing a comprehensive technology "infusion" program which goes beyond the mere publication of technological findings to an active encouragement of its use by industry; in part, if one sees this as a piece of the larger problem of spreading the findings of technology to the underdeveloped world, it is a cultural and technical aid program.

The pace of knowledge. If knowledge and new disciplines are differentiating at a more rapid rate, how can the teaching of these subjects keep up with these developments? Is there not a need to assess the nature of curriculum in terms of "structures of knowledge," to use Jerome Bruner's phrase, or "conceptual innovation," along the lines I have argued before.[100]

The strains of change. Insofar as this society, like every other, is undergoing multiple revolutions of a diverse yet simultaneous

---

[99] See the symposium on "The Financing of Higher Education," in *The Public Interest*, no. 11 (Spring 1968), with contributions by Clark Kerr, David Truman, Martin Meyerson, Charles Hitch, *et al.*

[100] See Daniel Bell, *The Reforming of General Education;* and Jerome Bruner, *The Process of Education* (Cambridge, Mass., 1960).

character—the inclusion of disadvantaged groups *into* the society; the growth of interdependence and the creation of national societies; the increasing substitution of political for market decision-making; the creation of fully urbanized societies and the erosion of an agricultural population; the multiple introductions of technological items, and so on—do we not need more conscious means of "monitoring" social change and the creation of mechanisms for anticipating the future? [101]

Let us return to our parable. The tower of Babel was foretold in *Genesis* at the dawn of human experience. "And the Lord said: 'Behold, they are one people, and they have all one language; and this is what they begin to do; and now nothing will be withholden from them, which they purpose to do. Come, let us go down, and there confound their language, that they may not understand one another's speech.' "

Cast out from the Eden of understanding, the human quest has been for a common tongue and a unity of knowledge, for a set of "first principles" which, in the epistemology of learning, would underlie the modes of experience and the categories of reason and so shape a set of invariant truths. The library of Babel mocks this *hubris:* like endless space, it is all there and is not all there; and, like Gödel's theorem, knowing that it is a contradiction makes it not a contradiction. In the end, said the poet, is the beginning. This is the curvilinear paradox, and the necessary humility, in the effort to measure knowledge.

---

[101] This question is discussed in chap. 5, on the idea of a social report.

CHAPTER
4

*The Subordination of
the Corporation: The
Tension between the
Economizing and
Sociologizing Modes*

IN the post-industrial society, as the previous chapters have indicated, there will be an enormous growth in the "third sector": the non-profit area outside of business and government which includes schools, hospitals, research institutes, voluntary and civic associations, and the like. Yet with all that, the business corporation remains, for the while, the heart of the society. About 55 percent of the Gross National Product originates in the corporate sector; about 9.5 percent of Gross National Product is invested annually by non-financial corporate firms for new plants and equipment.[1]

When we speak of the corporation in any familiar sense, we usually think of the industrial giants and of the "magic number" 500 that *Fortune* magazine has popularized. And there are clear reasons for this focus. Actually, there are, in round numbers, about 1,500,000 corporations in the United States. But if we break down the total, they are distributed in this fashion:

> Retail and wholesale trade—450,000
> Finance, real estate and insurance—400,000
> Services—200,000
> Manufacturing—195,000
> Construction—115,000
> Agriculture and mining—45,000

If we take the manufacturing sector as the prototype of industrial America, we find that these 195,000 corporations have about $500 billion in assets. But about 192,000 corporations (or 98 percent of the total) are under $10 million in asset size, and this group of 98 percent of all corporations owns only 14 percent of all industrial corporate assets. Slightly more than 500 firms, with more than $25 million in assets, account for 83 percent of all corporate assets; 200 firms, each

---

[1] All the data are from the *Statistical Abstract of the United States* (1971).

with more than $250 million in assets, account for 66 percent of all industrial assets, while 87 firms, each holding more than a billion dollars in assets, account for 46 percent of the total $500 billion assets.

These 500 industrial corporations, which, in 1970, employed 14,600,000 workers, or more than 75 percent of all employment in manufacturing, symbolize a degree of power which has been a source of recurrent concern for public policy. This concern is evident, once again, today; but for reasons far different than those, say, of thirty years ago, when a firm such as General Motors would spend millions of dollars for thugs, tear gas, and guns to fight the violence of labor organizing. Corporate power, clearly, is the predominant power in the society, and the problem is how to limit it. The concern for public policy, summed up in the phrase "social responsibility," derives from the growing conception of a communal society and the controls which a polity may have to impose on economic ventures that generate unforeseen consequences far beyond the intentions, or powers of control, of the initiating parties.

Over the last few years, there has been a notable change in public attitudes toward the corporation. Only fourteen years ago, writing in Edward S. Mason's magisterial compendium on *The Corporation in Modern Society*, Eugene V. Rostow could comment:

In reviewing the literature about the current development of [the large, publicly-held] corporations, and about possible programs for their reform, one is struck by the atmosphere of relative peace. There seems to be no general conviction abroad that reform is needed. The vehement feelings of the early thirties, expressing a sense of betrayal and frustration at a depression blamed on twelve years of business leadership, are almost entirely absent.[2]

The reason for that tolerant and even benign attitude toward the corporation in the 1950s is not hard to find. Apart from the general sense of social peace induced by the Eisenhower administration (a peace maintained, in part, by the mobilization of the sentiments of society against an external enemy), a new and seemingly satisfactory conception of the role of the corporation in the society had arisen.

For seventy-five years, going back to 1890 when Congress passed the Sherman Antitrust Act, the corporation had been viewed with populist suspicion because of its size. Size, in the American lexicon, means power, and the bigness of business was perceived as both an economic and political threat to democracy. Economic size was

---

[2] E. V. Rostow, "To Whom and for What Ends is Corporate Management Responsible," in *The Corporation in Modern Society*, ed. Edward S. Mason (Cambridge, Mass., 1959), p. 59.

equated with market power, or the ability to control (within limits) the price of products offered for sale. Large-scale assets were equated with undue influence, either in a local community or state, or in the nation itself.

But in the more than half century's experience with antitrust, a new economic sophistication had been developed. One was the important distinction between size and market control, and the realization that the two are not completely related. The two biggest manufacturing companies today are Standard Oil of New Jersey and General Motors, with $20.5 billion and $18.2 billion respectively in assets. GM has about 55 percent of United States' automotive production; but Standard Oil, though larger than GM, has only about 9 percent of domestic oil refining and an even smaller percentage of production.

Size, clearly, is not a good predictor of market control. Market control is measured by "concentration ratios," i.e. the sales of the largest four companies, in a product line, as a percentage of total product sales. But it seems reasonably clear that, since the turn of the century, the concentration ratios have gone down considerably and that, in most industries, there is not increasing concentration but rather a ceaseless flux.[3]

But the more important shift was a change in ideology. The idea took hold that "size" was less relevant than "performance." Performance itself is an elusive criteria. It embraces the idea of receptivity to innovation; willingness to expand capacity (one of the chief charges by liberal economists in the 1940s against such "oligopolistic" industries as aluminum and steel was that they were unwilling to expand capacity); the reflection of increased productivity in better quality, higher wages, and steady, if not lower, prices; and similar indices of responsiveness to the needs of the society.

The clearest mark of performance was growth. The fear of the 1930s, after all, was stagnation. Liberal economists such as Alvin

---

[3] The stereotype that the big company has a big market share is obviously supported by many examples. Only it is refuted by even more. If one looks at the "symbolic" examples of concentration, it is quite clear that in no industry today is concentration at a comparable level with the period after the great wave of consolidations, from 1898 to 1902. As pointed out by Professor Segall of the University of Chicago: In 1900, International Harvester produced 85 percent of the nation's harvesting machines. In 1902, National Biscuit controlled 70 percent of the biscuit output. In 1901, American Can turned out 90 percent of its industry's output. In 1902, Corn Products had 80 percent of its industry's capacity. In 1902, U.S. Leather accounted for more than 60 percent of leather output; Distillers Securities provided more than 60 percent of whiskey output; International Paper produced 60 percent of all newsprint. In 1900, American Sugar Refining refined virtually all the sugar in the country. For a comprehensive discussion of the contemporary degree of concentration see M. A. Adelman, "The Two Faces of Economic Concentration," *The Public Interest*, no. 21 (Fall 1970).

Hansen had predicted, in fact, that the economy had achieved such a state of "maturity" that there was no longer the possibility of expansion. The facts belied these fears. New technological frontiers opened up after the war; and the large corporations took the initiative.

A vigorous, large company could present its case to the public that size was immaterial, so long as the corporation displayed those hallmarks of dynamism that added up to "performance." In fact, as J. K. Galbraith argued in his book, *American Capitalism*, size was an asset because it enabled the large corporation to underwrite technological progress.

It is admirably equipped for financing technical development. Its organization provides strong incentives for undertaking development and for putting it into use. . . . The power that enables the firm to have some influence on price insures that the resulting gains will not be passed on to the public by imitators (who have stood none of the costs of development) before the outlay for development can be recouped. *In this way market power protects the incentive to technical development.* (Italics in the original.)[4]

Here was a strong and sophisticated defense of bigness by the criteria of performance. And, to a considerable extent, the ideology of American business in the postwar years became its ability to perform. The justification of the corporation no longer lay primarily in the natural right of private property, but in its role as an instrument for providing more and more goods to the people. Because the corporation seemed to be performing this role adequately, criticism of it did, indeed, become muted, so that by the end of the 1950s the corporation had established a new legitimacy in American life.

The New Criticism

Today that legitimacy is being challenged, or at least the tolerant and benign attitude toward the corporation has receded. The paradox is that the ground of the new criticism is no longer size or bigness (though some old populist echoes persist), but performance itself. A feeling has begun to spread in the country that corporate performance has made the society uglier, dirtier, trashier, more polluted, and noxious. The sense of identity between the self-interest of the corporation and the public interest has been replaced by a sense of incongruence.

---

[4] John Kenneth Galbraith, *American Capitalism: The Concept of Countervailing Power* (Boston, 1952), pp. 91, 93.

The Subordination of the Corporation

Any issue that becomes ideological becomes distorted. The facts of spoliation of countryside and the reduction of various amenities are obvious; the reasons less so. One evident cause is the sheer increase of numbers of persons in the society and a change in social habits. Take, for example, the national parks: in 1930, the number of visitor-days (one person staying twelve hours) was 3 million in a population of 122 million; by 1960, it was 79 million, in a population of 179 million; and in 1968, there were 157 million visitor-days in a population of 200 million. The results are described vividly in an account in *The New York Times*:

Yosemite, only a day's drive from San Francisco and Los Angeles, is generally considered the most overcrowded park. Congestion reaches its peak on major holidays and this Labor Day weekend was no exception.

The constant roar in the background was not a waterfall but traffic. Transistor radios blared forth the latest rock tunes. Parking was at a premium. Dozens of children clambered over the rocks at the base of Yosemite Falls. Campsites, pounded into dust by incessant use, were more crowded than a ghetto. Even in remote areas, campers were seldom out of sight of each other. The whole experience was something like visiting Disneyland on a Sunday.

Moreover, if we take pollution of the air and water as the criterion of social ill, then clearly all sections of the society are at fault: The farmer who, by seeking to increase food production, uses more nitrate fertilizer and thus pollutes the rivers of the country; the individual automobile owner who, seeking greater mobility, spews noxious gas into the atmosphere; the Atomic Energy Commission which, in seeking to expand nuclear power, may be responsible for thermal pollution of the waters; and the corporation whose smokestacks emit smog-creating gases in the air, or whose waste products pollute the lakes.

But if one takes the attitude that everyone is to blame—and simply ends with the moral exhortation for each person to restrain his behavior—then one misses the important point. Such a situation itself points to the fact that the allocative mechanism of society, the proper distribution of costs and resources, is not working. In a free society, the socially optimal distribution of resources and goods exists where the market reflects the true economic cost of an item. But where private costs and social costs diverge, then the allocation of goods becomes skewed. When the owner of a factory has no incentive to take account of costs to others of the pollution he generates because these costs are not charged to him, factory output (or automobile mileage in the case of a car owner) will be at a higher level than is socially optimal.

The growing problem for modern society is this increasing diver-

gence of private costs and social costs (what economists call technically an "externality," because such costs are not "internalized" by a
firm in its own cost accounting). But along with this awareness there
arises, too, the question whether the strict conception of costs—
and return on investment—that is the rationale of the accounting
procedures of the firm is at all adequate today. In other words, perhaps the older definition of "performance" is too narrow. The question that then arises involves, not just the "social responsibility" of
any particular corporation, but the "rightness" of the broader pattern
of social organization and of the social goals of the society. And, to
the extent that the corporation has been the institution integral to the
existing pattern, it becomes the starting point of a new inquiry.

Perhaps we can see the quite radical difference between these two
perspectives by setting up two models, which I shall call the *economizing* mode and the *sociologizing* mode, as polar extremes within
which the actions of the corporation can be estimated and judged.

The Economizing Mode

Beginning little more than 150 years ago, modern Western society
was able to master a secret denied to all previous societies—a
steady increase of wealth and a rising standard of living by peaceful
means. Almost all previous societies had sought wealth by war, plunder, expropriation, tax-farming, or other means of extortion. Economic life, in the shorthand of game theory, was a zero-sum game;
one group of winners could benefit only at the expense of another
group of losers. The secret mastered by modern Western society was
productivity, the ability to gain a more than proportional output
from a given expenditure of capital, or a given exertion of labor; or,
more simply, society could now get "more with less effort or less
cost." Economic life could be a non-zero-sum game; everyone could
end up a winner, though with differential gains.

In the popular view, productivity was made possible by the introduction of machinery or, more specifically, the discovery of new
forms of power, mechanical or electrical, hitched to an engine.
Clearly much of this view is true. But productivity, as a concept, became possible only through a new "supporting system" which dictated the placement of machines in a new way. To put the matter less
abstractly, modern industrial society is a product of two "new men,"
the engineer and the economist, and of the concept which unites the
two—the concept of efficiency. For the engineer, the design of a
machine and its placement vis-à-vis other machines is a problem of

finding the "one best way" to extract maximum output within a given physical layout. The economist introduces a calculus of monetary costs, within the framework of relative prices, as a means of finding the most appropriate mix of men and machines in the organization of production.

Modern industrial life, in contrast with traditional society, has been revolutionized by these innovations. The new sciences have introduced a distinctive mode of life. We call it *economizing*. Economizing is the science of the best allocation of scarce resources among competing ends; it is the essential technique for the reduction of "waste"—as this is measured by the calculus stipulated by the regnant accounting technique. The conditions of economizing are a market mechanism as the arbiter of allocation, and a fluid price system which is responsive to the shifting patterns of supply and demand.

Economics itself, over the past one hundred years, has developed a rigorous and elegant general system of theory to explain the relative prices of goods and services and of the factors in production, the allocation of those factors to various uses, the level of employment, and the level of prices. With economics, comes a rational division of labor, specialization of function, complementarity of relations, the use of production functions (the best mix of capital and labor at relative prices), programming (the best ordering of scheduling of mixed batches in production, or in transportation), etc. The words we associate with economizing are "maximization," "optimization," "least cost"—in short, the components of a conception of rationality. But this conception of rationality, it should be pointed out, was intended by its utilitarian founders as a rationality of *means*, a way of best satisfying a given *end*. The ends of life themselves were never given; they were seen as multiple or varied, to be chosen freely by the members of society. Economics would seek to satisfy these choices in the "best way," i.e. the most efficient means possible in order to "maximize" satisfaction.

For an understanding of the economizing mode, this distinction between rational means and a plurality of ends must be emphasized. Modern industrial society, being a liberal society, has never felt the need to define its ends or to establish priorities within some set of ends. It has always eschewed such collective decision-making. No conscious social decision was made to "transform" society two hundred years ago. No conclave met, as in a French constituent assembly or an American constitutional convention, to declare a new social order. Yet it is quite clear what the new goals of the new industrial society were to be—the ends that became "given" all involved the rising material output of goods. And other, traditional modes of life (the existence of artisan skills and crafts, the family hearth as a site of work) were sacrificed to the new system for the attainment of these economic ends.

Commonplace as this history may be, the singular fact needs to be emphasized. Unlike political change, no one "voted" for these decisions in some collective fashion, no one assessed (or could assess) the consequences of these changes. Yet a whole new way of life, based on the utilitarian calculus or the economizing mode, gradually began to transform the whole of society.

The Corporation: A New Social Invention

Productivity is a technique, steadily rising output of goods is an end; for the two to be realized they have to be institutionalized in some renewable system of organization. That institution was the corporation.

Much of economic history and some of economic theory has focused on the entrepreneur as the singularly important person who, sensing new opportunities, breaks the cake of custom and innovates new areas of economic life. Much of contemporary sociological theory has dealt with the manager as the faceless technocrat who runs a routinized operation. But to understand the corporation, one has to turn not to the entrepreneur (and the myths about him) or the manager (and the caricatures that are drawn of him), but to a figure historically and sociologically intermediate between the two—the organizer.

The church and the army have been the historic models of organizational life. The business corporation, which took its present shape in the first decades of the twentieth century, was the one new social invention to be added to these historic forms. The men who created that form—Theodore N. Vail who put together AT&T, Walter Teagle of Standard Oil of New Jersey, Alfred P. Sloan of General Motors—designed an instrument which coordinates men, materials, and markets for the production of goods and services at least cost with the best possible return on capital investment. They did so by introducing the idea of functional rationality, of *economizing*, as a new mode of ordering social relations.

Of the three, only Alfred P. Sloan has put down directly the principles he employed. His account, *My Years With General Motors*, is fascinating, and one can take his sketch as prototypical of the corporate mode of mid-century America. The most striking aspect of Mr. Sloan's book is its language. Sloan's key terms are *concept, methodol-*

ogy, and *rationality*. Throughout the book, Sloan uses these terms to explain the innovations he made in General Motors: "Durant had no systematic financial methodology. It was not his way of doing business." "The spacing of our product line of ten cars in seven lines in early 1921 reveals its irrationality." "In product variety only Buick and Cadillac had clear divisional concepts of their place in the market."

The language is not an accident or an affectation. It is surprising only to those who associate such language with the academy and not with the analytical necessities of organization. The language derives in part from Sloan's training as an engineer (he took a degree at MIT in 1895); but more, it derives directly from the revolution in organization that Sloan introduced: the initiation of detailed planning, of statistical methods, and of financial controls. In explaining why he relied on market research and forecasting rather than salesmen's intuition, he remarked: ". . . In the automobile industry you cannot operate without programming and planning. It is a matter of respecting figures on the future as a guide." [5]

The reasons for the success of General Motors can be attributed, in simplified fashion, to two elements: a market strategy based on a "clear concept" of product lines and an organizational form which combined decentralization of operations with coordination of policy.[6] The organizational structure of General Motors is commonplace now, and has been widely copied by most large corporations. At the time of its innovation, it was a novelty. Stated most simply, the principle of organization is to have a complete breakdown of the costs of each unit, and to exercise control of operating divisions through stringent budgets. Before the system was instituted, divisions in GM sold their parts to other divisions (e.g. a battery division to a car division) on the basis of cost plus a predetermined percentage. But the corporation at the top did not know which units were profitable and which not. "It was natural for the divisions to compete for investment funds," Sloan wrote, "but it was irrational for the general

---

[5] Alfred P. Sloan, Jr., *My Years with General Motors* (New York, 1964), pp. 135–136.

[6] This market strategy and organizational form allowed GM to come from behind to oust Ford, a genius at production techniques, from the leading position in the market. In 1921, Ford had 60 percent of the car and truck market and almost complete control of the low-price field. Chevrolet, GM's entry in the low-price field, had only 4 percent of the market. To meet Ford head-on in price competition would have been suicidal. Sloan's strategy was not to undercut the Ford price but to *top* it somewhat, seeking to skim off that layer of buyers who would be willing to go to a higher price on the assumption they were getting a better car. By successive "upgrading" of items, largely through annual model changes, GM won the larger share. In effect, GM countered "style" to "utility" and won.

officers of the company not to know where to place the money to best advantage."

What Sloan did was to treat each division as a separate company, with the corporate group at the top acting as a "holding company," and to measure the performance of each division by the rate of return on investment consistent with attainable volume. The rate of return is thus a measure of performance and a means of ranking each division, not on the basis of its absolute profit alone, but on the rate of return on capital invested. The measure, in short, is the margin of profit multiplied by the rate of turnover of invested capital. Through these measures, the corporate group at the top could determine how to allocate the corporation's money in order to achieve a maximum return for the whole.

All aspects of corporate policy became subordinated to that end. In specifying the corporation's philosophy, Sloan was explicit:

To this end [he writes] we made the assumptions of the business process explicit. We presumed that the first purpose in making a capital investment is the establishment of a business that will pay satisfactory dividends and preserve and increase its capital value. The primary object of the corporation, therefore, we declared, was to make money not just motor cars. Positive statements like this have a flavor that has gone out of fashion; but I still think that the ABC's of business have merit for reaching policy conclusions.[7]

The economizing system of each corporation locks with each other to create a social system. Earnings per share of common stock becomes the balance wheel around which the system turns. If the earnings of a firm drop, it may find it difficult to attract capital, or may have to pay more for capital vis-à-vis other firms. Thus, the allocation of capital in the economy follows the same principle as it does within the corporation. Locked thus into competition, the degree of freedom of any single corporation to break away from this measuring rod—the rate of return on investment—is limited. Any change in the system has to be a change in the entire system.

Profitability and productivity, thus, are the indices of corporate success. They are the tests of meeting the demands of the marketplace and the demand for the efficient distribution of resources within the firm and between members of the society. This is the rationale for the *economizing* mode for the corporation, as for the economy.

---

[7] Sloan, op. cit., p. 64.

Limits of the Economizing Mode

The theoretical virtue of the market is that it coordinates human interdependence in some optimal fashion, in accordance with the expressed preferences of buyers and sellers (within any given distribution of income). But what ultimately provides direction for the economy, as Veblen pointed out long ago, is not the price system but *the value system of the culture* in which the economy is embedded. The price system is only a mechanism for the relative allocation of goods and services within the framework of *the kinds of demand* generated. Accordingly, economic guidance can only be as efficacious as the cultural value system which shapes it.

The value system of industrial society (communist as well as capitalist) has been centered around the desirability of economic growth; and the cultural value of Western society, particularly American society, has been the increase of private-consumption economic goods. There are, however, three drawbacks (at least) to this system.

The most important consideration is that it measures only *economic* goods. But as E. J. Mishan has pointed out, and as a once popular refrain once had it, "the best things in life are free." Clean air, beautiful scenery, pure water, sunshine, to say nothing of the imponderables such as ease of meeting friends, satisfaction in work, etc.— they are "free goods" either because they are so abundant that there is little or no cost, or because they are not appropriable and saleable. Such free goods contribute greatly to our total welfare. But in our present accounting schemes, priced at zero, they add nothing to the economist's measure of wealth. Nor, when they disappear, do they show up as subtractions from wealth.

The second consideration is that growth, as measured by our present economic accounting, tends to generate more and more "spillovers" which become costs borne directly by other private parties or distributed among the society as a whole. These are what economists call "externalities." Externalities (or "external costs"), as economists define the term, are the unintended or unplanned impact, the "fallout" on Third Party C (and often D, E, and F, as well), of a private transaction between parties A and B. The result is a social cost (though frequently a social benefit, too). The most obvious example of a social cost is air pollution—the result, in part, of the increasing number of private cars in the society. In every elementary economics textbook, air was once the classic illustration of the "free good." Yet the irony is that in the next 30 years one of the most scarce resources we may have (in the sense of proportionately sharply rising costs) will be clean air. The costs of automobile disposal are not charged to the automobile owner; similarly, the costs of salvaging a depressed coal mining community are not charged to the companies selling the competing fuels which may have driven coal off the market. Moreover, because air and water belong to no one, the market economy treats them as free resources. Firms pay for raw materials and labor, but until now they have not had to pay for the discharge of effluents into the air and water. Thus their prices have not reflected the true costs of their activities.

The third problem with the economizing mode is that the value system of American society emphasizes, as the primary consideration, the satisfaction of individual private consumption; the result is an imbalance between public goods and private goods. In the popular psychology, taxes are not considered as the necessary purchase of public services that an individual cannot purchase for himself, but as money "taken away from *me* by *them*." Taxes, thus, are not considered as an addition to welfare, but as subtractions from it. This is reinforced by politicians who claim that taxes are too "high" (but by what standard?) rather than asking: Are there needs which can be met only by public goods, and what are the taxes buying?

Thus, if one is trying to assess welfare (or the quality of life) in some optimal fashion, the problem is not only the simple commitment to economic growth, but the nature of the accounting and costing system of the economizing mode which has served to mask many of its deficiencies. Our fascination with Gross National Product is a good illustration.

GNP, Private Costs, and Social Costs

Conventionally we measure economic welfare primarily through the figures of Gross National Product. These accounts allow us to sketch the macroeconomic levels of activity in the society, and through them to measure economic shortfalls, the potentials of full employment revenues and the like, as a means of deciding on economic policy. But there are several drawbacks as well, particularly if we are concerned not only with wealth but the welfare of the society.

GNP measures the value of goods and services bought and sold in the market. But the measure itself is only "additive." It does not discriminate between a genuine addition to welfare and what, in effect, may be a subtraction but is counted as an economic plus. Thus, in the conventional example, the output of a steel mill is a value added to GNP. But if the steel mill pollutes a lake, and then uses additional resources to clean up the lake, that new expenditure is also added to GNP. Similarly an increase in environmental deterioration over time would not show up as a decline in real output because the flow of benefits from the environment is not counted as an output to begin with (e.g. the usability of a lake or river for swimming). But expenditures designed to reduce environmental deterioration would show up as increased real output.

More important, however, is the fact that in assessing *public* services we do not have a means of estimating actual benefits or values. In items that are sold in the market, such as automobiles or clothing, we have market prices as the value individuals place on the products. But how do we value publicly provided services such as health, or education, or protection? Our accounting system does so only by the "input" costs, not by the output values. Thus the "output" of police services is measured by salaries paid to members of the police department, the costs of police cars, etc., not by the social and economic value of crimes prevented or violators apprehended; the value of health services is measured by the costs of doctor's fees and drugs, not by the reduction of time lost on account of illness; the value of education is measured by the cost of teachers' salaries, equipment, etc., not by the value imputable to the gain in pupil knowledge.

This is a central problem in the question of how much money should be spent on "public goods." People grumble over taxes, but there is no way, at present, of showing that the benefits received for these services may be far greater than the costs. And while there is no way of knowing, it is likely that public services of this kind are "under valued," and therefore less appreciated.

The second limitation of the accounting system, which derives from the growing existence of externalities, is the divergence between private and social costs. The idea of social costs is an old one, going back one hundred and fifty years to the socialist economist Sismondi. But it was not until about fifty years ago, when A. C. Pigou wrote his *Economics of Welfare*, that the phenomenon of social costs was integrated into the conceptual system of neoclassical equilibrium economics. Pigou pointed out that the investment of additional resources may throw costs "upon people not directly concerned" such as the "uncompensated damage done to surrounding woods from railway engines." [8]

---

[8] In his book, Pigou gave dozens of examples of similar "disservices": the destruction of neighborhoods by the construction of factories in residential districts; the costs to the consumers of competitive advertising; the increase in expenditures for police and prisons because of the rising sale of liquor; the overrunning of a neighbor's land by rabbits originating from game preserves; the costs of diplomacy and armies because of the rise of foreign investments, etc.

In this country the theme was elaborated by John Maurice Clark of Columbia,

But for almost half a century, this idea of divergence between private cost and social cost was almost completely neglected. Now with the rising concern with environmental spoliation, the second-order consequences of technological change and the increase in "externalities," the problem has moved into the center of social policy. In the next decade one of the major social questions will be the determination of who is to pay the costs of such externalities, and how the amounts will be assessed. Which costs ought to be borne by the parties that generate the costs, and which, legitimately, should be borne by the society as a whole, will be one of the most difficult questions in the political economy of the future. What we have now is only the beginning awareness of the problem. What we lack is a genuine total cost matrix which, for particular instances, would be able to assess the costs and benefits of particular actions and policies.[9]

The Sociologizing Mode

Important as all these issues are, they do not go to the heart of the matter, which is that the economizing mode is based on the proposition that *individual* satisfaction is the unit in which costs and benefits

who, in his *Economics of Overhead Costs* (1923), drew a distinction between social and market values and between social and market costs. For Clark, as Allan Gruchy points out, the business concept of cost excluded many important social costs such as communal health hazards, unemployment, and other costs associated with business fluctuations. Clark's concern was to bring commercial efficiency closer to social efficiency, and with making the economic system account for social values, clean air, scenic beauty, etc., as well as market values.

[9] I do not minimize the technical and political difficulties of establishing such a matrix. Let me provide a "homely" example of a problem which, many years ago, first brought the social cost problem to my personal attention.

In New York City when I was a boy, snow was removed from the streets by the hiring of extra trucks which would cart mounds of it away and dump it in the river. Many years later, Paul Screvane, who was the Commissioner of Sanitation, ordered his men to push the snow into the middle of the streets, where it was churned into slush by passing cars. Perhaps he did it because the costs of hiring trucks had gone up exorbitantly, or because he wanted to demonstrate an outstanding record in office so that he could run for mayor. The sanitation department showed a commendable record of economy. But (as I figured out from the records of the Industry and Commerce Association), after each snowfall the cleaning and dyeing bills in the city went up substantially, because the passing cars would splatter the clothes of the innocent bystander.

Now, which was the "rational" solution? One could say that Screvane's method was highly irrational, because it passed the costs of snow removal onto the backs of the unfortunate pedestrians, and if the cleaning and dyeing bills were higher than the cost of hiring additional trucks, it was truly a misallocation of resources. Yet one could also say that if the trucks had been hired, direct city expenses would have been increased and taxes would have to go up, increasing the resentments of the taxpayers in the city, so that the system of "Russian roulette" whereby a random group of bystanders bore the costs might have a greater "political" rationality than economic cost-benefit analysis.

are to be reckoned. This is an atomistic view of society and reflects the utilitarian fallacy that the sum total of individual decisions is equivalent to a social decision. Yet the aggregate of individual decisions has collective effects far beyond the power of any individual to manage, and which often vitiate the individual's desires. Thus, every individual may value the freedom and mobility which a personal automobile provides, yet the aggregate effect of so many autos on the roads at once can lead to clogged transportation. We might all accept, in the abstract, the principle that the automobile has become a vehicle of uglification; yet lacking a social decision about which alternative modes of transportation might best serve an area, I might have, willy-nilly, to go out and buy a car. Each of us, individually, may see the consequences of an individual action, but lacking a social mechanism to assess it, we become helpless, drift, and thereby accelerate it.

In effect, in contrast to the economizing mode of thought, one can specify—I apologize for the heavy-handed clumsiness—a sociologizing mode, or the effort to judge a society's needs in more conscious fashion,[10] and (to use an old-fashioned terminology) to do so on the basis of some explicit conception of the "public interest."

Two fundamental questions are involved.

First, the conscious establishment of social justice by the inclusion of all persons *into* the society. If the value system of a society is made more explicit as a means of guiding the allocative system (pricing) of a society, this value system must also establish, however roughly, the "right" distribution of income in the society, the minimum income available to all citizens, etc.

The second is the relative size of the public and the private sector. Economic goods, to put it in textbook fashion, are of two types, individual and social. Individual goods are "divisible"; each person buys the goods or services he wants—clothes, appliances, automobiles—on the basis of free consumer choice. Social goods are not "divisible" into individual items of possession, but are a communal service—national defense, police and fire protection, public parks, water resources, highways, and the like. These goods and services are not sold to individual consumers and are not adjusted to individual tastes. The nature and amounts of these goods must be set by a single decision, applicable

---

[10] One can say, theoretically, that the price system could manage the problem, e.g. when the costs of individual congestion became high it would then become profitable for alternative modes of transportation to compete with the private car. But the price system, in this instance, relies on *trial and error* to assess the result. The difficulty is that such assessments, *after the fact*, are likely to be futile—an enormous amount of resources would have been misallocated, and a preemptive "system" of transportation will have been established. Under such a system, clogged highways will eventually result in the building of more highways.

jointly to all persons. Social goods are subject, therefore, to communal or political, rather than individual demand.

A man cannot ask for and individually buy in the marketplace his share of unpolluted air, even if he were willing to pay extra for it. These are actions that have to be taken in coordinated fashion through public channels. We can assign the costs of air pollution to its source, whether industrial, municipal, or individual, in order to force culprits to reduce the pollution, or we can use the money for remedial measures. In the same way, the laying out of roads, the planning of cities, the control of congestion, the organization of health care, the cleaning up of environmental pollution, the support of education—all these, necessarily, become matters of public policy, of public concern, and often (though not necessarily) of public funding.

To say, in effect, that the public sector of the society has to be expanded, is not to assume, naively, that the failures of the market will now be remedied. Each arena has its own problems, and the beginning of political wisdom is to recognize the ineluctable difficulties in each. Public decision-making can easily be as irrational and counterproductive as private decision-making. The major sociological problem ahead will be the test of our ability to *foresee* the effects of social and technological change and to *construct alternative courses* in accordance with different valuations of ends, at different costs.

Varieties of Planning

A considerable amount of planning goes on already. Every major corporation today necessarily operates in accordance with a one-year fiscal plan and a five-year market strategy in order to meet competition or to expand its size. Each company plans singly and each introduces its own new technologies—yet no one monitors the collective effects. The same is true of the planning of various government agencies. In considering social effects, one finds this kind of planning unsatisfactory.

The first flaw is the fallacy inherent in single-purpose planning itself.[11] Most engineers, developers, industrialists, and government officials are single-purpose planners. The objective they have in mind is related almost solely to the immediate problem at hand—whether

---

[11] For an elaboration of this point, see Harold Gilliam, "The Fallacy of Single-Purpose Planning," in the *Daedalus* issue on America's Changing Environment (Fall 1967).

it be a power site, a highway, a canal, a river development—and even when cost-benefit analysis is used (as in the case of the Army Corps of Engineers) there is little awareness of, and almost no attempt to measure, the multiple consequences (i.e. the second-order and third-order effects) of the new system.

The second is the failure to make the necessary distinction between, as Veblen put it, the technological and institutional processes, or, in the terminology used by a panel of the National Academy of Sciences, between the "technologies" and "the supporting system." The automobile, the SST, pesticides, drugs—all these are technologies in the physical engineering sense of the term. The support system is the organization of production and distribution, or more generally the economic and legal matrix in which the technology is embedded. The simple point is that there is no "technological imperative," no exact one-to-one correspondence between a particular technology and a specific supporting system. As Jack Burnham pointed out in a pungent way: "When we buy an automobile we no longer buy an object in the old sense of the word, but instead we purchase a three-to-five year lease for participation in the state-recognized private transportation system, a highway system, a traffic safety system, an industrial parts-replacement system, a costly insurance system. . . ." [12]

One may, therefore, depending on the problem, seek to change either the technology (the gasoline engine) or the support system (unrestricted private use of the roads). But what this allows us to do is to compare alternative modes, at alternative costs, and to design better systems to serve social needs. This, in turn, underlines a need for national "technology assessment." [13] With few exceptions, the decision about the future use of a technology today is made by the economic or institutional interests who will primarily benefit from it. But as the panel of the National Academy of Sciences argues: "Decisions concerning the development and application of new technologies must

---

[12] Jack Burnham, *Beyond Modern Sculpture* (New York, 1968). If one asks what a sculptor is doing in discussing the automobile system, his argument is cast in the context of the disappearance of "objects" in contemporary society and its replacement by "systems."

[13] The idea of technology assessment grew largely out of the studies of the House Science and Astronautics Committee under the leadership of Congressman Daddario. Two panels, one in the National Academy of Sciences and one in the National Academy of Engineering, were set up to test the feasibility of the idea. The National Academy of Sciences Panel, under the direction of Harvey Brooks, agreed that assessment was possible and proposed a number of ways in which the process could be implemented in government. The Engineering panel undertook three studies—of subsonic aircraft noise, of computer-assisted instruction, and of multiphasic health screening—to further this idea. Both reports on technology assessment were published by the House Committee in July 1969.

not be allowed to rest solely on their immediate utility to their sponsors and users. Timely consideration must be given to the long-term sacrifices entailed by their use and proliferation, and to potentially injurious effects upon sectors of society and the environment often quite remote from the places of production and application."

In rather inchoate fashion, assessment and decisional systems already exist in the federal government. The Federal Water Pollution Control Administration, the National Air Pollution Control Administration, and the Environmental Control Administration, all are empowered to make studies of consequences; but they have less power to establish controls. Some agencies, such as the Atomic Energy Commission both promote new technology (e.g. nuclear power) and assess the consequences. But what may be needed are *independent* boards to make assessment and propose remedial actions to the executive or to Congress. Whatever the final structures may be, it is clear that some social decision mechanisms will have to emerge in the next few years to make such assessments of second-order effects of technological and social change. New and large powers will be vested in administrative boards. New and complex tasks will confront the Congress.

And for the private corporation, a new principle in the relation of corporations to public policy will soon be emerging. Just as it has been public policy to provide tax inducements to help corporations expand plant capacity (by investment credits, or more rapid depreciation allowances), so it will be public policy to provide tax penalties either to force corporations to bear the burdens of social costs generated by the firm, or to favor an alternative technology or supporting system if the social costs can be minimized by the alternative system or the social benefits enhanced. Given the collective effects of private decisions, this involvement of public policy in corporate policy is inescapable.

Just as we may be moving into technology assessment, so we shall have to cope with social assessments as well. For example, the social map of the United States was redrawn after World War II by the rapid expansion of the suburbs and the extraordinary rise in suburban home ownership. But all this was made possible only as a matter of public policy: by federal guarantee of mortgages; by low downpayments by veterans (often as little as 10 percent down on a purchase price) so that "owning" became cheaper than renting; and by the policy of permitting the deduction of interest payments on mortgages from income taxes. But no one questioned the existing "support system" of large numbers of small developers creating tracts of unattached houses in mechanical grids.

There can be, let us say, three alternative models of suburban development: one, a pattern of detached homes with private walkways and separate garages; the second, a set of "cluster houses" with the sharing of common auxiliary facilities (e.g. garaging); and third, high-rise apartment houses with large green spaces. Each of these developments has vastly different "social costs" which are borne by the community, not by the developer (the pattern of roads, auxiliary land use, the location of schools, etc.). Yet these social costs are rarely, if ever, taken into consideration. There is no "total cost matrix" to make a buyer aware of what the alternative styles could cost him in terms of the secondary costs he and the community would have to pay as a result of his choice. Nor has public policy ever sought to make such a determination.

Now, I am not arguing that consumers should be required to take one or another of the patterns. But intelligent public policy—because it is public monies that are facilitating this social change—should inquire into the alternative total cost matrices of the different patterns, and of the consequences of maintaining or changing existing institutional patterns of home building and development. It is not a matter of "interference" or "non-interference" in the society; *any* action (including non-action) is bound to strengthen or weaken one or another vested interest. It is a matter of making the choices and consequences explicit.

The Corporation As a Sociological Institution

In traditional corporate law, property is defined as things (*res*), but the major lesson which corporations have learned in the last thirty years is that a corporation, while producing things, is made up of people, and that one cannot treat people—at least managerial and white-collar personnel!—as things.

Corporations are institutions for economizing; but they are also ways of life for their members. Until the early years of the twentieth century, the life of most Americans was bounded by the isolated small town, the church, and the family. The small town has virtually disappeared; the church has lost much of its emotional hold on people; and the tight bond between family and occupation, which gave a unity to life—the family farm, the family business, or the family occupation which the son inherited—has been sundered. The breakup of that traditional way of life, and the consequent sense of uprootedness and disorientation, is the source of what sociologists call *anomie*.

Emile Durkheim, the French sociologist who coined that term, thought that for *anomie* to be resolved there must be a group which could provide a sense of kindredness and common purpose for its members. Political society, he thought, was too amorphous and too distant. The answer, he said, lay in the occupational group, the profession, which could provide a new ethic for society. One of Durkheim's chief expositors, Elton Mayo of the Harvard Business School, thought that this purpose could be most effectively realized in the business corporation.

For a significant number of persons, this has necessarily become the case. The "four wishes" which the late sociologist W. I. Thomas thought were basic to human experience—the wish for security, for new experience, for response, and for recognition—can for these men only be obtained within the corporate milieu. Much of this led, twenty years ago, to the creation of the derogatory expression, "the organization man," as signifying a new kind of conformity. If the image were meant to suggest that previously men had been free and individualist and now were uniform and identical, the history was mythical and the irony was simply a new ideology. For life in the small town had been largely narrow and bigoted—one has only to recall Sinclair Lewis's *Main Street*—and the world of organizations offered an authentic, fresh challenge and opportunity. Corporations can be forces for conformity; and they can equally be arenas for personal initiative.

A business corporation, like a university, or a government agency, or a large hospital—each with its hierarchy and status system—is now a lifetime experience for many of its members. Necessarily, therefore, it can no longer be an instrument satisfying a single end —in the case of the business corporation, only turning out its goods and services—but it has to be a satisfactory way of life for its members. It not only has to satisfy its customers; it has to be agreeable to its "self."

A business corporation, however, is subject to different constraints, and has a somewhat different ethos, from a university or a government agency or a hospital. Corporations, unlike the other three, are competitive and have to be profitable. (And the profits, moreover, are often a major support—through taxes—of the other three.) Even so, if we set up a continuum, with *economizing* at one end of the scale (in which all aspects of organization are single-mindedly reduced to becoming means to the goals of production and profit) and *sociologizing* at the other (in which all workers are guaranteed lifetime jobs, and the satisfaction of the work force becomes the primary levy on resources), then in the last thirty years the corporation has been moving steadily, for almost all its employees, towards the *sociologizing* end of the scale. One has only to note, in the rising percentage of "fringe benefit costs," the index of that shift—vacations, disability pay, health insurance, supplementary unemployment benefits, pensions, and the like.

All of this, historically, was inescapable. To the extent that the traditional sources of social support (the small town, church and family) have crumbled in society, new kinds of organizations, particularly the corporation, have taken their place; and these inevitably become the arenas in which the demands for security, justice, and esteem are made. To think of the business corporation, then, simply as an economic instrument is to fail totally to understand the meaning of the social changes of the last half century.

The Balance of Obligation

When one uses the phrase the "social responsibility" of the corporation, one is not indulging in rhetoric (though many corporate officials are), or thinking of *noblesse oblige* (which fewer corporate officials do), or assuming that some subversive doctrine is being smuggled into society (as some laissez-faire economists suggest), but simply accepting a cardinal socio-psychological fact about human attachments. Unless one assumes that loyalty and identification are simply monetary transactions, or that employment is simply a limited relation of service-for-payment, then the corporation is a social world, with social obligations to its members, as well as an economizing instrument competitively providing goods at least cost to an economic world of consumers.

But what is the balance of obligation, and how far can one go in either direction? Perhaps the best way of trying to deal with this question is to confront some questions which have already emerged or which may be emerging in the next decade.

Satisfaction on the job. The trite observation from the "human relations" literature of twenty years ago was that a man more satisfied with his job was likely to have higher morale and be more productive. Thus, the mechanical layout of work, set down by the engineer, was modified to take into account the findings of industrial psychologists and sociologists. The increase in costs could be justified by the more than proportional increase in productivity.

But what if a change in job patterns increases satisfaction but does *not* increase productivity? What is the corporation to do? The conventional answer is that the primary obligation of the corporation is to profits and that marginal increases in costs can only be justified by marginal increases in productivity. But let us take a variant of this problem. When a corporation hires more women, and these women ask for child-care centers to be paid for and maintained by the company, is it obligated to do so? The question is not just of treating such centers as a necessary cost to attract female labor when one has a tight labor market, but of a change in social values which would permit women who want to work to go back to work during the years when their children are young. A child-care center is a necessary component of job satisfaction for young women, even though it may add costs to a company far beyond the "gains" in productivity from such women. Does the conventional principle still hold?

Minority employment. Does a corporation have a special obligation to take on a larger proportion of persons from minority groups which have suffered historical disadvantage—even if such persons are less able than a competitor for the job? And if the employment of such a person increases training costs and may lead to lower productivity? The problem, in principle, is no different from that of a university which may have to set aside a special quota and, sometimes, given the limited number of places, exclude "majority" group persons who on the formal criteria of merit (e.g. test scores, grades) may be more qualified. The question of merit versus social justice is, as most complex moral problems, a question of "right" versus "right," rather than right versus wrong. Where there is such a conflict of right, how does one balance one's obligations?

Relative pay. How does one decide what a man is worth? A pure market principle, of competing supply and demand, only reflects relative scarcities, but relative scarcity is not identical with social justice. In most American industry, a distinction is still maintained between blue-collar work, wherein a man is paid by the piece or the hour, and white-collar work wherein a man is paid by the week or month. A few corporations—IBM, Texas Instruments—have abolished the distinction, but not many have followed that lead. What is the rationale for this invidious status distinction?

Within the corporation itself, the differential between the lowest paid (often the common labor rate) and the average of the top executive group may be about 25:1 or higher. On what basis is this spread justified? The original rationale was the market. But increasingly the market becomes less relevant for the determination of the relative differences between "grades" of labor and persons. Elliot Jaques, the English industrial psychologist, has sought to work out a principle of "equitable" pay on the basis of differential responsibility between jobs—as measured, for example, by the amount of independent time a man has to do a job and the degree of supervision. There may be other such "formal" systems. But because human beings want and need a clear rationale for the differences in reward among them, some principle of social justice for social distinctions will have to be articulated.

Responsibility to a community. An old problem, but one that recurs as increasingly the corporation becomes the way of life for its members. Beyond the payment of taxes, what obligations does a corporation have to the local community where it locates its plants and headquarters? What are its responsibilities in creating amenities and a more satisfactory social and cultural environment?

Responsibility for the environment. In the last few years, the corporation, along with the rest of the society, has learned that the environment cannot be treated as a "free good." How the costs are to be divided will be, as I have already indicated, one of the most difficult technical-political issues of the decade.

The confrontation with moral issues. The corporation, like the university, has always pleaded that on moral questions it is "value-neutral." As a corporation, its obligation is to seek the best return on investment. But value neutrality is no longer so easily possible. The difficulty arising from American private investment in South Africa illustrates the problem. In the classic morality tale of fifty years ago, the example was one of the local church which gained an income from properties on which brothels were located. The church could always claim a trade-off by arguing that it saved as many souls as it lost bodies. Such a calculus was never entirely convincing. A corporation's claim that it saves as many bodies as it loses souls is not likely to be more so.

What all this adds up to is that, on the continuum I have drawn of the *economizing* and *sociologizing* modes, the balance of attention shifts more and more to the latter. And, while on the particular questions I have cited which the corporation will face in the next decade, there are no exact answers or ready-made formulae, the standpoint from which the decisions will be considered will, more and more, be made from the sociological viewpoint.

The Turning Point for the Corporation

The question of "social responsibility" is, I believe, the crux of a debate that will become crucial in the next few years. One position has been put forth by Milton Friedman:

What does it mean to say that the corporate executive has a "social responsibility" in his capacity as businessman? If this statement is not pure rhetoric, it must mean that he is to act in some way that is not in the interest of his employers. For example, that he is to refrain from increasing the price of the product in order to contribute to the social objective of preventing inflation, even though a price increase would be in the best interests of his corporation. Or that he is to make expenditures on reducing pollution beyond the amount that is in the best interests of the corporation or that is required by law in order to contribute to the social objective of improving the environment. Or that, at the expense of corporate profits, he is to hire "hard-core" unemployed instead of better qualified available workmen to contribute to the social objective of reducing poverty. . . .

In a free-enterprise, private property system, a corporate executive is an employee of the owners of the business. He has direct responsibility to his employers. That responsibility is to conduct the business in accordance with their desires, which generally will be to make as much money as possible while conforming to the basic rules of the society, both those embodied in law and those embodied in ethical custom.[14]

There are two different kinds of answers to Friedman. Both were given recently by Alden Clausen, the new president and chief executive officer of the Bank of America, the biggest bank in the world.

For Clausen, one crucial question is: In what social context does the corporation operate today? As an article in *Fortune* by John Davenport reported: "To keep this giant money machine profitably growing is the first business of Alden Winship (Tom) Clausen. . . . It is of some significance that . . . his thoughts turn often to: how to alleviate if not cure the blight now spreading at Hunter's Point and south of Market Street [in San Francisco]; how to crack the city's hard-core unemployment; how to cope with student unrest at Berkeley or down the peninsula at Stanford."

In defending these objectives, Clausen confronted directly the views of Friedman. As the article in *Fortune* reported:

At the moment Clausen and his associates are less interested in modifying their bank's capital structure than in charting a course through a period when capitalism itself is under intense attack. . . .

. . .Business, he argued, has to concern itself with nonbusiness problems today if it wants to be around tomorrow. The Friedman view is okay in the short pull. "But in the long pull, nobody can expect to make profits—or have any meaningful use for profits—if the whole fabric of society is being ripped to shreds."

There is, equally, a different question, apart from social expediency: Below the surface of this clash of views, there lies an important but seldomly explicated or confronted question about the nature of the corporation. Friedman sees the corporation as fundamentally an "artificial person" and the corporate manager as simply an agent of individual sharehold-

---

[14] From "The Social Responsibility of Business Is to Increase Its Profits," in *The Sunday Times Magazine* (September 13, 1970). The argument is elaborated in Friedman's book, *Capitalism and Freedom*.

ers. Clausen sees the corporation as having a kind of life of its own, and hence having a certain freedom of choice in balancing its contribution to the long-range needs of the community against the immediate demands of owners.

And, as the writer John Davenport, himself a distinguished conservative, comments: "There may be dangers lurking in Clausen's view of corporate autonomy, but there is surely something unrealistic in the view that society is just an atomized collection of individuals." [15]

The heart of the matter is the question of the nature of the corporation. Is the corporation primarily an instrument of "owners"—legally the stockholders—or is it an autonomous enterprise which, despite its particular history, has become—or should become—an instrument for service to society in a system of pluralist powers?

A classic debate on that question was initiated forty years ago in the pages of the *Harvard Law Review* by A. A. Berle and Merrick Dodd. Berle held to the view at the time (he later revised his views) that all corporate powers are powers in trust for the benefit of the stockholders. Dodd argued that legally such was the case, but the use of private property was deeply affected with a public interest and that the directors should be viewed as trustees for the enterprise as a whole—for the corporation viewed as an institution—and not merely as "attorneys for the stockholders." Berle responded that, since one could not offer "a clear and reasonably enforceable scheme of responsibilities to someone else," Dodd's proposal would place the control of the organization entirely in the hands of management. The problem, as he saw it, was: If there is not a prior legal statement of responsibility to the stockholders, how does one prevent management from exercising arbitrary social and political power, or from becoming overreaching and self-seeking?

This legal—and sociological—issue remains. Is the manager primarily a trustee for absentee investors? Or is the role of the manager, as Frank Abrams, when he was chairman of the board of Standard Oil of New Jersey, put it, to conduct his affairs "in such a way as to maintain an equitable and working balance among the claims of the various directly interested—stockholders, employees, customers and the public at large."

Private Property or Private Enterprise?

The modern business corporation has lost many of the historic features of traditional capitalism, yet it has, for lack of a new rationale, retained the old ideology—and finds itself trapped by it.

---

[15] John Davenport, "Bank of America Is Not for Burning," *Fortune* (January 1971).

Unhappy is a society that has run out of words to describe what is going on. So Thurman Arnold observed in connection with the language of private property—the myths and folklore of capitalism —which even thirty years ago was hopelessly out of date. *The point is that today ownership is simply a legal fiction.*

A stockholder is an owner because, in theory, he has put up equity capital and taken a risk. But only a minor proportion of corporate capital today is raised through the sale of equity capital. A more significant portion of capital comes through self-financing, by the success of the enterprise itself. In the last decade, more than 60 percent of the capital investment of the nation's 1,000 largest manufacturing firms was financed internally. Retained capital is the basis of the rise in net assets of large corporations. And the growth of retained capital is the product of managerial skill. (Equally, a large portion of new capital is raised by debentures, which become a fixed charge against earnings, rather than through floating equity or risk stock. Debentures hinge on the stability of the company and the prospect of repayment—again a managerial problem.)

If one were to follow the logic of Friedman's argument, as he does—it is his strength and weakness that he always follows the logic of his argument, to the very end—one would have to outlaw or at least discourage self-financing. Under the "pure" theory of market capitalism, a firm risks a stockholder's capital and then pays back any profits—in the form of dividends—to its legal owners, the stockholders. If it seeks to risk that money again, it should ask those stockholders to reinvest that money, rather than withhold it from them and reinvest it by managerial decision. Friedman argues that it is only the "double taxation" (through corporate and personal income tax) of dividends that prevents such a desirable state of affairs from emerging. But I should say that such a state of affairs is neither desirable nor possible. Given the pattern of stock ownership today —particularly with the growth of mutual funds, pension funds and trust funds—the stockholder is often an "in-and-out" person with little continuing interest in the enterprise. Such an in-and-out procedure may be a useful discipline for management and a measure of economic performance—but then it becomes a form of countervailing power, not ownership. True owners are involved directly and psychologically in the fate of an enterprise; and this description better fits the employees of the corporation, not its stockholders. For these employees, the corporation is a social institution which they inhabit. It is politically and morally unthinkable that their lives should be at the mercy of a financial speculator.

In other words, the corporation may be a *private enterprise* institution, but it is not really a *private property* institution. (If the assets of the enterprise are primarily the skill of its managerial employees, not machinery or things—and this is preeminently true in the science-based industries, in communications, and in the so-called "knowledge industries"—then property is anyway of lesser importance.) And if ownership is largely a legal fiction, then one ought to adopt a more realistic attitude to it. One can treat stockholders not as "owners" but as legitimate claimants to some fixed share of the profits of a corporation—and to nothing more.[16]

The Meaning of "a Corporation"

What then is a corporation? If one goes back to the original meaning of the term, as a social invention of the late Middle Ages to meet some novel problems, a corporation was an instrument for self-governance for groups carrying on a common activity (artisan guilds, local boroughs, ecclesiastical bodies); it often had common economic assets, and its existence would persist beyond the lives of its individual members. Those who were "members" of the corporation were those directly responsible for its activities, those who were the legatees of the past members, and those chosen to carry on the work.

A business corporation today—like a university today—can be viewed in this original sociological conception of the term. Indeed, if one begins to look on the business corporation more and more on the model of the university, then the fallacy of ownership becomes more apparent. Who "owns" Harvard or the University of Chicago? Legally the "corporation," as composed by the overseers or the trustees. But in any sociological sense this is meaningless. The university is a self-selective ongoing enterprise of its members (administration, faculty, students, and alumni, with differential responsibilities and obligations) who seek to carry out its purposes with due

---

[16] There are about 31 million shareholders in the United States most of whom have only a small holding in the enterprise. The New York Stock Exchange survey of shareownership (1970) showed that of 30,520,000 shareholders surveyed (out of a total of 30,850,000) about 12,500,000 had portfolios worth less than $5,000, and 6,400,000 had between $5,000 and $10,000. Thus a total of 18,900,000 shareholders, or 62 percent, had portfolios of less than $10,000.

Institutional investors generally now hold an increasing proportion of the outstanding equity securities of major American corporations. As of the end of 1970, the New York Stock Exchange estimated that $161.9 billion or 25.4 percent of all equity securities of companies listed on the Exchange were held by institutional holders. If one includes unregistered mutual funds, investment partnerships, nonbank trusts and foreign institutions, the Exchange estimated that the total of all institutional holdings would exceed 40 percent. (I am indebted to Professor Philip Blumberg of the Boston University Law School for the data.)

regard to the interests of the particular community which constitutes the university—and also to the larger community that makes the university possible.

As a business institution, the "corporation" is the management and the board of directors, operating as trustees for members of the enterprise as a whole—not just stockholders, but workers and consumers too—and with due regard to the interests of society as a whole. But if this view is accepted, there is a significant logical corollary—that the constituencies which make up the corporation themselves have to be represented within the board of corporate power.[17] Without that, there is no effective countervailing power to that of executive management. More important, without such representation, there would be a serious question about the "legitimacy" of managerial power.

How such constituencies might be represented is a question to be explored. A dozen years ago, Bayless Manning, Jr., until recently the Dean of the Stanford Law School, sought to picture the corporation as if it were in law what it often is in fact, as a kind of "voting trust" wherein the stockholder delegates all his rights, except that of collecting dividends, to the directors. In order to establish some check on the board of directors, he proposed a "second chamber," an "extrinsic body," which would review decisions of the board where conflicts of interest arose—such as compensation of officers, contributions to other enterprises (universities, community efforts, etc.) not directly related to a company's business, clashes with a public interest, etc.

It is beyond the scope of this essay, and the competence of the author, to estimate the viability of these—or other—specific pro-

---

[17] The growth of institutional holdings by political entities, such as municipal pension funds, colleges, foundations, churches, and other groups which are subject to direct political pressure may itself create a small force, in certain circumstances, for changes in corporate policy. Thus in the General Motors campaign initiated by Ralph Nader, Mayor Lindsay of New York instructed the trustees of the New York City pension funds to vote their 162,000 General Motors shares in favor of the Campaign GM proposals, as did Mayor White of Boston, Mayor Alioto of San Francisco, and the Wisconsin and Iowa state retirement funds.

At the same time, corporations have moved to widen representation on their boards. As of 1970, blacks had been elected to the Boards of Directors of such leading corporations as:

Chase Manhattan Bank	Columbia Broadcasting
Commonwealth Edison	Equitable Life Assurance
First National City Bank	General Motors
Girard Trust Bank	Great Atlantic & Pacific Tea
International Business Machines	Michigan Consolidated Gas
Pan American Airways	Prudential Life Insurance
Standard Oil of Ohio	Westinghouse Broadcasting
W. T. Grant	

posals. The problem is there; it is not going to go away; and discussion of possible resolutions is anything but premature.

From Bitterness to Banality

As a debate on these issues continues, one important consideration should be kept in mind—the bitterness of one generation is often the banality of another. Who, today, gives a second thought to savings bank life insurance? Yet this idea, authored by Louis D. Brandeis in Massachusetts, was fought for five months in passage through the legislature and was marked by one of the bitterest fights ever witnessed on Beacon Hill. (One line of attack was that people would not voluntarily seek insurance, and that they would not take it out at all if the expensive system of soliciting by agents were done away with.) The issue gave Brandeis a national reputation, and eventually brought him to the Supreme Court. The reputation remained, but the issue itself soon faded.

The lesson, however, was not, and is still not wholly learned— reforms will never be as sweeping in their effects as their proponents hope, and the results will rarely be as damaging and apocalyptic as the opponents fear. Workmen's compensation was an issue that inflamed a generation of radicals and was fought by industry on the ground that it would relieve the workman of "individual responsibility" for his actions; yet who today would deny that industrial safety is a legitimate cost of factory operations?

Such reforms are always an expression of a revision—implicit or explicit—in the American "public philosophy." This kind of "revisionism" is inevitable as men and societies change, and as the dominant values assume a new shape. The private enterprise system has been the primary institution of Western society not because of its coercive power but because its values—economizing and increasing output of material goods—were congruent with the major consumer values of the society. With all its obvious imperfections the system "worked." Today, however, those values are themselves being questioned, not in the way socialists and radicals questioned them a generation ago—that they were achieved at the cost of exploiting the worker—but at the very core, the creation of more private goods at the expense of other social values. I return to a point made earlier that unlike the polity, no one, meeting collectively "voted in" our market economy. But now votes are being taken.

It seems clear to me that, today, we in America are moving away from a society based on a private-enterprise market system toward one in which the most important economic decisions will be made at the political level, in terms of consciously defined "goals" and "priorities." The dangers inherent in such a shift are familiar enough to anyone acquainted with the liberal tradition. In the past, there was an "unspoken consensus," and the public philosophy did not need to be articulated. And this was a strength, for articulation often invites trials by force when implicit differences are made manifest. Today, however, there is a visible change from market to non-market political decision-making. The market disperses responsibility: the political center is visible, the question of who gains and who loses is clear, and government becomes a cockpit.

But to be hypnotized by such dangers is little less than frivolous. No social or economic order has a writ of immortality, and the consumer-oriented free-enterprise society no longer satisfies the citizenry, as once it did. So it will have to change, in order that something we still recognize as a liberal society might survive.

Whether such a change will represent "progress" is a nice metaphysical question that I, for one, do not know how to answer. This is a society that has rested on the premises of individualism and market rationality, in which the varied ends desired by individuals would be maximized by free exchange. We now move to a communal ethic, without that community being, as yet, wholly defined. In a sense, the movement away from governance by political economy to governance by political philosophy—for that is the meaning of the shift—is a turn to non-capitalist modes of social thought. And this is the long-run historical tendency in Western society.[18]

---

[18] This essay has dealt with the business corporation in the American context, but in the Soviet Union many of the same problems occur in the relation of the bureaucratic state enterprise to the society as a whole. Under the Soviet planning system, each enterprise is responsible for meeting the production and profit goals of the central plan. Where the enterprise "overfulfills" the plan it is allowed to retain a portion of the profits for its social investment fund, which is used to build housing for its workers, expand clubhouse facilities, and the like. Thus there is an incentive to "economizing," since the enterprise does not want to absorb the social costs that it generates. The large Soviet paper plants at the edge of Lake Baikal, for example, dangerously polluted the lake but strenuously resisted the idea of "internalizing" those additional costs. Insofar as the Soviet Union is committed so singlemindedly to the idea of "economic growth" and the "economizing" mode in the way I have used it, one can say that the Soviet system is actually state capitalism in which the maximization of production of each enterprise is the primary goal of the society. Yet, inevitably, in a complex society no enterprise can run its show in a single-purpose fashion, and protests do arise; and the state must also confront the problem of how to allocate the social costs. For a discussion of this problem in the Soviet Union, see Marshall Goldman, *The Spoils of Progress: Environmental Pollution in the Soviet Union* (Cambridge, Mass., 1972).

CHAPTER
5

Social Choice and
Social Planning:
The Adequacy of Our
Concepts and Tools

"THE intellectual life of man," William James once remarked, "consists almost wholly in his substitution of a conceptual order for the perceptual order in which his experience originally comes."[1] A conceptual scheme is a set of consistent terms which group together diverse attributes or properties of objects or experiences, in a higher order of abstraction, in order to relate them or distinguish them from other objects or experiences. To some extent, our intellectual—and political—problems derive from the fact that we use intellectual concepts and paradigms that are products or summations of an older order of experience. In economics, we have the "theory of the firm," but the modern corporation is not simply the firm writ large, and we have no coherent intellectual model to account for its behavior. We still think of the individual as the unit of social decision (and on such questions as the number of children to have, or on consumer purchases in the market, he—and she—is the unit) but on most of the questions which affect major allocation of resources or the social map of the country, the unit is the group, or the government, and we have no adequate theory of public goods and social choice. We all know that problems of scale completely distort the shape of the society, yet in discussing our governmental structures we still use the language, and often the assumptions, of two hundred years ago.

The first order of questions, therefore, is the adequacy of our concepts as related to the purposes at hand. In dealing with the changes in American life, I intend to set forth some propositions which question the older formulations and, in part, to propose a number of new ones which may be more adequate in understanding some perplexities about American life.

---

[1] See "Percept and Concept," in William James, *Some Problems of Philosophy* (New York, 1916), p. 51.

These questions, some of them rhetorical, some of them ambiguous (as are all true questions), are presented here in the guise of "notes." Notes are often a difficult form for a reader. He wants a tidy exposition which makes its points in linear fashion (ideally with some elegance of expression) and which comes to a specific conclusion. In a curious sense, this is a peculiarly "American" demand. The presumption is usually made that every problem has a solution, and one can march toward it in direct, linear fashion. Indirection is irritating. It suggests ambiguity or complexity, which, in the American vernacular, becomes translated as evasiveness or hesitation. American life is based on experience, not sensibility; and this, too, is an aspect of the "national style."

SOCIAL CHOICE AND SOCIAL VALUES:
THE NEED FOR A NEW CALCULUS [2]

"The great society"—that is, in the occurrence of the phrase—has many forebears, but none, perhaps, as startling as Adam Smith. In *The Wealth of Nations,* he wrote:

According to the system of natural liberty, the sovereign has only three duties to attend to; three duties of great importance, indeed, but plain and intelligible to common understandings: first, the duty of protecting the society from the violence and invasion of other independent societies; secondly, the duty of protecting, as far as possible, every member of the society from the injustice or oppression of every other member of it, or the duty of establishing an exact administration of justice; and thirdly, the duty of erecting and maintaining certain public works and certain public institutions, which it can never be for the interest of any individual, or small number of individuals, to errect and maintain; because the profit could never repay the expense to any individual or small number of individuals, though it may frequently do much more than repay it to a great society.[3]

---

[2] In this and in some of the succeeding sections I have drawn on memoranda I prepared for the National Commission on Technology, Automation and Economic Progress and for the Commission on the Year 2000 of the American Academy of Arts and Sciences.

[3] Adam Smith, *The Wealth of Nations* (New York, 1937), p. 651. The phrase "the great society" appears in three places in *The Wealth of Nations* by my count (pp. 651, 681, and 747), but its meaning is to be found at the conclusion of book V, chap. 1—which deals with the revenues of the sovereign or Commonwealth—and, in context, the phrase "great society" means here the "whole society" (see p. 767). It is a point of considerable relevance for the discussion above. The capitalized phrase "The Great Society" occurs as the title of the book by Graham Wallas. That book (published in 1914) grew out of a course that Wallas gave at Harvard in 1910, and though the initial theme is the growing interdependence of peoples, and an ensuing change of social scale, the book itself is not an effort to assess the sources or consequences of this change, but an effort to use the findings of the newer social psychology for the rational pursuit of social affairs.

To encounter the phrase "a great society" in the context of what are, for Adam Smith, the legitimate functions—and indeed the limitations—of government is striking in the light of the problems of the great society today. For Adam Smith was one of the men—the other was John Locke—who "planned" the United States of America. I use the word "planned"—awkward in this context—quite deliberately. For both Smith and Locke laid down the conditions—derived from some specific philosophical assumptions—for the operation of the society that was to emerge in the United States.

The key proposition for Smith, of course, was that every individual, by pursuing his own ends, helps society as a whole. Adam Smith argued:

As every individual, therefore, endeavours as much as he can . . . to direct that industry that its produce may be of the greatest value; every individual necessarily labours to render the annual revenue of the society as great as he can. He generally, indeed, neither intends to promote the public interest, nor knows how much he is promoting it . . . by directing that industry in such a manner as its produce may be of the greatest value, he intends only his own gain, and he is in this, as in many other cases, led by an invisible hand to promote an end which was no part of his intention. Nor is it always the worse for the society that it was no part of it. By pursuing his own interest he frequently promotes that of the society more effectually than when he really intends to promote it.[4]

To put the case briefly and baldly in the modern jargon, Smith's conditions for a free and productive society are: individualism, rationality, perfect information, and rational choice; the good of the society is the aggregate of individual utilities. In fact, Smith here laid down a proposition that was almost entirely new in the history of civil society: in a free exchange, both parties to a transaction could gain. In previous times, it was well understood that wealth was in some way acquired largely through exploitation: conquest, tax-farming, tolls, tithes, and so on. Economic life was thus a zero-sum game; one could win only at the expense of a loser. Under the conditions laid down by Smith, economic life could be a non-zero-sum game.[5]

We come to the problem raised by the two quotations from Adam Smith, for economic goods are not of one type, but two: individual goods and social goods. Individual goods are divisible and each per-

---

[4] *The Wealth of Nations*, Book IV, chap. 11, p. 423.

[5] In actual fact, it was not the existence of free exchange but the existence of technology, with its promise of rising productivity, that created the possibility of economic life remaining a non-zero-sum gain. For an instructive book on the means whereby technology has been the chief means of promoting social equality, see Jean Fourastie, *The Causes of Wealth* (Glencoe, Ill., 1960).

son or household buys particular objects and individual service on the basis of free consumer choice. Social goods are not divisible into individual items of possession but are part of a communal service (e.g. national defense, education, beautification of landscape, flood control and so on). These goods and services are not sold to individual consumers nor adjusted to individual tastes. The nature and amount of goods must be set by a single decision, applicable jointly to all persons. Social goods, therefore, are subject to communal or political, rather than individual, demand.[6]

The singular point is that in "the great society" more and more goods necessarily have to be purchased communally. Defense apart, the planning of cities and the rationalization of transit, the maintenance of open spaces and the extension of recreational areas, the elimination of air pollution and the cleaning up of the rivers, the underwriting of education and the organization of adequate medical care, all are now "public institutions" which cannot be undertaken by individuals, though their creation would "more than repay it to a great society."

Now, individuals have their own scale of values, which allow them to assess relative satisfactions against costs, and to make their purchases accordingly. Yet, as I have argued in the previous chapter, there is no mechanism which allows us to consider, in terms of costs and benefits, the varying combinations of private consumption and public purchases of goods.

These are practical, political problems. But at this point a theoretical thorn intrudes. For in recent years economists and mathematicians have been able to supply a "rational proof" of the individual utility preference model, but not that of the group welfare function model. Let us turn to what might be called Adam Smith I. In the famous beginning of *The Wealth of Nations* Smith remarks that only human beings engage in truck or barter. An animal who wants attention fawns or seeks to be engaging. While human beings are sometimes equally servile, they do better by trying to strike a bargain. (". . . it is in vain for him to expect [help of his brethren] from their benevolence only. He will be more likely to prevail if he can interest their self-love in his favour, and shew them that it is for their own advantage to do for him what he requires of them.")

In effect, one offers another man a rationally calculable advantage. But how does one make such calculations? What is the value of an object or a service to a person, and how does he compare one object to another? For a man to choose rationally, there must be some un-

<hr>

[6] For one of the first discussions of this problem, see Howard Bowen, "The Interpretation of Voting in the Allocation of Economic Resources," *Quarterly Journal of Economics*, vol. LVIII (November 1943), pp. 27–48.

derlying standard of value against which he can rate all alternatives. Money is a rough and ready measure. But the "value" of money diminishes as one's hoard of it increases. Ten dollars means much less to a millionaire than to a pauper. (This is one of the difficulties, as well, in applying a theory of equality to punishments. Two men may be fined $100 for speeding, but for the millionaire the $100 means much less than for a worker who pays the same fine. Is equality then the "same" punishment, or an equal ability to bear punishment?) Jeremy Bentham proposed the concept of "utility" as the unit for a model of rational choice, in which individuals would rank their preferences in an orderly way. But there was little way of comparing utilities (i.e. how much more one wanted one preference rather than another— its intensity quotient, so to speak) or of working out optimal combinations when one wants different proportions of different things. Utility, like value, came to be regarded as a metaphysical concept, and price alone was taken as the indicator of exchange and comparability.

The publication of *The Theory of Games and Economic Behavior* by von Neumann and Morgenstern, in 1944, rehabilitated the concept of utility by dealing with the conditions of choice, or decision-making under risk. One does not know for certain the consequences of a given choice, but one does know the alternatives, and a certain gamble can be built into the choices in which the value of the probability of winning is put against the probability of losing. (A simple game: under conditions of a gamble you can win a Cadillac, but if you lose you get a bicycle; if you decide not to play you get a Volkswagen. Thus, if the chances are 50–50, will you take the gamble or take the consolation prize? What if the chances are 40–60, 30–70, 20–80, 10–90? At what point will you stop taking the risk?) Under such conditions it is possible to assign numerical values to utility which allow you to scale (like a temperature gauge, rather than just rank) the preferences individuals may have.[7] It is equally possible, using the various techniques of linear programming, to work out "optimal" solutions in the combination of resources, the maximizing of utilities and the like.

But when one turns from individual decision-making to that of groups, when one considers the problem, quoting Luce and Raiffa, "of how best to amalgamate the discordant preference patterns of the

[7] John von Neumann and Oskar Morganstern (Princeton, N.J., 1953). For a simple mathematical proof of the possibility of scaling utilities, see Jacob Marschak, "Scaling of Utilities and Probabilities," in *Game Theory and Related Approaches to Social Behavior*, ed. Martin Shubik (New York: Wiley, 1964). For a more general discussion of utility theory, and decision-making under certainty, risk, and uncertainty, see Duncan Luce and Howard Raiffa, *Games and Decisions* (New York, 1958), chap. 2.

members of a society to arrive at a compromise preference pattern for society as a whole," we seem to be at an impasse. In the first major effort to formulate the problem, Kenneth Arrow demonstrated, in his *Social Choice and Individual Values*, written in 1951, that the five requirements of "fairness" for social welfare functions are inconsistent (i.e. no welfare function exists which satisfies all of them.) [8] Even the principle of majority rule, which satisfies three and possibly four of the conditions, is subject to the logical contradiction, first formulated by Condorcet, of the paradox of the cyclical majority.

What is paradoxical, therefore, is that while one can now, for the first time perhaps, set up a rational "model" of the Smith-Bentham world, the basic conditions for social rationality become less and less a possibility for the "players" in the communal society.

The proof can be demonstrated by an elementary theorem. Supposing there are three voters, A, B, and C, whose preferences on issues x, y, and z are ordered in the following pattern, we find:

PREFERENCES	VOTERS		
	A	B	C
First	x	z	y
Second	y	x	z
Third	z	y	x

Clearly, x is preferred to y by a majority (voters A and B); y is preferred to z by a majority (voters A and C); from the principle of transitivity (i.e. if an individual prefers x to y, and y to z, we assume he would also prefer x to z) we should predict that x is also preferred to z, and that x, therefore, is the choice of the majority of the voters: but in fact, z is preferred to x by voters B and C, so that no single majority can be formulated on these three issues.[9]

There have been numerous attempts both to modify the original conditions Arrow put forth as necessary to organize a group welfare function and to resolve the voting paradox (by conceptions of logrolling, bargains, or the creation of what Anthony Downs has called "passionate majorities"). But so far, at least to the extent that I can

---

[8] A revised edition appeared in 1963 (New York).

[9] The most comprehensive effort to deal with the problem is that of Duncan Black, *The Theory of Committees and Elections* (Cambridge, Eng., 1958). Further discussion can be found in James M. Buchanan and Gordon Tullock, *The Calculus of Consent* (Ann Arbor, Mich., 1962). Some earlier discussions are in Robert A. Dahl and Charles E. Lindblom, *Politics, Economics and Welfare* (New York, 1953), and Anthony Downs, *An Economic Theory of Democracy* (New York, 1957). For a symposium on Arrow's "impossibility theorem," see Sidney Hook, ed., *Human Values and Economic Policy* (New York, 1967).

follow the technical literature, no satisfactory solutions have been forthcoming.[10]

This problem—of seeking to produce a single social ordering of alternative social choices which would correspond to individual orderings—is academic, in the best sense of the word. In the "real" world the problem of social priorities, of what social utilities are to be maximized, of what communal enterprises are to be furthered will be settled in the political arena, by "political criteria"—i.e. the relative weights and pressures of different interest groups, balanced against some vague sense of the national need and the public interest. But it is precisely at this point that the theoretical thorn may begin to prick. For increasingly, one of the issues of a great society—one which can be defined as a society that seeks to become conscious of its goals—is the relationship, if not the clash, between "rationality" and "politics." Much of contemporary social theory has been addressed to the rigorous formulation of rational models of man, in which optimizing, maximizing, and minimizing provide models of behavior that are rationally normative. But we seem to be unable to formulate a "group theory" of economic choice. The impasse of social theory, in regard to social welfare, is a disturbing prospect at this stage of the transition to a communal society.

I have raised a problem—the lack of an ordering mechanism to make social choices—and quickly taken it to a level of abstraction which is meaningless to practical men.[11] For theorists, the implications are quite drastic, for these logical conundrums strike at the assumptions of those who think that the general will will emerge out of necessity in democratic debate, and those rationalists—as we all may be—who assume that the public interest is discoverable simply by a summation of preferences. Practical men can take heart, for in all this an intuitive idea is reinforced; namely, that differences between persons are best settled, as are so many differences, by bargaining. As Robert Dahl has observed:

Many Americans are frequently dismayed by its paradoxes; indeed, few Americans who look upon our political process attentively can fail,

---

[10] See Arrow, op. cit. In an appendix to a new edition of his book (New Haven, 1963) Arrow has sought to counter some discoveries of errors in his proofs by reformulating the conditions to show that the inconsistencies in the conditions still remain and that no logical foundations for a complete social welfare function are possible.

[11] But theory does have a way sometimes of confounding practical men. William H. Riker has illustrated the relevance of hidden voting paradoxes through an analysis of the rules for amending bills in the committees of the House of Representatives. He has shown that under a number of rules, amendments might be adopted which are not favored by a majority—without this fact ever being known! Thus,

at times, to feel deep frustration and angry resentment with a system that on the surface has so little order and so much chaos.

For it is a markedly decentralized system. Decisions are made by endless bargaining; perhaps in no other national political system in the world is bargaining so basic a component of the political process. . . . [Yet] with all its defects, it does nonetheless provide a high probability that any active and legitimate group will make itself heard effectively at some stage in the process of decision. This is no mean thing in a political system.[12]

And this is, perhaps, as it should be. But if we are to rest our case on the legitimacy of the group interest process—and this was the contribution, initially, of Arthur F. Bentley—some less rarefied but still theoretical questions arise.[13]

---

for example, when a paragraph of an amendment and an amendment to an amendment are before a committee, the first vote is on the amendments. If the amendment to a paragraph is passed, it replaces the original paragraph without further vote. Because it votes only twice on three issues, the House does not discover any intransitivity, and a choice may become law which was favored only by a minority. Riker concludes that various situations of this sort may be expected to occur, *in practice*, slightly more than 10 percent of the time—which should make some practical men uneasy.

This is not to say that "majority voting" is impossible. If one returns to the original example of the cyclical majority it will be seen that the intransitivity of preferences is evident only on a third vote. Thus, to uncover intransitivities, one has to initiate a complete "round robin" matching each proposal with every other, but as Riker notes no legislatures require such matching procedure for groups of more than three proposals. Once the intransitivities are uncovered, one can, as Duncan Black has demonstrated, proceed to a system of "exhaustive voting," which matches candidate against candidate, or issue against issue, to obtain the majority decision in each instance. And, in a more theoretical vein, as Arrow and Black have demonstrated, by ranking preferences on a graph, one can obtain "single-peaked" profiles of each voter; and when all the profiles for a given group are represented as a single-peaked preference curves on one set of axes, a single majority choice can be obtained—if the group is odd in number, or if the chairman votes in case of a tie.

But practical men can take heart from the fact that, in practice, where such disparities of preferences or intensities do occur, some form of log-rolling or bargaining takes place, and, as Tullock and Buchanan have shown, one can fit such procedures into the theoretical resolutions of the voting paradoxes. This still leaves open, again it should be noted, the larger theoretical question of finding a rational solution to a social welfare function. Majority voting is preferred because it satisfies three or possibly four of the five conditions which Arrow has established as necessary for validation, and therefore is the most sensible of "compromises." On some occasions, however, fearing a "tyranny of the majority," one might want to consider some of the more complicated means which have been suggested by Black and Arrow to arrive at a social welfare function. And, finally, there is the point that any solution—at least those suggested so far—does not fulfill the complete logical conditions of arriving at a true social choice.

For further discussion see William H. Riker, *The Theory of Political Coalitions* (New Haven, 1962).

[12] Robert A. Dahl, *A Preface to Democratic Theory* (Chicago, 1956), p. 150.

[13] Nag that I am, I would still like, at the conclusion of this section, to return to the justification of the theoretical problem; for even a pragmatist like myself has to

GROUP POLITICS AND INDIVIDUAL LEADERSHIP

If rationality and individual choice operating through the market were the theoretical contributions of eighteenth-century economics, the idea of representation and interests was the addition of nineteenth-century politics; and the fusion of the two resulted in a social theory of the free society. The most comprehensive formulation of the political idea was offered, perhaps, by John Stuart Mill, in his essay on "Representative Government." Mill wrote:

The meaning of representative government is, that the whole people, or some numerous portion of them, exercise through deputies periodically elected by themselves the ultimate controlling power, which, in every constitution, must reside somewhere . . .

A place where every interest and shade of opinion in the country can have its cause even passionately pleaded, in the face of the government and of all other interests and opinions, can compel them to listen, and either comply, or state clearly why they do not, is in itself, if it answered no other purpose, one of the most important political institutions that can exist anywhere, and one of the foremost benefits of free government.

The theory of representative government reflected a picture of society as a "balance of forces." The legislature, in this conception, was supposed to contain representatives of the various social divisions and all the class interests in the country, for, as Mill noted in appealing for the right of the working class to be represented in Parliament, "in the absence of its natural defenders, the interest of the excluded is always in danger of being overlooked." Mill, in fact, was so intent on the idea of the representation of minorities that he gave enthusiastic endorsement to Thomas Hare's proposal for proportional representation, "a scheme which has the almost unparalleled merit of carrying out a great principle of government in a manner approaching to ideal perfection as regards the special object in view. . . ." [14]

---

recognize the necessity for some rational system (if only as yardstick), of what social choices *could be*. One can carry the argument forward, perhaps, with this consideration: one might, today, with mathematical models and high-speed computers, write a single economic plan for a country that would show, through input-output matrices, the optimal distribution of economic resources, with products valued at full economic costs. But the administrative difficulties in implementing such a plan might be so enormous that, in practice, one would have to resort to the market or some quasi-bargaining system for the actual operation of the economy. Yet the value of such a theoretical construction is that it could serve as a yardstick, establishing "shadow allocations" and "shadow prices" for the system and allowing us to intervene at those points where discrepancies show up. In an analogous sense, one would want a theoretical social choice model in order to have an optimal social welfare function.

[14] John Stuart Mill, *Utilitarianism, Liberty and Representative Government* (New York, 1936), pp. 209, 228, 240, 261. The theory of representation and interests, it should be noted, is normative. It is part of Mill's concern to define the "best form of

This normative theory was refined by what might be called the "realist" school of political thought, from Arthur F. Bentley on (one should note, of course, that Bentley's original formulations in 1908, ignored for many years, were restated three decades later by V. O. Key, David Truman, and Earl Latham), to describe the empirical nature of political reality. If a "group theory" was lacking in economics, it certainly made its appearance, in full flower, in American political thought in the twentieth century. V. O. Key put it most succinctly:

At bottom, group interests are the animating forces in the political process. . . . Whatever the bases of group interest may be, the study of politics must rest on an analysis of the objectives and composition of the interest groups within a society. . . . The chief vehicles for the expression of group interest are political parties and pressure groups. Through these formal mechanisms groups of people with like interests make themselves felt in the balancing of political forces.[15]

And, in this conception, the role of the politician was to be a broker:

The problem of the politician or the statesman in a democracy is to maintain a working balance between the demands of competing interests and values. . . . Within limits . . . special interests in a democracy are free to express their demands and their disagreements. . . . The politician in a democracy . . . must be able to hold together enough of these special interests to retain power; he must yield here, stand firm there, delay at the next point, and again act vigorously in a confusing complex of competing forces and interests. . . . The politician . . . must play the part of arbitrator and mediator, subject to the criticism of all. To avoid or mitigate conflict, he compromises.[16]

Whatever the truth of this "model" as a description of the "nineteenth century inheritance," [17] it is astonishingly out of date for an understanding of politics in the second half of the twentieth century, for it fails to take into account the three most decisive characteristics, or shaping elements, of national policy today: the influence of foreign

---

government." Practice, of course, might be entirely different. As Mill notes: "Politically speaking, a great part of all power consists in will . . . Opinion is itself one of the greatest active social forces. One person with a belief is a social power equal to ninety-nine who have only interests." Ibid., p. 183.

[15] V. O. Key, *Politics, Parties and Pressure Groups* (New York, 1942), pp. 23–24.

[16] Ibid., pp. 10–11.

[17] The "group theory of politics," it should be noted, has been challenged on theoretical grounds by Mancur Olson, Jr., who, applying an "economic analysis" to the nature of aggregate choice, argues that interest groups do not represent best the interests of their members. See Mancur Olson, Jr., *The Logic of Collective Action: Public Goods and the Theory of Groups* (Cambridge, Mass., 1965).

policy, the "future-orientation" of society, and the increasing role of "technical" decision-making.

Foreign policy is not primarily formulated in response to the needs and pressures of domestic pressure groups (though once decisions are taken, some modifications may be made in reaction to their demands —e.g. to build airplanes in the Southwest rather than in the Northwest). Foreign policy is shaped in accordance with great power and ideological interests, and as responses to perceived threats from other great powers or ideological forces. But its consequence, under conditions of a cold war, is to force a "mobilized posture" on the society as a whole, to create some sense of national unity, and to centralize decision-making and enormous resources in the hands of a national administration.

The commitment to economic growth and the new dimensions of social change—its more rapid shock effects on larger and larger sections of the society and the consequent need to anticipate social change and, to a considerable extent, direct it—have brought with it a renewed emphasis on planning, on the need to become more conscious of national goals and with the "alternative futures" which a society with a steady productivity (a constant 3 percent rate of productivity will *double* national output in twenty-four years) can provide. "The process of innovation," write Dahl and Lindblom, "is both scientific and political. It is not enough that new social techniques be discovered; they must also be put to use. Invention and discovery are only the beginning of a process, the next step in which is innovation, a matter of politics. What we are suggesting is that this process taken as a whole is proceeding with astonishing rapidity— it is perhaps the greatest political revolution of our times." [18]

The combination of these two elements brings into play the increasing role of technical decision-making. The shaping of conscious policy, be it in foreign policy, defense, or economics, calls to the fore the men with the skills necessary to outline the constraints ahead, to work out in detail the management and policy procedures, and to assess the consequences of choices. The revolutions in military technology (the introduction of nuclear power, the replacement of manned aircraft by missiles) were initiated by scientists. The development of systems-analysis and cost-effectiveness techniques, which have revolutionized both the strategy process as well as the management structure of the Pentagon, was brought about by mathematicians and economists.[19] The management of the national economy, with its

---

[18] Op. cit., p. 8.
[19] See Charles J. Hitch and Roland N. McKean, *The Economics of Defense in the Nuclear Age* (Cambridge, Mass., 1960), and *Analysis for Military Decisions: The Rand Lectures on Systems Analysis*, ed. Edward S. Quade (Chicago, 1964).

close watch on the effects of government spendiing, requires the services of men skilled in the arts, and such crucial policy questions as when to have tax cuts or tax increases, how much to have and where to apply it, and what the wage-price guidepost should be, increasingly become technical decisions.[20]

But the most important political consequence of all this is the passing of effective power, in almost all political systems, from the legislative and parliamentary bodies to the executive, and the re-emergence of what Bertrand de Jouvenel has called, in his elegant fashion, *The Principate*. How could it be otherwise when, in the nature of modern politics, foreign policy is no longer "diplomacy" but an unceasing round of strategic maneuver in which crucial decisions have to be taken speedily, and when, because of the new patterns of social change, the very need to plan policies, rather than lay down laws, gives the initiative to the executive?

In the United States we have seen, in the past twenty-five years, the enormous transformation of the presidency to the Executive Office of the President, with the addition of new staff functions, such as the Bureau of the Budget, the Council of Economic Advisers, and the National Security Council, directly within that office. In the long run, it is not the growth of the personal powers and prestige of the President that is important, but the *institutionalization* of such crucial control and directing functions—as are now carried out by the Budget Bureau and the Council of Economic Advisers—in the executive which reinforces the structural shifts of power.

Although these essential changes—the new role of the executive (or the charismatic leader), the conflict between technocratic rationality with political bargaining, and the orientation to the future— have been variously described, political theory has not yet absorbed these new circumstances into a new conceptual structure. Although the interest-group model has less and less relevance in allowing us to understand the transformation of America into a mobilized polity, even the later, sophisticated versions of this model—cast in terms of systems, and inputs and outputs[21]—repeat the same assumptions, using equilibrium rather than "balance of forces" as the flywheel of

---

[20] As one quondam bureaucrat has earnestly argued, "the development of public policy and of the methods of its administration owe less in the long run to processes of conflict among political parties and social or economic pressure groups than to the more objective processes of research and discussion among professional groups." Don K. Price, *Government and Science* (New York, 1962)—a statement written little more than ten years after V. O. Key's and reflecting the differences, perhaps, of the pre-war and post-war experiences of political analysts.

[21] See, for example, David Easton, "An Approach to the Analysis of Political Systems," *World Politics* (April 1957), pp. 383–400, and *A Systems Analysis of Political Life* (New York, 1965). A more mechanical model is presented by William Mitchell, *The American Polity* (New York, 1962).

the model. Instead of models depicting government as a kind of umpire, mediating the inputs provided by conflicting interest groups and allowing them to issue forth in the output of decisions, a more adequate picture would have to see the presidency as a system capable of free action, even choosing which interests it allows to become inputs, and the executive itself bargaining—on the basis of technocratic decisions—with various interest groups in the society.[22]

Beyond the question of a more adequate empirical model there is the more difficult problem of formulating a normative theory, which—taking into account the ineluctable elements of centralized decision-making, the extension of social or communal choices, and the need for conscious social planning (not to "direct" the society, but to facilitate desired social changes)—can set forth rational criteria consonant with the values of a free society. In the construction of such a theory, other elements of re-conceptualization may have to be taken into account. Such re-conceptualizations, by grouping familiar facts in a new way, may help us identify new problems that will be arising in the communal society.

NUMBER, INTERACTION, DENSITY

A mass society is one which is characterized not by large numbers, or rather by numbers alone, but by concentration and density. Large land-mass societies may have large populations, but in the past they were spread out over immense areas of land and were mainly segmental rather than integral in social organization. It is when segmentation breaks down and people come into increasing contact and interaction with each other—in large urban concentrations in the past, or through mass communication today—that the features of a mass society appear.[23] Such features are (in the social structure) the divorce of the family from the occupational system, increased specialization, differentiation of function, multiplication of collectivities, hierarchies, formalization of rules, extension of universalism, and (in the culture) the secularization of beliefs, the emphasis on individual experience, the search for novelty and sensation, the syncretism of creeds and forms.[24]

The mass society, in short, reflects what I have called in another context "the eclipse of distance." While the initial changes are cre-

---

[22] An extreme version of this, perhaps, would be Gaullist France, where for a period of time almost the entire political system (concentrated in the administrative structure) had become "independent" of the society, initiating the changes (demands, inputs) and making decisions on the basis of technocratic criteria.

[23] For the classic statement of the problem, see Emile Durkheim, *On the Division of Labor in Society* (New York, 1933), book II, chap. 2.

[24] These themes are elaborated by Talcott Parsons in several works. See *Structure and Process in Modern Societies* (Glencoe, Ill., 1960).

ated by the new forms of transportation and communication which bring people into ready contact with each other in innumerable ways, the "eclipse of distance" is not only the foreshortening of time and space in flying across continents, or in being in instant communication with any part of the globe by television or radio, it is also, as regards the *experienced* time of the person, an eclipse of social, esthetic and psychic distance as well.[25]

The United States, with all its historical particularity, has in many ways acquired these features of a mass society. Regionalism as a form of cultural segmentation has largely broken down, though some political influences remain. The family-based enterprise (farms, retail establishments, small manufacturing businesses) is of minor importance in the economy. The mobility of individuals, social and spatial, is unprecedented in history, and stupendous.[26]

The effects of the increase in number, interaction, and density of population are enormous. Here, taking the communication pattern as a single variable, I shall seek to illustrate it, with two problems.

The loss of insulating space. If one looks at American history, what strikes one immediately is the tremendous amount of violence, particularly labor violence, that took place over a period of sixty-five years (from 1877, beginning with the railroad strikes, and ending with the outbreak of war at the end of 1941). From any rough set of

---

[25] Though the changes in culture and social structure derive from a common source, the contrasting demands or impulses in each realm clearly impose an agonizing tension whose consequences, important as I believe they are for locating crucial strains in the society, are beyond the purview of this essay. I discuss this, to some extent, in "The Disjunction of Culture and Social Structure," in *Science and Culture*, ed. Gerald Holton (Boston, 1965).

[26] The continuous movement of persons into, out of, between, and within labor markets in any one year is one index of such mobility. Thus, in 1964, the average number of persons in the labor force was 74 million, with about 70 million employed and 3.9 million unemployed. But hidden beneath these national averages, one finds that: 87 million people were in the labor force at some time during the year; 85 million different people held jobs; 43 million entered or re-entered the labor force; 42 million left the labor force for temporary periods or permanently; and 14.1 million different persons experienced some period of unemployment. (Data from the Bureau of Labor Statistics for the National Commission on Technology, Automation and Economic Progress.)

Between 1955 and 1960, slightly more than *half* of the population (about 80 million persons) changed residences, about 47 million to different homes in the same county, the remainder to different counties or states. In a single year (1969) about 36 million persons changed homes, about a third of these out of the original counties. See the *Statistical Abstract of the United States* (1971), p. 34.

The most recent comprehensive study of social mobility, based on inter-generational moves of occupation, shows a continuing movement of upward class mobility into salaried, technical, and professional employments. See Peter Blau and Otis Dudley Duncan, *The American Occupational Structure* (New York, 1967).

indicators one chooses—the number of times troops were called out, the number of riots, the number of individuals killed, the amount of sabotage, the number of man-days of work lost, the amounts of money spent by corporations in fighting trade unions—it is highly likely that America suffered more violence than any country in Europe. Yet the United States did escape the political holocausts that wracked European society, and some basic accommodation (formalized in the labor representation on the War Production Board and institutionalized later in the union security clauses established by the War Labor Board) was reached.

One can identify many factors which account for this difference between American and European society, but surely an important one, particularly before World War I, was what one can call the factor of "insulating space." One of the distinguishing features of political violence in Europe is that most of it took place close to or at a political center. (What would have happened in France, for example, if the Constituent Assembly had met at Dijon rather than at Versailles, twenty miles from Paris and subject to the pressures of the Paris crowds? Clearly all such *if* questions are unanswerable, but their formulation allows one to see the possibility of alternative variables.) In the United States, that early violence took place largely at the "perimeters" of the society (in isolated coal-mining communities, in the Chicago and Rocky Mountain areas), and the shock effects had small radial range.

The introduction of modern mass communication allows us, in many cases forces us, to respond directly and immediately to social issues. To take the first instance of its kind in the 1960s: There is little question that the presence of the television cameras in Selma, Alabama, showing the use of crude violence (snarling police dogs, electrified cattle prods) against the black marchers, aroused an immediate national response which was reflected in the presence of thousands of persons who poured into Selma the following week from all over the country. Without television, it is likely that the shock effect, even if transmitted through news photos and newsreels, would have been dissipated (and that before the rise of the mass media this incident would have never had a national impact).

One can see this by a crude comparison of two incidents. In the winter of 1893–1894, growing economic distress and mass unemployment brought about the formation of scattered groups of jobless men into "armies" that declared for a "march on Washington" to demand relief. The best known of these was Coxey's Army, led by the populist "general" Jacob S. Coxey. Although detachments of the armies started out from various parts of the country, and Coxey led his contingent from Massillon, Ohio, only 400 persons reached the national capital, and the "armies" were easily dispersed.[27]

In the summer of 1963, black civil-rights leaders called for a March on Washington to bring pressure upon the Administration for the passage of a civil-rights bill, and by plane, bus, rail, and car 250,000 persons descended on the capital in an extraordinary demonstration of political purpose. Differences of issue apart, it is clear that the one incident is a product of a regional society, the other of a mass society.

One may applaud the fact that the nature of the mass media increases the likelihood of a spectacular rise in "participatory democracy," but these instances are also more likely to arise out of emotional issues (drawing therefore from the extremes), so that the loss of insulating space may itself permit the setting off of chain reactions which may be disruptive of civil politics and reasoned debate.

Communications overload. Whatever else may be said about the twentieth century, it has produced the greatest bombardment of aural and visual materials that man has ever experienced in his history. To the linotype, camera, typewriter, telephone, and telegraph, the twentieth century has added radio (and radio telephone), teletype, television, microwaves, communication satellites, computers, xerography, and the like. Transistors and miniaturization not only facilitate an incredible packaging of communication senders, receivers, and recorders in the confines of a space ship, they also allow automobile telephony, walkie-talkies, portable radio and television sets, and finally, on the agenda, person-to-person communication by "wristwatch" radio anywhere in the country (and soon the world?). Radar and loran have taken over most of the air-sea guidance of transport, and an incredibly deployed watching system like SAGE (already obsolete) permitted a national command-control system, using real-time computers, to patrol the continental defense from the distant-early-warning lines.

George Miller, the Harvard psychologist, once demonstrated in a marvelous article, "The Magical Number Seven Plus or Minus Two," the finite limits in the number of different "bits" (or signals) that a human channel could encompass at one time.[28] Yet the problem is not the single instant, but the total number of sensations that an individual is subject to. Some random sampling of the communication media illustrates, in a cursory way, the growth of the networks

---

[27] Longevity, it should be pointed out, is a different variable from distance. Coxey, who was born in 1854, ran for President in 1932 on a Farmer-Labor ticket, and died in 1951.

[28] See George A. Miller, "The Magical Number Seven, Plus or Minus Two: Some Limits on Our Capacity for Processing Information," *The Psychology of Communication: Seven Essays* (New York, 1967), chap. 2.

of interaction. In 1899, there were one million telephones in the United States, or 13.3 per 1000 population; in 1970, there were 120 million telephones, or 583 per 1000 population. (Over 380 million local calls are made daily.) In 1899, 6,576,000 pieces of mail were moved in the United States; in 1970, 84,882,000,000 pieces of mail were sent (more than 60 percent of them first-class). In 1924, 1,250,000 families had radio sets, and 530 stations were on the air; by 1970, more than 99 percent of families had radio sets and 6,983 stations (AM and FM) were on the air. In 1949, 940,000 families had television sets and 17 stations were sending pictures; by 1970, more than 95 percent of all families had television sets and 666 television stations were broadcasting regularly.[29]

The extension of the range of communication has brought the entire world to the instant attention of any listener. Consider only the multiple geography lessons that each of us has had to learn in the last twenty-five years, from a knowledge of the strategic value of the Chagos archipelago as an equatorial staging area halfway between Aden and Singapore, to the distinction between the Congo Republic (Leopoldville), formerly Belgian, and the Republic of the Congo (Brazzaville), formerly French, and then the changing of the Congo Republic to Zaire, and its capital to Kinshasa. And consider, too, the number of different political figures and the bewildering number of political parties that we have to learn about to keep abreast of the news.

For the society and the political process there are enormous problems which arise from this communications overload. At a time when, in our psychological values, we place a greater emphasis on individuation, where is the possibility of privacy, a "psycho-social moratorium" (the term used by Erik Erikson to describe the need of sensitive adolescents to escape the pressures of schools, career choice, and the like), the finding of open spaces (consider the desecration of Lake Tahoe), and a relief from the stresses created by these incessant "messages" out of the blue?

And for the political process, consider only one image: the problems, terrifying in number, which automatically flow today to Washington as a political center, and the multifarious issues which the President therefore has to confront, and often decide upon, in "real time." Can such a system continue without breakdown?

Numbers alone, of course, are not the problem. But thinking about them leads us to our next topic.

---

[29] These data are taken from the *Historical Statistics of the United States* (Chapter R), and the *Statistical Abstract of the United States*, 1971, section 18.

DIFFUSION AND CHANGE OF SCALE

While we hear much of the *acceleration* of social change today, the idea, as I argued in Chapter 3, is a difficult one to define.[30] For sociological analysis it is preferable to speak of diffusion, which can be measured—the diffusion of products, ideas, styles, values.

The point about diffusion is the critical one for any consideration of social change—and for prediction about the future. For it is not the spectacular innovations (crucial though they may be as turning points) which are the important elements in changing the social map of a country, but the diffusion of products—and privileges—and the rate of such diffusion in a country. For diffusion is not automatic. In the case of products, it rests upon certain entrepreneurial talents and the ability to break through the cake of custom or the barriers of entrenched interests. In the case of privileges, it rests upon the ability of disadvantaged groups to mobilize political pressures. And both of these are operative only within the framework of the value system of a society.

One of the reasons why the predictions of Tocqueville, made more than 130 years ago, are still so cogent is that he had hit upon the great "master key" to American society—the desire for equality.[31] In effect, what has been the property or privilege of the few can be demanded, legitimately, by the many. For example, the enormous change in the character of higher education is due not to any sweeping technological innovation (though there is a greater need for more professionally and technically trained manpower) but to the extension of higher education from the few to the many. In 1935, for example, 12.2 percent of the 18–21 age group attended college, while in 1970, more than 40 percent of the 18–21 age group was enrolled in college.

Out of the same impulses, there is a constant set of rising expectations about what the society can produce. It has been estimated, for

---

[30] The theme of the acceleration of social change has been popularized by Alvin Toffler in his best-seller *Future Shock*. I think the idea is deceptive. In terms of *daily life* of individuals, more change was experienced between 1850 and 1940—when railroads, steamships, telegraph, electricity, telephone, automobile, motion picture, radio, and airplanes were introduced—than in the period since when the future is supposed to be accelerating. In fact, other than television, there has not been one major innovation which has affected the daily life of persons to the extent of the items I enumerated.

[31] Tocqueville had a penchant, like many great theorists, for seeking such "prime movers." Thus, he also predicted an eventual clash between the United States and Russia because large land-mass societies with great natural resources would inevitably expand their living space. For a discussion of this, as well as other modes of prediction, see my essay, "Twelve Modes of Prediction," *Daedalus*, XCIII (Summer 1964), 845–880.

example, that about 20 percent of our people live in poverty. But this is a definition of poverty by 1964 standards. If we applied, say, 1947 standards, only about 15 percent of the people, perhaps, would be considered poor today.[32] It is the nature of the American experience to "upgrade" constantly the notion of what constitutes a decent minimum, and correspondingly of poverty. As Herman Miller, the assistant to the director of the Census, points out in his book *Rich Man, Poor Man*,[33] according to the Bureau of Labor Statistics a "modest but adequate living standard" in New York City in 1947 (as distinct from poverty) required a family income (in 1961 dollars) of $4,000 a year. This criterion rose in 1961 to $5,200, a 28 percent increase. At this rate, by 1975, the new "decent minimum" for a family will be (in 1961 dollars) $7,000. As Mr. Miller concludes: Our standards will be lifted a little higher, our belts will be opened another notch, and there will still be a large block of families living under new and higher substandard conditions.

It is this aspect of social change which gives rise to a curious discrepancy of social perception. The national output will double, or individuals will find that their own incomes have doubled over a period of time, yet there will be compliants that people are not living *twice* as well as before. The entry of more and more disadvantaged persons *into* the society, as claimants for goods and privileges, clearly changes the nature of privileges and services themselves.[34] In seeking for clues to social change, therefore, the important task is to be able to identify which aspects of privilege or advantage today will be demanded by the many tomorrow. (More travel, travel to more distant places, winter vacations, summer houses?) And it is the diffusion of these privileges, in terms of increasing number, that provides the clue to the kinds of social and political demands of the coming years.

But changes in number also mean a change in scale. If relationships were linear, there would be no problem; but increased size changes the nature of organizations, results in multiple hierarchies, introduces new problems of coordination, and poses new questions of order and planning. The question of the size and scope of the social unit—the appropriate size of governmental units, the optimal size of organizations, the decentralization of function, and the creation of a "human scale" in a mass society—is the most crucial sociological problem

[32] See Robert J. Lampman, *The Low Income Population and Economic Growth* (Washington, D.C.: Joint Committee on the Economic Report, U.S. Congress, 1961).

[33] New York, 1964.

[34] A noted British novelist in a recent travel book complained bitterly of the lack of amenities in New York, as evidenced by her inability to get someone to carry her groceries from a supermarket, whereas in Mexico City there were dozens of little boys who, for a few pesos, would be clamoring to help her. By the same logic, it is easier for a person in India, with a smaller income, to hire servants than it is for a person in New York.

that arises out of a consideration of the two conceptual frameworks that have been sketched out above: the influence of number, density, and interaction, and the consequences of diffusion and change of scale.

THE APPROPRIATE SIZE AND SCOPE OF THE SOCIAL UNIT

The United States today, as I have observed, is for the first time genuinely a "national society." Many of the domestic problems we confront do not arise out of such hoary formulations as "capitalism" and "socialism," but from the fact that a multiplicity of problems—education, transportation, welfare, urban renewal, air and water pollution, medical care and the like—no longer are manageable on the state and local level but are now passed on to the national society for solution.

This development, in its own way, dramatizes more than any other single question the problem of the appropriate size of the social unit, in the political as well as the sociological sense. This question can be looked at along four dimensions: the adequacy of the political structure; the question of centralization and decentralization; the distinction as to what is "public" and what is "private"; and the optimal size of bureaucratic structures, private and public. The first two questions are discussed in this section, the other two in the one following.

The adequacy of political structures. It should strike anyone, on momentary reflection, that in a society confronting the kind of problems we have, the existing organization of fifty states makes no economic, political, or social sense. What is the rationale for the boundaries of New Jersey, Delaware, Rhode Island, or Maryland? Under the Constitution, such concerns as education, welfare, local services, and the like are powers reserved to the states and municipalities. But these entities are no longer able to perform such services. Their tax bases are inadequate, their administrative structures archaic and inefficient.

Our problems are compounded when we go to a lower-level unit of government. In the past, advances in transportation technology served as the strategic variable in determining the scale of urbanization. The limits to urban growth in the nineteenth century were set, at first, by natural waterways and canals, later by railroads and steamships. Since World War I the automobile and the truck have advanced the pace of urbanization and changed its nature. With them have come the central city, the suburb, and the metropolis. By 1975, it is estimated that three-fourths of all Americans will be living an urban life. As suburbs spread farther away from the central city, the expanding metropolitan areas merge to form a new social and economic unit—the megalopolis. The skeletal outlines of a northeast megalopolis from Boston to Washington are already visible. The large crescent around Lake Michigan forms another. The stretches from San Francisco to San Jose and from Los Angeles to San Diego already form ribbon cities. The development of the megalopolis intensifies the need to organize the common use of water, land, recreational resources, and transportation systems for large areas that cut across the boundaries of existing state and local governments.

Yet the situation at the local level is chaotic. There is no decentralization—just disarray. The proliferation of government at the local level gives rise to serious problems in the coordination of public programs, in reducing public accountability, in making decisions affecting multi-unit areas, and in contributing to the wide disparities between available financial resources and community and human needs. The complexity of the problem can be seen from the fact that in 1962 the San Diego metropolitan area had 11 municipalities; Phoenix, 17; Houston, 25; Cleveland, 75; St. Louis, 163; Chicago, 246; and the New York metropolitan region, 1,400 local governments—small villages, school districts, sewerage districts, health districts, park districts, police districts, each with its own restrictive powers. These boundaries, historic growths, once adaptive to local needs, are no longer meaningful.[35] Air pollution, waste disposal, and mass transportation are at least metropolitan in scope. Adequate housing can be obtained only if mass-production techniques are introduced into the industry, but the research and development of new materials and methods of construction, or the creation of markets large enough to warrant mass production, are not possible so long as there are thousands of different local building codes—often as many as fifty in a single metropolitan area—in the United States.

Centralization and decentralization. Clearly what is necessary in the next several decades is a comprehensive overhaul and modernization of governmental structures to find the appropriate size and scope of units which can handle the appropriate tasks. No one expects, of course, that the existing state boundaries will be abolished—for historic, traditional, or political reasons they are likely to be retained. But all sorts of functions can be "detached" and lodged in multi-state or regional "compacts" which can take over such functions. Clearly there are no pat answers. Even the favorite theme of regionalism is not an easy solution, for the definition of what is a region varies not on the basis of geography but on the function to be performed: A water region, a transport region, an educational region, and even an economic region have different "overlays" on the map. One has to

---

[35] For an excellent discussion of the problems see John C. Bollens and Henry J. Schmandt, *The Metropolis: Its People, Politics, and Economic Life* (New York, 1965).

define first what it is that one wants to centralize, and what to decentralize.

If a single principle can be established it would be this: that the function of the federal government should be primarily in the areas of policy and funding, and that operative functions be in the hands of regions, metropolises, and non-profit corporations whose size and scope would be appropriate to the function that had to be performed. It is a principle that leads us to the next distinction we seek to make.

THE PUBLIC AND THE PRIVATE

The conventional model of the economy concentrates on the private, profit-seeking center. Yet what is public and what is private, and what is profit and what is not-for-profit, is no longer an easy distinction. The aerospace companies are private, yet the federal government purchases 94 percent of their entire output. Instead of retaining as profits their revenues above costs, all profits above a negotiated sum are returned to the government; the government, rather than the competitive market, determines their profitability, and even their survival. The New York Port Authority and the Triborough Bridge Authority are non-profit public corporations, yet they make enormous profits which, though they do not go to stockholders, are reinvested in new enterprises far beyond the original charter of these corporations. In practical effect, they differ little from private utilities which pay off a fixed sum of their indebtedness and use profits for reinvestment. The Battelle Institute is a non-profit research foundation, the Arthur D. Little Company is profit-seeking, yet the activities of the two are quite similar and they are competitive. (Battelle did the development work on xerography and now reaps large royalties; Arthur D. Little does a considerable amount of public service work at no fee.) Mutual insurance companies and mutual savings banks are non-profit, yet their rates, salaries, and practices are virtually identical with capital stock insurance companies and savings banks. The University of California at Berkeley is a state university, yet it receives large amounts in corporate gifts and other private contributions. Columbia University is a private school, yet more than half of its annual $160 million budget comes from federal contracts and grants. The medical and health service field, the largest "growth industry" in the country, is a commingling of private, profit, nonprofit, and government activities. Most physicians are self-employed and operate within the private sector, yet are connected with hospitals, most of which are non-private, while the federal government increasingly underwrites a large share of hospital construction, medical care for the aged, and the overwhelming portion of research funds in medicine.

It is, in the main, the distinctive role of government as the "funder," but not the operator, of activities that makes for these confusions. One can take as a specific instance the emergence in the ten years after World War II of the non-profit "systems research and development" corporations as a paradigm. The archaic civil service rules and the rigid bureaucratic structure made it almost impossible for the government to develop quickly a necessary "in-house" capacity in a number of scientific and defense fields. The creation of Rand (an acronym for Research and Development), housed originally in the Douglas Aircraft Corporation, as a "think factory" for the air force provided a model which was quickly used by the Defense Department and other government agencies to create what is, essentially, a new social form. In some instances, these new groupings are independent corporations, in other instances they are housed in universities or are managed by a consortium of universities. The Lincoln Laboratory of MIT, under contract to the Defense Department, worked out the feasibility of a distant-early-warning signal system for continental defense, and then set up MITRE (MIT Research and Engineering) to do some of the necessary design work on the system. Since MITRE did not involve any fundamental research, and was not intrinsic to the purposes of the university, it was "spun off" as an independent non-profit corporation. The need to train thousands of persons quickly to manage new computer systems involved in continental defense led the air force to create the Systems Development Corporation (a spin-off from Rand), and this organization, having pioneered new systems of programmed learning and of computer capabilities, has extended its effort into the educational field, seeking contracts from many organizations far outside the Defense Department. It would take one too far afield here to trace the complicated pattern of relationships that emerged between the government—principally through the Defense Department, the Atomic Energy Commission, the National Science Foundation, the National Aeronautical and Space Administration, and the National Institutes of Health—and the different kinds of research and development organizations, public and private.

If one looks at the non-profit sector as a whole, taking into account the wide range of government, educational, and health services, the striking fact is that about one-fourth of GNP and "not less than one-third and possibly almost two-fifths of all employment" *is accounted for by the activities* of that sector.[36] In the 1950–1960 decade, in fact, nine out of every ten *new* jobs added to the economy

---

[36] These and subsequent figures are taken from Eli Ginzberg, Dale L. Hiestand, and Beatrice G. Reubens, *The Pluralistic Economy* (New York, 1965).

were generated in the non-profit sector—i.e. by the vastly enlarged role of the federal government in connection with the cold war, the expanded activities of state and local governments in providing community services, and the growth of the education and health and welfare fields.

The growth of the non-profit sector brings into focus as employers of significant amounts of manpower a whole array of organizations whose structure and form differ to a considerable extent from the usual model of "bureaucracy." These are universities, research laboratories, hospitals, community welfare organizations, and the like. The "received" doctrine, as drawn from Max Weber and accepted by most students of stratification theory, posits a bureaucracy as having a division of labor based on functional specialization, a well-defined hierarchy of authority, recruitment, selection, and promotion based on technical criteria, impersonal, "bureaucratic" rules of behavior, and so on. This is the "ideal type" model which is often best exemplified in corporate business structure. Yet the variety of new kinds of organizations that are emerging (particularly ones with a high component of technical and research personnel) indicates that the older models, patterned on pyramidical structures, may no longer be applicable, and that in the coming decades the "traditional" bureaucratic form will have given way to organizational modes more adaptive to the needs for initiative, free time, joint consultation, and the like.[37] The emergence of new structural forms of non-bureaucratic organization is one more item on the long agenda of new problems for the post-industrial society.

A SYSTEM OF SOCIAL ACCOUNTS

We have learned in recent years how to chart economic growth and thus to identify at various points the kinds of policies that may be necessary to stimulate growth. We have begun to perfect an economic reporting system and to establish economic indicators that give us a measure of national performance. But as yet we do not have a continuous charting of social changes and we have been ill-prepared (in such matters as housing, education, or the status of the black) to determine our needs, establish some goals, and measure our performance. We have had no coherent accounting of our results, no assessment of gaps or short-falls, no reckoning of social costs and social gains. Lacking any systematic assessment, we have few criteria which allow us to test the effectiveness of present policies or weigh alternatives regarding future programs.

---

[37] For a comprehensive list of the vast literature on the problem see James G. March, *Handbook of Organizations* (Chicago, 1965).

The development of national economic accounting provides us with an instructive picture of the workings of a modern economy. There are at present, for example, four types of accounting systems which allows us to measure different kinds of economic phenomena and transactions: National Income and Product Accounts sums up the total value of goods and services transacted in the economy and the allocation of net income among households, government, business, and foreign units; National Moneyflow Accounts traces the flow of funds between financial and non-financial units, including households and government; National Inter-Industry Accounts sets forth the value of purchases and sales of goods and services among variously "disaggregated" units of business, government, household and foreign sectors; and National Wealth Accounting, in effect a national assets inventory, evaluates the reproducible assets and resources of the nation.

Yet these economic instruments, particularly the GNP, are limited in their use, and sometimes—more by popular opinion than by professional economists—give us a distorted picture of the social economy. The GNP measures the sum total of goods and services transacted in the *market* economy. It is immediately apparent that services performed within a household by a wife, for example, are not "valued." (The British economist A. C. Pigou, the pioneer of welfare economics, once remarked that if a widowed vicar paid his housekeeper a weekly wage, this was an addition to the national income; if he married her, it became a subtraction.) The point at issue is that "income" in rural areas (where a substantial amount of food may be produced at home) is often "undervalued" as against urban income—a fact neglected not only in some discussions about poverty in the United States, but in the international comparisons between the United Sates and some well-to-do agrarian countries (e.g. Denmark and New Zealand), which on the scale of GNP rank lower than their real income would put them.[38]

---

[38] One can point to other "methodological" problems which limit the use of the GNP as an accounting measure. Professor Fritz Machlup, in *The Production and Distribution of Knowledge in the U. S.* (Princeton, N.J., 1962), writes: "The fact that the production of knowledge of several types is paid for by others than the users of the knowledge and that these types of knowledge have no market prices, raises questions of their valuation for national income accounting as well as for welfare-economic considerations." The question of what the GNP can measure thus becomes an important one.

In a similar vein, Victor Fuchs of the National Bureau of Economic Research, in writing of the expansion of the service sector of the economy, remarks: "There has been a presumption [among economists] that [the real GNP] becomes more useful as a measure the more highly developed the economy is. . . . But the trend may be in the other direction because at high levels of GNP per capita a large fraction of productivity effort will be devoted to service [where output is very difficult to measure] and to other activities that are presently not measured at all." Many government services are not measured today since these cannot be valued at market prices.

One can have a meaningful sense of progress only by knowing its costs, direct and indirect. A difficulty in national economic accounting today is that of directly assigning the costs generated by one group which often are borne by others (e.g. the costs to the community of strip mining, gouging out a countryside). But the problem is not only the social costs, unfairly generated and widely borne, but the broader cost matrix which would allow us to balance gains against costs.

What we need, in effect, is a System of Social Accounts which would broaden our concept of costs and benefits, and put economic accounting into a broader framework. The eventual purpose would be to create a "balance sheet" that would be useful in clarifying policy choices.[39]

What would a system of social accounts allow us to do? The word "accounts," as it stands now, is perhaps a misnomer. Sociologists have been able to establish few completely consistent sets of relationships. Even where sophisticated social analysis can establish relationships it is difficult to do so in measurable terms. But we can begin by seeking to establish a conceptual framework.

A System of Social Accounts would begin with a series of social indicators that would give us a broader and more balanced reckoning of the meaning of economic progress as we know it. This effort to set up a System of Social Accounts would move us toward measurement of the utilization of human resources in our society in four areas: (1) the measurement of social costs and net returns of innovations; (2) the measurement of social ills (e.g. crime, family disruption); (3) the creation of "performance budgets" in areas of defined social needs (e.g. housing, education); and (4) indicators of economic opportunity and social mobility.

The following elaborations of the four areas referred to above are meant to be illustrative rather than prescriptive. They are intended to suggest the range of problems and the scope of application.

Social costs and net returns. Technological advances create new investment opportunities. These investments are expected to be paid out of the enhanced earnings they produce. But clearly there are losses as well. The major loss is the unemployment created by technological change, particularly in those instances where the advanced age of the worker whose particular skill is displaced makes it difficult for him to find new employment. Or a new plant in an area may create new employment opportunities, yet its by-products—water

---

[39] The section here is taken from the report *Technology and the American Economy*, U.S. Commission on Technology, Automation and Economic Progress (U.S. Government Printing Office, February 1966). I was the author of that section of the report.

pollution and air pollution—may create additional costs for the community.

The question of which costs should be borne by the firm and which by the community is clearly a matter of public policy. Increasingly, for example, the firms responsible for polluting the waters of a river are asked to bear the costs of filtration. The Ruhr, flowing through West Germany's densest industrial region, is at present less polluted than it was twenty years ago. Swimming and boating are commonplace. This happy circumstance is the result of a cooperative arrangement between 259 municipalities and 2,200 industries along the river which have developed a system of effluent fees calculated to encourage the construction of waste-disposal systems. In this case the entire cost of pollution is assigned to the source. On the other hand, certain costs of severance pay or maintenance of an older labor force on a firm's payroll may be so huge as to inhibit the introduction of useful technological devices and such costs might better be borne by the community than by a firm itself. But these questions of public policy can only be decided when we have a clearer picture of the actual social costs and returns of innovations.[40]

The measurement of social ills. Every society pays a huge price for crime, juvenile delinquency, and disruption of the family. The costs of child care and mental health are also high. There are no simple causes, such as unemployment, of such social ills. Yet such ills and social tensions have measurable effects on the economy (from the loss of able-bodied workers because of mental illness, to direct losses of property because of thefts and riots). Although data on crime, on health, dependent children, and the like are collected by government agencies, there is rarely any effort to link these problems to underlying conditions; nor is there a full measure of the cost of these ills. Systematic analysis of such data might suggest possible courses of remedial action.

Performance budgets. America is committed not only to raising the standard of living but to improve the quality of life. But we have few yardsticks to tell us how we are doing. A system of social accounts would contain "performance budgets" in various areas to serve as such yardsticks. A national housing budget, for example, would indicate where we stand in regard to the goal of a "decent home for every American family." It would also enable us to locate,

---

[40] Andrew Shonfield, in *Modern Capitalism* (London, 1965), pp. 227–229, points out that the construction of a new subway line in London was held up for over a decade on the premise that it couldn't pay its way until someone demonstrated that the secondary benefits resulting for people *not* using the line—in speeding vehicular flow and the like—would result in a true return on investment which was 10 percent over the capital cost of the project.

by city and region, the areas of greatest needs and so provide the basis for effective public policy. A series of community health indices would tell us how well we are meeting the medical needs of our people.

Indicators of economic opportunity and social mobility. More than thirty years ago, in *An American Dilemma,* Gunnar Myrdal wrote: "We should . . . have liked to present in our study a general index, year by year or at least decade by decade, as a quantitative expression of the movement of the entire system we are studying: the status of the Negro in America. . . . But the work of constructing and analyzing a general index of Negro status in America amounts to a major investigation in itself, and we must leave the matter as a proposal for later research." [41]

Three decades later, we still have no "general index" of the status of the black in America. In a strict methodological sense, perhaps no "comprehensive indexes" are possible, but we can assemble specific indicators. Thus, where once it seemed impossible to conceive of a "value" figure for human assets, the creation in recent years of a "lifetime-earning-power index" gives us a measure to reflect the improvements in income associated with increased education, improvement in health, and reduction of discrimination. Data on social mobility, developed by sociologists, can tell us whether there is a genuine equality of opportunity in the United States and can identify the barriers (e.g. inadequate school opportunities) to that equality. Economists have a term, "opportunity costs," which allows us to calculate not only direct costs but the gains forgone from the use of those resources if they had been employed elsewhere. "Social opportunity" costs may allow us to reckon the possible gains by the utilization of hitherto unused human resources and to weigh, in terms of social costs and social benefits, alternative social policies.

These proposals have an underlying assumption: that the society would be in a better position to appraise its achievements, its needs, and its shortcomings by being able to specify broad national goals. The definition of such goals has to be a continuing process in which a system of social accounts would serve as a tool to identify the greatest areas of needs.

---

[41] Gunnar Myrdal, *An American Dilemma* (New York, 1942), p. 1,068.

The Tools of Planning

On January 20, 1968, the very last day of the Democratic administration, Wilbur Cohen, Secretary of Health, Education and Welfare, quietly released a document called *Toward a Social Report*. It was the first effort by any government to set up a set of social indicators for measuring the performance of the society in meeting social needs. Despite the awkward symbolism of making the report public in the waning hours of the Great Society, it is clear that the idea of a social report is one whose time is coming. No society in history has yet made a coherent and unified effort to assess those factors that, for instance, help or hinder the individual citizen in establishing a career commensurate with his abilities, or living a full and healthy life equal to his biological potential; an effort to define the levels of an adequate standard of living, and to suggest what a "decent" physical and social environment ought to include. The document *Toward a Social Report* is the first step in the effort to make that assessment.

Inevitably, the idea of a Social Report brings to mind the Economic Report and raises questions about parallels and differences. Each January, the Council of Economic Advisers produces its annual report, whose economic indicators chart growth, productivity, employment, and inflation, and whose accounting scheme measures the distribution of income and spending among government, firms, and private individuals in terms of investment and consumption. The economic report has become a necessary tool for public policy-making. But for social policy it is highly inadequate, and in some ways even deceptive. The economic report, though presenting data on the incidence of poverty, understandably says little about the social attitudes—apathy, alienation, or resentments—bred by deprivation. It cannot, in its self-limiting scope, deal with the quality or amenities of life, such as better health, the degree of congestion, the availability of social services, and the invasion of privacy. These gaps, and the need to find measures that could chart their extent, have prompted the effort to set up social indicators as a necessary complement of economic measures. Without such social indicators, policy-making becomes increasingly deficient in its ability to judge alternatives.

The movement to set up social indicators, though recent, has a long history as an idea and appears in the earliest reflections on the consequences of private economic activities, principally in the recognition of the divergence between the private costs borne by a firm or individual entrepreneur and the costs to others, or to the community, which such individuals generate but do not bear. Though the idea of social costs is implicit in the writings of the classical economists, it was the socialist writer Sismondi who first made the idea explicit, and formulated some remedies. In his *New Principles of Political Economy* (1819), Sismondi argued that the true object of economics is man, not wealth. Observing the costs of unemployment that were borne by the community in the form of poorhouses and hospitals, he proposed that employers guarantee their workmen security against intermittent work, sickness, and destitution in old age. As Schumpeter remarks, in his *History of Economic Analysis:*

The more limited modern idea of the "guaranteed wage" may with justice be said to have been visualized by [Sismondi]. The originality of his suggestions stands out in one point: his idea was to turn the social costs of labor-saving improvements into business costs of employers.

It was not until a hundred years later, as I pointed out previously, when A. C. Pigou wrote his *Economics of Welfare* (1920), that the phenomenon of social costs was integrated into the system of neo-classical economics. Yet, except for the work of K. William Kapp, later formulations in welfare economics tended to play down the idea of social costs that Pigou had emphasized. This was due to the fact that the "new" welfare economics, taking up a different issue from Pigou, conceived of the welfare of the community in terms of the sum total of utilities of *individuals*, and denied even the possibility of a combined or a communal welfare function similar to the ordering principle of individual preferences. Kapp's work, *The Social Costs of Private Enterprise* (1950) (the first of this scope that I know of), returned to the earlier examples of Pigou, and in comprehensive fashion sought to assess, in quantitative and money terms, the social costs of work (occupational injuries, disease, and the like), air pollution, water pollution, the depletion of natural resources and energy resources, erosion and deforestation, technological change, unemployment, and advertising. The book was written within the framework of "institutional" economics, and had a normative (i.e. political) intent; given the mood of the economists of the time about refined mathematical models, it was neglected. But the concept is clearly laid out, and the idea of measuring social costs (or what economists today call "externalities" and "diseconomies") is an important dimension of the effort to set up social indicators.

A second, different source of the interest in social indicators goes back to the work of the sociologist William F. Ogburn and his desire to measure the rates of social change. Ogburn was intent on establishing statistical series that would improve the methods of extrapolation and correlation as means of predicting the future.[42] But his broader interest was in social planning, and he realized that one needed an accurate "fix" on social trends in order to do any useful social planning. The benchmark work in this respect (neglected for nearly thirty-five years) was the volume *Recent Social Trends* (1933), consisting of twenty-nine chapters, many of them summarizing monographs of greater length, which covered every facet of American life.

The volume was an outgrowth of the President's Research Committee on Social Trends, which had been established by President Hoover in 1929, under the chairmanship of Wesley Clair Mitchell, with Ogburn as director of research. The intention was to issue an annual report on social trends, but during the depression this effort was abandoned.[43]

What is remarkable about the volume *Recent Social Trends* is how well a number of the analyses stand up. The chapter on medicine, for example, dealt with the rise of specialized medical practice, the divergence between research and general practice, and the consequences of geographical concentration; if heeded, it would have gone far to avert the present crisis in the delivery of health care. The chapter on metropolitan communities was an accurate foreshadowing of postwar suburban problems.

In the late 1930s, a governmental agency, the National Resources Planning Board, prompted by Louis Brownlow and Charles Merriam, undertook substantial monographic studies on technology, population, and the cities, which were intended as guides for the preparation of public policy. These were published, but were ignored because of World War II. None of these efforts was resumed after the war.

In one sense, it is surprising how belated the movement for social indicators has been. Despite the New Deal, and despite the apparent interest in social trends before World War II, they received scant attention afterward. One reason was the shift within the sociological profession itself. The kind of "institutional" sociology practiced by Ogburn at the University of Chicago, as well as "institutional eco-

---

[42] See, for example, the chapter "On Predicting the Future," in Ogburn's *The Social Effects of Aviation* (1946).

[43] Five volumes appeared, under the editorship of Ogburn, as annual reports, entitled *Social Changes in 1928, in 1929, in 1930, in 1931, in 1932*. In addition there was a preparatory volume entitled *Recent Social Changes Since the War and Particularly in 1927*, and two postludes, *Social Change and the New Deal* and *Social Changes During Depression and Recovery*, all published by the University of Chicago Press. An effort was made to continue the index of social trends for the next three years (1935–1937) in essays in the *American Journal of Sociology*. A bibliography of Ogburn's voluminous writings appears in a volume of his selected papers, *William F. Ogburn on Culture and Social Change*, ed. Otis Dudley Duncan (Chicago, 1964).

nomics," was displaced by an interest in abstract theory; in sociology, notably, by "structure-functionalism" and its preoccupation with the problems of order and integration in society, rather than with change.

A second reason, perhaps, was the preoccupation in government with economic indicators and the development of macroeconomics. Though the ideas of national income, GNP, and economic accounting go back to the "political arithmetic" of Sir William Petty in the seventeenth century and the *tableau économique* of François Quesnay in the middle of the eighteenth century, their development in quantitative and aggregative form—by such men as J. R. Hicks and Simon Kuznets—came only in the 1930s, when economic theory began to shift its attention from the firm to the national economy. It was only in 1942 that the U.S. Department of Commerce, at the instigation of Robert R. Nathan, began publishing national-income data, whereas the concept of GNP was first broached by Franklin D. Roosevelt in his budget message in 1944.

Thus, during the late 1940s and the 1950s, the sociologists neglected social-trend analysis, while on the government level the chief interest was in the shaping of macroeconomic data and the formulation of the economic advisory process in the Council of Economic Advisers.

It was only in the Kennedy years and after, as concern with domestic social problems increased—poverty, race, health, environmental pollution, persistent unemployment (which some alarmists attributed to "automation"), housing, and the like—that interest in social measurement and social-trend analysis reawakened. Economists began to apply cost-benefit analysis to some of these problems and became aware of the immense difficulty in measuring social costs and social benefits. Political scientists and economists began to formulate Program Planning Budget Systems as a means of rationalizing diverse government programs and of weighing the effectiveness of alternative systems. Sociologists became interested in urban planning, education, race, and long-range forecasting for purposes of social planning. The new interest in social indicators arises from a merger of all of these concerns.

In 1966, John Gardner, the Secretary of Health, Education and Welfare, became sufficiently intrigued with the idea of social indicators to convince the President that the idea was worthwhile, and an official message from the President formally assigned this task to HEW.[44] In the fall of 1966, a Panel on Social Indicators was set up,

[44] The Presidential Message to Congress on Domestic Health and Education stated: "To improve our ability to chart our progress, I have asked the Secretary to establish within his office the resources to develop the necessary social statistics and

chaired by William Gorham, Assistant Secretary of HEW in charge of program evaluation, and myself. When Gorham left HEW in 1968 to become head of the new Urban Institute, he was replaced by Alice Rivlin, an economist from the Brookings Institution, as Assistant Secretary and co-chairman of the panel. The Deputy Assistant Secretary, Mancur Olson, was in charge of the creation of the social indicators. The panel, composed of forty-one social scientists and an equal number of government statisticians and technicians, prepared a large volume entitled "Draft Materials for a Social Report." The major task of preparing the final document was the responsibility of Dr. Rivlin and Mancur Olson.

WHAT IS A SOCIAL INDICATOR?

Given the initial comparisons with the Economic Report, and the hope of sociologists that the development of social indicators would lead to a system of social accounts, it is important to stipulate the nature—and limits—of the document *Toward a Social Report*. The document was not trying to achieve some kind of definitive assessment of American society. For as the first pages of the introduction and the appendix on the deficiency of existing statistics indicate, no one is in a position to make any such assessment because we do not have the measures to do so. If anything, a close reading of the document would caution anybody against using the existing data to make any authoritative statements, hopeful or pessimestic, about "the state of American society." *Toward a Social Report* is only a first step in developing measures that might allow us to do so.

The primary point is that the existing government data—which are all that are available to anybody—are organized primarily for administrative purposes, and not for analysis; from such data it is difficult to draw conclusions which are of normative value. Take the question of health. Given the increasing amounts of money we have been spending, is the country healthier or not? We do not know. No one knows. Our statistics tell us the amount of money *spent* on health care, how many doctors, nurses, and hospitals we have, but there is no measure of any *result*. Part of the difficulty is that our data collection is oriented to "inputs" and not to evaluation. The larger difficulty is a conceptual one, because there has been no agreement on *how* one measures health. Traditionally, the government has used a measure of "life-expectancy." But on reflection it is clear that this is hardly adequate, because such a simple index does not take into account the number of sick days or days in bed that a person experi-

indicators to supplement those prepared by the Bureau of Labor Statistics and the Council of Economic Advisers. With these yardsticks we can better measure the distance we have come and plan the way ahead."

ences. In fact, and paradoxically, as a larger and larger percentage of the population lives out its full years, the amount of sickness may be expected to increase, because old age has its inescapable infirmities; and the increase in the number of the aged has been a sizable factor in the rise of hospital costs. One of the things that the Panel on Social Indicators sought to do was to establish a more sophisticated index of health by estimating the number of "free-of-bed-disability" days a person has during the year. In creating, for the first time, such an index, two questions remain: How valid is it (and this is a technical question for the demographers and health scientists to argue about)? And if such an index is valid, what is the historical time period for meaningful comparisons? But so far no one can say with any precision what kind of correlation exists between various expenditures on health and the actual state of the nation's health.

A second, and equally obvious, area is that of crime. Any literate person is aware of the monstrous deficiencies of the FBI crime "index." For one thing, it does not "deflate" for changes in price (a $50 larceny of twenty years ago and a $50 larceny today are counted under the rubric of "major crimes," even though a stolen item costing $50 today was worth $30 twenty years ago and therefore such thefts were not counted then: in effect an inflationary bias is built into the index, making comparison hopeless); nor does the FBI relate crime to age-specific rates (about 70 percent of all crimes are committed by the young, and if there are more young people in the population, as is the case today, the number of crimes will increase). Aside from such deficiencies, there is the most difficult fact of trying to make sense of the FBI "index"—it jumbles murder, rape, assault, burglary, larceny, car theft, and the like to produce a gross total that inevitably, because of the larger number of car thefts and such, will always tell us that there is more "crime" today than ever before. This tells us, in effect, almost nothing—and for the purpose of telling us exactly what is happening, it is misleading.

The problem of constructing a relevant crime index highlights the general problem of constructing social indicators. The chief virtue of the national income statistics, for example, is that they are aggregative. Over any period of time, the output of some goods increases whereas that of other goods decreases, but the national income account summarizes this diversity into a single number and tells us, on balance, whether an economy has grown or declined over time. It does so because there is a single linear measure—money—into which these changes can be aggregated, and the different economic items can be "weighted" by relative price. But how does one compare murders (which until recently were decreasing in the United States) with car thefts (which have been soaring)? How does one aggregate them into a single meaningful figure? What is needed is a common measure, and in this case the panel (utilizing the work of Marvin Wolfgang of the University of Pennsylvania) sought to do so by "weighting" each crime by the relative legal penalties associated with it, and also by the discernible opinion of the public on the relative heinousness of different crimes. (Interestingly, the most comprehensive opinion survey correlates .97 with the average length of prison sentences for the same crime.) Thus, it may be that rapes are given a weight of "30" and car thefts "2," so that length of prison sentence—the *penalty time*, like money—becomes the linear basis for an aggregative index. If this new index is valid, then in time we might be able to say whether crime is actually increasing in the country or not, and by how much.

But not all questions can now be solved, even in this primitive fashion. In the 1968 yearbook of the Department of the Interior, Stewart Udall wrote: "Gross National Product is our Holy Grail . . . but we have no environmental index, no census statistics to measure whether the country is more livable in from year to year." Mr. Udall asks for a "tranquility index, a cleanliness index, a privacy index." Such things are easy to ask for, but how does one define tranquility (is it simply the absence of noise, or is it "peace of mind"?) and how does one measure it? The social indicators panel did work out a "materials balance framework" to set up a combined air-pollution index (which aggregates five different kinds of air pollutants), a water-pollution index, and a measure of pollution by solid wastes. And again these become, for the first time, benchmarks available for the purpose of *future* comparisons. But we have no way of knowing whether air pollution is worse now than before, when cities burned coal in industrial plants and in the cellars of homes, while rail engines belched smoke into the skies. Similarly, on such questions as participation (is there an increase or decrease in memberships in voluntary associations?) and alienation (how does one compare the unrest of some affluent youth against the material satisfactions of blue-collar workers owning their own homes?) we simply do not have any easy answers to whether things are worse or better than before.

In the area of social mobility—thanks to the work of Otis Dudley Duncan and Peter Blau, who recently published a study of *The American Occupational Structure* based on the very first national sample of intergenerational mobility ever drawn in the United States—we can say with some certitude that, despite various apprehensions, the American class structure has not become rigid, and that the occupational achievements of sons are not in any significant degree (only 16 percent of the variation of occupational scores) explained by the socio-economic position of their fathers. Thus a considerable degree of equality of opportunity does exist in the United States—but largely for whites. From the Duncan data it is also possible to measure the "mobility gap" between black and white, and to estimate the role of discrimination in maintaining that gap.

In short, *Toward a Social Report*—and the word "toward" was chosen deliberately—is not a prototypical social report; nor is it an assessment of the society. It indicates what data are already available to start on such an assessment; it makes the necessary start on the creation of social indicators that may allow us, in the future, to make relevant comparisons of changes over time.

THE PERSPECTIVE OF TIME

Americans, more than other people (as a *national style*, not on individual comparison), are an impatient lot. A problem emerges and people want answers—quickly. There are, in fact, two simplistic notions in the American temper: that all problems are soluble, and that the way to solve a problem is to pour men and money into it. (Do you want to go to the moon? Build a NASA. Do you want to raze the slums? Mount a huge housing program. The fact that the problems are not wholly congruent, that one case is a technical "game against nature," and the other a "game between people who have discordant aims," rarely enters into such considerations.)

The extraordinary fact, in relation to the huge range of social problems that confronts us, is the recency of the simple tools we have for dealing with them. The Council of Economic Advisers, as a research, analysis, and policy body for the nation, was created only twenty-five years ago, and not until a dozen years ago did it begin to function in the way it was intended. Just recently were the techniques of input-output analysis and that of linear programming developed so that only now are we able to lay out an adequate *tableau économique* and plot the varying combinations of resources and requirements in accordance with different values assumptions. And only with these techniques is a model of economic planning actually possible. We still lack any adequate forecasting models of the economy, either for short-run or long-run purposes. Efforts, as at Brookings, to test econometric models for quarterly economic forecasts have only just begun; efforts, such as those of James Tobin and Robert Solow, to set up a mathematical model for longer-range forecasting have been abandoned as too difficult.

In the areas of social planning we are woefully behind. The economic data collected and disseminated by the federal government, and the economic models based on them, are highly relevant to economic policy. Unfortunately they are less applicable to the new problems of social change. National economic and census statistics, aggregated as they are, tell us little about pockets of poverty, depressed communities, sick industries, or disadvantaged social groups. The national data, averaged out, provide few clues to, or relevant information about, regional or local problems. In respect to the integration crises and anti-poverty programs of the 1960s, the federal government found itself lacking the necessary information for making effective policy decisions in response to these new social problems. The need for this kind of data is urgent. The socio-economic crisis in the 1930s led the government to establish national income and product accounts and thus facilitated macro-economic analysis and economic models on an aggregate national basis. In effect, the government's decision of several decades ago about the type of data to be collected, made on the basis of its own need for information, shaped in considerable measure the direction of economic theory and practice. The new type of social data collection, which is so urgently needed now, undoubtedly will influence the development of social science for the next generation.

But, in the end, the problems of the communal and post-industrial society are not technical, but political, for even though in the nature of the new complexities a large kind of new social engineering is involved, the essential questions are those of values. Only when men can decide what they want, can one move to the questions of how to do the jobs. The central question of the post-industrial society, therefore, is the relation of the technocratic decision to politics, and that is the theme of the next chapter.

CHAPTER
6

"Who Will Rule?"
Politicians and
Technocrats in the
Post-Industrial
Society

T HE rational is real and the real is rational" is a famous phrase of Hegel's. By this he did not mean that the existent was real. As a post-Kantian philosopher, he accepted the proposition that the empirical reality was a flux, and that knowledge is gained only through the application of the a priori categories necessary to organize it. Thus, the "real" is the underlying structure of concepts that makes sense of the confusing froth of the present. For Hegel, the "real" was the unfolding of rationality as the self-conscious reflective activity of mind that gave men increasing power over nature, history, and self.

In a fundamental sense, the theme of rationality is also the major underpinning of sociological theory. For Durkheim, as he argued in his *Division of Labor*, the tendency of civilization is to become more rational, and this was a product of the greater degree of interdependence in the world and the syncretism of culture or secularization, which broke down parochial forms. In the writings of Max Weber, the concept of the rational moves to the very center of sociology. In his last lectures, given in the winter of 1919–1920, Weber points out that modern life is made up of "rational accounting, rational technology, rational law, and with these a rationalistic economic ethic, the rational spirit and the rationalization of the conduct of life." [1] Indeed, as Talcott Parsons points out, "the conception of a law of increasing rationality as a fundamental generalization about systems of action . . . is the most fundamental generalization that emerges from Weber's work." And, drawing a curious parallel— or is it a prophecy?—Parsons concludes: "Rationality occupies a logical position in respect to action systems analogous to that of entropy in physical systems." [2]

[1] Max Weber, *General Economic History* (London, n.d.), p. 354.
[2] Talcott Parsons, *The Structure of Social Action* (New York, 1937), p. 752.

These conceptions of rationality are rooted in nineteenth-century ideas of man's relation to nature and society, and they are extensions, in one sense, of the conceptions of progress that had emerged at the end of the eighteenth century. Whatever their philosophical overtones, the concepts of rationality received a practical embodiment in industry—and in war. The development of every advanced industrial society, and the emergence of the post-industrial society, depends on the extension of a particular dimension of rationality. But it is precisely that definition of rationality that is being called into question today, and what I seek to do here is to trace the vicissitudes of that conception—the technocratic—as it relates to politics.[3]

The Paradigm

More than a hundred and fifty years ago, the wildly brilliant, almost monomaniacal technocrat, Claude Henri de Rouvroy, Lecomte de Saint-Simon ("the last gentleman and the first socialist" of France), popularized the word *industrialism* to designate the emergent society, wherein wealth would be created by production and machinery rather than seized through plunder and war. The revolution that ended feudal society—the French Revolution—could have ushered in the industrial society, said Saint-Simon, but it did not do so because it had been captured by metaphysicians, lawyers, and sophists—men with a predilection for abstract slogans. What was needed, Saint-Simon added, was a breed of "new men"—engineers, builders, planners—who would provide the necessary leadership. And since such leaders require some concrete inspiration, Saint-Simon, shortly before his death, commissioned Rouget de l'Isle, the composer of "The Marseillaise," to write a new "Industrial Marseillaise." This "Chant des Industriels," as it was called, had its première in 1821 before Saint-Simon and his friend Ternaux, the textile manufacturer, at the opening of a new textile factory in Saint-Ouen.[4]

---

[3] The tension between the technocratic and the cultural is equally a major problem for modern society.

[4] The episode takes on a somewhat comic air, especially when we read that a number of the Count's followers established a new religious cult of Saint-Simonianism to canonize his teachings. (In the monastic castle to which the followers of Saint-Simon retreated, garments were buttoned down the back so that, in socialist fashion, each man would require the help of another in dressing. Thus was pedagogy reinforced by ritual.) And yet many of these very followers of Saint-Simon were also the men who, in the middle of the nineteenth century, redrew the industrial map of Europe.

It is not too much to say, Professor F. H. Markham has written, "that the Saint-Simonians were the most important single force behind the great economic expan-

We may leave the story of Saint-Simon and his followers to the curiosa of the history of ideas, but since Saint-Simon was, in a sense, the father of technocracy, we may, in his spirit, sum up now the features of post-industrial society and its technocratic foundation.

We are now in the first stages of a post-industrial society. We have become the first nation in the history of the world in which more than half of the employed population is not involved in the production of food, clothing, houses, automobiles, and other tangible goods.

The character of work has been transformed as well. In a paper read to the Cambridge Reform Club in 1873, Alfred Marshall, the great neoclassical economist, posed a question that was implicit in the title of his paper "The Future of the Working Classes." "The question," he said, "is not whether all men will ultimately be equal—that they certainly will not be—but whether progress may not go on steadily, if slowly, till, by occupation at least, every man is a gentleman." And he answered his question: "I hold that it may, and that it will."

Marshall's criterion for a gentleman—in the broad, rather than the traditional genteel, sense—meant that heavy, excessive, and soul-destroying labor would vanish, and the worker would then begin to value education and leisure. Apart from any qualitative assessment of contemporary culture, it is clear that Marshall's question is well on the way to being answered. The manual and unskilled worker class is shrinking in the society, while at the other end of the continuum the class of knowledge workers is becoming predominant.

In identifying a new and emerging social system, it is not only in the portents and social trends, such as the move away from manufacturing or the rise of new social relationships, that one seeks to understand fundamental social change. Rather it is in the defining characteristic of a new system. In the post-industrial society, what is crucial is not just a shift from property or political criteria to knowledge as the base of new power, but a change in the *character* of knowledge itself. What has now become decisive for society is the new centrality of *theoretical* knowledge, the primacy of theory over empiricism, and the codification of knowledge into abstract systems of symbols

---

sion of the Second Empire, particularly in the development of banks and railways." Enfantin, the most bizarre of the Saint-Simonians, formed the society for planning the Suez Canal. Former Saint-Simonians constructed many of the European railways—in Austria, Russia, and Spain. The brothers Emile and Isaac Pereire, who promoted the first French railway from Paris to Saint-Germain, also founded the Crédit Mobilier, the first industrial investment bank in France, as well as the great shipping company the Compagnie Générale Transatlantique (the CGT today sails the *Flandre* and the *France*), which gave its first ships the names of Saint-Simonian followers, including the *Saint-Simon* (1987 tons). See F. M. H. Markham, *Henri Comte de Saint-Simon: Selected Writings* (Oxford, 1952).

that can be translated into many different and varied circumstances. Every society now lives by innovation and growth, and it is theoretical knowledge that has become the matrix of innovation. With the growing sophistication of simulation procedures through the use of computers—simulations of economic systems, of social behavior, of decision problems—we have the possibility, for the first time, of large-scale "controlled experiments" in the social sciences. These, in turn, will allow us to plot alternative futures in different courses, thus greatly increasing the extent to which we can choose and control matters that affect our lives. And, just as the business firm was the key institution of the past hundred years because of its role in organizing production for the mass creation of products, the university —or some other form of a knowledge institute—will become the central institution of the next hundred years because of its role as the new source of innovation and knowledge.

If the dominant figures of the past hundred years have been the entrepreneur, the businessman, and the industrial executive, the "new men" are the scientists, the mathematicians, the economists, and the engineers of the new intellectual technology. This is not to say that the majority of persons will be scientists, engineers, technicians, or intellectuals. The majority of individuals in contemporary society are not businessmen, yet one can say that this has been a "business civilization." The basic values of society have been focused on business institutions, the largest rewards have been found in business, and the strongest power has been held by the business community, although today that power is to some extent shared within the factory by the trade union, and regulated within the society by the political order. In the most general ways, however, the major decisions affecting the day-to-day life of the citizen—the kinds of work available, the location of plants, investment decisions on new products, the distribution of tax burdens, occupational mobility—have been made by business, and more recently by government, which gives major priority to the welfare of business.

In the post-industrial society, production and business decisions will be subordinated to, or will derive from, other forces in society; the crucial decisions regarding the growth of the economy and its balance will come from government, but they will be based on the government's sponsorship of research and development, of cost-effectiveness and cost-benefit analysis; the making of decisions, because of the intricately linked nature of their consequences, will have an increasingly technical character. The husbanding of talent and the spread of educational and intellectual institutions will become a prime concern of the society; not only the best talents but eventually the entire complex of prestige and status will be rooted in the intellectual and scientific communities.

The Time Machine

It was once exceedingly rare to be able to observe the formation of institutions *de novo*. Social change was crescive and slow-moving. Adaptations were piecemeal and contradictory, the process of diffusion halting, the spread of rationalization difficult and cumbersome. Thirty-five years ago in his reflections on history, Paul Valéry, the quintessential Frenchman of letters, remarked:

There is nothing easier than to point out the absence from history books, of major phenomena which were imperceptible owing to the slowness of their evolution. They escape the historian's notice because no document expressly mentions them. . . .

An event which takes shape over a century will not be found in any document or collection of memoirs. . . .

Such was the discovery of electricity and the conquest of the World by its applications. Events of this nature, unparalleled in human history, appear in it—only as something less noticeable than some more spectacular happening, some happening, above all, more in conformity with what traditional history usually reports. Electricity in Napoleon's day had about the same importance as, in the days of Tiberius, could have been ascribed to Christianity. It is gradually becoming apparent that the general innervation of the world by electricity is more fraught with consequences, more capable of modifying life in the near future, than all of the so-called "political" events which have happened from Ampère's day to the present time.[5]

Today, not only are we aware of trying to identify processes of change, even when they cannot be dated, but there has been a speeding up of the "time-machine," so that the intervals between the initial forces of change and their application have been radically reduced.

Perhaps the most important social change of our time is a process of direct and deliberate contrivance. Men now seek to anticipate change, measure the course of its direction and its impact, control it, and even shape it for predetermined ends. "The transformation of society" is no longer an abstract phrase but a process in which governments are actively engaged on a highly conscious basis. The industrialization of Japan by the old Samurai class was an action aimed at transforming an agrarian economy from the top, and it succeeded re-

---

[5] Paul Valéry, *Reflections on the World Today* (New York, 1948), p. 16.

markably because of the disciplined nature of social relationships that had existed in post-Meiji restoration society. The extraordinary upheavals in the Soviet Union, more ruthless and more concentrated in time than the changes in any other society in history, were carried out on the basis of specific plans, in which the movements of the population, as well as industrial targets, were plotted on social charts. The breakdown of the old colonial system has brought about, since the end of World War II, the creation of almost fifty new countries, many of them committed abstractly to the idea of "socialism," in which the creation of new industrial and urban economies is the fundamental agenda of the new elites. And in the older Western societies we have seen the emergence of planning in more differentiated forms, whether it be target plans, indicative planning, induced investment, or simply economic growth and full employment.

The Birth-Years

It is foolhardy to give dates to social processes (when, and by what criteria, can one say that capitalism eclipsed feudalism, at least in the economic sphere?), but our self-consciousness about time, which is itself an aspect of modernity, urges us to seek some symbolic points that mark the emergence of a new social understanding. Alfred Whitehead once remarked that the nineteenth century was dead by the 1880s, and the 1870s was its last lush decade. One could also say that the period from 1880 to 1945 was the period in which the old Western ideologies exploded, culminating in the dreadful travails of fascism and communism as they rode the new Leviathan.

The period since the end of World War II has produced a new consciousness about time and social change. One might well say that 1945 to 1950 were the "birth-years," symbolically, of the post-industrial society.

To begin with, the transformation of matter into explosive energy by the creation of an atom bomb in 1945 made the world dramatically aware of the power of science.[6] With it came the potentialities

---

[6] Contrast the role of science in World War II with that in World War I. In *Modern Science and Modern Man*, James Bryant Conant, who before becoming a distinguished educator was a prominent chemist, tells the story that when the United States entered World War I, a representative of the American Chemical Society called on Newton D. Baker, then Secretary of War, and offered the services of the chemists to the government. He was thanked and asked to come back the next day, when he was told that the offer was unnecessary since the War Department already had a chemist.

When President Wilson appointed a consulting board to assist the Navy, it was

of nuclear energy for human use. In 1946, the first digital computer, the ENIAC, was completed at the government proving grounds in Aberdeen, Maryland, and it was soon followed by the MANIAC, the JOHNNIAC, and, within a decade, ten thousand more. Never in the history of invention has a new discovery taken hold so quickly and spread into so many areas of use as the computer. In 1947, Norbert Wiener published his *Cybernetics*, which spelled out the principles of self-regulating mechanisms and self-adjusting systems. If the atom bomb proved the power of pure physics, the combination of the computer and cybernetics has opened the way to a new "social physics"—a set of techniques, through control and communications theory, to construct a *tableau entière* for the arrangement of decisions and choices.

In those years, the basic relationships between science and government were laid out with the creation of the Atomic Energy Commission and the National Science Foundation. Through these agencies, commitments have led to enormous government spending in research and development, and to the underwriting of large laboratories and research stations through a variety of creative new social forms—university facilities, non-profit corporations, university consortiums, and the like.

If we turn from the dramatic change in science to the prosaic realm of political economy, new techniques and new commitments were forged during those crucial years from 1945 to 1950. The concept of Gross National Product (GNP), the basic tool for all macroscopic economic analysis, was first used in 1945. In 1946, Congress passed a Full Employment Act, which established a Council of Economic Advisers and stated, as a matter of national policy, that each man had a right to a job, and that society had the responsibility of maintaining full employment. By 1950 Wassily Leontief had outlined his input-output tables, which provide a planning grid for the entire economy. Mathematicians and economists at Rand, such as George Dantzig, had worked out the techniques of linear and dynamic programming to give us queuing techniques in production decisions. Technical economics had become inextricably intertwined with public policy, especially through the Council of Economic Advisers.

---

chaired by Thomas Edison, and this appointment was widely hailed for bringing the best brains of science to the solution of naval problems. The solitary physicist on the board owed his appointment to the fact that Edison, in choosing his fellow members, had said to President Wilson: "We might have one mathematical fellow in case we have to calculate something out." In fact, as R. T. Birge reports (in his study "Physics and Physicists of the Past Fifty Years," in *Physics Today* [1956]), during World War I there was no classification of physicist; when the armed forces felt the need of one, which was only occasionally, he was hired as a chemist.

If one looks beyond the provincial horizon of one's own country, one also sees in these years the emergence of an entirely new world system, with the creation of the *tiers monde* and the fateful relationship of former colonial countries to once imperial powers; the self-conscious recognition of the idea of development—economic, political, and social; the beginning awareness that such social-system terms as capitalism and socialism may be part of a more inclusive social process within the rubrics of industrialization and bureaucratization, and even that these societies, as variants of industrial systems, may be converging in the pattern of their economies into some new kind of centralized-decentralized market-planning system.

Finally, there has occurred what is perhaps the most pervasive change in moral temper—a new "future-orientation" on the part of all nations and social systems. Some observers have seen the dawn of a new universal history in the fact that all societies, for the first time, are creating common technological foundations. Of course, economic, political, and cultural diversities among nations are still far too great for us to be able to see a single world society, at least within this next century. And yet common foundations are being laid, particularly in the establishing of international scientific communities, and common aspirations are being voiced. The common thread is the orientation to the future and the recognition that men have the technological and scientific possibility of controlling the changes in their lives consciously, and by social decision. But such conscious control does not mean the "end of history," the escape, so to speak, from necessity, which Hegel and Marx emphasized in man's relation to nature, but the beginning of vastly more complicated problems than men have ever faced before.

In all these diverse activities, the fundamental themes are rationality, planning, and foresight—the hallmarks, in short, of the technocratic age. The vision of Saint-Simon seemingly has begun to bear fruit.

The Technocratic Mind-View

In France, where the idea of technocracy has been more widely talked about than in any other country, it has been defined as "a political system in which the determining influence belongs to technicians of the administration and of the economy," and a technocrat, in turn, is "a man who exercises authority by virtue of his technical competence." [7]

---

[7] *Dictionnaire alphabétique et analogique de la langue française* (Paris: Société de nouveau Littre, 1964); and *Grand Larousse Encyclopédique* (Paris, 1964).

But a technocratic mind-view, one can say with some sense of paradox, is more than just a matter of technique.[8] In its emphasis on the logical, practical, problem-solving, instrumental, orderly, and disciplined approach to objectives, in its reliance on a calculus, on precision and measurement and a concept of a system, it is a world-view quite opposed to the traditional and customary religious, esthetic, and intuitive modes. It draws deeply from the Newtonian world-view, and the eighteenth-century writers who inherited Newton's thought did indeed believe, as Hume has Cleanthes say in his *Dialogues Concerning Natural Religion,* that the author of Nature must be something of an engineer, since Nature is a machine; and they believed, further, that within a short time the rational method would make all thought amenable to its laws.[9] Bernard de Fontenelle, the popularizer of Cartesianism, precipitated a gory conflict with the humanists (reflected in Jonathan Swift's *Battle of the Books*) when he declared: "The geometric spirit is not so bound up with geometry that it cannot be disentangled and carried into other fields. A work of morals, of politics, of criticism, perhaps even of eloquence, will be the finer, other things being equal, if it is written by the hands of a geometer."[10]

---

[8] The word *technocracy* itself was first coined in 1919 by William Henry Smyth, an inventor and engineer in Berkeley, California, in three articles published in the *Industrial Management* of February, March, and May in that year. These were reprinted in a pamphlet, and later included with nine more articles, written for the *Berkeley Gazette*, in a larger reprint.

The word was taken over by Howard Scott, a one-time research director for the Industrial Workers of the World (I.W.W.), and was popularized in 1933–34, when Technocracy flashed briefly as a social movement and a panacea for the depression. The word became associated with Scott, and through him retrospectively with Thorstein Veblen, who, after writing *The Engineers and the Price System*, was briefly associated with Scott, in an educational venture at the New School for Social Research in 1919–1920. Interestingly, when the word became nationally popular through Scott, it was repudiated by Smyth, who claimed that Scott's use of the word fused *technology* and *autocrat*, "rule by technicians responsible to no one," whereas his original word implied "the rule of the people made effective through the agency of their servants, the scientists and technicians."

For the origin of the term, see William H. Smyth, *Technocracy Explained by its Originator* (San Francisco, 1933), and J. George Frederick, ed., *For and Against Technocracy: A Symposium* (New York, 1933). For a discussion of the relations between Veblen and Scott, see my introduction, "Veblen and the New Class," to the Harbinger edition of *The Engineers and the Price System* (New York, 1965).

[9] It should be pointed out, however, that de la Mettrie, the author of the famous book *Man the Machine*, died of overeating and gout; he stoked the machine too well.

[10] Mindful, perhaps, of some of the *hubris* of the past, Norbert Wiener, thirteen years after the publication of his *Cybernetics*, warned his readers not against the inadequacies of the machine but against its possible success. "We have already made very successful machines of the lowest logical type with a rigid policy," he wrote. "We are beginning to make machines of the second logical type, where the policy itself improves with learning. In the construction of operative machines, there is no

The most comprehensive statement of this world-view was made by an unexpected precursor of the technocratic ideology, the nineteenth-century mathematician Augustin Cournot, who is better known for his applications of mathematics to economics than for his writings on history. But as he interpreted the rise of technological civilization, Cournot saw a general movement in history from the vital to the rational. He foresaw an era of mechanization which would be "post-historic," since universal rationalization would provide a stability to society that resulted from the erosion of instincts and passions and the perfection of administration. In this post-historic era, statistics would more and more be substituted for history as a means of studying human events.[11]

Man's progress toward greater rationality was, of course, the theme of Max Weber, but in the parallel with the second law of thermodynamics, Weber also saw a running down of the system. Societies, Weber said, are changed when there is an infusion of charismatic energy which breaks the bounds of old traditional constraints, but in the "routinization of charisma" the stock of energy is consumed until, at the end, there is only a dead mechanism, and, as Weber wrote of the exhaustion of the Protestant ethic and the transformation of capitalism, the administrators of the system become "sensualists without spirit, specialists without heart, a nullity. . . ."[12]

It is in this conception of rationality as functional, as rationalization rather than "reason," that one confronts the overriding crisis of the technocratic mode. The virtue of the belief in History was that some law of reason was operative: History had either a teleology as defined by Revelation, or some powers of emergence or transcend-

---

foreseeable limit with respect to logical type, nor is it safe to make a pronouncement about the exact level at which the brain is superior to the machine." But even though a completely "intelligent" machine is still far off in the future, the immediate problem, Wiener said, is that while machines do not transcend man's intelligence, they do transcend men, in the performance of tasks. "We have seen," he pointed out, "that one of the chief causes of the disastrous consequences in the use of the learning machine is that man and machine operate on two distinct time scales, so that the machine is much faster than man and the two do not gear together without some serious difficulties. Problems of the same sort arise whenever two control operators on very different time scales act together, irrespective of which system is faster and which system is slower." (See Norbert Weiner, "Some Moral and Technical Consequences of Automation," *Science* [May 1960]).

The point would seem to be that when a machine is constructed to absorb its incoming data at a pace faster than it can be fed, we may not, like the sorcerer's apprentice, think of turning it off until it is too late.

[11] On Cournot, see Georges Friedmann, "Les technocrates et la civilisation technicienne," in *Industrialisation et Technocratie*, ed. Georges Gurvitch (Paris, 1949).

[12] The most comprehensive discussion of Weber's "increasing law of rationality" can be found in Talcott Parsons, *Structure of Social Action*. The phrase at the end of the paragraph is from Weber's conclusion to *The Protestant Ethic* (London, 1930), p. 182.

ence that were implicit in man's creativity. In Hegel, the "cunning of reason" was the evolution of man's self-consciousness—the end of the mystery of "objectification" wherein men made things, idols, gods, societies "outside" of themselves, and often worshipped them as fetishes—so that, finally, he could "recognize himself in a world he has himself made." Thus the end of history—the overcoming of nature, and the overcoming of the duality of subject and object which divided the "self"—was the beginning of freedom, of impulses of individual and social action that would no longer be subject to any determinism. However metaphorical these sentiments were—though they were quite realistic in their picture of man's slavish dependencies in the past—they did posit some ends to the march of rationality.

Things Ride Men

Saint-Simon had a vision of the future society that made him a utopian in the eyes of Marx. Society would be a scientific-industrial association whose good would be the highest productive effort to conquer nature and to achieve the greatest possible benefits for all. Men would become happy in their natural abilities. The ideal industrial society would be by no means classless, for individuals were unequal in ability and in capacity. But social divisions would follow actual abilities, as opposed to the artificial divisions of previous societies, and individuals would find happiness and liberty in working at the job to which they were best suited. With every man in his natural place, each would obey his superior spontaneously, as one obeyed one's doctor, for a superior was defined by a higher technical capacity. In the industrial society, there would be three major divisions of work, corresponding, in the naive yet almost persuasive psychology of Saint-Simon, to three major psychological types. The majority of men were of the motor-capacity type, and they would become the laborers of the industrial society; within this class, the best would become the production leaders and administrators of society. The second type was the rational one, and men of this capacity would become the scientists, discovering new knowledge and writing the laws that were to guide men. The third type was the sensory, and these men would be the artists and religious leaders. This last class, Saint-Simon believed, would bring a new religion of collective worship to the people and overcome individual egoism. It was in work and in carnival that men would find satisfaction and, in this positivist Utopia, society, in the famous vision of Saint-Simon, would move from the governing of men to the administration of things.

But in the evolution of technocratic thinking, things began to ride men. For Frederick W. Taylor, the founder of scientific management, who was perhaps most responsible for the translation of technocratic modes into the actual practices of industry, any notion of ends other than production and efficiency of output was almost nonexistent. Taylor believed strongly that "status must be based upon superior knowledge rather than nepotism and superior financial power," and in his idea of functional foremanship he asserted that influence and leadership should be based on technical competence rather than on any other criteria.

Out of Taylor's reflections (and his own compulsive character) came the idea of scientific time-study and, more broadly, the measurement of work—for it is with the measurement of work and the idea of unit cost, rather than with the introduction of the factory as such, that modern industry gained distinctive meaning as a new way of life. Taylor's principles were based upon the following: the time it takes to do a specific job; incentives and bonus systems for exceeding norms; differential rates of pay based on job evaluation; the standardization of tools and equipment; the fitting of men to jobs on the basis of physical and mental tests; and the removal of all planning and scheduling from the work floor itself into a new planning and scheduling department, a new superstructure, the responsibility for which was in the hands of the engineer.

By setting "scientific" standards, Taylor felt that he could specify the "one best way" or the "natural laws" of work, and so remove the basic source of antagonism between worker and employer—the question of what is "fair" or "unfair." [13] But in his view of work,

---

[13] See *The Principles of Scientific Management*, by Frederick W. Taylor, p. 10, reprinted in the compendium *Scientific Management* (New York: Harper & Bros., 1947).

Interestingly enough, Taylor's condemnation of "waste and confusion" made him seem progressive to many young engineers, and one of Taylor's chief disciples, Morris L. Cooke, became a link with Veblen.

Cooke was lured by Taylor's gospel declaration that "the same principles [of scientific management] can be applied with equal force to all social activities: to the management of our homes; the management of our farms; the management of the business of our tradesmen large and small; of our churches, our philanthropic institutions, our universities, and our governmental departments."

In short, the engineer was to be the hierophant of the new society. Cooke, in 1919, became the head of the American Society of Mechanical Engineers, and it was the ferment created by Cooke, principally the severing of the ties with business and trade associations and the statement that the first professional obligation of the engineer was to the profession not the employer, which led Veblen to believe, in the memorandum he wrote for *The Dial*, that the engineers could become the basis of a "soviet of technicians." After the formation of the CIO, Cooke became an advisor to

man disappeared, and all that remained was "hands" and "things" arranged on the basis of minute scientific examination along a detailed division of labor wherein the smallest unit of motion and the smallest unit of time became the measure of a man's contribution to work.

In Marxism, another great source of technocratic thought, the same dissolution of ends and concentration on means alone also appear. Hegel had seen man's growth as an ideational process in which self-consciousness triumphed over limited dependencies of subjectivity and objectification. Marx naturalized this historic process by seeing man's growth in material and technical powers, in the growth of his means over nature. But what would this lead to? In his earlier works Marx had envisioned socialism as a state where a man would be a hunter in the morning, a fisherman in the afternoon—and perhaps a superior lover at night; in which there would be no distinction between mental and physical work or between town and country. The single image of socialism for Marx, by and large, was the end of the division of labor, which he saw as one of the sources, along with private property, of the alienation of men from society. But in his later writings these naive ideas had vanished, and Marx, in his conception of man as "emergent," assumed that new powers would be created and new visions of life would be achieved which his own generation, limited by nature and human frailty, could not yet envisage. And so, the ends of history were left ambiguous.

In Lenin, who bears the same relation to Marx that Taylor does to Saint-Simon, the conception of ends disappears almost completely. Lenin was the superb technician of power. The creator of the disciplined party and the cadre, Lenin was able to create a flexible instrument of revolution and subversion which could lash hundreds of thousands, even millions, of persons into action. But once the power had been won, only a fumbling and incoherent vision of the future could be detected. In *State and Revolution*, written as the first manual of socialism, Lenin assumed that running a society would be as simple as running the post office, and administration would become so simple that any shoemaker could be an executive.

When the power had finally been secured in a war-torn, broken-down country, Lenin's formula for socialism turned out to be only Soviet

---

Philip Murray, the head of the Steel Workers Organizing Committee, and together with Murray wrote a book, *Organized Labor and Production*, which laid out a work rationalization for industry.

For Cooke's relation to Veblen, and the background of events which led Veblen to think that the engineers might be the basis for a revolutionary new class, see my introduction to the Harbinger edition (1965) of Veblen's *The Engineers and the Price System*. For a biography of Cooke, see Kenneth E. Trombley, *The Life and Times of a Happy Liberal* (New York, 1954).

power plus electrification.[14] The irony is that today in the Soviet Union, as in the other communist countries, the chief demand of individuals is for private cars, individual homes, and other personal possessions. But the nature and conditions of work represent no flowering of socialist humanism as it was envisaged in the past. Work, like all production, has become geared to a consumption society and to turning out larger and greater quantities of goods.

In the technocratic mode, the ends have become simply efficiency and output. The ends have become means and they exist in themselves. The technocratic mode has become established because it is the mode of efficiency—of production, of program, of "getting things done." For these reasons, the technocratic mode is bound to

---

[14] Lenin, as is well known, was strongly attracted to the ideas of Frederick W. Taylor. In an address in June 1919 on "Scientific Management and the Dictatorship of the Proletariat," he stated: "The possibility of socialism will be determined by our success in combining Soviet rule and Soviet organization or management with the latest progressive measures of capitalism. We must introduce in Russia the study and teaching of the Taylor system and its systematic trial and adoption." See the citation and the discussion in *The End of Ideology* (Glencoe, Ill., 1960), p. 253. More of this can be gleaned from some newly discovered materials in Lenin's archives.

During 1969, in preparation for the 1970 centenary of Lenin's birth, the Soviet press devoted considerable space to this material from Lenin's archive on the first few months of the new Soviet government. In an article in *Komsomolskaya Pravda* for January 11, 1969, V. Chikin takes off from a "unique Lenin album," which is being completed by scholars from the central party archives, on Lenin's efforts to work out "just principles and a judicious system of government management," and the author draws on some "rough notes and instructions, newspaper articles and detailed reports" to make the following observation:

Ilyich [Lenin] sets himself the special goal of teaching practicality to the Bolshevik leaders who had not yet broken out of the sweet captivity of revolutionary romanticism. He notes to himself: "Practicality and efficiency as a slogan." And knocking the "romantics" right out, he advances a completely unexpected formula for socialism: "To scoop up with both hands the best from abroad: Soviet power + the Prussian railway system plus American technique and the organization of trusts + American education, etc., etc. + + = Σ = socialism." True, to judge from the evidence of eyewitnesses, the first efforts to "Americanize" the office work in the CPC [Council of Peoples Commissars] had no success. (I am indebted to Paul Zinner for the citation and to Colette Shulman for the translation.)

A technocratic mind-view, one might say, is not only a doctrine but also a temperament. Just as one can observe the awesome obsessiveness in Taylor, so one sees the compulsive orderliness in Lenin. A recently published memoir by Nikolay Valentinov, who spent several months with Lenin in Geneva in 1904, provides a vivid picture of his personality:

In his "normal" condition, Lenin tended towards an orderly life, free from all excesses. He wanted it to be regular, with precisely fixed hours for meals, sleep, work, and leisure. He did not smoke or drink, and looked after his health doing physical exercises every day. He was order and neatness incarnate. Every morning, before he settled down to read the newspapers, write, and work, Lenin, duster in hand, would put his desk and his books in order. He sewed any loose buttons on his coat or trousers himself, without bothering Krupskaya (his wife). If he found a stain on his suit, he immediately tried to remove it with petrol. He kept his bicycle as clean as a surgical instrument. In this "normal" condition Lenin would have appeared to any observer as the most sober, balanced, and well-disciplined of men,

spread in our society. But whether the technocrats themselves will become a dominant class, and how the technocratic mode might be challenged, are different questions, which we must now consider.

Soldiers Ride Things

It was the root idea of Saint-Simon, August Comte, and Herbert Spencer, the theorists of industrial society, that there was a radical opposition between the industrial spirit and the military spirit. The one emphasized work, production, rationality, the other display, waste, and heroics. Out of technology, economizing, and investment would come productivity as the basis of increasing wealth for all, rather than exploitation and plunder as the means of seizing wealth from others. In ancient society, work was subordinated to war and the warrior ruled; in industrial society, life would become pacific and the producer would rule.

The irony is that although the economizing spirit—the deployment of limited resources to attain maximum results—has indeed spread throughout society as Schumpeter and others have argued, war rather than peace has been in large part responsible for the acceptance of planning and technocratic modes in government. The rise of the mass army, beginning with the Conscription Act passed in 1789 by the French revolutionary government—a system followed by every major power in the nineteenth century except Great Britain and the United States—set forth new modes of organization and supply. War and the mass army have supplied the model, too, for the most curious of social schemata. In 1795, for example, Gracchus Babeuf, the fiery conspiratorial leader of the extreme left-wing of the Jacobin movement, outlined his picture of collective economic plan-

---

without passions, repelled by slovenliness, and in particular by Bohemian ways. "I have already got used to the way of life in Cracow: it is limited, quiet and sleepy," he wrote to his relatives in 1913. "No matter how god-forsaken this town may be, I like it better here than in Paris."

Lenin's didactic utilitarian yardstick is also revealed in a comment of another Russian revolutionist, Vorovsky, to Valentinov:

. . . Lenin knows none of Goethe's works except *Faust*. He divides literature into two parts: what he needs, and what he doesn't need. . . . He has managed to find time to read all the volumes of *Znanie* (Knowledge) [a popular literary miscellany] while he has consciously ignored Dostoyevsky: "I haven't got time for this rubbish!!" After reading *Memoirs from the House of the Dead* and *Crime and Punishment*, he felt no desire to read *The Possessed* and *The Brothers Karamazov*. "I know the subject of both of those malodorous works. . . . I looked through [*The Possessed*] and threw it away. I don't read such literature—what good is it to me?" Nikolay Valentinov, *Encounters with Lenin* (New York: Oxford University Press, 1968), pp. 147 and 49–50.

ning as follows: All workers would be classified according to the type of work. Society would have exact information on what everyone was doing so that there would be neither underproduction nor overproduction. Society would determine the number of persons to be employed in any particular branch of industry. All would be apportioned to the needs of the present, and to the requirements of the future in the light of probable increases in population. All real needs would be exactly investigated and fully satisfied, thanks to the swift transport of goods to all localities and over all distances. And where was all this drawn from? From the experience of Revolutionary France at war, from the logistical plan for the organization of supplies for an army of 1,200,000 men divided into twelve widely dispersed points.

Instead of peace, every industrial society has a *Wehrwirtschaft*, a term for which, significantly, there is no adequate English translation, but which we could call, perhaps, a "preparedness economy," or a mobilized society. A mobilized society is one in which the major resources of the country are concentrated on a few specific objectives defined by the government. In these sectors, private needs are in effect subordinated to the mobilized goals and the role of private decision is reduced almost to nothing. The Soviet Union is a mobilized society par excellence. Most of the "new states," in their quest for modernization, have become mobilized: The basic resources of the society—capital and trained manpower—are geared to planned economic change.

In recent years, America has taken on the features of a mobilized polity in that one of the crucial scarce resources, that of "research and development"—and more specifically the work of most of the scientists and engineers in research and development—is tied to the requirements of the military and of war preparedness. The United States has not done this by outright commandeering of talents, or by restricting the right of non-governmental units to engage in R & D. But since R & D is always a risk, in that no immediate payoffs or profits are assured, and the costs of R & D have become astronomical, few institutions other than the government can underwrite such expenditures. And the government has been compelled to do so because of the extraordinary revolutions in the art of war that have occurred since 1945.

In one sense, as Herman Kahn has pointed out, military technology has supplanted the "mode of production," in Marx's use of the term, as a major determinant of social structure. Since the end of World War II there have been almost three total revolutions in military technology, with complete and across-the-board replacement of equipment, as older weapons systems were phased out without being used. Neither World War I nor World War II represented such complete breaks in continuity.

The sources of these accelerated revolutions—changes in the character of atomic weapons, from manned bombers to missiles, from fixed missiles to roving missiles and from medium-range to inter-continental missiles—has been the concentration on research and development and concerted planning for new systems of weaponry. And the technology of "custom-crafted" missile construction, as against bombers, was a chief element in changing the "production-mix" of the aerospace industry labor force, so much so that the Budget Bureau Report on Defense Contracting (the David Bell Report of 1962) estimated that the ratio of engineers and scientists to production workers in the aerospace industry was roughly one-to-one.

But it is not only in the engulfing of technology that a significant change has taken place, but in the modes of decision-making as well. The McNamara "revolution" of 1960–1965 transformed military logistics, and for this reason one can say that McNamara joins Saint-Simon and Frederick W. Taylor as a hierophant in the pantheon of technocracy.

What McNamara did was to introduce a new way of assessing costs and choices in relation to strategy. In the days before the revolutions in military technology, an airplane might be designed by the air force and farmed out to a private contractor. It was common practice in the 1950s for the air force to pay the development costs of four or five planes and then choose one for quantity production. All of this was possible so long as the development costs (designs, tools, mockups) of a single prototype were about $100 million. By 1956 this cost had increased by a factor of five, and over the same period the estimated cost of a single missile had increased by a factor of fifty. By the time Robert McNamara became Secretary of Defense, costs had risen so enormously that some system of "value engineering"— computing the cost-effectiveness ratios of alternate weapons systems—had to be introduced.

The McNamara "revolution" represented a rationalization of governmental structure. The key idea, of course, is not just cost-effectiveness, but to assess the value of the weapons system in different kinds of programs and objectives. In the system of program budgeting, the entire structure of line-item budgets, which had been traditionally organized, was overhauled to serve "functional" programs.[15]

---

[15] Thus, the American defense effort was organized not along the traditional lines of army, navy, and air force, but in nine basic programs: Strategic Retaliatory Forces, Continental Air and Missile Defense Forces, General Purpose Forces, Airlift and Sealift Forces, Reserve and National Guard Forces, Research and Development, down into "program elements" (there are now 800 such elements in the Defense

The system that McNamara introduced was called the Program Planning Budget System (PPBS).

In a technical sense, there can be little quarrel with an effort to regroup in some logical fashion the scattered efforts of government programs and put them down in some systematic form. In the fiscal 1965 budget, for example, funds for education were dispersed through more than forty agencies. The expenditures of the U. S. Office of Education constituted only one-fifth of the total federal education budget. A program-budgeting system can thus unify what constitutes the education program of the American government. The difficulty arises, however, when one goes one step further and tries to discover, within a narrow economic calculus of cost-effectiveness techniques, the social value of one program as against another. Expenditures for defense may constitute the first line on a federal budget because, in the language of utility theory, defense constitutes a "single-peaked preference curve" in which the society, by and large, is agreed on the importance—and priority—of these efforts. But what about the situations in which there is no such agreement—such as science policy, or social policy, or welfare policy? How does one decide? When men have different valuations, how does one choose? For this the technocratic view has no answer.

Who Holds Power?

Decisions are a matter of power, and the crucial questions in any society are: *Who* holds power? and *how* is power held? How power is held is a *system* concept; who holds power is a *group* concept. How one comes to power defines the base and route; who identifies the persons. Clearly, when there is a change in the nature of the system, new groups come to power. (In the tableau of pre-industrial, industrial, and post-industrial societies, the major differences can be shown schematically—see Table 6–1 on Stratification and Power.)

In the post-industrial society, technical skill becomes the base of and education the mode of access to power; those (or the elite of the group) who come to the fore in this fashion are the scientists. But this does not mean that the scientists are monolithic and act as a corpo-

Budget) which are intended to accomplish common missions. The original rationale is laid down in a book by Charles Hitch and Roland McKean, *The Economics of Defense in the Nuclear Age* (Cambridge, Mass., 1960). A more extended application of the concept is contained in the Rand volume, edited by David Novick, *Program Budgeting—Program Analysis and the Federal Budget* (Cambridge, Mass., 1965).

TABLE 6–1
Stratification and Power

	PRE-INDUSTRIAL	INDUSTRIAL	POST-INDUSTRIAL
Resource	Land	Machinery	Knowledge
Social locus	Farm Plantation	Business firm	University Research institute
Dominant figures	Landowner Military	Businessmen	Scientists Research men
Means of power	Direct control of force	Indirect influence on politics	Balance of technical-political forces Franchises and rights
Class base	Property Military force	Property Political organization Technical skill	Technical skill Political organization
Access	Inheritance Seizure by armies	Inheritance Patronage Education	Education Mobilization Co-optation

rate group. In actual political situations scientists may divide ideologically (as they have in the recent ABM debate), and different groups of scientists will align themselves with different segments of other elites. In the nature of politics, few groups are monolithic ("the" military, "the" scientists, "the" business class), and any group contending for power will seek allies from different groups. (Thus, in the Soviet Union, for example, where the interest groups are more clear-cut in functional terms—factory managers, central planners, army officers, party officials—and the power struggle more naked, any faction in the Politburo *seeking* power will make alliances *across* group lines. Yet once *in* power, the victors will have to make decisions *between* groups and affect the relative distribution of power of the functional units and shift the weights of the *system*.) In the change of the system in the post-industrial society, two propositions become evident:

1. As a *stratum*, scientists, or more widely the technical intelligentsia, now have to be taken into account in the political process, though they may not have been before.

2. Science itself is ruled by an ethos which is different from the ethos of other major social groups (e.g. business, the military), and this ethos will *predispose* scientists to act in a different fashion, politically, from other groups.

Forty-five years ago Thorstein Veblen, in his *Engineers and the Price System*, foresaw a new society based on technical organization and industrial management, a "soviet of technicians," as he put it in the striking language he loved to use in order to scare and mystify the academic world. In making this prediction, Veblen shared the illusion of that earlier technocrat, Henri de Saint-Simon, that the complexity of the industrial system and the indispensability of the technician made military and political revolutions a thing of the past. "Revolutions in the eighteenth century," Veblen wrote, "were military and political; and the Elder Statesmen who now believe themselves to be making history still believe that revolutions can be made and unmade by the same ways and means in the twentieth century. But any substantial or effectual overturn in the twentieth century will necessarily be an industrial overturn, and by the same token, any twentieth-century revolution can be combatted or neutralized only by industrial ways and means."

If a revolution were to come about in the United States—as a practiced skeptic Veblen was highly dubious of that prospect—it would not be led by a minority political party, as in Soviet Russia, which was a loose-knit and backward industrial region, nor would it come from the trade-union "votaries of the dinner pail," who, as a vested interest themselves, simply sought to keep prices up and labor supply down. It would occur, he said, along the lines "already laid down by the material conditions of its productive industry." And, turning this Marxist prism to his own perceptions, Veblen continued: "These main lines of revolutionary strategy are lines of technical organization and industrial management; essentially lines of industrial engineering; such as will fit the organization to take care of the highly technical industrial system that constitutes the indispensable material foundation of any modern civilized community."

The heart of Veblen's assessment of the revolutionary class is thus summed up in his identification of the "production engineers" as the indispensable "General Staff of the industrial system." "Without their immediate and unremitting guidance and correction the industrial system will not work. It is a mechanically organized structure of the technical processes designed, installed, and conducted by the production engineers. Without them and their constant attention to the industrial equipment, the mechanical appliances of industry will foot up to just so much junk."

This syndicalist idea that revolution in the twentieth century could only be an "industrial overturn" exemplifies the fallacy in so much of Veblen's thought. For as we have learned, no matter how technical social processes may be, the crucial turning points in a society occur in a political form. It is not the technocrat who ultimately holds power, but the politician.

The major changes that have reshaped American society over the past thirty years—the creation of a managed economy, a welfare society, and a mobilized polity—grew out of political responses: in the first instances to accommodate the demands of economically insecure and disadvantaged groups—the farmers, workers, blacks and the poor—for protection from the hazards of the market; and later because of the concentration of resources and political objectives following the mobilized postures of the cold war and the space race.

All of this opens up a broader and more theoretical perspective about the changing nature of class and social position in contemporary society. *Class, in the final sense, denotes not a specific group of persons but a system that has institutionalized the ground rules for acquiring, holding, and transferring differential power and its attendant privileges.* In Western society, the dominant system has been property, guaranteed and safeguarded by the legal order, and transmitted through a system of marriage and family. But over the past twenty-five to fifty years, the property system has been breaking up. In American society today, there are three modes of power and social mobility, and this baffles students of society who seek to tease out the contradictory sources of class positions. There is the historic mode of property as the basis of wealth and power, with inheritance as the major route of access. There is technical skill as the basis of power and position, with education as the necessary route of access to skill. And finally there is political office as a base of power, with organization of a machine as the route of access.

One can, in a simplified way, present these modes in a reduced model:

Base of Power:	Property	Political Position	Skill
Mode of Access:	Inheritance Entrepreneurial Ability	Machine Membership Co-optation	Education
Social Unit:	Family	Group Party	Individual

The difficulty in the analysis of power in modern Western societies is that these three systems co-exist, overlap, and interpenetrate. While the family loses its importance as an economic unit, particularly with the decline of family-firms and the break-up of family capitalism, family background is still advantageous in providing impetus (financial, cultural and personal connections) for the family member. Ethnic groups, often blocked in the economic access to position, have resorted to the political route to gain privilege and wealth. And, increasingly, in the post-industrial society, technical skill becomes an overriding condition of competence for place and position. A son may succeed a father as head of a firm, but without the managerial skill to run the enterprise, the firm may lose out in competition with other, professionally managed corporations. To some extent, the owner of a firm and the politician may hire technicians and experts; yet, unless the owner or politician themselves know enough about the technical issues, their judgments may falter.

The rise of the new elites based on skill derives from the simple fact that knowledge and planning—military planning, economic planning, social planning—have become the basic requisites for all organized action in a modern society. The members of this new technocratic elite, with their new techniques of decision-making (systems analysis, linear programming, and program budgeting), have now become essential to the formulation and analysis of decisions on which political judgments have to be made, if not to the wielding of power. It is in this broad sense that the spread of education, research, and administration has created a new constituency—the technical and professional intelligentsia.

While these technologists are not bound by a sufficient common interest to make them a political class, they do have common characteristics. They are, first, the products of a new system in the recruitment for power (just as property and inheritance were the essence of the old system). The norms of the new intelligentsia—the norms of professionalism—are a departure from the hitherto prevailing norms of economic self-interest which have guided a business civilization. In the upper reaches of this new elite—that is, in the scientific community—men hold significantly different values, which could become the foundation of the new ethos for such a class.

Actually, the institution of property itself is undergoing a fundamental revision, in a significant way. In Western society for the past several hundred years, property, as the protection of private rights to wealth, has been the economic basis of individualism. Traditionally the institution of property, as Charles Reich of the Yale Law School has put it, "guards the troubled boundary between individual man and the state." In modern life property has changed in two distinctive ways. One of these is elementary: Individual property has become corporate, and property is no longer controlled by owners but by managers. In a more subtle and diffuse way, however, a new kind of property has emerged, and with it a different kind of legal relationship. To put it more baldly, property today consists not only of visible things (land, possessions, titles) but also of claims, grants, and contracts. The property relationship is not only between persons but between the individual and the government. As Reich points out, "The valuables dispensed by government take many forms, but they all share one characteristic. They are steadily taking the place of the traditional forms of wealth—forms which are held as private property. Social insurance substitutes for savings, a government contract replaces a businessman's customers and goodwill. . . . Increasingly, Americans live on government largess—allocated by government on its own terms, and held by recipients subject to conditions which express 'the public interest.' "[16]

While many forms of this "new property" represent direct grants (subsidies to farmers, corporations, and universities) or are contracts for services or goods (to industry and universities), the most pervasive form is claims held by individuals (social security, medical care, housing allowances) which derive from a new definition of social rights: claims on the community to ensure equality of treatment, claims legitimately due a person so that he will be able to share in the social heritage. And the most important claim of all is full access to education, within the limits of one's talent and potential.

The result of all this is to enlarge the arena of power, and at the same time to complicate the modes of decision-making. The domestic political process initiated by the New Deal was in effect a broadening of the "brokerage" system—the system of political deals between constituencies—although there are now many participants in the game. But there is also a new dimension in the political process, which has given the technocrats a new role. Matters of foreign policy have not been a reflex of internal political forces, but a judgment about the national interest, involving strategy decisions based on the calculation of an opponent's strength and intentions. Once the fundamental policy decision was made to oppose the communist power, many technical decisions, based on military technology and strategic assessments, took on the highest importance in the shaping of subsequent policy. Even a reworking of the economic map of the United States followed as well, with Texas and California gaining great importance because of the electronics and aerospace industries. In these instances technology and strategy laid down the requirements, and only then could business and local political groups seek to modify, or take advantage of, these decisions so as to protect their own economic interests.

In all this, the technical intelligentsia holds a double position. To the extent that it has interests in research, and positions in the universities, it becomes a new constituency—just as the military is a distinct new constituency, since this country has never before had a permanent military establishment seeking money and support for science, for research and development. Thus the intelligentsia be-

---

[16] Charles Reich, "The New Property," *The Public Interest*, no. 3 (Spring 1966), p. 57.

comes a claimant, like other groups, for public support (though its influence is felt in the bureaucratic and administrative labyrinth, rather than in the electoral system or mass pressure). At the same time, the technicians represent an indispensable administrative staff for the political office holder with his public following.

The Cockpit of Politics

Though the weights of the class system may shift, the nature of the political system, as the arena where interests are mediated, will not. In the next few decades, the political arena will become more decisive, if anything, for the two fundamental reasons I have indicated in previous chapters: We have become, for the first time, a national society, in which crucial decisions, affecting all parts of the society simultaneously (from foreign affairs to fiscal policy), are made by the government, rather than through the market; in addition, we have become a communal society, in which many more groups now seek to establish their social rights—their claims on society—through the political order.

In the national society, more and more projects (whether the clean-up of pollution or the reorganization of the cities) must be undertaken through group or communal instruments. In a tightly interwoven society, more decisions have to be made through politics and through planning. Yet both mechanisms, paradoxically, increase social conflict. Planning provides a specific locus of decision, as against the more impersonal and dispersed role of the market, and thus becomes a visible point at which pressures can be applied. Communal instruments—the effort to create a social choice out of the discordance of individual personal preferences—necessarily sharpen value conflicts. Do we want compensatory education for blacks at the expense, say, of places for other students when the number of positions is limited? Do we want to keep a redwood forest or provide a lucrative industry to a local community? Will we accept the increased noise of jets in communities near the airports, or force the reduction of weight and payloads, with a consequent increased cost to the industry and the traveler? Should a new highway go through old sections of a community, or do we route it around the section with a higher cost to all? These issues, and thousands more, cannot be settled on the basis of technical criteria; necessarily they involve value and political choices.

The relationship of technical and political decisions in the next decades will become, in consequence, one of the most crucial problems of public policy. The politician, and the political public, will have to become increasingly versed in the technical character of policy, aware of the ramified impact of decisions as systems become extended. As Robert Solow has pointed out: The views of Adam Smith may have been popularly digestible; an econometric study of alternative public-investment programs is not. And the technical intelligentsia must learn to question the often unanalyzed assumptions about efficiency and rationality which underlie their techniques.

In the end, however, the technocratic mind-view necessarily falls before politics. The hopes of rationality—or, one should say, of a particular kind of rationality—necessarily fade. There may still be, in the language of Max Weber, a *Zweckrationalität*, a rationality of means that are intertwined with ends and become adjusted to each other. But this is possible only when the ends are strictly defined and the means, then, can be calculated in terms of the end.[17]

Politics, in the sense that we understand it, is always prior to the rational, and often the upsetting of the rational. The "rational," as we have come to know it, is the routinized, settled, administrative and orderly procedure by rules. Much of life in a complex society necessarily has this character. In going by plane or train to Washington one does not haggle with the airline company or railroad over the fare, as one might with a taxi driver in the Levant. But politics is haggling, or else it is force. In Washington one haggles over the priorities of the society, the distribution of money, the burden of taxation, and the like. The idea that there is a "social decision" which can satisfy everyone has been annihilated by Kenneth Arrow, who in his "impossibility theorem" has demonstrated that no social decision can amalgamate the diverse preferences of a group in the way a single individual can amalgamate his own. Thus, theoretical economics, in its denial of a communal welfare function, which would be similar to the ordering principles of individual utility, undermines the application of rationality to public decisions. In a practical sense, this is something every politician knows in his bones. What is left is not rationality as the objective scaling of social utilities but bargaining between persons.

As for politics, what is evident, everywhere, is a society-side uprising against bureaucracy and a desire for participation, a theme summed up in the statement, already a catch-phrase, that "people ought to be able to affect the decisions that control their lives." To a considerable extent, the participation revolution is one of the forms of

---

[17] In the terminology of Weber, rationality is of two kinds, *Wertrationalität* and *Zweckrationalität*. *Wertrationalität* is the rationality of "reason" whose ends are to be considered by themselves as valid, independent of means. *Zweckrationalität* is the rationality of function.

reaction against the "professionalization" of society and the emergent technocratic decision-making of a post-industrial society. What began years ago in the factory through the trade unions has now spread to the neighborhood—because of the politicalization of decision-making in social affairs—and into the universities; in the next decades it will spread into other complex organizations as well. The older bureaucratic models of hierarchically organized centralized organizations functioning through an intensive division of labor clearly will be replaced by new forms of organization.

Yet "participatory democracy" is not the panacea that its adherents make it out to be, no more so than efforts of fifty years ago at creating plebiscetarian political mechanisms such as the initiative, the referendum, and the recall. With all the furor about "participatory democracy," it is curious that few of its proponents have sought to think through, on the most elementary level, the meaning of the phrases. If individuals are to affect the decisions that change their lives, then under those rules segregationists in the South would have the right to exclude blacks from the schools. Similarly, is a neighborhood group to be allowed to veto a city plan which takes into account the needs of a wider and more inclusive social unit? But at that point one would have to say that the South is not an independent entity but part of a larger polity, and must comply with the moral norms of the more inclusive society, and so does the neighborhood. In short, participatory democracy is one more way of posing the classical issues of political philosophy, namely, Who should make, and at what levels of government, what kinds of decisions, for how large a social unit?

The conception of a rational organization of society stands confounded. Rationality, as a means—as a set of techniques for efficient allocation of resources—has been twisted beyond the recognition of its forebears; rationality, as an end, finds itself confronted by the cantankerousness of politics, the politics of interest and the politics of passion. Faced with this double failure, the adherents of rationality—in particular the planners and designers—are now in the difficult position of having to rethink their premises and to understand their limits. And yet, the recognition of those limits is itself the beginning of wisdom.

In the end is the beginning, as T. S. Eliot wrote, and we return to the question that is the root of all political philosophy: What is the good life that one wants to lead? The politics of the future—for those who operate within the society, at least—will not be quarrels between functional economic-interest groups for distributive shares of the national product, but the concerns of communal society, particularly the inclusion of disadvantaged groups. They will turn on the issues of instilling a responsible social ethos in our leaders, the demand for more amenities, for greater beauty and a better quality of life in the arrangement of our cities, a more differentiated and intellectual educational system, and an improvement in the character of our culture. We may be divided on how to achieve these aims, and how to apportion the costs. But such questions, deriving from a conception of public virtue, bring us back to the classical questions of the polis. And this is as it should be.

CODA

An Agenda for the Future

1. *How Social Systems Change*

SOCIAL systems take a long time to expire. In the 1850s Marx thought that the "historical revolutionary process" was already undermining bourgeois society and bringing Europe to the verge of socialism. He feared that the final upheaval would come before he had completed his grand demonstration in *Capital*, and he wrote to his friend Dr. Kugelmann at the end of 1857, "I am working like mad all through the nights at putting my economic studies together so that I may at least have the outlines clear before the deluge comes." [1] But it was a still older social order that was dying at the time, and even then that order had another half-century of life ahead. [2] In our foreshortening of social time we forget that a powerful monarchical sys-

---

[1] In a speech in 1856, he used a geological metaphor: "The so-called revolutions of 1848 were but poor incidents—small fractures and fissures in the dry crust of European society. However, they announced the abyss. Beneath the apparently solid surface, they betrayed oceans of liquid matter, only needing expansion to rend into fragments continents of hard rock." And yet it is also good Marxism—a view he developed in later years—that no social system ever disappears until all its potential for development has been realized, a view Marx argued against the Utopians, leftists, and political adventurers who thought that "will" alone could create a social revolution.

The speech of 1856 was given at the anniversary of the Chartist organ, the *People's Paper*, and is reprinted in *Karl Marx: Selected Works*, vol. 2 (Moscow, 1935); the quotation is on p. 427. The letter to Dr. Kugelmann is cited in the editor's notes in *The Correspondence of Marx and Engels* (New York, 1936), pp. 225–226.

[2] In his memoirs *Gesichter und Zeiten*, published two years before his death in 1935, the German count and noted publisher Harry Kessler, who was born in 1868, looked back to the eighties and recalled a widespread feeling that

something very great, the old cosmopolitan, yet still mainly agricultural and feudal Europe, the world of beautiful ladies, gallant kings, dynastic arrangements, the Europe of the eighteenth century and the Holy Alliance, had become old and sick, and was declining to its death; and something new, young, strong, as yet unimaginable, would make its appearance. (Cited by Naomi Bliven, *The New Yorker* [January 15, 1972].)

tem lasted until 1918 in Germany, Russia, Austria-Hungary (which included large parts of central Europe) and Italy, while in England a small upper class, whose members knew each other intimately, still governed the society. A Communist Revolution may have arisen out of the ashes of World War I, but that conflagration did not so much kill capitalism as finally destroy the political remnants of feudalism.

Ninety years after the death of Marx, capitalism was still dominant in the Western world while, paradoxically, communist movements had come to power almost entirely in agrarian and pre-industrial societies, where "socialist planning" was largely an alternative route to industrialization, rather than the succession to capitalism. To predict, thus, the close demise of capitalism is a risky business and, barring the breakdown of the political shell of that system because of war, the social forms of managerial capitalism—the corporate business enterprise, private decision on investment, the differential privileges based on control of property—are likely to remain for a long time.

And yet the functional basis of the system is changing, and the lineaments of a new society are visible. The historical change is taking place along two axes. One is the relation of the economic function to the other major functions of society. Marx, in his view of capitalist society, had focused on class division as the source of tension—the exploitation of the workers within the economic system—and predicted a political upheaval and a new social order as the succession of classes. But from the perspective of industrial society, Emile Durkheim saw the lack of restraint on the economic function itself as the source of anomie and the disruption of social life. As Durkheim first wrote in 1890:

. . . It is not possible for a social function to exist without moral discipline. Otherwise nothing remains but individual appetites, and since these are by nature boundless and insatiable, if there is nothing to control them they will not be able to control themselves.

And it is precisely due to this fact that the crisis has arisen from which the European societies are now suffering. For two centuries economic life has taken on an expansion it never knew before. From being a secondary function, despised and left to inferior classes, it passed on to one of first rank. We see the military, governmental and religious functions falling back more and more in face of it. The scientific functions alone are in a position to dispute its ground, and even science has hardly any prestige in the eyes of the present day, except in so far as it may serve what is materially useful, that is to say, serve for the most part the business occupations. That is why it can be said, with some justice that society is, or tends to be industrial.[3]

[3] Emile Durkheim, *Professional Ethics and Civic Morals* (Glencoe, Ill., 1958), pp. 10–11. These lectures, unpublished during Durkheim's lifetime, were first published in Turkey, by the Faculty of Law of Istanbul, and the Presses Universitaire de

The major problem for modern society, thus, was not class conflict, which was a subsidiary aspect of unrestricted competition in regard to wages, but the unregulated character of the economic function itself—even when aided by the state.

The decisive social change taking place in our time—because of the interdependence of men and the aggregative character of economic actions, the rise of externalities and social costs, and the need to control the effects of technical change—is the subordination of the economic function to the political order. The forms this will take will vary, and will emerge from the specific history of the different political societies—central state control, public corporations, decentralized enterprises and central policy directives, mixed public and private enterprises, and the like. Some will be democratic, some not. But the central fact is clear: The autonomy of the economic order (and the power of the men who run it) is coming to an end, and new and varied, but different, control systems are emerging. In sum, the control of society is no longer primarily economic but political.

The second major historical change is the sundering of social function (or place in society, primarily occupational) from property. In Western society, and particularly under capitalism, function in society could be turned into property (land, machinery, stocks, franchises), which was conserved as wealth and transferred to one's heirs, to create a continuity of rights—privileges formalized as a social system. In the new society which is now emerging, individual private property is losing its social purpose (i.e. to protect one's labor in the Lockean sense, to control or direct production, to be a reward for risk) and function stands alone.

The autonomy of function, or technical competence, was the root of the technocratic vision of Saint-Simon. It was the basis for the moral view of the eminent English economic historian and socialist R. H. Tawney. In his influential tract, *The Acquisitive Society*, Tawney argued that ownership of property had lost its moral claim for reward and therefore was less the criterion of esteem or place than function, which he defined "as an activity which embodies and expresses the idea of social purpose." [4]

France in 1950. These lectures were first given in 1890 and 1900 at Bordeaux and repeated at the Sorbonne in 1904 and 1912. The passage cited above appears in slightly reduced form in Durkheim's preface to the second edition of *The Division of Labor*, which appeared in 1902 under the title "Quelque Remarques sur les Groupements Professionels." See *The Division of Labor*, trans. George Simpson (New York, 1933), p. 3. In the quotation above, I have in the last two lines used the wording from the preface to *The Division of Labor*, since it strengthens Durkheim's essential meaning.

[4] R. H. Tawney, *The Acquisitive Society* (New York, 1920), p. 8. See especially chap. 6, "The Functional Society," and chap. 10, "The Position of the Brain Worker."

What Tawney defined is *professionalism,* and if this vision is correct, the heart of the post-industrial society is a class that is primarily a professional class. As with any status group, the boundaries of definition are fluid and often indistinct, yet certain core elements are obvious.[5] A profession is a learn*ed* (i.e. scholarly) activity, and thus involves formal training, but within a broad intellectual context. To be within the profession means to be certified, formally or informally, by one's peers or by some established body within the profession. And a profession embodies a norm of social responsiveness. This does not mean that professionals are more charitable or high-minded than their fellows, but that expectations about their conduct derive from an ethic of service which, as a norm, is prior to an ethic of self-interest.[6] For all these reasons, the idea of a profession implies an idea of competence and authority, technical and moral, and that the professional will assume an hieratic place in the society.

In Chapter 6 I discussed the transformations of class and power in industrial society. From those foundations, one can speculate about the future. If one turns, then, to the societal structure of the post-industrial society considered along these two historical axes, two conclusions are evident. First, the major class of the emerging new society is primarily a professional class, based on knowledge rather than property. But second, the control system of the society is lodged not in a successor-occupational class but in the political order, and the question of who manages the political order is an open one. (See "Schema: The Societal Structure of the Post-Industrial Society," p. 375.)

In terms of status (esteem and recognition, and possibly income), the knowledge class may be the highest class in the new society, but in the nature of that structure there is no intrinsic reason for this class, on the basis of some coherent or corporate identity, to become a new economic interest class, or a new political class which would

---

[5] For a classic discussion of the subject, see A. M. Carr-Saunders and P. A. Wilson, *The Professions* (Oxford, 1933; reprint edition, London, 1964), especially part 4, "Professionalism and the Society of the Future." For a summation of the concept, see the article "Professions," by Talcott Parsons, in the *International Encyclopedia of the Social Sciences* (New York, 1968), vol. 12. For some recent discussions on what can be professionalized, see Harold Wilensky, "The Professionalization of Everyone," in the *American Journal of Sociology*, vol. 70, no. 2 (September 1964), and *Professions and Professionalization*, ed. J. A. Jackson (Cambridge, Eng., 1970).

[6] One might say that business is called to account by its customers through the market, whereas a professional is called to account by his peers through the professional group. Property is associated with wealth, which can be passed on through legal title directly; a profession is defined by skill which can be passed on only indirectly through cultural advantage that the children of professionals may gain.

Coda: An Agenda for the Future

bid for power. The reasons for this are evident from an inspection of the Schema.

Schema: The Societal Structure of the Post-Industrial Society (U.S. Model)

I. *Statuses: Axis of Stratification—Based on Knowledge* (Horizontal Structures)
   A. The professional class: the four estates
      1. Scientific
      2. Technological (applied skills: engineering, economics, medicine)
      3. Administrative
      4. Cultural (artistic and religious)
   B. Technicians and semi-professional
   C. Clerical and sales
   D. Craftsmen and semi-skilled (blue-collar)
II. *Situses: Locations of Occupational Activities* (Vertical Structures)
   A. Economic enterprises and business firms
   B. Government (bureaucratic: judicial and administrative)
   C. Universities and research institutions
   D. Social complexes (hospitals, social-service centers, etc.)
   E. The military
III. *Control System: The Political Order*
   A. The directorate
      1. Office of the President
      2. Legislative leaders
      3. Bureaucratic chiefs
      4. Military chiefs
   B. The polities: constituencies and claimants
      1. Parties
      2. Elites (scientific, academic, business, military)
      3. Mobilized groups
         a) Functional groups (business, professional, labor)
         b) Ethnic groups
         c) Special-focus groups
            (1) Functional (mayors of cities, poor, etc.)
            (2) Expressive (youth, women, homosexual, etc.)

The professional class as I define it is made up of four estates: the scientific, the technological, the administrative, and the cultural.[7]

---

[7] The suggestion of four estates is derived, of course, from Don K. Price's fruitful book *The Scientific Estate* (Cambridge, Mass., 1965). Price defines four functions in

375

While the estates, as a whole, are bound by a common ethos, there is no intrinsic interest that binds one to the other, except for a common defense of the idea of learning; in fact there are large disjunctions between them. The scientific estate is concerned with the pursuit of basic knowledge and seeks, legitimately, to defend the conditions of such pursuit, untrammeled by political or extraneous influence. The technologists, whether engineers, economists, or physicians, base their work on a codified body of knowledge, but in the application of that knowledge to social or economic purposes they are constrained by the policies of the different situses they are obedient to. The administrative estate is concerned with the management of organizations and is bound by the self-interest of the organization itself (its perpetuation and aggrandizement) as well as the implementation of social purposes, and may come into conflict with one or another of the estates. The cultural estate—artistic and religious—is involved with the expressive symbolism (plastic or ideational) of forms and meanings, but to the extent that it is more intensively concerned with meanings, it may find itself increasingly hostile to the technological and administrative estates. As I noted in the introduction, the axial principle of modern culture, in its concern with the self, is antinomian and anti-institutional, and thus hostile to the functional rationality which tends to dominate the application of knowledge by the technological and administrative estates. Thus in the post-industrial society one finds increasingly a disjunction between social structure and culture which inevitably affects the cohesiveness if not the corporate consciousness of the four estates.[8]

While the classes may be represented, horizontally, by *statuses* (headed by the four estates), the society is organized, vertically, by *situses*, which are the actual loci of occupational activities and interests. I use this unfamiliar sociological word *situses* to emphasize the fact that in day-to-day activities the actual play and conflict of interests exist between the organizations to which men belong, rather than between the more diffuse class or status identities. In a capitalist so-

---

government—the scientific, professional, administrative, and political—and converts each function, as an ideal type, into an estate. My differences with Price are twofold: I think the estates can be represented more accurately as social groups, rather than functions; more importantly, I do not consider the *political* function coeval logically with the others, for I see the political as the control system of the entire societal structure. Terminologically, I have substituted the word "technological" (for the applied skills) where Price uses "professional," since I would reserve "professional" for the larger meaning of the entire class, and I have added a cultural estate, where Price has none. Nonetheless, my indebtedness to Price is great.

[8] One might note that the more extreme forms of the "new consciousness" such as Theodore Rozsak's *The Making of a Counter-Culture* and Charles Reich's *The Greening of America* manifest a distinct hostility not only to scientism, but to science as well.

ciety, the property owner or businessman, as a class, is located exclusively in the business firm or corporation, so that status and situs are joined. In the post-industrial society, however, the four estates are distributed among many different situses. Scientists can work for economic enterprises, government, universities, social complexes, or the military (though the bulk of the "pure" scientists are to be found in the university). And the same distributions hold for the technologists and the managers. Because of this "cross-cutting," the likelihood of a pure "estate" consciousness for political purposes tends to diminish.

Finally, if the major historical turn in the last quarter-century has been the subordination of the economic function to societal goals, the political order necessarily becomes the control system of the society. But who runs it, and for whose (or what) ends? In one respect, what the change may mean is that traditional social conflicts have simply shifted from one arena to another, so that what the traditional classes fought out in the economic realm, where men sought comparative advantage in place, privilege and domination, is now transferred to the political realm, and as that arena widens, the special foci and ethnic groups (the poor and the blacks) now seek to gain through politics the privileges and advantages they could not obtain in the economic order. This is what has been taking place in recent years, and it will continue. The second, and structurally more pervasive, shift is that in the post-industrial society the *situses* rather than the *statuses* would be the major political-interest units in the society. To some extent this is evident in the familiar phenomenon of pressure groups. But in the post-industrial society it is more likely that the *situses* will achieve greater corporate cohesiveness vis-à-vis one another and become the major claimants for public support and the major constituencies in the determination of public policy.[9] And yet the very forces which have re-emphasized the primacy of the political order in a technical world make it imperative to define some coherent goals for the society as a whole and, in the process, to articulate a public philosophy which is more than the sum of what particular situses or social groups may want. In the efforts to forge some such coherence one may find the seeds of the cohesiveness of the professional class in the post-industrial society.

---

[9] The limitation of this analysis is that while the post-industrial society, in its societal structure, increasingly becomes a *functional* society, the political order is not organized in functional terms. Thus the continuing existence of the traditional geographical districts and the dispersal of persons in this fashion means that the political issues at any one time are much more diffuse than the interests of the particular statuses or situses. It would also indicate that the situses would, like the pressure groups, operate primarily through the lobbying of the legislative and executive branches, rather than work directly through the electoral process. Reality complicates immeasurably any ideal-type schemas.

A new social system, contrary to Marx, does not always arise necessarily within the shell of an old one but sometimes outside of it. The framework of feudal society was made up of noblemen, lords, soldiers, and priests whose wealth was based on land. The bourgeois society that took hold in the thirteenth century was made up of artisans, merchants, and free professionals whose property lay in their skills or their willingness to take risks, and whose mundane values were far removed from the fading theatrics of the chivalric style of life. It arose, however, outside the feudal landed structure, in the free communes, or towns, that were no longer seignorial dependencies. And these self-ruling small communes became the cornerstones of the future European mercantile and industrial society.[10]

So, too, the process today. The roots of post-industrial society lie in the inexorable influence of science on productive methods, particularly in the transformation of the electrical and chemical industries at the beginning of the twentieth century. But as Robert Heilbroner has observed: "Science, as we know it, began well before capitalism existed and did not experience its full growth until well after capitalism was solidly entrenched." And science, as a quasi-autonomous force, would extend beyond capitalism. By this token, one can say that the scientific estate—its ethos and its organization—is the monad that contains within itself the imago of the future society.[11]

2. The Future of Science

THE ETHOS OF SCIENCE

Though the idea of science goes back to Greek times, the organization of scientific work begins largely in the seventeenth century with the rise of academies, or scientific societies, funded by wealthy

---

[10] Paradoxically, the growth of that society came about only after the self-contained economic life of the commune—its roots—was broken by the rise of larger-scale industry which, in branching out, could buy its raw materials in one town and sell in another, and which made its way, against both the older feudal society and the regulative restrictions of the commune, in alliance with the monarchical centralization of the newly emerging national state.

[11] This is, indeed, Heilbroner's suggestion. See Robert Heilbroner, *The Limits of American Capitalism* (New York, 1966), p. 115. He states:

. . . like the first manifestations of the market in the medieval era, science and its technology emerge as a great underground river whose tortuous course has finally reached the surface during the age of capitalism, but which springs from far different sources. But that is not where the resemblance ends. As with the emergent market forces, the river of scientific change, having now surfaced, must cut its own channel through the existing social landscape—a channel that will, as in the case of the money orientation in medieval life, profoundly alter the nature of the

patrons and developing outside the universities, to foster scientific experiments. The institutionalization of scientific work, however, develops only with the formalization of national academies, as in France in the late eighteenth century, and the absorption of science into the university, beginning in Germany in the nineteenth century, and the creation of scientific laboratories in the universities which became centers of world-wide scientific communities in their fields.[12]

Despite the fact that it often functioned within state systems—in Germany and in France the universities and academies were state institutions and professors were civil servants—the overriding fact about science was its *autonomy* as a self-directed community: in the decisions about what research would be undertaken, in the debates about what knowledge was valid, in the recognition of achievement and the granting of status and esteem. This very autonomy is the heart of the ethos—and organization—of science.

And yet, while the moral strength of science lies in the ethos of a self-regulating commune, the growth of this estate since World War

---

existing terrain. Indeed, if we ask what force in our day might in time be strong enough to undercut the bastions of privilege and function of capitalism and to create its own institutions and social structures in their place, the answer must surely be the one force that dominates our age—the power of science and of scientific technology (ibid., pp. 116–117).

I believe that while the initial proposition may be correct, Mr. Heilbroner neglects the transformation of science itself when it becomes "Big Science," and becomes intertwined with the government in dealing with the social and political issues of the day. It is this transformation—as my ensuing discussion argues—that makes problematic the utopian component of the post-industrial society.

[12] For a short but lucid discussion of the early organization of science, see A. R. Hall, *The Scientific Revolution, 1500–1800* (London, 1954), chap. 7, "The Organization of Scientific Inquiry." On the institutionalization of science in the last two centuries, see Joseph Ben-David, *The Scientist's Role in Society* (Englewood Cliffs, N.J., 1971). As Professor Ben-David describes the new role of the universities:

. . . the laboratories of some German universities became the centers and sometimes virtually the seats of world-wide scientific communities in their respective fields starting about the middle of the nineteenth century. Liebig at Giessen, and Johannes Müller at Berlin were perhaps the first instances of a master and a considerable number of advanced research students working together over a period of time in a specialty until they obtained, by sheer concentration of effort, an edge over everyone else in the world. Toward the end of the century the laboratories of some of the professors became so famous that the ablest students from all over the world went there for varying periods of time. The list of students who worked in such places often included practically all the important scientists of the next generation. . . .

These unplanned and unexpected developments were an even more decisive step in the organization of science than the early nineteenth century reform. Research started to become a regular career, and scientists in a number of fields started to develop into much more closely knit networks than ever before. Their *nuclei* were now university laboratories training large numbers of advanced students, thus establishing between them personal relationships, highly effective means of personal communication, and the beginnings of deliberately concentrated and coordinated research efforts in a selected problem area (ibid., pp. 124–125).

II, the birth-years of the post-industrial society, has transformed science in such extraordinary fashion as to create a radical disjunction between the traditional image, both in ethos and organization, and the reality of its structure and role as "Big Science." It is this disjunction which raises the question whether the paradox of the rise of capitalism (noted in footnote 10) may not be repeated in the intertwining of science and government, and whether the traditional ethos and image of science may not have a different function in the post-industrial society.

The community of science is a unique institution in human civilization.[13] It has no ideology, in that it has no postulated set of formal beliefs, but it has an ethos which implicitly prescribes rules of conduct. It is not a political movement that one joins by subscription, for membership is by election, yet one must make a commitment in order to belong. It is not a church where the element of faith rests on belief and is rooted in mystery, yet faith, passion, and mystery are present, but they are directed by the search for certified knowledge whose function it is to test and discard old beliefs. Like almost every human institution, it has its hierarchies and prestige rankings, but this ordering is based uniquely on achievement and confirmation by peers rather than on inheritance, age grading, brute force, or contrived manipulation. In totality, it is a social contract but in a way never foretold by Hobbes or Rousseau, for while there is a voluntary submission to a community and a moral unity results, the sovereignty is not coercive and the conscience remains individual and protestant. As an imago, it comes closest to the ideal of the Greek *polis*, a republic of free men and women united by a common quest for truth.

Science, almost like a religious order, defines the stages along life's way. "One enters civil society by mere birth, and one becomes a citizen by mere coming of age. Not so in the Republic of Science, wherein membership must be diligently sought and is selectively granted." Thus Bertrand de Jouvenel has described the beginning of the process. One lives within a great tradition shaped out of the errors and advances of the past. The first forcing ground is the university. In a lower school a student may have learned the received doctrine, the scientific verities, the "dead letter" of science. A university

---

[13] In this sketch of the traditional imago—and rationale—of science, I have relied principally upon Michael Polanyi's *The Logic of Liberty* (London, 1951), part I; Max Weber's "Science as a Vocation," in *From Max Weber*, ed. Gerth and Mills (New York, 1946); and Robert K. Merton's *Social Theory and Social Structure* (revised edition, Glencoe, Ill., 1957), chaps. 15 and 16.

This imago is an ideal type and, like any such construct, is sometimes contradicted in practice. For a skeptical note, see Robert A. Rothman, "A Dissenting View on the Scientific Ethos," *British Journal of Sociology*, vol. xxiii, no. 1 (March 1972).

seeks to make the student realize its uncertainties and its eternally provisional nature.

To be a scientist is to serve an apprenticeship. As in art, there are few primitives or self-taught; one achieves competence by serving under a master. "In the great schools of research," Polanyi writes, "are fostered the most vital premises of scientific discovery. A master's daily labors will reveal these to the intelligent student and impart to him also some of the master's personal intuitions by which his work is guided. . . . This is why so often great scientists follow great masters as apprentices. Rutherford's work bore the clear imprint of his apprenticeship under J. J. Thomson. And no less than four Nobel laureates are found in turn among the personal pupils of Rutherford. . . ."

If there is apprenticeship, there is also fellowship. One has only to read a book like Werner Heisenberg's *Physics and Beyond* to get the sense that, in the 1920s, nuclear physics had all the excitement of an avant-garde movement. The young physicists flocked to Göttingen, Berlin, Copenhagen, and Cambridge to study with the masters and participate in the exciting reconstruction of the physical universe. They had a self-conscious feeling of belonging to a special order, and their relationships were intimate and personal. One is struck by the cooperative, yet competitive, ambience in which men working on the frontiers of physics, such as Bohr, Dirac, Schrödinger, Heisenberg, Pauli, and others, sought each other out to exchange ideas and talk physics, and masters like Bohr quickly sensed the quality of younger men and invited them to work with him, or went with them on long, extended walks and talks, in order to test and clarify their ideas.[14]

The heart of science lies in the definition of inquiry. It is an effort to solve a question which is not "given" but is problematic. The inception of an inquiry rests upon the guess that an unknown yet underlying pattern links together apparently diverse phenomena, and the scientific method narrows the models to a few alternatives which permit of testing. A theory is not a mechanical algorithm which runs down every possible permutation and combination, but an insight

---

[14] In this respect, science is like many an intellectual or artistic community where painters or writers seek each other out and, when they are united by a common interest, will reinforce each other's work. One can take an analogous movement such as abstract painting in the 1950s when such artists as Hoffman, Pollock, de Kooning, Still, and Motherwell extended the qualities of "painterliness"—i.e. the effects of the *texture* of paint as a dimension of the painting itself—to the formal limits of painting, and thus, in a sense, exhausted a paradigm. And yet while they all talked with each other (though Still was a recluse), they were not engaged in a *cooperative* enterprise to master a problem or complete a phase in an intellectual tradition. For science is the testing of *coordinate* knowledge within a coherent paradigm. However individual the explorations, the results dovetail to provide a comprehensive description, if not explanatory answer, of a theoretical question.

which is subject to verification. If a man fails to pursue this testing with great rigor, he may still possibly have hit upon a truth, but he will have fallen from the standards of scientific inquiry.

For this knowledge to be accredited, it must run the gauntlet of criticism. There are the initial "referees" whose judgment permits publication in the scientific journals. There are the seniors whose words command respect. In the scientific estate, as in other institutions, there are the elders, grouped often in an academy or some other formal body of official recognition, who are the unofficial governors of the scientific community. "By their advice [as Polanyi puts it] they can either delay or accelerate the growth of a new line of research. . . . By the award of prizes and of other distinctions, they can invest a promising pioneer almost overnight with a position of authority and independence. . . . Within a decade or so a new school of thought can be established by the selection of appropriate candidates for Chairs which have fallen vacant during that period. The same end can be advanced even more effectively by setting up new Chairs."

Along with this process goes an ethos which is based on the norm of free inquiry. It is accepted as a commitment not because it is technically and procedurally efficient in promoting scientific work, which it is, but because it is deemed morally right and good. This ethos, as codified by Robert K. Merton, has four elements: universalism, communalism, disinterestedness, and organized skepticism.

Universalism demands that careers be open to anyone with talent. It rejects claims dependent upon the personal or social attributes of the individual, such as race, nationality, birth, or class. Communalism implies that knowledge is a social product, drawn from the common heritage of the past and given freely to the inheritors of the future. In science, an eponymous acclaim (such as Boyle's law of gases) is a commemorative device, not a property right. One can patent an invention and derive a profit, but not the theory which has guided the invention.[15] Scientific theory is in the public domain, and to this extent full and open communication is a necessary condition for the advance of knowledge.

Disinterestedness is not a matter of individual motivation (scientists are as jealous of their own claims to fame as other persons—if not more so, since fame is their major reward) but of normative imperatives. The virtual absence of fraud in the annals of science, an exceptional record when compared with other spheres of activity, is due

---

[15] Thus I. I. Rabi, with his work on molecular beams, and Charles Townes, with his theory of radiation emission, did the theoretical work which led directly to the principle of the laser. Though industrial corporations may reap profits, the reward of Rabi and Townes is scholarly recognition; they both won Nobel Prizes.

less to the personal qualities of the scientists than to the nature of scientific inquiry itself. "The demand for disinterestedness [writes Merton] has a firm basis in the public and testable character of science and this circumstance, it may be supposed, has contributed to the integrity of the men of science."

Organized skepticism emphasizes its detached scrutiny, its "willing suspension of belief," its dissolution of the wall between the sacred and profane. Scientific knowledge is not ideology (though it may be distorted for such purposes) but a public explanation subject to renewed tests of verification. Einsteinian physics, according to Soviet ideologists (circa 1930), may have been bourgeois idealism, but it is Soviet ideology and not Einsteinian physics that crumbled. If science makes an absolute claim for autonomy and freedom, it does so by emphasizing the non-partisanship of its results.

Science is a special kind of social arrangement designed to achieve, in John Ziman's phrase, "a consensus of rational opinion." So, ideally, does a polity. Yet the processes differ. In science, "truth" is achieved through controversy and criticism, in which a single answer has to be forthcoming. In the polity, a consensus is achieved through bargaining and trade-offs, and the answers are a compromise.

Because no committee of outsiders can forecast the future progress of science, other than the routine extensions of existing paradigms, it can only be directed by the men of science themselves. Thus the community of science is a group of dedicated individuals, recognized by each other, working within a self-governing commune, responsible less to society as a whole than to its own ideals.

The process and ethos add up to a "calling." It is a calling because, as Max Weber put it, "Science . . . presupposes that what is yielded by scientific work is important in the sense that it is 'worth being known,' " even though that very statement cannot be proven by scientific means and must be related, by each in his own way, to the ultimate values that each holds. But the dedication to science has a hallowed quality, and because this partakes of the "sacred" we can say that the ethos of science describes a "charismatic community."

The controlling term in this description is a *community* of science. And that very term highlights the distinctive sociological disjunction which has emerged in the last quarter of a century. A community, in the sociological term, is a *Gemeinschaft*, a primary group bound by intimate ties regulating itself through the force of tradition and opinion. But as against the *Gemeinschaft*, in the familiar sociological dichotomy, is the *Gesellschaft*, the large, impersonal society of secondary associations regulated by bureaucratic rules and tied together by the sanctions of dismissal. Today, science is both *Gemeinschaft* and

Gesellschaft. There is the community of science, the recognition by peers of outstanding achievement, which partakes of the charismatic quality of the undertaking and maintains the norms of disinterested knowledge. There is also the "occupational society," a large-scale economic enterprise whose norms are "useful returns" to the society or the enterprise (non-profit or profit-making) and which grows larger and larger and tends to dwarf the first.

The features of the "occupational society" are clear. Internally, there are the common features of bureaucratization: size, differentiation, and specialization—the risks of what Hans Magnus Enzenberger has called "the industrialization of mind." The enterprise is regulated—less in the universities, more in the research laboratories—by formal hierarchy and impersonal rules. One loses the sense of the whole in the allocation of minute tasks; one loses control of the process of work. What we have is the common prescription of alienation in the workplace itself.

Externally there is the dependence on government for financial support ("Without doubt," writes Derek Price, "the abnormal thing in this age of Big Science is money") and the demand that science be subordinated to "national needs," be these weapons research, promotion of technology, the cleanup of the environment, and the like. Instead of self-direction there arises "science policy," which inevitably becomes another name for the "planning" of science, a planning which becomes inevitable with economic questions such as the degree of support for science as a proportion of GNP, the relative allocations among fields, the statement of priorities in research, and so on. A community can demand autonomy, but any large-scale bureaucratic structure becomes subject to public scrutiny or to governmental controls or, like any regulated or funded enterprise, it seeks on its own to influence political decisions for its self-interest and becomes a claimant in the political system.

Along a different dimension, this transition in social structure poses a set of crucial questions for the norms and ethos of science. The community of science has been one of the most remarkable instances of the institutionalization of vitalized charisma. Charisma, as we know, is one of the major modes for legitimating change and innovation, especially revolutionary change. Charismatic authority, lodged usually though not necessarily in compelling figures, becomes the moral sanction for the breakup of established and traditional systems. In religion and politics one finds, historically, that the period after the eruption of charisma is usually followed by routinization, in which the original charismatic impulse (Christianity, communism) itself becomes established and resists change. This is not so in science. In the community of science the accepted norm is that of permanent revolution through codified rules. It is the fate of scientific knowledge to submit to constant testing, and while individuals, understandably, may resist the overthrow of a particular theory or paradigm, the community as a whole must accept the wheel of revolutionary fate.[16] This "charismatic community" has been an operative reality in the history of science, guarding the chalice of revolution and acting as a set of guardians to bestow legitimacy on new paradigms and recognition and reward to individuals.[17]

But with the growth of Big Science, especially since World War II, the distinguishing feature of the "occupational society" is that few people "do" science, and many carry on research. Necessarily the "occupational society" creates its own structures of representation which function either politically, to mediate with government, or as lobbies (like trade associations), to guard the occupational interests of science. The major problem for science in the post-industrial society will be the relation between the "charismatic community" (the "invisible college"), which bestows recognition and status, and the bureaucratized institutions (scientific and technical societies, research institutions, engineering associations, and the like) of the occupational society, which wrestles not only with the more mundane facts of careers, promotions, and the availability of money, but with the inevitable process of the planning of science, which derives from the fact that the laissez-faire relation between science and government has vanished, and the question of *what* science should do (if it asks

---

[16] As Max Weber wrote, in "Science as a Vocation":

In science, each of us knows that what he has accomplished will be antiquated in ten, twenty, fifty years. That is the fate to which science is subjected; it is the very *meaning* of scientific work. . . . Every scientific "fulfilment" raises new "questions"; it *asks* to be "surpassed" and outdated. Whoever wishes to serve science has to resign himself to this fact. Scientific works can last as "gratifications" because of their artistic quality, or they remain important as a means of training. Yet they will be surpassed scientifically—let that be repeated—for it is our common fate and, more, our common goal. We cannot work without hoping that others will advance further than we have. In principle, this progress goes on ad infinitum . . . (p. 138).

[17] I owe the suggestion and the phrase to Joseph Ben-David, though I suspect he might not approve of my own idiosyncratic usage; see his essay, "The Profession of Science and Its Powers," *Minerva* (London, July 1972).

The operative character of the community of science as a recognition and reward mechanism has been demonstrated in a number of research studies by Robert K. Merton and his associates. See Harriet Zuckerman and Robert K. Merton, "Patterns of Evaluation in Science: Institutionalisation, Structure and Functions of the Referee System," *Minerva* (London), vol. IX, no. 1 (January 1971); Stephen Cole and Jonathan R. Cole, "Scientific Output and Recognition: A Study in the Operation of the Reward System in Science," *American Sociological Review*, vol. 32, no. 3 (June 1967); Harriet Zuckerman, "Stratification in American Science," in Edward O. Laumann, ed., *Social Stratification: Research and Theory for the 1970s*, (Indianapolis, 1970). A collection of Merton's papers, *The Sociology of Science—Theoretical and Empirical Investigations*, ed. Norman Storer, was published by the University of Chicago Press in 1973.

for public support and money) becomes a matter of negotiation.[18]

Any social system is ultimately defined by an ethos—the values enshrined in creeds, the justifications established for rewards, and the norms of behavior embodied in character structure. The Protestant ethic was the ethos of capitalism and the idea of socialism the ethos of Soviet society. In the same way, the ethos of science is the emerging ethos of post-industrial society. Yet in the past instances the ethos diverged from reality. Bourgeois individuals became motivated by mundane acquisitive drives and hedonistic rewards rather than a sanctified calling of work; communist society today maintains large differentials of privilege which are now inherited despite the formal commitment to egalitarianism. In the end, both the Protestant ethic and the idea of socialism became ideologies, a set of formal justifications masking a reality, rather than imperatives for conduct. So, too, may the ethos of science. Formulated in an earlier age of innocence, it risks becoming the ideology of post-industrial society: a creed which establishes the norm of disinterested knowledge, but which is at variance with the reality of a new bureaucratic-technological order that is meshed with a centralized political system struggling to manage a complex and fractionated society. Whether this will happen—or under what conditions it might—is the subject of the next section.

THE POLITICS OF SCIENCE

In his novel *The Shape of Things to Come*, written forty years ago, H. G. Wells pictured a war-wasted world, where crudely clad Neanderthalers fight with club and spear among the mute ruins of a wrecked technological civilization. Finally this world is redeemed by a glitteringly dressed group of scientists who, having withdrawn a few decades before to some remote Eurasian wastes to build a rational civilization, now fly back and, with super-weapons of their own invention, impose universal peace on the bickering nations of the world.[19]

---

[18] As Jean-Jacques Solomon has observed: "In these days . . . if there is a conflict between science and government, such a conflict does not take place under the old banner of truth, but under that of productivity. This claim for the quickest output possible is the modern, industrialized version of the threats which dogma's authority has exercised in the past. Conceived in this instrumental manner, science is only one among other tools that a society uses for achieving certain goals, and decision-making here cannot be dissociated from the decision-making process in other fields such as economics or defense." "Science Policy in Perspective," *Studium Generale*, no. 24 (1971), p. 1,028.

[19] The final scene of the book—and the movie which starred Raymond Massey as the chief scientist—shows the older generation of scientists, now tremulous, watch with awe and pride as the next generation takes the next great stride of science—to the moon!

Technocratic eudaemonism has always bred fantasies of science imposing its conceptions of order on the chaos of society. This messianism comes in part from the charismatic dimension of science and the original *Weltanschauung* which saw science as enlightenment, combatting both magic and religion. The theme first appears in Bacon's *New Atlantis*, which created the image of the truths of science redressing the ignorance and superstitions of mankind. The head of Solomon's House tells his visitors: "We have consultations which of the inventions and experiences we have discovered shall be published, and which not; and take all an oath of secrecy for the concealing of those we think fit to keep secret: though some of these we do reveal sometime to the State and some not." [20] It receives its most complete contemporary expression in the fantasy *The Voice of the Dolphins*, written in 1961 by that marvelous busybody-genius Leo Szilard, the man who initiated the chain of events that led to the atom-bomb project. Written from the vantage point of the year 2000, the book tells how world disarmament has been achieved through the intervention of the *scientists ex machina*. In this fantasy, a group of American and Russian scientists claims to have learned how to communicate with dolphins, whose larger brain capacity suggests a superior intelligence. They obtain from the dolphins solutions of various biological problems which result in the winning of multiple Nobel Prizes and the development of commercially profitable products. Of course, there is no such marine communication. The dolphin plan was necessary to mask the pooling of American and Russian scientific effort by men who, sacrificing personal fame, are able to accumulate large sums of money which are then used politically to buy out corrupt politicians. This political movement, centered in an institute named *Amruss*, finally succeeds in getting the world powers to disarm by 1988.

The striking thing about Szilard's fantasy was not any idea of technological gadgetry but two messianic images. One was the idea of the power of a few. It was derived from the thought that Werner Heisenberg expressed after the war: "In the summer of 1939 twelve people might still have been able, by coming to mutual agreement, to prevent the construction of atom-bombs." Second was the contempt for politicians and the belief that only scientists, not politicians, could provide the rational solutions to the world's problems. In Szilard's fantasy, the narrator, looking back in time, remarks: "Political issues were often complex, but they were rarely as deep as the scientific problems which had been solved in the first half of the twentieth cen-

---

[20] Bacon, *New Atlantis*, in *Famous Utopias*, ed. Charles M. Andrews (New York, n.d.), p. 171.

tury. This was because a scientist discussed a question with another scientist on the issue only 'whether it is true,' whereas a politician suspiciously asks, 'why did he say it?' " [21]

The messianic role of science, however, though given powerful literary attention, rarely tempted many scientists. The majority of them, understandably, have preferred to "do" science and remain aloof from politics. Historically, in fact, the public liberties of the universities and the autonomy of science were guaranteed by the state in an implicit bargain, a viewpoint which was justified philosophically by Max Weber in his distinction of *fact* and *values* and his relegation of values (and politics) to the status of "ultimate" questions

[21] Few contemporary scientists have had such an intensely messianic vision of their role as Szilard, who, with John von Neumann, was one of the last Renaissance men of science. Physicist, biologist, a founder of information theory, he made original contributions to almost any subject that caught his restless attention.

In his fascinating memoirs, Szilard relates that while in Berlin in 1932 he read a book by H. G. Wells, *The World Set Free*, written in 1913, in which Wells predicts the discovery of artificial radioactivity (which he places in 1933, one year before it actually occurred), the liberation of atomic energy, the development of atomic bombs, and a world war fought by England, France, and America against Germany—in 1956—in which all the major cities of the world are destroyed by atomic bombs

A year later Szilard was a refugee in England, and a speech by Lord Rutherford pooh-poohing the possibility of liberating atomic energy on an industrial scale led Szilard to think of Wells's predictions. The idea of a self-sustaining chain reaction so dominated his thinking that in 1934 he worked out the theoretical equations which could govern it. Having read Wells, and fearing that the knowledge would become public, Szilard assigned the documents to the British Admiralty in order to keep them secret.

When Lise Meitner reported on the Hahn-Stasseman experiment in uranium fission, Szilard was among the first to realize its possibilities. He participated in the early explorations of chain reactions at Columbia in 1939. And he initiated the letter to President Roosevelt (through the mediation of Albert Einstein and Alexander Sachs) which led to the Manhattan Project and the technology of the atom bomb. When the bomb was successfully tested, Szilard took the lead, with the Nobel laureate James Franck, in the unsuccessful effort to dissuade the government from using the atom bomb against Japan.

After the war, Szilard was active in the scientists' effort to wrest control of atomic energy from the military, and he organized a political lobby, the Council for a Livable World, to influence public and congressional opinion. He died in 1964.

Szilard's reminiscences, put together by his wife from taped interviews, are in *The Intellectual Migration*, ed. Donald Fleming and Bernard Bailyn (Cambridge, Mass., 1969). A remarkable memoir of Szilard by Edward Shils appeared in *Encounter* (December 1964), pp. 35–41.

The official account of the development of the atom bomb, the Smyth Report, is revealing on the initial innocence of American science. Smyth writes:

The announcement of the hypothesis of fission and its experimental confirmation took place in January 1939. . . . At that time American-born nuclear physicists were so unaccustomed to the idea of using their science for military purposes that they hardly realized what needed to be done. Consequently the early efforts both at restricting publication and at getting government support were stimulated largely by a small group of foreign-born physicists centering on L. Szilard and including E. Wigner, E. Teller, V. F. Weisskopf, and E. Fermi. (Henry D. Smyth, *Atomic Energy for Military Purposes* [Princeton, 1946], p. 45.)

on which science could not pronounce. At the other end of the spectrum, there was also a small group of scientists who, out of a sense of public responsibility or patriotism (mixed inevitably with the personal lure of power), served their governments as advisors or as links with the scientific community.

Before World War II, these were largely personal choices which did not affect the status of the enterprise of science itself. But in consequence of World War II, the situation has changed completely. Science has become an inextricable adjunct to power because of the nature of the new weaponry. Science has become integral to economic development. The rated power of a country no longer rests on its steel capacity but on the quality of its science and its application, through research and development, to new technology. For these obvious reasons the new relation of science to government (or, in the more fancy formulations, of truth to power) completely affects the structure of science both as "charismatic community" and as "occupational society." What becomes central, therefore, is the question, Who speaks for science and for what ends?

"The notion of an American science policy, a policy with which the scientists are to be influentially identified, requires the scientists to have leaders who can act as their representatives in that bargaining with public officials and other groups which accompanies the policy-making process," Wallace Sayre has written. But Professor Sayre doubts that there are such accredited spokesmen, and he is skeptical even of the idea of a community of science as anything other than a rhetorical phrase.[22]

Who are to be considered scientists? he asks. Are there "hard scientists" whose membership is taken for granted and "soft scientists" who are accepted on sufferance? Are physicists and chemists members by right while other natural scientists have to submit additional claims? Do all engineers qualify, or only certain types? Do doctors of medicine have entrée or only those engaged in medical research? In numbers, are they a small elite group—for example, the approximately 96,000 persons named in *American Men of Science*—or do they number several million (if all engineers, doctors, and social scientists are admitted)?

"The difficulties raised by these questions," Sayre writes, "suggest that 'the scientific community' is most often used as a strategic phrase, intended by the user to imply a larger number of experts where only a few may in fact exist, or to imply unity of views where

---

[22] Wallace Sayre, "Scientists and American Science Policy," *Science* (March 24, 1962).

disagreement may in fact prevail. The phrase may thus belong in that class of innovations, so familiar to the political process, which summons up members and legitimacy for a point of view by asserting that 'the American people' or 'the public' or 'all informed observers' or 'the experts' demand this or reject that."

The difficulty with such nominalism is that its disingenuousness would debar almost all political analysis. By the same token, who speaks for "business" or "the blacks" or "the poor"? It is true that few constituencies in the American polity are "corporative" in that some single chosen spokesman acts for the interest of the whole—with the possible exception of labor, where a single body, the executive council of the AFL-CIO, formulates over-all policy, and George Meany expresses its opinion. But the heart of the political process is the recognition of roughly bounded constituencies and the existence of representative figures as influential. Do Richard C. Gerstenberg (General Motors) or Reginald Jones (General Electric) or Frank Cary (IBM) or John D. DeButts (AT&T) speak *for* business? Perhaps not; no one elected them. But when they speak *as* businessmen, their views carry weight in government because of their leading positions. Who speaks for the blacks? No single person or organization. But Martin Luther King and Whitney Young had weight, and Roy Wilkins and Jesse Jackson have influence, because of their positions or their ability to mobilize a following.

In this sense, science has become a polity in that there are coherent bodies of opinion and representative figures. In order to identify a constituency and its leaders, we can admit as "members" those who have come into the arena publicly *as* scientists or who are represented by scientific bodies. These are of three kinds. There is, first, to use the current metaphor, a scientific establishment. It is composed, in overlapping layers, of the outstanding figures in the major universities, the heads and leading figures of the major government-sponsored laboratories (Brookhaven, Oak Ridge, Argonne, Livermore), the main science administrators from such industrial laboratories as Bell Telephone or IBM, the editors of the general science journals, and the leaders of such general associations as the National Academy of Science and the American Association for the Advancement of Science. This is the political elite, which is not necessarily unified and which often plays the mediating role between government and science. There is, second, the "occupational society" which is made up of the more than 1,800 professional associations, such as the American Physical Society, the American Chemical Society, the American Institute of Biological Sciences, the Engineers Joint Council, the Institute of Radio Engineers, etc. While concerned with such intellectual problems as the publication and dissemination of research, and such educational issues as standards and training, they function more and more as "trade associations" for the professions, particularly in relation to government funds and policies for these fields.

And finally there are a small number of individuals whose moral authority is drawn from their standing in the "charismatic community" and whose stature rests on their intellectual contributions— Einstein, Bohr, Fermi, von Neumann, and, in a wider penumbra, those who have received Nobel Prizes or other marks of intellectual distinction. When men from this body philosophize about science and society or speak out on moral and political issues, they are regarded, symbolically, as spokesmen for "science."

In this, however, are confused two very different kinds of sociological issues. The first is the role of science in speaking *to* the moral and political issues that confront society. Should it so speak in the name of science? Should it seek to remain outside government or within? If within, with what role and with what voice? As Szilard sardonically remarked, would scientists be on top or on tap? The second is the question of government policy *for* science: the degree of control or the direction of research, the level of spending and the allocation between fields, and the like. In the decade between 1945 and 1955, the first set of questions predominated; in the next decade it was the second.

In the period immediately following World War II, a new scientific elite was intimately involved with questions of national power in a way unique to the history of science. There were those who believed that scientists would become a new priesthood of power, and those, of a more utopian bent, who regarded scientists as prophets pointing the way to a new world society. In the end both visions faded, and the role of scientists as members of a power elite diminished. And yet it is that experience which has been crucial for the political fate of science and the question of what role science can play in a post-industrial society.

In World War II, science was joined to power in a radically new way. In the United States (as in almost every country) every major scientist (principally physicists and chemists) was involved in the development of weapons of war.[23] And this included, pre-eminently,

---

[23] The organization of science for the war effort was centralized in the Office of Scientific Research and Development, headed by Vannevar Bush, a former professor of electrical engineering who was known for his work in applied mathematics, particularly the differential analyzer which became one of the foundations of the electronic computer. Bush had been vice-president of MIT, and when the war broke out, was president of the Carnegie Institution of Washington, the prestigious research institution.

Under Bush there was a National Defense Research Committee which included

the elders of the "community of science." While scientists were involved in hundreds of research programs, the major effort, as fact and symbol, was the creation of the atomic bomb.

The men who created these new weapons of war quickly stepped into positions of power not only as scientific advisors to government, but as shapers and makers of policy, particularly what to do with these weapons—and weapons were power. Rarely has a new power elite emerged so quickly. (Recall the marginal role of science in World War I.)

Scientists came to the fore for two reasons. By cracking the powers of nature they had evoked deep mythological and atavistic fears —the apocalyptic destruction of the world—and were thus held in awe as the men who had unleashed these forces. On a more mundane level, these weapons involved a technical knowledge far beyond the competence of the military, and the military now seemed largely dependent on science. But the military, too, was a new elite. For the first time the United States had a large-scale military establishment which, it was clear, would be retained permanently. And the military did not like its dependence on science. From 1945 to 1955 a hidden war was waged between these two elites in the bureaucratic labyrinths of Washington, a struggle which ended in the political defeat of science.[24]

K. T. Compton, president of MIT, James B. Conant, president of Harvard (both scientists), Richard C. Tolman, dean of the graduate school of the California Institute of Technology, Frank B. Jewett, president of the National Academy of Science, C. P. Coe, U.S. Commissioner of Patents, and several others. The aforementioned five each became the head of a division dealing with a class of problems. Thus Conant became the chairman of Division B, bombs, fuels, gases, and chemical problems, and became the effective liaison between the laboratories working on the atom bomb and Washington.

In the first experimental efforts at producing fissionalbe material, the physicists were grouped under three program chiefs, Arthur H. Compton, Ernest O. Lawrence, and Harold C. Urey, all Nobel Prize winners. The work on a sustained chain reaction was carried out at the University of Chicago by Enrico Fermi. The final assembly of the bomb was done at Los Alamos under the direction of J. Robert Oppenheimer with a group that included such men as Hans Bethe, George Kistiakowsky, Robert F. Bacher, and Edward Teller, with advice and help from such luminaries as Niels Bohr, Eugene Wigner, I. I. Rabi and others.

For a brief, official history of the Office of Scientific Research and Development, see James Phinney Baxter 3rd, *Scientists Against Time* (Boston, 1946).

[24] Clearly the struggle was not simply a matter of "the" scientists versus "the" military. The scientists were not a monolithic block, and as the cold war developed, a number of prestigious figures like von Neumann, Wigner, and Teller took a hard political line which often allied them with the military. But as the ensuing discussion argues, what counted—and this was recognized by all—was that the debates—on control of atomic energy, on the internationalization of control, on the H-bomb, and on civilian defense versus SAC—*symbolically* pitted science (particularly in some of its messianic conceptions) against the military, representing traditional political control, even though there was no unanimity of opinion.

Coda: An Agenda for the Future

For the nuclear physicists, a rupture of history occurred on that morning when the first atom bomb was exploded in the experimental area of the Alamogordo Air Base known as the *Jornade del Muerto* (The Death Tract). The news was officially reported in the incredibly pompous prose of a War Department handout: "Mankind's successful transition to a new age, the Atomic Age, was ushered in July 16, 1945, before the eyes of a tense group of renowned scientists and military men gathered in the desert-lands of New Mexico to witness the first end results of their $2,000,000,000 effort. . . ." [25]

Paradoxically, some of the men who had initiated the steps leading to the "transition" were at that moment engaged in a desperate effort to prevent the final leap. "They believed," as Eugene Rabinowitch wrote ten years later, "that mankind was entering, unawares, into a new age fraught with unprecedented dangers of destruction. In spring 1945 this conviction led some scientists to an attempt—perhaps the first one in history—to interfere *as scientists* with the political and military decisions of the nation." [26]

The group was headed by the Nobel laureate James Franck, one of the great figures at the University of Göttingen in the 1920s, and it included Szilard, Glenn Seaborg, Eugene Rabinowitch, and others. The Franck Committee presented a memorandum to the Secretary of War, Henry L. Stimson, arguing that the chief reason for the bomb had been the fear that Germany would develop one, and would have no moral scruples about its use. With the war in Europe ended, any military advantages and American lives saved by using the bomb against Japan would be outweighed, they warned, by "the ensuing loss of confidence and by a wave of horror and revulsion" that would engulf the rest of the world.[27]

Stimson referred the report to the panel of scientific experts—Oppenheimer, Fermi, Lawrence, and Compton—and as Oppenheimer later wrote of their negative decision: "We said that we

---

[25] The release is reprinted as appendix 6 of the Smyth Report, *Atomic Energy for Military Purposes*, by Henry DeWolf Smyth, the official report of the Manhattan District Project (Princeton, 1946), p. 247.

[26] "Ten Years That Changed the World," by Eugene Rabinowitch, *Bulletin of the Atomic Scientists* (January 1956; emphasis in the original). The Bulletin was launched largely through efforts of that early group at the University of Chicago to provide a public platform for the scientists' views.

[27] The Franck Committee memorandum, "A Report to the Secretary of War, June 1945," was printed in *The Bulletin of Atomic Scientists* (May 1, 1946). The primary political-military aim of the United States in the postwar world, the authors went on, should be the prevention of an atomic-arms race, which could be brought about only through the international control of atomic energy. To this end, if international control were deemed possible, the United States should use the bomb only for demonstration effect; but if this seemed unlikely, the United States should renounce any advantage to be gained by the "immediate use of the first and comparatively inefficient bombs" in order to prevent a postwar nuclear-arms race.

didn't think that being scientists especially qualified us how to answer this question of how the bombs should be used or not; opinion was divided among us as it would be among other people if they knew about it."

But for the scientists who had worked on the bomb, the accounts of the explosions at Hiroshima and Nagasaki became an existentialist nightmare, forcing many of them to relive compulsively the forebodings which had haunted them throughout the years of their work. These feelings crystallized into a spontaneous movement to do things: to put atomic energy under the control of civilian authority[28] and to seek for international agreements to abolish any further use of the bomb.

The strategy adopted, however, was a cautious one. They realized that their proposal—the partial surrender of American sovereignty to an international body—would be difficult to "sell" to the Congress. And many were becoming aware of the hostility of the military leaders, who felt that their prerogatives in the formulation of

---

[28] The campaign was carried out on two "levels." A number of organizations (the Federation of Atomic Scientists, the Emergency Committee of Atomic Scientists, and the National Committee on Atomic Education) were formed under the leadership of younger project scientists from Los Alamos and Chicago to lobby in Congress and to educate the public. The leaders of the scientific community who had been the "directorate" of the wartime research—Oppenheimer, Rabi, Du Bridge, Conant, and others—had assumed important policy roles within the administration and they were voices within the executive branch.

It was not, in fact, a coordinated campaign. An uneasy sense had developed among the younger scientists that the "directorate" was too close to the administration and unwilling to confront the military overtly. This produced an amorphous division among the politically active scientists between those who were "out" as against those who were "in," a distinction in part generational, in part between those who had worked primarily at Chicago, as against those in Cambridge, Los Alamos, and Washington, who had quickly become the establishment. As is so often the case, those who did not participate in the decisions felt themselves to be more "principled" than those on the inside, while the directorate used the arguments of "realism" and "responsibleness" to justify the accommodations and compromises with the other contending forces within the administration.

On the first issue, the future of atomic energy, the initiative was taken by the younger outside scientists. The administration had submitted a bill, prepared mainly by the War Department, which would have reduced the government's role in the peaceful development of atomic energy, turning it over, in great measure, to private industry and concentrating largely on military purposes. This bill, the May-Johnson bill, became the target of a frenetic campaign by scientists, led largely by the Chicago group, who "with missionary fervor" flocked to Washington to lobby in Congress, join "the voices of doom on radio," and present capsule courses in nuclear physics to mass magazine readers. In the end, the administration bill was defeated and the McMachon Act was passed instead. It set up an independent Atomic Energy Commission which was charged with the dual responsibility of weapons development and peaceful uses of atomic energy.

The history of this campaign is told in detail in Alice Kimball Smith, *A Peril and a Hope: The Scientists' Movement in America 1945-47* (Chicago, 1965).

strategic doctrine were being undermined by the newly emerging elite. The scientists, therefore, decided to tone down the moral basis of their argument, to deny they were the advocates of a decidedly political point of view, and to present their case on "technical" grounds.

The American position on international control of atomic energy had been shaped by the scientists, particularly J. Robert Oppenheimer.[29] It was prepared by a panel headed by Dean Acheson and David Lillienthal, and was presented to the United Nations in 1946 by Bernard Baruch. The Baruch Plan proposed an international Atomic Development Authority which would hold a monopoly on all the world's "dangerous" fissionable materials and production plants. No nation could build its own atomic weapons, and sanctions would be applied against the offenders. The Atomic Development Authority would also seek to develop the peaceful uses of atomic energy for underdeveloped countries.[30]

But the Baruch Plan became mired in the complex negotiations with the Soviet Union, which offered one objection after another to the pooling of weapons. In October 1949, the United States announced that the Soviet Union had exploded its first atomic bomb. That single shot shattered the hopes for the international control of atomic energy. It was a signal that the cold war, which had been rumbling since 1947 when the United States began to confront the Soviet Union on such questions as the guerilla war in Greece, the Soviet pressure on Turkey, and the stalemate on the unification of Germany, had become an open reality.

---

[29] Oppenheimer, in addition to presenting some of the ideas, functioned also as "scientific coach" for the panel. As he related at one point: ". . . my job was that of teacher. I would go to the blackboard and say you can make energy this way in a periodic table and that way and that way. This is the way bombs are made and reactors are made. I gave in other words a course. I gave parts of this course also to Mr. Acheson and Mr. McCloy at night informally." *In the Matter of J. Robert Oppenheimer*, Transcript of Hearing before Personnel Security Board, United States Atomic Energy Commission, 1954. This volume, almost a thousand pages long, is an invaluable source for the politics of science during this early period and is basic to understanding the bureaucratic battle between the scientists and the military which is discussed later in this section.

[30] As Robert Gilpin has pointed out: ". . . the Baruch Plan also provided for an open scientific world in that all the research laboratories under the Authority, wherever they were located, would be open to the scientists of all nations and scientists in nuclear physics would be free to communicate with other scientists. The political significance of such freedom of communication would be that nations would be prevented from taking secret advantage of new knowledge. Scientific breakthroughs which would enable a nation to infringe on the control system established under this plan would be known to all and the control system could be improved as fast as knowledge developed. Every nation would thus be assured that no other was secretly advancing its nuclear weapon technology." Robert Gilpin, *American Scientists and Nuclear Weapons Policy* (Princeton, 1962), p. 54.

The unity of scientific opinion was also shattered. Fear of Russia on the part of many scientists (notably Teller, Wigner, and Lawrence), and the rising power of the Strategic Air Command, began to pose many different kinds of problems. The division of opinion among scientists was no longer derived solely from "technical" assessments. Scientists who were taking strategic stands now had to justify themselves in political terms as well.

The explosion of the Soviet A-bomb transferred the discussion of policy issues from the public realm to the private arena required by military security. Thus from 1949 to 1955, the political role of the scientists was played out in secret, and participation was restricted to the elites in advisory or administrative positions in the government. During those years a number of savage "guerilla wars" were fought in Washington, but little reached the public at that time.

Three issues were involved: the decision to build the hydrogen bomb, the creation of tactical nuclear weapons for "limited war" instead of relying on "massive retaliation," and the possibility of an extended continental air defense. Among the scientific elite then in government, there was no real disagreement about the need to confront the Soviet Union. The question was how to do it. The issues were primarily strategic and political, though technical matters were inextricably linked with policy, as the scientists emphasized, while the military sought to make the issue almost entirely political and strategic.

At the center was the doctrine of "massive retaliation" developed by the Strategic Air Command, which flew long-range bombers such as the B-36 and later the B-52. The Strategic Air Command argued that in a future war it would be increasingly difficult for bombers to penetrate enemy air defenses, and it would thus be better to gamble on delivering a few large bombs with overwhelming power to kill rather than many small bombs. When the Soviet shot was revealed in October 1949, the air force began pressing for the development of a super-bomb, and on this proposal a radical cleavage developed within the administration.[31]

The issue was referred to the General Advisory Committee of the Atomic Energy Commission, which was composed of the leading scientists who had been the organizers of wartime research, including

---

[31] During the work on the nuclear bomb at Los Alamos, a number of scientists had speculated on the possibility of a thermonuclear weapon, a so-called fusion bomb based on the heat generated by the fission of small atomic bombs. Hans Bethe, the head of the theoretical-physics division, had written some studies of solar explosions as the prototype of thermonuclear reactions, and Edward Teller had initiated studies at Los Alamos on the possibility of a fusion bomb. Now Teller, supported by a number of physicists at Berkeley, principally Ernest Lawrence and Luis Alvarez, began to press for a crash program to develop an H-bomb.

Conant, Du Bridge, Rabi, Fermi, and Oppenheimer, who was chairman. After considerable debate the committee voted 6–3 that it would be unwise to undertake such a program. Oppenheimer opposed the H-bomb largely on the grounds of wastefulness and danger, and supported George Kennan's view that the country was placing undue reliance on strategic air power and that a containment policy, based on the capability of waging a limited war, would be politically more effective.[32]

After protracted debate in high government circles, President Truman in January 1951 ordered a crash program to develop an H-bomb. (The decision, as was noted later, was made against the background of the announcement that Klaus Fuchs, a physicist who had worked at Los Alamos, had confessed in Great Britain to turning over secret information to the Soviet Union.) The strategic debate now shifted to different grounds. Oppenheimer sought to show that Europe could be defended by small-scale tactical nuclear weapons and, with the support of the National Security Council, set up Project Vista at the California Institute of Technology, under the direction of Lee Du Bridge, to assess the feasibility of this argument. At MIT, Zacharias and Wiesner argued that the United States should set up a distant early warning system and an adequate civil defense, on the theory that if we could be made impregnable to Soviet attack, negotiations could be then opened to halt the arms race.[33] Subsequently Project East River was set up at Brookhaven to study the practical possibilities of civil defense and Project Lincoln at MIT to study continental air defense.

In 1953, the new Eisenhower administration endorsed the policy of massive retaliation as official strategic doctrine.[34] The Strategic Air

[32] Fermi and Rabi, in a minority statement, opposed the bomb "on fundamental ethical principles," warning that it would be a "danger to humanity as a whole." (In this they were influenced by Hans Bethe, who had warned that the H-bomb had a special radiation hazard because of the long half-life of Carbon-14.) But they also added that if the cold war could not be halted, there was no recourse but to go ahead with the H-bomb.

[33] Ironically, these strategic positions were completely reversed in subsequent years. In 1963, the Kennedy administration proposal to strengthen civil defense was held to be the hallmark of a "tough" policy, i.e. giving the public a false sense of security against Soviet missiles and thus encouraging a hard response to Soviet policy. In 1969, the Nixon administration proposal to build an Anti-Ballistics Missile (ABM) was attacked on the ground that such actions simply escalated the arms race. Yet in the early 1950s, civil defense had been the rallying point for the opponents of "big bomb" doctrine.

[34] It was a strategy which peculiarly matched the temperament of the new regime, reflecting the "admonitory" manner of the new secretary of state, John Foster Dulles, and reinforcing the illusion of omnipotence that had been so characteristic of the American national style. It fitted the demand for economy and the reduction of military expenditures, voiced by the new secretary of treasury, George Humphrey, who promised, with characteristic American buncombe, "a bigger bang for a buck."

Command, as the striking arm of the air force, now became the dominant voice in military policy. But the reports emerging from the science study groups continued to challenge its doctrine. The Vista report declared that Western Europe could be best defended by tactical atomic weapons, rather than an all-or-none strategy which might allow the Russians to nibble away at small pockets. A summer study group of Project Lincoln suggested not only that a continental air defense was feasible but that a distant early warning line was a matter of highest priority. Moreover, the scientists, now excluded from policy decisions, began to urge public discussion of these issues. In a direct challenge, Oppenheimer wrote an article for *Foreign Affairs* in July 1953 calling for a public debate on the new weapons policy. With that challenge, the die was cast.

When theurgic springs are touched—and what other event in the recorded history of man is comparable to the diremption of matter itself?—men need some personifications of these frightening powers in order to make them bearable. Because he was the genie who had conjured up the bomb, J. Robert Oppenheimer had become for the world the Janus-faced symbol of science as creator and destroyer. And it was as the symbol of science that the military now moved against him.

J. Robert Oppenheimer was a gnostic figure about whom legends gathered for the reason that he seemed to have stepped more from the world of thaumaturgy than of science, or because his very presence hinted at the magical springs which join the two when one intends to tamper with the forces of the universe. A physicist and a poet, his mind was seemingly focused upon that far-distant zero point where mathematics and mysticism merge to dissolve the cosmos into the numerological void of oneness. A slim man, head carried high, his bony features and translucent eyes were set in a face that seemed to have been etched by inner anguish. On the surface, he was a strange choice for directing the refractory task of making the bomb.

Yet in any gathering of scientists his intellectual authority was quickly apparent. And with his brilliance he could systematically and coldly drive the scientific teams along the single track toward solving all the difficult equations which led to the final assembly of the bomb itself. At the end, when the mushroom cloud rose ever higher over Alamogordo, its blinding light enveloping the skies, other men could only fumble for words, but a passage from the Bhagavad-Gita, the words of Sri Krishna, lord of the fate of mortals, came to Oppenheimer's lips: "I am become Death, the shatterer of worlds."

The man himself was of softer clay. Though rarely polite to fools, he could be swayed by tougher characters of the world of power, which led him in the late 1930s to contribute to communist causes and, during the war, to crumble before some of the security officers who demanded that he name former associates who had been communists. Power tempted him and, as it often does, in some ways corrupted him. Though he sometimes spoke like a prophet, he had become a priest; he spoke *for* power, rather than *to* power. On the specific moral and political issues that confronted scientists in the early postwar years, Oppenheimer had not sided with the crusaders, such as Szilard and the younger scientists at Chicago; in fact, he had often disappointed them. He had not opposed dropping the atom bomb; he had not opposed the May-Johnson bill; and even though he had opposed the H-bomb he later withdrew his opposition. When the curtains on policy were drawn after 1949, he had entered the corridors of power rather than remain outside, and the issues for which he fought were primarily political. A troubled man, he had committed himself to an "ethic of responsibility" and on this he took his moral stand.

In December 1953, after the meeting of a small White House committee,[35] President Eisenhower issued an order directing that a "blank wall" be placed between Robert Oppenheimer and any secret information until a security hearing had been held. The basis of the action against Oppenheimer was a letter written in November 1953 to J. Edgar Hoover by William L. Borden, a former air force pilot who, until July of that year, had served as executive director of the Congressional Joint Committee on Atomic Energy. In that letter, Borden declared that "more probably than not J. Robert Oppenheimer is an agent of the Soviet Union." Hoover then assembled a file on Oppenheimer and turned it over to the White House.

The basis of the charges against Oppenheimer—that in the late 1930s he had been sympathetic to communist causes—had long been known to security agencies and to General Groves, Oppenheimer's superior in the Manhattan District Project. Not one new item of evidence was presented at the 1954 hearings that had not been known in 1943, when Oppenheimer had taken charge of the bomb-construction project. But what was clear from the testimony was that the real inspiration for the action was the air force, which feared Oppenheimer's influence and drew sinister conclusions from his political positions.[36] Thus, Major General Roscoe C. Wilson, the former chief

---

35 At the meeting were President Eisenhower, Secretary of Defense Charles Wilson, Attorney General Herbert Brownell, Director of Defense Mobilization Arthur S. Flemming, White House special assistant for national security Robert Cutler, and Lewis Strauss, chairman of the Atomic Energy Commission. For the background of this discussion see Lewis L. Strauss, *Men and Decisions* (New York, 1962), chap. 14.

36 The tipoff was an article in *Fortune* of August 1953 written by Charles J. V. Murphy, a *Fortune* editor but also a colonel in the Air Force Reserve and former

of the Air War College, testified that he once "felt compelled to go to the Director of Intelligence to express concern over what I felt was a pattern of action . . . not helpful to the national defense." The items cited included Oppenheimer's interest in the "internationalizing of atomic energy" and his insistence that it was technically premature to build a nuclear-powered aircraft. David Griggs, the chief scientist of the air force, also testified to a "pattern of activities," in which he included support for Project Vista and a belief attributed to Oppenheimer that it was necessary "to give up . . . the strategic part of our total air power" in order to achieve world peace, which led him "to a serious question as to [Oppenheimer's] loyalty." In the final decision of the AEC, Oppenheimer's loyalty was reaffirmed, but in the light of his past associations and his opposition to the hydrogen bomb he was judged a "security risk" and denied access to classified material.[37]

The Oppenheimer case is now long past, a shameful instance of national folly. The specific strategic issues are now obsolete. The rise of missile technology has brought the engineer and the political scientist as well as the theoretical physicist into the arena of weapons policy and has given a new complexity to the meaning of strategy. In recent years, scientists have continued to play important roles in connection with technical questions about arms control. But what the Oppenheimer case signified was that the messianic role of the scientists—as conceived by themselves and feared by their opponents—was finished, and different questions had come to the fore.

The ever-increasing growth of science and the introduction of scientists into the administrative and policy levels of government have

---

assistant to Air Force General Hoyt Vandenberg. The article hinted for the first time in public print at Oppenheimer's pre-war communist associations and attacked the scientists active in the Lincoln summer study group and Project Vista, implying that a cabal known as ZORC (from the initials of Jerrold Zacharias, Oppenheimer, Rabi, and Charles Lauristen) had masterminded a plot to subvert the Strategic Air Command. The source of the charge, it was revealed later, was David Griggs, chief scientist for the air force, who told the AEC Security Board that he had seen Zacharias write these initials on a blackboard during a meeting of the Lincoln summer study group in 1952. Under oath, Zacharias denied the charge. See *In the Matter of J. Robert Oppenheimer*, pp. 750, 922. A detailed account of these episodes, with much useful background material, can be found in Philip Rieff's essay "The Case of Dr. Oppenheimer," in *On Intellectuals*, ed. Philip Rieff (New York, 1959).

[37] The literature on the Oppenheimer case is vast. The best source is still the transcript of the hearings themselves. A comprehensive review, favorable to Oppenheimer, can be found in Philip M. Stern, with Harold Green, *The Oppenheimer Case: Security on Trial* (New York, 1969). A biographical account of Oppenheimer, contrasting him with Ernest O. Lawrence, can be found in Nuel Pharr Davis, *Lawrence and Oppenheimer* (New York, 1959). There is also a useful review article on the issue by Sanford Lakoff, "Science and Conscience," *International Journal* (Autumn 1970).

raised questions to which we still have few answers. It is doubtful whether we shall find recapitulated the story told by C. P. Snow of the intense personal feud between Henry Tizard and F. A. Lindemann, which dominated the British scene during World War II, or the duel between Edward Teller and Robert Oppenheimer, which captured some of that flavor in the mid-1950s, simply because the arena of science politics has widened so considerably. It is no longer a question of personalities—though dominant figures and highly placed cliques will always play decisive roles—but of institutional arrangements and divisions of responsibility. There is a federal council of science and technology, made up of policy officials of government agencies which include science as a principal operating function. There is a National Science Foundation, charged with the funding of basic science and research. And there are the many agencies which together disburse the billions of dollars for research and development.

Robert Gilpin has posed these questions: Does the scientist-advisor have the right to initiate advice or must he speak only when spoken to? Ought the scientist-advisor concern himself with the political, strategic, and moral implications of technical questions or must he refrain from stepping outside his technical competence? Should the science advisor be given broad policy matters on which to give advice or must he be restricted to narrowly prescribed questions?

Such formulations, unfortunately, are still redolent of the simple days when "technical" matters were left to the expert and "policy" to the responsible political officials. But technical decision-making in all spheres is inextricably linked with policy questions. The recent debate on the Anti-Ballistics Missile is a case in point. Here scientists (physicists and political scientists) were divided on both technical and political questions. But the crucial point is that as against the period of the 1950s, when these questions were settled in closed bureaucratic labyrinths, the issue was thrashed out openly in the Congress so that all its dimensions, technical and political, could be openly explored. As Paul Doty has observed, "The debate preceding the Senate vote was a milestone in the history of scientific and technical advising related to military decision making." In the wake of the debate, one of the proponents of the ABM system, Albert Wohlstetter, a political scientist and operations research specialist at Rand and the University of Chicago, charged his opponents with misusing quantitative data, and a special panel of the Operations Research Association (ORSA) upheld his point of view. But this report, too, has been subject to vigorous open debate, and as Doty has remarked in his essay, three different issues were involved—the assessment of the need for a defense system, the assessment of the solution, and the political value of the solution. The proponents of ABM had concentrated on the first issue and its opponents on the second, but the differences in quantitative methodology (technical issues) actually disguised a doctrinal difference—and where doctrinal differences are involved, as has long been evident in the history of the church or of university faculties, science has to adopt a self-denying ordinance regarding accusations of misconduct or bad faith lest it became a party to the imposition of orthodoxies and (as in the case of Robert Oppenheimer) the branding of dissidents as heretics who are to be either dismissed or put to death.[38]

The fact is that technical issues cannot easily be separated from political ones, and scientists who come into the policy arena will necessarily be advocates as well as technical advisors. But one facet cannot be a shield for the other. And on issues which affect a nation's security, health, economy, or way of life—be it an ABM system or a supersonic transport—any technical policy has to be arrived at only after open and informed political debate. A banal conclusion —but what is often agreed to in rhetoric is rarely achieved in practice.

It is a truism of sociology that the initial patterns of any social system, like the first tracks through a virgin forest, shape its future modes. Traditions become established, routines are set, vested interests develop, innovations are either resisted or must conform to the adaptive patterns laid down at the start, and an aura of legitimacy surrounds the existing ways and becomes in time the conventional wisdom of the institution. In short, "structure" is not only a response to past needs but itself becomes a shaping tool of the future.

The first organizational forms of science developed after the war were ad hoc responses to the sudden urgencies precipitated by the tensions of the cold war and the new awareness of the centrality of science and the need to support research: the expansion of the universities as research institutions, the creation of large scientific laboratories at universities supported by government (the jet propulsion lab at Cal Tech, the Argonne atomic lab at the University of Chicago, MITRE and Lincoln lab at MIT, the Riverside electronics lab at Columbia, and the like), the growth of "consortiums" such as the Brookhaven lab on Long Island managed by a half-dozen universities. After these have come the large government health-research centers, such as those at the National Institutes of Health, the major National Science Foundation-supported laboratories, the creation of a vast

---

[38] Paul Doty, "Can Investigations Improve Scientific Advice? The Case of the ABM," *Minerva* (London), vol. X, no. 2 (April 1972).

number of non-profit research "think tanks" such as Rand, the Institute of Defense Analysis, the Aerospace Corporation, and so on.

As yet, no coherent science policy has emerged and, given the huge, diverse and complex patterns that have sprouted in topsy-turvy fashion, it is unlikely that any "rationalization" will take place for a long time, if ever. In one fundamental sense, such a sprawl is an advantage. The very diversity of structures means that it would be difficult, if not impossible, to establish a single czar or impose a pattern of central direction such as exists, to a considerable extent, in the Soviet Union, where the Academy of Science is a directing agency for science. Yet the very dependency of science on government for financial aid leads to vagaries of support for different fields: at times according to the whims of fashion, or the strength of organized lobbies, or the shifting emphasis on what constitutes "national needs." Such vagaries have played havoc with the universities, bringing about enormous expansion in the decade of the 1960s and a threatening contraction in the 1970s. Beginning with the close of the Johnson administration and carried over into the Nixon administration, the old scientific elite was kept at arm's length from the formulation of top government policy. Nixon, in fact, abolished the Office of Science and Technology and during his administration "science policy" became a shamble. (In 1975, President Ford proposed the creation of a new science advice office.) Thus one finds, a quarter of a century after the onset of a new age, that while the interdependencies of science and government have been sealed, there is still no real structure or consistent policy in the relations between the two. Yet, given the strategic role of science for military power and of technology for economic advantage, at some point the government will have to face up to the problem of what constitutes a policy for science.

In the last decade, there have been three major structural changes in the character of science's relation to government:

1. The old, closely bound elite structures are dissolving. The old political elites of science derived from close personal associations in wartime experiences—at the radiation lab at MIT, at Chicago, Berkeley, and Los Alamos—and even the cliques that were subsequently formed had their source in differences going back to those old associations and conflicts. The original political elite was drawn largely from the physicists, because of their centrality in wartime research. There is no central elite today, and the multiplication of scientific fields, principally the diverse branches of biology (molecular biology, population biology, and environmental biology), has greatly broadened the top group.

2. The military, today, has its own weapons labs and is less directly dependent on university science than it was twenty-five years

ago. The military-industrial complex, though its influence has been exaggerated, has given the military a broad research capacity it never had before.

3. The growth of research and development funds, particularly after 1956, has multiplied the claimants of funds *for* science. Universities have become active political entities in the search for money. Scientists and engineers have started hundreds of profit and non-profit companies to do research and evaluation. The number of scientific and technical associations with headquarters in Washington to represent their constituents has multiplied enormously. This is the broad base of the bureaucratization of science.

In this context, then, who speaks for science? There are three different kinds of spokesmen:

1. The individuals—Nobel laureates or those recognized by their peers—who derive their authority from the charismatic community of science. Inevitably, however, some of the luster is gone simply because of the realization, owing to the events of the last twenty-five years, that *as individuals* scientists are neither better nor worse at judgment or moral stricture than other leaders of society and that individual scientific achievement is not a guarantee of mosaic wisdom.

2. Movements like that of the young radicals in science, or ecological reformers such as Rachel Carson or Barry Commoner, who invoke the institutional charisma of science in making moral or political judgments. What we have here is the resumption of the prophetic claims of science as setting forth truth against self-interest.

3. Institutional associations such as the National Academy of Science or the National Academy of Engineering. In the last two decades, the National Academy of Science—whose membership, by self-selection, is limited to the achieving elite in science—has come to the fore as a quasi-official agency for two reasons. First, since cooperation among governments involves the selection of a single scientific body to negotiate exchanges and cooperation, the academy has more and more become a government conduit for such official transactions. And second, attached to the National Academy of Science is the National Research Council, a body which, under the impetus of the academy or the government, undertakes research on policy questions which often becomes the basis for measures taken by the President or Congress. To the extent that the "advice process" on technical questions has become formalized, it is the National Academy of Science—and in recent years a comparative body, the National Academy of Engineering, set up in 1964—which becomes a spokesman for science.

Given the large-scale growth of science, the huge number of persons involved, the enormous amounts of money needed for support, and its centrality in the post-industrial society, the bureaucratization of science is inevitable. And the problem of creating representative structures will be one of the most difficult political problems for science in the coming decades. In the past, some persons have talked of a "parliament of science"[39] which would be a formal representative body for the drafting of coherent science policies, but it is highly unlikely that such a formal body will ever be established. And yet some greater coordination than now exists is probable, and some clearer identification of the "spokesmen" for science may be necessary.

Bureaucratization is a problem in every complex society, and the fear of a bureaucracy as a new administrative class both throughout a society and within a large organization has bedeviled the hopes of socialistic and utopian writers. For science, bureaucratization imposes a number of severe risks. Within the organization of science, bureaucratization may impede the "recognition system" of work and persons which has been the heart of the community of science through the subordination of individual achievement to the over-all goals of a laboratory, or by appropriating the work for the credit of the "bureau" itself. In the over-all organization of science, the creation of a centralized bureaucracy—and centralization is an invariable tendency in these instances—could mean the stifling of inquiry, the demand that scientific work be responsive to stipulated national or social needs and the priority of political goals over scientific work.

Inevitably, thus, tensions will arise between the bureaucratic tendencies of large-scale science and the charismatic dimension of science, which sees its activities as ends in themselves that should not be subordinated to other goals. These tensions are bound to be of two sorts. One is the demand, voiced most recently by Jacob Bronowski, for the "disestablishment of science."[40] In this argument, government should refrain from any statement of scientific goals and provide only a sum of money, which would be distributed within scientific endeavors by committees of scientists in accordance with their own criteria. In a curious way this demand reopens a debate that took place thirty years ago among leading scientists about the planning of science. In the later 1930s, there was a movement in Great Britain, under the leadership of the Marxist scientist J. D. Bernal, which called for the "planning of science" to meet the practical needs of society. The movement was opposed by another group of scientists,

---

[39] In 1958, the American Association for the Advancement of Science—a loose body with a membership of 135,000 and two hundred and eighty-seven affiliated scientific societies—sought to assert its leadership as the spokesman for science by convening a Parliament of Science to consider the proposal of a federal cabinet department of science. Nothing came of the move.

[40] See J. Bronowski, "The Disestablishment of Science," *Encounter* (July 1971).

headed by Michael Polanyi and Percy Bridgman, which denied that advances in science arose, as Marxists claimed, in response to material needs and that there was no essential distinction between science and technology. For Bernal, the need for scientific planning was on the same footing as the need for economic planning, in order to achieve greater efficiency in research. Ironically, the very financial needs of science have imposed a rough measure of planning, and the demands to create the weapons of war, and later material production, have brought science close to the point Bernal had thought it should reach. Yet in answer to Bernal, Polanyi argued a different credo. "We must reassert," he wrote, "that the essense of science is the love of knowledge and that the utility of knowledge does not concern us primarily. We should demand once more for science that public respect and support which is due it as a pursuit of knowledge and knowledge alone. For we scientists are pledged to values more precious than material welfare and to a service more urgent than that of material welfare." [41] To some extent, we have here the reassertion of Max Weber's idea of "science as a vocation" and the exemption of science from the mundane aspects of the world because of its "sacred" character. It is likely that the move for the "disestablishment of science" will spread.

The second tension is the inherent confrontation of science with any arbitrary power. In this view, the fate of science is tied to the fate of intellectual freedom, and science must necessarily speak out actively against any efforts to impose an official ideology or doctrinal view of truth. This is a faith which derives from the ethos of science. This is a view which has received its most vigorous emphasis in recent years in the Soviet Union itself. For Soviet science the most damning example of the havoc created by *partiinost*—the doctrine that the party must direct all aspects of science and literature—was the Lysenko affair. As a reviewer in the *Times Literary Supplement* observed: "The Lysenko affair has been aptly described as perhaps the most bizarre chapter in the history of modern science. For thirty years, until 1964, Soviet genetics was dominated by an illiterate, neu-

---

[41] Michael Polanyi, *The Logic of Liberty* (London, 1951), p. 6. As Professor Polanyi writes further:

What technical inventions were the discoveries of the Nobel Laureates Planck, Einstein, Perrin, Millikan, Michaelson, Rutherford, Aston, Chadwick, Barkla, Heisenberg, Compton, Franck, G. Hertz, Rubens, Laue, Joliot, Fermi, Urey, Anderson, W. H. and W. L. Bragg, Schrödinger, Dirac, etc., unconsciously intended to produce? No one can tell—so the new theory of science must pass them over.

One wonders how the great physicists in the list above would have fared if, before embarking on their investigation, they had to get a certificate of its social usefulness from a scientific directorate, as contemplated by Marxist scientists and their friends. To what conflicts may not have led their "arrogant pretence" to be the sole judges of their own preference! (Pp. 82–83.)

rotic charlatan who was allowed absolute dictatorship over both biological research and agricultural practice. Hundreds of scientists lost their jobs, and the outstanding Russian geneticist N. I. Vavilov, Lysenko's main opponent, died in one of Stalin's prisons. All genetics teaching in universities was stopped, laboratories were closed or taken over by Lysenko's supporters, and research came to a halt." Behind this bizarre episode was an ideological doctrine that the Lamarckian hypothesis of the inheritance of acquired characteristics was truer than Mendelian genetics; environment, not heredity, could be the most powerful force shaping a society. This was accompanied by the political bosses' arrogant belief that they knew better than scientists how to increase farm yields.

The shame of the Lysenko affair spurred the Russian biologist Zhores Medvedev to write *The Rise and Fall of T. D. Lysenko,* which was published abroad, and to send out a book, *The Medvedev Papers,* which is a record of his efforts to establish full and free communication with scientists abroad, to end censorship, and to be able to travel freely to scientific congresses. It is the necessity for intellectual freedom and international cooperation that underlies the document *Progress, Coexistence and Intellectual Freedom,* by Andrei Sakharov.

Andrei Sakharov, most brilliant of the younger Soviet physicists, was at the age of thirty instrumental in creating the Russian hydrogen bomb. (At thirty-two he was elected to the Soviet Academy of Science, the youngest Russian scientist ever to be given this honor.) Like the physicists who created the first atomic bomb, the threat of thermonuclear war has disturbed him deeply, as has Stalin's terrible destruction in the Soviet Union. The document which Sakharov issued, after circulating it among leading Soviet scientists and intellectuals, has two theses: the need for international agreements to outlaw nuclear weapons, and the fact that "intellectual freedom is essential to human society." But the fundamental premise, contained in the opening page, is that the method of science—"presupposing unprejudice, unfearing open discussion and conclusions"—has not become a reality and must be employed. What is perhaps most important of all is the implicit thesis that an international community of science is a reality and that its moral foundations compel all men who believe in science to support the conditions of cooperation and intellectual freedom.[42]

[42] On the history of the Soviet biology issue, see David Joravsky, *The Lysenko Affair* (Cambridge, Mass., 1971). The book by Zhores Medvedev was published by Columbia University Press in 1970 and *The Medvedev Papers* by Macmillan in 1971. The TLS quotation is from November 5, 1971, p. 1,388. Sakharov's book was published in 1968, with an introduction and notes by Harrison Salisbury. The quotation is from p. 26.

All of this leads to a set of classic conundrums. Is science to be only "pure" science, serving knowledge and truth as defined by the community of science? Or is science to be of "service to the society"? If science is to be "pure," how does it justify the vast sums that are necessary for modern research, and how are the levels to be established? And does the purity of science mean that it has to be apolitical to justify government support? If science is to serve society, how is this to be determined? By the scientists themselves, or does the polity have the decisive voice in deciding what kind of scientific and technological enterprises—military or social service—take priority? In practice, none of these stark divisions make complete sense, for in the very way science is intertwined with military, technological, and economic development, there will be forces at work arguing for all these positions. Yet by the very fact that science is so strategic and the sums involved are so large, state intervention is inevitable, either in the tight and direct form of the Soviet Union, or the loose and pluralistic monetary controls of the United States.

The defense of science—against bureaucratization, against political subjugation, against totalitarianism—derives eventually thus from the vitality of its ethos. The charismatic aspect of science gives it its "sacred" quality as a way of life for its members. Like Christianity, this charismatic dimension has within it a recurrent utopian and even messianic appeal. It is the tension between those charismatic elements and the realities of large-scale organization that will frame the political realities of science in the post-industrial society.

3. *Meritocracy and Equality*

In 1958, the English sociologist Michael Young wrote a fable, *The Rise of the Meritocracy*.[43] It purports to be a "manuscript," written in the year 2033, which breaks off inconclusively for reasons the "narrator" failed to comprehend. The theme is the transformation of English society, by the turn of the twenty-first century, owing to the victory of the principle of achievement over that of ascription (i.e. the gaining of place by assignment or inheritance). For centuries, the elite positions in the society had been held by the children of the nobility on the hereditary principle of succession. But in the nature of modern society, "the rate of social progress depend[ed] on the degree to which power is matched with intelligence." Britain could no

---

[43] Michael Young, *The Rise of the Meritocracy, 1870–2033* (London, 1958).

longer afford a ruling class without the necessary technical skills. Through the successive school-reform acts, the principle of merit slowly became established. Each man had his place in the society on the basis of "IQ and Effort." By 1990 or thereabouts, all adults with IQs over 125 belonged to the meritocracy.

But with that transformation came an unexpected reaction. Previously, talent had been distributed throughout the society, and each class or social group had its own natural leaders. Now all men of talent were raised into a common elite, and those below had no excuses for their failures; they bore the stigma of rejection, they were known inferiors.

By the year 2034 the Populists had revolted. Though the majority of the rebels were members of the lower classes, the leaders were high-status women, often the wives of leading scientists. Relegated during the early married years to the household because of the need to nurture high-IQ children, the activist women had demanded equality between the sexes, a movement that was then generalized into the demand for equality for all, and for a classless society. Life was not to be ruled by "a mathematical measure" but each person would develop his own diverse capacities for leading his own life.[44] The Populists won. After little more than half a century, the Meritocracy had come to an end.

Is this, too, the fate of the post-industrial society? The post-industrial society, in its initial logic, is a meritocracy. Differential status and differential income are based on technical skills and higher education. Without those achievements one cannot fulfill the requirements of the new social division of labor which is a feature of that society. And there are few high places open without those skills. To that extent, the post-industrial society differs from society at the turn of the twentieth century. The initial change, of course, came in the professions. Seventy years or so ago, one could still "read" law in a lawyer's office and take the bar examination without a college degree. Today, in medicine, law, accounting, and a dozen other professions, one needs a college degree and accrediting, through examination, by legally sanctioned committees of the profession, before one can practice one's art. For many years, until after World War II, business was the chief route open to an ambitious and aggressive person who wanted to strike out for himself. And the rags-to-riches as-

---

[44] A theoretician of the Technicians party, Professor Eagle, had argued that marriage partners, in the national interest, should consult the intelligence register, for a high-IQ man who mates with a low-IQ woman is wasting his genes. The activist women, on the other hand, took romance as their banner and beauty as their flag, arguing that marriage should be based on attraction. Their favorite slogan was "Beauty is achievable by all."

cent (or, more accurately, clerk-to-capitalist, if one follows the career of a Rockefeller, Harriman, or Carnegie) required drive and ruthlessness rather than education and skills. One can still start various kinds of small businesses (usually, now, by franchise from a larger corporation), but the expansion of such enterprises takes vastly different skills than in the past. Within the corporation, as managerial positions have become professionalized, individuals are rarely promoted from shop jobs below but are chosen from the outside, with a college degree as the passport of recognition. Only in politics, where position may be achieved through the ability to recruit a following, or through patronage, is there a relatively open ladder without formal credentials.

Technical skill, in the post-industrial society, is what the economists call "human capital." An "investment" in four years of college, according to initial estimates of Gary Becker, yields, over the average working life of the male graduate, an annual return of about 13 percent.[45] Graduation from an elite college (or elite law school or business school) gives one a further differential advantage over graduates from "mass" or state schools. Thus, the university, which once reflected the status system of the society, has now become the arbiter of class position. As the gatekeeper, it has gained a quasi-monopoly in determining the future stratification of the society.[46]

Any institution which gains a quasi-monopoly power over the fate of individuals is likely, in a free society, to be subject to quick attack. Thus, it is striking that the populist revolt, which Michael Young foresaw several decades hence, has already begun, at the very onset of the post-industrial society. One sees this in the derogation of the IQ and the denunciation of theories espousing a genetic basis of intelligence; the demand for "open admission" to universities on the part of minority groups in the large urban centers; the pressure for increased numbers of blacks, women, and specific minority groups such as Puerto Ricans and Chicanos in the faculties of universities, by quotas if necessary; and the attack on "credentials" and even schooling itself as the determinant of a man's position in the society. A post-industrial society reshapes the class structure of society by creating new technical elites. The populist reaction, which has begun in the 1970s, raises the demand for greater "equality" as a defense against being excluded from that society. Thus the issue of meritocracy versus equality.

[45] Gary S. Becker, *Human Capital* (New York, 1964), p. 112. Later writers have suggested this figure may be too high; the point remains that a college degree does provide an investment "yield."

[46] For a comprehensive discussion of this major social change, see Jencks and Riesman, *The Academic Revolution* (New York, 1968). For a survey of the reaction, see Stephen Graubard and Geno Ballotti, eds., *The Embattled University* (New York, 1970).

Coda: An Agenda for the Future

In the nature of a meritocracy, as it has been traditionally conceived, what is central to the assessment of a person is the assumed relation of achievement to intelligence, and of intelligence to its measurement on the Intelligence Quotient scale. The first question, therefore, is what determines intelligence. In the received social science and biology opinion, the number of talented persons in a society, as measured by IQ, is a limited pool; and this is reflected in the bell-shaped curve of a normal distribution of test scores in a particular age category. By the logic of a meritocracy, these high-scoring individuals, no matter where they are in the society, should be brought to the top in order to make the best use of their talents.[47] This is the basis of the liberal theory of equality of opportunity and of Jefferson's belief in the "natural aristoi" against the ascriptive nobility.

All this makes the question of the relation of intelligence to genetic inheritance very touchy. Is intelligence largely inherited? Can one raise intelligence by nurture? How does one separate native ability and drive from improvements in skill acquired through education? The average IQ of college graduates is 120, while that of high-school graduates is only 107. As Fritz Machlup, the Princeton economist, has commented: "The greater earning capacity of college graduates, compared with high-school graduates, is, no doubt, to a large extent [the figure is about 40 percent] the result of superior native intelligence and greater ambition; it would be quite wrong to attribute all of the incremental earnings to the investment in college education."[48]

---

[47] As Michael Young describes the rationale in his fable:
The proportion of people with IQs over 130 could not be raised—the task was rather to prevent a fall—but the proportion of such people in work which called upon their full capacities was steadily raised. . . . Civilization does not depend upon the stolid mass, the *homme moyen sensuel*, but upon creative minority, the innovator who with one stroke can save the labour of 10,000, the brilliant few who cannot look without wonder, the restless elite who have made mutation a social, as well as a biological, fact. The ranks of the scientists and technologists, the artists and the teachers, have been swelled, their education shaped to their high genetic destiny, their power for good increased. Progress is their triumph; the modern world their monument. (Pelican edition, 1961, p. 15.)

[48] Fritz Machlup, *Education and Economic Growth* (Lincoln, Nebraska, 1970), p. 40. Machlup cites a study by Edward Denison, which assumes that two-fifths of the income differentials of persons with more schooling was due to natural ability, while three-fifths was the result of additional schooling. Gary Becker, in *Human Capital* (New York, 1964), examined samples of persons for whom IQ and grades in primary and secondary school were available, and could be correlated with later income returns, and found that differential ability "might well have a larger effect on the estimated rate of return" than simply the effect of schooling, but that, by the college level, "education itself explains most of the unadjusted earnings differential between college and high-school graduates" (pp. 88, 124). The Denison data are in his essay, "Measuring the Contribution of Education to Economic Growth," *The Economics of Education*, ed. Robinson and Vaizey (London

The logic of the argument has been pushed further by the Harvard psychologist Richard Herrnstein. Using data assembled by Arthur Jensen of Berkeley—that 80 percent of a person's IQ is inherited, while environmental factors account for only 20 percent—Herrnstein then proceeds to extend the implication:

1. If differences in mental abilities are inherited, and
2. if success in society requires those abilities, and
3. if the environment is "equalized,"
4. then social standing will be based to some extent on inherited differences.[49]

Herrnstein's argument mixes up two different situations: the assertion that in American society today occupational position *is* largely a function of IQ, and the model of a meritocracy, whose stratification system would *be* determined by IQ. Herrnstein concludes, however, that if all persons are given an equal start, and equality of opportunity is fully realized, then heredity will become the decisive factor, since the social environment would be the same for all. And he draws a dismal picture of the new poor:

. . . there will be precipitated out of the mass of humanity a low-capacity (intellectual and otherwise) residue that may be unable to master the common occupations, cannot compete for success and achievement and are most likely to be born to parents who have similarly failed.[50]

---

and New York, 1966). The figures on college and high-school IQ are from Machlup, p. 40.

For a review of studies that question the relation of IQ to economic success, see Samuel Bowles and Herbert Gintis, "I.Q. in the U.S. Class Structure," *Social Policy*, vol. 35, nos. 4 & 5 (November/December 1972).

[49] Richard Herrnstein, "I.Q.," *The Atlantic Monthly* (September 1971). Technically, one cannot say that within any single person, 80 percent of his IQ is inherited. In a large sample, 80 percent of the variance between scores would be attributed by Jensen to inheritance.

[50] Ibid., p. 63. Herrnstein's arguments are paralleled by a school of ethologists who see in "the breeding process" the basis of the political struggle in human society. Thus, anthropologists Lionel Tiger and Robin Fox write, in their book, *The Imperial Animal:*

Analogies are often drawn between human and ant societies. There are, to be sure, striking similarities—such as division of labor, caste system, and domestication of other creatures—but the analogy breaks down at one fundamental point: human societies are political, and ant societies are apolitical. The social order of an ant colony is genetically fixed. Workers are workers, drones drones, queens queens, soldiers soldiers, and so on. Workers cannot usurp power in the colony, because they are genetically programmed to be workers and nothing else. There can be no redistribution of power, of place, and, most importantly, of breeding ability, and therefore of contribution to the genetic pool. This is a crucial difference. Politics involves the possibility of changing the distribution of resources in a society—one of which is the control over the future that breeding allows. The political process—the process of redistributing control over resources among the individuals of a group—is, in evolutionary terms, a breeding process. The political system is a breeding system. When we apply the word "lust" to both power and sex,

Coda: An Agenda for the Future

The relation of genetics to intelligence to social-class position involves five different kinds of disputed questions. The first is the question whether one can ever fix with any exactness the proportions of genetic inheritance and environment to intelligence. (This is possible only if one assumes they are *causally* independent, i.e. that biological endowment does not influence the environment; but this is highly unlikely.) Second is the question of what the IQ tests actually measure, whether only particular skills or some more general and unified underlying intelligence. Third is the question whether IQ tests are "culture-bound," including even the self-styled "culture-*fair*" tests which do not deal with school-taught knowledge but ask the child to deduce relations and correlates within simple non-representational drawings. Fourth, the question whether the social class of the parent is more important than IQ in determining entry into college or occupational position in the society. Finally, the crucial question whether these relationships—between intelligence, social class background and other factors—have changed over time at all and, to that extent, whether the society *is* becoming more meritocratic.[51]

---

we are nearer the truth than we imagine. In the struggle for reproductive advantage, some do better than others. It is this that changes the distribution of genes in a population and affects its genetic future. This is a world of winners and losers, a world of politics—of the haves and the have-nots, of those who have made it and those who sulk on the sidelines.

[From the beginning of human time] the species has been irretrievably concerned with who can marry whom and with the relationship between position, property and productive copulation.

The result of the reproductive struggle is a social system that is profoundly hierarchical and competitive. And if human politics exhibits a constant tension between the commonly valued ideal of equality and the privately valued aim of happy inequality, then this is simply a reflection of our evolutionary history. (New York, 1971, pp. 24–25.)

What makes this formulation even more striking is the character of the "new biology," which now allows the human species control of breeding by transferring frozen sperm by "donors" to different women, the placing of the embryo in "host" *vitro*, and cloning, which allows one to reproduce the exact genetic code of an organism. For a thoughtful discussion of the disquieting social and ethical questions raised by the new biology, see Leon Kass, "Making Babies," *The Public Interest*, no. 26 (Winter 1972).

[51] For a discussion of the argument that society is not becoming more meritocratic see Christopher Jencks and associates, *Inequality: A Reassessment of the Effect of Family and Schooling in America* (New York, 1972).

Jencks argues that there is no evidence that (a) the correlation between education and occupational status has changed over the past 80 years; (b) the correlation between IQ and occupational status has changed over the past 50 years; (c) the correlation between education and income has changed over the past 30 years; (d) or that the correlation between IQ and income has changed.

Equally, says Jencks, there is no evidence for a decline in the effects of family background either on occupational status or income, at least since World War I. The work of Stephan Thernstrom, *Poverty and Progress: Social Mobility in a Nineteenth-Century City* (Cambridge, Mass., 1964), suggest mobility rates as high in the nineteenth century as in the twentieth.

What the parties to these disputes mix up, however, are two very different kinds of issues. One, whether the society—because of either social-class privilege or cultural advantage (e.g. the selective biases of IQ tests)—does or does not provide genuine equality of opportunity, or a fair start for all; and two, whether a society in which genuine equality of opportunity did prevail, but a new form of income and status inequality based on merit resulted, would be desirable? *In other words, is it a more genuine equality of opportunity that is wanted, or an equality of result?* It is the shuttling from one to another of these positions that has marked the populist argument in recent years and created a confusion in the political demands raised in its wake.

Initially, equality of opportunity was the main preoccupation. The explicit fear created by a post-industrial society is that the failure to get on the educational escalator means the exclusion from the privileged places in society. A meritocratic society is a "credentials society" in which certification of achievement—through the college degree, the professional examination, the license—becomes a condition of higher employment. Education thus becomes a defensive necessity. As Lester Thurow has observed:

As the supply of educated labor increases, individuals find that they must improve their educational level simply to defend their current income po-

"In what sense, then, can we say that society is becoming more meritocratic, if the importance of family background and educational credentials is constant over time?" writes Jencks. "Why should we accept Herrnstein's thesis if (a) education is no more important, and (b) there is not a shred of evidence that IQ is more important than it used to be, and (c) all the indirect evidence suggests no change in the importance of IQ as against other factors in determining success?" (Private communication, July 25, 1972.)

Jencks is somewhat skeptical, as well, of the argument about family background as the primary factor in determining the correlation between schooling and occupational status. "Samuel Bowles has an essay in the Spring 1972 *Journal of Political Economy* arguing that family background is a major factor in the observed relationship, although I think he greatly overstates his case. I can easily imagine that personality differences (persistence, discipline, etc.) may explain most of the differences between the educated and the uneducated, and that these may not be caused to any significant extent by schooling, but may simply affect the amount of schooling people get" (ibid).

Drawing upon the work of Jencks et al., a collaborator, David K. Cohen of the Harvard Education School, has stressed the large role of contingent factors in going to college. Cohen writes:

A comparison of IQ and social and economic status of college students reveals that being rich is nearly as big a help in increasing a student's chances of going to college as being smart. The most important fact, however, is that *ability and status combined explain somewhat less than half the actual variation in college attendance.* As in the case of curriculum placement, we must turn to other factors—motivation, luck, discrimination, chance, and family encouragement or lack of it—to find likely explanations. "Does I.Q. Matter?" *Commentary* (April 1972), p. 55 (emphasis added).

sitions. If they don't, others will, and they will find their current job no longer open to them. Education becomes a good investment, not because it would raise people's incomes above what they would have been if no one had increased his education, but rather because it raises their income above what it will be if others acquire an education and they do not. *In effect, education becomes a defensive expenditure necessary to protect one's "market share."* The larger the class of educated labor and the more rapidly it grows, the more such defensive expenditures become imperative.[52]

The logical outcome of these fears on the part of disadvantaged groups is a demand for "open admissions" to universities. The underlying rationale of the demand has been the argument that social-class origin of the parent was the primary factor skewing selection in the occupational system, and that open admission to colleges, despite low grades, would enable minority groups to compete more fairly in the society. To that extent, open admissions is no more than the historic American principle that everyone should have a chance to better himself, no matter where he starts. It is also the optimistic American belief that giving *any* student more education will do him more good. This was the logic behind the land-grant college acts; it was the long-standing practice of the public universities, outside the East, even before World War II.[53]

But for some, the extension of this demand has become an attack on the meritocratic principle itself. As one proponent writes: "As long as open admissions remains limited to a few institutions, it poses no threat to the meritocracy. Recruitment into the elite will be based not on *whether* one went to college, but on *where* one went to college. Universal open admissions, however, would destroy the close articulation between the meritocracy and the system of higher education; further, by the very act of abolishing hierarchy in admissions, it would cast doubt on hierarchy in the larger society."[54]

---

[52] Lester Thurow, "Education and Social Policy," *The Public Interest*, no. 28 (Summer 1972), p. 79 (emphasis in the original).

[53] But there was usually some kind of sorting device. In the midwestern systems, anyone with a C average or better in high school could enter the state university, but a ruthless examination system would weed out the poorer students by the end of the first or second year. In the California system, any high school graduate could go on to higher education, but a grade tracking system put the top 10 to 15 percent directly into the universities (e.g. Berkeley, UCLA), the next 25 percent into the state colleges, and the remainder into junior or community colleges.

[54] Jerome Karabel, "Perspectives on Open Admission," *Educational Record* (Winter 1972), pp. 42–43.

"The philosophical rationale for open admissions," Mr. Karabel writes, "is that the educational mission of the institution is not . . . to serve as a talent scout for future employers but rather to foster growth in the student." And in that light, Mr. Karabel quotes approvingly the remark of B. Alden Thresher: "There is no such thing as an unfit or unqualified seeker after education." Mr. Thresher's remark is in

That argument, however, if pushed to its logical conclusion, would mean that admission to all higher schools in the country, from Parsons College to Harvard, should be by lot. And the further conclusion, since elite schools would still be defined by their faculty, would be to make teaching assignment in the national university system a matter of lot as well.

Open admissions is a means of widening equality of opportunity for disadvantaged students by broadening access to the university. But there is also the question of place in the university structure itself—in the faculty, staff, and administration. In their comprehensive study of the American occupational structure, Peter Blau and Otis Dudley Duncan have shown that almost all the different minority groups have been able to achieve commensurate status, power, and economic rewards—with the exception of women and blacks. Clearly, if there is discrimination—on the basis of sex, or color, or religion, or any criterion extraneous to the stated one of professional qualification—there is no genuine equality of opportunity. The second effort to widen equality has been the effort to expand the number of places of minorities in the system.

In the 1960s, the government declared it a matter of public policy that "affirmative action" had to be taken to rectify the discrimination against minorities. The policy of affirmative action was first proclaimed by President Johnson in an executive order of 1965. It stated that on all federal projects, or in any employment situation that used federal money, employers had to prove they had sought out qualified applicants from disadvantaged groups; had to provide special training where necessary, if qualified applicants could not be found immediately; and had to hire preferentially from among minority groups when their qualifications were roughly equal to those of other applicants. This program, combined with others such as Head Start and compensatory education programs, was designed to redress a historic cultural disadvantage and, quite deliberately, to give minority-group members, especially blacks, an edge in the competition for place.

In the first years of the government affirmative-action program, the efforts were directed primarily within the skilled trades—especially the building trades, where there had been a deliberate policy of racial exclusion. In the early 1970s, the Nixon administration, acting through the Department of Health, Education and Welfare (HEW), extended the program to universities, and each school with federal contracts was asked to provide data on the number of minority persons in each position, academic and non-academic, and to set

---

"Uses and Abuses of Scholastic Aptitude and Achievement Tests," *Barriers to Higher Education* (New York: College Entrance Examination Board, 1971), p. 39.

specific goals for increasing the number of minority-group persons in each classification. As Edward Shils summarized the order:

Universities were informed that for each category of employee in the university it would be necessary to specify rates of renumeration and number in each category by "racial breakdown, i.e. Negro, Oriental, American Indian, Spanish-surnamed Americans. . . ." This had to be accompanied by an "Affirmative Action Program which specifically and succinctly identif[ies] problem areas by division, department location and job classification, and includes more specific recommendations and plans for overcoming them." The "Affirmative Action Program" must "include specific goals and objectives by division, department and job classification, including target completion dates on both long and short ranges as the particular case may indicate. Analytical provision should be made for evaluating recruitment methods and sources; the total number of candidates interviewed, job offers made, the numbers hired with the number of minority group persons interviewed, made job offers and hired." . . .[55]

The initial intention of the Executive Order was to eliminate *discrimination*. But discrimination is difficult to prove, especially when the qualifications required for a job are highly specific. And the government's test became: Are the members of the minority groups to be found in employment, at every level, in numbers equal to their proportion in the population? Or, if women earned 30 percent of the Ph.D.s, are 30 percent of the faculty women? What this meant, in theory, was to set "target" figures for women and blacks. In practice, this has meant, quotas, or priorities in hiring, for persons from these groups.

What is extraordinary about this change is that, without public debate, an entirely new principle of rights has been introduced into the polity. In the nature of the practice, *the principle has changed from discrimination to representation*. Women, blacks, and Chicanos are to be employed, as a matter of right, in proportion to their number, and the principle of professional qualification or individual achievement is subordinated to the new ascriptive principle of corporate identity.[56]

The implications of this new principle are far-reaching. One can, "logically," insist on quotas where the skill is homogeneous, where

[55] Edward Shils, "Editorial," *Minerva* (April 1971), p. 165.

[56] In full acknowledgment of this principle, the Union Theological Seminary on June 1 voted that blacks and other minority groups would henceforth make up one-third and women one-half of all students, faculty, staff, and directors. (At the time, blacks made up 6 percent of the 566 number student body and 8 percent of the 38 member faculty; women 20 percent of the student body and 8 percent of the faculty.) "It is unrealistic," said the Seminary, "to educate people in a pluralistic society in an environment that is overwhelmingly white and male-oriented." The figure of 50 percent women was chosen to reflect their representation in society; the one-third minority as a "critical mass" to give them presence. *New York Times* (June 1, 1972).

one person can readily substitute for another. But by focusing on group identity rather than the person, by making the mechanical equation of number of women Ph.D.s to number of positions they should hold, the government assumes that "educated labor" is "homogeneous"—that individual talent or achievement is less important than the possession of the credential. This may be true in many occupations, but not in university teaching and research, where individual merit is the singular test. Putting someone in a tenure position, which is capitalized at three-quarters of a million dollars, is very different from hiring a black rather than a white plumber; simply having the degree is not necessarily the qualification for the high position.

Furthermore, quotas and preferential hiring mean that standards are bent or broken. The inescapable assumption of the ascriptive criterion as regards tenured university positions is that minority persons are less qualified and could not compete with others, even if given a sufficient margin. What effect does this have on the self-esteem of a person hired on "second-class" grounds? And what effect does it have on the quality of a university, its teaching and research and morale, if its faculties are filled on the basis of quotas?

But quotas themselves are no simple matter. If "representation" is to be the criterion of position, then what is the logic of extending the principle only to women, blacks, Mexicans, Puerto Ricans, American Indians, Filipinos, Chinese, and Japanese—which are the categories in the HEW guideline? Why not to Irish, Italians, Poles, and other ethnic groups? And if representation is the criterion, what is the base of representation? At one California state college, as John Bunzel reports, the Mexican-Americans asked that 20 percent of the total work force be Chicanos, because the surrounding community is 20 percent Mexican-American. The black students rejected this argument and said that the proper base should be the state of California, which would provide a different mix of blacks and Chicanos. Would the University of Mississippi be expected to hire 37 percent black faculty because that is the proportion of blacks in the population of Mississippi? And would the number of Jews in most faculties of the country be reduced because the Jews are clearly overrepresented in proportion to their number?

And if ethnic and minority tests, why not religious or political beliefs as the criteria of balanced representation? Governor Reagan of California has said that conservatives are highly underrepresented in the faculties of the state universities, a fact evident when the political coloration of those faculties is compared with voting results in California; should conservatives therefore be given preference in hiring? And should particular communities be asked to support the teaching of certain subjects (or the presence of certain books in school libraries) which are repugnant to the beliefs of that community?—a question first raised in the Virginia House of Burgesses in 1779 and a principle restated by the Tennessee legislature in the 1920s in barring the teaching of evolution in that Fundamentalist state.

The historic irony in the demand for representation on the basis of an ascriptive principle is its complete reversal of radical and humanist values. The liberal and radical attack on discrimination was *based on its denial of a justly earned place to a person on the basis of an unjust group attribute.* That person was not judged as an individual, but was judged—and excluded—because he was a member of a particular group. But now it is being demanded that one must have a place primarily because one possesses a particular group attribute. The person himself has disappeared. Only attributes remains. The further irony is that according to the radical critique of contemporary society, an individual is treated not as a person but as a multiple of roles that divide and fragment him and reduce him to a single dominant attribute of the major role or function he or she plays in society. Yet in the reversal of principle we now find that a person is to be given preference by virtue of a role, his group membership, and the person is once again "reduced" to a single overriding attribute as the prerequisite for a place in the society. That is the logic of the demand for quotas.

DE-SCHOOLING

From a different direction there has come another attack on the idea of meritocracy: the argument that all schooling is being subordinated to the demands of technocratic thinking and that the school is assuming a disproportionate influence in the society. The argument is made most sharply by Ivan Illich:

The hidden curriculum teaches all children that economically valuable knowledge is the result of professional teaching and that social entitlements depend on the rank achieved in a bureaucratic process. The hidden curriculum transforms the explicit curriculum into a commodity and makes its acquisition the securest form of wealth. Knowledge certificates —unlike property rights, corporate stock or family inheritance—are free from challenge . . . . school is universally accepted as the avenue to greater power, to increased legitimacy as a producer, and to further learning resources.[57]

For Illich—whose mysterious role as both Catholic heresiarch and prowler in the corridors of power has made him a figure of cul-

---

[57] Ivan Illich, "After Deschooling, What?" *Social Policy* (September/October 1971), p. 7.

tural curiosity [58]—there is a distinction between schooling and education. Schooling is an instrument that enables a person to accumulate a "knowledge stock," just as business once allowed individuals to accumulate a "capital stock." [59] Education is the "free determination by each learner of his own reason for living and learning—the part that his knowledge is to play in his life." Since schooling has become completely instrumental, and a barrier to education, one must eliminate schools and create a process whereby each person can pursue the education he wants and needs.

For Illich, schooling creates a new hierarchy in which the hierophants of knowledge maintain their position by arcane and technical knowledge that is closed off from the rest of society.[60] "Effective access" to education requires "a radical denial of the right of facts and complexity of tools on which contemporary technocracies found their privilege, which they, in turn, render immune by interpreting its use as a service to the majority."

In place of institutions—which only develop vested interests to maintain the privileges of its administrators—Illich would substitute "learning webs" made up of skill-exchanges, peer-matching and Educators-at-Large, intellectual sadhus or gurus, wandering scholars, available at call. There would be no compulsory attendance, no credentials, just education *pour le gout* in the street bazaars of learn-

---

[58] Illich, who was a Monsignor in the Catholic Church, burst rather suddenly onto the American intellectual scene in the late 1960s with essays in the *New York Review of Books* and the *New York Times* on his theories of "de-schooling society." These essays were published as *Deschooling Society* (New York, 1970), and a second collection of essays, *Celebration of Awareness*, with an introduction by Erich Fromm, appeared a year later. Illich came to attention within the Catholic Church as the organizer of the center in Cuernevaca, Mexico, for training priests for work in Latin America. Though the center was set up with support from the Vatican hierarchy, after a few years it began to espouse unorthodox doctrines. A profile of Msgr. Illich—who has since resigned his church title—appeared in *The New Yorker* (April 25, 1970) by Francine DuPlessix Gray, and is reprinted in her book, *Divine Disobedience* (New York, 1971).

[59] "The more learning an individual consumes, the more 'knowledge stock' he acquires. The hidden curriculum therefore defines a new class structure for society within which the large consumers of knowledge—those who have acquired large quantities of knowledge stock—enjoy special privileges, high income, and access to the more powerful tools of production. This kind of knowledge-capitalism has been accepted in all industrialized societies and establishes a rationale for the distribution of jobs and income." Ivan Illich, "The Alternative to Schooling," *Saturday Review* (June 19, 1971), reprinted in *Deschooling Society*.

[60] Illich writes:

Science will be kept artificially arcane so long as its results are incorporated into technology at the service of professionals. If it were used to render possible a style of life in which each man would enjoy housing, healing, educating, moving, and entertaining himself, then scientists would try much harder to retranslate their discoveries made in a secret language into the normal language of everyday life. ("After Deschooling, What?" p. 13.)

ing.[61] And all of it financed by the tax money hitherto spent on the schools.

The distinction between education and schooling is a relevant one. At one time, the two were joined. We then lived, as James Coleman has put it, in an "information-poor" society.[62] The degree of direct experience on a farm or in the small town may have been large, but the range of vicarious experience—the acquaintance with the world of art, or cultures or politics outside the immediate region— was limited to books and school. School was the central organizer of experience and the codifier of values. Today the situation has changed enormously. Whether the amount of direct experience of the child has shrunk is moot; it is perhaps romantic fallacy to believe that the child today, with the increased mobility of travel and the variety of urban stimuli available to him, has fewer direct experiences than before. But the range of vicarious experience, with the spread of communication and the wider windows onto the world offered by television, diverse magazines, picture books and the like, has broadened enormously. Education takes place outside the school, in the multifarious influence of media and peer group, while schools, because of their gatekeeper roles, have become more vocational and specialized.

The question, however, is whether this changed relationship requires the de-schooling of society or a very different conception of education and schooling. Illich is a romantic Rousseauian. His picture is drawn from *Emile*, and has the same farrago of rhetoric, the emphasis on the "authenticity of being"—those cant words of modernity which can never be defined. There is the same idea that a person should not obey social convention but "make up his mind for himself," as if there are hundreds of millions of independent truths

---

[61] As Richard Wollheim, a friendly critic, pictures the idyll:
Little vignettes of what would ensue are scattered through *Deschooling Society*. If a student wanted to learn Cantonese, he would be put on to a Chinese neighbour whose skill in his native language had been certified and whose willingness to impart it expressed. If he wanted to learn the guitar, he could rent not only a guitar but also taped guitar lessons and illustrated chord charts. If he wanted to find someone much in his own position with whom to discuss a disputed passage in Freud or Aquinas, he might go to a specially identified coffee shop, place the book by his side, and stay with whoever turned up as long a time as it took to satisfy his curiosity, or as short a time as it took to finish a cup of coffee. With the streets freed of private cars, individuals might wander freely through the city and explore the profuse teaching materials that exist not only in museums and libraries but in laboratories, storefronts, zoos, tool shops, cinemas and computer centres. And meanwhile the true teachers, the intellectual masters, would wait, presumably at home, for their self-chosen disciples to call on them. Richard Wollheim, "Ivan Illich," *The Listener* (December 16, 1971), p. 826.

[62] See James Coleman, "Education in Modern Society," in *Computers, Communications and the Public Interest*, ed. Martin Greenberger (Baltimore, 1971).

rather than multiple subgroups of socially circumscribed conventicles of thought. There is the same anti-intellectualism which regards experience alone as truth, rather than disciplined study. There is even the same manipulation by the master—the "noble lie" which Illich tells, in order to destroy institutions—to re-create the "state of nature" in order to align desires and powers. But in the end, as in *Emile*, the search is not for knowledge, or an education, but for an identity, the identity of lost innocence, the identity of the naif.[63]

The difficulty with the exoteric argument of Illich—as with so much of modernism—is that it confuses experience, in all its diversities, with knowledge. Experience has to be made conscious, and this is done, as Dewey remarked, "by means of that fusion of old meanings and new situations that transfigures both." [64] Knowledge is the selective ordering—and reordering—of experience through relevant concepts. Reality is not a bounded world, "out there," to be imprinted on the mind as from a mirror, or a flux of experience to be sampled for its novelties according to one's inclination (or its relevance for "me"), but a set of meanings organized by mind, in terms of categories, which establishes the relations between facts and infers conclusions.

Nor need there be, in principle, a contradiction between a cognitive and an aesthetic mode in which, as alleged, the technocratic orientation is concerned only with the functional and the adversary culture with sensibility—much as this may be true in sociological fact. In the very nature of knowledge, as Dewey observed, there has to be an interplay of the two: The cognitive makes the variety of experience more intelligible by its reduction to conceptual form; the aesthetic makes experience more vivid by its presentation in an expressive mode. The two reinforce each other in a singular way.

What has to be common to both is a reliance on judgment—the making of necessary distinctions and the creation of standards which allow one to sort out the meretricious from the good, the pretentious from the enduring. Knowledge is a product of the self-conscious and renewable comparison and judging of cultural objects and ideas in order to say that something is better than something else (or more complex, or more beautiful, or whatever the standard one seeks to

---

[63] This is Rousseau's portrait of Emile at the end of his childhood:
He does not know the meaning of habit, routine and custom; what he did yesterday has no control over what he is doing today; he follows no rules, submits to no authority, copies no pattern, and only acts or speaks as he pleases. So do not expect set speeches or studied manners from him, but just the faithful expression of his thoughts and the conduct that springs from his inclinations. *Emile* (New York, 1911), p. 125.

[64] John Dewey, *Art as Experience* (New York; Capricorn edition, 1958; original publication, 1934), p. 275.

apply), and that something is truer. Inevitably, therefore, knowledge is a form of authority, and education is the process of refining the nature of authoritative judgments. This is the classic, and enduring, rationale of education.

But to this is added a special burden of the post-industrial society. One need not defend the technocratic dimensions of education—its emphasis on vocationalism and specialization—to argue that schooling becomes more necessary than ever before. By the very fact that there are now many more differentiated ways in which people gain information and have experiences, there is a need for the self-conscious understanding of the processes of conceptualization as the means of organizing one's information in order to gain coherent perspectives on one's experience. A conceptual scheme is a set of consistent terms which groups together diverse attributes of experience or properties of an object, in a higher order of abstraction, in order to relate them to, or distinguish them from, other attributes and properties. To see what is common and what is different about modes of experience—the theme I raised in the introduction on the need for prisms for the comparison of societies—is the function of education. And just as the resolution of an identity crisis for individuals is the amalgamation of discordant aspects of growing up into a coherent whole, so is knowledge an organization of experiences, tested against other patterns of experience, in order to create consistent standards of judgment.

The function of the university, in these circumstances, is to relate to each other the modes of conscious inquiry: historical consciousness, which is the encounter with a tradition that can be tested against the present; methodological consciousness, which makes explicit the conceptual grounds of inquiry and its philosophical presuppositions; and individual self-consciousness, which makes one aware of the sources of one's prejudgments and allows one to re-create one's values through the disciplined study of the society. Education is the "reworking" of the materials of the past, without ever wholly surrendering its truths or bending to its pieties. It is a continuing tension, "the tension between past and future, mind and sensibility, tradition and experience, [which] for all its strains and discomforts, is the only source for maintaining the independence of inquiry itself." It is the affirmation of the principle of intellectual and artistic order through the search for relatedness of discordant knowledge.[65]

---

[65] I have presented these ideas, in larger historical and philosophical detail, in my book, *The Reforming of General Education* (New York, 1966). See, especially, chap. 4, "The Need for Reform: Some Philosophical Presuppositions," and chap. 6, "A New Rationale." The quotation is from the Anchor edition (1968), p. 151.

II

THE REDEFINITION OF EQUALITY

The issues of schooling, of income, of status all have become matters of social policy because equality has been one of the central values of the American polity. But there has never been a clear-cut meaning to equality, and the earliest form of the idea in the seventeenth century was quite different than what it assumed in its popular form by the third decade of the nineteenth century. Those who founded the colonies—in New England, at least, beginning with the Pilgrim Fathers of the Mayflower Compact—had an image of themselves as a "community of virtuous men who understood themselves to be under sacred restraints." There was equality, but in the Puritan sense of an equality of the elect. Among the Constitutional Fathers, the idea of virtue, and election by ability (if no longer by grace), dominated their thinking. A curious blend of Roman republican imagery and Lockean thinking—since both emphasized agrarian virtues and labor—informed their language. The central theme was independence, and the conditions whereby a man could be independent. But in the very use of Lockean language there was an implicit commitment to a hierarchy—the hierarchy of intellect. Since thought was prized, it was assumed that some men "thought" better than others, were more able, more intelligent—and so formed the natural aristocracy.

The singular changeover was symbolized by the "Jacksonian persuasion" (to use Marvin Meyer's phrase). Thought was replaced by sentiment and feeling, and each man's sentiments were held to be as good as any others. This is what gives point to the striking observations of Tocqueville. The opening lines of Tocqueville's *Democracy in America* are:

No novelty in the United States struck me more vividly during my stay than the equality of conditions. It was easy to see the immense influence of this basic fact on the whole course of society. It gives a particular turn to public opinion and a particular twist to the laws, new maxims to those who govern and particular habits to the governed.

And, reflecting on the power of this new principle, Tocqueville concluded:

Therefore the graduate progress of equality is something fated. The main features of this progress are the following: it is universal and permanent, it is daily passing beyond human control, and every event and every man helps it along. Is it wise to suppose that a movement which has been so long in train could be halted by one generation? Does anyone imagine that democracy, which has destroyed the feudal system and vanquished kings, will fall back before the middle classes and the rich? Will it stop now, when it has grown so strong and its adversaries so weak? [66]

In nineteenth-century America, however, the notion of equality was never sharply defined. In its voiced assertions it boiled down to the sentiment that each man was as good as another and no man was better than anyone else. What it meant, in effect, was that no one should take on the airs of an aristocrat and lord it over other men. To this extent, it was a negative reaction to the highly mannered society of Europe, and travelers to this country at the time understood it in those terms. On its positive side, equality meant the chance to get ahead, regardless of one's origins—that no formal barriers or prescribed positions stood in one's way. It was this combination of attributes—the lack of deference and the emphasis on personal achievement—which gave nineteenth-century America its revolutionary appeal, so much so that when the German '48ers came here, including such members of Marx's Socialist Workers Club as Kriege and Willich, they abandoned European socialism and became Republicans instead.

What is at stake today is the redefinition of equality. A principle which was the weapon for changing a vast social system, the principle of equality of opportunity, is now seen as leading to a new hierarchy, and the current demand is that the "just precedence" of society, in Locke's phrase, requires the reduction of all inequality, or the creation of equality of result—in income, status, and power —for all men in society. This issue is the central value problem of the post-industrial society.

The principle of equality of opportunity derives from a fundamental tenet of classic liberalism: that the individual—and not the family, community, or the state—is the singular unit of society, and that the purpose of societal arrangements is to allow the individual the freedom to fulfill his own purposes—by his labor to gain property, by exchange to satisfy his wants, by upward mobility to achieve a place commensurate with his talents. It was assumed that individuals will differ—in their natural endowments, in their energy, drive, and motivation, in their conception of what is desirable—and the institutions of society should establish procedures for regulating fairly the competition and exchanges necessary to fulfill these individually diverse desires and competences.

As a principle, equality of opportunity denies the precedence of

---

[66] Alexis de Tocqueville, *Democracy in America*, ed. J. P. Mayer and Max Lerner (New York, 1966), Author's Introduction, pp. 3, 5–6.

birth, of nepotism, of patronage or any other criterion which allocates place, other than fair competition open equally to talent and ambition. It asserts, in the terms of Talcott Parsons, universalism over particularism, achievement over ascription. It is an ideal derived directly from the Enlightenment as codified by Kant, the principle of individual merit generalized as a categorical imperative.

The social structure of modern society—in its bourgeois form as the universalism of money, in its romantic form as the thrust of ambition, in its intellectual form as the priority of knowledge—is based on this principle. Estate society—that of the eighteenth century and earlier—had given honorific precedence to land, the army, and the church, and only the birthright of inheritance could provide access to these institutions. Even where there was nominal mobility—the institutions of the Red and the Black—commissions in the army (as in England up to the middle of the nineteenth century) were open only by purchase, and benefices in the church available through family connection. Modernity meant the uprooting of this stratified order by the principle of openness, change, and social mobility. The capitalist and the entrepreneur replaced the landed gentry, the government administrator took power over the army, and the intellectual succeeded the priest. And, in principle, these new positions were open to all men of talent. Thus there occurred a complete social revolution: a change in the social base of status and power, and a new mode of access to place and privilege in the society.

The post-industrial society adds a new criterion to the definitions of base and access: Technical skill becomes a condition of operative power, and higher education the means of obtaining technical skill. As a result, there has been a shift in the slope of power as, in key institutions, technical competence becomes the overriding consideration: In industry, family capitalism is replaced by managerial capitalism; in government, patronage is replaced by civil service and bureaucratization; in the universities, the exclusiveness of the old social elites, particularly WASP domination of the Ivy League colleges, breaks up with the inclusion of ethnic groups, particularly the Jews. Increasingly, the newer professional occupations, particularly engineering and economics, become central to the technical decisions of the society. The post-industrial society, in this dimension of status and power, is the logical extension of the meritocracy; it is the codification of a new social order based, in principle, on the priority of educated talent.

In social fact, the meritocracy is thus the displacement of one principle of stratification by another, of achievement for ascription. In the past—and this was the progressive meaning of liberalism—

this new principle was considered just. Men were to be judged—and rewarded—not by attributes of birth or primordial ties but on individual merit. Today that principle is held to be the new source of inequality and of social—if not psychological—injustice.

THE CASE AGAINST MERITOCRACY

The sociological and philosophical objections to the meritocracy are of a contradictory and overlapping nature:

1. Genetics and intelligence: If one assumes that a meritocracy is purely a selection by intelligence, and that intelligence is based on inherited genetic differences, then one obtains privilege on the basis of a genetic lottery, and this is an arbitrary basis for social justice.

2. Social class: There can never be a pure meritocracy because, invariably, high-status parents will seek to pass on their positions either through the use of influence or simply by the cultural advantages their children would possess. Thus, after one generation a meritocracy simply becomes an enclaved class.

3. The role of chance: There is considerable social mobility in the United States, but it is less related to schooling or ability or even to family background than to intangible and random factors such as luck and competence in the particular job one falls into. Christopher Jencks and his associates, in a review of the effect of family and schooling on mobility, conclude:

Poverty is not primarily hereditary. While children born into poverty have a higher than average chance of ending up poor, there is still an enormous amount of economic mobility from one generation to the next. There is nearly as much economic inequality among brothers raised in the same homes as in the general population. . . .

. . . there is almost as much economic inequality among those who score high on standardized tests as in the general population. Equalizing everyone's reading scores would not appreciably reduce the number of economic "failures." . . .

Our work suggests, then, that many popular explanations of economic inequality are largely wrong. We cannot blame economic inequality primarily on genetic differences in men's capacity for abstract reasoning, since there is nearly as much economic inequality among men with equal test scores as among men in general. We cannot blame economic inequality primarily on the fact that parents pass along their disadvantages to their children, since there is nearly as much inequality among men whose parents hold the same economic status as among men in general. We cannot blame economic inequality on differences between schools, since differences between schools seem to have very little effect on any measurable attribute on those who attended them. Economic success seems to depend on varieties of luck and on-the-job competence that are only moderately related to family background, schooling or scores on standardized tests.[67]

Thus, a situation of inequality exists which is justified on the basis of achievement or meritocracy but does not actually derive from them, so that the rewards of mobility, or, at least, the degrees of inequality in reward, are not justified.

4. The principle—or illusion—that a meritocracy instills a competitive feeling into society which is damaging to those who succeed and even more so to those who fail. As Jerome Karabel writes: "A meritocracy is more competitive than an overtly-based class society, and this unrelenting competition exacts a toll both from the losers, whose self-esteem is damaged, and from the winners, who may be more self-righteous about their elite status than is a more traditional ruling group. Apart from increased efficiency, it is doubtful whether a frenetically competitive inegalitarian society is much of an improvement over an ascriptive society which, at least, does not compel its poor people to internalize their failure." [68]

5. The principle of equality of opportunity, even if fully realized on the basis of talent, simply re-creates inequality anew in each generation, and thus becomes a conservative force in society.[69] In its most vulgar form, this is the argument that equality of opportunity has been the means of some (e.g. the Jews) to get "theirs" in society, and deny latecomers (e.g. blacks) a fair share of the spoils. This is the argument used in New York City, for example, where it is charged that in the school system Jews "used" the merit system to dispossess the Catholics, who had risen through patronage, but that the merit system was now a means of keeping out blacks from high place in the system. In its pristine form, this argument states that social justice should mean not equality at the start of a race, but at the finish; equality not of opportunity but of result.

---

[67] Christopher Jencks et al., *Inequality*, p. 8.

[68] Jerome Karabel, "Perspectives on Open Admissions," p. 42.

[69] This was an argument made more than sixty years ago by W. H. Mallock, a British skeptic about democracy and perhaps the most able conservative thinker of the late nineteenth century. In *The Limits of Pure Democracy* (1917) Mallock argues that civilization proceeds only from the ability of a creative few and that complete equality would mean the end of economic progress and culture. In this respect, he writes: "The demand for equality of opportunity may, indeed, wear on the surface of it certain revolutionary aspects; but it is in reality—it is in its very nature—a symptom of moderation, or rather of an unintended conservatism, of which the masses of normal men cannot, if they would, divest themselves. . . . The desire for equality of opportunity—the desire for the right to rise—is a desire [for] some position or condition which is not equal, but which is, on the contrary, superior to any position or condition which is achievable by the talents of all." Cited in Raymond Williams, *Culture and Society* (London, 1958), pp. 164–165.

Coda: An Agenda for the Future

This change in social temper—the distrust of meritocracy— occurred principally in the last decade. The Kennedy and Johnson administrations, as a double consequence of the civil-rights revolution and the emphasis on higher education as a gateway to better place in the society, had made equality the central theme of social policy. The focus, however, was almost completely on widening equality of opportunity, principally through the schools: on compensatory education, Head Start programs, manpower training to improve skills, school integration, bussing ghetto children to suburban schools, open admissions, and the like. It was clear that black and poor children were culturally disadvantaged, and these handicaps had to be eliminated. It was felt that these programs would do so. In justifying them, the image that President Johnson used, in proclaiming the policy of affirmative action, was that of a shackled runner:

Imagine a hundred yard dash in which one of the two runners has his legs shackled together. He has progressed 10 yards, while the unshackled runner has gone 50 yards. At that point the judges decide that the race is unfair. How do they rectify the situation? Do they merely remove the shackles and allow the race to proceed? Then they could say that "equal opportunity" now prevailed. But one of the runners would still be forty yards ahead of the other. Would it not be the better part of justice to allow the previously shackled runner to make up the forty yard gap; or to start the race all over again? That would be affirmative action towards equality.[70]

The change in attitude, however, began with the realization that schooling had little effect in raising the achievement or reducing the disparate standing of black children relative to white. In 1966, Professor James Coleman of Johns Hopkins University, carrying out a mandate of the Civil Rights Act of 1964, concluded a massive survey of 4,000 schools and 600,000 students. The Office of Education, which sponsored the research, and Coleman himself, had expected to find gross inequality of educational resources between black and white schools and to use this finding as an argument for large-scale federal spending to redress the balance. But the report—*Equality of Educational Opportunity*—found that there was little difference between black and white schools in such things as physical facilities, formal curricula, and other measurable criteria. It also found that a significant gap in the achievement scores between black and white children was already present in the first grade, and that despite the

---

[70] Executive Order 11246, September 1965, cited in Earl Raab, "Quotas By Any Other Name," *Commentary* (January 1972), p. 41.

rough comparability of black and white schools, the gap between the two groups of children had widened by the end of elementary school. The only consistent variable explaining the differences in scores *within* each racial or ethnic group was the educational and economic attainment of the parents. As Coleman wrote:

First, within each racial group, the strong relation of family economic and educational background to achievement does not diminish over the period of the school, and may even increase over the elementary years. Second, *most of the variation in student achievement lies within the same school, very little of it is between schools.* The implication of these last two results is clear: family background differences account for much more variation in achievement than do school differences.

But there was no consistent variable to explain the difference between racial groups, not even measured family background— which is why some persons have fallen back on genetic explanations.

The Coleman findings dismayed the educational bureaucracy, and at first, received little attention. Issued in July 1966, the document was scarcely reported in *The New York Times* or the news weeklies. But as the explosive findings gradually became known, the Coleman Report became the center of the most extensive discussion of social policy in the history of American sociological debate, and the source of vehement public recrimination on such questions as compulsory integration, school bussing, and the like.[71]

---

[71] The document is formally known as "Equality of Educational Opportunity," Report of the Office of Education to the Congress and the President, U.S. Printing Office (July 1966), pp. 731.

The first discussion of the report was in *The Public Interest*, no. 4 (Summer 1966), where Coleman summarized his conclusions in an article, "Equal Schools or Equal Students." The quotation above is from p. 73 (emphasis added). As the debate widened, Coleman discussed the implications of the report in *The Public Interest*, no. 9 (Fall 1967), in the article "Toward Open Schools." He argued for the utility of integration on the following grounds:

The finding is that students do better when they are in schools where their fellow students come from backgrounds strong in educational motivation and resources. The results might be paraphrased by the statement that the educational resources provided by a child's fellow students are more important for his achievement than are the resources provided by the school board. This effect appears to be particularly great for students who themselves come from educationally-deprived backgrounds. For example, it is about twice as great for Negroes as for whites.

But since family background is so important, Coleman warned

The task of increasing achievement of lower-class children cannot be fully implemented by school integration, even if integration were wholly achieved—and the magnitude of racial and class concentrations in large cities indicates that it is not likely to be achieved soon (pp. 21–22).

The most comprehensive discussion of the Coleman Report took place in a three-year seminar at Harvard University initiated by Daniel P. Moynihan. The various papers analyzing the report, and Coleman's reply to his critics, are in *On*

Coda: An Agenda for the Future

Much of the controversy over the Coleman Report dealt with integration: some interpreted it, as did Coleman himself, in part, as a mandate to mix lower-class black schoolchildren with middle-class white to provide stronger peer-group pressures for achievement; black-power advocates saw it as justification for black control of black schools in order to strenghten the black child's control over his own destiny; and still others felt that additional money spent on schools was a waste since schools were ineffective in reducing the achievement gaps between the races or between social classes.

But in the long run the more important aspect of the report was not its findings but its major thesis, which was the redefinition of equality of opportunity.[72] Coleman had been charged, by explicit congressional directive, to determine the extent of inequality in the educational *resources* available to black and white children, the assumption being that social policy had to equalize the "inputs" into the educational process. But what Coleman took as his criterion was achievement, or *results*. In effect, he redefined equality of opportunity from *equal access to equally well-endowed schools (inputs)* to *equal performance on standardized achievement tests (equality of outcomes)*. As he put it in the title of his *Public Interest* essay, the focus had to shift from "equal schools to equal students."

Coleman was saying that the public schools—or the process of education itself—were not the social equalizers American society imagined them to be. Children achieved more or less in relation to family background and social class, and these were the variables that would have to be changed. Equality would not be attained until an average public school in Harlem produced as many high achievers as one in Scarsdale.

The argument has been pushed one step further by Christopher Jencks. If the focus was on the "equal student," then the problem was not even the distinction between Harlem and Scarsdale. In re-analyzing the Coleman data, Jencks found that students who performed best on achievement tests "were often enrolled in the same schools as the students who performed worst," and this, he declared, was potentially the most revolutionary revelation in the report. "In the short run it remains true that our most pressing political problem is the achievement gap between Harlem and Scarsdale. But in the long run it seems that our primary problem is not the disparity between Harlem and Scarsdale but the disparity between the top and bottom of the class in both Harlem and Scarsdale."

Equality of Educational Opportunity, ed. Frederick Mosteller and Daniel P. Moynihan (New York, 1972).

[72] I have profited here from Diane Ravitch's acute reading of the Mosteller and Moynihan book in *Change* (May 1972).

One can carry this still another step to the disparity among children of the same family. And as Jencks argues, in fact, "There is nearly as much economic inequality among brothers raised in the same homes as in the general population. This means that inequality is recreated anew in each generation, even among people who start life in essentially identical circumstances." For Jencks, inequality is not inherited. There is no single consistent variable which explains who gets ahead and why. It is as much luck as anything else.

The logic of this argument is developed by Jencks in his book *Inequality*. Not only can one not equalize opportunity, but even if one could, equalizing opportunity does not appreciably reduce the inequality in results. He concludes quite bluntly: "Instead of trying to reduce people's capacity to gain a competitive advantage on one another, we will have to change the rules of the game so as to reduce the rewards of competitive success and the costs of failure. Instead of trying to make everybody equally lucky or equally good at his job, we will have to devise 'insurance' systems which neutralize the effects of luck, and income sharing systems which break the link between vocational success and living standards." [73] The aim of social

---

[73] *Inequality*, pp. 8–9.

Jencks's key argument, to repeat, is that "economic success seems to depend on varieties of luck and on-the-job competence that are only moderately related to family background, schooling, or scores on standardized tests." And, as he concludes, "Nobody seems able to say exactly what 'competence' in this sense entails, including employers who pay huge sums for it, but it does not seem to be at all similar from one job to another. This makes it hard to imagine a strategy for equalizing such competence. A strategy for equalizing luck is even harder to conceive."

Since the factors which make for success are, for Jencks, simply wayward, there is no ethical justification for large disparities in income and status, and since one cannot equalize luck in order to create equal opportunity, one should seek to equalize results.

While Jencks's findings are important against the vulgar Marxist notion that inheritance of social class background is all-important in determining the place of the child—since there *is* social mobility in the U.S., about one-third of all children end up below their parents—and they disprove, once again, the stilted American myth that each person of ability finds a place commensurate with his merit, the inability to find a consistent set of relationships leads Jencks to emphasize "luck" as a major factor. But in his analysis, "luck" is really only a *residual factor* which is inserted because all other variables do not correlate highly. In and of itself, luck cannot be measured as a positive variable. While it may be true, as many studies show, that there is a low correlation between the career one thinks a man is educating himself for and the final outcomes, and that there is a measure of "luck" about the job one finds in relation to one's talents, the fact remains, nevertheless, that to keep that job, particularly at the professional level, a high degree of talent and hard work is required to succeed.

By emphasizing "luck" Jencks seeks to use the randomness of a roulette occupational wheel to minimize the *earned* quality of success. And it may be that there is much more luck to the occupational system than Marxists or meritocrats would like to admit. Yet "common observation" (that other residual category of analysis) would indicate that—again on the professional level at least—hard work is a necessary condition for success, and that if a rough equality of opportunity has allowed one

policy, thus, has to be equality of result—by sharing and redistributive policies—rather than equality of opportunity.

If equality of result is to be the main object of social policy—and it is the heart of the populist reaction against meritocracy—it will demand an entirely new political agenda for the social systems of advanced industrial countries. But no such political demand can ultimately succeed—unless it imposed itself by brute force—without being rooted in some powerful ethical system, and for this reason the concept of equality of result has become the Archimedean point of a major new effort to provide a philosophical foundation —a conception of justice as fairness—for a communal society.

In the nature of human consciousness, a scheme of moral equity is the necessary basis for any social order; for legitimacy to exist, power must be justified. In the end, it is moral ideas—the conception of what is desirable—that shapes history through human aspirations. Western liberal society was "designed" by Locke, Adam Smith, and Bentham on the premise of individual freedoms and the satisfaction of private utilities; these were the axioms whose consequences were to be realized through the market and later through the democratic political system. But that doctrine is crumbling, and the political system is now being geared to the realization not of individual ends but of group and communal needs. Socialism has had political appeal for a century now not so much because of its moral depiction of what the future society would be like, but because of material disparities within disadvantaged classes, the hatred of bourgeois society by many intellectuals, and the eschatological vision of a "cunning" of history. But the normative ethic was only implicit; it was never spelled out and justified.[74] The claim for "equality of result" is a socialist ethic (as equality of opportunity is the liberal ethic), and as a moral basis for society it can finally succeed in obtaining men's allegiance not by material reward but by philosophical justification. An effort in politics has to be confirmed in philosophy. And an attempt to provide that confirmation is now underway.

---

man to go further than another, he has *earned* the unequal reward—income, status, authority—which goes with that success. The important question of justice —as I argue later—is really "how much" unequal reward, in what dimensions, and for what.

[74] Classical Marxism always eschewed the task of creating a normative ethic for socialism. Kautsky, for example, in his *Ethics and the Materialist Conception of History*, argued that socialism was a "necessary" outcome of human evolution, and did not have to be justified in moral terms. It was dissatisfaction with this view which led a number of pre-World War I socialist philosophers, principally Max Adler, to provide a neo-Kantian argument—the superior use of Reason in a socialist order —as the basis of its desirability. The victory of Bolshevism after 1917, and the spread of Marxism-Leninism, reasserted the eschatological vision as the basis of socialism.

III

The starting point for the renewed discussion of inequality—as for so much of modern politics—is Rousseau. In his *Discourse On the Origin and Foundations of Inequality Among Men* (the "Second Discourse") Rousseau sought to show that civil society ineluctably generates inequality.

For Rousseau, the state of nature was a psychological construct that showed what men would be like without society. In nature and in society, there are two kinds of dependence. As he wrote in *Emile*, there are "dependence on things, which is the work of nature; and dependence on men, which is the work of society. Dependence on things, being non-moral, does no injury to liberty and begets no vices; dependence on men, being out of order, gives rise to every kind of vice, and through this master and slave become mutually depraved." [75] The movement from nature to society is a change in the character of dependence.

For Rousseau, there are also two kinds of inequality: One is natural or physical (such as age, health, strength); the other moral or political inequality is based on convention and established by the consent of men. [76] Inevitably, however, as society developed, the first led to the second:

Each one began to look at the others and to want to be looked at himself, and public esteem had a value. The one who sang or danced the best, the handsomest, the strongest, the most adroit or the most eloquent became the most highly considered; and this was the first step toward inequality and, at the same time, toward vice.

Since mind, beauty, strength, skill, merit, and talent established the rank and fate of men, it was necessary to have these qualities, or to dissemble:

. . . for one's advantage, it was necessary to appear to be other than what one in fact was. To be and to seem to be became two altogether different things; and from this distinction came conspicuous ostentation, deceptive cunning, and all the vices that follow from them. . . . Finally, consuming ambition, the fervor to raise one's relative fortune less out of true need than in order to place oneself above others, inspires in all men a base inclination to harm each other, a secret jealousy all the more danger-

---

[75] *Emile*, op. cit., p. 49.
[76] *The First and Second Discourses*, ed. Roger D. Masters (New York, 1964), p. 101.

ous because, in order to strike its blow in greater safety, it often assumes the mask of benevolence. . . .

Vanity, thus, was one source of inequality. The other was material differences rooted in property. Property in and of itself is good and productive. Labor gives a person the right to the soil, and continuous possession is transformed into property, thus establishing "the first rules of justice." Things in this state "could have remained equal if talents had been equal . . . but this proposition was soon broken; the stronger did more work; the clever turned his to better advantage; the more ingenious found ways to shorten his labor." And so one man had more than another.

Thus, does natural inequality imperceptibly manifest itself along with contrived inequality; and thus do the differences among men, developed by those circumstances, become more perceptible, more permanent in their effects, and begin to have a proportionate influence over the fate of individuals. . . . Thus, as the most powerful or most miserable made of their force or their needs a sort of right to the goods of others, equivalent to them to the right of property, the destruction of equality was followed by the most frightful disorder. . . .

Inequalities of various kinds become formalized, "but in general, wealth, nobility or rank, power and personal merit [are] the principal distinctions by which one is measured in society." Of these four types of inequality,

as personal qualities are the origin of all the others, wealth is the last to which they are reduced in the end because, being the most immediately useful to well-being and the easiest to communicate, it is easily used to buy all the rest: an observation which can permit a rather exact judgement of the extent to which each people is removed from its primitive institution, and of the distance it has traveled toward the extreme limit of corruption.

Thus, "from the extreme inequality of conditions and fortunes . . . come scores of prejudices equally contrary to reason, happiness and virtue." This is what one finds "in discovering and following . . . the forgotten and lost routes that must have led man from the natural state to the civil state. . . ." [77]

Since man cannot live in the state of nature, the problem is how to reduce the dependence of man upon man and yet make him a social

---

[77] Ibid., in seq., pp. 149, 155–156, 157, 155, 174, 176, 178. Cf. Rousseau's comments on wealth with Marx on the power of money, in the *Economic-Philosophical Manuscripts:* "Money is the alienated ability of *mankind*. That which I am unable to do as a *man* . . . I am able to do by means of money. Money thus turns each of these powers into something which in itself it is not—turns it, that is, into its *contrary*." (Moscow, 1969), p. 139. (Emphasis in the original.)

person, instead of a natural person. Rousseau's answer, of course, is the social contract, the tie by which men forswear both natural liberty and conventional liberty to gain moral liberty. One renounces one's self—one's vanity and the desire to dominate others—by becoming a member of the community; and the community itself is a single personality, a whole of which each citizen is a part.

These clauses [of the social contract], rightly understood, are reducible to one only, viz. the total alienation to the whole community of each associate with all his rights; for, in the first place since each gives himself up entirely, the conditions are equal for all; and the conditions being equal for all, no one has any interest in making them burdensome to others.

The price of equality, thus, is that "an individual can no longer claim anything"; he has no individual rights, "his person and his whole power" are dissolved into the general will.[78] Equality is possible only in community through the eclipse of the self. Thus, Rousseau pursued one logic of the meaning of equality.[79]

MILL AND THE LOGIC OF REPRESENTATION

For Rousseau, who sees social nature as ruled by passion and vice, equality is not an end in itself but a means of achieving civic virtue and making virtuous men; in his hierarchy of purposes, he retains the classical view of the goals of society. For a second, more diffuse kind of political thought, the purpose of equality is social peace, and its guiding principle is utility.

Democracy is by nature contentious because men constantly covet what other men have. Not all societies invite invidious comparisons. The peasant did not compare his lot with the lord; he had his allotted place in the scheme of things and accepted it fatalistically. Democracy, with its normative commitment to equality, inevitably provides an evaluative yardstick for measuring discrepancies in status, wealth, and power. Where one is barred from modifying these discrepancies, the result is often—in Nietzsche's term—*ressentiment*, or envy, anger, and hatred toward those at the top. As Max Scheler has noted:

---

[78] *The Social Contract*, book I, chap. 6, ed. H. J. Tozer (London, 1948), pp. 109–110. In this context, one can see *The Second Discourse* and *The Social Contract* as a unified social cosmology which lays out an Arcadia and a Utopia based on man's past, present, and future:

Past	Present	Future
State of Nature	Civil Society	Community
Natural Liberty	Conventional Liberty	Moral Liberty

[79] Any single conclusion drawn from a thinker as protean, complex, and contradictory as Rousseau is manifestly unfair. This is *one* reading, and one which various writers since the French Revolution have given Rousseau. It is borne out both in text and in history.

Ressentiment must therefore be strongest in a society like ours, where approximately equal rights (political and otherwise) or formal social equality, publicly recognized, go hand in hand with wide factual differences in power, property and education. . . . Quite independently of the characters and experiences of individuals, a potent charge of *ressentiment* is here accumulated by the very structure of society.[80]

Since *ressentiment* is the chief psychological fuel of disruption and conflict, the problem for the society is how to reduce it. And since inequality is not random but patterned—the discrepancies are grouped—all groups have to be included in the society and enabled to use the political system as a means of redressing other forms of inequality. Thus, the chief instrument of social peace is representation.

The rationale for this system was laid down by John Stuart Mill in his *Representative Government.* "The interest of the excluded is always in danger of being overlooked," he wrote.[81] The group he had in mind, at the time, was the working class. Although the other classes no longer "deliberately" sought to sacrifice the interests of the working class to themselves, the very fact that the workers were excluded meant that questions were never regarded from their viewpoint. Mill went so far as to argue that representative government can only exist when there is proportional representation, and one chapter of his book, entitled "Representation of Minorities," explores the Hare system for this kind of election, "a scheme which has the almost unparalleled merit of carrying out a great principle of government in a manner approaching to ideal perfection as regards the special object in view. . . ." What is good about that principle of government is that "it secures a representation, in proportion to numbers, of every division of the electoral body: not two great parties alone, with perhaps a few large sectional minorities in particular places, but every minority in the whole nation, consisting of a suffi-

---

[80] Max Scheler, *Ressentiment* (New York, 1961), p. 50. Emphasis in the original. Compare Tocqueville, in *Democracy in America:*

> One must not blind himself to the fact that democratic institutions most successfully develop sentiments of envy in the human heart. This is not because they provide the means for everybody to rise to the level of everybody else but because these means are constantly proving inadequate in the hands of those using them. Democratic institutions awaken and flatter the passion for equality without ever being able to satisfy it entirely. This complete equality is always slipping through the people's fingers at the moment when they think to grasp it, fleeing, as Pascal says, in an eternal flight; the people grow heated in search of this blessing, all the more precious because it is near enough to be seen but too far off to be tasted. They are excited by the chance and irritated by the uncertainty of success; the excitement is followed by weariness and then by bitterness. In that state anything which in any way transcends the people seems an obstacle to their desires, and they are tired by the sight of any superiority, however legitimate (p. 183).

[81] John Stuart Mill, *Representative Government* (Everyman Library edition), p. 209.

ciently large number to be, on principles of equal justice, entitled to a representative." [82]

The logic of minority representation is the quota. Any polity, to obey the dictates of equal justice, would have to insist that its representative body be made up of social units equal in proportion to the diverse composition of its membership. The Democratic Party, in its new rules for the 1972 convention, did exactly this in stipulating that all state parties had to take "affirmative steps" to make their delegations representative of their respective state populations in terms of minority groups, women, and young people (those from 18 to 30). [83]

But this raises two serious problems. First, how does one define a legitimate "interest," or social unit, or minority corporate group? In the early years of the Republic, it was argued that the states were the legitimate units of representation, and the Constitution, before it was amended, gave state legislatures the duty of electing each state's two senators. In the 1930s and after, the legitimate units seemed to be the "functional groups"—business, farmers, and workers. In the sixties and seventies, the units came to be biologically defined (sex, color, age) and culturally defined (ethnic, religious) groups. Yet if one sits in a representative body on the basis of age, sex, ethnic group, religion, or occupation, is that single corporate identity to be the overriding attribute which guarantees one's place? [84] It is an elementary sociological fact that a person has not a single identity but a multiple number of roles. Does a black women under thirty have three votes rather than one? Or must she choose a single attribute to be quotaed for?

Second, if political bodies are composed entirely of corporate groups, what happens to numerical majority rule? Do the few larger

---

[82] Ibid., pp. 261, 263.

[83] Thus, women made up about 38 percent of the delegates (as against 13 percent four years earlier), blacks 14 percent of the delegates (as against 5.5 percent in 1968), and delegates under thirty 22 percent (as against 4 percent in 1968). Yet the Daley delegation from Chicago, which was denied its seats on the ground that it was "unrepresentative" claimed that the rules were undemocratic since they had been freely elected by majority vote. What, then, is democracy—majority vote or representation by social group?

[84] The mind boggles at the logic of minority representation carried to its policital conclusion. If one observes the present claimants in the polity, a legislature on Mill's principle would be composed of three sexes: men, women, and homosexuals; three age groups: young people, middle-aged and senior citizens; four religions: Protestant (assuming no division by sect), Catholic, Jews, and Muslim (and what of Jehovah's Witnesses, Amish, and the like?); four disadvantaged minority groups: blacks, Mexican-Americans, Puerto Ricans, and American Indians; five middle-America ethnic groups: Irish, Italian, Polish, German, and Slavs; eight occupational groups, from the standard census classification. This leaves WASPs and "others" as only residual categories.

Though this to some extent caricatures Mill's argument in *Representative Government*, I have taken one crucial aspect to its logical conclusion.

corporate bodies outvote the smaller ones? The blacks, for example, one of the most disadvantaged groups in American society, make up about 11 percent of the population. In a few cities they are a majority, but these cities do not have sufficient financial resources for rehabilitation or improvement. The sociologist Herbert Gans has argued that no numerical majority will ever tax itself, or redistribute its wealth, to aid a minority, so that in a majoritarian society the lot of the blacks will never be greatly improved. In consequence, he argues that if equality is to be achieved, minority groups should be given special veto rights in the society.[85] This is, in effect, the principle of the "concurrent majority" which John C. Calhoun sought before the Civil War to protect the Southern states from being outvoted by the North.[86] It is also the logic behind the idea of "community control" over social resources, such as schools, housing, and the like. But is there, then, any wider social or public interest? If corporate or community groups are to control the decisions which affect their lives, by what right can one deny a Southern community the right to practice segregation? And if a local group vetoes the passage of a highway through its neighborhood, does it not thus impose a higher tax cost on its neighbors by insisting on this relocation?

The purpose of inclusive representation of all minorities is to reduce conflict, yet the history of almost all societies shows that when polities polarize along a single overriding dimension—be it class, religion, language, tribe, or ethnic group—there is bound to be violent conflict, and when there are numerous "cross-cutting" identities—in Holland, where there are both class and religious political parties, Catholic and Protestant workers divide so that neither religion nor class wholly captures a single allegiance—there is a greater degree of check and veto power in the society.[87] In short, can the principle of quota representation in the polity, defined along communal or particularistic lines, escape either the polarization or the fragmentation of the polity, and the fate of ataxia for the society?

---

[85] Herbert Gans, "We Won't End the Urban Crisis Until We End Majority Rule," *New York Times Magazine* (August 3, 1969).

[86] Calhoun argued that agreement requires a consensus of all the major interests or factions, rather than a simple majority of people which cuts across such natural or social lines as regions, groups, or classes. This was a caricature, though a brilliant one, of the Madisonian model. It was a philosophical argument about representation in a heterogenous rather than a homogeneous society, in order to sustain human inequality, white supremacy, states' rights, anti-majoritarianism, and minority power. It came, one should also note, at a time when American parties had begun to splinter. See James McGregor Burns, *The Deadlock of Democracy* (New York, 1963), chap. 3, esp. p. 57.

[87] For a comprehensive summation of this problem, see Lipset, Lazarsfeld, Linz, and Barton, "The Psychology of Voting: An Analysis of Political Behavior," in *Handbook of Social Psychology,* ed. Gardner Lindzey, vol. II (Cambridge, Mass., 1954).

RAWLS AND FAIRNESS

If Rousseau sought equality of result for the sake of virtue, and Mill equal representation proportionate to one's interest for the purpose of utility, the contemporary philosopher John Rawls wants to establish the priority of equality for reasons of justice. As he elegantly declares, "justice is the first virtue of social institutions, as truth is of systems of thought." [88]

What is justice? It cannot be the greatest good for the greatest number, for the price of those magnitudes may be injustice for the lesser number. It has to be a distributive principle for judging competing claims—i.e. the appropriate division of social advantages. For Rawls, this is justice as fairness,[89] and the foundation of fairness rests, initially, on two principles:

First: each person is to have an equal right to the most extensive basic liberty compatible with a similar liberty for others.

---

[88] John Rawls, *A Theory of Justice* (Cambridge, Mass., 1971), p. 3.

Justice, for Rawls, does not encapsulate all the energies of the society; it is a principle of distributive standards, and is itself part of a larger social ideal to which a society commits itself. He writes:

A conception of social justice, then, is to be regarded as providing in the first instance a standard whereby the distributive aspects of the basic structure of society are to be assessed. This standard, however, is not to be confused with the principles defining the other virtues, for the basic structure, and social arrangements generally may be efficient or inefficient, liberal or illiberal, and many other things, as well as just or unjust. A complete conception defining principles for all the virtues of the basic structure, together with the respective weights when they conflict, is more than a conception of justice; it is a social ideal. The principles of justice are but a part, although perhaps the most important part of such a conception. A social ideal in turn is connected with a conception of society, a vision of the way in which the aims and purposes of social cooperation are to be understood. . . . Fully to understand a conception of justice we must make explicit the conception of social cooperation from which it derives (ibid., pp. 9–10).

(All citations in this section are from Rawls's book; page citations appear at the end of each quotation.)

[89] The idea of fairness necessarily assumes a social *tabula rasa*. Rawls writes:

In justice as fairness the original position of equality corresponds to the state of nature in the traditional theory of the social contract. This original position is not, of course, thought of as an actual historical state of affairs, much less as a primitive condition of culture. It is understood as a purely hypothetical situation characterized so as to lead to a certain conception of justice. Among the essential features of this situation is that no one knows his place in society, his class position or social status, nor does anyone know his fortune in the distribution of natural assets and abilities, his intelligence, strength and the like. I shall even assume that the parties do not know their conceptions of the good or their special psychological propensities. The principles of justice are chosen behind a veil of ignorance. This ensures that no one is advantaged or disadvantaged in the choice of principles by the outcome of natural chance or the contingency of social circumstances. Since all are similarly situated and no one is able to design principles to favor his particular condition, the principles of justice are the result of a fair agreement or bargain (p. 12).

Second: social and economic inequalities are to be arranged so that they are both (a) reasonably expected to be to everyone's advantage, and (b) attached to positions and offices open to all (p. 60).[90]

The first principle deals with equal liberties of citizenship—freedom of speech, vote, and assembly; eligibility for office; and so on. The second deals with social and economic inequalities—the distribution of income and wealth, differences in the degree of authority, and the like. It is with the second principle that we are concerned. The controlling terms in the propositions are the ambiguous phrases "to everyone's advantage" and "equally open to all." What do they mean?

Rawls's argument is complex, yet lucid. "Equally open to all" can mean either equal in the sense that careers are open to the talented, or equal in the sense of "equality of fair opportunity." The first simply means that those who have the ability and the drive are entitled to the place they have earned. This is the conventional liberal position. But Rawls notes that it does not account for the distortion by social contingencies. "In all sectors of society," Rawls writes, "there should be roughly equal prospects of culture and achievement for everyone similarly motivated and endowed. . . . Chances to acquire cultural knowledge and skills should not depend upon one's class position, and so the school system, whether public or private, should be designed to even out class barriers" (p. 73).

The liberal principle accepts the elimination of social differences in order to assure an equal start, but it justifies *unequal result* on the basis of natural abilities and talents. For Rawls, however, "natural" advantages are as arbitrary or random as social ones. It is not "fair opportunity." "There is no more reason to permit the distribution of income and wealth to be settled by the distribution of natural assets than by historical and social fortune. . . . The extent to which natural capacities develop and reach fruition is affected by all kinds of social conditions and class attitudes. Even the willingness to make an effort, to try, and so to be deserving in the ordinary sense is itself dependent upon happy family and social circumstances. It is impossible in practice to secure equal chances of achievement and culture for those similarly endowed, and therefore we may want to adopt a principle which recognizes this fact and also mitigates the arbitrary effects of the natural lottery" (p. 74).

Therefore, Rawls concludes that one cannot equalize opportunity, one can only bend it towards another purpose—the equality of re-

---

[90] A final formulation by Rawls, having to do with priority and rankings, appears on his pp. 302-303. For the purposes of our argument we can stay with the initial formulations.

sult. "No one deserves his greater natural capacity nor merits a more favorable starting place in society. But it does not follow that one should eliminate these distinctions. There is another way to deal with them. The basic structure can be arranged so that these contingencies work for the good of the least fortunate. Thus we are led to the difference principle if we wish to set up the social system so that no one gains or loses from his arbitrary place in the distribution of natural assets or his initial position in society without giving or receiving compensating advantages in return" (p. 102).[91]

The question thus turns from "equally open to all," i.e. the distribution of chances for place, to the distribution of primary social goods or values, i.e. to the meaning of "everyone's advantage." That latter phrase, for Rawls, can be defined in terms of either the "principle of efficiency" or the "difference principle."

The efficiency principle is congruent with what welfare economics calls "Pareto optimality." The allocation of goods or utilities is efficient when one reaches the point where it is impossible to change an existing distribution pattern so as to make some persons (even one) better off without at the same time making some other persons (at least one) worse off. A utilitarian principle, "Pareto optimality" is interested only in a range of choices and is indifferent to actual bargains. For Rawls the difficulty with the principle of efficiency is that, as a matter of fairness, it cannot specify *who* should be better off or not worse off.

The "difference principle" simply means that if some persons are to be better off, the lesser advantaged are also to be better off, and in some circumstances even more so. If one gains, so must the others. "The intuitive idea is that the social order is not to establish and secure the more attractive prospects of those better off unless doing so is to the advantage of those less fortunate" (p. 75).[92]

---

[91] As Rawls further notes, "The naturally advantaged are not to gain merely because they are more gifted, but only to cover the costs of training and education and for using their endowments in ways that help the less fortunate as well" (p. 101). See, too, the discussion on p. 104 about whether individuals "deserve" the advantage of natural capacities.

[92] In an interesting comparison, Rawls (like Rousseau) takes the metaphor of the family as the model for this principle. "The family in its ideal conception, and often in practice, is one place where the principle of maximizing the sum of advantages is rejected. Members of a family commonly do not wish to gain unless they can do so in ways that further the interests of the rest. Now wanting to act on the difference principle has precisely this consequence" (p. 105). The difficulty with this argument —if one regards society as the family writ large—is that the family, as Freud has argued, holds together by love, which is specific. One loves one's wife and children —and tries to pass on one's advantages to them. Where love is generalized to the society, it becomes "aim-inhibited" (because one loves all) and is consequently weak and ineffective. For this reason, Freud argued that communism is impossible in the larger society. See *Civilization and Its Discontents, Standard Edition of the Com-*

This leads Rawls to his more general conception of social justice, or the social ideal:

All social primary goods—liberty and opportunity, income and wealth, and the bases of self-respect—are to be distributed equally unless an unequal distribution of any or all of these goods is to the advantage of the least favored (p. 303).[93]

For this reason, too, Rawls rejects the idea of a meritocracy. Although the meritocratic idea *is* democratic, it violates the conception of fairness:

The [meritocratic] social order follows the principle of careers open to talents and uses equality of opportunity as a way of releasing men's energies in the pursuit of economic prosperity and political domination. There exists a marked disparity between the upper and lower classes in both means of life and the rights and privileges of organizational authority. The culture of the poorer strata is impoverished while that of the governing and technocratic elite is securely based on the service of national ends of power and wealth. Equality of opportunity means an equal chance to leave the less fortunate behind in the personal quest for influence and social position. Thus a meritocratic society is a danger for the other interpretations of the principles of justice but not for the democratic conception. For, as we have just seen, the difference principle transforms the aims of society in fundamental respects (p. 107).

The difference principle has two implications for social policy. One is the principle of redress for individuals:

This is the principle that undeserved inequalities call for redress, and since the inequalities of birth and natural endowment are undeserved, these inequalities are to be somehow compensated for. Thus, the principle holds that in order to treat all persons equally, to provide genuine equality of opportunity, society must give more attention to those with fewer native assets and to those born into the less favorable social position. The idea is to redress the bias of contingencies in the direction of equality. In pursuit of this principle greater resources might be spent on the education of the less rather than the more intelligent, at least over a certain time of life, say the earlier years of school (pp. 100–101).

The second is the more general principle that talent is to be regarded as a social asset, and its fruits should be available to all, especially the less fortunate:

---

plete *Psychological Writings of Sigmund Freud*, vol. xxi (London, 1961), pp. 112–113.

[93] An earlier, slightly variant, version by Rawls appears on p. 62. The later version, emphasizing the advantage to the least favored, is more relevant to my argument. One can say in this context that utilitarianism, which is the logic of bourgeois economics, follows the indifference principle in that each person pursues his own goods independent of the others, and the invisible hand coordinates the society.

[The difference principle] transforms the aims of the basic structure so that the total scheme of institutions no longer emphasizes social efficiency and technocratic values. We see then that the difference principle represents, in effect, an agreement to regard the distribution of natural talents as a common asset and to share in the benefits of this distribution whatever it turns out to be. Those who have been favored by nature, whoever they are, may gain from their good fortune only on terms that improve the situation of those who have lost out (p. 101).

We have here a fundamental rationale for a major shift in values: Instead of the principle "from each according to his ability, to each according to his ability," we have the principle "from each according to his ability, to each according to his need." And the justification for need is fairness to those who are disadvantaged for reasons beyond their control.

With Rawls, we have the most comprehensive effort in modern philosophy to justify a socialist ethic. In this redefinition of equality as equity, we can observe the development of a political philosophy which will go far to shape the last part of the twentieth century, just as the doctrines of Locke and Smith molded the nineteenth. The liberal theory of society was framed by the twin axes of individualism and rationality. The unencumbered individual would seek to realize his own satisfactions on the basis of his work—he was to be rewarded for effort, pluck, and risk—and the exchange of products with others was calculated by each so as to maximize his own satisfactions. Society was to make no judgments between men—only to set the procedural rules—and the most efficient distribution of resources was the one that produced the greatest net balance of satisfactions.

Today we have come to the end of classic liberalism. It is not individual satisfaction which is the measure of social good but redress for the disadvantaged as a prior claim on the social conscience and on social policy.[94] Rawls's effort in *A Theory of Justice* is to establish the principle of fairness, but he pays little attention, other than using the generic term "disadvantaged," to *who* is to be helped.[95] His argument

---

[94] The claims of the poor are, of course, among the oldest traditions in Western thought and are central to the idea of Christian love. But Christian love—charity as *caritas*—accepted the poor as worthy in themselves and loved the poor as poor without endowing them with higher qualities than they possessed. In that sense, classic Protestant liberalism—with its sympathy and humanitarianism, rather than love—corroded the social conscience of the Catholic world. From a different source, the romanticizing of the poor, a tradition going back to Villon, also led to the erosion of *caritas* toward poor. (For a defense of Christian love as the basis of society, and a biting attack on English moral philosophy, i.e. Hutcheson, Adam Smith, Hume, see Max Scheler, op. cit., section IV, pp. 114–137.)

[95] It is striking that Rawls, like Jencks, does not discuss either "work" or "effort"—as if those who had succeeded, in the university, or in business or gov-

is set in social contract terms, and his "constitution of justice" is a bargain agreed to by individuals. Yet in contemporary society, inevitably, the disadvantaged are identifiable largely in group terms, and the principle of equity has become linked with the principle of quota representation.

The claim for group rights stands in formal contradiction to the principle of individualism, with its emphasis on achievement and universalism. But in reality it is no more than the extension, to hitherto excluded social units, of the group principle which has undergirded American politics from the start. The group process—which was the vaunted discovery of the "realists" of American political science (see the discussion in Chapter 5)—consisted largely of economic bargaining between functional or pressure groups operating outside the formal structure of the party system. What we now find are ethnic and ascriptive groups claiming formal representation both in the formal political structure and in all other institutions of the society as well.

These claims are legitimated, further, by the fact that America has been a pluralist society, or has come to accept a new definition of pluralism rather than the homogeneity of Americanism. Pluralism, in its classic conceptions,[96] made a claim for the continuing cultural identity of ethnic and religious groups and for the institutional autonomy of cultural institutions (e.g. universities) from politics. Pluralism was based on the separation of realms. But what we have today is a thoroughgoing politicizing of society in which not only the market is subordinated to political decision but all institutions have to bend to the demands of a political center and politicize themselves in group representational terms. Here, too, there has been another change. In functional group politics, membership was not fixed, and one could find cross-cutting allegiances or shifting coalitions. Today the groups that claim representation—in the political parties, in the

---

ernment, had done so largely by contingent circumstances of fortune or social background. There is a discussion of meritocracy, but not of merit. This itself is a measure of how far we have moved from nineteenth-century values.

It is equally striking that, in the "social-attention cycle," the policy concern a decade ago was with "excellence." The Stern Fund sponsored a major study on the identification of excellence; John Gardner wrote a book entitled *Excellence: Can We Be Equal and Excellent Too?* (New York, 1961). At that time, meritocracy was a positive word—so much so that Merrill Peterson, in his magisterial biography of Thomas Jefferson, said that, had Jefferson known the term, he would have used it to define his "natural aristocracy." Today the concern is almost entirely with equality and the disadvantaged. Will the "social-attention cycle" come full circle in the future?

[96] See, for example, the work of R. M. MacIver, *The More Perfect Union: A Program for the Control of Inter-group Discrimination* (New York, 1948), and on the religious side, John Courtney Murray, *We Hold These Truths: Reflections on the American Proposition* (New York, 1960).

universities, in the hospitals and the community—are formed by primordial or biological ties, and one cannot erase the ascriptive nature of sex or color.

And yet, once one accepts the principle of redress and representation of the disadvantaged in the group terms that were initially formulated, it is difficult for the polity to deny those later claims. That is the logic of democracy which has always been present in the ambiguous legacy of the principle of equality.

THE REDEFINITION OF MERITOCRACY

Any principle inevitably has its ambiguities, for no moral situation is ever clear-cut, particularly in the case of equal opportunity versus equal result, since the conflict is between right versus right, rather than right versus wrong. What, then, are the difficulties and the contradictions in Rawls's principle of fairness, and are they of sufficient weight as to render it nugatory?

First, what is the meaning of disadvantage? What is the measure of fairness? Is it objective or subjective? Often a sense of unfairness depends upon expectation and the degree of deprivation. But by whose standard? One measure, Rawls writes, "is a definition solely in terms of relative income and wealth with no reference to social position. Thus, all persons with less than half the median income and wealth may be taken as the least advantaged segment. This definition depends only upon the lower half of the distribution and has the merit of focusing attention on the social distance between those who have the least and the average citizen." [97]

But for most persons the question of unfairness or deprivation is not some fixed or absolute standard but a comparison with relevant others. We know from many sociological studies that large disparities of income and status are accepted as fair if individuals feel that these are justly earned, while small differences, if arbitrary, will often seem unfair. Orderlies in a hospital compare their income with that of a nurse but not that of a doctor. Thus relative deprivation and reference group (to use the sociological jargon) at each point stipulate the degree of disparity.[98] But are we to accept the subjective evaluations of individuals as the moral norm, or an objective standard, and on what basis? [99] The point is not clear.

[97] Rawls, op. cit., p. 98. The criterion of using half of the median was also advanced by Victor Fuchs in "Redefining Poverty," *The Public Interest*, no. 8 (Summer 1967).

[98] For an elaboration of these two concepts and their application to the subjective sense of fairness, see W. G. Runciman, *Relative Deprivation and Social Justice* (London, 1966).

[99] In classical ethical theory, the good is defined as independent of individual satisfaction. Aristotle distinguished between "being good" and "feeling good." A person having an adulterous affair feels good but is not being good.

If disadvantage is difficult to define, there is a different kind of problem in the identification of "the least fortunate group." Rawls writes: "Here it seems impossible to avoid a certain arbitrariness. One possibility is to choose a particular social position, say that of the un-skilled worker, and then to count as the least advantaged all those with the average income and wealth of this group, or less. The ex-pectation of the lowest representative man is defined as the average taken over this whole class" (p. 98).[100]

Problems of borderlines and shadings apart—and in practical terms these are great—the identification of social position in this fashion raises a serious psychological question. One of the important considerations of moral philosophy has been to avoid labelling, or public stigmatization, of the disadvantaged. This is one of the reasons why reformers have always fought a "means test" as the criterion for public aid and tried to provide help as a right. It is one of the reasons (administrative matters aside) why proposals for the redistribution of income have suggested that a stipulated sum be given to all persons, and that money above a certain level be recouped by taxation. Yet Rawls writes: ". . . we are entitled at some point to plead practical considerations in formulating the difference principle. Sooner or later the capacity of philosophical or other arguments to make finer dis-criminations is bound to run out." But it is exactly at those points where principle has to be translated into rule and case that the prob-lems of public policy and administration begin.

The question of labelling and redress leads back to a more general contradiction, the relation of equality to a principle of universalism. One of the historical gains of equality was the establishment of a principle of universalism so that a rule—as in the rule of law—applied equally to all, and thus avoided the administrative determi-nation between persons. As in the Constitution, this meant the out-lawing of bills of attainder which are aimed at one person; a law has to be written with a sufficient degree of generality so as to cover all persons within a category. In criminal law, we apply *equal punish-ment* to those who have violated the same law, regardless of the ability to bear punishment, and two men convicted of speeding are fined

---

[100] What if the "least fortunate" are there by their own choice? Christopher Jencks points out while "we have already eliminated virtually all economic and aca-demic obstacles to earning a high school diploma . . . one student in five still drops out." And while one may guarantee working-class families the same educational op-portunities as middle-class families, what happens if they don't want to use this op-portunity. Society may have an obligation to those who are kept down or cannot advance because it is not their fault. But if individuals—for cultural or psychologi-cal reasons—do not avail themselves of opportunities, is it the society's responsibility—as the prior obligation—to devote resources to them? But if not, how does one distinguish between the genuinely disadvantaged and those who are not? This is the inextricable difficulty of social policy.

twenty-five dollars each though one is a millionaire and the other a pauper. The law does not inquire into their status differences; there is equal liability. And the court is enjoined from so prying in order to avoid the enlargement of judicial power which would enable the judge to make determinations between persons; his function is solely to find out whether they are guilty or not.

Yet, in instances where wealth and income are concerned, we have gone far in the opposite direction. Under the income-tax law, which was adopted in this century, not only do individuals not pay an equal amount (e.g. $500 each), they do not even pay equal proportions (e.g. 10 percent each, which would lead to different absolute amounts on varying incomes). In principle they pay progressively higher proportions, as incomes rise. Here ability—the ability to pay—becomes the measure. It may well be that in the area of wealth and income one wants to establish the principle "from each according to his ability to each in accordance with another's needs"; the principle of justice here applies because *marginal* amounts must be compared. (If two persons pay the same amount, in one case it comes to half his income, in the other case only a tenth, and the same principle is at work in proportionate taxes.) But, in the larger context, the wholesale adoption of the principle of fairness in all areas of social values shifts the entire slope of society from a principle of equal liability and universalism to one of unequal burden and administrative determination.

The ground of fairness, says Rawls, is a generalized social norm founded on a social contract. It is based on the theory of rational choice whereby individuals declare their own preferences, subject to the principle of redress and the principle of difference; and this rational choice would push the societal balance toward the social norm. Now, utility theory can order the preference of an individual and define the rational conduct of that individual; and in utility theory society is rightly arranged when we have a net balance of individual gains or losses on the basis of the persons' own preferences in free exchange. But here we run up against a difficulty. If rationality is the basis of the social norm, can we have a social-welfare function that amalgamates the discordant preferences of individuals into a combined choice which recapitulates the rationality of the individual choice? If one accepts the theoretical argument of the Arrow impossibility theorem (observing the conditions of democracy and majority choice), we cannot have such a social-welfare function.[101] What the

<hr/>

[101] For the previous discussion of the Arrow theorem, see chap. 5. Rawls avoids the difficulty of the Arrow impossibility theorem by rejecting the condition of majority rule. As he writes:

It is evident from the preceding remarks that the procedure of majority rule, how-social norm is to be then becomes a political question, subject to either consensus or to conflict—extortion by the most threatening, or collective bargaining in which people eventually accept some idea of trade-off. But if the decision is political, there are then no clear theoretical determinations, set by principles of rational choice, of what the social norm should be—unless, in the Rousseauian sense, the body politic is a "single" personality. We may want a social norm for reasons of fairness, but in the structure of rational choice procedures we cannot define one.

If the definition of a social norm, then, is essentially a political one, the principle of helping the least fortunate as the *prior* social obligation may mean—in a sociological as well as statistical sense—a regression toward the mean. If it is assumed that we have reached a post-scarcity stage of full abundance, this may be a desirable social

---

ever it is defined and circumscribed, has a subordinate place as a procedural device. The justification for it rests squarely on the political ends that the constitution is designed to achieve, and therefore on the two principles of justice. . . . A fundamental part of the majority principle is that the procedure should satisfy the conditions of background justice. . . . When this background is absent, the first principle of justice is not satisfied; yet even when it is present, there is no assurance that just legislation will be enacted.

There is nothing to the view, then, that what the majority wills is right. . . . This question is one of political judgment and does not belong to the theory of justice. It suffices to note that while citizens normally submit their conduct to democratic authority, that is, recognize the outcome of a vote as establishing a binding rule, other things equal, they do not submit their judgment to it (p. 356).

Rawls is right of course, as with most traditional conceptions of justice, that the action of a majority does not make any decision just. The tyranny of a majority has long been recognized as a source of injustice, as much as the tyranny of a despot. The procedural question, however, is whether, as a *consistent* rule there is any better method than majority vote, subject to the democratic check of a minority having the right and ability to change the decision and become a majority, in reaching consensus.

Rawls seeks to avoid the Arrow dilemma by specifying a "veil of ignorance" when the initial social contract is bargained. Since each man does not know how well he might do, it is to his interest to gain at least a minimum prize. Thus, each man would accept a set of rules that maximizes the chance of winning at least a minimum prize, and he would therefore also want to make that minimum prize as large as possible. Presumably, such veiled bargaining should move the prizes (i.e. the primary social goods, such as income, self-respect, etc.) to the mean. Yet as Lester Thurow points out:

Although maximizing the minimum prize seems egalitarian, it need not be. . . . Rawls believes that the trickle-down effect is so large that it would be impossible to design economic activities that concentrated income gains among high income groups. As an economist I do not share this faith. There are many economic activities with marginal amounts of trickle-down. To be really egalitarian social rules would have to state that individuals must choose those economic activities with the largest trickle-down effects ("A Search for Economic Equity," *The Public Interest*, [Spring 1973]).

Thus, some coercive device may be necessary to achieve the desired outcome of a set of rules that will maximize the minimum prize, or give priority to the disadvantaged.

policy. But if this is not so—and it is questionable whether it can ever be so—and if one defines society, as Rawls does, "as a cooperative venture for mutual advantage," why not, just as logically, allow greater incentives for those who can expand the total social output and use this larger "social pie" for the mutual (yet differential) advantage of all?

It is quite striking that the one society in modern history which consciously began with a principle of almost complete equality (including almost no wage differentials)—the Soviet Union—gradually abandoned that policy, not because it was restoring capitalism but because it found that differential wages and privileges served as incentives and were also a more rational "rationing" of time. (If a manager's time is worth more than that of an unskilled worker, since he has to make more decisions, should he be expected to wait in line for a crowded tram or be given a car of his own to get to work?) Even those societies which have had relatively small differentials in income and incentives in the post-World War II years, such as Israel and Yugoslavia, have gradually widened these differences in order to stimulate productivity. And one of the chief pieces of advice which sympathetic economists have given to Fidel Castro to restore his stumbling economy (which has been largely organized on the basis of moral exhortation and the donation of extra labor time) is to make greater use of material incentives and wage differentials.[102] In the United States, the major period when social programs could be most easily financed was from 1960 to 1965, when the increase in the rate of economic growth, not the redistribution of income, provided a fiscal surplus for such programs.[103]

The United States today is not a meritocracy; but this does not discredit the principle. The idea of equality of opportunity is a just one, and the problem is to realize it fairly. The focus, then, has to be on the barriers to such equality. The redress of discrimination by representation introduces arbitrary, particularistic criteria which can only be destructive of universalism, the historic principle, won under great difficulty, of treating each person as a person in his own right.

The difficult and thorny question, in the end, is not just priority —who should be helped first—but the degree of disparity among persons. How much difference should there be in income between

---

[102] See Wassily Leontieff, "The Trouble with Cuban Socialism," *New York Review of Books* (January 7, 1971).

[103] For a review of the data, and the argument, see Otto Eckstein, "The Economics of the '6os, A Backward Look," *The Public Interest*, no. 19 (Spring 1970).

the head of a corporation and a common laborer, between a professor at the top of the scale and an instructor? The differences in pay in a business firm are on the order of 30:1, in a hospital of 10:1, and a university of 5:1. What is the rationale for these differences? What is fair? Traditionally, the market was the arbiter of differential reward, based on scarcity or on demand. But as economic decisions become politicized, and the market replaced by social decisions, what is the principle of fair reward and fair differences? Clearly this will be one of the most vexing questions in a post-industrial society.

A striking fact of Western society over the past two hundred years has been the steady decrease in the disparity among persons—not by distribution policies and judgments about fairness, but by technology, which has cheapened the cost of products and made more things available to more people.[104] The irony, of course, is that as disparities have decreased, as democracy has become more tangible, the expectations of equality have increased even faster, and people make more invidious comparisons ("people may suffer less but their sensibility is exacerbated"), a phenomenon now commonly known as the "Tocqueville effect." [105] The revolution of rising expectations is also the revolution in rising *ressentiment*.

The real social problem, however, may be not the abstract question of "fairness" but the social character of *ressentiment*, and the conditions which give rise to it. The fascinating sociological puzzle is why in democratic society, as inequality decreases, *ressentiment* increases. That, too, is part of the ambiguous legacy of democracy.

IV

A JUST MERITOCRACY

The difficulty with much of this discussion is that inequality has been considered as a unitary circumstance, and a single principle the measure of its redress, whereas in sociological fact there are different kinds of inequality. The problem is not *either/or* but what *kinds* of inequality lead to what *kinds* of social and moral differences. There are, we know, different kinds of inequality—differences in income

---

104 This is by now a commonplace argument, used tediously, often by apologetic propagandists for free enterprise. But this does not make it—as an historical fact —less true. For some striking comparisons on the exact amount of decrease of disparity, see Jean Fourastie, *The Causes of Wealth* (Glencoe, Ill. 1960), previously cited.

105 For Tocqueville's discussion of this phenomenon, see *The Old Regime and the French Revolution* (New York, 1955), part III, chaps. 4 and 5, esp. pp. 176–181, 186–187.

and wealth, in status, power, opportunity (occupational or social), education, services, and the like. There is not one scale but many, and the inequalities in one scale are not coupled completely with inequality in every other.[106]

We must insist on a basic social equality in that each person is to be given respect and not humiliated on the basis of color, or sexual proclivities, or other personal attributes. This is the basis of the civil-rights legislation outlawing modes of public humiliation such as Jim Crow laws, and setting forth the principle of complete equal access to all public places. This principle also makes sexual conduct a purely private matter between consenting adults.

We should reduce invidious distinctions in work, whereby some persons are paid by the piece or the hour and others receive a salary by the month or year, or a system whereby some persons receive a fluctuating wage on the basis of hours or weeks worked and others have a steady, calculable income.

We should assert that each person is entitled to a basic set of services and income which provides him with adequate medical care, housing, and the like. These are matters of security and dignity which must necessarily be the prior concerns of a civilized society.

But one need not impose a rigid, ideological egalitarianism in all matters, if it results in conflict with other social objectives and even becomes self-defeating. Thus, on the question of wage or salary differentials, there may be good market reasons for insisting that the wages of a physician and dentist be greater than those of a nurse or dental technician, for if each cost the patient roughly the same (if one could for the same price have the services of a better qualified person) no one would want to use a nurse or dental technician, even in small matters. The price system, in this case, is a mechanism for the efficient rationing of time. If as a result of differential wages the income spread between the occupations became exceedingly high, one could then use the tax laws to reduce the differences.

---

[106] Rawls writes: "One is not allowed to justify differences in income or organizational powers on the ground that the disadvantages of those in one position are outweighed by the greater advantages of those in another. Much less can infringements of liberty be counterbalanced in this way" (op. cit., pp. 64–65).

His argument is puzzling. In any interdependent society one forgoes certain liberties—in traffic and zoning regulations—to enhance others. Nor is it clear why one has to redress inequalities in every sphere rather than allow individuals to choose which sphere represents the most nagging inequality to them.

As a political principle, it is unlikely that any single rule can dominate a polity without disruption. Aristotle distinguished between two kinds of justice, numerical equality (equality of result) and equality based on merit. As he concluded: "To lay it down that equality shall be exclusively of one kind or another is a bad thing, as is shown by what happens in practice; no constitution lasts long that is constructed on such a basis." *Aristotle's Politics*, trans. T. A. Sinclair (London, 1966), pp. 191–192.

But the point is that these questions of inequality have little to do with the issue of meritocracy—if we define the meritocracy as those who have an *earned* status or have achieved positions of rational authority by competence. Sociologists have made a distinction between power and authority. Power is the ability to command, which is backed up, either implicitly or explicitly, by force. That is why power is the defining principle of politics. Authority is a competence based upon skill, learning, talent, artistry or some similar attribute. Inevitably it leads to distinctions between those who are superior and those who are not. A meritocracy is made up of those who have earned their authority. An unjust meritocracy is one which makes these distinctions invidious and demeans those below.

Contemporary populism, in its desire for wholesale egalitarianism, insists in the end on complete levelling. It is not *for fairness*, but *against elitism*; its impulse is not justice but *ressentiment*. The populists are for power ("to the people") but against authority—the authority represented in the superior competence of individuals. Since they lack authority, they want power. In the populist sociology, for example, the authority of doctors should be subject to the decisions of a community council, and that of professors to the entire collegiate body (which in the extreme versions include the janitors).

But there cannot be complete democratization in the entire range of human activities. It makes no sense, in the arts, to insist on a democracy of judgment. Which painting, which piece of music, which novel or poem is better than another cannot be subject to popular vote—unless one assumes, as was to some extent evident in the "sensibility of the sixties," that all art is reducible to experience and each person's experience is as meaningful to him as anyone else's.[107] In science and scholarship, achievement is measured and ranked on the basis of accomplishment—be it discovery, synthesis, acuity of criticism, comprehensive paradigms, statements of new relationships, and the like. And these are forms of intellectual authority.

All of this underscores a confusion between a technocracy and a meritocracy. Because the technocratic mode reduces social arrangements to the criterion of technological efficiency, it relies principally on credentials as a means of selecting individuals for place in the society. But credentials are mechanical at worst, or specify minimum achievement at best; they are an entry device into the system. Meritocracy, in the context of my usage, is an emphasis on individual achievement and earned status as confirmed by one's peers.

Rawls has said that the most fundamental good of all is self-respect.

---

[107] For a discussion of the context of this anti-intellectualism, see Lionel Trilling, *Mind in the Modern World*, The 1972 Jefferson Lecture in the Humanities (New York, 1973).

But the English sociologist W. G. Runciman has made a useful distinction between respect and praise. While all men are entitled to respect, they are not all entitled to praise.[108] The meritocracy, in the best meaning of that word, is made up of those worthy of praise. They are the men who are the best in their fields, as judged by their fellows.

And just as some individuals are worthy of praise, so are certain institutions—e.g. those engaged in the cultivation of achievement, the institutions of science and scholarship, culture and learning. The university is dedicated to the authority of scholarship and learning and to the transmission of knowledge from those who are competent to those who are capable. There is no reason why a university cannot be a meritocracy, without impairing the esteem of other institutions. There is every reason why a university has to be a meritocracy if the resources of the society—for research, for scholarship, for learning—are to be spent for "mutual advantage," and if a degree of culture is to prevail.

And there is no reason why the principle of meritocracy should not obtain in business and government as well. One wants entrepreneurs and innovators who can expand the amount of productive wealth for society. One wants men in political office who can govern well. The quality of life in any society is determined, in considerable measure, by the quality of leadership. A society that does not have its best men at the head of its leading institutions is a sociological and moral absurdity.

Nor is this in contradiction with the principle of fairness. One can acknowledge, as I would, the priority of the disadvantaged (with all its difficulty of definition) as an axiom of social policy, without diminishing the opportunity for the best to rise to the top through work and effort. The principles of merit, achievement, and universalism are, it seems to me, the necessary foundations for a productive—and cultivated—society. What is important is that the society, to the fullest extent possible, be a genuinely open one.

The question of justice arises when those at the top can convert their authority positions into large, discrepant material and social advantages over others. The sociological problem, then, is how far this convertibility is possible. In every society, there are three fundamental realms of hierarchy—wealth, power, and status. In bourgeois society, wealth could buy power and deference. In aristocratic society, status could command power and wealth (through marriage). In military and estate societies, power could command wealth and

---

[108] W. G. Runciman, " 'Social' Equality," *Philosophical Quarterly*, XVII (1967), reprinted in his *Sociology In Its Place* (London, 1970).

status. Today it is uncertain whether the exact relations between the three any longer hold: Income and wealth (even when combined with corporate power) rarely command prestige (who knows the names, or can recognize the faces, of the heads of Standard Oil, American Telephone, or General Motors?); political office does not make a man wealthy; high status (and professors rank among the highest in prestige rankings) does not provide wealth or power. Nor does the existence of a meritocracy preclude the use of other routes —particularly politics—to high position and power in the society.

But even within these realms, the differences can be tempered; and the politics of contemporary society makes this even more likely in the future. Wealth allows a few to enjoy what many cannot have; but this difference can—and will—be mitigated by a social minimum. Power (not authority) allows some men to exercise domination over others; but in the polity at large, and in most institutions, such unilateral power is increasingly checked. The most difficult of all disparities is the one of status, for what is at stake is the desire to be different and to *enjoy* the disparity. With his usual acuteness into the passions of the human heart, Rousseau observed: "[It is] the universal desire for reputation, honors and preferences, which devours us all, trains and compares talents and strengths . . . stimulates and multiplies passions; and making all men competitors, rivals or rather enemies, how many reverses, successes and catastrophes of all kinds it causes. . . ." [109]

Yet, if vanity—or ego—can never be erased, one can still observe the equality of respect due to all, and the differential degree of praise bestowed upon some. As Runciman puts it, "a society in which all inequalities of prestige or esteem were inequalities of praise would to this extent be just." [110] It is in this sense that we can acknowledge differences of achievement between individuals. It is to that extent that a well-tempered meritocracy can be a society if not of equals, then of the just. [111]

---

[109] *The Second Discourse*, pp. 174–175. In his economic lottery, Rawls would be forced to rule out the envious man. As Lester Thurow puts it: "Suppose the worst-off man were envious. In this case anything that lowers the income of better-off people faster than it lowers the income of the worst-off man maximizes the minimum prize. If envy were not ruled out, maximizing the minimum prize could lead to zero incomes for everyone."

Pareto, in his discussion of utility, argued that when income disparities are reduced, individuals seek to increase the inequalities in status and power (*The Mind and Society* [New York, 1935], vol. IV, sect. 2128–2145). For a further discussion of this question in relation to scarcity and abundance, see the next section, particularly the argument in footnote 126.

[110] " 'Social' Equality," p. 211.

[111] This essay has concentrated principally on the United States, but the question of meritocracy and equality is, quite clearly, central to all advanced industrial societies. It is no accident, perhaps, that the fable of the meritocracy was written in En-

4. *The End of Scarcity?*

For a number of writers, as I noted in the Introduction, the idea of a post-industrial society is equated with a post-scarcity society. David Riesman, when he first used the term "post-industrial" in 1958, was thinking of a "leisure society" and the sociological problems that might arise when, for the first time in human history, large numbers of persons had to confront the use of leisure time rather than the drudgery of work. Anarchist writers such as Paul Goodman and Murray Bookchin envisage a post-scarcity society as one in which technology has freed men from dependence on material things and thus provides the basis for a "free" relation to, rather than dependence on, nature. The elimination of scarcity, as the condition for abolishing all competitiveness and strife, has been the axial principle of all utopian thinking.

The postulate of scarcity has underlain the dismal view of society held by many philosophers. For Hobbes, "in the nature of men we find three principal causes of quarrel. First, competition; secondly, diffidence; thirdly, glory. The first maketh man invade for gain; the second for safety; and the third for reputation." [112] Thus men are

gland, where the social disparities (reflected in such things as language, accent, and dress) have been most acute, and where equality of opportunity was a revolutionary thrust of the technicians emerging from the middle class. But England, with its strong Labour Party (which has been acutely strained by the dilemma of either favoring a meritocracy, to increase technical progress and growth, or favoring policies that reduce inequality), will in all likelihood move toward increasing redress. In Sweden, Rawls's philosophy of "fairness" is likely to become the quasi-official philosophy. In the United States, the influence of the meritocracy has been exaggerated. Politics remains the major mode of popular control, and there are few codified systems of esteem to give any meritocracy an elite position in the society.

The country where the "meritocracy" will be the greatest problem is the Soviet Union. In its initial ideology, all social strata and social groups were declared to be equal in social status. But over the past two decades there has been a systematic effort to reward the elite, both political and scientific; and it is the scientific elite which has the greatest security of tenure. The political and scientific elites live in special sections, have special shops for foods, and even have special hospitals reserved for them. (Under Stalin, there were even specially privileged concentration camps for the scientists, a situation described in Solzhenitsyn's *The First Circle*.) Those elites are now passing on their privileges directly to their children, and one even finds, *mirabile dictu*, that official ideology keeps pace. Thus, in the authoritative Academy Journal *Voprosy Filosofi*, no. 2 (1972), two philosophers write that the hereditary tendencies of the Soviet System are a positive feature of the "period of highly developed socialism," as this aids the general and continuous rise in the welfare of all social groups. The sociological question for the Soviet Union is whether it will have a just or unjust meritocracy, alongside its unjust power. (This citation, as well as detailed data on the transmission of privileges in the Soviet Union, is in the study of Zev Katz, "Patterns of Social Mobility in the USSR" (mimeographed), Center for International Studies, MIT (April 1972).

[112] Thomas Hobbes, *Leviathan*, ed. Michael Oakeshott (Oxford, n.d.), p. 81.

constantly at war with one another for a greater share of the scarce values. For Malthus, scarcity is willed by Providence. Resources are limited, men's appetites are limitless; men must therefore learn to live prudently rather than prodigally lest their unchecked lust lead to over-population, famine, disease, and war. For Rousseau, scarcity is an artificial restriction which allows some men to flaunt their possessions before those who are kept from having them: ". . . if one sees a handful of powerful and rich men at the height of grandeur and for-tune, while the crowd grovels in obscurity and misery, it is because the former prize the things they enjoy only insofar as the others are deprived of them; and because, without changing their status, they would cease to be happy if the people ceased to be miserable." [113]

In his reworking of Marxism, in the *Critique de la Raison Dialec-tique*, Jean-Paul Sartre makes scarcity the central postulate of the "negation" which rules men's nature, and the *practico-inerte*, the "inert practicality," which is the failure of society to comprehend it-self *as* society. Because men begin in an environment of scarcity, each man takes his needs as the starting point for the social image of so-ciety; scarcity pits men against each other in the competitive struggle for survival. Each man sees in his fellow man the *other* who is a con-stant threat to him. Scarcity is "the negation within man of man by matter," the "negative unity" imposed by matter on society through labor and social conflict. War is the "inhumanity of human conduct as interiorized scarcity . . . which causes everyone to see everyone else as other and as the principle of Evil." It is only because everyone sees in his neighbor primarily the other—a generalization by Sartre of the lord-bondsman theme of Hegel's phenomenology—that his-tory developed as it did. History is the conjunction of *alterité* (other-ness) and alienation. History is the effort to overcome scarcity, and with it the blind operation of social forces—the *practico inerte*—that has bent men to others. [114]

Marx, as we know, rarely speculated on what the future society would be like. Yet it is clear from every aspect of his work that the condition for socialism, for genuine equality, was economic abun-dance. In the so-called *Economic-Philosophic Manuscripts*, written in 1844, Marx writes that the simple abolition of private property, and the equal sharing of goods, would only be "crude" or "raw" communism, only a form of levelling. [115] More than thirty years later, in a letter criticizing the program of the newly formed German So-

---

[113] Rousseau, *Second Discourse*, p. 175.

[114] For the discussion of Sartre's views I have followed George Lichtheim's "Sartre, Marxism and History," in *The Concept of Ideology* (New York, 1967), esp. pp. 301–306.

[115] Marx, *Economic and Philosophical Manuscripts of 1844* (Moscow, n.d.), p. 101.

cial Democratic Party, Marx returned to the theme and spelled out the difference between "equal right," with its inescapable degree of inequality, as a transitional phase of socialist society, and the kind of equality that would be possible under communism. Marx's most famous phrase about the character of communism occurs in this letter:

. . . equal right here is still in principle—*bourgeois right*—although principle and practice are no longer at logger-heads. . . .

This *equal* right is an unequal right for unequal labour. It recognizes no class differences, because everyone is only a worker like everyone else; but it tacitly recognizes unequal individual endowment and thus productive capacity as natural privileges. *It is, therefore, a right of inequality, in its content, like every right.* Right by its very nature can consist only in the application of an equal standard; but unequal individuals (and they would not be different individuals if they were not unequal) are measurable only by an equal standard in so far as they are brought under an equal point of view. . . . Further, one worker is married, another not; one has more children than another, and so on and so forth. Thus, with an equal performance of labour, and hence an equal share in the social consumption fund, one will in fact receive more than another, one will be richer than another, and so on.

To avoid all these defects, right instead of being equal would have to be unequal. . . .

In a higher phase of communist society, after the enslaving subordination of the individual to the division of labour, and therewith also the antithesis between mental and physical labour, has vanished; after labour has become not only a means of life but life's prime want; after the productive forces have also increased with the all-round development of the individual, and all the springs of co-operative wealth flow more abundantly—only then can the narrow horizon of bourgeois right be crossed in its entirety and society inscribe on its banners: From each according to his ability, to each according to his needs! [116]

The possibility of abundance, of course, lay in the extraordinary accomplishments of the bourgeoisie. In 1848, in a startling panegyric in the Communist Manifesto, Marx wrote:

[The bourgeoisie] has been the first to show what man's activity can bring about. It has accomplished wonders far surpassing Egyptian pyramids, Roman aqueducts, and Gothic cathedrals. . . .

The bourgeoisie, during its rule of scarce one hundred years, has created more massive and more colossal productive forces than have all the proceeding generations together. Subjection of nature's forces to man, machinery, application of chemistry to industry and agriculture, steam navigation, railways, electric telegraphs, clearing of whole continents for cultivation, canalization of rivers, whole populations conjured out of the

---

[116] *Critique of the Gotha Programme*, in Karl Marx, *Selected Works*, vol. II (Moscow, 1935), pp. 564–566 (emphasis in the original).

ground—what earlier century had even a presentiment that such productive forces slumbered in the lap of social labour.[117]

The achievement of the socialist society is the taking over of these productive forces and organizing them with conscious coordination for social ends. In the famous formulation of Engels:

Man's own social organization, which in the past confronted him as something imposed by nature and history, now becomes his own free act. The outside, objective forces which until now governed history, pass under the control of man himself. Only from then on, will man make his own history with complete consciousness. . . . It is the leap of mankind from the kingdom of necessity into the kingdom of freedom.[118]

Writing in 1930, during a worldwide depression, John Maynard Keynes quixotically asked, "What can we reasonably expect the level of our economic life to be a hundred years hence? What are the economic possibilities for our grandchildren?" The depression, he pointed out, was not the "rheumatics of old age" but the "growing-pains of over-rapid changes . . . between one economic period and another." The "disastrous mistakes" we have made "blind us to what is going on under the surface—to the true interpretation of the trend of things." The underlying trend of things could be seen in two innovations: the discovery of technical efficiency or productivity, and the sustained means for the accumulation of capital.

From the earliest times, back to two thousand years before Christ, down to the eighteenth century "there was no very great change in the standard of life of the average man living in the civilized centres of earth." But with the combination of technical efficiency and capi-

---

[117] *Selected Works*, vol. I, pp. 208, 210.

[118] Frederick Engels, *Anti-Dühring* (Chicago, 1935), p. 295, Marx, always more complicated and subtle than Engels, never went this far. In a parallel passage, in vol. 3 of *Capital*, Marx stated that the realm of freedom does not simply replace that of necessity—even the most rational organization of the economy can never wholly abolish labor—but retains it as in ineluctable fact to be shaped by men in that realm where "human energy is . . . an end in itself." (Moscow, 1965), pp. 799–800. For a discussion of these differences, see Alfred Schmidt, *The Concept of Nature in Marx* (London, 1971), pp. 134–136.

Yet there always was a romantic tinge to Marx, as one sees in the vision of Communism of *The German Ideology* (Moscow, 1964) written in 1845–46:

. . . as soon as the distribution of labour comes into being, each man has a particular, exclusive sphere of activity, which is forced upon him and from which he cannot escape. He is a hunter, a fisherman, a shepherd, or a critical critic, and must remain so if he does not want to lose his means of livelihood; while in communist society, where nobody has one exclusive sphere of activity, but each can become accomplished in any branch he wishes, society regulates the general production and thus makes it possible for me to do one thing today and another tomorrow, to hunt in the morning, fish in the afternoon, rear cattle in the evening, criticize after dinner, just as I have a mind without ever becoming hunter, fisherman, shepherd or critic (pp. 44–45).

tal accumulation, mankind had discovered the "magic" of "compound interest," of growth building on growth. "If capital increases, say, 2 per cent per annum, the capital equipment of the world will have increased by a half in twenty years, and seven and a half times in a hundred years. Think of this in terms of material things—houses, transport and the like." And to Keynes this meant "in the long run *that mankind is solving its economic problem.* I would predict that the standard of life in progressive countries one hundred years hence will be between four and eight times as high as it is today. There would be nothing surprising in this even in the light of our present knowledge. It would not be foolish to contemplate the possibility of a far greater progress still." [119]

On the basis of compound interest, an economy that grows at the rate of 3 percent a year doubles its gross national product in twenty-four years; one that grows at a 4 percent rate doubles it in eighteen years. During the 1960s most of the industrialized countries were growing at about a 3 percent rate, West Germany and Italy were doing better at 4 percent, and Japan was growing at a startling rate of 7 percent a year. On the basis of these rates, Herman Kahn and his associates, during the mid-sixties, made projections of the world's economies to the year 2000. Taking income levels as the criterion of division between types of societies, Kahn divided the world into five spheres:

1. Pre-Industrial	$50 to $200 per capita
2. Partially Industrialized	$200 to $600 per capita
3. Industrial	$600 to $1,500 per capita
4. Mass Consumption or Advanced Industrial	$1,500 to $4,000 per capita
5. Post-Industrial	$4,000 to perhaps $20,000 per capita

In 1965, only the United States and Western Europe (and possibly Japan) could be called mass-consumption or advanced industrial societies. By the year 2000, Kahn estimated, twelve countries would be "visibly post-industrial," and nine countries "early post-industrial." Seventeen more countries would have achieved the mass-consumption stage.[120] Of a world population of six billion persons, about

---

[119] John Maynard Keynes, "Economic Possibilities for Our Grandchildren" (1930), in *Essays in Persuasion* (New York, 1932). Quotations from pp. 359–364; emphasis in the original.

[120]   Economic Groupings in the Year 2000
         (The number in parenthesis refers to the income level in the text.)

Visibly Post-Industrial (5)	*Early Post-Industrial* (5)
United States, Japan, Canada, Scandinavia, Switzerland, France, West Germany, Benelux	United Kingdom, Soviet Union, Italy, Austria, East Germany, Czechoslovakia, Israel, Australia and New Zealand

a billion would be above the $4,000 income level, almost a half-billion above $1,500, and slightly more than a half-billion above $600, the industrial level. About three billion persons would be in a transitional stage, and the remaining billion in the pre-industrial stage. As Kahn points out, until the last two or three centuries no large human society has ever produced more than the equivalent of $200 per capita annually. By the year 2000, more than five-sixths of the world will have broken out of the historical range.

For the United States, Kahn drew an even more effulgent picture. By the year 2000, income would be tripled, reaching to more than $10,000 a person (in 1965 dollars) as against $3,550 per capita in 1965; and in a lesiure-oriented world each person would work no more than 1,100 working hours a year, broken down schematically as follows:

7.5	hour working day
4	working days
39	working weeks a year
10	legal holidays
13	weeks a year vacation.

Presumably, since many enterprises—automated production firms, utilities, hospitals, service institutions, retail stores, and the like—would operate more than 2,000 hours a year, or even round the clock, there would probably be two-shift arrangements, and "double heads" of operations who would take turns in managing the enterprises. In short, there would be a much more complex and differentiated pattern of work and responsibility in the post-industrial world.

This technological euphoria reached its vertex in 1964 with the statement of a group calling itself "The Ad Hoc Committee on the Triple Revolution." "A new era of production has begun," the Com-

---

Mass Consumption (4)
Spain, Portugal, Poland, Yugoslavia, Cyprus, Greece, Bulgaria, Hungary, Ireland, Argentina, Venezuela, Taiwan, North and South Korea, Hong Kong, Malaysia, Singapore

Industrial (3)
Union of South Africa, Mexico, Uruguay, Chile, Cuba, Colombia, Peru, Panama, Jamaica, North and South Vietnam, Thailand, Philippines, Turkey, Libya, Lebanon, Iraq

Early Industrialization (2)
Brazil, Pakistan, China, India, Indonesia, Egypt, Nigeria

Pre-Industrial (1)
Rest of Africa, Arab World, Asia, Latin America

The classifications in this section are taken from the first formulations by Herman Kahn and Anthony Wiener, in "The Next Thirty-Three Years: A Framework for Speculation," *Toward the Year 2000: Work in Progress, Daedalus* (Summer 1967), pp. 716–718. A later formulation, with more elaborate justification, appears in Kahn and Wiener, *The Year 2000* (New York, 1967). A somewhat different set of projections appears in Fremont Felix, *World Markets of Tomorrow* (London, 1972), which modifies the Kahn-Wiener extrapolations.

mittee declared; indeed, a new "cybernation revolution" was underway whose "principles of organization are as different from the industrial era as those of the industrial era were different from the agricultural." Cybernation—a term invented by Donald Michael —is "the combination of the computer and the automated self-regulating machine." The increased efficiency of machine systems "is shown in the more rapid increase in productivity per man-hour since 1960, a year that marks the first visible upsurge of the cybernation revolution." Cybernation results "in a system of almost unlimited productive capacity which requires progressively less labor." An "industrial economic system postulated on scarcity [is] unable to distribute the abundant goods and services produced by a cybernated system." The major change must occur in the relation between work and reward. "It is essential to recognize that the traditional link between jobs and incomes is broken. The economy of abundance can sustain all citizens in comfort and economic security whether or not they engage in what is commonly reckoned as work." Thus, the rise of a post-scarcity society marks a turning point in the most fundamental historical experience of man, the rootedness of his social character in work. Man will have been replaced by machines, and he will have to find a new purpose in the world.[121]

This was Keynes's theme, too, when he said that in the future the "economic problem" may be solved. "Why, you may ask, is this so startling? It is startling because—if, instead of looking into the future, we look into the past—we find that the economic problem, the struggle for subsistence, always has been hitherto the primary, most pressing problem of the human race. . . ." If the economic problem is solved, "mankind will be deprived of its traditional purpose. . . . I think with dread of the readjustment of the habits and instincts of the ordinary man, bred into him for countless generations, which he may be asked to discard within a few decades. . . ." Thus, "for the first time since his creation man will be faced with his real, his permanent problem—how to use his freedom from pressing

---

[121] The initiating individual of the Ad Hoc Committee on the Triple Revolution was W. H. Ferry, at the time a vice-president of the Center for the Study of Democratic Institutions at Santa Barbara, a Socratic Academy headed by Robert M. Hutchins. Much of the thinking behind the statement was shaped by Robert Theobold, an economist whose books (e.g. *The Challenge of Abundance* [New York, 1961]; *The Guaranteed Income* [New York, 1966]) had proposed the severance of the link between jobs and income predicted on the technological revolution he saw in the post-scarcity society. Among the signers of the statement were Michael Harrington, Tom Hayden, Gerard Piel, H. Stuart Hughes, Linus Pauling, John William Ward, A. J. Muste, Robert Heilbroner, Irving Howe, Bayard Rustin, Dwight MacDonald, and Norman Thomas. The coloration, as is evident, came largely from the socialist circles of the time. Quotations above are from the pamphlet issued by the Committee in April 1964.

economic cares, how to occupy his leisure, which science and compound interest will have won for him, to live wisely, agreeably and well." [122]

Has the economic problem been solved? Will scarcity disappear? Put in the terms which socialist and utopian thinkers have used—nineteenth-century terms—the answer is no, or not for a long time. For one thing, the cybernetic revolution quickly proved to be illusory. There were no spectacular jumps in productivity. The detailed study by the President's Commission on Technology, Automation and Economic Progress showed that for the past two decades there had been no sharp changes in the rate of productivity and, if one looked ahead ten years—the period for which one could identify oncoming technological developments—there were no increases in the offing. In fact, the prospects for the economy were quite the reverse. The expansion of the service sector—a significant feature of the post-industrial society—had become a drag on productivity, so much so that, as *Fortune* estimated, by 1980 the American growth rate would decline from 3 percent to 2.8 percent, a difference, in 1970 prices, of $40 billion worth of output a year.[123] Cybernation had proved to be one more instance of the penchant for overdramatizing a momentary innovation and blowing it up far out of proportion to its actuality. (One forgets that in a trillion-dollar economy, even a new one-billion-dollar industry is only one-thousandth of GNP). The image of a completely automated production economy—with an endless capacity to turn out goods—was simply a social-science fiction of the early 1960s.

Paradoxically, the vision of Utopia was suddenly replaced by the spectre of Doomsday. In place of the early-sixties theme of endless plenty, the picture by the end of the decade was one of a fragile planet of limited resources whose finite stocks were being rapidly depleted, and whose wastes from soaring industrial production were polluting the air and waters. Now the only way of saving the world was zero growth.

What is striking in this change is the shift in attention from machinery to resources, from man's mastery of nature to his dependence upon its bounty, from Harrod-Domar-Solow growth economics to Malthusian-Ricardian scarcity economics. And the principle of diminishing returns, rather than increasing yields to scale, becomes the analytical motif. A group of computer scientists at MIT, students of

[122] Keynes, op. cit., pp. 366–368.
[123] See *Technology and the American Economy* (U.S. Government Printing Office, 1966), and Gilbert Burck, "There'll Be Less Leisure Than You Think," *Fortune* (March 1970).

Jay Forrester, published a simulation of the world's growth, at current rates of use, in which the model traced the interconnections of four basic variables: resources, population, industrial production, and pollution. Their first projections showed a collapse of economic growth in a one hundred years because of a shortage in natural resources; food supplies would fail since fertilizer requirements could not be met. Second, they doubled the amount of resources, but in the next simulation the economy collapsed because of the rise in wastes. Third, assuming a three-quarter reduction in pollution by 1975, the model showed a continuation of economic growth, but the consequent expansion of cities and industries used up agricultural land so that food supply often ran short. Finally, when they assumed a doubling of agricultural yields, there was a huge industrial expansion, followed by a new collapse because of unmanageable pollution.

The admonition was clear. Societies had to limit their growth.[124] A hundred years ago, contemplating the vision of a cramped and depleted earth, on a smaller scale, John Stuart Mill had urged human society to limit its population and wealth and seek "the stationary state." Now Mill's injunction had been resuscitated. For the new ecological radicals, Mill replaced Marx as the prophet for the times.

The difficulty with the Forrester model is its simplified quantitative metric. The exponential growth of any factor in a closed system inevitably reaches a ceiling and collapses. (See the discussion in Chapter 3 on logistic curves.) It assumes that no qualitative change in the behavior of the system takes place, or is even possible. But this is clearly not so. Materials can be recycled. New sources of energy (e.g. solar energy) can be tapped. We do not yet have a full inventory of the mineral and metal resources of the earth (in the oceans, in Siberia, the Amazon basin, etc.). And technology makes possible the transmutation of resources. Taconite, once thought to be worthless, is now a vast source of iron ore; aluminum oxide, once a curiosity, has now become a source of hundreds of millions of tons of metal reserve because industrial chemistry reduced the cost of extraction. The ecological models take the physical finiteness of the earth as the ultimate bound, but this is fundamentally misleading. Resources are properly measured in economic, not physical, terms, and on the basis of relative costs new investments are made which can irrigate arid land, drain swampy land, clear forests, explore for new resources, or stimulate the process of extraction and transmutation. These methods of adding to the supplies of "fixed resources," as Carl Kaysen has

---

[124] D. H. Meadows et al., *The Limits to Growth* (New York, 1972). The logic of the model was first laid out by Jay Forrester in his book *World Dynamics* (Cambridge, Mass., 1971).

pointed out, have been going on steadily throughout human history.[125]

If in the foreseeable future—say for the next hundred years—there will be neither Utopia nor Doomsday but the same state that has existed for the last hundred years—namely, the fairly steady advance of "compound interest"—the banality of this fact (how jaded we soon become of the routinization of the spectacular!) should not obscure the extraordinary achievement Keynes called attention to. For the first time in human history, he reminded us, the problem of survival in the bare sense of the word—freedom from hunger and disease—need no longer exist. The question before the human race is not subsistence but standard of living, not biology but sociology. Basic needs are satiable, and the possibility of abundance is real. To that extent, the Marx-Keynes vision of the economic meaning of industrial society is certainly true.[126]

But this is to define the future in nineteenth-century terms which, it was hoped, would be realizable in the twentieth or twenty-first

---

[125] See Carl Kaysen, "The Computer That Printed Out W*O*L*F," *Foreign Affairs* (July 1972).
For a general examination of the apocalyptic hysteria of the ecology movement, see John Maddox, *The Doomsday Syndrome* (London, 1972).

[126] Yet, the fact that the problem is not primarily economic but sociological, as Keynes insisted, however, makes the resolution of scarcity that much more difficult. If we accept the arguments of thinkers as diverse as Adam Smith, Thorstein Veblen, and Georg Simmel, the fundamental impulse in human behavior is the desire to be different. And the urge to assert those differences in a visible way—the possibility of large discretionary income, the ability to fashion a standard of living to personal desire—all this leads to the pursuit of scarce and rare items as a means of emphasizing those differences invidiously.
For Adam Smith, in *The Theory of Moral Sentiments*, men's primary motives are not economic, since most persons could live on a small amount, but sociological: the desire to be applauded and to be considered superior. Men crave social prestige and social rank, and by this "cunning of social nature," civilization has been improved by the enterprises men have created to emphasize their distinction.
For Thorstein Veblen, the impulse toward "conspicuous consumption," which he describes in *The Theory of the Leisure Class*, is the expression of the desire for status differentiation which motivates all social behavior. In this quest, individuals seek "status-conferring goods," and those who seek to share that status emulate their styles. This is the basis of fashion as a fundamental fact in social behavior.
For Georg Simmel, human beings are impelled to seek what they do not have, as a way of gaining ego-satisfaction, and "the difficulty of attainment . . . is thus the element that peculiarly constitutes value. Scarcity constitutes only the outer appearance of this element, only its objectification in the form of quantity." Georg Simmel, "Exchange," in *Georg Simmel on Individuality and Social Forms*, ed. Donald Levine (Chicago, 1971), p. 69.
The dialectic of scarcity and abundance that we find in Marx and Sartre assumes that the economic needs of men are primary, and that social conflict, from individual strife to national wars, arises out of this scarcity. Yet the sociological argument emphasizes status differentiation as the primary motive, and here competition is largely unrestricted. As society expands its production of goods—and more means of differentiation are possible—the status race would be intensified.

century. The overcoming of scarcity, as it was conceived in the nineteenth century, was the problem of meshing machinery and resources, technics and nature, for *the production of goods*. But the post-industrial society, because it is not a design between man and fabricated nature but a game between persons, brings in scarcities of a kind scarcely envisaged by any social thinker before the present day. It is the new kind of scarcities which poses such vastly different problems for human society.

THE NEW SCARCITIES

The difficulty with the nineteenth-century conception of scarcity, which has carried over to the twentieth, is its definition of scarcity in physical terms; it was for this reason that abundance became counterposed to scarcity. But scarcity is not a "zero-sum" term of have or have-not. It is a measure of relative differences of preference at relative costs. In this sense the postulate of scarcity as an analytical concept underlies all of contemporary social science. It states axiomatically that all values (esteem, power, wealth) are scarce relative to desire; that all resources are scarce relative to wants. Economics deals with the allocation of scarce goods, political sociology with the regulation of competition among men for scarce values. To economize is to make the "best" use of limited resources among competing ends: the specification of the best mix of factors of production (at relative costs) with the most productive techniques (highest utilization) within the most efficient scheduling (programming) of the flow of items; the outcome is the largest output at the least cost. For this reason, the axial principle of economics is functional rationality. Political sociology is the study of the rules that regulate competition among men for wealth, power, and esteem. But men have to accept these rules as fair and right if this competition is to proceed; men seek just authority. For this reason, the axial principle of political life is legitimacy.

Central to all this is the postulate that any good has a *cost*, that there are few, if any, free goods. *For this reason, the measure of scarcity is the estimate of relative costs.*

We have had rising pollution because the polluters treat the abundant air and water as a free good; it costs them nothing to discharge their wastes into these places. But with the rising costs of cleaning up these elements, clean air and water are scarcer now than ever before. Relative scarcity is the measure of cheapness and dearness. Abundance does not necessarily mean that goods are more plentiful in physical terms, but that they are cheaper, because they cost less to make, or the yield at fixed costs is higher. (Land was always abundant, but the yields

466

were far less than they are today; it is the greater output at less cost that constitutes abundance.) To achieve one good means offsetting different (though not always measurable) costs in the price of other goods or values. There are no costless remedies. The reduction of unemployment may be at a cost in lowered productivity because of the employment of marginal resources or skills, or there may be a trade-off in the cost of inflation, or there may be a cost in the restriction of individual freedom. In a technical sense, the elimination of scarcity means a situation of zero cost, and this is impossible. In sum, the concept of the abolition of scarcity is an empirical absurdity.

If we think of scarcity in terms of cost, the post-industrial society brings with it a whole new set of scarcities for the society. Schematically, these are: the costs of information; the costs of coordination; and the costs of time.

Information. The post-industrial society is an information society, as industrial society is a goods-producing society. But the centrality of information creates some new, and different, problems for the society to manage. These are:

1. The sheer amount of information that one has to absorb because of the expansion of the different arenas—economic, political, and social—of men's attention and involvement. Classical utility theory assumed that the individual, as *homo economicus*, had complete information about the different goods available to him, estimated the costs, and made his choice to maximize his preferences. But *more* information is not complete information; if anything, it makes information more and more incomplete. In the political world one must keep up with the changing fortunes of several dozen countries and pay consistent attention to political situations in a half-dozen areas of the world simultaneously. And the cost of gathering relevant information necessarily goes up.[127]

---

[127] As Martin Shubik points out:

Rational economic man in the economists' model is one who knows what he wants, what his choices are, what his resources are. His value system is assumed to be well defined; his cool, consistent mind quickly and costlessly scans the myriads of alternatives facing him. His flawless discernment enables him to spy subtle differences in quality. He even calculates the value differences between the giant economy size and the regular pack. . . .

[But] man lives in an environment about which his information is highly incomplete. Not only does he not know how to evaluate many of the alternatives facing him, he is not even aware of a considerable percentage of them. His perceptions are relatively limited; his powers of calculation and accuracy are less than those of a computer in many situations; his searching, data processing, and memory capacities are erratic. As the speed of transmission of stimuli and the volume of new stimuli increase, the limitations of the individual become more marked relative to society as a whole. "Information, Rationality and Free Choice," *Toward the Year 2000*, p. 772.

2. The information becomes more technical. Today the discussion of international affairs involves a knowledge of balance of payments, of first- and second-strike nuclear capabilities, and the like; to judge economic policy on unemployment and inflation, one has to understand the intersects of the Phillips curve, the relation of monetary to fiscal policy, and the like. Information thus becomes more arcane, and one must study a subject more intensively than ever before.

3. There is a greater need for mediation, or journalistic translation: News is no longer reported but interpreted. There is the question of selection from the vast flow of information; there is the question of explaining because of the technical nature of the information. Not only do journalists have to become more specialized but the journals themselves become more differentiated—including the rise of a large number of "mediating" journals (from sophisticated analysis to vulgar simplification) that explain the new theories to intermediate and mass audiences.[128] The differentiation of journalism inevitably becomes a rising "cost" to the society.

4. The sheer limits of the amount of information one can absorb. In an essay I have referred to, George Miller showed that the "magical number 7 ± 2" is the outer limit to the span of control of the "bits" of information an individual can "process" at one time. There is equally an outer limit to the amount of information about events one can absorb (or the fields or interests one can pursue), and with the "exponential" growth of knowledge and the multiplication of fields and interests, the knowledge that any single individual can retain about the variety of events or the span of knowledge inevitably diminishes. More and more we know less and less.[129]

Coordination. The post-industrial society, as I have said, is a "game between persons," but a game between persons requires increasing

---

[128] One of the "structural" features of journalism in the past two decades has been the rise of such mediating journals—*Scientific American, The Listener, Psychology Today, New Society, The Public Interest, Transaction/Society*—and the decline and even demise of "general" magazines such as *Saturday Evening Post, Colliers, Look,* and *Life.* Increasingly *Time* and *Newsweek* devote sections to "Behavior," the "Environment," and the like, and such high-class literary magazines as the *Times Literary Supplement* and the *New York Review of Books* carry extensive *hautes vulgarisations* of the new work in linguistics, structural anthropology, and so on.

[129] On Miller's formulation, see "The Magical Number Seven, Plus or Minus Two—Some Limits on Our Capacity for Processing Information," *Psychological Review,* vol. 63, no. 2 (1956), reprinted in his book *The Psychology of Communication* (New York, 1967).

On the multiplication of cultural fields, and their consequences for knowledge, see my essay, "Modernity and Mass Society: On the Varieties of Cultural Experience," in *Studies in Public Communication,* no. 4 (Autumn 1962), reprinted, in part, in Arthur M. Schlesinger and Morton White (eds.), *Paths of American Thought* (Boston, 1963).

amounts of coordination, especially when that game is carried on in a visible political arena rather than through the "invisible hand" of the economic marketplace. The costs of coordination can be deduced from this change in the locus of decision-making.

1. *Participation.* The expansion of the political arena and the involvement of a greater number of persons simply means that it takes more time, and more cost, to reach a decision and to get anything done. More claimants are involved, interests multiply, caucuses have to meet, demands have to be bargained over, differences have to be mediated—and time and costs mount up as each person or interest wants to have his or its say. Often one hears the statement that individuals or groups feel "powerless" to affect affairs. But there is probably more participation today than ever before in political life, at all levels of government, and that very increase in participation leads to the multiplication of groups that "check" each other, and thus to the sense of impasse. Thus increased participation paradoxically leads, more often than not, to increased frustration.[130]

2. *Interaction.* In the expansion of the world sensorium, we exchange more telephone calls, travel more often, go to more conferences, meet more people. But with what result? Emile Durkheim, who first plotted the consequences of more interaction among persons, thought this would lead to a greater "moral density" in society, that individuals would become more free and independent and that "a greater development of psychic life comes from his greater sociability." [131] But at what cost? Either one accepts the fleeting nature of such encounters, or one encounters an "upper bound" which limits the degree of personal interaction. As Martin Shubik has observed:

In spite of growth in communications, has there been any considerable change in the number of individuals that a person can get to know well? Since spatial distribution has changed, the individual may select his friends from a larger set. Yet regardless of the growth of modern science and the speeds of transportation, an evening with a friend, except for the transportation factor, will still call for the same amount of time to be expended in the twenty-first century as in the nineteenth. . . .

Taking a few crude calculations we observe that if half a day a year is needed to maintain contact with a relatively good friend, then there is an upper bound of seven hundred people with whom we could have much personal interaction. How many cases can the judge handle? How many patients can the psychiatrist treat? Is personal interaction becoming a lux-

---

[130] For an acute case study of the consequences of this state of affairs, see Daniel P. Moynihan, *The Politics of a Guaranteed Income* (New York, 1973).

[131] *The Division of Labor* (New York, 1933), p. 347.

ury that the modern mass society cannot afford, or are there new social forms and institutions that will foster and preserve it? [132]

On this basis—720 persons, each with a span of seven—5,040 citizens would be the optimum size for the city-state of phila-delphia. What happens, of course, is that the number of contacts and interactions often increases at the expense of one's relatively good friendships. Increasingly, one goes through "cycles" of friendship while at a particular job or place, and then these end or become attenuated as one moves on to a different job or place. Thus, the increase of mobility, spatial and social, itself has its costs in the multiplication of interactions and networks that one has experienced.

3. *Transaction*. In our definition of freedom, we attach a high value to easy mobility and freedom from schedules. We seek to have rapid and easy access from our homes to any other point along the radius of the roads. Living further apart, we need to ship more goods—and to ship ourselves—across larger distances. As a result, we incur an increasing amount of what one might call *transaction costs*, especially in the form of goods and space devoted to communication and transportation.[133] Two cars per family no longer represent an increase in the standard of living. These are part of the rising transaction costs of the newer affluent life-styles—and they give rise to larger social costs in the congestion on the roads, the need for more parking space, air pollution, and the like. The costs of freedom and mobility in the end become quite high and must be regulated, or the life-style becomes self-defeating.

4. *Planning*. Inevitably a complex society, like the large, complex organizations within it, becomes a planning society. The large corporations engage in five-year and even longer-range planning in order to identify new products, estimate capital needs, replace obsolescent plants, train labor, and so on. Necessarily, government begins to plan—in dealing with such questions as renewal of cities, building of housing, planning of medical care, etc. The costs of planning, involving as they do research and consultation, inevitably become more expensive as more and more factors—and claimants—enter into the planning process. In the building of government-sponsored housing, for example (and almost all housing for low-income families in America today is government housing), the processes of planning—site selection, consultation, government approval—are so expensive that the overhead cost of starting a small housing project is al-

---

[132] Shubik, op. cit., p. 773.
[133] I am indebted for this term to Paul Hohenberg, from his talk on "Space, Economic Activity and Environment," before the Columbia University seminar on Technology and Social Change, March 9, 1972.

most as great as building a large one, which is why the government tends to foster massive housing projects rather than small scatter-site projects. *The paradox is that the economies of scale become the diseconomies of space.*

5. *Regulation.* The more income and the greater the abundance in a society, the greater becomes the need for regulation, and for an increase in the costs of regulation. It may well be, as Herman Kahn has predicted, that private income in the year 2000 will be $10,000 a person, as against $3,550 in 1965, but that person will not be three times better off, just as a person today, whose income is twice as high as it was twenty years ago, is not twice as well off as then. As incomes rise there is a greater demand for goods or amenities which are by their nature limited: access to parks, to beaches, to vacation homes, to travel. Forty years ago, the French Riviera was relatively uncrowded; today almost every French worker gets a month's vacation—usually in August—and the coastline is a jagged silhouette of high-rise hotels and apartment houses; the interstices are filled in with campsites. Unless vacations are staggered, or access to the area regulated, the amenities diminish. Yet this involves more planning, scheduling, and regulation.

Thomas Schelling has outlined a variety of interesting cases in which each individual may be acting completely rationally, but the result, without coordination, is irrational collective decisions. Because it is rational for each of us to work from nine to five, free choice leads to everyone working in those hours, though everyone is worse off than they would be if the hours of work were staggered. The example illustrates the universal dilemma of individual decision and collective interest. As Schelling writes: " 'Human nature' is easily blamed; but accepting that most people are more concerned with their own affairs than with the affairs of others . . . we may find human nature less pertinent than social organization. These problems often do have solutions. The solutions depend on some kind of social organization, whether that organization is contrived or spontaneous, permanent or ad hoc, voluntary or disciplined." [134]

---

[134] Thomas C. Schelling, "On the Ecology of Micromotives," *The Public Interest*, no. 25 (Fall 1971), p. 67.

Schelling also cites the homely example of an accident on the southbound lane of a major highway. Some drivers on the northbound lane slow down for a look, backing up all the traffic behind them. If there were a by-pass, most of the drivers might speed by, but lacking one, they are forced to wait for those ahead of them.

Everybody pays his ten minutes and gets his look. But he pays ten seconds for his own look and nine minutes, fifty seconds for the curiosity of the drivers ahead of him.

It is a bad bargain. More correctly, it is a bad result because there is no bargain. As a collective body, the drivers might overwhelmingly vote to maintain speed, each foregoing a ten second look and each saving himself ten minutes on

The moral is clear: Without appropriate organization, the results are apt to be unsatisfactory. But organization, too, has its costs, not only in time, personnel, and money, but in the degree of coercion required. As Mancur Olson, in his pathbreaking book *The Logic of Collective Action*, pointed out several years ago, the nature of collective goods or benefits is such that they apply to all in the group, and it is impossible to exclude any member of the group from the benefits. But for this very reason, there is often an incentive for each individual not to make a payment of his own accord since he will receive the benefit once it is extended. This is why, for example, trade unions seek to impose a closed shop or obligatory union membership on all workers in a plant in order to bar a "free ride" for those who do not pay the union dues. For a collective action to be fair, everyone must be required to join the agreement.

Again, greater abundance and more time for leisure create wider choice and more individual options, but also, and paradoxically, the greater need for collective regulation. If all people are to coexist in the world, there is a greater need for a social contract, but for that contract to work it must also be enforceable—which is also a greater cost.[135]

Time. Benjamin Franklin, that practical Yankee, used to say that "time is money," a remark that Max Weber regarded as the heart of the Protestant ethic of calculation. We usually think of time as a cost when applied to production. When a machine is idle—or "downtime"—costs mount up; an efficient manager seeks to get full use of the time of the machine. But the fact is, as Staffan Linder has pointed out in an intriguing work, consumption also requires time. In the modern economy, which is one of growing abundance, time paradoxically becomes the scarcest element of all.[136] Unlike

---

the freeway. Unorganized, they are at the mercy of a decentralized accounting system according to which no gawking driver suffers the losses that he imposes on the people behind him (ibid., pp. 65–66).

[135] See Mancur Olson, *The Logic of Collective Action* (Cambridge, Mass., 1965). For a discussion of this problem in the post-industrial society, see Francois Bourricaud, "Post-Industrial Society and the Paradoxes of Welfare," *Survey* 16, no. 1 (London, Winter 1971).

The problem of "collective action" applies particularly to the willingness of people to vote for "public goods," i.e. government measures which apply to all. For an important discussion of this problem, see Anthony Downs, "Why the Government Budget is Too Small in a Democracy," *World Politics* (July 1960), and R. Joseph Monsen and Anthony Downs, "Public Goods and Private Status," *The Public Interest*, no. 23 (Spring 1971).

[136] See Staffan Burenstam Linder, *The Harried Leisure Class* (New York, 1970). The theory of the scarcity of time was first given rigorous analytical treatment by Gary Becker, in "A Theory of the Allocation of Time," *Economic Journal* (September 1965).

For a useful exposition of these ideas, see Max Ways, "Why Time Gets

other economic resources, time cannot be accumulated. As Linder puts it: "We cannot build up a stock of time as we build up a stock of capital." In economic terms, there is a limited "supply" of time. And like any limited supply, it has a cost.

The poorest societies are those with most time on their hands. Productivity is so low that even a considerable amount of time on work yields little marginal increment. In such societies there is little need for punctuality or the measuring of time. There is always mañana. In societies where productivity is high, the allocation of time becomes a pressing economic problem, and efficient rationing is necessary to get the best use of time. The principle, thus, is simple: When productivity is low, time is relatively cheap; when productivity is high, time becomes relatively expensive. In short, economic growth entails a general increase in the scarcity of time.

In industrial society, the relation of time and work is analyzed in minutest detail. As I wrote many years ago in my essay "Work and Its Discontents," scientific management goes far beyond the old rough computations of the division of labor, and instead divides time itself. Working time, highly fractionated (in many industrial plants workers are paid, after an initial call-in guarantee, on the basis of tenths of an hour worked), is subject to measurement and allocation. Time, outside of work, is "free time" for play or leisure. But in the post-industrial society that "free time" also becomes subject to measurement and allocation, and the "yield on time" in those activities is brought into parity with the yield on working time.

There are three areas in which this calculus begins to take hold:

1. *Services.* Most of the consumption durables we buy—TV sets, autos, houses—have costs in the form of time required for maintenance. An individual can either take these costs out of his own time (e.g. paint the house himself) or engage a service man to do the work. When only a small proportion of people own many goods it is easy to farm out the maintenance cost. But as productivity rises and the high yield on time spreads throughout the whole society, the price of maintenance services rises too. Thus, as Max Ways points

Scarcer," *Fortune* (January 1970). Albert Hirschman, in his imaginatively titled *Exit, Voice and Loyalty*, has pointed out that when individuals confront overwhelming situations they can respond by leaving, speaking up for change, or remaining quiet. But each option has a calculus, and when the costs of one mount up it becomes a costly strategy. When too many people participate, others simply quit. As Hirschman puts it more formally: "As voice tends to be costly in comparison to exit, the consumer will become less able to afford voice as the number of goods and services over which he spreads his purchases increases—the cost of devoting even a modicum of time to correcting the faults of any one of the entities he is involved with is likely to exceed his estimate of the expected benefits for a large number of them." *Exit, Voice and Loyalty* (Cambridge, Mass., 1970), p. 40.

out, the consumer finds he needs more income to buy the maintenance time required for his consumer goods.

2. *Consumption.* The pleasures of consumption take time: the time to read a book, to talk to a friend, to drink a cup of coffee, to travel abroad. In "backward countries" with fewer goods to enjoy, there is more time. But when a man has a sailing boat, a sports car, or a series of concert tickets he finds that his "free time" is his scarcest resource. If he wants to go to the concert, he may have to rush through his dinner, and since good cooking takes time he may buy frozen dinners which can be cooked quickly (microwave ovens halve cooking time). If he goes to a concert, and takes his dinner afterwards, he may have to stay up too late and thus lose sleep in order to get to work "on time." If he could cut down the "on time" requirements, he would have more time; but then he would have to be quite wealthy or retired. So he must ration and allocate his time.

3. *Time-savers.* Since "free time" becomes more and more precious, the consumer will tend to buy those items that require relatively little of his non-work time and relatively more of his income from work. He will buy items that he can use and then throw away. He will "contract out" various services or maintenances (as he now sends clothes to the dry cleaners). And to do this he may have to work longer in order to acquire the kinds of goods and services that give him a high yield on his non-work time. But the cost may be too high and he has to begin to reckon his trade-offs. He must calculate relative prices and yields from different allocations of time and money. He may find that because of high maintenance cost he will do his own laundry or dry cleaning in a self-service store, thus spending part of his time to save money. Or he may want to spend money to save time. In balancing these considerations he begins to plot (without knowing that he is doing technical economics) an indifference curve of differential scales of substitution (of time and money) and the marginal utility of each unit of satisfaction in the different sectors of his expenditures. Low yields have to be transferred to high yields until, at the end, his resources have been so efficiently distributed as to give him an equal yield in all sectors of use. Economic abundance thus reintroduces utility by the back door of time. Man, in his leisure time, has become *homo economicus.*

In cruel fashion, Utopia thus stands confounded.[137] The end of scarcity, as it was envisaged by nineteenth-century writers, would

---

[137] Nicholas Georgescu-Roegen has devised a very different kind of theoretical argument against the idea that scarcity can ever be eliminated. This argument, generalized as the Entropy Law, states that energy is not reversible: If the energy of a piece of coal or of uranium could be used over and over again, scarcity would then

bring such a plethora of goods that man would no longer need to delay his gratifications or live like a calculating machine. Men could throw prudence to the winds, indulge their prodigal appetites, and live spontaneously and joyously with one another.

And yet it has all been turned around. Industrial society is spectacularly devoted to the production of things (and man's dependence upon them). But in the post-industrial society, the multiplication of things, and their rising custodial costs, brings time into the calculus of allocating one's personal activities; men become enslaved to its measurement through marginal utility.

In Utopia (as in the market economy) each man was free to pursue his own interest, but in the post-industrial society—where the relation among men (rather than between man and nature, or man and things) becomes the primary mode of interaction—the clash of individual interests, each following its own whim, leads necessarily to a greater need for collective regulation and a greater degree of coercion (with a reduction in a personal freedom) in order to have effective communal action. And when individuals demand full participation in the decisions that affect their lives, the consequence is an increase in information costs and in the time required for bargaining each against each in order to reach agreement on action.

The end of scarcity, it was believed—the leap from the kingdom of necessity—would be the freeing of time from the inexorable rhythm of economic life. In the end, all time has become an economic calculus. As Auden put it, "Time will say only, I told you so."

5. *Culture and Consciousness*

What is common to all sociological thought today is the sense of a profound transformation in industrial society. Some writers have focused on structural and social combinations—the new science-based technology, the change in sectors of the economy, the shifts in the occupational system and the like—and see in these permuta-

---

hardly exist. Even the re-use of scrap materials involves "a greater amount of low entropy than the difference between the entropy of the finished product" and that of the scrap. As Georgescu-Roegen points out, this illustrates the thesis that "thermodynamics is a blend of physics and economics." Professor Georgescu-Roegen's examples are in the context of an argument against the "equilibrium models" of economics, based on classical mechanics; he seeks to establish, analytically, an evolutionary model based on irrevocable qualitative change. And the "running down" process of energy—the idea of entropy—becomes an argument, too, against the idea that scarcity can be eliminated. See *The Entropy Law and the Economic Process* (Cambridge, Mass., 1971), chap. 10, esp. 277–282.

tions the major source of all other shifts in the society. From this viewpoint, the changes in values and attitudes, particularly the anti-scientism of the youth and the intellectuals, are seen as "counter-rev-olutionary." Other writers—Norman O. Brown, Michel Fou-cault, R. D. Laing, and their *epigones* such as Charles Reich and Theodore Roszak—place the transformation of the society in con-sciousness: a new polymorph sensuality, the lifting of repression, the permeability of madness and normality, a new psychedelic awareness, the exploration of pleasure.

Formulated in these contrasting ways, the changes invariably raise the question, Which of these changes is primary—social structure or culture—and which is the initiating force? Paradoxically, those who emphasize the economic and structural changes, in the tradi-tional Marxist method, are labelled conservative and technocratic, while those who emphasize the autonomy of consciousness—the realm of ideology—are called revolutionary.

The difficulty with this confrontation is not the correctness of each description—to considerable degree both are right—but the effort to force a conclusion. Such efforts, methodologically, derive from the prevailing view in sociology that society is integral: in He-gel's sense, an organic whole; or as Marx put it, that a single organiz-ing institution (e.g. commodity production) frames the entire society; or that, as Weber would have it, a common mode of life (e.g. ration-alization) permeates all aspects of behavior.

For Hegel, every society is a structurally interrelated whole, orga-nized through a single "moment" (a state of historical development) of consciousness. No aspect of that whole can be understood as an isolated phenomenon. Marx, in his famous formulation, declared that "The sum total of [the] relations of production constitutes the eco-nomic structure of society—the real foundation, on which rise legal and political superstructures and to which correspond definite forms of social consciousness. The mode of production in material life determines the general character of the social, political and spiri-tual processes of life." [138] And Weber believed that "In the last resort the factor which produced capitalism is the rational permanent enter-prise, rational accounting, rational technology and rational law, but again not these alone. Necessary complementary factors were the ra-tional spirit, the rationalization of the conduct of life and a rationalis-tic economic-ethic. [139]

---

[138] Marx, "Author's Preface," *Contribution to the Critique of Political Economy* (Chicago, 1904), p. 11.
[139] Weber, *General Economic History* (London, n.d.), p. 354. Weber was so im-pressed with the pervasiveness of rationalization in Western life that in 1910 he wrote an essay entitled "The Rational and Social Foundations of Music," in which

Of the great synoptic efforts in contemporary sociology to create a theory of society, we find Sorokin emphasizing the role of unitary "mentalities" (e.g. the "sensate" and the "ideational"), or Parsons emphasizing values as the ordering principle which in hierarchical fashion shapes all the other components of social structure, namely norms, collectivities, and roles. Thus, all the major sociological figures have, in one way or another, understood society as a unity of social structure and culture.

Contrary to these conceptions, what has been happening in Western society for the past hundred years, I believe, is a widening disjunction between the social structure (the economy, technology, and occupational system) and the culture (the symbolic expression of meanings), each of which is ruled by a different axial principle. The social structure is rooted in functional rationality and efficiency, the culture in the antinomian justification of the enhancement of the self.

The sources of each impulse are quite different. The "life-style" of the social structure was shaped by the principle of calculation, the rationalization of work and of time, and a linear sense of progress. All of this derived, fundamentally, from the effort to master nature by technics, to substitute wholly new rhythms of life for those bound to the regularities of the season and the diminishing returns of the soil. Technical mastery was in turn fused with a character structure which accepted the idea of delayed gratification, of compulsive dedication to work, of frugality and sobriety, and which was sanctified by the morality of service to God and the proof of self-worth through the idea of respectability. To this extent, bourgeois society of the nineteenth century was an integrated whole in which culture, character structure, and economy were infused by a single value system. This was the civilization of capitalism at its apogee.

Ironically, all this was undermined by capitalism itself. Through mass production and mass consumption, it destroyed the Protestant ethic by zealously promoting a hedonistic way of life. By the middle of the twentieth century capitalism sought to justify itself not by work or property, but by the status badges of material possessions and by the promotion of pleasure. The rising standard of living and the relaxation of morals became ends in themselves as the definition of personal freedom.

The result has been a disjunction within the social structure itself. In the organization of production and work, the system demands

---

he compared the Western organization of the division of the octabe with the musical forms of China, Japan, Arabia, Islam, and Black Africa, to show the distinctiveness of Western modes in the rise of polyphony and counterpoint as the basis of the rationalization of music.

477

provident behavior, industriousness and self-control, dedication to a career and success. In the realm of consumption, it fosters the attitude of *carpe diem*, prodigality and display, and the compulsive search for play. But in both realms the system is completely mundane, for any transcendent ethic has vanished.

If the modern social structure—based as it is on technics and metrics—is a distinctively new kind of social organization in human history, then contemporary culture, in its concern with the self, combines the deepest wellsprings of human impulse with the modern antipathy to bourgeois society.

The antinomian dimension of culture has been a recurrent feature of human society, in which the dialectic of restraint and release was played out originally in religion and then in the secular moral order itself. The antinomian attitude, in fact, is the repeated effort of the self to reach out "beyond": to attain some form of ecstasy (*ex-stasis*, the leaving of the body); to become self-infinitizing or idolatrous; to assert immorality or omnipotence. Its source is the finitude of creaturehood and the denial by the self of the reality of death. It is the radical "I" asserting its imperishable survival against imperious fate. One finds this expressed in ancient times in the Dionysian revels, and in early Christian times in a gnosticism which thought itself absolved of obligation to the moral law. In modern society this psychological solipsism reacted most sharply against the efforts of bourgeois society to impose repressive constraints on the spontaneous acting-out of impulsive desires. The nineteenth-century antinomian impulse found its cultural expression in such anti-bourgeois attitudes as romanticism, "dandyism," "estheticism," and other modes that counterposed the "natural man" to society, or the "self" against society. The theme expressed most radically in such writers as Baudelaire, Lautrèamont, and Rimbaud is that of the "authentic" self, free to explore all dimensions of human experience and to follow those impulses regardless of convention and law.

What in the nineteenth century was private and hermetic has become, in the twentieth-century effulgence of modernism, public and ideological. Contemporary culture, with the victory of modernism, has become anti-institutional and antinomian. Few writers "defend" society or institutions against the "imperial self," to use Quentin Anderson's citation. The older artistic imagination, however wild or perverse, was constrained by the shaping discipline of art. The new sensibility breaks down all genres and denies that there is any distinction between art and life. Art was formerly an experience; now all experience is to be turned into art.

These anti-bourgeois values, on the levels of ideology and consciousness, go hand in hand with the expansion of a new intellectual class huge enough to sustain itself economically *as* a class, and with the emergence of a large new youth movement which seeks expression and self-definition in altered states of consciousness, cultural rebellion, and enormous personal freedom. What has emerged, coincident in time, is both an "adversary culture" and a "counter-culture."

The adversary culture derives historically from the modernist movement and carries the flag of anti-bourgeois values. It draws upon the realm of imagination and art, and particularly the different kinds of experimental and "difficult" art which gave such vitality to literature, music, painting, and poetry in the first decades of the twentieth century. What such art does, primarily, is to break up the "rational cosmology" of ordered time and space, of sequence and proportion, of foreground and background, of distance and control, which had been the esthetic modes of organizing experience from the fifteenth to the nineteenth centuries. Through modernism, the antinomian impulse has captured the highbrow culture of literature and the arts.

The counter-culture is a revolution in life-style which sanctions the acting-out of impulse, the exploration of fantasy, the search for polymorphic pleasure in the name of liberation from restraint. It proclaims itself "daring" and in revolt against bourgeois society. But in fact bourgeois culture vanished long ago. What the counter-culture has done is to extend the double tendencies of cultural modernism and capitalist marketing hedonism initiated sixty years ago. It seeks to take the creed of personal freedom, extreme experience, and sexual experimentation into areas where the liberal culture—which would accept such ideas in art and imagination—is not prepared to go. Yet the liberal culture finds itself at a loss to explain its reticence. It approves a basic permissiveness, but cannot with any certainty define the bounds. And it leaves the moral order in a state of confusion and disarray. For this reason liberalism may yet suffer a reaction.

Ideas and cultural styles do not change history—at least, not overnight. But they are the necessary preludes to change, since a change in consciousness—in values and moral reasoning—is what moves men to change their social arrangements and institutions.

This is the cultural dilemma of capitalist society: it must now acknowledge the triumph (albeit tempered) of an adversary "ideology," the emergence of a new class which sustains this ideology, and the collapse of the older value system which was, ironically, undermined by the structural transformation of capitalism itself. The inimical ideology is not the secular socialism of the working class—if anything, the working class covets ever-expanding goods and production—but the cultural chic of "modernism" which retains its subversive thrust however much it is absorbed by the system. This new class, which dominates the media and the culture, thinks of itself less as radical than "liberal," yet its values, centered on "personal freedom," are profoundly anti-bourgeois. The value system of capitalism repeats the old pieties, but these are now hollow because they contradict the reality, the hedonistic life-styles promoted by the system itself.

Like any chiasmus in culture, the cross-over cannot be pinpointed at a particular moment of time. The ideological roots go back to the literary cenacles of a hundred or more years ago, the changes in the life-style promoted by capitalism fifty years ago, and the expansion of the new intellectual class within the last decade. A cultural crisis cannot be resolved, like a political problem, by the inclusion or exclusion of a particular social group; it lies deep in the character of the values which sustain or fail to sustain a system. For this reason the cultural paradox is a continuing crisis of capitalist society.

In a post-industrial society, the disjunction of culture and social structure is bound to widen. The historic justifications of bourgeois society—in the realms of religion and character—are gone. The traditional legitimacies of property and work become subordinated to bureaucratic enterprises that can justify privilege because they can turn out material goods more efficiently than other modes of production. But a technocratic society is not ennobling. Material goods provide only transient satisfaction or an invidious superiority over those with less. Yet one of the deepest human impulses is to *sanctify* their institutions and beliefs in order to find a meaningful purpose in their lives and to deny the meaninglessness of death. A post-industrial society cannot provide a transcendent ethic—except for the few who devote themselves to the temple of science. And the antinomian attitude plunges one into a radical autism which, in the end, dirempts the cords of community and the sharing with others. The lack of a rooted moral belief system is the cultural contradiction of the society, the deepest challenge to its survival.[140]

THE POLITY AS ARBITER

The post-industrial society is a crescive, unplanned change in the character of society, the working out of the logic of socio-economic

---

[140] These themes are explored in a work in progress on the character of contemporary culture. Parts of this work have appeared in several publications in recent years. The essay "The Cultural Contradictions of Capitalism," *The Public Interest*, no. 21 (Fall 1970), reprinted in Daniel Bell and Irving Kristol, eds., *Capitalism Today* (New York, 1971), deals with the emergence of the "adversary culture" in relation to the changes of capitalist ethos; the essay "Sensibility in the Sixties," *Commentary* (June 1971), discusses the break-up of traditional methods in painting, literature, and criticism in the search for novelty and experience in the arts; the essay "Religion in the Sixties," *Social Research* (Fall 1971), argues that "when religions fail, cults appear," and analyzes the rise of different cults in the sixties. An earlier formulation of the theme of the "disjunction of culture and social structure" is in the volume *Sci-*

organization, and a change in the character of knowledge. At some point, the major social groups in society become conscious of the underlying social transformation and have to decide, politically, whether to accept the drift, accelerate it, impede it, or change its direction.

Politics, in contemporary society, is the management of social structure. It becomes the regulative mechanism of change. But any political decision necessarily involves some conception of justice, traditional, implicit, and now increasingly explicit. Men accept different principles of justice, or different hierarchies of value, and seek to embody them in social arrangements. Ultimately the differences between social systems lie not in their social structures (the arrangements of reward and privilege around the organization of the economy) but in their ethos. Capitalism was not just a system for the production of commodities, or a new set of occupations, or a new principle of calculation (though it was all of these), but a justification of the primacy of the individual and his self-interest, and of the strategic role of economic freedom in realizing those values through the free market. This is why the economic function became detached from other functions of Western society and was given free rein.

The political ethos of an emerging post-industrial society is communal, insofar as social goals and priorities are defined by, and national policy is directed to, the realization of those goals. It is sociologizing rather than economic (in the sense discussed in Chapter 4), insofar as the criteria of individual utility and profit maximization become subordinated to broader conceptions of social welfare and community interest—particularly as the ancillary effects of ecological devastation multiply social costs and threaten the amenities of life.

For this reason, the political system in post-industrial society can never be wholly technocratic. In a highly technical society, the "technicians"—using that word in the broad sense of those having specialized knowledge—will be the main source of innovation because of their professional expertise. The power to initiate—to direct the attention of society to particular possibilities of action—becomes enormously important: Like the scientists who during World War II created nuclear weapons, they are aware of the potentials in the changes in theoretical knowledge and the specialized technologies that flow from these discoveries; they can codify knowledge, direct new invention, create new methods of analysis, calculate the costs and consequences of policies and the like. The "power" to innovate, as Herbert Simon has pointed out, does not fit the classical

---

ence and Culture, ed. Gerald Holton (Boston, 1965). An earlier exploration of the break-up of formal syntax in the arts is in my essay "The Eclipse of Distance," *Encounter* (May 1963).

categories of power or influence; and it is a real force in the society.[141] But it is not the power to say "yes" or "no," which is where real power lies.

The onset of a communal society, combined with the transformation of personal morality, brings with it a new "cross-over" of political and cultural roles for the regulative mechanisms of society. In the nineteenth century there was economic freedom and the social regulation of the person. In the economic market, individuals and corporations were largely free to pursue goals, so much so that when the state of New York once sought to regulate the conditions of hazardous work, the Supreme Court, in *Lochner vs. New York* (1905), struck down the statute, leading Justice Holmes to say, in a dissenting opinion, that the Court was seeking to write Herbert Spencer's "social statics" into the law of the land. But in the realm of personal conduct, various "blue laws" severely limited what could be printed, or performed on the stage; and, with Prohibition, what could be drunk. One could say that the lack of a regulatory ethic in economics was over-compensated for in the sphere of morality.

Today there is personal freedom and economic regulation. The location of industry is subject to community check, the design of cars is subordinated to government-imposed safety standards, the pollution of the environment is restrained by government penalties, the hiring of individuals (particularly minorities) must follow government guidelines, and, extraordinary for a peace-time economy, wage and price increases are limited by government commission. Yet in the cultural sphere, nudity is common in the movies, pornography on the newsstands, and group sex a subject for attentive media discussion. Almost anything goes. The change has been so great that cultural issues are transformed into political issues as women press for the repeal of anti-abortion laws, young people for the legalization of marijuana, and sexual deviants for the end of discrimination—all of these issues featured in the Democratic National Convention of 1972. The paradox is that in the nineteenth and early-twentieth centuries we had, in America, individualism in the economy and regulation in morals; today we have regulation in the economy and individualism in morals.

Inevitably, the politicization of decision-making—in the economy and in the culture—invites more and more group conflict. The crucial problem for the communal society is whether there is a common framework of values that can guide the setting of political policy. The one major impulse at the moment is that of redress—

---

[141] Herbert A. Simon, "The Changing Theory and Changing Practice of Public Administration," in *Contemporary Political Science*, ed. Ithiel Pool (New York, 1967).

providing for the disadvantaged and seeking some redistribution of the income shares in the society. To some extent, this may satisfy one criterion of justice—as fairness. But it does not create any positive ideal of the kind of individual a society wishes to have. The simplistic notion that one should be "free" to follow one's individual impulse comes into conflict with the increasing pressure for communities to regulate the material conditions of life—including the development of recreation, of access to beaches or wild lands, or the multifarious ways in which the increasing interdependence of life forces each individual to subordinate his desires because they have an adverse effect on others. Politically, there may be a communal society coming into being; but is there a communal ethic? And is one possible?

THE INTERNATIONAL CONTEXT

The concept of post-industrial society is an *analytical construct,* not a picture of a specific or concrete society. It is a paradigm or social framework that identifies new axes of social organization and new axes of social stratification in advanced Western society. Social structures do not change overnight, and it may often take a century for a complete revolution to take place. Any specific society is a combination of many diverse social forms—mixes in the character of the economy, different kinds of political structures, and the like —and this is why one needs multi-conceptual prisms to show, from different standpoints, the analytical frameworks, and their weights, embedded in any society. As a social system, post-industrial society does not "succeed" capitalism or socialism but, like bureaucratization, cuts across both. It is a specification of new dimensions in the social structure which the polity has to manage.

By the end of the century, the United States, Japan, Western Europe, and the Soviet Union will take on aspects of the post-industrial society and have to confront the management of these new dimensions. How this is done will vary from country to country. The organization of science, the character of education, the positions and privileges of the new technical elites, the balance of meritocracy and equality necessarily will be handled within the framework of the different political structures of these countries—the respective ideologies, the amount of resources available, the strength of competing groups, the degree of openness and flexibility of these societies. What a venture in social forecasting can do is to pose an agenda of questions, not a panoply of answers.

In political terms, the problems, in principle, are no different than the kinds of challenges—urbanization, the claims of a working class, mass education—which the new capitalist and industrial nations faced in the hundred years between 1850 and 1950. And yet by the end of the twentieth century one major new feature will have intervened to change the character of the answers—the increased interdependence of the world economy and the rise, with new telecommunications and jet transport, of the world business corporation. The context of all decisions today is truly international.

There are today about 300 colossal multi-national corporations whose production of goods and services adds up to about $300 billion a year, a figure higher than the gross national product of every country except the United States. If one takes the 100 largest economic units in the world, only 50 of them are nation-states; the other 50 are the largest of these 300 multi-national companies.

Of the 300 multi-national corporations, 187 are American; half of the remaining third are British and Dutch, and the other half European and Japanese.[142] The majority of these American giants do more than a half-billion dollars in sales a year. General Motors, the largest, has total annual sales of $25 billion, which exceeds the net national income of all but a dozen countries.

But it is not size and income alone which are important, but the change in the control pattern of the "product cycle." In the past, countries found that once a new product or technique had been created, its initial advantage was overtaken by other countries which, with cheaper labor or newer machinery, could turn out the product cheaper and thus undersell the original country. The textiles industry is perhaps the classic case in point. But the multi-national corporation not only transfers capital and managerial know-how abroad; it has become an organizational mechanism for the transfer of manufacturing production to low-wage countries and its managerial techniques and technology to the advancing industrial countries while retaining control—and earnings—at both ends. In the last five years, overall employment in electronics in the United States declined by some 219,000 jobs as American firms located their new plants in Singapore, Hong Kong, Taiwan, and Mexico. In the nature of the product cycle, more and more manufacturing of the standardized sort will move to the poorer sections of the world while the post-industrial societies concentrate on knowledge-creating and knowledge-processing industries. But the control of the product, in many industries, will remain with the multi-national corporation.

For the United States the salient fact is that the multinational cor-

---

[142] See Raymond Vernon, *Sovereignty at Bay* (New York, 1971). About 4,000 U.S. firms have a total of 17,000 foreign affiliates, but most of these are simply sales offices or some other loose trading relation. The 500 largest firms in the United States own about 2,500 manufacturing firms, but the largest 187 own more than 80 percent of these. For a lucid summary of the statistics and a fanciful speculation about the fate of these firms, see Norman Macrae's supplement, "The Future of International Business," *The Economist* (January 22, 1971).

porations are now increasingly dependent on earnings abroad, a factor completely new in American economic history. A study by *Forbes* magazine of fifty major U.S. corporations showed that, on the average, 40 percent of their total revenue comes from overseas. In the case of Standard Oil of New Jersey, 52 percent of whose net income comes from foreign operations, the dependence on foreign oil is understandable. In the case of IBM, which also earned 50 percent of its net income from worldwide operations, its technological lead gives it an advantage. But one finds that standard manufacturing companies are also heavily dependent on operations outside the United States. Goodyear Tire and Rubber, a $3.6-billion corporation, operates plants in twenty-four countries and earns one-third of its net income from overseas operations. Firestone Tire and Rubber earns 39 percent abroad, and Uniroyal 75 percent. The same is true of processing companies. H. J. Heinz receives 44 percent of its income from worldwide operations, Colgate-Palmolive does 55 percent of its business abroad, chemical and drug companies such as Dow, Pfizer, and Union Carbide do between 30 and 55 percent of their business abroad. Even the largest U. S. manufacturing giants have become increasingly dependent: General Electric receives 20 percent of its profits, Ford 24 percent (excluding Canada), and General Motors 19 percent (excluding Canada) from overseas operations.[143] The headquarters and staff operations remain in the United States, as directing and service facilities, while manufacture and operations are extended abroad.

In short, what is happening as a post-industrial cycle within the national economy is repeating itself on the larger stage of the world economy. New York, in relation to the rest of the American economy, is a headquarters city. More than a third of the largest 500 corporations in the country have their headquarters there, or in the environs, and the concentration of financial, legal, advertising, and marketing services provides the basis of the white-collar employment in the city. But as American management and capital find their most efficient use abroad, and the employment of foreign labor for manufacturing, the United States, too, as Paul Samuelson points out, might become a "headquarters economy."

In the future, it would be normal for the United States to enjoy an unfavorable balance of merchandise trade, but this deficit would be financed by the "invisible" items of interest, dividends, repatriated profits and royalties. In such a situation two political problems would rise. Though total American GNP might be larger, because of this mobile flow of capital and investment, the competitive share of prop-

---

[143] *Forbes* (November 15, 1971), p. 77.

erty income flow (i.e. profits, dividends, etc.) would rise at the expense of labor's share, and pose a domestic problem for the welfare state—the greater need to expand tax and transfer programs for the redistribution of income. But the larger question is the new relation of the United States to the rest of the world. As Samuelson writes: "Suppose that economic equilibrium did dictate our becoming a service economy, living like any rentier on investment earnings abroad. . . . Can one really believe that in the last three decades of the twentieth century the rest of the world can be counted on to permit the continuing flow of dividends, repatriation of earnings and royalties to large corporations owned here? " [144]

We thus find the paradox of the spread of a world capitalist economy as in each nation-state the economic order becomes more subordinate to the wider context of political decision.

But this problem is set in a wider context, the relation between the advanced industrial societies and the rest of the world. Estimates of the disparities between rich and poor vary, and such statistics are notoriously inexact. Yet it has been roughly estimated that the gross value of world production in 1971 was about $3,875 billion. Assuming a world population of 3,600 million, the average income in the world was thus about $1,075 a head. But if one takes the polar cases, the United States produced a trillion-dollar GNP (almost a fourth of the world's total), which, for its 200 million persons, meant an income of $5,000 per capita. The poor countries of the world, whose population numbers 2,300 million, produced 500 billion GNP (or half the production of United States alone) for an income of $212.50 per capita.[145]

Arnold Toynbee once wrote of the rise of an "external proletariat," the poor perimeter of the world encircling the central heartland of the rich. It was a theme sounded ominously in 1965 by Lin Piao, Mao Tse-tung's former Number Two man, when he warned that the "class struggles" of the end of the twentieth century would be between nations rather than within them.[146] Given the pattern of economic development, such a "class struggle," if it ever develops, might become a color struggle as well. But that is the outer limit of our trajectory—a problem for the twenty-first century.

---

[144] Samuelson's observations are from a talk reprinted in the *Sunday Times* financial section (July 30, 1972), p. 12.

[145] Adapted from *The Economist* (January 22, 1971), p. xvii.

[146] Lin Piao, "Long Live the Victory of the People's War" (Peking, New China News Agency, September 2, 1965), reprinted in Samuel B. Griffiths, *Peking and Peoples' War* (New York, 1966), pp. 51–114.

Conclusion

The post-industrial society, as I have emphasized several times, is primarily a change in the character of social structure—in a dimension, not the total configuration of society. It is an "ideal type," a construct, put together by the social analyst, of diverse changes in the society which, when assembled, becomes more or less coherent when contrasted with other conceptual constructs. In descriptive terms, there are three components: in the economic sector, it is a shift from manufacturing to services; in technology, it is the centrality of the new science-based industries; in sociological terms, it is the rise of new technical elites and the advent of a new principle of stratification. From this terrain, one can step back and say more generally that the post-industrial society means the rise of new axial structures and axial principles: a changeover from a goods-producing society to an information or knowledge society; and, in the modes of knowledge, a change in the axis of abstraction from empiricism or trial-and-error tinkering to theory and the codification of theoretical knowledge for directing innovation and the formulation of policy. Any massive set of social changes poses new problems of social management, and in this Coda I have attempted to suggest the agenda of issues which emerges with the onset of post-industrial society: the new hierarchies of technical elites and the bureaucratization of science; meritocracy and equality; the antinomian thrust of an adversary culture, the communal society and the difficulty of consensus. These run the gamut from ethos and values to politics and social organization.

Yet, in an intangible way, there may be more—a change in consciousness and cosmology, the dark tinge of which has always been present at the edges of man's conception of himself and the world, which now moves to the phenomenological center.

In existentialist terminology, man is "thrown" into the world, confronting alien and hostile powers which he seeks to understand and master. The first confrontation was with nature, and for most of the thousands of years of man's existence, life has been a game against nature: to find shelter from the elements, to ride the waters and the wind, to wrest food and sustenance from the soil, the waters, and other creatures. The coding of much of man's behavior has been shaped by his adaptability to the vicissitudes of nature. In the nature of societal design, most of the world's societies still live in this game against nature.

Man as *homo faber* sought to make things, and in making things he dreamt of remaking nature. To be dependent on nature was to bend to its caprices and acknowledge its tyrannies and diminishing returns. To rework nature, to make fabricated things, was to enhance man's powers. The industrial revolution was, at bottom, an effort to substitute a technical order for the natural order, an engineering conception of function and rationality for the haphazard ecological distributions of resources and climates. In the industrial society, the cosmological vision was the game against fabricated nature.

The post-industrial society turns its back on both. In the salient experience of work, men live more and more outside nature, and less and less with machinery and things; they live with and encounter one another. The problem of group life, of course, is one of the oldest difficulties of human civilization, going back to the cave and the clan. But of necessity the context has changed. The oldest forms of group life were within the context of nature, and the overcoming of nature gave an external purpose to the lives of men. The group life that was hitched to things gave men a huge sense of power as they created mechanical artifacts to transform the world. But now these older contexts have been routinized, indeed have almost disappeared from men's view. In the daily round of work, men no longer confront nature, as either alien or beneficent, and fewer now handle artifacts and things. The post-industrial society is essentially a game between persons.

Will this changed experience create a change in consciousness and sensibility? For most of human history, *reality was nature*, and in poetry and imagination men sought to relate the self to the natural world. Then *reality became technics*, tools and things made by men yet given an independent existence outside himself, the reified world. Now *reality is primarily the social world*—neither nature nor things, only men—experienced through the reciprocal consciousness of self and other. Society itself becomes a web of consciousness, a form of imagination to be realized as a social construction. Inevitably, a post-industrial society gives rise to a new Utopianism, both engineering and psychedelic. Men can be remade or released, their behavior conditioned or their consciousness altered. The constraints of the past vanish with the end of nature and things.

But what does not vanish is the duplex nature of man himself— the murderous aggression, from primal impulse, to tear apart and destroy; and the search for order, in art and life, as the bending of will to harmonious shape. It is this ineradicable tension which defines the social world and which permits a view of Utopia that is perhaps more realistic than the here-and-now millennium on earth that modern man has sought. Utopia has always been conceived as a design of harmony and perfection in the relations between men. In the wisdom of the ancients, Utopia was a fruitful impossibility, a conception of the desirable which men should always strive to attain but which, in the nature of things, could not be achieved. And yet, by its very idea, Utopia would serve as a standard of judgment on men, an ideal by which to measure the real. The modern *hubris* has sought to cross that gap and embody the ideal in the real; and in the effort the perspective of the ideal has become diminished and the idea of Utopia has become tarnished. Perhaps it would be wiser to return to the classic conception.

Men in their imagination will always seek to make society a work of art; that remains an ideal. Given the tasks that have to be solved, it is enough to engage in the sober construction of social reality.

NAME INDEX

Name Index

Buckley, Walter, 10n
Bunzel, John, 418
Burck, Gilbert, 463n
Burckhardt, Jacob, 50, 85
Burnham, Jack, 285
Burnham, James, 14, 96n; on managerial revolution, 90–94
Burnier, Michel-Antonio, 79n
Burns, James McGregor, 439n
Burns, Tom, 54n
Bush, Vannevar, 391n

Calhoun, John C., 439
Cannon, James P., 90n
Carr-Saunders, A. M., 374n
Carson, Rachel, 404
Cartter, Allan M., 235, 237
Cary, Frank, 390
Castro, Fidel, 76n, 450
Cavendish, Henry, 179
Challis, J., 186
Chaplin, Charlie, 162
Chatelier, Henri Le, 21
Chikin, V., 354n
Churchman, C. W., 208
Clapham, John H., 124
Clark, Colin, 14, 35; on industrial society, 75
Clark, John Maurice, 281n
Clarke, Arthur C., 199
Clausen, Alden Winship (Tom), 292, 293
Coe, C. P., 391n
Cohany, Harry P., 141n
Cohen, David K., 413n
Cohen, Wilbur, 329
Cole, Arthur, 35
Cole, Jonathan R. and Stephen, 385n
Coleman, James, 421, 429, 430, 431
Commoner, Barry, 404
Compton, Arthur H., 391n, 393
Compton, K. T., 391n
Conant, James Bryant, 346n, 391n, 394n, 397
Comte, August, 49, 55, 74, 78, 355
Condorcet, M. J. A. N., 306
Cooke, Morris L., 352n
Corey, Robert, 170
Coser, Lewis, 162n
Cournot, Augustin, 263n, 350
Coxey, J. S., 315
Crick, Francis, 170
Croner, Fritz, 69n
Cutler, Robert, 399n

Dahl, Robert A., 306n, 307–308, 311
Dahrendorf, Ralf, 37, 51, 52, 54n, 70n, 79n
Daley, Richard J., 438n
Dantzig, G. B., 30n, 76n, 347
Davenport, John, 292, 293

Davis, Nuel Pharr, 400n
Debray, Regis, 148
DeButts, John D., 390
Denison, Edward, 151–152, 211
Dewey, John, 10, 164, 422
Dewey, Lucretia M., 141n
Dilthey, W., 12
Dirac, P. A. M., 381
Djilas, Milovan, 95–97, 105
Dodd, Merrick, 293
Domar, Evsey, 194, 463
Dorfman, Robert, 30n
Doriot, Jacques, 96n
Doty, Paul, 401
Downs, Anthony, 306, 472n
Draper, Hal, 96n
Dreyfuss, Carl, 69n
Du Bridge, Lee, 394n, 397
Dulles, John Foster, 397n
Dunayevskaya, Raya (Forest), 90n
Duncan, Otis Dudley, 8n, 314n, 335, 336, 416
Dunlop, John, 93–94
Durkheim, Emile, 173, 287–288, 313n, 341, 372, 469; on industrial society, 74, 75

Easton, David, 83n, 312n
Easton, Lloyd, 80n
Eckstein, Otto, 450n
Edison, Thomas A., 20, 346n
Ehrenberg, Richard, 63n
Einstein, Albert, 9, 111, 388n, 391
Eisenhower, Dwight D., 246, 258, 270, 397, 399
Eisenstadt, S. N., 54
Eliot, T. S., 366
Ellul, Jacques, 54n
Enfantin, B. P., 342n
Engel, Christian, 128
Engels, F., 60n, 76, 77, 101n, 108n, 123, 459
Englehard, Erich, 69n, 71n
Enns, John N., 24n
Enzenberger, Hans Magnus, 384
Epstein, M., 64n
Erikson, Erik, 317
Etzioni, Amitai, 52–53, 263n

Fainsod, Merle, 100n
Fallada, Hans, 72
Farber, Eduard, 21n
Farrell, Robert, 237
Feldman, Arnold, 113n
Felix, Fremont, 460n
Fermi, Enrico, 186, 388n, 391, 393, 397
Ferry, W. H., 462n
Feuer, Lewis, 54
Flemming, Arthur S., 399n

SUBJECT INDEX